The International Economy

The International Economy

SIXTH EDITION

P. T. Ellsworth

PROFESSOR EMERITUS,
UNIVERSITY OF WISCONSIN

J. Clark Leith

PROFESSOR OF ECONOMICS,
THE UNIVERSITY OF WESTERN ONTARIO

MACMILLAN PUBLISHING COMPANY
NEW YORK

COLLIER MACMILLAN PUBLISHERS
LONDON

Macmillan Publishing Company
866 Third Avenue, New York, New York 10022

Collier Macmillan Canada, Inc.

Library of Congress Cataloging in Publication Data

Ellsworth, P. T. (Paul Theodore), DATE:
    The international economy.

    Includes bibliographies and index.
    1. International economic relations.   2. Commerce.
I. Leith, J. Clark.   II. Title.
HF1411.E424   1984   377   83-12057
ISBN 0-02-332770-7

Printing: 2 3 4 5 6 7 8   Year: 4 5 6 7 8 9 0 1 2

ISBN 0-02-332770-7

PREFACE

Developments in the international economy and the theory of international economics during the past several years have made it essential that this revision be thoroughgoing. The task of revision has been made easier by teamwork. P. T. Ellsworth and J. Clark Leith continue as full collaborators in preparation of this edition.

The text continues to provide the reader with a balanced coverage of all important topics in international economics. The approach blends theory, history, institutions, and policy. The level of difficulty in the theoretical material assumes only that the reader has had two semesters of principles of economics. Some of the more complex material in the previous edition has been omitted, and some transferred to appendixes.

Starting from a general equilibrium model of prices and production, the factor proportions basis for international trade is developed, as in earlier editions, as the dominant but not unique basis for trade. These chapters have been rewritten with the aim of simplifying the explanation of difficult material without a loss of rigor. The revision of later chapters on trade theory has been thorough, including the introduction of considerable new material. The balance-of-payments chapters have been totally redone. The approach emphasizes the fundamental importance of the simultaneous determination of income, expenditure, and asset changes. A systematic general framework permits both Keynesian and monetary approaches to be considered and then integrated.

As in earlier editions, history is employed to complement theory by showing the changes in institutional environment conditioning the principles developed in the analytical portions of the text. These chapters provide illustrations of how abstract principles apply in an ever-changing world. Recent changes in the international economy necessitated a thoroughgoing revision of the treatment of the evolution of the international monetary system to reflect the past decade.

We are indebted to numerous discussions of the issues to Leith's colleagues in international economics at Western Ontario and to Joseph D. Coppock and Ray Boddy in San Diego. In addition we would like to thank John Adams, University of Maryland; Dennis Appleyard, University of North Carolina—Chapel Hill; Lance Girton, University of Utah; and Lawrence H. Officer, Michigan State University, who reviewed the penultimate draft and provided valuable suggestions. A special note of thanks goes to Rubén Suarez and Brenda Gonzalez-Hermosillo, research assistants to Leith, and to Diane MacDonald and Judy Purves, who typed the manuscript.

Finally, on many occasions the patience of both the authors' wives and the Leith children was severely tried by our preoccupation with the manuscript. For their unfailing and cheerful support in our labors, we dedicate this edition to Frieda, Carole Ann, Jim, Deb, and Jonathan.

P. T. E.
J. C. L.

CONTENTS

vii

Part 2   The Theory of International Trade: Bases of Specialization and Trade

Part 3 Tariffs and Protection

The International Economy

Introduction

As a social science, economics focuses on one major aspect of social life: the activities related to maintaining life and to improving its condition. These activities encompass both consumption, whose pattern and composition determine the standard of living of an individual or of a group, and production, whose sole purpose is to provide the means for consumption.

In its analysis of these activities, economics has concerned itself with three major areas: the allocation of productive resources to the various branches of production, the degree of utilization (full or partial) of those resources, and the forces underlying their growth over time. In an unregulated economy, resources are allocated primarily through the operation of the price system. The task of studying this complex system falls to price theory, or microeconomics. Macroeconomics encompasses the analysis of the forces determining the level at which resources are employed, whereas growth theory, as its name implies, relates to problems of growth and development.

International economics is concerned with these same problems in their international setting. Thus the allocation of resources among several economies or nations, rather than within a single one, is studied. As far as unregulated economies are concerned, this means an examination of the way in which a number of distinct national price systems are interrelated. On the side of macroeconomics, the international transmission of the forces affecting the employment of resources must be analyzed. The same can be said of the problems of growth. In summary, international economics simply moves on from a study of the operation of a single economy to an analysis of the interrelation of two or more economies, and this with respect to their price systems, the forces affecting the level of employment, and the forces determining growth.

1

As any student of elementary economics knows, the prices of goods in a given economy are determined in the various markets for those goods by the interaction of the forces of demand and supply, stemming respectively from the needs and desires of consumers, on the one hand, and from the firms engaged in production, on the other. The prices of the factors used to produce these goods are similarly determined in the factor markets.

The principal way in which a number of economies are linked together into an international economy is through the extension of markets from the national to the international level. National prices are compared in these broader markets, with the business of supplying a particular commodity normally going to the cheapest supplier. Another link between economies is provided by movements of some of the factors of production. But commodities also move in trade within the boundaries of each nation. So do the movable factors of production: labor, capital, and enterprise. And as we just noted, the basic principles of microeconomics and macroeconomics form the theoretical foundation of international economics, as they do in the study of a national economy. Why, then, should the economic transactions between nations require a separate study?

INTERNATIONAL ECONOMICS AS A DISTINCT FIELD OF STUDY

Two reasons are generally advanced for distinguishing international economics as a special field. One is that such international movement of factors as occurs is, in general, far less free than movement within a single country. Thus factor prices can differ widely among nations. Wages need not be the same in Italy as in the United States, nor the return to capital the same in Britain, India, and Argentina. But within each country, the rewards of each factor tend strongly toward equality. Since payments to the productive factors are the ultimate costs of producing commodities, such national differences in factor prices suggest that international trade requires a different explanation from that of domestic trade.

Another reason for undertaking a separate study of international economics is that the economic activity we seek to analyze operates within a framework of laws and institutions that vary widely from country to country. That each country has its own money is of particular importance. Since the nationals of each country execute their transactions, whether domestic or foreign, in their own national money, this raises the problem of foreign exchange—of translating international payments and receipts from one currency into another. A closely related problem is the ways and means of bringing international payments and receipts into balance.

The major task of international economics is to provide an understanding of the basis for trade among nations, and of how a nation's international payments can be brought into balance with its receipts. These aspects of our study are the theoretical core, which make it possible to perceive regularity and order in the multitude of transactions among 150 or so nations, involving thousands of commodities, a wide variety of financial instruments, and services ranging from insurance to the leasing of patents.

By its very nature, the theory of international trade and finance is abstract. Yet this theory, when put to use, must always be applied to a concrete situation, one that is shaped by the laws and institutions of the nation or nations involved. And such institutional differences can, through their effect on a nation's development, strongly influence the character of its economy and therewith the role it plays in the world economy.

HISTORY AS A COMPLEMENT TO THEORY

It is considerations such as the preceding that make it desirable to complement the analytical tools of theory with a study of relevant aspects of history.

Thus the near absence in most of Latin America until recently of a middle class accounts in large part for a slow rate of growth, whereas the existence of such a class in the United States and Canada was an important factor in their rapid progress in the last century and a half. This striking difference can be traced to the character of the settlers in the two regions and the institutions they brought with them. To North America came people mainly from the lower middle classes, who brought with them a tradition of individual striving, a questioning of authority, and a desire for economic improvement. In South America, on the other hand, the Spanish *conquistadores* who dominated the early settlements introduced feudal ideas and institutions and imposed the *hacienda* system on the native Indian population. A concentration of land ownership and wealth resulted, which made for a rigid social structure, a continued predominance of agriculture, and a slow and tardy appearance of modern industry.

But institutional differences alone do not account for differences in the structure and operation of national economics. Laws and institutions are not immutable, but undergo constant change. As they change, they may greatly alter, not the operative economic principles themselves, but their impact on a society and hence upon the economic policies it adopts. Thus the gold standard, the international monetary system that tied national currencies together at fixed exchange rates, worked relatively well in the nineteenth century because the environment was favorable. But with increasing industrialization and urbanization, and with the changes in social attitudes that these developments caused, the deflationary bias of the gold standard condemned it as a satisfactory international monetary framework. In recent years, attention has therefore been directed toward alternative types of international arrangements.

THE CHANGING CHARACTER OF THE INTERNATIONAL ECONOMY

Looked at more broadly, the international economy—the system of trade relationships and the system of monetary arrangements that link nations with one another—has gone through at least four phases, each of considerable duration. The earliest phase, economic nationalism or mercantilism, was one of aggressive struggle, with each nation pitted against its rivals. Despite the seeming anarchy, international economic relations conformed to a unique kind of order, with trade regulated in great detail. Then, following deep-seated changes in methods of production and in the growth of social and economic classes, the nineteenth century witnessed a period of rapid growth under an international system based on freedom of trade. This phase endured down to 1914. Then the shocks of World War I, the Great Depression of the 1930s, and finally World War II brought the international economy near to disintegration. Fortunately, the lessons of that period led to rapid reconstruction and to a substantial degree of deliberate international cooperation. Whether, with the worldwide recession of 1982–1983 and the associated protectionist pressures, that phase is coming to an end, it is too soon to tell. In any event, changes of great moment appear to be upon us. These changes will be interesting to watch and, for those who can, exciting to help guide.

THE PLAN OF THIS BOOK

The preceding discussion gives some indication of the structure of this book. We start in Part 1 with an account of the beginnings of an international economic system in the preindustrial era, of the economic ideas that guided statesmen, and of the manner in which trade was conducted and regulated. There follows a chapter on the rise of liberalism in economic thought and of the social and economic consequences of the Industrial Revolution, two developments that were to shape events for well over a century. The third and final chapter of this section presents the theories on international trade of Adam Smith, David Ricardo, and John Stuart Mill, theories that were powerful weapons in the struggle to free trade from its mercantilist restrictions. Part 2 consists of six chapters that present, in a sequence running from the simple to the complex, the modern analysis of international trade. The trading equilibrium is set out and bases for trade are developed, followed by an empirical evaluation of the theories. We also take into account changing conditions—changes in technology and in supplies of productive factors, from sources that are either internal or external to the domestic economy.

Part 3 deals with the issues arising from the restriction of trade. In the first pair of chapters we undertake an analysis of the nature and effects of tariffs, and an evaluation of the case for protection. In a second pair of chapters we take up some international institutional arrangements that have been designed to free-up trade: economic integration among a group of countries, and multilateral tariff reductions. The final chapter of Part 3 considers the case put forward by developing countries for special treatment in the international economic system.

Part 4 picks up the historical narrative. It opens with a description of the development in the nineteenth century of a closely interwoven world trading system, with Britain at its center. The next chapter goes on to show the reemergence of expansive nationalism, which ended with World War I.

Part 5 moves from microeconomics to macroeconomics in eight chapters devoted to the monetary and financial relations among nations. The stage is set by establishing a simplified framework of real production, consumption, and trade. This provides a link between the pure theory of trade and the balance of payments. The simultaneity of the determination of income, expenditure, and asset changes is emphasized to assist the reader in understanding the fundamentals of the balance of international payments of a country. This system approach is taken from the very beginning to guard against treating balance-of-payments policy issues as the sum of unconnected parts.

To keep the analysis simple at this early stage, only one asset is assumed but is not identified specifically. Further, the complication of different currencies is left until a later chapter.

The accounting of the various elements of the balance of payments is added in the next chapter.

Complications are then added one at a time. Chapter 19 adds the first major complication: different currencies and the concept of exchange rates.

Chapter 20 introduces a pair of well-known simple models that attempt to explain the balance-of-payments adjustment behavior. The simple Keynesian and monetary approaches to the balance of payments are developed, still assuming in both cases that there is a single asset. The models are elucidated, and then used to explore the differences between fixed and flexible exchange rates. (To develop the monetary model, the single asset is explicitly assumed to be money.)

In Chapter 21 we introduce the second asset. Note that until this is done we have avoided treatment of anything involving interest rates. This chapter is designed to explore issues associated with asset choice and the effect of such choices on the balance of payments, depending on whether or not bonds are tradeable.

In Chapter 22, using the idea of asset choice, we are ready to introduce the *IS–LM* framework. We then add a foreign balance (*FB*) curve in Chapter 23, including interest-sensitive capital flows. The full-blown *IS–LM–FB* framework of short-run adjustment integrates many of the elements from the earlier chapters. The Keynesian and monetary adjustment mechanisms plus the choice between two assets are handled simultaneously. The contrast between fixed and flexible exchange rates in this full-blown model is explored, and the well-known internal versus external balance literature is introduced and employed to set up the debate between policy activists and passivists.

Chapter 24 addresses what happens when balance-of-payments adjustments are blocked. The frequency with which individual countries resort to this solution for a balance-of-payments problem and the substantial difference in the consequences make it important to understand the nature and consequences of blocked adjustment.

Part 6 takes up the review of historical developments, focusing on the institutional consequences for the international monetary system in the twentieth century. Two chapters review the changes wrought by World War I, the severest depression in modern history, and other disruptive forces. In further chapters we examine the evolution of the postwar fixed exchange rate system from the establishment of the Bretton Woods framework, through the dollar shortage, to the emergence of flexible exchange rates among many industrial countries. Specific attention is paid to some important concepts associated with the floating rate system, including real exchange rates, purchasing power parity, effective exchange rates, and optimum currency areas. Finally, in Chapter 30 the modern International Monetary Fund is examined.

PART
1

FROM RESTRICTION TOWARD FREEDOM IN TRADE AND ENTERPRISE

1
CHAPTER

Regulated Trade: Mercantilism

It may seem strange to begin a study of the international economy with a chapter on mercantilism, yet there are many reasons for doing so. The system of thought known by that name developed during the early modern period (1500–1750) when the nation-state as we know it first made its appearance. The new nations—notably England, France, and Spain—commanding the allegiance of comparatively large populations and ruling over sizable territories, developed a system of economic thought and economic policies that reflected the peculiar circumstances of the times—bitter rivalry for trade and colonies, a scramble for gold, and almost constant wars. Although these narrow-minded views underwent a softening during the nineteenth century, the protectionist sentiment underlying them was never far from the surface and tended to reappear whenever times grew hard. One of the worst outbursts of neomercantilism occurred in the 1930s, when to widespread crude trade restrictions were added many ingenious refinements. Their principal effect was to intensify the severe depression of those years and make matters worse. Now in the early 1980s, with the world economy flat and unemployment severe, proposals to tax or otherwise limit trade are again becoming common.

Will we never learn that policies to choke off the natural flow of trade are essentially useless? Surely it would help if people were better informed about the character of such policies, about the circumstances of their origin, and about the kind of thought upon which they rest. This book provides such information.

SOCIAL AND ECONOMIC CHARACTERISTICS OF THE MERCANTILIST PERIOD

Europe in 1500

What was the Western world like in 1500, the threshold of modern times? Probably Europe west of the Urals had a population of no more than 60 million, 80 to 90 percent of it tilling the soil as serfs on the large estates of the nobility or as independent peasant farmers. Of the remainder, most were employed as craftsmen, shopkeepers, servants of the relatively small number of nobles, higher clergy, and well-to-do merchants who enjoyed ample incomes and who held the reins of political and economic power.

Society was thus preponderantly agrarian. Only four cities had attained a population of about 200,000: London, Paris, Naples, and Milan. Perhaps a half dozen could count as many as 100,000: Antwerp, Amsterdam, Lisbon, Seville, Rome, and Palermo. There were many towns of a few thousand to 50,000 people, but even these were widely scattered.

Moreover, the rate of population growth appears from scattered figures to have been very slow. Until the eighteenth century the average rate of increase seems to have been well below 1 percent, and at times even negative.[1]

Manufactures

In the scattered cities and towns of western Europe, industry as we know it today did not exist. With few exceptions, manufacturing processes took place in the shop of the craftsman employing a few journeymen and apprentices, or in the home of the peasant. This was true of furniture, kitchen utensils, pottery, candles, hardware, and clothing. But in the manufacture of woolen textiles, which was the dominant industry of the thriving commercial cities of northern Italy and Flanders, and of England as well, the craft gild system had given way to the "domestic" or "putting-out" system. Here the trader or merchant–capitalist purchased raw wool; placed it in the homes of spinners and weavers to be worked up; collected the crude cloth and put it out with other workers for fulling, dyeing, and finishing; and marketed the completed product. Only rarely did the capitalist provide not only the raw materials but also the tools and a large building where he employed as

---

[1] Karl F. Helleiner, "The Population of Europe from the Black Death to the Eve of the Vital Revolution," Chapter 1 in E. E. Rich and C. H. Wilson, eds., *The Cambridge Economic History of England*, Vol. 4 (New York: Cambridge University Press, 1967).

many as several hundred workers on the various process of textile manufacture. In some other industries, principally mining, the capitalist had achieved a position of dominance. Otherwise, the craft method of the Middle Ages continued relatively unchanged.

Trade

Because of the widespread poverty, trade at the beginning of the sixteenth century was mainly local, confined to the towns and their immediate countryside. Long-distance trade could be divided into the movement of such staples as grains and timber from the Baltic regions and salt fish from the Baltic and North Seas to supplement the food requirements of city dwellers, and the flow of luxuries to supply the wants of the comparatively rich. The latter included the long-established trade with the East in fine cotton and silk fabrics, spices, drugs, dyes, and perfumes, the movement northward of the wines and fruits of the Latin countries, and the exchange for these of the famous woolens of northern Italy, Flanders, and England.

During the sixteenth century itself, world trade experienced rapid expansion. The intra-European trade in staples continued a steady increase, owing mainly to the development by the Dutch of efficient specialized ships and by their opening of new herring fisheries. As for the trade of the East in luxuries, the great geographical discoveries of the last decade of the fifteenth century acted as a strong catalyst.

Vasco da Gama's discovery of the ocean route to India and the Spice Islands via the Cape of Good Hope (1498) enabled Portugal, and later Holland, to rival and then displace Venice in trade with these areas. For da Gama's achievement meant that commerce was no longer confined to the Mediterranean galleys of Venice, to the camel caravans of the Near East, and to the pack trains winding their way northward over the Alps. Now commerce could take to the high seas in vessels of increasing size, at a diminishing cost of operation.

The discovery of the Americas was soon followed by the Spanish conquest of Mexico and Peru. From their art treasures and mines flowed a swelling stream of gold and silver that bulwarked Spain's power for over a century. But the Spanish economy remained backward; for supplies for its growing American colonies, Spain had to depend increasingly on purchases from other European sources. With the consequent seepage of the precious metals into the rest of western Europe, prices rose steadily if somewhat irregularly, while wages lagged behind. The mild but steady inflation continued until about 1650, sustaining profits and stimulating both the accumulation of capital and the growth of trade. And beginning early in the sixteenth century, colonial expansion in North America by the English, Dutch, and French added another dimension to Europe's trade.

The Rise of the Commercial Class

One of the most significant developments of the period was the rise of the new capitalist class to positions of prominence and power. All the influences to which we have called attention worked in this direction: the geographical discoveries by providing new trading opportunities for men of enterprise; the fresh supplies of precious metals by making profits more abundant and secure and capital accumulation easy; and colonial expansion by creating new markets and sources of raw material supplies. Reinforcing these influences, the Renaissance brought a shift in scholarly interest from the study of established doctrine to the examination of the actual world. This laid the foundations of modern science, contributed many inventions that, like the telescope, barometer, and sextant, aided navigation, and generated a secular outlook on life that was favorable to commercial activity.

The capitalist organizer expanded his activities in all directions. He increased his trade in such staples as grain, fish, and timber. The need for nails, chains, and miscellaneous hardware, such as locks, keys, hinges, and lanterns, stimulated the rise of many small industries making these articles in Birmingham as early as 1538. Sugar, which in the Middle Ages appeared only on the tables of the very rich, by the middle of the seventeenth century became a common article of diet for all but the poor. Sugar, molasses, and rum were mainstays of the trade with the West Indies at that time. The closely associated traffic in Negro slaves, which began in 1510, rose to a volume of 15,000 a year in the seventeenth century and 30,000 in the eighteenth.

The Rise of National States

Complementing the economic expansion of the sixteenth century and the accompanying rise to power and influence of the merchant–capitalist was the outstanding political fact of the period—the appearance in western Europe of powerful national states. Until after the middle of the fifteenth century, the terms "England," "France," "Spain," and "Netherlands" had principally geographical and linguistic significance—they carried little political meaning. Although there had been kings of England and France since at least the Norman Conquest, their power to command the loyalty of their subjects was constantly in dispute, ever challenged by the strong feudal nobility. Spain was divided into Castile, Aragon, and regions still dominated by the Moors, while the Low Countries were principalities of the dukes of Burgundy.

Yet during the late medieval period, even while authority remained dispersed among countless feudal nobles, the bases of their power were being gradually eroded. The slow but steady growth of trade brought with it and was supported by an increase in the supply of money. Towns grew and multiplied, expanding the numbers and influence of the wealthy burgher class. The use of money spread, invading even the institutions of feudalism, where it led to the conversion of mutual rights and obligations between lord and vassal into contractual payments. With the spread of the money economy, royal monarchs no longer had to depend on feudal levies of armed knights for military support, but could hire mercenaries, using the proceeds of the taxes that replaced contributions in kind. And in the rising burgher class, they found men experienced in business and finance to administer their increasingly complex affairs and to provide, when needed, substantial loans. Finally, the introduction of gunpowder from China, together with the invention of muskets and cannon, destroyed the impregnability of the castle stronghold and relegated chain mail and plate armor to quiet corners of museums.

In spite of these developments favorable to centralized authority, it required the firm hand and strenuous efforts of Henry VII (1485–1509) to establish the royal power and to unify England. His work of national unification was strengthened and consolidated by his great successors, Henry VIII (1509–1547) and Elizabeth I (1558–1603). In France, it was not until the end of the Hundred Years' War in 1453, when the English claims to almost half of France were liquidated, that it became possible to weld the numerous duchies and counties into a national state subject to a single ruler. Then, building on the long struggle of his predecessors to subdue the feudal nobles, Louis XI (1461–1483) used shrewdness and treachery to consolidate the kingdom. From his time on, the authority of the French king was never in serious doubt, and France became one of the major powers of Europe.

Spain's entry upon the international scene was sudden. Although the separate feudal kingdoms of Castile and Aragon spent several centuries in pushing back the Moors, national unity came all at once with the marriage in 1469 of Ferdinand of Aragon and Isabella of Castile. In the same year that Columbus discovered America, his royal master's troops were engaged in the conquest of Granada, the last remaining stronghold of the Moors. Thereby all the Iberian peninsula, with the exception of independent Portugal, came under the rule of a single Spanish king.

The Dutch Republic, the fourth of the great powers of Europe in the early modern period, did not emerge until more than a century later. By a succession of marriages, the Low Countries passed from the hands of the last of the dukes of Burgundy to those of Charles V, King of Spain. The intolerance and persecution that Charles's son Philip II visited upon the Dutch Protestants, culminating in the infamous cruelty and butcheries of his delegate, the Duke of Alva, provoked the Dutch into rebellion. For forty years, their bloody struggle against their Spanish oppressors continued, until in 1609 they won effective independence.

THE BASES AND CHIEF ELEMENTS OF MERCANTILIST THOUGHT

We come now to the economic ideas generated in this age of expanding trade and colonial settlement, of rising prices and increasing accumulation of capital, of the rise to prominence of the merchant–capitalist class, and of the emergence of nation-states. These ideas were not expressed by scholars engaged in research, but by active men of affairs: prominent merchants, lawyers, financial advisers to kings, and state officials. Dealing with practical problems of trade, manufactures, and shipping, and with the role of government in relation to these activities, the views they expressed were unsystematic and of widely varying quality. Yet they contained common threads of argument that constantly reappear, and warrant the title of "mercantilism." With one exception soon to be noted, these ideas expressed an outlook that today we call "economic nationalism," an outlook that regards other nations as rivals if not enemies and that turns the powers of government to the aggressive support of domestic industry, domestic trade, and domestic shipping. In the early day of mercantilism, its expression was highly chauvinist and bellicose, and it remained self-centered to the end.

With markets expanding and wealth increasing, it seems strange that such a belligerent economic philosophy should have emerged. But this was an age of violence.

> War was almost a normal relationship among national states. From 1494 to 1559 there was fighting nearly every year in some part of Europe; the seventeenth century enjoyed only seven calendar years of complete peace, and England was at war during eighty-four of the 165 years between 1650 and 1815.[2]

A Static View of the World

In part, no doubt, this prevalence of war can be attributed to the very human rivalry of ambitious monarchs, in part to religious zeal and

---

[2] Herbert Heaton, *Economic History of Europe* (New York: Harper & Row, Publishers, Inc., 1936), p. 228.

intolerance. Yet in large measure, what was responsible was an essentially static view of the world and its resources. There was no conception, until relatively late, of the immense size of the American continents, of the room for expansion, of the increase in wealth that all could hope to share. Within each country, on the other hand, the desire for growth was strong. Merchants, manufacturers, and shippers all wanted to increase the scope of their activities. The national states, however, were new and insecure. Kings and ministers of each nation sought to build up its strength and to improve its position. But if the resources available for expansion were strictly limited, as they were thought to be, the desires of one nation were bound to collide with those of others. International conflict was inevitable.

One of the leading students of mercantilism has described the situation this way:

> *Within* the state, mercantilism consequently pursued thorough-going dynamic ends. But the important thing is that this was bound up with a static conception of the total economic resources in the world; for this it was that created that fundamental disharmony which sustained the endless commercial wars. Both elements together implied that the position of a particular country could change and was capable of progress, but that this could only happen through acquisitions from other countries. This was the tragedy of mercantilism. Both the Middle Ages with their universal static ideal and *laissez faire* with its universal dynamic ideal avoided this consequence. Without grasping this it is impossible to understand mercantilism either in theory or practice.[3]

Only in the Low Countries, later the Dutch Republic, did mercantilist concepts and policies fail to take root. For there the governing authorities remained relatively weak and decentralized. Merchants early acquired riches and political power; their interest lay in freedom to expand and freedom from constraint and regulation. They kept their freedom and made good use of it; Holland became the richest country in Europe and the envy of others. But in England, France, and Spain, the monarch held the power, each distrusted his rivals, and each shared the common view that the growth and security of his nation could come only at the expense of his rivals. Hence, in these nations, to increase the power and wealth of the state became the primary national objective.

[3] August Heckscher, *Mercantilism*, Vol. 2 (London: George Allen & Unwin Ltd., 1936), pp. 25–26.

The Doctrine of State Power

The common desire of the new states of western Europe to expand their wealth, population, and territory, combined with the conviction that the opportunity for such growth was severely circumscribed, set the overriding goal of national policy. To increase the power of the state by all possible means must be a nation's primary objective.

This goal, and the world view on which it rested, gave shape and content to mercantilist ideas and practice. If national power was essential in a narrow and hostile world, how could it best be realized? Military strength is, of course, an important component of national power. Great stress therefore, was laid on the recruitment, training, and supplying of a sizable army. England in particular, as an insular power, stressed the need for a large navy, and for merchant vessels to carry the profitable cargoes of goods of all kinds. To support these forces a nation must have a strong agricultural and industrial base, and this, it was assumed, required the support and regulation of the state. Colonies furnished an outlet for a growing population and could supply timber, ship's spars, and other naval stores, as well as an ever-widening variety of raw materials for processing by the skilled workers of the mother country. Colonies were therefore important in their own right, and they also required the protection of strong naval forces.

The Balance-of-Trade Theory

In addition to their agreement on the goal of national power, on an abundance of riches as its essential support, and on regulation of economic activity as the best means of attaining national wealth, mercantilists also shared—what is of particular interest to us—a common theory of international trade. This may be summarily stated as follows: *that a nation could only gain through foreign trade if it had a favorable balance, or an excess in the value of exports over imports.* The gain arose from the fact that an excess of exports over imports had to be paid for with gold and silver, and for a nation to acquire those precious metals, or treasure, was the surest way of enriching itself. For a nation without gold and silver mines, it was the *only* way.

Clearly, the favorable balance-of-trade doctrine rested upon the conviction that the precious metals were of paramount importance. At least to the earlier and less sophisticated mercantilists, wealth consisted above all else in gold and silver. Clement Armstrong, an English mercantilist of the early sixteenth century, asserted that it is "better to have plenty of gold and silver in the realm than plenty of merchants and merchandizes," and Monchrétien, a Frenchman writing a century later, said, "We live not so much from trade in raw materials as from gold and silver."[4]

Why the Stress on the Precious Metals?   In part, this emphasis on gold and silver stems from an early confusion between wealth and money, but this confusion seems to have been confined largely to the cruder mercantilist writings. In part, too, the idea that, for trade to be profitable, it must show a net export balance to be settled in cash derived from the simple extrapolation of the individual merchant's experience. When he conducted his business successfully, his sales exceeded his purchases and brought in money. Why should not the same be true of the entire economy? This tendency to put private and public finance on the same footing is natural, so natural that even Adam Smith fell into this fallacy.

Even the more sophisticated mercantilist writers, however, regarded the precious metals as the most important form of wealth, making this view practically unanimous.[5] Such unanimity suggests that perhaps the main reason for their preference was the close association between the universal stress on national power, the consequent emphasis on military strength, and the usefulness of large stocks of ready money to buy the needed supplies. Having an ample supply of liquid assets was of special importance at a time when credit facilities were in their infancy.

The emphasis placed on the balance-of-trade doctrine varied considerably among the new nations. It was especially strong in England, which relied mainly on stringent policies to promote exports and to impede imports, but which also obtained important quantities of the precious metals through the piratical activity of privateers preying on the Spanish galleons bringing treasure from the Americas. France stressed the encouragement of domestic industry through subsidies, protection, and investment by the crown, and followed this up with the detailed regulation of industry.

Holland, unlike its rivals, showed little concern for its balance of trade, perhaps because its citizens were Europe's most efficient traders. Spain alone could obtain all the gold it needed by plundering the treasures of the Incas and the Aztecs they had conquered, and by forcing

---

[4] Ibid., p. 182.

[5] Thus Viner comments: "on the basis of my turning of the pages of English mercantilist literature I venture the conclusion that not ten per cent of it was free from concern, expressed or clearly implied, in the state of the balance of trade and in the means whereby it could be improved." Jacob Viner, *Studies in the Theory of International Trade* (New York: Harper & Row, Publishers, Inc., 1937), p. 56.

them to wrest more gold from their mines. Spain also introduced extremely tight regulations over its trade with its colonies.

Summary

Mercantilism can be briefly summarized by the following propositions: that the paramount goal of national policy must be to make the nation rich and powerful; that this requires a prosperous and productive agriculture, a wide variety of manufactures, and secure access to foreign markets and supplies; that the means to this end consist mainly in the protection of domestic industry and the regulation of trade; and that the test of success is to be found in a continuing favorable balance of trade.[6]

What this view implied in practice was vividly expressed in the work of an Austrian mercantilist, Von Hornick (1638–1712):

> All commodities found in a country, which cannot be used in their natural state, should be worked up within the country; since the payment for manufacturing generally exceeds the value of the raw material by two, three, ten, twenty, and even a hundred fold. . . .
>
> The inhabitants of the country should make every effort to get along with their domestic products, to confine their luxury to these alone, and to do without foreign products as far as possible (except where great need leaves no alternative, or if not need, wide-spread, unavoidable abuse, of which Indian spices are an example). . . . Such foreign commodities should in this case be imported in unfinished form, and worked up within the country, thus earning the wages of *manufacture* there. . . .
>
> Opportunities should be sought night and day for selling the country's superfluous goods to these foreigners in manufactured form, so far as this is necessary, and for gold and silver; and to this end, *consumption*, so to speak, must be sought in the farthest ends of the earth, and developed in every possible way. . . .
>
> Except for important considerations, no importation should be allowed under any circumstances of commodities of which there is a sufficient supply of suitable quality at home; and in this matter neither sympathy nor compassion should be shown foreigners, by their friends, kinsfolk, *allies*, or enemies. For all friendship ceases, when it involves my own weakness and ruin. And this holds good, even if the domestic commodities are of poorer quality, or even higher priced. For it would be better to pay for an article two dollars which remain in the country

---

[6] It should be noted that the "invisible items" in a nation's international receipts and payments, such as freight earnings, insurance payments, traveler's expenses, diplomatic and military expenditures abroad, and so on, were recognized early, and most of the leading mercantilists urged the necessity of including these in the calculation of a country's favorable balance. The balance that they had in mind was therefore what we today would call the balance of trade and services, or the balance on current account.

than only one which goes out, however strange this may seem to the ill-informed.[7]

MERCANTILISM IN ACTION: CONCRETE POLICIES

Regulation of Trade

Being convinced that in seeking the road to wealth and power, trade could not be left to itself, but must be regulated, the mercantilists applied their conviction with thoroughness. Scarcely any measure that would promote exports or diminish imports, no matter how petty or annoying, was overlooked.

Bullionism   One of the earliest, and certainly the crudest, of mercantilist restrictions consisted in the direct prohibition of exports of gold or silver bullion. Such restrictions go back to the Middle Ages, but became common in the sixteenth century. Spain, the recipient of most of the gold and silver from the Americas, applied these restrictions over the longest period and with the greatest severity; it imposed the death penalty for the export of bullion or coin, established rewards for informers, and prohibited the purchase of bullion by foreigners. Yet so great was the appetite for goods in her growing colonies, and even among her own citizens, and so feeble the ability of her backward economy to produce them, that in the face of the flood of gold and silver, prices of commodities soared. Importing became so profitable and corruption of officials so common that large amounts of specie moved surreptitiously into the hands of foreigners. Spain finally licensed limited exports of gold and silver. In England and Holland, bullionist restrictions virtually came to an end by about the middle of the sixteenth century.

The Monopoly of Trade   Prominent among mercantilist measures were those designed to exclude all foreigners from certain areas of trade. Portugal made the monopoly of trade with the East the backbone of her policy throughout the sixteenth century, even going so far as to capture or destroy the ships of interlopers. The king, moreover, kept the trade in his own hands; private traders could carry on only petty dealings, being limited to what they could transport in their cabins on royal ships.

---

[7] Phillip W. Von Hornick, "Austria over All If She Only Will," reprinted in Arthur Eli Monroe, *Early Economic Thought* (Cambridge, Mass: Harvard University Press, 1927), pp. 223–25.

Spain, too, attempted to monopolize the trade with its colonies, although, unlike Portugal, it did not try to keep all commerce in royal hands. Private traders bought goods in Spain and shipped them to the colonies to an agent, who sold them and shipped back specie or colonial produce. All goods had to be carried, however, in royal ships, and traders' activities were subject to the closest inspection and regulation. To make this control more effective, colonial trade was confined to one port in Spain, Seville, and to a limited number of American ports. For protection against pirates, privateers, or organized attack by other nations, after 1560 all westbound vessels sailed twice annually in great fleets accompanied by warships. When they arrived in the Indies, their shipments were sold at great fairs, the return cargo was loaded aboard, and the fleet sailed back to Spain.

This system worked quite well in the sixteenth century, in spite of considerable smuggling, but broke down in the seventeenth, owing to Spain's increasing economic weakness. Its land eroded by the overgrazing of sheep, its most industrious citizens and most skilled artisans—the Jews and Moors—expelled from the country, its economy ridden by inflation and by heavy taxation to support foreign wars, Spanish industry simply could not produce the goods demanded in its colonial markets. Dutch, English, and French traders, with the connivance of local governors, took over a large share of the trade with Spain's colonies by illegal methods.

Mercantilist ideas never took a firm hold in Holland. That nation's policies as to trade, too, generally favored freedom. The exception was the monopoly of the East India Company (founded in 1602). Its officials established trading posts in Java, Amboina, and other islands of the East Indies, drove out traders of other nationalities, and thereafter successfully bent every effort to keep them out. In addition to making the Indies its private preserve, the Company practiced every other device of monopoly. It limited the production of certain commodities, such as coffee, pepper, nutmeg, cloves, and indigo, to specific areas, destroying crops raised elsewhere; it used its strong bargaining power to hold to a minimum the prices it paid native growers. The artificially scarce but cheap goods were then sold at high prices in the European market. Small wonder that the Company established a dividend record unequaled in history.

Direct Regulation of Trade   Through their trading monopolies, the various nations sought to improve the balance of trade by obtaining needed supplies within an imperial area and by buying cheap—and selling dear—things needed by the rest of the world. This same objective was also pursued by the many detailed regulations applied to exports and imports. All the countries of western Europe, with the sole exception of Holland, used these measures extensively, but they were probably more widespread and more highly developed in England than elsewhere.

Thus British exports that could not meet foreign competition unaided were supported at the very least with refunds ("drawbacks") of taxes, internal or external, previously paid on raw materials. If more help was necessary, a subsidy was not hard to get. A more indirect stimulus to exports was sought in obstacles to the export of raw materials. It was thought that by keeping them at home they would be made abundant and cheap, to the advantage of the exporter of finished products. Export duties were levied on a long list of raw materials and semifabricated articles, but total prohibition of such exports was common. The English woolen textile industry, accounting in 1700 for half the country's exports, was thus favored; we find sheep, wool, woolen yarn, and worsted, as well as fuller's earth (used in cleaning wool) all on the list of prohibited exports. Enforcement of the law was Draconian in its severity; for the first offense the transgressor was to have his left hand cut off; the second offense carried the death penalty.

Measures aimed at imports paralleled those affecting exports. Practically every finished good imported into England paid a heavy duty, in a very large number of cases so high as to be prohibitive. As we might expect, direct prohibition of imports applied to England's most important manufactures, both woolen and silk textiles being so favored. Imports of raw materials, on the other hand, were permitted duty-free entry; some (principally naval stores and indigo from the American colonies) were even given bounties.

Each particular regulation, taken by itself, worked to the advantage of some specific industry. Special interests, therefore, worked unremittingly to maintain and extend the system that protected and favored them, yet in so doing they also worked to further the general interest, as it was understood in the mercantilist economic philosophy.

Here, with a reverse twist, is that coincidence of selfish and public interests that Adam Smith later attributed to the working of laissez faire. He denied it to mercantilism simply because he refused to accept either its principal goal, the increase of the power of the state, or what he regarded as its basic assumption, the supreme importance of the precious metals.

The Navigation System

If the complex system of trade regulation followed logically from the mercantilist balance-of-trade doctrine, so likewise did the laws adopted by various countries to foster a native shipping industry. For as it was early recognized, ocean freights could substantially add to or subtract from a country's balance of international payments. Reinforcing this contribution by a merchant fleet to a nation's economic strength was its equally important contribution to its physical strength. Merchant vessels—and the fisheries, too—reared up a force of seamen to man the navy, while the ships themselves could be converted into privateers or auxiliary men-of-war, or provide an assured means of bringing in needed foreign supplies. Laws affecting navigation, therefore, bulked large in mercantilist economic policy. Nowhere did this aspect of national power receive closer attention or fuller expression than in England, whose insular position from early times aroused keen interest in matters relating to the sea.

Although England took her first steps in the regulation of maritime traffic as early as the late fourteenth century, and imposed increasingly exclusive controls as her colonial system developed, two and a half centuries passed before they were strengthened and consolidated in the famous Navigation Acts of 1651 and 1660. The motive leading to the adoption of these laws was the severe inroads on the British carrying trade made by the Dutch while England was preoccupied with the Civil War of 1642-1646. The purpose and effect of the acts was to reserve, with as few exceptions as possible, the carriage of freight to and from British and colonial ports to British (including colonial) vessels.

The Navigation Acts succeeded in excluding foreign ships from the British coastal trade, from trade between the colonies and Britain, and from carrying imports from Asia, Africa, or the Americas to Britain or her colonies. British ships, moreover, had to be British built and three-quarters British manned. It was felt unwise, however, to prevent foreigners from taking English exports to noncolonial destinations, for this could mean larger exports, a goal at least as important as a monopoly of the shipping trade. Yet if foreign ships were to be allowed to call at English ports, they must be allowed to bring goods in. Hence imports into the British Isles from the continent were permitted, although they had to pay double duties on arrival.

The British reinforced their monopoly of the colonial trade by establishing a list of "enumerated" commodities, comprising the most important colonial products, which the colonies could export only to other British possessions. At first limited to a half dozen commodities, including sugar, tobacco, and cotton, this list was later expanded to a score of goods, and in 1776 to all colonial exports. Although Spain and France also endeavored to enforce a monopoly of trade with their colonies, their policy was less rigorous than the British, and less successful.

The Dutch, as usual, showed a liberality unusual for this period. Except in the cherished East Indies trade, they relied not on monopoly but on competition. They developed the light, easily handled flyboat to replace the clumsy, armed tub in general use, standardized its design, bought construction materials in bulk, and built it by methods resembling the modern assembly line. Besides cheap construction, the need for a small crew and a willingness to hire sailors of any nationality at the lowest possible wage—in contrast to the nationality requirements of their rivals—kept operating costs low and Dutch freight rates at levels one-half to two-thirds those of their competitors. No wonder that in the late seventeenth century perhaps half of Europe's shipping tonnage was Dutch, and that Holland was the shipbuilder to Europe.

The Old Colonial System

In the management of their colonies, the English felt that, since they furnished the people and the capital needed for colonial development, they had a right to guide this development in such a way as to serve their major political objective, the increase of national power. According to mercantilist doctrines, this meant using the colonies as a base of supplies needed by the mother country, as a source of raw materials that could be worked up into manufactures for export, and as a market for the products of English labor.

The means to this end of making colonies serve as the economic complement of the home country were numerous, and we have considered some of them already. Thus the navigation system, in addition to establishing a semimonopoly of the carrying trade for British subjects, also formed an integral part of the colonial system. The principle of enumerated commodities, in particular, guaranteed that England would have her pick of these major products of the colonies and that her merchants would secure the profits to be gained from the reexport of any surplus.

In addition to the close regulation of colonial trade contained in the navigation acts, controls were established over the development of colonial industry. Positive encouragement of colonial production of articles wanted in England for consumption or reexport took the form of bounties or of preferential duties on their import into the British Isles. Negative measures of control aimed at the suppression of colonial manufactures in favor of producers in the mother country; these included the prohibition of colonial exports of woolen products and hats and of colonial processing of iron.

In spite of the burdens to which Britain's colonial subjects had to submit, we must remember that the special privileges possessed by English merchants and shippers were shared equally with colonials. The colonial system most injured the interests of consumers: English consumers, like colonial consumers, were sacrificed to the requirements of mercantilism. Yet as the population and wealth of the colonies increased to the point where local manufacturing industries became significant, their suppression added one more element to the conflict of interests that led to the American Revolution.

The Internal Regulation of Industry

French mercantilism stressed the guidance and control of domestic industry. Policy in this field followed two principal lines: the deliberate encouragement of manufactures and the close regulation of almost every aspect of production.

In the seventeenth century, stimulation of manufactures first took the form of grants of tax exemptions, subsidies, and privileges and of the liberal investment of royal funds—as in the establishment of the raw silk and silk manufacturing industry and in many other luxury industries for which France is still famous.

Under Colbert, Louis XIV's great minister, the policy of fostering industrial development was intensified and expanded. Many businesses were made "royal manufactures" (the Gobelins' tapestry works is the best known), a title that carried with it the assurance of sales to the crown as well as the luster and prestige that went with royal patronage.

Colbert carried even further the second aspect of French industrial policy, the state regulation of industry. Building on existing gild controls, he drew up a comprehensive system of uniform regulations for each type of production, imposed them by decree, and tried—with indifferent success—to enforce them through local inspectors appointed from Paris.

England as well as France tried centralized regulation of industry. In the reign of Elizabeth, a major piece of legislation, the Statute of Artificers (1563), brought together and codified into a national system the workable parts of earlier national laws and local regulations. Its more important purposes were the provision of adequate training for industrial workers, who had suffered from the decay of the gilds and the spread of industry to villages and country districts; the ensurance of an ample supply of agricultural labor; and the establishment of greater security of employment. It met these goals by requiring, in every branch of industry, an apprenticeship of seven years; by prescribing in general terms a uniform training in each craft for all England; by making compulsory the employment in agriculture of all workers not engaged in some specific industry; and by setting up as the minimum hiring period the term of one year. In addition it continued the regulation of wages, established in the mid-fourteenth century to cope with the great shortage of labor resulting from the Black Death.

Labor Under Mercantilism

Trade, colonial, and navigation policies were, as we have stressed, shaped by the mercantilist balance-of-trade theory. So too were the views and policies of mercantilists toward labor, which in an age when capital equipment was limited mainly to comparatively simple tools, was clearly the chief factor of production, especially in manufacturing. Since exports of manufactures ranked high as a means of obtaining the precious metals, it is, therefore, only natural that mercantilists stressed the need for a large and growing population to ensure that mercantilists stressed the need for a large and growing population to ensure an ample supply of labor, or that they advocated measures to stimulate its increase, such as rewards for marriage, bounties for children, and penalties on the unmarried. Indeed, they even went so far as to concede labor "a position of strategic importance."[8] Expressions such as the following were common:

> The people are the riches and strength of the country. (Nicholas Barbon)
> Is not that country richest which has the most labor? (Josiah Tucker)
> That the strength and riches of a society consists in the numbers of the people is an assertion which hath attained the force of a maxim in politics. (Henry Fielding)

If the quantity of labor was important, its skill and industriousness were equally so, for these qualities would enable it to produce more and better exports. Almost without exception, economic writers of the mercantilist period emphasized the need for habits of industry and the acquisition of manufacturing skills.

But what of wages? It would appear that those who hold that "the people are the riches and strength of the country" should also want to see them well paid, comfortable, and satisfied with their lot. Most mercantilists, however, held quite the contrary view. To have a favorable balance of trade, it was necessary to be able to undersell the foreign rival. Labor, being the largest element in cost, therefore must be cheap. Large numbers of workers were needed not only to ensure a large volume of manufactures for export, but also to guarantee low wages, low cost, and strong competitive ability.

We know today that it does not necessarily follow that labor costs will be low only if wages are low. High wages are consistent with low labor costs if the productivity of labor is high. But among mercantilists

---

[8] Edgar S. Furniss, *The Position of the Laborer in a System of Nationalism* (Boston: Houghton Mifflin Company, 1930), p. 31. The quotations immediately following are from p. 22n.

the opinion was widespread that high wages induced not greater industry, but idleness and sloth. Thus, Arthur Young, a widely traveled and intelligent observer of the middle of the eighteenth century, merely expressed the common viewpoint of many other contemporary and earlier writers when he said;

> Every one but an idiot knows that the lower classes must be kept poor or they will never be industrious; I do not mean, that the poor of England are to be kept like the poor of France, but, the state of the country considered, they must (like all mankind) be in poverty or they will not work.[9]

A low opinion of the motives that stimulated the workman to effort thus combined with the balance-of-trade theory (and with the self-interest of the employing classes) to establish the necessity of low wages as a firmly held doctrine. At the same time, it was believed with equal conviction that labor was of vital importance in the national economy. There is no inconsistency in the two ideas, however. An abundance of labor, as a source of exports and thus of treasure, was a necessary condition of national wealth and power. But this labor must be industrious and productive; if poverty is essential to make the laborer work, low wages are just as much a necessary condition as an ample supply of labor.

If a paradox appears to lurk here between "the riches of the nation" and a people in rags and poverty, it could easily be reconciled. Since the worker was regarded as simply a means to the strategic end of national wealth and power, only his toil, not his welfare, was relevant.

SELECTED REFERENCES

HECKSCHER, AUGUST. *Mercantilism*, 2 vols. London: George Allen & Unwin Ltd., 1936. This is the most comprehensive study of mercantilism available, both with respect to theory and practice.

VINER, JACOB. *Studies in the Theory of International Trade*. New York: Harper & Row, Publishers, Inc., 1937. Chapters 1 and 2 provide an excellent discussion of the mercantilist theory of foreign trade as it was expressed in England.

WILSON, C. H. "Trade, Society and the State." Chapter 8 in *The Cambridge Economic History of Europe*, Vol. 4. New York: Cambridge University Press, 1967. A scholarly study of mercantilism in all parts of western Europe, which reappraises its doctrines and purposes.

[9] Arthur Young, *Eastern Tour* (1771), p. 361, cited in ibid., p. 118.

2
CHAPTER

The Transition to Economic Liberalism

Any period of history is transitional, in the sense that it is not static but is undergoing changes that foreshadow what is to come, while at the same time it clings to and only gradually sheds habits and institutions of an earlier age. Thus in the period from 1500 to 1750 mercantilist views were dominant, but were themselves permeated and also in conflict with medieval doctrines and practices. Simultaneously, the theory and practice of mercantilism underwent change, as the social class that spawned it, the merchant–capitalists, became more numerous, more powerful, and more confident. The parallel institution of princely rule was also drastically modified, especially in England, as the national state to whose needs it ministered became more firmly established and secure in its power. And both economic ideas and the principles and practices of government reflected the influence of the spread of the scientific spirit and the changes it wrought in men's outlook on the world.

The Continuity of History

In summary, the Middle Ages did not end in 1500, nor did the age of laissez faire begin with Adam Smith. The one extended its hold far into modern times; the other began as a seedling long before it came to flower. The historian G. M. Trevelyan clearly expresses this continuity of history in the following passage:

> It is indeed useless to look for any date, or even for any period, when the Middle Ages "ended" in England. All that one can say is that, in the Thirteenth Century, English thought and society were mediaeval, and in the Nineteenth Century they were not. Yet even now we retain the

27

mediaeval institutions of the Monarchy, the Peerage, the Commons in Parliament assembled, the English Common Law, the Courts of Justice interpreting the rule of law, the hierarchy of the established Church, the parish system, the Universities, the Public Schools and Grammar Schools. And unless we become a Totalitarian State and forget all our Englishry, there will always be something mediaeval in our ways of thinking, especially in our idea that people and corporations have rights and liberties which the State ought in some degree to respect, in spite of the legal omnicompetence of Parliament. Conservatism and Liberalism, in the broadest sense, are both mediaeval in origin, and so are trade unions. The men who established our civil liberties in the Seventeenth Century, appealed to mediaeval precedents against the "modernizing" monarchy of the Stuarts. The pattern of history is indeed a tangled web. No single diagram will explain its infinite complication.[1]

Just as no powerful social habits have suddenly lost their influence, so none has suddenly sprung into being. The individualistic age that was to follow mercantilism was not the creation of the "classical" economists, but was germinating and slowly taking shape in an environment of state regulation and of restrictions aiming at the maximum favorable balance of trade.

The problem of this chapter is to trace the major strands out of which there grew a new philosophy of government and a new economic viewpoint that were to achieve dominance for a time, and then become modified, qualified, and eventually, perhaps, superseded by still other philosophies of government and economics more suited to the changed society that they both shaped and mirrored.

THE INFLUENCE OF THE RISING CAPITALIST CLASS

The most important single contribution to the decline of the merchantilist system of ideas and regulations and to the rise of economic individualism came from the growth in the numbers, wealth, and influence of the rising class of businessmen. Comparatively few and unimportant as a class in the late fifteenth century, by the eighteenth they were numerous, rich, and powerful. They then dominated the affairs of cities and towns, were heavily represented in Parliament, and carried great weight in councils of state.

[1] G. M. Trevelyan, *English Social History* (London: Longmans, Green & Co., 1942), pp. 95–96.

Challenge and Response

The rise of the businessman was made possible by the rapid expansion to whose increasing opportunities he responded vigorously and successfully. We have seen how the great geographical discoveries opened up a new world of trade, both in the Americas and in the East. To the stimulus of an expanding trading area was added the further stimulus of rising prices, supported by the seepage of the precious metals out of Spain and by occasional large leaks engineered by the daring piracy of men such as Drake, Hawkins, and Frobisher. Trade offered rich rewards, capital accumulation proceeded in almost geometrical progression, and merchants, manufacturers, shippers, and bankers, English and Dutch above all, waxed prosperous and powerful.

As the older industrial organization of the craft gilds proved incapable of meeting the demands of an expanding economy, its place was taken, in industry after industry, by individual enterprise. The domestic system, with the merchant–capitalist in the central guiding role, became common and eventually predominant, not only in the woolen trade, but also in shipbuilding, iron production and manufacture, mining, and in occupation after occupation, until by the eighteenth century, this system, supplemented and sometimes overshadowed here and there by small factories, was typical, and gild organization was an occasional survival of the past.

The substitution of the individual businessman for the corporate gild led to a radical change in the ideals by which men measured their accomplishments. The new aim of getting rich quick replaced the older ideal of a "suitable" income. The medieval notion of the regulation of economic activity according to moral principles gave way to the pursuit of wealth for its own sake.

At first this led, as we have seen, to the excessive emphasis on the precious metals and to the regulation of trade so as to create a favorable balance of trade and an inflow of gold and silver.

Freedom Favors Expansion

Yet at the very time that mercantilist tendencies were strongest, individuals here and there perceived that their desire for gain would best be served by freedom. A free market, it became slowly but increasingly apparent, offered greater scope for individual initiative; and where individual initiative was least hampered, output could be most rapidly increased, costs could be lowered by using new methods and new sources of supply, and gain could be maximized. The desire of particular businessmen for freedom to expand their activities led to pronouncements and appeals in favor of the relaxation of mercantilist restrictions.

This dislike of regulation appeared early. Thus, in 1550, Sir John Masone, expressing himself with respect to a proclamation regulating the price of butter and cheese, said,

> I have seen so many experiences of such ordinances; and ever the end is dearth, and lack of the thing that we seek to make *good cheap*. Nature will have her course, ... and never shall you drive her to consent that a *penny*-worth of new shall be sold for a *farthing*. ... For who will keep a cow that may not sell the milk for so much as the merchant and he can agree upon?[2]

Another illustration, a half century later in date, is furnished by the comment of Sir Walter Raleigh on a bill making compulsory the sowing of a certain proportion of hemp:

> For my part, I do not like this constraining of men to use their grounds at our wills. Rather let every man use his ground to that which is most fit for, and therein use his own discretion.[3]

The slow accretion of such views as these went on steadily, building up, bit by bit, a widening sentiment in favor of freedom. At the same time, the belief that regulation and restriction of industry and of *internal* trade were necessary underwent gradual erosion.

The Decline of State Control

The spreading dislike of regulation was strongly reinforced by experience, especially in England. For state control of industry, in particular the system of monopoly grants, had worked badly. Partly to domesticate industries that had grown up abroad or to develop new industries, partly to obtain revenue, the crown had adopted the system of granting monopolies to individuals or groups in return for a lump payment or a share of the profits. During the late sixteenth and early seventeenth centuries, such English industries as glass, salt, soap, alum mining, pin manufacturing, the production of wire, and the sale of coal came under this system. The results, quite generally, were high prices, poor quality, and inadequate supplies. "Nearly all the monopolists promised to supply a better quality more cheaply. In no single case was this

---

[2] Cited in H. M. Robertson, *Aspects of the Rise of Economic Individualism* (New York: Cambridge University Press, 1933), p. 70.
[3] Ibid.

promise fulfilled."[4] But not only were the monopolies grasping; they were also inefficient and corrupt, frequently being given not to the most promising enterpriser, but to court favorites and their friends.

Public indignation mounted, became vocal, and expressed itself vigorously in meetings, pamphlets, and speeches in Parliament. Finally, with the establishment of that body's supremacy by the Revolution of 1688, the royal right of dispensation was abolished. Thereafter the individual was free to develop any industry to which he might be attracted.

But dislike of regulation did not stop at government-supported monopolies; it extended also to those survivals of the Middle Ages, wage and price regulations. The central agency that supervised and administered these ordinances was the Privy Council, a sort of supercabinet. Their local enforcement was in the hands of the Justices of the Peace. With the abolition of the Privy Council at the time of the Cromwellian Revolution (1642–1646), the whole system of regulation lost its head; its hands and feet continued to function as before for a time, but showed increasing feebleness and lack of coordination. The Justices of the Peace were overburdened with a multitude of duties; where opposition to the wage and price legislation was strong, they tended to permit it to become a dead letter. Its enforcement became more and more sporadic. By the eighteenth century, the system of regulation was in an advanced stage of decay.

Other aspects of state control also declined or disappeared in the latter part of the seventeenth or in the eighteenth century. Thus the regulation of the quality of various kinds of goods, which had been loosely enforced by agents of the crown, was abandoned when Parliament became the dominant institution of government. Even the Elizabethan Statute of Artificers, which regulated the conditions of apprenticeship, became more limited in its application, trade after trade being exempted by Parliament from its scope.

Thus by the end of the seventeenth century there had been a strong growth of sentiment in favor of economic freedom and a great increase in the actual area of freedom. These tendencies were the result of the rise of an important capitalist trading and industrial class, itself the response of the individualist side of human nature to the expanding opportunities that appeared after the great geographical discoveries.

The steady strengthening of the motive for commercial gain caused more than the erosion of official restrictions on individual freedom: It forced the Church to soften its opposition to the taking of interest (usury) as well as its long support of the doctrine of a "fair

---

[4] Herman Levy, *Economic Liberalism* (London: Macmillan Publishers Ltd., 1913), p. 30.

price." After the Reformation, the Protestant church became an active advocate of the doctrine of work, and emphasized the parallel virtue of frugality.[5]

THE BALANCE-OF-TRADE DOCTRINE MEETS THE QUANTITY THEORY OF MONEY

Responding to a rising volume of criticism, mercantilist writers gradually clarified their opinion as to the relative importance of money and other forms of wealth. Although the view that money was all-important continued to be expressed well into the eighteenth century, a broader understanding of the real nature of wealth became steadily more widespread.

What was needed to overcome the heavy stress most mercantilists placed on money was a coherent quantity theory. Although such a theory had been stated in simple terms several times during the seventeenth century, it had not been thoroughly incorporated into current thought; hence its inconsistency with an unqualified balance-of-trade doctrine was not perceived.

A series of writers provided the necessary corrective. John Locke, writing in the 1690s, gave a clear and emphatic statement of the quantity theory, but he failed to connect it with the balance of trade.[6] A contemporary of Locke's, Dudley North, contributed a statement to the effect that the supply of money adjusts itself automatically among nations according to the needs of trade.[7] But since he lacked a grasp of the quantity theory of money, the logical conclusion eluded him.

It was David Hume who, by bringing the quantity theory of money and the balance-of-trade doctrine into direct juxtaposition, effectively undermined the latter:

> Suppose four-fifths of all the money in Great Britain to be annihilated in one night . . . what would be the consequence? Must not the price of all labour and commodities sink in proportion . . . ? What nation could then dispute with us in any foreign market, or pretend to navigate or to sell manufactures at the same price, which to us would afford sufficient profit? In how little time, therefore, must this bring back the money which we had lost and raise us to the level of all the neighboring nations? Where, after we arrived, we immediately lose the advantage of the

[5] See R. H. Tawney, *Religion and the Rise of Capitalism* (New York: Harcourt Brace Jovanovich, Inc., 1926), especially Chapter 4.

[6] John Locke, *Some Considerations, etc.*, in *Works*, Vol. 5, p. 43.

[7] See James W. Angell, *The Theory of International Prices* (Cambridge, Mass.: Harvard University Press, 1926), pp. 16–18.

cheapness of labour and commodities; and the farther flowing in of money is stopped by our fullness and repletion.[8]

Here we have the essentials of what is known as the classical price–specie-flow analysis. Prices in any one country are determined by the quantity of money; prices in different countries are interdependent—a low-price country can undersell a high-price country; such underselling will lead to a flow of specie to the low-price country, raising prices there and lowering them in the other country. Equilibrium is finally reached with some common relationship between national price levels.

INDIVIDUALISM IN POLITICAL THOUGHT

Modern philosophy starts with Descartes, and with good reason. To him, writing at the time (the 1630s and 1640s) when scientific inquiry was replacing reliance on authority as the source of knowledge, the universe appeared ruled by laws discoverable by human reason. Since the use of reason was an individual matter, the independence and importance of the individual as a discoverer and interpreter of the world about him were vastly stimulated.

Locke and Limits on Government

This modern view of the world was accepted by and applied to the problems of politics by John Locke. In the state of nature, governed by its own laws, he assumed that all men were equal. Because of this equality, men were endowed with certain natural rights, which Locke identified—as a citizen of seventeenth-century England—with life, liberty, and the enjoyment of property. But since men, although equal in their rights, are unequal in intelligence, they will interpret natural law differently. The result is chaos and confusion. Government is necessary to ensure order and the peaceful pursuit by each man of his natural rights. Men instituted government by a social contract, endowing it with the power to make laws to secure life, liberty, and property, but no more. Government thus has a distinctly limited function—to permit individuals to live not as they would in a state of nature, but according to the underlying laws of nature.

Revolution against a tyrannical government is implicit in such a concept, for a tyrannical government oversteps the limits of the social

[8] David Hume, *Essay of the Balance of Trade*, cited in Arthur Eli Monroe, *Early Economic Thought* (Cambridge, Mass.: Harvard University Press, 1927), p. 325.

contract. But revolution, if necessary, should be the act of a majority. And to avoid tyranny, government should be democratic—it should reflect the will of the majority.

Thus Locke was the exponent of limited, democratic government, designed to serve the interest of individuals. His political liberalism, applied to the relations of Parliament and King in the English Revolution of 1688 and copied and elaborated by numerous followers, became the intellectual foundation of the British government, of the American Declaration of Independence, and, as interpreted by Rousseau, of the French Revolution.

ADAM SMITH AND THE NEW ECONOMICS

Production for the Market

By the middle of the eighteenth century, the commercial and political revolutions of early modern times had completed their work. In England and Holland, and to a lesser extent in other countries, a simple agricultural society had been transformed into a complex economy with a thriving industry and commerce. Trade, no longer confined mainly to local markets, was conducted on a national and worldwide scale. Instead of wool and wheat, England now exported textiles, wares of iron and pewter, shoes, hats, leather goods, and coal. The domestic system of industry, supplemented here and there by small mills and factories, was now predominantly capitalistic. Labor received its raw materials, its orders, and often its tools from a capitalist employer; it received a money wage, fixed mainly by market forces, for its skill and effort. A developed system of banking, involving the widespread use of bills of exchange and the issue of bank notes, and headed by the Bank of England (established 1694), had come into being to serve the needs of industry and trade.

Above all, the guidance of economic activity was no longer subject to the control of gild, town authority, church, or king. The questions of what to produce, by what methods, and at what price were now decided by the individual enterpriser serving an impersonal and evergrowing market.

Even in agriculture, production for the market had replaced the old communal system of the manor. Transfer of property had become increasingly free, and many small holdings had been bought up and consolidated by the more enterprising peasants. Serfdom had ceased with the reign of Elizabeth, and farming was now carried on by small freeholders and by tenants working the large- and medium-sized farms of the gentry. The numbers of the latter were steadily augmented by the purchase of farms by well-to-do businessmen desirous of acquiring the status of landowners. The enclosure movement, involving the union into a few large properties of the scattered small holdings of the manorial open-field system, had begun with the scarcity of labor after the Black Death (1348–1349). As the English woolen industry became more important, the demand for its raw materials became steadily greater, sheep raising became more profitable than arable farming, and enclosures increased rapidly under the Tudors. Yet the amount of land enclosed by the end of the seventeenth century was probably only a small proportion of the total.[9] The disappearance of the old open-field system awaited the tremendous burst of enclosures in the latter half of the eighteenth century.

The modern state, no longer new and untried, but secure and well established, had less need to shape every policy with an eye to the increase of its power. It could tolerate greater freedom of the individual to pursue his own interests. Moreover, in Holland the machinery of government had been taken over by the commercial classes, while in England they shared its control with landed proprietors. Mercantilist restrictions on internal trade and industry, together with those medieval survivals that mercantilism supported, disappeared with the declining interest of government in their retention and the rising interest of traders and manufacturers in their abolition.

Adam Smith and the "Invisible Hand"

Although the spirit of individualism was already dominant in the mid-eighteenth century and had received its political expression in the writings of Locke, it still awaited formulation as a rounded economic philosophy. This was the great task that Adam Smith was to perform. What Locke had done for government, Smith did for economics. Taking the prevalent view of the universe as ruled by natural law, and of individual enterprise as the most efficient means of getting goods produced, he constructed a thoroughgoing individualist economic system. The central core of his ideas may be summarized in the following propositions:

Each man is best fitted to be the judge of his own actions.

Individual interests are not in conflict, but are subject to a natural harmony.

Therefore, the selfish actions of individuals lead to the welfare of all, and the continuous regulation of government is unnecessary. The

---

[9] On the enclosure movement, see W. H. R. Curtler, *A Short History of English Agriculture* (Oxford: Clarendon Press, 1909), especially Chapters 7, 9, and 11.

best results can be obtained if the state follows a policy of let-alone, of laissez faire.

But let Adam Smith speak for himself:

> As every individual endeavors as much as he can both to employ his capital in the support of domestic industry, and so to direct that industry that its produce may be of the greatest value; every individual necessarily labours to render the annual revenue of the society as great as he can. He generally, indeed, neither intends to promote the public interest, nor knows how much he is promoting it. By preferring the support of domestic to that of foreign industry, he intends only his own gain, and he is in this, as in many other cases, led by an invisible hand to promote an end which was no part of his intention. Nor is it always the worse for the society that it was no part of it. By pursuing his own interest he frequently promotes that of the society more effectually than when he really intends to promote it.[10]

From this reasoning comes a major conclusion. The "Wealth of Nations" is best served not by minute regulation—of which there were many survivals, especially in the field of foreign trade—but by the greatest possible freedom of enterprise. The businessman's yearning for economic freedom is now entirely justified. Full release of his energies is the right prescription for a prosperous society.

No wonder that Adam Smith's philosophy of laissez faire received wide acceptance, becoming the ruling economic doctrine of the nineteenth century. For it told the rising commercial and industrial classes, who were soon to achieve political dominance, to do what they wanted to do.

Protection Survives

Adam Smith did not confine his recommendation of freedom to internal economic affairs; he also vigorously advocated a policy of free trade. But his prescription had little in the way of immediate, practical results. Beneficiaries of protection were loath to give it up, even though they did not need it, and even though they agreed with his basic philosophy. Moreover, the most significant restrictions on foreign trade, the very core and center of English protectionism, were the duties on grain, or, as they were generally known, the Corn Laws. The landowning classes, whose interests these served, were still the numerically dominant group in Parliament.

Not until the Reform Act of 1832, which gave wider representation to the urban middle class, was a frontal assault on the Corn Laws

---

[10] Adam Smith, *The Wealth of Nations*, Modern Library Edition, p. 400.

politically possible. And not until the interests of merchants and manufacturers in free trade were more clearly apparent than in 1776, when
Adam Smith wrote, could a powerful body of opinion be marshaled
behind a free trade movement. The growth of this opinion had to await
the impact of the Industrial Revolution.

THE INDUSTRIAL REVOLUTION: TECHNICAL ASPECTS

Although individualism was the dominating philosophy in politics, economics, and religion by the time Adam Smith wrote *The Wealth of
Nations,* the full consequences of the unleashing of the individual's energies were not brought out until the Industrial Revolution had transformed England from an economy of household industry, based on
skilled labor adept in the use of tools, to an economy of factories and
mills, based on machines and steam power.

Inventions: A Chain Effect

On the technical side, the Industrial Revolution was a series of interrelated inventions, each meeting some immediate and pressing industrial need, but upsetting the balance of industry so that additional inventions became an urgent necessity. Consider, for example, the
sequence of development in the cotton textile industry. The production
of cotton fabrics (actually fustians, a cloth half linen and half cotton)
had first been established in England about 1600 on the same household
basis as its older rival, the woolen industry. For a century, its growth
was very gradual until, in the opening years of the eighteenth century,
the importation of cotton prints, and even their wear, was prohibited.
These colorful prints, a product of Indian hand looms, had become so
popular that they aroused the strenuous opposition of the woolen and
silk industries. English-made fustians, however, met no such obstacles;
with the elimination of the competition of pure cotton fabrics, for which
they were a fairly satisfactory substitute, their production expanded
swiftly.

      The first of the textile inventions was a simple improvement in
the old loom designed to remedy a defect that hampered the expansion
of production. Hitherto, the width of the fabric that could be made by
a single workman had been limited by the length of his arms, for he
had to throw the shuttle containing the cross thread, or weft, from one
hand to the other. For wider fabrics, two or more men had to be employed. In 1733, John Kay, a weaver with mechanical talent, developed

the flying shuttle, fitted with wheels and propelled mechanically with sufficient force so that a much wider stretch of warp threads could be traversed.

Because the flying shuttle permitted a considerable expansion in the output of the weaving branch of the textile industry, it upset its balance. The spinning process had always required five or six men to supply one weaver with thread. Now the spinners found it impossible to keep up with the demand. The need for improvement in this stage of the industry became acute. The Society for the Encouragement of Arts and Manufacturers offered a prize for a suitable invention,[11] and many men worked intensely on the problem.

Finally, between 1769 and 1779, three inventions revolutionized spinning—Hargreaves' spinning jenny, Arkwright's water frame, and Crompton's mule. The jenny made possible the spinning by one operator of several threads of fine quality, but too weak to replace linen in the warp. Arkwright's water frame furnished a coarser but stronger thread, which could be spun by power-driven machinery and which permitted for the first time the manufacture in England of pure cotton goods.[12] The mule combined the principles of the jenny and the water frame and made a thread that was both fine and strong. It soon came to be fitted with three to four hundred spindles, so that a single machine did the work of that many individual spinners, each working with a single spinning wheel. Fortunately, at about the time that these advances in spinning made it possible to work up much larger quantities of the raw material, an American, Eli Whitney, developed his cotton gin (1793). By permitting the easy extraction of the rough seeds from the boll, his invention enabled the processing of enough cotton to keep up with rapidly expanding demand.

The new spinning machines gave a great impetus to factory production, since they could be operated most economically by water (later steam) power, and thus had to be brought together in large numbers where the power was available. Arkwright, whose claims as an inventor are at least dubious, was above all else a man of great business ability. He succeeded in raising capital, training workmen, and building and setting into operation a large number of factories, employing from 150 to 600 hands. His fame thus has a legitimate basis mainly in the fact that he was the first of the new class of industrial capitalists who, seizing upon the inventions of others, were to transform Britain's cottage industry in the next hundred years. Even in the cotton

[11] Paul Mantoux, *The Industrial Revolution in the Eighteenth Century* (New York: Harcourt Brace Jovanovich, Inc., 1927), p. 220. This book contains one of the best accounts available of the role played by inventions in the Industrial Revolution. We are much indebted to it.

[12] It was Arkwright's defense of his industry before Parliament that resulted in freeing it from the prohibition against cotton manufacturers.

textile industry, his example was soon followed by many others, while similar men-of-business made over the iron and steel trades.

By 1790, when the inventions in spinning were widely used, the different parts of the textile industry were again badly out of balance. Whereas thirty years earlier, thread had been scarce, now there were not enough weavers to work up all the thread streaming out of the spinning mills. A chance discussion set a country parson named Cartwright to proving that a power loom was not, as the company present had alleged, an impossibility. After several years of effort, he proved his point in 1795; but it took years more for his invention to make its way in industry, owing mainly to the violent opposition it met from handloom weavers. Not until about 1810 was the power loom widely used; but within a few years more, it was universal in the cotton industry.

In the manufacture of wool, the spinning inventions took hold rapidly, especially in Yorkshire, where wages rose from the competition of the neighboring Lancashire cotton districts and where abundant water power was to be found. The power loom, partly because of strenuous opposition to its introduction, partly because it was less adapted to weaving woolen fabrics, made much slower progress. In 1803, according to Mantoux, only one-sixteenth of the cloth production of the main Yorkshire woolen district was factory-made. Large numbers of handlooms continued to be operated until late in the nineteenth century.

As in the textile industries, a succession of inventions upset the balance of the iron industry, each leading to further development. Thus the opening years of the eighteenth century found the English iron industry quite incapable of meeting the demands of the Midland iron workers for pig iron; the industry was even on the point of disappearing. Ever since prehistoric man discovered how to extract the metal from its ore, iron manufacture had been dependent on charcoal for smelting. By 1720, almost all wooded areas near enough to iron mines to permit economic production had been destroyed. In that year, only sixty blast furnaces, producing only 17,000 tons of pig iron annually, were in operation in England.[13] The country was becoming increasingly dependent on imports of pig iron from Sweden, Germany, Spain, and the American colonies. Coal was abundant and was widely used as a fuel in many countries, but it could not be combined with iron ore to smelt pig iron because its sulfur content made the product too brittle for use. A method of making coal into a serviceable smelting agent had to be devised and was actively sought throughout the seventeenth century. Finally, about 1709, an English ironmaster named Abraham Darby succeeded in making a coke that could be used in the smelting process.

[13] Mantoux, op. cit., p. 278.

Apparently, in spite of its great utility, the manufacture of pig iron with coke did not become common until some seventy years had passed. By that time, the supply of pig iron outstripped the ability of refiners to make it into malleable iron, the type necessary in the many uses requiring a low carbon content. Research became actively stimulated, and in 1784 the process of "puddling," or heating and stirring molten pig iron mixed with iron mixed with iron oxide to burn out the carbon left by the coke, was invented by a contractor named Cort, together with a rolling mill that eliminated the tedious labor of hammering the refined metal.

Along with these basic discoveries, there were many auxiliary ones, such as the development of air pumps to deliver an adequate blast in the blast furnace, the invention of the steam hammer, and of metal-turning lathes. They made possible a rapid expansion in the output of iron and a lowering of its cost, as well as greater precision in machine manufacture. The use of machines made of iron grew rapidly; the iron industry itself furnished an increasing number of applications of the new technique, while the superior strength, accuracy, and durability of machinery made of this material led, after a beginning was made in 1785, to the rapid replacement of the early wooden spinning mules and water frames.

The Advent of the Steam Engine

The invention that removed all limitations to the spread of machinery, and which, combined with the chemical discoveries of coking and puddling, laid the foundations of England's industrial greatness, was the steam engine. At about the beginning of the eighteenth century, two primitive steam engines had been developed in England, and these became quite widely used. Owing to mechanical defects, however, and to the lack of any means of transmitting power from the engine to a driving wheel, their use was limited mainly to pumping water.

The problems of designing an engine of sufficient power and accuracy and of translating the straight thrust of a piston into rotary motion were solved by James Watt. His person united scientific training, intelligence, and a rare intellectual curiosity. A maker of scientific instruments at the University of Glasgow, a student, and the friend of distinguished scientists, he devoted years of study and patient research to making the inefficient Newcomen engine an effective source of motive power. Success came in 1769 when he registered his first patent. A great gap, however, separates an invention from its effective application to industry. In Watt's case this gap was overcome by a fortunate partnership with Boulton, a Birmingham manufacturer of small metal wares. His financial aid brought the new engine past the test stage, his business connections established its first market, and his exceptionally well-equipped and well-managed shops furnished the accuracy of construction required for a satisfactory engine. After initial difficulties, the partnership throve, and the firm of Boulton and Watt became the producer of steam engines for all of Britian. By 1800, when their patents expired, steam power was really beginning to displace water power.

> With this new great event, the invention of the steam engine, the final and most decisive stage of the industrial revolution opened. By liberating it from its last shackles, steam enabled the immense and rapid development of large-scale industry to take place. For the use of steam was not, like that of water, dependent on geographical position and local resources. Wherever coal could be bought at a reasonable price a steam engine could be erected. England had plenty of coal, and by the end of the eighteenth century it was already applied to many different uses, while a network of waterways, made on purpose, enabled it to be carried everywhere very cheaply: the whole country became a privileged land, suitable above all others for the growth of industry. Factories were now no longer bound to the valleys, where they had grown up in solitude by the side of rapid-flowing streams. It became possible to bring them nearer the markets where their raw materials were bought and their finished products sold, and nearer the centres of population where their labour was recruited. They sprang up near one another, and thus, huddled together, gave rise to those huge black industrial cities which the steam engine surrounded with a perpetual cloud of smoke.[14]

THE INDUSTRIAL REVOLUTION: SOCIAL AND ECONOMIC ASPECTS

The mechanical inventions in the textile and iron industries, the chemical discoveries in the use of coal and the manufacture of iron, set in motion a technological revolution, a revolution that was to alter completely the physical bases of industry. From its dependence for thousands of years upon wood as a material and as a fuel, upon water, animals, and men for power, and upon human dexterity and skill for the scope of its processes, it now became liberated. Coal, iron, and machinery replaced these less reliable, less accurate resources and opened up a century of industrial growth and process that made earlier periods of expansion look stagnant.

The Factory System

If the Industrial Revolution had had no other effects than these, it would have earned its title. But it was at least as revolutionary in the

[14] Ibid., pp. 344–45.

social and economic sphere as in the purely technical. The new industrial machinery and methods could be used effectively only in establishments where large numbers of machines could be assembled, both because of the close relationship of the various processes of manufacture and because of the large volume of power made available by a single steam engine. This meant, of course, the grouping together under a single roof of hundreds of workmen and the development of a system of factory discipline that tolerated little deviation from a standard norm, whether in the matter of hours, of shop practice, or of quality of performance. Paradoxically, the industrial changes that gave the freest rein to the individual, provided he belonged to the managing and directing class, imposed an iron conformity of behavior on the great mass of the workers.

The new working environment came gradually, since the factory system supplanted the old cottage industry only in the course of decades. But by 1830, the cotton textile industry had become thoroughly mechanized, the production of iron was a relatively large-scale operation, and even in iron manufacturing, the small shop of the skilled craftsman was fast disappearing. Not until after the middle of the century, as we have noted, were the handloom weavers of woolen fabrics finally vanquished.

What is important is not the time required for the spread of the factory system, but its inevitability. With minor exceptions, the progress of the steam engine, the machine, and the new factory discipline was remorseless. Within the span of a century, most men who earned their living by making things ceased to work in their own homes, at hours they themselves set, and often with their own tools, but instead entered the factory gates at a set hour, took their places before expensive machines in which they had no share of the ownership, and worked for a period, in a manner, and at a speed determined by the iron constitution of an inhuman engine. Machine and steam power spawned a new class, the industrial proletariat, with a new way of life, and in so doing gave a tremendous impetus to the growth of cities.[15]

[15] If we put the figure for the population of a town at 2000, in 1801 there were in England and Wales 283 towns containing approximately 31 percent of the total population. By 1841 these towns contained 46 percent of the people. This later figure may exaggerate the situation somewhat, but it is probably not excessive. G. P. Jones and A. G. Pool, *A Hundred Years of Economic Development in Great Britain* (London: Gerald Duckworth & Co. Ltd., 1940), p. 19.

For the United States, comparable figures are available for the period 1820–1940. In 1820, 82 percent of the country's labor force was engaged in agriculture, only 18 percent in nonagricultural pursuits. In 1940 the figures were exactly reversed—18 percent of the labor force was employed in agriculture, 82 percent in nonagricultural pursuits. (The latter include, besides industry, also transportation, trade, government, the professions, and so on, all of which have expanded with the expansion of industry.)

Industrial Leadership

Urbanization and the growth of an urban industrial proletariat were two of the social consequences of the Industrial Revolution. Still another was a tremendous increase in the importance of capital and the capitalist. We have seen that even the earlier cottage or domestic system of industry was dominated by the capitalist, who organized and directed the various processes of manufacture. He was, however, essentially still a merchant, and was generally so called, even though he might direct extensive manufacturing operations. With the replacement of tools by machines, and of hand or water power by the steam engine, thousands of pounds or dollars had to be invested in plant and equipment where hundreds or tens had formerly sufficed. The men who raised these vaster sums and who directed their use were a very different type from the earlier merchants.[16] Besides a knowledge of markets, they had to know a good deal about the technology of industry, they had to possess organizing ability, and, if they were to succeed, they had to have, or to understand how to raise, large amounts of capital. Men like Arkwright, the cotton manufacturer, and the ironmasters Boulton and Wilkinson were typical of the new "captains of industry," who became the innovators, the entrepreneurs, of the new age of iron and coal.

What made the innovating activity of this class of industrial capitalists possible was an inheritance of the previous century—the "liberal" view of society that had arisen out of the constant pressure of business interests seeking to take advantage of expanding opportunities, and out of the stimulus to individual freedom of thought and action furnished by the rise of scientific thought and the parallel decline in the hold of religion and authority. Without the favorable climate of opinion known today as political and economic liberalism (formulated in the writings of Locke, Hume, Adam Smith, and Jeremy Bentham), the freedom necessary for introducing the radical changes in industry required by the mechanical inventions would have been lacking. Bound by old rules of handicraft manufacture, industry would have continued along lines laid down in the Middle Ages. Evasion of these rules had made possible the rise of the domestic system; their continued evasion, and the repeal of the restrictions introduced during the mercantilist period, was essential to the rise of the new industry.

---

[16] At first, the capital income came from accumulations already made in trade or industry, frequently pooled in partnerships containing from two to several partners. As the profits of the new enterprises mounted, large sums were ploughed back into the expansion of old or the erection of new plants. It was not until after the middle of the nineteenth century that the corporate form of organization, with its limited liability and its power of attracting many small streams of savings, became at all common in England.

The Combination Act

So far had the philosophy of individualism gone by the end of the eighteenth century that intervention by the state was largely discredited, and laissez faire was widely accepted as the foundation of economic relations. In the Combination Act of 1799, all combinations of workmen to improve their condition of labor were outlawed. Henceforth, it was assumed, individual pursuit of individual interest would ensure economic justice to all. Forbidden to unite their strength to offset the greater bargaining power of the employer, workers tried to obtain remedy for low wages, long hours, and wretched working conditions by appealing for enforcement of such old laws as the Elizabethan Statute of Artificers. But though many such laws remained on the books of Parliament or were technically in force in various towns and trades, the spirit that had created them was dead. Besides, fixed numbers of apprentices and regulation of methods of production were inconsistent with the needs of a rapidly changing industry and with the interests of its owners and directors. The old laws were suspended, then repealed.[17] The "simple system of natural liberty" had prevailed. The character of industry and the status of labor were to be determined in a free market by free competition. Government was to combat ignorance by providing instruction, to stimulate progress by encouraging science and invention, and to protect the unsuspecting against fraud. With government thus limited, all restraints on the spread of the factory system vanished.

Conclusion

In closing, it is important to stress the fact that the Industrial Revolution was, initially at least, a British affair and that the changes that took place in industry and in society were limited to that country until well into the nineteenth century. Yet the ground had been laid for the transformation of the Western world into a true international economy as the new industrial techniques spread abroad. Especially important in this respect were the revolution in transport that came with the application of the steam engine to land and ocean transport, and the innovations in banking that were still to come. We shall consider these developments later (see Chapter 15).

---

[17] The Statute of Artificers was repealed in 1809, thus finally doing away with national regulation of apprenticeships and of wages.

SELECTED REFERENCES

HALÉVY, ELIE. *The Growth of Philosophic Radicalism.* London: Faber & Faber Ltd., 1928. Chapter 3, Section 1, has a good discussion of the views of Adam Smith, especially his principle of the natural identity of interests.

MANTOUX, PAUL. *The Industrial Revolution in the Eighteenth Century.* New York: Harcourt Brace Jovanovich, Inc., 1927. One of the outstanding studies of the Industrial Revolution.

POLANYI, KARL. *The Great Transformation.* New York: Holt, Rinehart and Winston, 1944. A provocative study of the development of the market economy in the eighteenth and nineteenth centuries, and of its subsequent decline.

SMITH, ADAM. *The Wealth of Nations.* Chapters 1–3, on the division of labor, and its relation to the extent of the market, are well worth reading.

3
CHAPTER

The Classical Doctrine of Comparative Cost

State regulation of internal industry and trade within England had, as we have seen, a limited scope and a relatively short life. After the Cromwellian Revolution, it expired. By the end of the eighteenth century, businessmen possessed almost unlimited freedom in the choice of their field of activity and the manner in which they carried it out; the philosophy of individualism permeated the intellectual classes and was beginning to influence both statesmen and leaders of industry.

From this time on, the controls of mercantilism affected chiefly the country's external trade by means of tariffs, bounties, prohibitions, and the colonial and navigation systems. Although a beginning had been made, in the Eden Treaty of 1786 with France, toward the relaxation of restrictions on foreign trade, commercial and industrial opinion was divided on this topic; during the long interval, from 1793 to 1815, of wars with France, further progress in this direction was impossible.

Yet during these war years expansion and mechanization of England's newer industries, cotton, iron and steel, coal, and engineering, continued rapidly, and new machine processes began to take hold in the old woolen textile industry. On the continent of Europe, the war retarded development in these lines. With the end of the military conflict, therefore, Britain's leading industries held an unchallengeable position. No one anywhere was in a position to offer them effective competition. On the other hand, the termination of the war brought with it a collapse of markets. Steel was no longer needed for muskets and cannon, the demand for soldiers' uniforms and blankets vanished, and prostrate Europe was in no position to buy large quantities of English goods. Concern for markets, therefore, caused a strengthening of sentiment in favor of freer trade among merchants and manufacturers, a

46

change in opinion that was to have important consequences, as we shall see.

ADAM SMITH

At the same time that economic developments were preparing the ground for an attack on mercantilist foreign trade policies, the intellectual weapons necessary for this attack were being sharpened and improved. Adam Smith stressed the absurdities of mercantilist restrictions and had laid the groundwork for the free trade argument when he showed that trade between nations enables each to increase its wealth—in the sense of real income—by taking advantage of the principle upon which all increase of wealth rests, the division of labor.

> It is the maxim of every prudent master of a family, never to attempt to make at home what it will cost him more to make than to buy. The taylor does not attempt to make his own shoes, but buys them of the shoemaker. The shoemaker does not attempt to make his own clothes, but employs a taylor. The farmer attempts to make neither the one nor the other, but employs those different artificers. All of them find it for their interest to employ their whole industry in a way in which they have some advantage over their neighbours, and to purchase with a part of its produce, or what is the same thing, with the price of a part of it, whatever else they have occasion for.

> What is prudence in the conduct of every private family, can scarce be folly in that of a great kingdom. If a foreign country can supply us with a commodity cheaper than we ourselves can make it, better buy it of them with some part of the produce of our own industry, employed in a way in which we have some advantage. . . .

> The natural advantages which one country has over another in producing particular commodities are sometimes so great, that it is acknowledged by the world to be in vain to struggle with them. By means of glasses, hotbeds, and hotwalls, very good grapes can be raised in Scotland, and very good wine too can be made of them at about thirty times the expense for which at least equally good can be bought from foreign countries. Would it be a reasonable law to prohibit the importation of all foreign wines, merely to encourage the making of claret and burgundy in Scotland? But if there would be a manifest absurdity in turning towards any employment, thirty times more of the capital and industry of the country, than would be necessary to purchase from foreign countries an equal quantity of the commodities wanted, there must be an absurdity, though not altogether so glaring, yet exactly of the same kind, in turning towards any such employment a thirtieth, or even a

three hundredth part more of either. Whether the advantages which one country has over another, be natural or acquired, is in this respect of no consequence. As long as the one country has those advantages, and the other wants them, it will always be more advantageous for the latter, rather to buy of the former than to make. It is an acquired advantage only, which one artificer has over his neighbor, who exercises another trade; and yet they both find it more advantageous to buy of one another, than to make what does not belong to their particular trades.[1]

Absolute Advantage Assumed

This statement, vigorous and clear though it was, lacked something in sharpness. Excellent as far as it went, it did not go far enough. It assumed without argument that international trade required a producer of exports to have an *absolute* advantage; that is, an exporting industry must be able to produce, with a given amount of capital and labor, a larger output than any rival.

But what if a country had *no* line of production in which it were clearly superior? Suppose a relatively backward country whose "capital and industry" in the broadest sense (compared with its more advanced neighbors) were inefficient, capable of producing less in all lines of activity—a not too hypothetical case. Would it be forced to insulate itself against more efficient outside competition or see all its industry and agriculture subjected to ruinous competition? Adam Smith's analysis was incapable of dealing with this kind of situation, and it was not until David Ricardo undertook a more precise formulation of the theory of international trade (*Principles of Political Economy*, 1817) that a *general* theory of the subject became available.

DAVID RICARDO

Throughout the nineteenth century, two men stood out in the field of international trade theory above all the rest: David Ricardo and John Stuart Mill. Many other writers, it is true, made noteworthy contributions to the subject, but these were only in the form of qualifications and elaborations. Both Mill and Ricardo were primarily concerned with and did most to advance the understanding of that aspect of our subject hitherto largely ignored: the causes governing the movements and exchange ratios of internationally traded goods. Because of the

---

[1] Adam Smith, *The Wealth of Nations*, Modern Library Edition, pp. 424–26.

mercantilists' emphasis on gold and silver as the type of wealth most useful to the state, attention had long been focused on the monetary factors involved in international transactions. When, with Adam Smith, the individual replaced the nation as the arbiter of economic activity, goods useful in satisfying human wants naturally assumed the position of central importance. This shift in emphasis was responsible for the greater concern shown thereafter for the goods side of international economic relationships.

Labor Cost

The logical point of departure for considering Ricardo's explanation of international trade is his labor theory of value. According to this, the value of any commodity is determined by its labor cost: "The value of a commodity . . . depends on the relative quantity of labour which is necessary for its production."[2] In the internal trade of a country, this principle of relative labor cost determines value in exchange. Thus if it takes 10 days of labor to produce a pair of shoes, and 5 days to produce a hat, one pair of shoes will command two hats.

It should be noted that Ricardo made no effort to prove the validity of his labor theory of value. This is because in effect he assumed it by giving to labor alone any importance in determining the value of a commodity. Ricardo was, of course, well aware of the need for capital and land in production. But he assumed either that capital was of little importance, or that it was combined with labor in proportions that were the same for all goods. Moreover, according to Ricardo, labor was a homogeneous factor. While granting that skilled labor contributed more than common labor to the value of a commodity, he regarded the various kinds of skilled labor as fixed multiples of common labor. As for land, in Ricardo's system it plays no direct role in the determination of value.

Comparative Cost

Although in the internal trade of a nation the value of commodities is determined by their labor cost, matters are different when it comes to trade between nations.

> The same rule which regulates the relative value of commodities in one country does not regulate the relative value of the commodities exchanged between two or more countries. . . . The quantity of wine which [Portugal] shall give in exchange for the cloth of England is not deter-

[2] David Ricardo, *Principles of Political Economy*, Everyman's Edition, p. 9.

mined by the respective quantities of labour devoted to the production of each, as it would be if both commodities were manufactured in England, or both in Portugal.[3]

What, then, does determine values in international exchange? According to Ricardo, it is the *relative* or *comparative* labor cost of commodities in the two countries, instead of the *absolute* labor cost or amount of labor required for their production. Here is an example, similar to but simpler than the one Ricardo used, that illustrates the point:

| | Labor Costs of Producing (days): | |
Country	Wine (one cask)	Cloth (one bolt)
Portugal	3	4
England	6	5

Costs of producing both commodities are lower in Portugal. In spite of this, it will pay Portugal to specialize in the production of wine and to exchange it for cloth made in England. By so doing, at an exchange ratio of 1 unit of wine for 1 unit of cloth, as assumed by Ricardo, Portugal would procure for an outlay of three days of labor a bolt of cloth, which would cost her four days to produce at home. England would also gain from the exchange, for by concentrating on the production of cloth and exchanging it for wine, she could get for a cost of five days' labor a cask of wine, which in the absence of trade would cost her six days' labor.

Factor Immobility and Comparative Cost

Why should there be such a remarkable difference in the principles regulating exchange within and between countries? The explanation is simple.

> The difference in this respect, between a single country and many, is easily accounted for, by considering the difficulty with which capital moves from one country to another, to seek a more profitable employment, and the activity with which it invariably passes from one province to another in the same country.

[3] Ibid., pp. 81–82.

It would undoubtedly be advantageous to the capitalists of England, and to the consumers in both countries, that under such circumstances the wine and the cloth should both be made in Portugal and therefore that the capital and labour of England employed in making cloth should be removed to Portugal for that purpose. . . .

Experience, however, shows that the fancied or real insecurity of capital, when not under the immediate control of its owner, together with the natural disinclination which every man has to quit the country of his birth and connections, and intrust himself, with all his habits fixed, to a strange government and new laws, check the migration of capital. These feelings, which I should be sorry to see weakened, induce most men of property to be satisfied with a low rate of profits in their own country, rather than seek a more advantageous employment for their wealth in foreign nations.[4]

In more modern terms, it is the immobility of labor, capital, and enterprise that tends to keep them at home, and thus to prevent production from taking place where labor costs are absolutely lowest.[5] The localization of production as between different countries follows the principle of comparative costs: Each country will tend to specialize in the production of those goods for which its (labor) costs are comparatively lowest.

Basically, this is simply an extension of the principle of the division of labor. In general terms, applicable to both nations and individuals, competence should specialize where competence counts most, and incompetence where incompetence counts least. As Ricardo expressed the matter in an illustration:

Two men can both make shoes and hats, and one is superior to the other in both employments, but in making hats he can only exceed his competitor by one-fifth or 20 per cent, and in making shoes he can excell him by one-third or 33 per cent—will it not be for the interest of both that the superior man should employ himself exclusively in making shoes, and the inferior man in making hats?[6]

It is clear that the doctrine of comparative cost makes a real advance over Adam Smith's position. A nation may be at an absolute disadvantage in all lines of production, yet be able to participate in

---

[4] Ibid., p. 83.

[5] It is, of course, true that only natural resources such as fertile land and mineral deposits are completely immobile. Although labor and capital can and do move internationally, their mobility (except in recent times for short-term capital) is far from perfect. As we shall soon see, factor immobility need only be sufficient to cause an appreciable difference in its price in order for it to be significant.

[6] Ricardo, op. cit., p. 83.

gainful trade. It can do so provided only that its costs are comparatively lower for some type of production. It need have only a comparatively smaller disadvantage, not an absolute advantage. Similarly, of course, a nation having an absolute advantage in every product can gain from trade if it has a greater comparative advantage in some products.

Having attained his goal of providing a convincing proof that relative differences in supply or cost conditions establish the basis for gainful trade, Ricardo carried the analysis no further. He left undetermined the question of the division of the gains, simply assuming, in his famous illustration, that Portugal and England would share the gains in the proportions determined by the exchange of 1 unit of wine for 1 unit of cloth. The answer to this question awaited the attention of Ricardo's illustrious successor, John Stuart Mill.

JOHN STUART MILL

After restating Ricardo's doctrine of comparative cost in a clearer fashion, Mill continued the analysis with an illustration that focused attention on the unsolved question of the terms of trade, which required consideration not only of the supply side of the problem, but also demand. Instead of taking as given the output of each commodity in two countries, with the labor costs different, he assumed a given amount of labor in each country, but different outputs per unit of labor. Thus his formulation ran in terms of comparative advantage, or comparative effectiveness of labor, which is the inverse of Ricardo's comparative labor cost.

Instead of converting Ricardo's illustration into a comparative advantage rather than a comparative cost form, let us construct a new one, with numbers more suited to our purpose. We assume two countries, called simply I and II, and two goods, food and clothing, with production subject to the following conditions:

Input of Labor	Country	Output of:	
		Food	Clothing
1 man-year	I	20	20
1 man-year	II	4	16

Country I has an absolute advantage in the production of both goods, but a clear comparative advantage in food: 5 to 1 as compared to 5 to 4 in clothing. Country II's least comparative disadvantage is in clothing.

In the absence of trade, food will exchange for clothing in country I at domestic terms of trade of 1*F* for 1*C*, since the unit labor cost of these goods is the same. In country II, 1*F* will exchange for 4*C*, again because the labor cost of these quantities of the two goods is identical.

Possible Terms of (International) Trade

Given these domestic terms of trade, it is clear that the opening of trade between the two countries will benefit country I if for 1 unit of food it can obtain any *more than* 1 unit of clothing, while country II will gain if it can obtain 1 unit of food for anything *less than* 4 units of clothing. That is, *the limits to the possible barter terms of trade* (the international exchange ratio) *are set by the domestic exchange ratios established by the relative efficiency of labor in each country*. The range of possible barter terms can therefore be shown as follows:

Units of Food	Units of Clothing	
1	1	(Domestic exchange ratio in I)
1	1.3	Possible international exchange ratios
1	2	
1	4	(Domestic exchange ratio in II)

Within this range of commodity price ratios or barter terms, any single one may rule. The question Mill sought to answer was: What factors determine the *actual terms* at which the commodities will trade?

Reciprocal Demand

Stated briefly, Mill's answer was that the actual ratio at which goods are traded will depend on the strength and elasticity of each country's demand for the other country's product, or upon *reciprocal demand*. Here it is important to note that demand is *not* expressed in the manner to which you are accustomed, as an offer of money for goods, but in barter terms, as an offer of quantities of an export good for quantities of an import good. When each country's demand is brought into contact with the other's in the market, we have reciprocal demand—a pair of interacting demands.

How the international demands of two countries interact to establish equilibrium in their trade can be shown by a simple illustration.

Since our country I will gain from trade at terms better than even, its traders might stand ready to offer, at such slightly better terms as $1F$ for $1.1C$ (or, to avoid decimals, $10F$ for $11C$), as much as $10,000F$ for $11,000C$. Such terms would be relatively far more advantageous for country II, however, since they would enable it to obtain 1 unit of food for far less than 4 units of clothing, its home trade ratio. Perhaps it would offer as much as $110,000C$ for $100,000F$ at such an advantageous "real price." Perceiving the huge excess in the clothing demand for food shown by such an offer by II's traders, those of country I would surely raise their price from $10F = 11C$ to one more favorable to them, say $10F = 13C$, at which they might offer as much as $40,000F$ for $52,000C$. Confronting such less advantageous terms, II's traders would presumably back off a bit, reducing their offer at such possible terms to $104,000C$ for $80,000F$. By such a process of offer and response, mutual agreement might be reached at such terms as $1F = 2C$, with $100,000F$ exchanging for $200,000C$. Since I's exports of food would just pay for its imports of clothing, and vice versa, this would be an equilibrium situation, subject to change only when the demand of either country for imports in terms of its exports changed.[7]

Division of the Gains from Trade

From this illustration of how reciprocal demands operate to determine terms of trade that yield equilibrium, we can proceed directly to the question of how the gains are divided between the trading partners. As we have already noted, Mill's answer was: according to the relative strength and elasticity of the demands of the two countries.

Continuing our illustration, clearly each country will gain the most, the better the real price it can obtain for its export good. This will be when the international terms of trade are close to the domestic terms of trade of its trading partner. For country I a highly advantageous real price for its food would be somewhere close to $1F = 4C$. With I's demand schedule given, this would require a very strong demand for food in terms of clothing. The final terms in our illustration of $1F = 2C$ might be pushed up to $1F = 3C$ or higher if at $1F = 2C$ country II were willing to offer substantially more than its actual offer of $200,000C$. Symmetry in the demand schedule would imply larger offers of clothing for food throughout that schedule. A similar result would occur were country I's demand weaker, amounting, say, to an offer of only $80,000F$ for $160,000C$ at the $1F/2C$ ratio.

What about elasticity of demand, the other element suggested by

----

[7] It is common practice to represent such a bargaining situation by a diagram representing each country's demand in the form of an "offer" curve. Discussion of this refinement is postponed to Chapter 4 and Appendix 2 of Chapter 5, where the formal derivation of an offer curve is given and its properties discussed.

Mill? Just as with the more familiar demand for a good in terms of money, here too elasticity means responsiveness of quantity demanded to a change in price, with the difference that an offer of exports for imports replaces an offer of money for a good. As with an ordinary demand curve, it is a matter of the rate of movement along the curve rather than the position of the entire curve. A strong demand is relatively large at each point of its entire schedule; elasticity is responsiveness to price changes at various points along the schedule.[8]

THE ADEQUACY OF CLASSICAL THEORY

Constant Cost and Complete Specialization

In his famous illustration of Portuguese wine and English cloth, Ricardo quite clearly assumed that the number of days specified as the labor cost of producing each of those goods was to be considered to remain the same whatever the output. That is, he assumed constant cost of production as the rule.[9] From this it follows that, given a situation of comparative differences in cost, specialization in each country will be complete. With the opening of trade, Portugal will produce all the wine for both countries, while England will produce all the cloth. If either country failed to do this, continuing to produce for local consumption some of the import good, it would be using part of its labor force inefficiently. In any event, the competition of cheaper imports would quickly bring such inefficient production to an end.

Ricardo's assumption of constant costs was a drawback of his theory; it is both highly unrealistic and unnecessary. In ensuing chapters, we use an increasing-cost model, which permits domestic production and imports of the same good to go on side by side.

What Underlies Comparative Advantage?

A more important deficiency of the classical theory is that it fails to explain the *basis* for comparative advantage. Such an advantage is shown to rest on relative differences in the productivity of labor among nations, but attempts to indicate the reasons for such differences were fragmentary and unsupported by any body of evidence. Thus Ricardo

[8] These matters are considered more fully in Appendix 2 of Chapter 5, where some technical aspects of offer curves are discussed.

[9] If all units of labor are in effect the same, and no other factor contributes as Ricardo assumed, then it follows that increasing the output of a good by increasing the input of labor will leave the unit labor cost unchanged as long as there are constant returns to scale (see Chapter 4).

seems to have appealed either to national differences in the quality of labor or to differences in the technology used. Thus, to explain why labor was relatively more efficient in one of two countries in manufactures as compared with agriculture, Ricardo mentions "greater skills" and "better machinery."[10] At a later date, in a modern formulation of classical theory, Taussig suggested differences in "climate, soil, the stores of minerals" and "inventiveness and ingenuity" in the use that managers make of natural resources and of capital equipment.[11]

But such suggestions as to what underlies the relative efficiency of labor seem to hint at a number of possible explanations. These include national differences in the quality of labor, differences in the techniques of production available, and even differences in the use made of factors other than labor. In other words, when it came to accounting convincingly for comparative advantage, Ricardo and later classical writers were content with rather vague and unsupported suggestions. There was no doubt in their minds about the existence of comparative differences in the efficiency of labor, but they showed relatively little interest in going behind those differences.

Despite its serious shortcomings, the classical theory of international trade, modified and qualified by successors of Ricardo and Mill,[12] served until well into the twentieth century as a convincing demonstration of the gains from trade. It therefore served admirably to support the fight for the abolition of mercantilist restrictions on trade and the later efforts to combat a revival of protectionism.

SELECTED REFERENCES

MILL, JOHN STUART. *The Principles of Political Economy.* Book 3, Chapter 18, contains Mill's theory of reciprocal demand.

OHLIN, BERTIL. *Interregional and International Trade.* Cambridge, Mass.: Harvard University Press, 1933. Appendix 3 is a vigorous criticism of the classical theory.

RICARDO, DAVID. *Principles of Political Economy and Taxation.* Chapter 7 contains the famous statement of the doctrine of comparative cost.

VINER, JACOB. *Studies in the Theory of International Trade.* New York: Harper & Row, Publishers, Inc., 1937. See Chapter 8, Sections 1, 7, 8, 10, 11, and 12, for a defense of the real cost approach to the theory of international trade.

[10] Ricardo, op. cit., p. 98.

[11] F. W. Taussig, *International Trade,* New York: Macmillan Publishing Company, 1927.

[12] Taussig, in particular, devoted attention to the role of noncompeting groups of labor and of differing costs of capital in different industries. See Taussig, op. cit., Chapter 6. Jacob Viner, in his *International Trade and Development* (New York: The Free Press, 1952), pp. 28–29, has interesting comments on qualitative differences in labor.

PART 2

THE THEORY OF INTERNATIONAL TRADE: BASES OF SPECIALIZATION AND TRADE

4
CHAPTER

The Basis for a Modern Trade Theory

We have just seen that Ricardo was the first to show convincingly that the immediate basis for trade among nations is relative differences in commodity prices, and that each nation gains from trade by specializing in the production of those goods it can produce relatively cheaply and exchanging them for those produced more cheaply elsewhere. Such specialization and exchange enables each nation to enjoy a larger real income than if it tried to make everything for itself.

Ricardo's theory, especially as refined and elaborated later by Mill, served as an effective weapon against the lingering restrictions of mercantilism and as a strong support of the free trade movement,[1] and later as a defense against resurgent protectionism.

Although the simple doctrine of comparative advantage served admirably to advance the cause of free trade, it was quite inadequate for other tasks. Thus it left virtually untouched the problem of what elements lie behind national differences in the efficiency of labor. Because of this, it could not go beyond its broad demonstration that trade in general is good for all nations. Yet trade is highly complex; it consists of a huge number of extremely varied items: raw materials of many kinds, agricultural products ranging from wheat to asparagus, manufactures that include heavy industrial equipment and fine watches, and services such as banking, insurance, and advertising. Countries specialize in some of this wide array of specific items but not in others, which in turn determines the composition or pattern of each nation's trade.

A trade theory that is adequate to its tasks must be able to explain international specialization in some detail: why particular in-

[1] Ricardo published his *Principles* in 1817, while Mill's appeared in 1848. Free trade came first in England in the 1840s.

59

dustries locate where they do, and therefore why trade patterns are what they are. The classical theory of international trade was unable to throw any light on these matters, for two reasons. First, it had nothing significant to say about what forces lie behind differences in the relative efficiency of labor, so these differences went unexplained. Second, the theory assumed that labor was the only factor of economic importance.

Both these deficiencies have been overcome in the last century or so. Investigation has shown that many elements, including among others technology, education, and health, combine to determine the efficiency of labor, with notable differences among nations. As for the labor theory of value which resulted from Ricardo's single factor assumption, that has been long discarded in favor of a more modern theory. We now turn to the relation between this theory and the theory of international trade.

PRICE THEORY AND TRADE THEORY

During the latter half of the nineteenth century, there gradually evolved a theory of value, the general equilibrium theory, which was far more sophisticated than Ricardo's labor theory. This modern theory, which explains the price-determining process in a single market, brings together the forces of demand and supply in a complex system of general equilibrium. Supplies of the productive factors, their combinations as inputs in the production of goods and services, the cost of those outputs, the incomes of buyers, their tastes, and the demands that result, all interact with one another in a system of mutual interdependence to determine the prices of final output.

Although these forces operate in a similar fashion in all countries, it is logical to suppose that prices will differ when there are significant national differences in the relative importance of one or more of the component forces. Such commodity price differences could originate on the side of demand, because of dissimilar consumers' tastes or disparities in income, or on the side of supply, because of national differences in factor endowments or in the technology that prescribes their use.

The leading modern theory of international trade derives from the work of two Swedish economists, Eli Heckscher and Bertil Ohlin.[2] As the elements of the pricing system responsible for international price

---

[2] Eli Heckscher sketched the outline of this theory in his seminal article, "The Effect of Foreign Trade on the Distribution of Income," *Ekonomisk Tidskrift,* **21,** (1919); reprinted in 1949 as Chapter 13 in *Readings in the Theory of International Trade* (Philadelphia: Blakiston). Bertil Ohlin expanded and systematized the new "factor proportions" theory in his *Interregional and International Trade* (Cambridge, Mass.: Harvard University Press, 1933). Later, Paul A. Samuelson made further notable contributions.

differences and thus for mutually beneficial trade, the Heckscher–Ohlin or H-O theory focuses on national differences in factor endowments, together with differences among industries in the proportions in which these factors are combined. Briefly summarized, the theory states that, given differences in the endowment of nations with land, labor, and capital, a nation will export those goods whose production requires relatively large amounts of its abundant and therefore cheap factors and will import those requiring relatively large amounts of its scarce and expensive factors.[3]

This statement of the H-O or factor proportions theory is no more than a thumbnail sketch. Before we undertake its fuller development, it is essential to review with some care the main features of its foundation, modern price theory. We shall consider first a simple model of production (supply), and then a similarly simple model of consumption (demand). Having done this, we can show how the two sides interact to yield equilibrium in an economy closed to trade. We conclude the chapter by showing how the economy reacts to the opening of trade, as well as precisely how it gains from that trade. In Chapter 5 we undertake a systematic presentation of the H-O theory. Chapter 6 allows for the fact that many goods, not just two, must be taken into account, that international trade involves costs of transportation, and that in the short run, capital goods are highly specific. Several alternatives to the H-O theory receive attention in Chapter 7. To help sort out the relative significance of these competing hypotheses, we shall review some of the extensive literature on the empirical testing of international trade theory (Chapter 8). Finally, having studied trade under a specified set of conditions, we allow in Chapter 9 for the fact of change. This includes growth in the supplies of the factors of production as well as international movements of labor and capital.

Returning to the present chapter, so as to make a complex subject manageable, we set out a very simple model of production and consumption. We shall follow the usual practice, and assume only two goods, food (F) and clothing (C), and two factors, labor (L) and capital (K). Since our analysis rests on certain key assumptions, to which we shall adhere in this and the following chapter, we state them explicitly now:

1. The markets for goods and factors of production are perfectly competitive.

---

[3] It is interesting to note that in this theory, differing national endowments with the productive agents play a role similar to that of natural or acquired aptitudes among individuals in Adam Smith's explanation of the division of labor, or interpersonal specialization. Just as the possession of manual dexterity or great physical strength gives a worker a cost advantage in occupations requiring these qualitites, so abundant land gives a nation a cost advantage in wheat or corn production, ample supplies of capital favor industries such as petroleum refining, while countries with relatively abundant labor attract industries such as the manufacture of clothing.

2. Factors of production are perfectly mobile within the country.
3. There are no external economies or diseconomies.[4]
4. The supply of each factor's services per period is given and remains constant.
5. All units of each factor are homogeneous, or qualitatively identical.
6. In equilibrium, the income and expenditure of an economy are equal.

THE PRODUCTION FUNCTION AND ISOQUANTS

We begin our examination of the forces of supply with that most basic of concepts, the production function. This is simply a statement of the technically most efficient relationships between inputs and outputs in the production of a single commodity. In the production of most goods, there is normally a number of alternative ways in which the factors can be combined. A production function formulates those factor combinations that are technically most efficient, usually in the form of a mathematical equation. Thus the equation

$$Q_c = f(K, L)$$

is such an equation in its most general form. It states that the maximum attainable output of C is some function (f) of the inputs of capital and labor (K, L) required to produce C. A concrete example could be

$$Q_c = \sqrt{K \cdot L}$$

For values of K and L, the quantity of output is the square root of their product. Thus $2K$ and $50L$, $4K$ and $25L$, $10K$ and $10L$, $25K$ and $4L$, or $50K$ and $2L$, yield an output of $10C$.

Such a single value of a production function, together with all the combinations of inputs that will yield it, can be shown diagrammatically as an *isoquant*, or equal product curve. Its essential feature is that every point on the curve represents the same output. Output is constant, or $dQ = O$.

---

[4] External economies are economies that are external to the firm and that arise from the growth of the industry as new firms enter. Such external economies cause the long-run costs of all firms to decline. A common illustration is the improvement in the availability and training of skilled labor brought about by such expansion of an industry. Diseconomies raise an industry's long-run costs, as when growth causes traffic congestion in facilities (such as a road) used in common by a number of firms.

In Figure 4.1, the isoquant C_1 represents the 10-unit level of C production for the equation just used. C_2 is the 20-unit level. An unlimited number of such isoquants could be drawn, one for each specified level of output, each higher level being located farther from the origin than the preceding one.

As one moves downward along any such isoquant, say C_2, labor is substituted for capital. The slope of the tangent at any point, such as m, expresses the marginal rate of substitution (*MRS*) between the factors at that point, or dK/dL (ignoring the negative slope of the isoquant). A very small amount of labor is substituted for an equally small amount of capital. The total loss of output due to the smaller input of capital (dK) is equal to this quantity multiplied by the marginal product of capital, or $dK \cdot MP_k$. To get back on the isoquant and thus avoid any loss in output, a minute quantity of labor (dL) must replace the reduced input of capital. Output is thereby increased by the marginal product of labor multiplied by dL, or $dL \cdot MP_L$. The initial loss in output is matched by the gain, and the definition of an isoquant is obeyed:

$$dQ_c = dK \cdot MP_K + dL \cdot MP_L = 0$$

If we leave out dQ_c as redundant, simple algebraic manipulations give us

$$\frac{dK}{dL} = \frac{MP_L}{MP_K}$$

We shall use this relationship shortly.

Figure 4.1   Isoquants

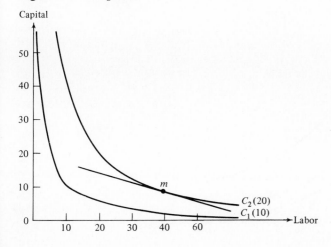

Economic Efficiency

Since an isoquant represents all equally efficient input combinations corresponding to a specific level of output, any combination is technically as good as any other. From the economic rather than the technical viewpoint, however, there is only *one* combination that will be efficient. This combination depends on what it costs to employ the productive factors, or upon their prices. Thus suppose that a typical producer of *C* has available $1000 to spend on factor inputs, and that he confronts a price of $10 a unit for capital and of $20 a unit for labor. He can then buy 100 units of *K*, 50 units of *L*, or any intermediate combination of his expenditure or isocost line K_1L_1 in Figure 4.2. The largest output obtainable for this expenditure is that whose isoquant is tangent to K_1L_1—in this instance, C_2. Any higher level of output (such as C_3) is unattainable, while any greater outlay would be uneconomic. *Thus tangency of an isocost or expenditure line to an isoquant represents economic efficiency or minimum cost.*

Note that the slope of the isocost line is the exchange ratio or relative real price of the factors: OK/OL, in this instance 100/50 or $2K/1L$. Since the slope of any tangent to an isoquant is also the marginal rate of factor substitution, dK/dL, which we know is equal to the inverse ratio of marginal productivities, MP_L/MP_K, we have by substitution

$$\frac{OK}{OL} = \frac{MP_L}{MP_K}$$

Figure 4.2   Economic Efficiency

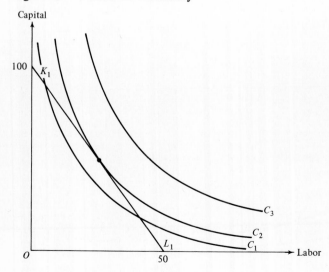

If we replace relative real prices by their inverse, the money prices of K and L,[5] we have

$$\frac{P_L}{P_K} = \frac{MP_L}{MP_K}$$

or

$$\frac{MP_L}{P_L} = \frac{MP_K}{P_K}$$

That is, if the marginal product of each factor is proportional to its costs, economic efficiency is attained. In simpler terms, if the amount of output obtained from the last dollar spent on labor is the same as that obtained from the last dollar spent on capital, production is economically efficient.

Factor Intensities

Differing factor intensities can be shown diagrammatically by a comparison of isoquants that express different production functions.[6] Figure 4.3 exhibits two isoquants, one for food and one for clothing, each at the 10-unit level of output. That for food corresponds to the equation $Q_F = \sqrt[3]{K^2 \cdot L}$, which is capital-intensive, since the equation gives relatively greater weight to capital than to labor. The clothing isoquant corresponds to the equation $Q_C = \sqrt[3]{K \cdot L^2}$, which is labor-intensive. The factor combinations prescribed by these production functions are such that at all relevant factor prices, food production is always more capital-intensive than the production of clothing. At the relative factor prices represented by OK_1/OL_1, the slope of the price line K_1L_1, which is tangent to both isoquants, food is more capital-intensive

---

[5] A word needs to be said about the use of money prices and real prices. In the preceding chapter, international price differences were expressed in real terms, as commodity exchange ratios, or the price of one good in terms of another. The more familiar money prices are the inverse of these relative (real) prices. Thus if the relative price of food in terms of clothing is $1F/4C$, then if the money price of clothing in both of two countries were $1, the money price of food would be $4. Since relative prices have certain advantages, expecially in the use of diagrams, we shall continue to use them, but when it is more convenient to use money prices, you will be notified.

[6] Comparison of factor intensities in this manner is possible only for certain types of production functions: those that are homogeneous. Of these, constant returns to scale is the simplest case. Homogeneity is a property of a production function (a mathematical equation) such that, if the variables of the equation are multiplied by a constant, the value of the equation is multiplied by some power of that constant. Thus for the general case, $Q = f(K, L)$, if the inputs K and L are multiplied by the constant t, so that $Q = f(tK, tL)$, this converts to $Q = t^n(K, L)$. For constant returns to scale, homogeneity is linear; $n = 1$. Thus if inputs are doubled or tripled, output is also doubled or tripled.

Figure 4.3   Differing Factor Intensities

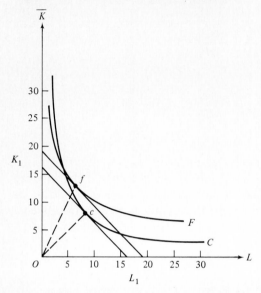

than clothing, as shown by the slope of the ray Of as compared with that of the ray Oc. Other factor price combinations could be represented by (parallel) lines of different slopes than that of K_1L_1. It is clear that at their (separate) points of tangency with the two isoquants, all Of lines would be steeper than the Oc lines.

PRODUCTION FRONTIERS AND COST CONDITIONS

Constant Costs

A concept that is useful in the analysis of production and which lends itself to diagrammatic representation is the production frontier. It expresses the maximum output of all goods from a given supply of the productive factors in a given country during a specific period under conditions of full employment. The simplest illustration of this concept is provided by the Ricardian model we encountered in Chapter 3. Recall that in an example we used, for one of our countries we assumed that 1 man-year of labor could produce either 4 units of food or 16 units of clothing. Since Ricardo assumed that labor was the only factor of economic importance and that labor was homogeneous, the cost of producing either food or clothing would remain constant regardless of output. Moreover, given that the labor cost of 4 food or 16 clothing is the same, 4 units of food can always be transformed into 16 units of clothing, and vice versa. That is, the marginal rate of transformation (*MRT*) between food and clothing is constant, with a value of 1*F*/4*C*.

From this information we can construct a diagram showing the country's production frontier. In Figure 4.4(a), the vertical axis represents food production, the horizontal axis the output of clothing. If our small country has a labor force of 100 workers, then if all are employed for a year in the production of food, output will be 400 units,

Figure 4.4   Production Frontier

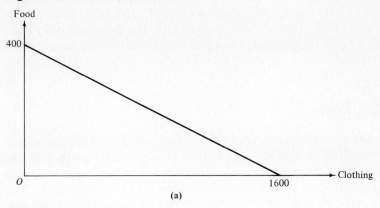

(a)

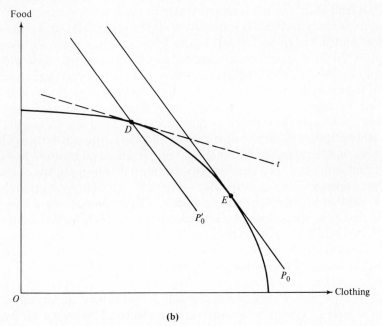

(b)

whereas if all employed in clothing production, output will be 1600 units. Indicate these amounts on the respective axes, and connect these points by a straight line. This is the country's production frontier or production possibilities "curve." It is also referred to as the transformation "curve," and in this instance is a straight line because *MRT* is constant at 1*F*/4*C*, the slope of the frontier.

The introduction of the marginal rate of transformation suggests the use of a concept with which you are no doubt familiar, that of opportunity cost. This considers the cost of producing one commodity to be the amount of another commodity that could be produced with the same input of resources. Since in our illustration the cost of 1*F* or 4*C* is the same, the opportunity cost of 1*F* is 4*C*, and vice versa. Moreover, this cost is constant. Finally, each point on the production frontier represents the maximum output of the country's resources when fully employed, at all possible combinations of food and clothing output.

Increasing Costs

Consider now a model that involves more than one factor of production. The outcome will be different from that of the Ricardian model just presented, even if each factor (labor or capital) is homogeneous, provided only that factor intensities differ in the two industries.

Continuing with the two-factor model used earlier in this chapter, we find that the movement of resources from the capital-intensive food industry to the labor-intensive clothing industry will cause costs to rise in the latter and to fall in the former. The reason for this result is that the food industry releases factors in proportions different from those required in clothing production. Less labor moves than is suitable to input–output relations in the clothing industry. As a result, the demand for labor exceeds the supply at existing wage rates; wages are bid up. Although the return to capital, which is in excess supply in the clothing industry, will fall, the cost of producing clothing will rise because of the disproportionate weight of labor compared with capital in that industry. For similar reasons, with declining production in the food industry, costs will fall. (Capital, the factor of greater weight in food production, is now cheaper.) With money costs thus moving in opposite directions, each increment by which food production is reduced will command smaller and smaller amounts of clothing. The production frontier or production possibilities curve will be concave or hollow toward the origin, as in Figure 4.4(b), whose axes measure units of food and clothing.

Finally, the rise in wages and the fall in the return to capital in the clothing industry, which because of intersectoral mobility of the factors will be communicated to the food industry, is just what is needed to bring production in both sectors into equilibrium. The relative rise in wages will stimulate the substitution of capital for labor at the margin in the production of both food and clothing. Such substitution will continue until the output obtained in each industry from the last dollar spent on labor or on capital is the same. Thus the condition for economic efficiency is attained, as well as equalization of wages and of the return to capital in both industries.

The Production Frontier Summarizes the Conditions of Equilibrium

The production frontier summarizes the conditions that exist when equilibrium is attained in an economy conforming to the assumptions stated on pages 61–62. Production in each industry satisfies the condition essential to survival under perfect competition: the realization of economic efficiency. With intersectoral mobility of the factors, both wages and the return to capital are brought to a common level throughout the economy. And there is full employment of both labor and capital, implied by their mobility and consequent competition for employment. This means that the production frontier represents the maximum attainable real national income, and that production must take place at *some* point on it. Points outside the frontier are unattainable with the resources available, while points inside it reflect either less than full employment or inefficient production. (For a fuller and more technical proof of the foregoing argument, see Appendix 1 of Chapter 5.)

Equilibrium in the Production of Two Commodities

At precisely what point on the production frontier or transformation curve equilibrium is realized depends on the relative prices of food and clothing—their exchange ratio in the market. This must be the same as the rate at which producers transform food into clothing. In terms of geometry, the slope of the price line must be the same as the slope of the transformation curve. Given relative prices as represented in Figure 4.4(b) by the price line P_0 with the slope of $1F/2C$, equilibrium will occur at point E. For there alone is the marginal rate of transformation of food into clothing, the slope of the tangent to the transformation curve, equal to the relative price of food and clothing.

Suppose that production took place at D, with relative prices (shown by line P_0') the same as at E. At that point the marginal rate of transformation is indicated by the much flatter dashed line t, with a slope of $1F/10C$. This means that the resources used to produce 1 unit of food can be used instead to produce 10 units of clothing. But in the market, $1F$ exchanges for only $2C$. It would be most attractive for producers to shift resources from food to clothing to take advantage of the highly favorable market terms. But this shift of resources will move the production point toward E, where MRT in production and the market exchange ratio are brought to equality. Then

$$MRT = \frac{dF}{dC} = \frac{P_c}{P_f}$$

By cross multiplication, we get

$$dF \cdot P_f = dC \cdot P_c$$

or

$$VMP_f = VMP_c$$

That is, the value of the marginal produce is the same in both industries, so production is in equilibrium.

CONSUMPTION AND DEMAND

In the preceding discussion of equilibrium in production, we have simply assumed the existence of market-determined prices of our two commodities. We can now go ahead and consider briefly the side of demand and its interaction with the supply side of our economy to establish relative prices that satisfy the requirements of both producers and consumers. Such a result represents a condition of general equilibrium in a single nontrading economy. We will then have a firm base from which to carry forward our study of international trade theory.

Consumption Indifference Curves

Our procedure in the analysis of production in a two-commodity world has been to consider those commodities as alternatives in the use of the productive factors. In a similar fashion, demand can be studied as a choice between alternatives in consumption. In our analysis of production, we expressed the relation between the output of a commodity, the goal of production, and the inputs of the factors, its source, in an equation of the general form $Q_c = f(K, L)$. In dealing with demand, which in a two-commodity world is the quantity of each of those goods desired at each of a series of relative prices, we can use a similar equation which expresses the quantitative relationship between the goal of demand, the satisfaction derived from consumption, and the source of that satisfaction—alternative combinations of the two goods. The general form of this equation is $U = g(F, C)$, where F and C are quantities of the goods being compared, U the total satisfaction derived from their consumption, and g expresses the functional relationship between them. (This is the relative preference of the consumer for the two goods at all relevant prices.) An important difference between a production function and a consumption function should be noted: Whereas the quantities of output in a production equation can be measured directly and expressed as cardinal numbers, the satisfaction or utility derived from consumption is intangible, incapable of direct measurement. It can be expressed only in terms of more or less, as an ordinal number.

Just as we were able to represent production functions in diagrammatic form, we can do the same with relationships in consumption. Thus production isoquants, any one of which reflects a single value of output, is paralleled in consumption by consumption indifference curves. Any one such curve indicates a single level of satisfaction—it is an equal-satisfaction curve. Thus in Figure 4.5 the curve U_1 represents a given level of satisfaction derived by a particular individual from the consumption of varying combinations of food and clothing. Again as with isoquants, a family of indifference curves reflects different (but ordinal) values that rise as one moves outward from

Figure 4.5   Consumption Indifference Curves

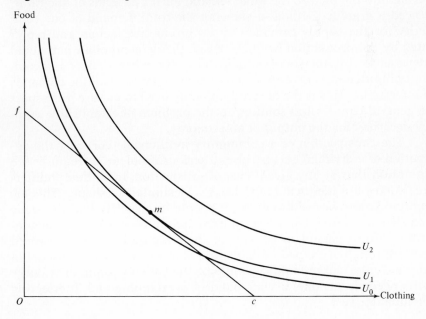

the origin. Thus U_0 indicates a lower, U_2 a higher level of satisfaction than U_1 from similar combinations of the two goods. Finally, a tangent to an indifference curve at any point measures the marginal rate of substitution in consumption, just as the tangent to an isoquant measures the marginal rate of substitution in production.

In production, output is limited by the expenditure available to a producer. An individual's consumption is similarly limited by his income. If relative commodity prices are given, the consumer will maximize his satisfaction by attaining the highest possible indifference curve, which is the one tangent to the expenditure or income-and-price line. At the point of tangency in Figure 4.5, we have $\mathrm{MRS}_c = dF/dC = Of/Oc = P_c/P_f$. If we select from this the relation $dF/dC = P_c/P_f$, then cross multiplication gives us $dF \cdot P_f = dC \cdot P_c$. This translates into the value of an increment of food and of clothing at a common margin, or $\mathrm{VMU}_f = \mathrm{VMU}_c$. In words, in equilibrium, when satisfaction is maximized, the last dollar spent on food yields the same satisfaction as the last dollar spent on clothing.

Community Indifference Curves

In our discussion of production, we used the production frontier as a means of representing the maximum production possibilities of a two-commodity economy, or the total annual supply of goods. To demonstrate how an equilibrium price for that output is established, we need to bring into the picture the total demand for it. In terms of diagrams, we need a graphic method of showing the total demand of our community for the supply provided by its productive factors and represented by the production frontier. Since the demand of an individual is represented by a personal indifference curve, what we need is a community indifference curve that sums into a single total all the demands of individuals. This is the device commonly used to picture this aspect of a general equilibrium solution to the problem of establishing equilibrium prices for the output of an economy.

The construction of a community indifference curve by the aggregation of individual curves raises a serious problem. It requires the assumption that at any given level of satisfaction, individual indifferences curves are identical (or at least very similar) in shape. This assumption would be valid only if all people in a society had the same tastes. Unfortunately, however, in most communities tastes differ substantially from person to person, so their indifference curves would have very different shapes. Aggregation of any considerable number of such dissimilar curves would yield, not the smooth community curve that is needed, but only a wide band of overlapping and intersecting individual curves.

How can this dilemma be resolved? One suggested solution, adopted by many, is to resort to the principle of compensation. According to this principle, if those who gain from a change can compensate the losers and still be better off, whereas the losers cannot buy off the gainers, the change should be approved. Applied to the aggregation of individual indifference curves, this principle permits one to construct a smooth community indifference curve, since in principle the gains and losses of individuals affected by price changes can be known, and the losers appropriately compensated by the gainers (see also p. 79). This is admittedly a very terse statement of this solution to the problem, made because an adequate statement would require excessive space.[7]

Community indifference curves are a very useful device in explaining a number of problems that we shall confront, especially those related to the gains from trade. We shall use them, assuming, in the light of the principle of compensation, that they accurately reflect the preferences of the community to which they refer.

GENERAL EQUILIBRIUM BEFORE TRADE

We can now bring together the information derived from our review of the supply and demand sides of our closed economy to show how a general equilibrium of production and consumption is reached. One result, the establishment of relative prices for the two goods produced, will provide the point of departure for the opening of the economy to a given set of world prices. We shall consider the reactions through which a new equilibrium with international trade is established, as well as the nature of the gains from that trade. In the next chapter we shall examine in more detail the Heckscher–Ohlin theory as a rational explanation of international trade.

Assembling the Parts

The two sets of curves we have been considering—the production frontier or transformation curve and the community indifference curves—summarize the information needed for the establishment of general equilibrium in production and consumption. All points on the transformation curve (Figure 4.6) are *possible* points of equilibrium in production. The *actual* equilibrium point will be where the price line is

---

[7] If you are interested in the problem, see Richard E. Caves, *Trade and Economic Structure* (Cambridge, Mass.: Harvard University Press, 1960), pp. 195–200, for a brief explanation. For a more thorough discussion, see Akira Takayama, *International Trade* (New York: Holt, Rinehart and Winston, 1972), Chapter 17.

Figure 4.6   General Equilibrium in a Single Economy

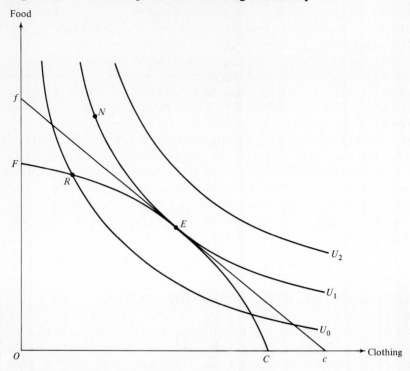

tangent to the transformation curve, since at that point the trade-off between food and clothing in production will be the same as the trade-off provided by the market.

   Equilibrium in consumption will exist when consumption takes place on the highest possible community indifference curve. This is the one that is tangent to the production transformation curve, since that curve represents production of full employment, or the largest possible national income. In Figure 4.6, this is at point E, where the community indifference curve U_1 is tangent to the transformation curve FC. The income constraint prohibits reaching any higher indifference curve, while moving to a higher point on U_1, such as N, yields no increase in satisfaction. (That point is also unattainable, not being on the production possibilities curve.) A point on any lower indifference curve, such as R on U_0, is feasible but less desirable. (Test your knowledge by proving that R cannot be a point of competitive equilibrium.)

   We know that the slope of a tangent to the transformation curve measures a relative price that is satisfactory to producers, since the trade-off between food and clothing in the market is the same as in production. For the same reason, a price line tangent to a community indifference curve is acceptable to consumers. Therefore, the price line *fc*, with the slope *Of/Oc*, represents a condition of equilibrium in both production and consumption. In symbols, we have

$$MRT = \frac{dF}{dC} = \frac{Of}{Oc} = \frac{P_c}{P_f} = \frac{dF}{dC} = MRS$$

Therefore,

$$dF \cdot P_f = dC \cdot P_c \quad \text{or} \quad VMU_f = VMU_c$$

EQUILIBRIUM IN A SMALL OPEN ECONOMY

Having established the conditions for equilibrium between production and consumption in an economy closed to trade, we are ready to see how that economy adjusts to its opening to trade. The impetus to trade comes from confrontation with a set of international prices different from those ruling in the isolated economy. We assume that our economy is relatively small, not large enough to alter the international prices with which it is confronted. We also retain the assumptions of a competitive model, in particular the assumption that in equilibrium a nation's income and expenditure are equal. Now, however, that equality is at *international prices*.

Starting with the pretrade exchange ratio between food and clothing represented by price line P_0 in Figure 4.7, equilibrium exists at *E*, with production (real national income) equal to consumption. Removal of previous restraints on trade confronts traders with the international exchange or price ratio represented by the line P_i. Since its slope is steeper than that of P_0, a larger quantity of food now exchanges for a given quantity of clothing. The price of clothing in terms of food, and in terms of money, too, is higher. With the production of clothing relatively more profitable, producers shift resources from food to clothing and move from the pretrade equilibrium point *E* to a new equilibrium at *S*, where the *MRT* in production is the same as the rate of transformation in the market, the slope of P_i.

At the new set of international prices, consumers face a different budget constraint, line P_i. Their expenditure can occur anywhere along this line, and because of trade, it is no longer limited to what is produced domestically. They will maximize satisfaction at *T*, where their

Figure 4.7   Equilibrium with Trade

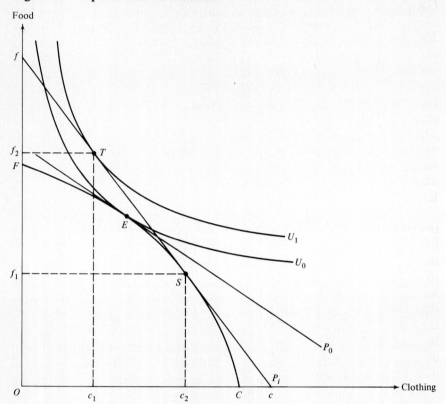

expenditure line is tangent to the indifference curve U_1, higher than U_0, and *MRS* in consumption is equal to the international price ratio.

With the new equilibrium for consumers at T and for producers at S, production and consumption of each of the two commodities is no longer equal. Nonetheless, although the physical composition of income and expenditure is no longer the same, the two are equal. Referring to Figure 4.7, expenditure is $Oc_1 + Of_1 + f_1f_2$, and income derived from production is $Oc_1 + c_1c_2 + Of_1$. But c_1c_2 of clothing is exported in exchange for f_1f_2 of food. Exports pay for imports, so $c_1c_2 = f_1f_2$. Income and expenditure are equal.

One further point should be mentioned. In the Ricardian model, with constant opportunity costs, when international trade becomes possible, specialization is complete. In the present model, because of increasing costs, specialization is only partial. Output of the export good expands and of the import good contracts, but import-competing production of clothing continues.

GAINS FROM TRADE

The classical theory of international trade was eminently successful in one area: It established convincingly the gains from international specialization and trade. These it attributed to the existence of a comparative advantage, which provides the opportunity for a country to import those goods for which its pretrade costs are relatively high in exchange for exports of goods that it can produce relatively cheaply. The country thus economizes in the use of resources, obtaining for a given amount thereof a larger total income than if it attempted to produce everything itself. Since this gain in real income results from relative differences in prices, the gain will be greater, the greater the difference between its pretrade prices and international prices.

The incorporation of trade theory into modern price and welfare theory has permitted a precise specification of the nature of the gains from trade. In addition, the conditions necessary for their full realization can be set out. These may be briefly summarized as follows. Before trade, output, and consumer satisfaction are maximized when, with each factor receiving the value of its marginal product and with that reward the same in all uses, the marginal rate of transformation in production and the marginal rate of substitution in consumption are both equal to the domestic commodity price ratio and thus to each other. The introduction of international trade permits the realization of a gain consisting of two parts—a gain from exchange and a gain from specialization. When equilibrium is established and these gains are maximized, the new marginal rate of transformation in production and the new marginal rate of substitution in consumption are equal to the international price ratio. Consumers enjoy a higher level of satisfaction, partly owing to more favorable terms of exchange, partly because of more specialized use of the country's resources.

To differentiate clearly the *gain from exchange* and the *gain from specialization*, consider the two-step shift from isolation to free trade illustrated in Figure 4.8. From the pretrade position of point E, confront the consumers of the country with the international price ratio depicted by P_i. (Ignore for the moment the reaction of producers.) With no change in production, but allowing consumers to purchase at international prices, the consumers are able to move to a higher level of satisfaction from point E on the community indifference curve U_0 to point E_1 on the curve U_1. This movement reflects the *gain from exchange* with no change in production.

But producers are not going to remain idle in the face of a change in the relative price of their products. At the new international price represented by P_i, producers respond to the higher price of clothing.

Figure 4.8   Gain from Trade

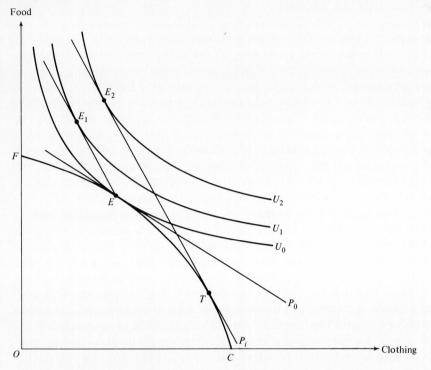

Its production expands and that of food contracts, which moves the production point along the transformation curve to point T, where MRT equals the new exchange ratio.

This shift in production results in increased efficiency. The country is now producing more of the good that is higher priced in a world market. The fruits of this higher efficiency are seen in the shift in consumption from E_1 on U_1 to E_2, where the level of satisfaction is reflected in the higher indifference curve U_2. This movement from E_1 to E_2 measures the *gain from specialization* in production. The sum of the gain from exchange and the gain from specialization is the total gain in satisfaction.[8]

A qualification needs to be entered at this point. Allowance needs to be made for the possibility that in the movement to a higher level of satisfaction, consumers with a preference for one of the goods

[8] It is worth noting that the existence of gain from trade does not depend on the direction of the change in relative prices from the pretrade position, but only on the fact of change. Thus, if international demands were such as to establish an international price ratio with a slope even flatter than that of P_0, and thus tangent to the transformation curve to the left of E in Figure 4.8, gain from trade would be possible.

may suffer some loss from the fact that at the international price ratio, they may consume less of their favored product than before trade. This can be seen in Figure 4.8 in the fact that the point E_1 lies not only above the point E, but to its left. This means that although total consumption of food is greater after the opening of trade, that of clothing is less. Consumers who prefer clothing to food will be worse off than before, although consumers of food will be substantially better off. This ambiguity would not exist if the consumption point with trade were not only above the point E, but also to the right of a perpendicular through it. For then, consumption of *both* food and clothing would be greater than before the opening of trade. Yet even with the trading equilibrium at E_1, the principle of compensation (p. 73) can be invoked. It would be possible for those who gain from trade to compensate the losers by an appropriate redistribution of income, leaving a net gain to the former and thus to society as a whole. This transfer of income need not actually be made; it is sufficient that if it were made, a net gain to the community would remain.

A final caution: Recall that this analysis of the gains from trade rests on certain explicit assumptions, the most important being the assumption of perfect competition in all markets. When trade theory is modified and extended to include influences such as those we deal with in Chapter 6, the optimal conditions underlying the gains from trade may not hold. The possibility then exists that the gains from trade may be reduced or even, in extreme cases, eliminated. Despite these possibilities, we shall see that a strong presumption remains: *Some trade is better than no trade.*

SELECTED REFERENCES

BHAGWATI, JAGDISH. "The Pure Theory of International Trade: A Survey." No. 7 in American Economic Association and Royal Economic Society, *Surveys of Economic Theory*, Vol. 2. New York: St. Martin's Press, 1965. A thorough and advanced discussion of modern theory, dealing in Sections 6 and 7 with welfare aspects of international trade.

CAVES, RICHARD E. *Trade and Economic Structure*. Cambridge, Mass.: Harvard University Press, 1960. See Ch. 8 for a good review of theoretical discussion of welfare aspects of international trade.

CHIPMAN, JOHN S. "A Survey of the Theory of International Trade." *Econometrica*, **33, 34** (July 1965; Oct. 1965; Jan. 1966). Three articles that review the theory of international trade, the third dealing with the modern version; technical and difficult.

CORDEN, W. M. *Recent Developments in the Theory of International Trade*. Princeton, N.J.: International Finance Section, Princeton University, 1965. Chapter 4 reviews contributions to trade and welfare theory.

LEONTIEF, W. "The Use of Indifference Curves in the Analysis of Foreign Trade." *Quarterly Journal of Economics*, **67** (May 1933). Reprinted in American Economic Association, *Readings in the Theory of International Trade*, New York: McGraw-Hill Book Company, 1949. An early introduction of community indifference curves into the theory of international trade.

MEADE, J. E. *A Geometry of International Trade.* George Allen & Unwin, Ltd., London, 1952. A compact book containing most of the geometry subsequently used in *Trade and Welfare*.

———. *The Stationary Economy.* Aldine-Atherton, Inc., Chicago, 1965. A useful rigorous nonmathematical statement of the basic equilibrium principles considered in these chapters.

———. *Trade and Welfare.* London: Oxford University Press, Inc., 1955. The standard work on this general area of study.

5
CHAPTER

Factor Endowments and International Trade

We have just shown how, in a setting of modern price and production theory, the existence of price differences between countries leads to gainful trade. Our next step is to go behind those price differences and show why they come into existence.

In general, a difference between countries in *any one* of the underlying supply or demand conditions is adequate to yield different pretrade or autarky prices and hence a basis for profitable trade. Of the various possibilities, we have indicated that the leading explanation, the Heckscher–Ohlin theory, focuses on the supply side, specifically on national differences in factor endowments. But before providing a detailed statement of this theory, it will be useful to establish as a starting point a set of conditions where before trade, relative prices in two countries would be identical and no trade would take place even if free trade were allowed. Then the introduction of any difference causing those prices to differ will stand out stark and clear.

EVERYTHING THE SAME

In general terms, there will be no basis for trade when supply and demand conditions in each of two countries are identical, including perfect competition in all markets.

More specifically, such conditions will exist on the supply side when (in our simple model) supplies of capital and labor are identical

81

in both countries and when the production functions (embodying constant returns to scale, or linear homogeneity), although different for food and clothing, are the same in both countries. Then the production frontiers for the countries compared will in turn be identical.

Demand conditions will be the same if the nations' community indifference maps are identical and if the proportions in which goods are consumed depend only on relative commodity prices.[1]

With identical supply and demand conditions and with perfect competition in all markets, pretrade equilibrium between production and consumption will be established in both countries at the same set of relative prices. In diagrammatic terms, the production frontiers and the indifference maps of the two countries will be identical. Therefore, the points of tangency and the slope of the price lines will also be the same. There is no basis for trade.

DIFFERENT FACTOR ENDOWMENTS

Now let us introduce the specific supply-side difference postulated by the factor proportions theory: a difference in the relative endowments of nations with the productive factors. This postulate rests on the readily observable fact that some nations, such as the United States, Germany, and Japan, possess relatively large accumulations of capital, whereas others, such as India and Egypt, are heavily endowed with labor.

How do such differences in relative factor endowments provide a basis for trade? The key lies in the fact that relative factor abundance means that a country's resource endowment is relatively better suited to the production of the good that uses relatively large amounts of the abundant factor. Hence, in isolation, with everything else equal, a commodity whose production requires more intensive use of the more abundant factor will be cheaper than in the other country. Autarky price differences then provide a basis for profitable trade.

The precise relationships among factor intensities, factor abundance, commodity supplies, and hence commodity prices need to be developed more explicitly. Instead of our "everything the same" model, let us consider two countries, of approximately equal size, which differ only in the fact that I is relatively well endowed with capital, II with labor. Food and clothing are the commodities produced in both countries, according to production functions that yield different factor intensities for the two goods but that are the same in both countries.

---

[1] That is, price levels are ruled out of consideration. In technical terms, the indifference curves are homothetic.

We continue to assume that food is the capital-intensive product, clothing the labor-intensive one.

The immediate consequence of introducing differences in national factor endowments is the appearance of corresponding differences in the ability of our two countries to produce food and clothing. When country I devotes all its resources to the production of food, its relatively abundant supply of capital will enable it to produce a far larger quantity of food than can country II. The latter, on the other hand, with all its resources put into the production of clothing, will produce a much larger amount than its rival.

These differences show up in contrasting production frontiers, as in Figure 5.1. By devoting all its resources to the production of food, country I will be able to produce a relatively larger amount than II, as indicated by the greater length of *OF* compared with *OF'*. (Unprimed letters refer to country I, primed letters to II.) Country II, with abundant labor, can produce substantially greater amounts of clothing: *OC'* is longer than *OC*. In general terms, national differences in the relative

Figure 5.1   Differing Factor Endowments as a Basis for Trade

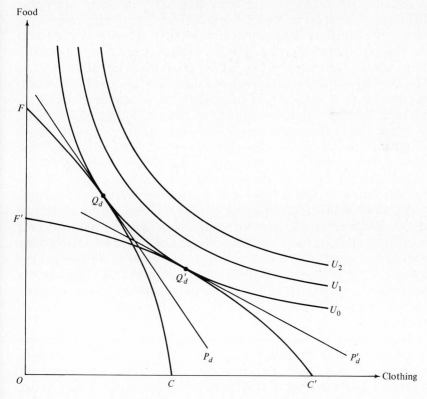

supply of the productive factors result in comparable differences in the supply of the goods they are able to produce.

Since we are deliberately introducing only a single change, a difference in relative factor endowments, tastes in our two countries and therefore their indifference maps remain identical. Three sample community indifference curves are shown in Figure 5.1, with U_0 tangent to both production frontiers—to FC at Q_d and to $F'C'$ at Q_d'. These are the respective points of equilibrium in production and consumption in the two countries. But note that domestic price lines P_d and P_d', which are tangent to the two production frontiers at Q_d and Q_d', have different slopes, chosen to fit the diagram. That of P_d is $2.33F/1C$, while that of P_d' is $0.69F/1C$. Thus food, being intensive in country I's relatively abundant factor, is relatively cheap there, while labor-intensive clothing is relatively cheap in II. The basis for trade exists.

This outcome is shown in Figure 5.2, where the initial situation existing in Figure 5.1 is repeated, but with the countries separated, part (a) being allocated to country I and (b) to II. In addition, the international price line as determined by the interaction of reciprocal demands is introduced as P_i and P_i'. At this price of $1.2F$ to $1C$, the production point in country I, where capital is the relatively abundant factor and food the capital-intensive product, moves from Q_d to Q_i, where P_i is tangent to the transformation curve and the MRT in production is equal to the market exchange ratio. Output of food expands to Of_2, while clothing output contracts to Oc_1. (Output at Q_d is not indicated, to avoid complicating the diagram.) Consumption, on the other hand, shifts from Q_d to E, where P_i is tangent to the indifference curve U_1, higher than U_0. Consumption of the now cheaper clothing rises to Oc_2, with production of Oc_1 supplemented by imports of c_1c_2, or RE. Since the relative price of food has risen, its consumption declines to Of_1. The excess of production over consumption, f_1f_2 or RQ_i, is exported.

Similar but opposite changes take place in country II. At the new production point Q_i', in Figure 5.2(b), clothing production is greater (Oc_2') and food smaller (Of_1') than before trade. Consumption of the two goods is now at E' on the higher indifference curve U_1', with clothing consumption at $O'c_1'$, food consumption at $O'f_2'$. Exports of clothing amount to $c_1'c_2'$, or $R'Q_i'$, identical to country I's imports of RE. Imports of food are $f_1'f_2'$ or $R'E'$, also identical to I's exports of RQ_i. This identity of the trade triangles Q_iRE and $Q_i'R'E'$ reflects equilibrium in the trade of the two countries, brought about by the interaction of their reciprocal demands.

It is important to note that in such an equilibrium free trade situation as that just described, the commodity prices are the *same* in both countries. The basis for the trade exists because there is some difference that, *in the absence of perfectly free trade*, would result in price

Figure 5.2   Factor Proportions Basis for Trade

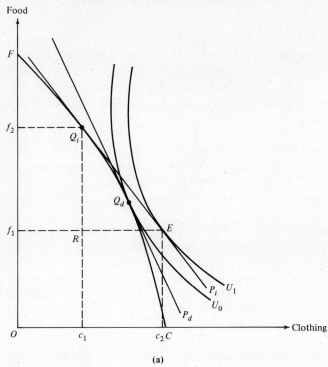

(a)

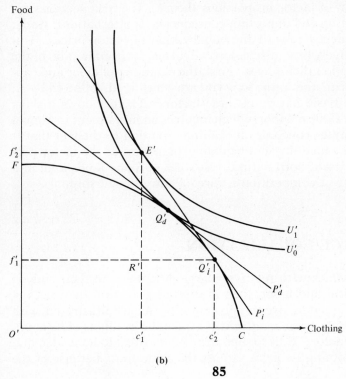

(b)

85

differences. In the presence of free trade, however, the price differences disappear, and we are left to infer what they would be if we did not have free trade.

The key elements underlying the changes in production and consumption that occur when isolation or autarkay gives way to trade can be briefly summarized:

1. Commodities that use a factor intensively cost less when that factor is relatively cheap, and more when it is expensive.
2. Countries differ with respect to their factor endowments. Abundant factors are relatively cheap, scarce ones relatively expensive.
3. Hence a particular price before trade will be relatively low in a country with abundant and cheap supplies of the factor used intensively in that commodity's production.
4. With trade based on price differences before trade, each country will export goods that use its relatively abundant factor intensively and import those that use its relatively scarce factor intensively.

This concludes our presentation of the basic model of the Heckscher–Ohlin of factor proportions theory. The next section considers an interesting and important consequence of international trade: a persistent tendency toward the equalization of factor prices. Following this relatively brief discussion, we turn to an examination of the factors of production themselves. First, the character of labor and capital in the short run and in the long run are considered, followed by an inquiry into the basic nature of these factors. There follows a short discussion of the skills of labor, which involves an investment in human capital. The chapter concludes by calling attention to the fact that it is necessary to include, in an adequate explanation of the factor proportions theory itself, both natural resources of many kinds and, in a world where perfect competition is rare, of entrepreneurship.

FACTOR PRICE EQUALIZATION

Given two economies with relatively large differences in their endowments with capital and labor, then in pretrade isolation the prices of those factors will tend to diverge substantially. As just illustrated, with the opening of trade, each country will export the products of its abundant and cheap factor. Thus foreign demand is added to home demand for this factor, forcing its price up. At the same time, because of the purchase of output of its trading partner's cheap factor, home demand in each country partially deserts its scarce factor, causing its price to fall. With each country's cheap factor rising and its scarce factor falling in price, there is a strong tendency for factor prices to be brought to a common level in both countries.

Logically, the equalization of factor prices is more than a tendency—it is a certainty. Under free trade, given the usual assumptions of perfect competition and the absence of transport costs and taxes, commodity prices are bound to be equal everywhere. Moreover, if technology is identical for all countries, production functions are also everywhere the same. There is therefore a one-to-one relationship between commodity prices and factor prices. Hence the only set of factor prices consistent with identical production functions and identical commodity prices in different countries is a set that is equal.

This can be shown clearly with the aid of Figure 5.3. Assume that in our familiar two countries, free trade has brought the prices of food and clothing to a common international level, with food at 10 cents a unit and clothing at 20 cents. Since production functions are the same everywhere, isoquants that represent them will also be the same for every country. Therefore, we can draw a unit-value isoquant—one that stands for a single dollar's worth of output in both I and II at the *free trade prices* just mentioned. This is 10 physical units of food and 5 of clothing.

Figure 5.3   Factor Price Equalization

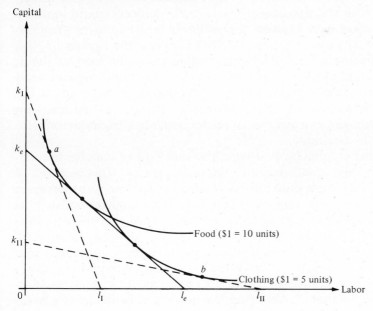

Now draw the $1 isocost line $k_I l_I$ representing the outlay of $1 on capital and labor in country I at their prices *before the opening of trade*. Because capital is then the cheap factor in I, a dollar will buy a relatively large amount, as indicated by the greater length of Ok_I than of Ol_I. Show the *different* factor prices in II, where labor is relatively cheap, by the isocost line $k_{II} l_{II}$. Since $k_I l_I$ is tangent to the food isoquant at point a, country I can produce $1 worth of food by using the factor combination indicated by that point. For country I to produce a dollar's worth of clothing, however, would require a large outlay, since its isocost line is well below the $1 clothing isoquant. Country II's isocost line, on the other hand, is tangent to the clothing isoquant at b, indicating that it can produce a dollar's worth of clothing with the factor combination corresponding to that point. But II cannot produce a dollar's worth of food with a dollar's worth of factors; it would have to spend more. The only set of factor prices consistent with identical production methods and identical commodity prices is the set represented by the isocost line $k_e l_e$, common to both countries.

This outcome would be ensured by the effects of trade. With its opening, country I would export its cheap product, food, while country II would export clothing. Adding production for export to each country's initial output for home consumption would raise the demand for the abundant factor—capital in I, labor in II—tending to increase its relative price. At the same time, clothing imports into I and food imports into II would cause domestic production of these goods to decline, reducing the demand for each country's scarce factor and thus its relative price. With no impediments to trade, this process would continue until factor prices were brought to equality in both countries. You can visualize this process in Figure 5.3 by imagining the isocost line $k_I l_I$ gradually rotating counterclockwise, sliding along the food isoquant, and $k_{II} l_{II}$ rotating clockwise, sliding along the clothing isoquant until the two isocost lines coincide at $k_e l_e$. Thus our argument leads to the basic conclusion: Given that commodity prices and production methods are the same in any two countries under free trade, factor price equalization is inevitable.

We must emphasize that complete factor price equalization depends on the prior equalization of commodity prices. This requires, of course, free trade under competitive conditions, with no transportation costs or other impediments to commodity price equalization, such as taxes. Other conditions, however, are also necessary for the equalization of factor prices. For one, factors of production must be qualitatively identical. Obsolete machinery is not the same as up-to-date machinery, nor is ill-nourished labor the same as well-fed labor. Moreover, the opening of trade must not lead to complete specialization in each country, for that would bring the process of factor price equalization to a halt before it was completed. A technical requirement of a mathematical character stipulates that the number of factors must not exceed the number of commodities, for then the relationship between relative factor and relative commodity prices breaks down. Finally, production functions must be such that, for any two goods compared, relative factor intensities remain the same for all relative factor prices. This means that, of goods F and C, it must not be possible for good F to be capital-intensive relative to C at one set of factor prices and labor-intensive at another set. This is known as the strong factor intensity assumption. We shall consider this assumption at a later, more appropriate point.

THE FACTORS OF PRODUCTION

We now turn to an examination of the character of the factors of production. Up to this point, we have considered only labor and capital, since to keep our model manageable, we have limited its scope to two goods and two factors. Later in this chapter, we shall introduce both land and entrepreneurship. Our immediate concern, however, is to look more closely at labor and capital. Our first inquiry will be into the way in which these factors differ in the short and in the long run and what this difference signifies. This leads to an examination of the basic nature of each of these factors.

Capital and Labor in the Short Run

We begin by drawing a sharp distinction: In the short run, capital and labor are specific; in the long run, they are homogeneous. The short run can vary from a few months to a good many years, depending on what industry we have in mind. We mean by "specific" that a factor's usefulness is generally limited to a particular type of operation, which in turn may be confined to a single industry. On the other hand, a factor is homogeneous when all units are alike and thus interchangeable. We shall see that in the long run, capital is homogeneous and that in a limited sense, so is labor.

In the short run, most forms of capital are highly specific. Only a limited number of relatively simple tools are useful over a wide range of industries; the heavy equipment and complex machinery that comprise most capital cannot be shifted from one industry to another. Much labor, too, because it possesses distinct skills, must be classified as specific; it cannot readily be transferred from one kind of work to another. Yet the extent of labor's specificity is far less than that of capital. Many industries require relatively large amounts of unskilled or semiskilled workers. Moreover, many if not most of the skills needed in most industries can be acquired in the relatively short period of two to three years.

The most important consequence of the short-run specificity of capital and labor is that during the period for which they are specific, their mobility ranges from low to zero. On the practical side, this means that adaptation to change is likely to be difficult and time consuming. The shift in demand from large to small cars occasioned by the huge rise in petroleum prices in the 1970s left American manufacturers in particular with large amounts of fixed equipment with no further use. The introduction of the pocket calculator meant the demise of the slide rule, a sharp decline in the demand for adding machines, and obsolescence of many kinds of facilities required for their production.

In the ideal world of theory, with its assumptions of perfect competition and perfect mobility of the factors within a country, adjustment to change takes place promptly, ensuring that factors are so reallocated that the value of the marginal product of each factor is the same in all uses. The required perfect mobility, however, implies that even in the short run, capital and labor must either be completely homogeneous or capable of instant transformation from one form into another.

In the real world, as we have seen, neither of these requirements of lightning mobility is met. Capital is frozen into concrete forms that endure for longer or shorter periods, while skilled labor cannot shed skills and acquire new ones overnight.

Adjustment to change nonetheless takes place. All forms of concrete capital can be homogenized, so to speak, by means of depreciation accounts. Each year some part of the value of a capital good is set aside in such an account. At the end of its useful life, provision will have been made for its replacement by transforming it into the liquid form of investible funds. This is the homogeneous, long-run form of capital. If shifts in demand or technological change make it necessary or desirable to replace capital goods that become obsolete before depreciation reserves are adequate, new financing—the investment of readily available liquid capital—will be required. These supplies of liquid capital arise, of course, through the process of saving—of foregoing the consumption of income and accumulating it in the form of investible funds, or generalized command over resources. As you have doubtless noted, the establishment of depreciation reserves is really a type of saving, since it requires a decision to forego consumption so as to ensure the replacement of existing capital goods rather than provide for the creation of new ones.

Capital and Labor Compared

Economists frequently draw a sharp distinction between capital in its familiar short-run form of capital goods and other factors of production, such as labor and land, or natural resources. The latter are characterized as original means of production which exist in their own right to begin with and do not have to be produced. All forms of concrete capital goods, on the other hand, are regarded as produced means of production. They are created by the investment of money or liquid capital to bring about the cooperation of labor, natural resources, and previously existing capital goods to produce a machine or piece of equipment.

     This distinction has only qualified validity. Capital goods, it is true, are definitely produced means of production. As for labor and land, they are "original" only in their pristine state, before they are involved, along with capital, in productive activity—before, that is, they truly become factors of production. Even unskilled labor would be useless for production without even elementary education that enabled workers to speak, read, and write their native language, and education requires the investment of capital in buildings and in the training of teachers. Perhaps unimproved land should be regarded as a factor, but even such land requires access roads, and many areas of land must be cleared, drained, or otherwise improved. As for natural resources such as mineral deposits, before they enter into production, mine shafts must be dug, and hoists, elevators, cars, rails, and other equipment provided. In sum, most if not all original means of production require at least some investment of capital before they are ready for productive use. They are a blend of labor and capital or of land and capital. There is, however, one sense in which "original" means of production differ from capital: Their supply is limited by nature. The supply of any natural resource is not freely producible, but is limited to nature's endowment, as also is the supply of unskilled or any grade of labor at any given time. The relevance of this point for our subject is that the supply of capital is far more flexible than that of land or even of labor.

Skills as Human Capital

Our simple model of the factor proportions theory presented in the early part of this chapter limited the number of factors to two: labor and capital. Both were undifferentiated. In fact, labor consists of many groups with skills that vary widely. Moreover, their distribution among nations also varies greatly and since skills affect productivity, their distribution among nations is an important element in international competition. Instead of reckoning labor as a single factor, we need to take into account subfactors with different skills.

Most skills of economic importance are not inborn, but are acquired by expenditure on education, both general and technical, apprenticeships, and on-the-job training. Such expenditure, of course, is a form of investment—investment in human capital. Total expenditures in any modern industrial nation comprise a large share of gross national product.

Historical examples of the importance of specialized skills are legion. The supremacy of England in textile production throughout the nineteenth century is one; another is the lead of the United States in cameras from Civil War days until recently, and the transfer of much of this industry to Germany and Japan.

In the present age of high technology, the importance of refined skills is increasing rapidly. Mass-production industries, which depend on repetitive operations, routine management, and relatively simple skills, have been moving to nations with abundant unskilled or semi-skilled labor. Examples are steel fabrication, heavy chemicals, shipbuilding, radios, television sets, pressed plastics, and many types of electrical appliances. The capital needed to finance construction of the plants of these undertakings has become increasingly mobile since World War II, with multinational corporations and large banks providing the funds (see Chapter 21).

Areas of high technology, such as computers, integrated circuitry, fiber-optic cables, titanium alloys, and specialized chemicals, require highly technical skills based on training in mathematics, science, and engineering. Japan has made great advances in these areas and at present leads the world. West Germany has come on fast. The United States, although its "silicon valleys" near San Francisco and Boston are prospering, still lags behind. One important reason for this relatively poor record is surely the backward state of teaching in mathematics and science in U.S. high schools and colleges. Investment in human capital has become of critical importance to the United States.

MULTIPLE FACTORS

Let us now continue to modify the factor proportions theory by broadening still further the range of factors to be considered.

Land, or Natural Resources

We shall start with land, which in classical writings was always included in the triumvirate of land, labor, and capital. Even in the long run, however, land, unlike capital, does not consist of homogeneous units, but is made up of a wide variety of distinct kinds, each suitable for a different purpose. Agricultural land is one very broad category, divisible into such subcategories as the great grain-producing regions of the world (temperate, comparatively fertile areas, with moderate rainfall), the tropical lowlands (suitable for sugar, bananas, pineapples, cacao, coconuts), and the medium-altitude lands of the tropics (the premier tea- and coffee-producing regions).

Forest resources are a highly specific kind of land, as are mineral deposits. It is obvious that a concept even broader than land, such as natural resources, is needed. This includes all forms of land-based resources, and should be extended to include such additional resources as fisheries and water power.

All of these discrete types of natural resources are specific to particular uses, most particularly, mineral deposits. The relation of such highly specific resources to the explanation of international trade is obvious: To produce a particular natural-resource-based product such as nickel ore, deposits of that ore are essential. A catch of fish can be obtained only from those limited areas that are the natural habitat of fish, such as the Newfoundland Banks, the salmon fisheries of the northwest Pacific, or the shrimp beds of the Gulf of Mexico.

To explain the localization of production and thus specialization in international trade in terms of the presence of a highly specific natural resource seems trite and trivial. Yet for many if not all primary products and basic foodstuffs, it is impossible to escape this conclusion. In their production, natural resources play a dominant role. Although capital and labor are of course necessary as cooperating factors, they are generally subordinate in importance.[2]

But primary products, or raw materials, comprise only one class of goods. In the manufacturing industries, labor and capital process raw materials into finished goods. Although it is true that some land is essential for factory and warehouse sites, its importance is minimal. In these processing industries, which account for a vast range of products, the two-factor model of labor and capital, modified to take account of subfactors of skilled labor, serves quite well. The same can be said of such service industries as banking, insurance, travel facilities, and so on.

---

[2] This is not so true of the products of the broader types of natural resources, such as land suitable for wheat, corn, and other grains. With the techniques available today, these commodities are capital-intensive; the cost of capital is the predominant element in their cost of production. A century ago, however, when techniques were simpler, the availability of suitable land was relatively of much greater importance.

Entrepreneurship

Up to this point, we have said relatively little about the entrepreneur and his role in production. Yet as the person (or group of persons) who brings capital, labor, and resources together, fashions them into a productive organization, and faces the risks of an uncertain world, he occupies a strategic position. Yet as long as we adhere to the assumption of perfect competition, this oversight is not too important. For in an economy in which all firms are small in scale, as they must be under conditions of perfect competition, the tasks of organizing and managing an enterprise are comparatively simple, and pretty much the same everywhere. Moreover, the degree of entrepreneurial ability required would be quite modest, and probably relatively evenly distributed around the world.

But when production is dominated by huge business organizations, as has increasingly become the case in the last 100 years or so, the problems of organization and management are highly complex. Their solution demands quite a different order of ability from that required by the small firm of perfect competition. For this reason, we shall postpone consideration of the factor of entrepreneurship until we are ready to deal with some of the problems raised by conditions of highly imperfect competition (Chapter 7).

SUMMARY

This chapter presents the leading modern theory of international trade, the Heckscher–Ohlin or factor proportions theory. Using a two-factor, two-commodity model, this theory attributes the proximate cause of trade, previously existing differences in relative commodity prices, to relative differences in national supplies of the factors. Each nation exports the good whose production requires relatively large inputs of its abundant and cheap factor and imports the good requiring relatively large inputs of its scarce and expensive factor. The remainder of the chapter turns first to a striking consequence of the opening of nations to international trade: a strong tendency toward the complete equalization of factor prices.

The remainder of the chapter discusses various characteristics of the factors themselves. First, attention is directed to the fact that both capital and labor, especially capital, take on highly specific forms in the short run. This means that the perfect mobility within a country postulated by theory is absent. Adjustment to change is therefore difficult and prolonged, yet it takes place, being made possible by saving for depreciation and saving for new investment. Next comes a comparison of capital, labor, and land as to their basic nature. The widely held view that capital is a produced means of production, while labor and land are original factors, is shown to be of limited validity, since even the latter factors usually contain an admixture of capital. Nonetheless, supplies of capital are generally far more flexible than those of "original" factors. A brief section calls attention to the importance of the skills of labor, which warrant their being treated as distinct subfactors. Their increasing importance in recent years is emphasized. The chapter ends by calling attention to the fact that natural resources must be included with capital and labor as a group of factors to be reckoned with in a more complete theory, as well as entrepreneurship in models where competition is far from perfect.

SELECTED REFERENCES

BHAGWATI, JAGDISH. "The Pure Theory of International Trade: A Survey." No. 7 in American Economic Association and Royal Economic Society, *Surveys of Economic Theory*, Vol. 2. New York: S. Martin's Press, Inc., 1965. Section 2 deals with factor price equalization.

CAVES, RICHARD E. *Trade and Economic Structure; Models and Methods.* Cambridge, Mass.: Harvard University Press, 1960. See Chapter 3 for a good review of factor price equalization.

CLEMENT, M. O., R. L. PFISTER, and K. J. ROTHWELL. *Theoretical Issues in International Economics.* Boston: Houghton Mifflin Company, 1967. Chapters 1–3 provide an excellent review and evaluation of the literature dealing with the factor-proportions theory and with the terms of trade.

FORD, J. L. *The Ohlin-Heckscher Theory of the Basis and Effects of Commodity Trade.* New York: Asia Publishing House, 1965. Provides a brief statement of the factor proportions theory and of Ohlin's theory dealing with "subsidiary" matters, together with a critique.

HECKSCHER, ELI. "The Effect of Foreign Trade on the Distribution of Income." *Ekonomisk Tidskrift,* **31** (1919). Reprinted in American Economic Association, *Readings in the Theory of International Trade*, New York: McGraw-Hill Book Company, 1949. The first formulation of the factor proportions theory.

JOHNSON, H. G. "Factor Endowments, International Trade, and Factor Prices." *The Manchester School of Economic Studies,* **25**, No. 3 (Sept. 1957). Reprinted in American Economic Association, *Readings in International Economics*, Homewood, Ill.: Richard D. Irwin, Inc., 1968. An alternative diagrammatic representation of the effect of trade on factor prices and factor price equalization.

OHLIN, BERTIL. *Interregional and International Trade.* Cambridge: Harvard University Press, 1933. Parts 1 and 2 provide the essentials of the theory as formulated by Ohlin.

ROBINSON, ROMNEY. "Factor Proportions and Comparative Advantage," in American Economic Association, *Readings in International Economics.* Homewood, Ill., Richard D. Irwin, Inc., 1968. A vigorous critique of the factor proportions theory.

SAMUELSON, P. A. "International Factor-price Equalization Once Again." *Economic Journal*, **59**, No. 234 (June 1949). Definitive statement of factor price equalization theorem, with both an intuitive proof and a rigorous mathematical proof.

STOLPER, W. F., and P. A. SAMUELSON. "Protection and Real Wages." *Review of Economic Studies*, **9** (Nov. 1941). Reprinted in American Economic Association, *Readings in the Theory of International Trade*, New York: McGraw-Hill Book Company, 1949. Contains original statement of effect of protection on factor prices, which is simply the reverse of the effect of trade on factor prices.

APPENDIX 1: DERIVATION OF THE PRODUCTION FRONTIER

The production frontier or production possibilities curve has been defined in Chapter 4 as the locus of points of efficient production at full employment of a country's resources of capital and labor. To prove this, together with all its implications, we construct a box diagram (Figure 5A1.1)—a rectangle whose sides represent a country's total supplies of capital and labor. We shall assume that our small country possesses relatively large amounts of labor compared to the rest of the world. By using O_c as the origin for clothing production, distances measured to the right along the lower horizontal axis indicate the amount of labor devoted to its production, while distances measured upward along the left-hand side of the vertical axis indicate the amount of capital so allocated. Starting at O_c, there could be drawn any number of labor-intensive isoquants reflecting higher and higher levels of clothing production as one moved upward and to the right. Of the possible infinite array, we have drawn a sample number of C isoquants.

With O_f as the origin for food production, and using the upper horizontal axis to measure the amount of labor devoted to food production and the right-hand vertical axis to measure capital so allocated, any number of F isoquants could be drawn, with levels of production rising as the isoquants moved downward away from O_f toward O_c.

Because the dimensions of the box correspond to the given and unchanging endowments of capital and labor, any point in the box represents full employment of the factors in the production of both goods. Thus at point d, O_cL_1 of labor is employed in producing clothing and O_cK_1 of capital. Since resources not employed in one industry are

Figure 5A1.1   Optimal Factor Allocation: The Efficiency Locus

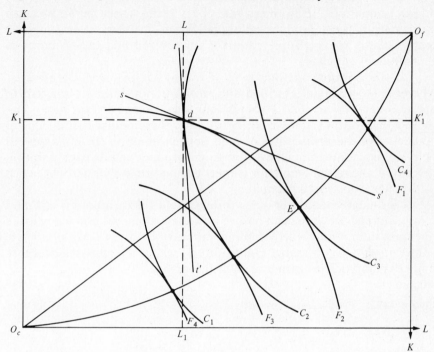

assumed to be employed in the other, $O_f L'_1$ of labor, measuring to the left (along the upper horizontal axis) is allocated to food production, and $O_f K'_1$ (along the right-hand vertical axis) of capital.

At d, which lies on both isoquants C_2 and F_2, these isoquants intersect, and as noted, both labor and capital are fully employed. This point, however, represents neither an optimal allocation of resources nor a position of equilibrium. The slope of the tangent tt' to isoquant C_2 is equal to the (inverse) ratio of marginal products in the production of clothing: $(dK/dL)_c = (MP_L/MP_K)_c$. The slope of the tangent ss' to the isoquant F_2 has the same relation to the marginal productivities in food: $(dK/dL)_f = (MP_L/MP_K)_f$. But the slopes of the two tangents are very different. That of the tangent to C_2 is much steeper and therefore has a higher numerical value than that of the tangent to F_2. Hence the ratio of marginal productivities is also different: $(MP_L/MP_K)_c > (MP_L/MP_K)_f$. Labor is relatively more productive in clothing, capital in the production of food. Labor should therefore be shifted from producing food to producing clothing, and capital from clothing to food until the ratios of marginal productivities are equal.

If this were done, the path of production would move along isoquant F_2 to E, with the level of food output remaining constant, while that of labor-intensive clothing rose to the level represented by the higher isoquant C_3. E is an optimal point in the sense that an increase in the output of one product cannot be obtained without decreasing the output of the other. Total output is maximized and the economy is economically efficient.

Point E is only one such point of technical efficiency. Others exist wherever isoquants of the food and clothing industries are tangent to one another. Figure 5A1.1 shows four such points of tangency. The curved line from O_c to O_f running through these points is the locus of efficiency in the production of food and clothing, it encompasses all points of economic efficiency or optimal production. At each point on this curve, the test of efficiency is met: The marginal productivity ratios in the two industries are equal.

Although the axes of our box diagram measure amounts of K and L, we can read off from each pair of isoquants along the efficiency locus the maximum obtainable combined outputs of F and C. We plot these values in a new diagram, Figure 5A1.2, whose coordinates measure units of commodities rather than of factors.

Figure 5A1.2   Production Frontier

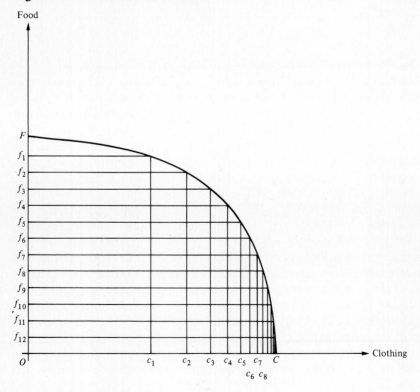

The resulting curve is the production frontier or production possibilities curve. It is concave to the origin for the reason given in the text. Starting with all resources devoted to food production, and gradually reducing output in this industry and shifting the released resources into clothing, the proportion of labor to capital in the transferred resources is inappropriate to the requirements of the clothing industry. The labor released is less than that called for by the labor-intensive production function of clothing, while capital becomes in excess supply. Wages rise, driving up the cost of clothing, while the return to capital falls. The unit cost of food declines.

In terms of quantities of clothing and food, equal reductions in the amounts of food produced will be accompanied by diminishing amounts of clothing. This is because the declining value of each decrement of food will purchase smaller and smaller increments of clothing.

APPENDIX 2: OFFER CURVES

In demonstrating the gain from trade (Chapter 4), we saw how a country responded to the establishment of a specific international price ratio. The diagram we used (Figure 4.7) showed simultaneously the production, consumption, and trade equilibria at that relative price. We shall find it useful to consider trade at various international prices. For this purpose, the offer curve or reciprocal demand curve is a very useful tool. An offer curve expresses the amounts of one commodity a country is willing to exchange for varying amounts of another over a range of international prices or terms of trade.

Derivation of an Offer Curve

The definition of an offer curve suggests that we confront consumers and producers in an economy with alternative international prices, and observe their reactions. This we do in the right-hand quadrant of Figure 5A2.1. We start with the situation existing before the opening of trade. Production and consumption of food and clothing are in equilibrium at E_0, at the domestic terms of trade represented by the slope of T_0. If the country were opened to trade and the international terms of trade were the same as the domestic, there would be no incentive for international trade to begin.

If, however, a price ratio somewhat more favorable to clothing were available abroad, as indicated by the steeper price line T_1, production would shift to P_1 while consumption would move onto the

Figure 5A2.1   Derivation of the Offer Curve

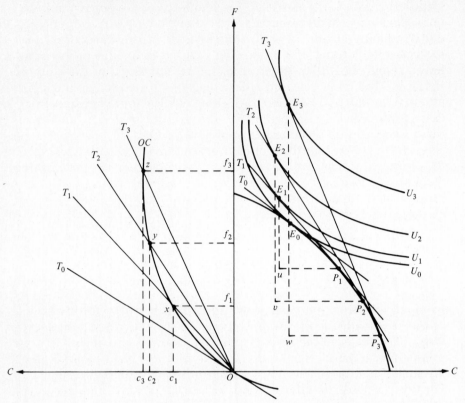

higher indifference curve U_1 at E_1, with the quantity uP_1 of clothing exported in exchange for uE_1 of food imports. Continuing this exercise, we confront the country with still better terms of trade for food, such as T_2 and T_3. For T_2 the volume of exports would rise to vP_2 of clothing and of imports to vE_2 of food. For T_3, exports offered would be wP_3 for imports of wE_3.

These data provide us with everything we need to construct the country's offer curve. In the left-hand quadrant of Figure 5A2.1, we draw the various terms of trade lines T_0, T_1, T_2, and T_3 with the same slopes as their counterparts in the right-hand quadrant. Enter exports on the horizontal axis at distances from the origin corresponding to uP_1, vP_2, and wP_3, giving the points c_1, c_2, and c_3. Imports are shown on the vertical axis as points f_1, f_2, and f_3, at distances above the origin corresponding to uE_1, vE_2, and wE_3 respectively. Run a dashed line from each of these pairs of points to its terms of trade line—from Oc_1 and Of_1 to x on T_1, etc.—then connect these points by a smooth curve, and we have the locus of equilibrium trade at various international prices. This curve (*OC*) is the country's offer or reciprocal demand curve. It shows the amounts of clothing the country is willing to offer in exchange for specific amounts of food at each of a series of relative prices. Our derivation makes clear that these amounts are not fortuitous, but are firmly anchored in the consumption preferences of the community and in its conditions of supply—its production possibilities.

Elasticity

Elasticity is a measure of the responsiveness of one variable to changes in a related variable. With an ordinary demand curve, it is the responsiveness of quantity purchased to changes in price, with both expressed in percentage terms. Elasticity is reflected in variations in total outlay or expenditure, $P \times Q$. As long as price reductions lead to an increase in total outlay, demand is elastic. When total outlay diminishes as price falls, demand is inelastic.

For an offer curve, outlay is not money expenditure but the quantity of export goods offered for imports, and the price is relative: the price of imports in terms of exports. Thus along the offer curve *OC* in Figure 5A2.1, elasticity is positive over the entire distance from *O* to *z*, since the amount of exports offered constantly increases as the relative price of imports falls. Elasticity is very great at first, from *O* to *x*, and from there on diminishes in value rapidly. At *z* elasticity is unity, since at this point exports offered cease to rise. Beyond *z*, if the offer curve turns towards the vertical axis, it becomes inelastic. Further reductions in the relative price of imports are accompanied by a reduction in exports offered.

6
CHAPTER

Modifications of the Basic Model

Having set forth the basic theory of international trade that has dominated discussion for some fifty years, we are now ready to begin relaxing some of its restrictive assumptions, so as to bring the theory more in line with the complexities of the real world. In the preceding chapter, besides considering the mobility of capital and labor in the long and in the short run, we extended our two-commodity, two-factor model by adding a third factor, natural resources. This in no way altered the conclusions of the factor proportions theory. Our next step will be to see how that theory is affected by allowing for trade in more than two goods. After exploring this topic, we shall take into account the fact, hitherto ignored, that transport costs are always present. Finally, beginning with the distinction made in the preceding chapter between the long-run mobility of capital and labor and the high degree of immobility, especially of capital, in the short run, we shall consider the process of adjustment to a disturbance of equilibrium. We shall focus on a particular type of disturbance, a rise in the price of an industry's product, and examine how this affects the distribution of income between capital and labor.

MANY GOODS

The only change we now make is to introduce several goods into our model. Otherwise, we continue to assume only two factors, capital and labor, and two countries, I and II. Labor is relatively abundant in I, capital in II. Instead of two goods, we shall consider five: a, b, c, d, and e. We assume that each country has full access to the available technology, and further, that the techniques of production embodied in the production functions differ from one good to another. That is, the capital–labor intensity is different for each of the five goods, but the same for each good in both countries. All goods can then be ranked in terms of their relative factor intensity. If we suppose that a is the most capital-intensive, and that each succeeding good is relatively less so, then in the absence of trade, a will be relatively the cheapest good in country II (with abundant capital), e relatively the cheapest in I, with the dividing line somewhere in between. For the sake of simplicity, let c be on the dividing line. Then a and b will be relatively cheaper in II, d and e in I, and c the same in relative price in both countries. Then upon the opening of trade, II will export a and b, while I will export d and e.

The situation just described can be illustrated diagrammatically. In Figure 6.1, the three straight lines are isocost lines, showing the quantities of capital and labor that can be purchased for a dollar, taken to be the common currency. The steepest of these, $k_{II}l_{II}$, with a slope of $2K/1L$, is the isocost line for country II before the opening of trade; capital is relatively cheap there. $k_I l_I$, with the relatively flat slope of $1K/3L$, is country II's isocost line. Finally, $k_e l_e$ is the isocost line for both countries under free trade, when factor prices have been equalized in the two countries.

The isoquants in the diagram are unit-value isoquants, which show the amounts of each good that can be produced for a dollar at prevailing factor prices.[1] Since we have ranked the goods in the descending order of their capital intensity, and since country II will specialize in the production of a and b, while country I specializes in d and e, we show dollar isoquants a' and b' tangent to II's isocost line, d' and e' tangent to I's, while c is tangent to both. (To avoid complicating the diagram, the dollar isoquants for d and e in I and a and b in II are not shown.) With the opening of trade, commodity prices will be brought to equality in the two countries, and factor prices will be equalized as well, as was shown in the preceding chapter. Both countries now share the common isocost line $k_e l_e$ and all five isoquants are tangent to that line.

The outcome of our five-commodity model thus turns out to be the same as with two commodities. Relative factor abundance determines in what goods each country will specialize. We are therefore entitled to conclude that the introduction of more than two goods into the model leaves it unimpaired. On the usual rigorous assumptions,

---

[1] Distances along lines radiating from the origin measure quantities of output; the slope of such lines measures relative factor intensity. Thus the ray Oa^*, the steepest of the rays in Figure 6.1, indicates high capital intensity relative to the other rays.

Figure 6.1   Factor Price Equalization with Several Goods

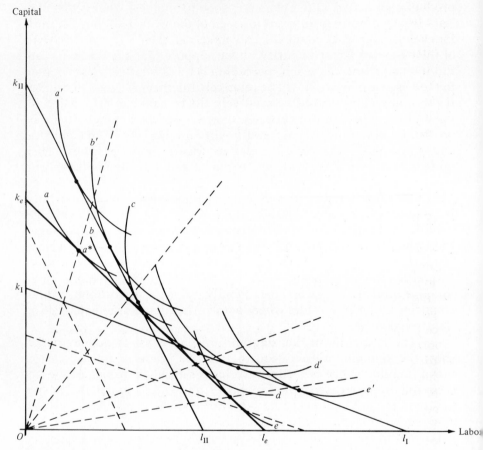

the prices of both goods and factors will be equalized. Moreover, because of increasing opportunity costs, each country will produce some of every commodity. Specialization will not be complete, as in a constant-cost model;[2] production of import-competing goods will continue.

Degrees of Specialization

If our model is allowed to become increasingly complex by enlarging the number of trading countries and the number of commodities traded, the possibility of intensified specialization increases, since a wider range of goods implies a wider range of factor requirements,

[2] Constant costs could exist either if there were only one factor of production, as in the Ricardian model, or if with two or more factors, all goods were produced according to a single production function and thus with identical factor intensities.

while with more countries, there is likely to be a considerable variety in relative factor endowments. Thus the correspondence between relative factor endowments and required factor proportions is almost certain to be spread over a large number of goods. This would allow many countries to concentrate their production on goods for which this correspondence was greatest. Finally, if allowance is made for the presence of several kinds of natural resources in addition to capital and labor, the range of pretrade price differences will obviously be greater. Nations with the greatest comparative advantage will specialize more intensively on their most favored export products, while those with the least comparative advantage will put up little competition with imports of such goods.

COSTS OF TRANSPORT

One of the assumptions underlying the equalization of commodity and factor prices is that there are no transport costs involved in the international exchange of goods. But in addition to freight charges, there are loading and unloading costs, cargo insurance, and interest on the cargo while in transit. When such costs are taken into account, the price of an imported good will be higher in the importing than in the exporting market by the amount of these costs. Equalization of commodity prices (and therefore also of factor prices) is prevented. The higher price of imports shelters producers of import-competing goods from foreign competition and permits production of those goods to be larger than it otherwise would. The extent of international specialization is therefore lessened. When costs of transport exceed the initial price spread, international trade will be unprofitable, and we have the extreme case of nontraded goods.

The most general aspect of transport costs is that they raise the delivered price of all goods, although as just indicated, in widely varying degree. A number of *special aspects* of these costs deserve attention. The most noteworthy is that the services of transportation are rendered *jointly* to a number of different goods. The same resources (such as a railway's roadbed, rolling stock, and terminal facilities) are used in carrying a large number of products. It is impossible to attribute specifically to a single commodity any of the large overhead costs of transport or more than a small proportion of operating costs. Given this costing difficulty, transportation services are generally priced on the basis of "what the traffic will bear." Rates per ton-mile are usually somewhat lower on bulky or heavy items with a low value per ton, such as coal, lumber, iron ore, grains, and crude oil, compared with compact, valuable articles, such as cameras, watches, and jewelry.

A further special feature of transportation charges is the phenomenon of *low "back haul" rates*. From every major shipping center, there radiates outward a network of rail, ship, plane, and truck lines. Each type of conveyance must make both an outbound and a return journey. If, at equal freight rates for inward and outward movement, the volume of traffic carried in each direction were about the same, there would be no problem. If rates were identical in both directions, however, more tonnage would often be carried in one direction than in the other. Without some specific inducement, such as especially low rates, trains or ships will have to make one voyage empty, or partially so. Their loads may be increased if transport charges are lowered. Hence the low rates on coal shipped from Cleveland or Erie to Duluth, as against the much higher rate on iron ore moving in the opposite direction.

Among other peculiarities of transport pricing, we may mention the practice of quoting lower rates for the long haul than for the short haul, which may result from the desire to stimulate increased traffic to outlying points, from the need to meet competition (as between rail and ship between Atlantic and Pacific coast ports of the United States), or simply because the long haul spreads some overhead costs thinner. And there is the advantage afforded canal and river barges by the fact that operating as distinct from overhead costs are unusually low for barges; once goods are loaded, the cost of transporting them is scarcely greater for a long than for a short journey. Hence the exceptionally low rates on long-distance barge traffic compared with rail or truck transport, where operating costs vary much more with distance.

Transport Costs and the Location of Industry

If transport costs bore with equal weight on all goods—that is, if they were an equal percentage of the cost of each commodity—they would raise the landed cost of imports and providing there were some natural protection to competing domestic producers of those goods, enable them to maintain their production at a higher level than in the absence of transport costs. They would not, however, affect the original location of industry. But since the relative burden of transport costs does vary widely, the location of industries among countries, and thus the pattern of international trade, is affected.

Of particular importance is the fact that all commodities require raw materials for their production, and that freight rates are generally lower on raw materials than on finished articles. Moreover, the manufacturing processes may by their very character eliminate much of the weight of the materials used, or, on the other hand, they may add to the weight or bulk of the finished goods at a rather late stage of processing.

These complexities increase the difficulty of determining the most economical point at which to locate production, and they lend themselves poorly to generalization. Nonetheless, even though one can derive no broad, simple rule, one can arrange commodities into three groups in terms of where their processing will tend to take place. Commodities may be materials or fuel oriented, market oriented, or neutral in their orientation.

Materials-Oriented Commodities When the cost of transporting the raw material (or fuel) to the market exceeds the cost of transporting the finished good, the processing or finishing industry will tend to locate near the site of raw-materials production. This will generally be the case if the raw material loses much weight in processing, for there is no sense in shipping waste matter to the point of manufacture. Thus lumber manufacture usually takes place near timber stands; the bark, sawdust, and other waste are left behind, and only the finished lumber is shipped to the market. Vancouver, British Columbia, is an important lumber-milling center. Spruce trees are felled in the woods some hundreds of miles to the north, formed into huge rafts at tidewater, and towed (cheaply) to Vancouver. There an adequate supply of labor, and the external economies available in an industrial city provide excellent conditions for milling. The finished lumber is then loaded on ships and carried to markets all over the world.

Cotton ginning and baling (but not spinning and weaving), the extraction of cane and beet sugar and turpentine and rosin, vegetable canning, and pottery manufacture are further examples of materials-oriented processes. Aluminum refining requires immense quantities of electric power (the fuel factor). Hence the processing occurs not at the source of the raw material (bauxite) in Jamaica and Guyana, but near the Grand Coulee Dam in the state of Washington, and in British Columbia and in Ghana, where cheap hydroelectric power is available.

Coal has immense drawing power, especially for the iron and steel and engineering industries, which are heavy users of this fuel. The greatest industrial area in western Europe arose in the coal deposits of the Ruhr—first iron and steel manufacture, drawing its ore from Lorraine and then northern Sweden, then industries fabricating heavy iron and steel products and needing coal for fuel, as well as heavy steel sheets, rods, and bars as intermediate inputs.

Market-Oriented Commodities Just as weight-losing commodities tend to be attracted to the supply of raw materials or fuel, so commodities that gain weight or bulk in processing are attracted to the market. Automobile assembly used to be of this character, especially in the era of large cars. In the United States, parts were made principally in Detroit or Flint, attracted originally by the availability of capital and enterprise and held there by ready accessibility of raw materials and fuel. Assembly in this area, however, was only for nearby markets. To serve more distant markets, both domestic and foreign, assembled parts, concentrated in small space, were shipped to widely scattered assembly plants. With the rapid increase in the popularity of small, compact cars, the element of bulk has become far less important. The new compacts are shipped assembled, both in the United States and from such major producers as Germany and Japan.

Coca-Cola extract is made in Atlanta. This is carried all over the world to local bottling companies, where carbonated water is added and the produce bottled. Beer and ink, like soft drinks, are weight-adding products. They, too, tend to be produced near their market areas.

Also market-oriented are perishable commodities, such as bread and baked goods, flowers, ice, and fresh milk. Fresh vegetables in season used to be in this category, but increasingly are shipped long distances, particularly in the United States, by refrigerated truck instead of by slower rail transport.

Neutral Commodities   Some commodities, or more accurately, processes, are neutral or indifferent to the pull of supply or of the market, and hence may locate at either point (or occasionally at intermediate points). This will be true when transport costs are unimportant in relation to processing costs, or when there is little gain or loss in weight or bulk during processing. In the former category are matches, plastic novelties, photographic equipment, cigarette lighters, and other small metal objects; in the latter, cotton and woolen textiles, cement, boots and shoes, and furniture.

When transport costs exert little influence, either because they are unimportant or because they exert a roughly equal pull toward materials and market, other elements, including relative factor costs, will be decisive in determining industrial location.

Even sheer accident can be important. This is well illustrated by the origins of the photographic industry of Rochester, New York, which can be traced to the accidental settling in that city in the first half of the nineteenth century of a small number of German lens grinders. With the outbreak of the Civil War, orders of telescope and binocular lenses poured in, requiring the training of additional workers and bringing prosperity and renown to Rochester. After the war, it was only natural that the photographic industry should locate in this city.

INCOME DISTRIBUTION AND THE SHORT-RUN IMMOBILITY OF CAPITAL

Up to now in this chapter we have undertaken one major modification of the basic two-factor, two-commodity model required to make it correspond more closely to the real world: We expanded the analysis to allow for the production of more than two goods. Then we examined the effect of taking into account the existence of transport costs, hitherto ignored. We now consider an interesting implication of the short-run immobility of capital.

You will recall that in the preceding chapter we stressed the fact that in the long run, capital and labor are both highly mobile within a country, but that in the short run, both factors, especially capital, are immobile. Capital is thus immobile because of its embodiment in specific forms that can only be rendered mobile very gradually through the establishment of depreciation reserves. We now consider a special aspect of this short-run immobility of capital: its effect on the distribution of income between the factors.

We shall use our familiar two-commodity, two-factor model, with food the capital-intensive and clothing the labor-intensive product. The only difference from our earlier discussion of this model is that capital in each industry takes specific concrete forms which are suited only to the industry in question. Whereas capital is thus immobile for a short run of unspecified length, labor is assumed free to move between the industries without restriction.[3]

The Basis for Increasing Opportunity Cost

As the heading of this entire section indicates, our concern is with the consequences for the distribution of the immobility of capital in the short run. Before entering upon that discussion, however, it is essential to establish an important point: the fact that although, like the long-run H-O model, our short-run model is one of increasing opportunity cost, the reason for this condition is very different in the two cases.

In the long-run model, with its assumption of factors freely mobile between industries, you will recall that increasing opportunity cost results from interindustry differences in factor intensities. As one industry, say clothing, which is labor-intensive, expands at the expense

---

[3] This differs from our discussion in Chapter 5, where we took into account the fact that for periods of perhaps two to three years, skilled labor should be considered relatively immobile.

of the capital-intensive food industry, the latter releases resources in proportions ill-suited to the current needs of clothing production. The capital content of the bundles of factors transferred to C is large relative to the proportion in actual use. Labor acquires more capital to aid it, so wages rise, while the increased abundance of capital drives its return down. Similar factor price changes occur in F because of the perfect long-run mobility of the factors. With wages higher, the cost of producing C will rise because of the greater weight of labor in its production, while that of producing F will fall. The opportunity cost of C in terms of F will therefore increase, and the production possibilities curve is concave toward its origin.[4]

Whereas in this long-run model, with both factors fully mobile, output in either industry can be increased by an interindustry flow of *both* factors, in our short-run model with capital frozen into place, output in one industry can be increased only by an interindustry movement of labor. Suppose that output of C is increased by the transfer of labor from F. The application of additional labor to the fixed amount of capital in industry C sets in operation the principle of diminishing returns. As the input of labor increases, so does the output of C, but at a constantly diminishing rate. Therefore, the marginal product of labor steadily declines. Meanwhile this principle operates in industry F in reverse: As labor leaves that industry, the marginal product of each remaining worker increases. The relative cost of producing C rises, which means increasing opportunity cost; the transformation curve has the typical shape, bowed outward from the origin.

Summarizing the argument, increasing opportunity costs in the short run, when capital is frozen into immobility, results from the operation of diminishing returns. Since this is a relationship between increments of a variable factor applied to a fixed factor, short-run increasing costs are the consequence of the assumption that capital is fixed and immobile. In contrast, in the long run, when both labor and capital are perfectly mobile, increasing costs are attributable to the fact that factor intensities differ among industries.

Adjustment to a Change in Relative Prices

We begin our analysis of short-run adjustment to change with our familiar model in equilibrium under free trade, with food and clothing prices in accord with international demands and with the value of the marginal product of capital and labor the same in both industries. Introduce now a fairly typical source of disturbance: a change in relative

---

[4] For a fuller account of the basis for long-run increasing cost, see pp. 68–69; also Appendix 1 of Chapter 5.

Figure 6.2 Short-Run Adjustment to a Change in Price

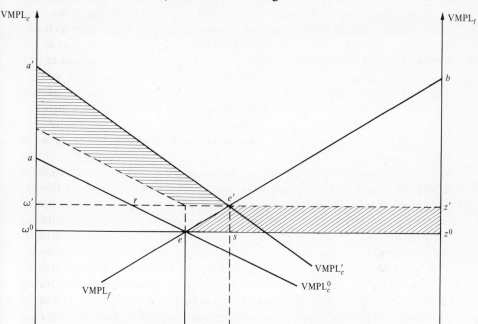

prices owing to an enduring change in international demand. Let this change involve a rise in the relative price of clothing.

The Short Run   A rise in the relative price of C will attract labor, the only mobile factor, away from industry F. The initial equality in the value of labor's marginal produce in the two industries will, because of its mobility, be preserved.

Both the initial conditions and those that develop as a result of the price change can be shown in a simple diagram. Figure 6.2 shows both the initial set of conditions and those that develop later.[5] The length of the horizontal axis represents the total supply of labor in the economy, which is assumed to remain constant. The value of labor's marginal product ($VMPL$) is measured on the vertical axis, that on the left referring to industry C, that on the right to industry F.

Starting from the initial equilibrium, with the price of C given,

[5] This diagram, and the analysis that follows, were first used by Michael Mussa in his article, "Tariffs and the Distribution of Income: The Importance of Factor Specificity, Substitutability, and Intensity in the Long Run," *Journal of Political Economy*, **82** (1974), and later by J. Peter Neary, "Short-Run Capital Specificity and the Pure Theory of International Trade," *Economic Journal*, **88** (Sept. 1978).

the line beginning at *a* represents $VMPL_c$ which declines as the quantity of labor employed in *C* increases. $VMPL_f$ is drawn similarly for the given initial equilibrium price of *F*, shown by the line starting at *b*. The two lines intersect at *e*, establishing an equilibrium wage of w^0, with O_cL^0 of the labor force employed in *C* and O_fL^0 in *F* production.

If the price of *C* now rises by some given percentage, this will be reflected in an equal proportional rise in the $VMPL_c$ line, say to $VMPL'_c$. There is now an excess demand for labor at w^0 because producers of *C* want to expand output. They do so by bidding labor away from producers of *F* in the amount L^0L'. Although capital, being specific to each industry cannot be reallocated, with the rise in the price of *C* and the increased employment of labor in its production, the return to capital employed there increases, while it falls in *F*. It will rise in *C* because the value of total output will increase in proportion to the rise in the price of *C*, which is greater than labor's increase in total wages.[6] The total return to capital in *F*, on the other hand, where the price of *F* remains constant, declines from the amount bez^0 to the amount $be'z'$, with the loss to capital in *F* measured by the shaded area on the right.

In contrast to capital, labor, whose money wage has risen, gains in terms of *F* but loses in terms of *C*, whose price has risen more than the wage. Whether labor enjoys a net *real* gain therefore depends on the relative importance of *C* and *F* in its consumption pattern. *These changes in the factoral distribution of income are the consequence of the assumption of sector-specific capital together with mobile labor.*

Suppose that we had assumed that production was capital-intensive instead of labor-intensive. The short-run result would have been no different. A rise in the price of *C* would, as before, raise *VMPL* in that industry, attracting labor from *F* and raising wages in both industries by an equal amount, an outcome guaranteed by the mobility of labor. Being immobile, only that capital in *C* will gain, while that in *F* suffers a decline in its return. Whether labor enjoys a net real gain from the rise in its money wages depends again on its consumption pattern.

What are the implications for economic policy of these short-run effects of a change in relative commodity prices? Clearly, since the return to capital increases in the industry whose price has risen (*C*), capitalists in that industry will tend to favor the policies that raise or maintain the price of their product. In practice, this means a favoring of tariff or a subsidy when price competition from abroad is intensive,

---

[6] In terms of the diagram, the gain to labor is easily shown. It is the rectangular area $w^0w'e's$. The difference between the return to capital in *C* before the price rise (the triangular area aw^0e) and its return after that rise (the larger area $a'w'e'$) is the shaded area to the left of and below $a'e'$.

and perhaps interest in measures to assist exports when the industry is competitive but has not yet developed export markets.

The interest of labor, on the other hand, is ambiguous, since any real gain depends on labor's consumption pattern. This is particularly true in a world of many commodities. Although a rise in the price of a single good could be seen to be advantageous to labor, since any one good is unlikely to carry a heavy weight in consumption, that advantage would be small, since the general rise in money wages would also tend to be small. With regard to the labor force in the particular industry whose price is directly involved, however, it would have a distinct interest in supporting measures that would raise the price of its product.

The Long Run   Since in the long run both labor and capital are completely mobile, the direction of change in income distribution depends entirely upon relative factor intensities. A rise in the price of one of two commodities will cause its production to expand, attracting resources from the other industry. If the expanding industry is labor-intensive, it will acquire relatively large amounts of capital from the capital-intensive industry, which will raise wages and depress the return to capital. If the expanding industry is capital-intensive, it will acquire relatively large amounts of labor, which will depress wages and raise the return to capital. Thus in the long run, a rise in the price of one of two goods will benefit the factor intensive in the good whose price rises.

The implication for long-term policy is thus that capitalists will benefit from a rise in the price of a capital-intensive good, labor from a rise in the price of a labor-intensive one. Foresight is uncertain, however, and it is the more so the longer the period involved. Hence short-run considerations generally prevail over long-run ones, and policies to effect a rise in the price of a good will probably be supported by investors in the industry in question rather than by labor.

SUMMARY

This chapter introduced one modification of the simple 2-2-2 model of the factor proportions theory: It extended the analysis to include several goods rather than only two. This model is based on the assumption, among others, that production functions, although differing from one good to another, are the same in all countries for each good. This means that one can rank any array of goods in the order of their relative factor intensities. With factor prices different in our countries, each will have lower costs in those goods that are intensive in its relatively abundant factor, and will specialize in and export those goods. In other words, the same principle of specialization applies for any number of goods. A second modification, unrelated to the basic model but applying to all theoretical discussions of international trade, involved taking into account the existence of transport costs. It was shown that in general, such costs raise the price of imports in importing countries, reducing the volume of trade, perhaps eliminating it. Equalization of commodity and of factor prices is made impossible. Because transport services are rendered jointly to a number of goods, it is impossible to attribute transport costs accurately to individual goods. Hence the principle generally adopted is: "Charge what the traffic will bear," which means low rates on bulky items and high rates on compact or valuable ones. Other rate differentials are low rates for "back hauling" and for long hauls. Such rate differentials can affect the localization of industry, as where low rates on raw materials or fuels attract processing to those sites rather than to the market.

A final section of this chapter extended the discussion of factor mobility taken up in Chapter 4. It showed that the short-run immobility of capital, frozen into highly specific forms of capital goods, means that a disturbance to equilibrium such as a rise in the price of a traded good would raise wages generally, and raise the return to capital in the affected industry, but lower it elsewhere.

SELECTED REFERENCES

MUNDELL, R. A. *International Economics.* New York: Macmillan Publishing Company, 1968, Chapter 5. A diagrammatic treatment of transportation costs in a general equilibrium model.

MUSSA, MICHAEL. "Tariffs and the Distribution of Income: The Importance of Factor Specificity, Substitutability, and Intensity in the Long Run," *Journal of Political Economy,* **82,** (Nov./Dec. 1974). Analysis underlying Figure 6.2 is contained in this article.

SAMUELSON, P. A., "International Factor Price Equalization Once Again," *Economic Journal,* **59** (June 1949). Definitive statement of the factor price equalization theorem, with an intuitive proof and a rigorous mathematical proof.

STOLPER, W. F., and P. A. SAMUELSON. "Protection and Real Wages," *Review of Economic Studies,* **9** (Nov. 1941). Reprinted in American Economic Association, *Readings in the Theory of International Trade.* New York: McGraw-Hill Book Company, 1949. Contains an original statement of the effect of protection on factor prices, which is simply the reverse of the effect of trade on those prices.

7
CHAPTER

Alternative Bases for Trade

Before examining alternatives to the Heckscher–Ohlin theory, which has occupied center stage in the explanation of the basis for international trade for some fifty years, let us review briefly the ground we have covered. We began by formulating a simplified two-factor, two-commodity, general equilibrium model of prices and production for a single market. In this model, commodity prices in an individual national market are determined by all the complex forces of demand and supply. Such prices will differ among nations and thus justify international trade when national differences in any of those forces exist. Heckscher and Ohlin stressed differences on the supply side, in particular, differences in national endowments of the factors of production.[1]

The factor proportions theory, however, as well as the general equilibrium theory of which it is a special adaptation, rests on a number of simplifying assumptions, necessary to reduce the complexity of the real world to manageable proportions. This is common practice in theoretical analysis, but any conclusions reached are valid only for the simplified model on which they are based. To ensure their validity for the real world, the restrictive assumptions must be removed.

We made a start on this process in Chapter 5, where we dealt with the assumption of the homogeneity of capital and labor, and with the limitation of their number to those two. Although complicating the analysis somewhat, these changes did no damage to the basic factor proportions theory. In the preceding chapter, we showed that ex-

---

[1] It is, of course, true that if two countries had identical relative factor endowments, price differences and thus a basis for trade would exist if tastes, and therefore demands, for factor services differed appreciably. Although a theoretical possibility, there has been little interest in it, either from an empirical or a theoretical point of view. We shall, therefore, devote no further attention to this possible basis for trade.

115

panding the simple model from two goods to several left its conclusions unharmed. An extended discussion of transport costs indicated that in general they reduce the overall volume of international trade by increasing its costliness, whereas with particular reference to goods that lose or gain weight in the process of manufacture, the location of certain processes and thus the pattern of trade may be affected but the basis for foreign trade itself is unaltered. Finally, having shown in Chapter 5 that the assumption of perfect internal mobility of labor and capital meant that the H-O theory was long-run in character, we took into account the fact that for considerable periods capital, in particular, may be frozen into specific forms suited only for employment in a particular industry. Again, this modification, while affecting the short-run distribution of income, provides no new basis for trade.

Among other simplifications that remain to be considered are the assumptions that factor supplies are given and remain constant, and that between countries, all factors are completely immobile. We shall take these fully into account in Chapter 9. There remain for discussion only three provisos. One, probably the most important, is the assumption of perfect competition in product markets, which we shall take up presently, and along with it, the hitherto ignored role of entrepreneurship. In the next section we shall consider briefly the proviso introduced by Paul Samuelson, that production functions, although varying from one good to another, are everywhere the same.[2]

DIFFERENCES IN TECHNOLOGY

In Chapter 4 we characterized a production function as a statement of the technically most efficient relationship between inputs and outputs in the production of a commodity. For any single good, its production can be expressed as a mathematical equation that gives the range of efficient combinations of inputs (say of capital and labor) at various prices of those inputs. At any given time and place, such production functions embody the known technology. If, as Samuelson assumed, production functions and therefore technology were everywhere the same, obviously international differences in technology could not be a basis for trade.[3] If there were no impediments to the transmission of such knowledge, there would be no reason why technology (and pro-

---

[2] This exhausts the list of assumptions, except for the one specifying that in equilibrium, income and expenditure are equal. This provision is irrelevant to the present discussion but will reappear in Part 5.

[3] This does not mean that all production functions are alike, but that although such functions differ among goods, they are the same in all countries.

duction functions) should not be the same everywhere. Even today, however, the transmission of technological knowledge to some parts of the world is highly imperfect. Certain primitive areas, such as Papua and New Guinea, have scarcely been touched by modern techniques, and in much of the Third World, cultural conditions such as poverty, poor educational facilities, inadequate communications, anti-Western feeling, and even religion stand in the way of easy transmission of modern technology.

Between modern industrial nations, on the other hand, the transfer of knowledge is extremely rapid. Patents, of course, reserve the use of certain processes and devices to their originators, but leasing of patents greatly extends their use. Therefore, in the industralized West, an approximation to a broad identity of technology could be said to exist. Insofar as the developed world is concerned, differences in technology (as distinct from technological change) provide no significant basis for international trade. As between the advanced industrial nations and less developed countries, however, differences in technology existing at any time are clearly responsible for a large volume of trade, especially in sophisticated manufactured goods.

Much more important than differences in technology is the dynamic element of change in technology, which we shall examine presently. But first it is important to consider the consequences of relaxing the assumption of perfect competition, together with the closely related matter of the nature of entrepreneurship in the modern world.

COMPETITION IN THE MODERN WORLD

The Meaning of Perfect Competition

For perfect competition to exist in any industry, four criteria must be met.

1. The number of firms producing a given good or service must be so large that the presence or absence of any one of them would have no influence on the price.
2. The product must be homogeneous, or consist of identical units.
3. New firms must be able to enter the industry without hindrance.
4. Decisions must be made independently, or without collusion.

A firm that meets these tests is a price taker; it can vary its output as much as it pleases without any concern about selling its product.

Ability to meet the price established in the market is the only criterion of success. Because of this, and because his product is like that of all his competitors, the individual producer has no incentive to advertise or to undertake sales campaigns. The entrepreneur's most onerous tasks would arise in connection with getting his business started: raising capital, investing it in plant and equipment, hiring the requisite labor force, contracting for supplies of raw materials or semifinished goods to be processed, and making arrangements for the sale of the output. Once the enterprise was under way, provided that it was efficient enough to cover its costs and show a normal profit, operation of such a firm would be routine. Its management would require little in the way of special aptitudes or training.

Restrictions on Competition

This description might have fitted the condition of industry in the time of Adam Smith, when the Industrial Revolution had scarcely begun, and possibly it could be applied to a large share of industry during most of the nineteenth century. But it does not correspond in any significant degree to market structure or industrial reality in the twentieth century. Throughout the industrialized nations, most major industries are either limited to a few large firms (oligopoly), or consist of a fairly large number of producers dominated by a relatively small number.[4] Large enterprises predominate, due partly to economies which are the accompaniment of large size (doubling the size of a truck motor more than doubles its power), or are due to the related indivisibility of certain large units of capital (a steel rolling mill).

Large-scale economies can arise, not only from the use of specialized machines, but also from spreading the cost of some kinds of labor over large output. Large firms can maintain relatively smaller inventories than small firms, thus reducing clerical labor costs. They can also make bulk shipments, which lessen storage, handling, and shipping charges. And some activities not directly related to current operations, such as research, planning, and public relations, increase in cost less rapidly than output.

Among the industrialized nations of the Western world, the industries of major importance—those that employ a large share of the labor force and that play a significant role in international trade—are of this oligopolistic character. They include the manufacture of aluminum, copper, iron and steel, industrial chemicals, pharmaceuticals,

---

[4] This is a sort of qualified oligopoly. It is not "monopolistic competition," which embodies a relatively large number of firms practicing some degree of product differentiation.

electrical equipment, automobiles, construction equipment, farm equipment, the refining and distribution of petroleum, much food processing, shipbuilding, and so on in a long list. In the United States, even a large share of agricultural products are dominated by large agribusinesses.

Product Versus Price Competition

If competition among the members of a perfectly competitive industry is focused entirely on price, among oligopolists such competition is carefully avoided. It is simply too dangerous, since it tends to become cutthroat in character. Despite their avoidance of price cutting, however, large firms do not enjoy an easy life. Their products do not sell themselves, as they do under perfect competition, where price is the only consideration. Competition can be fierce, since a major goal of every firm is to expand its sales and if possible gain a larger share of the market. Instead of focusing on prices, "competition among the few" centers on the product itself—on its real or fancied merits. This has consequences of great importance for the character of modern management, for the way in which it is organized, and for the process of technological change itself.

Management and Organization

Because of the very size of the firm so typical of modern industry, management of the production process itself is more complex and more important than in the small-scale plant of perfect competition. The switch from price competition to product competition, and the accompanying need to distinguish one firm's product from another's, creates the need for a whole range of different activities and for their effective coordination. Besides the personnel engaged in actual production, there are the sales promotion staff and the personnel required to service the product, including the financing of sales. Usually of great importance is the area of research and development, which has a particular need for individuals with technical training. Finally, most important is the coordination of all these diverse activities into a smoothly operating, unified organization. This requires what Harbison calls organization-building ability: the ability "to harness the ideas of innovators to the rest of the organization, . . . to select and develop persons who can properly manage a labor force" and "to stimulate initiative and enthusiasm in the accomplishment of the objectives of the organization."[5]

[5] Frederick Harbison, "Entrepreneurial Organization as a Factor in Economic Development," *Quarterly Journal of Economics*, **7**:367 (Aug. 1956).

The Development of Technology

Intimately related to the character of entrepreneurship and of competition in modern times has been the development of technology. Before the Industrial Revolution, small-scale production was universal, capital was unimportant relative to labor, and technology changed slowly. The Industrial Revolution greatly increased the importance of capital, and because of this, technological change became mainly a matter of change in the design and character of concrete capital goods. Indeed, the Industrial Revolution was essentialy a changeover from labor plus tools to labor plus power-drive machinery. (Recall the first wave of innovation: the steam engine, the power loom, the power lathe, and the blast furnace.) From that time on, technological change *meant* principally change in capital-intensive methods, a change that accelerated as productivity increased, costs fell, profits rose, and capital accumulated. With the spread of capital-intensive technology, the investment requirements of firms increased, and the scale of their operations grew, and industry became less and less competitive in the classical sense. The age of highly imperfect competition, of competition among the few, was ushered in.

It is, of course, true that innovation by the lone inventor or the small firm still goes on, accounting for a large number of inventions. Some of these innovations become highly successful, leading perhaps to the emergence of large and prosperous businesses. It is urged here only that in recent time, innovation that originates in the research departments of large firms has become by far the most typical. Moreover, innovations of the isolated kind tend to be brought up and developed by the industrial giants.

TECHNOLOGICAL CHANGE

In the modern economy of restricted competition, technological leadership has become extremely important. Among a small group of large rivals, any firm that first introduces an innovation, whether a new product or an improvement in an existing one, gains a distinct and often highly profitable market advantage. The need for technological leadership thus ensures a constant active search for new and improved products, a search that has become institutionalized in the allocation of a large share of corporate revenues to research and development (R & D).

New Products

When research leads to the discovery of a completely new product, we have technological change in its most extreme form: the creation of a new production function, different from any previous one. Obviously, technological change that leads to such a result provides a basis for specialization and trade additional to a favorable factor endowment. A new saleable commodity is created. Although initially its sales may well be limited to its home market, if the good has more than local appeal, it will probably soon become an object of international trade.

Because of the importance of capital in most manufacturing industries, technological innovation in that area is generally capital-intensive in nature, and is largely confined to the developed industrial nations. Deliberate attempts to stimulate labor-intensive innovation in less developed countries (LDCs), as a means of sharing the benefits of technological progress, have had little success. Yet as industries originating in advanced industrial nations mature and become standardized, they may become relatively labor-intensive compared to newer, emerging industries. If so, then factor proportions will tend to take over, leading to the transfer of the mature industries to countries where labor is relatively abundant. After a delay, the desired industrial development comes to the LDCs. (See also the discussion of the product cycle hypothesis on pp. 123–24.)

Many new products originate in the research departments of large corporations, especially when a line of goods is manufactured, as in pharmaceuticals. So does a large proportion of all new discoveries, owing to the constant, well-financed research effort maintained by such firms. As already noted, however, many innovations continue to emerge from the ranks of small business. If a newly invented product proves to be only of minor importance, its originator may well continue to produce and market it on a small scale. When, on the other hand, it appears to have a significant role to play, the originator may soon join the ranks of major corporations. This was the case with the silicon transistor, first produced by Texas Instruments in the 1950s, and followed by that corporation's development of the integrated circuit in the 1960s.

Product Differentiation

Objective Differentiation Anxious to avoid dangerous price competition, firms in industries of restricted competition resort to various methods of distinguishing their products from those of their rivals. The surest and most enduring form of product differentiation is the introduction of a tangible improvement. This gives the product a qualitative advantage over competing goods, an advantage that may last for some time, or be quickly challenged by the research activity of rival producers. Illustrations are legion. After its invention in the late nineteenth century, the typewriter underwent great improvement in this century, first with the application of electricity, later with the introduction by IBM of its changeable revolving type head, and other piecemeal improvements. Electric shavers come in various models with and without build-in batteries, with parallel or rotary blades, or with vibrating cutters.

Often product differentiation may extend over an entire line of goods, divided into a series of qualitative grades. Most notable in this respect is the automobile, with a wide price and quality range. These categories appeal to buyers of different income levels and with a wide variety of preferences as to comfort, style, speed, reliability, and workmanship.

Subjective Differentiation   Up to now, we have considered only product differentiation that is the result of real qualitative improvement—what we have termed objective differentiation. Yet the extent of improvement may vary over a wide range, at the lower end becoming virtually undetectable. This is certainly the case with women's cosmetics, where grandiloquent claims accompany minimal change.

Going beyond this area where the real merges into the imaginary, we come to what might be called subjective or psychological product differentiation: the creation in the buyer's mind of belief that a product is in some undemonstrable way superior or at least preferable to its rivals. To this end, all the persuasiveness of advertising, sales promotion techniques, and clever packaging work together. These devices are reinforced by stress on such auxiliary matters as servicing of the product and facilities for financing its purchase.

Despite its tenuous connection with reality, subjective product differentiation can be just as effective as the objective variety in leading the consumer to buy and thus to inaugurate trade. Therefore, subjective product differentiation, like its more authentic companion, is a basis for trade additional to and independent of price differences based on suitable factor proportions.

Most trade generated by product differentiation of whatever kind is probably two-way, the differentiated goods of one nation competing with different versions of the same good in other nations. Thus Cadillacs and Lincolns compete at home and abroad with the Rolls-Royce and the Mercedes, intermediate grades with one another, and the same is true with the compact cars of various countries. Both cultural differences and differences in national incomes have a bearing on this intraindustry trade. Small, inexpensive refrigerators may sell well and be the principal type produced in a relatively low-income country, while larger and more elaborate models may not be manufactured in that country at all, or produced in limited amounts, with exports negligible or nonexistent. A high-income country, on the other hand, would tend to concentrate on the production and export of more expensive models.

THE PRODUCT CYCLE

A version of the role of technology in international trade which stresses a cyclical pattern in its development has been presented by Raymond Vernon[6] and others under the label product cycle. In its simplest form this hypothesis is an attempt to explain why a country may have a technological advantage in a particular product at a particular time.

The product cycle idea begins by noting that for each product placed at a purchaser's door there are several different input costs: product development, marketing, materials, and primary factors. Each input has different characteristics, and over time the relative significance of each input will vary. Thus, because the comparative advantage in particular types of inputs differs among countries, comparative advantage in a product will change over the life of the product as the relative importance of particular inputs changes.

The product cycle literature suggests three product stages: new product, maturing product, and standardized product. At the new product stage, the technology is as yet undefined, and product development expenditures dominate the cost structure. A country with a comparative advantage in such activities is thus likely to be an exporter of the product at this stage. As the product matures and the technology is sorted out, marketing and capital costs (because of rapid obsolescence of equipment) become the dominant costs. Then, as the product becomes standardized, the technology stabilizes and production costs—largely materials, capital, and unskilled labor—become crucial in determining comparative advantage.

There appears to be no inconsistency between the product cycle hypothesis and the position advanced in this chapter. Yet if product development or innovation is typically undertaken by large, powerful, and relatively uncompetitive firms, this first stage of the product cycle will generally be carried out in one or another of the advanced indus-

---

[6] Raymond Vernon, "International Investment and International Trade in the Product Cycle," *Quarterly Journal of Economics*, **80**:190–207 (May 1966).

trial nations. Not only are such firms to be found there, but also the capital required and the type of management willing and able to foster research and development. During the second stage of maturing product, when marketing and capital costs predominate, the abundance of capital and managerial expertise and experience in marketing should tend strongly to keep the maturing industries in the countries where they originated.

As for the third stage, that of standardized product, when materials, capital, and unskilled labor become important, production of some commodities is likely to move. What industries will relocate in other countries will depend mainly on the relative importance of unskilled labor and of materials in total costs of production. As far as capital is concerned, its high international mobility, especially to centers such as Hong Kong and Singapore, probably counteracts any advantage that advanced industrial nations might have.

As for materials that must be imported, countries where they originate or countries closer to their source will enjoy some advantage from lower transport costs. If they or other nations possess abundant and cheap labor, this cost element will exert a powerful attractive force. Over the past century, many industries have migrated from their original sites in the industrial nations to certain less developed countries. Textiles, shoes and other leather products, plastic objects of many kinds, assembly operations, and many others have moved, if not in their entirety, at least in large part, from Europe, the United States, and even Japan to developing countries, especially South Korea, Taiwan, and Hong Kong.

TECHNOLOGICAL CHANGE, FACTOR PROPORTIONS, AND PERFECT COMPETITION

Before concluding this chapter, it will be instructive to consider how Ohlin treated technological change, and how the latter relates to a model of perfect competition.

Technological change received little attention in the factor proportions theory. Indeed, Ohlin discussed such change only near the end of his book, and treated it as amounting to "a change in the supply of technical labour."

> Variations in technique constitute another, and perhaps more important, sort of change in supply conditions. In this book they are regarded

as a change in the supply of technical labour, and are thus a parallel to those in the former case of new natural resources.[7]

The first thing to be said about this approach is that it is obviously a mere extension of the factor proportions theory. If technological change means an increase in the supply of one of the factors (technical labor), relative factor prices must change and therewith, the basis for trade. Changes in the volume and pattern of trade will follow. Nothing new, however, has been added to the basic theory: Relative factor endowments constitute the fundamental basis for trade.

In fact, technological change leads to the creation of a new production function, a new method of combining the factors of production to produce a new or improved product or to reduce the cost of an existing one. Technological advance originates in the laboratories, experiment stations, and workshops where research is carried out by scientists and engineers using specialized equipment; the activities of this technical labor are made possible by expenditure on research and development, on the employment of this labor, on its education and training in such fields as science, mathematics, and engineering, and on essential physical equipment. R & D expenditure is primarily investment in human capital (see pp. 136–37). It would involve little stretching of conceptual limits to regard R & D expenditure—the source of a special kind of human and related capital—as a special type of capital, and a factor in its own right.

An increase or decrease in the supply of this factor will, like changes in the supply of labor, capital, or natural resources, affect relative factor prices and therefore the pattern of trade. Our concern here, however, is with the nature of research and development. It is the primary engine of change in methods of production, its activities are being carried on continuously in many sectors of industry and agriculture, and even if the relative supply of R & D remained constant, it would have continuing effects on the composition of trade. That is, R & D is an independent basis for trade, on a par with changes in relative factor endowments.

A second point of interest in connection with Ohlin's treatment of technological change is its relation to the structure of industry. Throughout his study, Ohlin seldom departed from the assumption of perfect competition. A competitive order, however, is not one that would provide much encouragement for R & D expenditure or for technological change. Such an order implies that the number of firms is so large that the activity of any single one can have no effect on the

[7] Bertil Ohlin, *Interregional and International Trade* (Cambridge, Mass.: Harvard University Press, 1933), p. 517.

price of an industry's product. Because of his preoccupation with meeting the current market price, an individual small producer will have little time or inclination, even if he has the qualifications, for improving his product (i.e., introducing technological change). A more likely possibility would be for a lone inventor to come up with a new product, for which he undertakes to raise capital and organize production. Ruling out patents, which are inconsistent with perfect competition because they create a monopoly for a limited time, the original producer will certainly soon be imitated. Competition will establish a price equal to minimum average unit cost. All this would be very discouraging for further innovation.

It must be admitted that innovations enabling an entrepreneur to reduce his costs, lower his price, and thus expand sales and raise profits would have an appeal where price is the main consideration. Even here, however, the likelihood of rapid imitation would make such innovation risky and would tend to discourage it.

SUMMARY

This chapter begins with a review of the assumptions on which the H-O general equilibrium theory of trade is based, and shows how the removal of several assumptions has left that theory undamaged. The most important of all, however, the assumption of perfect competition in the markets for goods and factors, has not been touched. This assumption is now to be set aside and the consequences investigated.

Before undertaking this inquiry, however, attention is given to the possibility that national differences in technology might provide a basis for trade. The identity of individual production functions in different countries, assumed by Samuelson, appears to be true of the advanced industrial nations. Since production functions embody technical knowledge, technology in those nations is very similar, providing little if any basis for trade between them. On the other hand, because of severe cultural impediments to the flow of technical knowledge between developed and underdeveloped countries, great differences in technology exist. These differences underlie much trade between these regions, especially in sophisticated manufactured goods.

Coming now to the assumption of perfect competition, this condition is a rarity in the modern world. Industries of major importance are dominated by large-scale firms, their size being based partly on economies of scale and partly on the fact that, since competition centers on the appeal of the product rather than, as under perfect competition, entirely on price, the quality of entrepreneurship becomes of great importance, a consideration largely ignored in models of perfect competition. The development of technology has paralleled that of industrial organization, having become, since the Industrial Revolution, ever more capital-intensive in character. This reinforces the position of large firms with respect to innovation, since their well-financed R & D departments are properly equipped to cope with costly technological change.

When research activity leads to the creation of a new good, technological change obviously becomes a basis for international trade that is different from a favorable factor endowment. Improvements in existing goods, the most effective and enduring form of product differentiation, here termed objective differentiation, also gives rise to international trade. But products are also differentiated by advertising and sales promotion. Although artificial, such subjective differentiation leads to purchases and thus to trade, just as does objective product differentiation. Trade based on either type of differentiation, however, is mainly two-way trade, since it consists of the exchange between two countries of different versions of what is essentially the same commodity.

The product cycle hypothesis, which detects three stages in the production of a new good, is discussed briefly. Although not inconsistent with the argument of this chapter, less international migration of new industries is likely to occur than is suggested by this hypothesis.

A final section of this chapter considers how technological change is treated by Ohlin, as well as how it might fare under a regime of perfect competition. In the H-O theory, technological change is treated as merely an increase in the supply of technical labor, with effects no different from an increase in any other factor. In this view, technological change furnishes no independent basis for trade, as it does when regarded as changing a production function or giving rise to a new one and thus to a new product. Because of the likelihood of rapid imitation of a technological innovation in a competitive system, technological change appears unlikely to play a large role in such an environment.

SELECTED REFERENCES

GRUBEL, HERBERT G. "The Theory of Intra-Industry Trade," Chapter 4 in Robert E. Baldwin and J. David Richardson, *Readings in International Trade and Finance*, 2nd ed. Boston: Little, Brown & Co., 1974.

HABERLER, G. "Some Problems in the Pure Theory of International Trade." *Economic Journal*, **60**, No. 238 (June 1950). Reprinted in American Economic Association, *Readings in International Economics*, Homewood,

Ill.: Richard D. Irwin, Inc. 1968. Fundamental discussion of how non-competitive conditions affect pure theory model.

HUFBAUER, G. C. "The Impact of National Characteristics and Technology on the Commodity Composition of Trade in Manufactured Goods." In *The Technology Factor in International Trade.* New York: National Bureau of Economic Research, 1970. Contains several statistical tests.

LINDER, STAFFAN BURENSTAM, *An Essay on Trade and Transformation*, New York: John Wiley & Sons, Inc., 1961. An interesting attempt to relate national demands and income levels to the various locational aspects of international specialization.

MELVIN, J. R. "Commodity Taxation as a Determinant of Trade." *Canadian Journal of Economics*, **3**, No. 1 (Feb. 1970). Shows how domestic taxes can be a basis for trade, and more generally how the methodology of establishing bases for trade is employed.

————, and ROBERT D. WARNE. "Monopoly and the Theory of International Trade." *Journal of International Economics*, **3:** (May 1973). Treatment of monopoly in a general equilibrium model.

VERNON, RAYMOND. "International Investment and International Trade in the Product Cycle," *Quarterly Journal of Economics*, **80** (May 1966). Reprinted in Robert E. Baldwin, and J. David Richardson, *Readings in International Trade and Finance*, 2nd ed. Boston: Little, Brown & Co., 1974.

8
CHAPTER

Empirical Evaluation

The purpose of theory is to explain and to predict real-world events. If the explanation put forward by a theory is to be regarded as useful, it should correspond reasonably closely to the facts. Perfect correspondence or even extremely close correspondence between theory and reality is not normally to be expected, since a theoretical model is always more or less abstract: It specifies, in its assumptions, a world that often differs considerably from reality. This is certainly true of the factor proportions theory as we have presented it, since its assumptions are severely limiting. If, however, a theory's findings correspond even moderately to the facts, or show a fair correlation, a presumption is established in favor of the theory. The rough approximation of the theory could then be improved upon by taking into account those aspects of the real world set aside by its assumptions.

In this chapter we undertake a review of various attempts at verification in the area of international trade theory. Our discussion is organized by theories rather than by the testing techniques employed, except for the final section, in which we report the results obtained in a number of multivariate tests.

By far the largest part of the work on empirical evaluation of trade theories has focused on the determinants of a country's basis for trade, and within that discussion nearly all the work has implicitly, if not explicitly, assumed underlying competitive conditions. In other words, most attempts at verification reported here apply to the models that we examined in Chapters 6 and 7. Even within that subset, the major emphasis, as we shall see, has been on testing the factor proportions basis for trade. It will become clear that much testing remains to be done.

Despite the shortcomings of the existing state of knowledge, it will also become clear that an enormous effort has been applied to the task of testing the theory of international trade.

FACTOR PROPORTIONS

The factor proportions theory, initially developed by Heckscher and Ohlin, and refined by Samuelson, has been the focus of considerable empirical testing. We shall not attempt to review all the contributions to this major undertaking. Rather, we shall focus on the major highlights of over two decades of work by a great many researchers.

The Leontief Test

The first comprehensive and detailed examination of the factor proportions theory was that undertaken by Leontief.[1] Recall that the factor proportions theory predicts that a nation relatively abundant in capital will export relatively capital-intensive goods, and import goods for which domestic production requires relatively large amounts of its relatively scarce factor, labor. Thus, if we know a country's relative factor abundance, to test the theory, one simply has to compare the factor intensity of the country's export production with the factor intensity of its import-competing production. If it turns out that the country's export production is relatively intensive in its abundant factor, the prediction of the factor proportions theory holds.

Leontief observed that it is commonly agreed that the United States possesses a relatively large amount of capital and a comparatively small amount of labor vis-à-vis the rest of the world. It follows then that the factor proportions theory predicts that the United States would export capital-intensive products and import those that require relatively large amounts of labor when produced in the United States. To test this prediction, Leontief brought to bear data from his own input–output tables. These relate to 200 groups of industries, which he consolidated into fifty sectors, of which thirty-eight traded their products directly on the international market. His calculations of factor intensities take into account direct plus indirect factor requirements.

Leontief's startling findings are summarized in Table 8.1. His results show that import-competing products are relatively more capital-intensive than the export products. Thus, contrary to what the factor proportions theory of international trade would lead us to expect, the production of U.S. exports is labor-intensive relative to import-competing production, which is capital-intensive. As Leontief put it,

[1] W. Leontief, "Domestic Production and Foreign Trade: The American Capital Position Re-examined," *Proceedings of the American Philosophical Society*, **97** (Sept. 1953), reprinted in American Economic Association, *Readings in International Economics* (Homewood, Ill.: Richard D. Irwin, Inc., 1968).

Table 8.1 **Domestic Capital and Labor Requirements per Million Dollars of U.S. Exports and of Competitive Import Replacements (of Average 1947 Composition)**

	Exports	Import Replacements
Capital ($ in 1947 prices)	2,550,780	3,091,339
Labor (man-years)	182,313	170,004
Capital–labor ratio ($/man-year)	13,911	18,185

SOURCE: W. Leontief, "Domestic Production and Foreign Trade: The American Capital Position Re-examined," *Proceedings of the American Philosophical Society*, **97** (Sept. 1953); reprinted in American Economic Association, *Readings in International Economics* (Homewood, Ill.: Richard D. Irwin, Inc., 1968), p. 552. Page reference is the latter reprinting.

> America's participation in the international division of labor is based on its specialization on labor intensive, rather than capital intensive, lines of production. In other words, the country resorts to foreign trade in order to economize its capital and dispose of its surplus labor, rather than vice-versa.[2]

This conclusion was soon challenged.

Other Leontief-Type Tests

Leontief's paradoxical results stimulated similar studies for other countries, and alternative approaches, to test the validity of the Heckscher–Ohlin or factor proportions explanation of international trade.

Using an approach similar to Leontief's, two Japanese economists found that Japanese exports as a whole embody more capital and less labor than do Japanese import-competing goods.[3] Noting that Japan's capital-labor endowment is intermediate between the advanced and the underdeveloped nations, they suggested that that country should have a comparative advantage in labor-intensive goods in her trade with the former and in capital-intensive goods with the latter. By taking into account the destination of exports, they obtained results at least partially consistent with the factor proportions theory: Japanese exports to the United States turn out to be relatively labor-intensive, and those to the underdeveloped countries relatively capital-intensive.

Other direct tests of the Heckscher–Ohlin hypothesis similar in nature to Leontief's may be mentioned briefly. A study of East German

[2] Ibid., pp. 522–23.
[3] M. Tatemoto and S. Ichimura, "Factor Proportions and Foreign Trade: The Case of Japan," *Review of Economics and Statistics*, **41** (Nov. 1959).

trade,[4] of which 75 percent is with the communist bloc, showed exports to be relatively capital-intensive and imports labor-intensive. Since East Germany's relatively abundant factor, compared with others of this group, is probably capital, these results are consistent with the theory. An examination of Canada's trade with the United States,[5] however, found that Canada's exports embodied more capital and less labor than imports, which is not in accord with the theory. Finally, an investigation of Indian trade with the United States discovered exports to be capital-intensive and imports to be labor-intensive, also an unsatisfactory outcome.[6]

Tarshis, on the other hand, approached the problem indirectly.[7] He compared internal commodity prices in different countries and found that the price ratios of capital-intensive relative to labor-intensive products was lower in the United States and higher in other countries. Since the United States was presumed to be relatively well endowed with capital, this result tends to confirm the Hecksher–Ohlin hypothesis.

One more citation, this time of regional trade: Noting that factor mobility between the southeastern part of the United States and other regions is by no means perfect and that labor in the Southeast is relatively abundant—as evidenced by lower wages and other independent evidence—two American economists attempted to discover whether labor-intensive manufacturing industries tend to locate in that region.[8] That part of their study related to the *initial* location of industries was inconclusive, but a portion devoted to changes in the location of manufacturing industries between 1949 and 1957 showed a distinct tendency for the Southeast to attract those industries that were relatively labor-intensive. Moreover, three industries with a strong natural-resources base (petroleum and coal, chemicals, and paper products) showed a high concentration in the South. This led the authors to suggest that natural resources might be more important in determining initial location than the relative abundance of labor or capital. (Here again we see the need for a model with more than two factors.) Their

---

[4] W. Stolper and K. Roskamp, "An Input–Output Table for East Germany with Applications to Foreign Trade," *Bulletin of the Oxford University Institute of Statistics*, **23** (Nov. 1961).

[5] D. F. Wahl, "Capital and Labor Requirements for Canada's Foreign Trade," *Canadian Journal of Economics and Political Science*, **27** (Aug. 1961).

[6] R. Bhardwaj, "Factor Proportions and the Structure of Indian–U.S. Trade," *Indian Economic Journal*, **10** (Oct. 1962).

[7] L. Tarshis, "Factor Inputs and International Price Competition," in M. Abramowitz, ed., *Allocation of Economic Resources* (Stanford, Calif.: Stanford University Press, 1959).

[8] John R. Moroney and James M. Walker, "A Regional Test of the Heckscher–Ohlin Hypothesis," *Journal of Political Economy*, **74** (Dec. 1966).

final conclusion was that the Heckscher–Ohlin thesis is of at least some value in predicting regional patterns of industrial development.

Alternative Explanations

Not only did Leontief's results stimulate similar studies, they also brought forth a barrage of alternative explanations. Some were simply different bases for trade, which in effect concede that the factor proportions explanation is inadequate or inappropriate and attempt to test the different basis. Others concentrated on a factor proportions type of explanation but took into account elements that Leontief did not. We begin with a few examples of the latter type.

Investment in Human Capital   Numerous researchers have included investment in human, as opposed to tangible, capital employed in trade-related production. Kenen, for example, modified Leontief's estimate for the United States by adding in the human capital, and found that such a procedure can reverse the factor intensities Leontief found: In some cases, but not all, U.S. exports are human-plus-tangible-capital-intensive relative to U.S. import-competing production.[9]

Natural Resources   Some researchers have shown that natural resources and capital are complementary in production, and thus because the United States is relatively short of several natural resources, the Leontief paradox can be explained. The U.S. trade pattern conserves scarce natural resources, not capital.[10]

Although on theoretical grounds one would not expect such complementarity to affect the factor proportions model if factor price equalization is achieved,[11] the natural resource content of trade has been shown to be empirically significant. Naya's work,[12] for example, shows that natural resources had a significant influence in the capital–labor structure of the trade pattern of the United States, Japan, India, and Canada. In each country, several of the resource-intensive industries

---

[9] Peter B. Kenen, "Nature, Capital and Trade," *Journal of Political Economy,* **73:**437–60 (Oct. 1965).

[10] See J. Vanek, *The Natural Resource Content of U.S. Foreign Trade, 1870–1955* (Cambridge, Mass.: Harvard University Press, 1963). See also Seiji Naya, "Natural Resources, Factor Mix and Factor Reversal in International Trade," *American Economic Review,* **57** (May 1967).

[11] The theoretical argument is simply that where goods prices and production functions are identical, the factor proportions used to produce a commodity are the same in all countries. As a result, the factor proportions model predicts that a capital-abundant country would export products using even more capital than the resource-intensive products. For a discussion of this point, see Robert E. Baldwin, "Determinants of the Commodity Structure of U.S. Trade," *American Economic Review,* **61** (Mar. 1971).

[12] Naya, op. cit.

are also heavy users of capital. Hence trade based on natural-resources endowment gives the appearance of trade based on capital endowment. Furthermore, two types of resource use patterns emerged: agricultural resource use and extractive resource use. For Canada, agricultural- and raw-material-oriented exports are capital-intensive relative to its import-competing manufacturing production. Japan, on the other hand, conserves its scarce agricultural land by imports, but domestic production of agricultural products is very labor-intensive. Hence Japan's exports are capital-intensive relative to its import-competing production. There are thus two elements in Naya's explanation: complementarity of natural resources and capital, plus a reversal of factor intensity in the production of agricultural products in different countries. This leads us to an alternative explanation.

Factor Intensity Reversal   We noted in Chapter 5 that one of several conditions required for the equalization of factor prices was the validity of the strong factor intensity assumption. According to this assumption, relative factor intensities must, for any two goods compared, remain the same for the entire range of relative factor prices. To illustrate, this condition is satisfied in Figure 8.1(a), where F is the relatively capital-intensive good, C the labor-intensive one. At the relative factor price in country I of $k_1 l_1 (= k_1' l_1')$, good F is more capital-intensive than C, since the ray Of is steeper than the ray Oc. At the much higher

Figure 8.1   Unchanging Factor Intensity and Factor Intensity Reversal

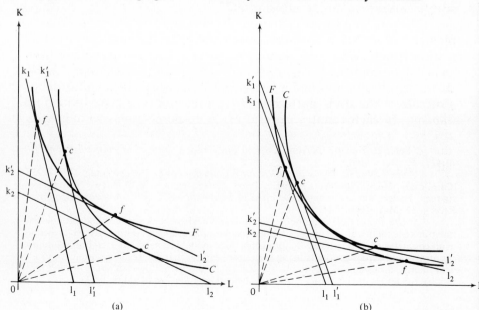

(a)   (b)

relative price of capital represented by country II's price line k_2l_2 (= $k_2'l_2'$), good F remains relatively capital-intensive. This condition would clearly hold for all other relative factor prices.

In contrast, this convenient result does not hold for Figure 8.1(b): isoquant F is relatively capital-intensive at the relative factor price k_1l_1, whereas at the different relative factor price k_2l_2, isoquant F is labor-intensive (relative to isoquant C). Factor reversal has occurred.

Visually, you can see that in part (b) the curvature of the two isoquants is very different, C being more sharply curved than F, although each retains a constant curvature throughout. In part (a), on the other hand, although each isoquant has constant curvature, the degree of curvature of the two is very similar—in fact, identical.

Underlying this matter of curvature is a technical feature of the two isoquants that is responsible for the factor reversal. When each of two isoquants can be unambiguously identified as either capital- or labor-intensive at all factor prices, the elasticities of substitution (defined in the Appendix to this chapter) of those isoquants are both constant and identical, as in part (a) of the diagram. On the other hand, factor reversal can occur if the elasticities of substitution of the two isoquants are constant but different.

The consequences of factor intensity reversal for the factor proportions theory are disturbing. Specialization and trade on the basis of differences in relative factor endowments may not be possible. A country with abundant capital could find that of two goods, it could produce relatively cheaply the one that was capital-intensive at its relative factor prices. If its potential trading partner, with abundant labor, could also produce the same good relatively cheaply, there would be no basis for trade. One or the other could specialize, but not both.

It seems only reasonable that, among the thousands of goods produced, and with a wide range of technological alternatives available, there would be some technologies whose elasticities of substitution differed, and thus gave rise to factor reversals. Naya's work has shown that this is so. Agricultural products in several countries exhibit reversal of factor intensity. Thus the United States exports rice produced with heavy mechanical equipment, while Burma, using much labor but little capital, competes in the sale of rice in world markets. And in Japan, a net importer of rice, this product is also produced by labor-intensive methods.

The question, however, is whether elasticities of substitution do in fact vary from industry to industry appreciably, and thus whether factor reversal is at all common. Minhas[13] investigated twenty-four industries for which comparable data could be obtained for nineteen

---

[13] B. Minhas, *An International Comparison of Costs and Factor Use*, Contributions to Economic Analysis No. 31 (Amsterdam: North-Holland Publishing Company, 1963).

different countries, and found factor reversals in five. In a critical review of Minhas' book, Leontief[14] points out that only 17 of 210 possible reversals occurred within a relevant range of factor prices. (Factor reversals that occur outside the range of relative factor prices found in the real world are of no practical importance.) Minhas also ranked twenty industries, common to the United States and Japan, in terms of their capital–labor ratio, and found that the correlation was low (+0.328). But as Moroney[15] points out, if the agriculture and food industries (which are more dissimilar internationally as to technological knowledge, natural resources, and relative efficiency) are omitted, the correlation is much higher (+0.765). And for eighteen "nonprimary" industries, it improves still more (+0.920). His own test of fourteen industries in six different regions of the United States yielded a high correlation (+0.9228) of the relative capital–labor rankings of those industries. Moroney concludes that Minhas' tests are not convincing enough to warrant our rejecting the strong factor intensity hypothesis, and that factor reversal "has much less empirical importance than theoretical interest."[16] In summary, the practical significance of factor reversal is very limited.

TECHNOLOGY: TECHNOLOGICAL CHANGE AND R & D EXPENDITURE

In our discussion of the role of technology, we identified technological change as providing a basis for international trade independent of, and additional to, a price advantage due to suitable factor endowment. Such change, in the form of new goods or improvements in existing ones, we saw as the product mainly of the research departments of large, oligopolistic firms that in the past century have come to dominate most major industries. By displacing the products of rivals and opening up an entirely new field, a firm expands its market, whether foreign or domestic, and thus alters the course and composition of trade. These innovations can be regarded as a consequence of the financial and managerial strength of large firms, which enables them to create and foster research and development. Since R & D expenditures provide a quantitative measure of the effort devoted to technological

---

[14] W. Leontief, "An International Comparison of Factor Costs and Factor Use," *American Economic Review*, **75**:343 (June 1964).

[15] J. R. Moroney, "The Strong Factor-Intensity Hypothesis: A Multisectoral Test," *Journal of Political Economy*, **75** (June 1967).

[16] Ibid., p. 247.

change, investigation of such expenditure should provide a useful empirical test of the importance of technological change as a basis for trade.

Empirical studies of R & D have focused on the relationship between R & D expenditures and various measures of export performance. One such test found that export performance of U.S. industries closely paralleled indicators of R & D effort.[17] Similar results have been found by other researchers. Although the test is somewhat indirect, for differences in technology are not established as a basis for trade, it does offer a reasonable explanation of the comparative advantage actually exhibited.

THE PRODUCT CYCLE

Louis Wells examined a number of pieces of evidence relating to the product cycle hypothesis in U.S. consumer durable exports.[18] Observing that U.S. producers would typically introduce high-income and sophisticated new products for the home market and then begin to export them, Wells performed two major tests. In one, he examined the relationship between the growth of U.S. exports and the effect of income on ownership of the products and found it to be significantly positive. In a second, he related prices to various versions of a product in the United States and in some European countries. He found that the United States had comparatively lower prices for the more sophisticated (and hence presumably newer) versions, while foreigners had comparatively lower prices for the more standardized, less sophisticated versions.

The work of Vernon and Wells is only a partial explanation, however. What remains is to integrate the product cycle theory carefully into the main body of international trade theory, and to subject it to further empirical tests.

PRODUCT DIFFERENTIATION

Product differentiation results from the efforts of large, oligopolistic firms to channel competition into a less disruptive form than price

[17] See William Gruber, D. Mehta, and R. Vernon, "The R & D Factor in International Trade and Investment of U.S. Industries," *Journal of Political Economy*, **75** (Feb. 1967).

[18] Louis T. Wells, "Test of a Product Cycle Model of International Trade: U.S. Exports of Consumer Durables," *Quarterly Journal of Economics*, **83** (Feb. 1969).

competition. These firms attempt to individualize their products by advertising and sales promotion so as to divide the market into separate segments. Since these techniques can influence decisions to buy, when successful they lead to increased exports to third countries, and between international rivals, to two-way trade in what is essentially a single product. Thus product differentiation, like technological change, can be a basis for international trade distinct from a price advantage.

Observing that there was substantial simultaneous import and export of goods in the same trade categories, Herbert Grubel examined the question of whether such specialization increased or decreased among the countries of the European Economic Community (EEC) as they moved toward free trade among themselves.[19] Grubel computed the ratios of exports to imports for net exporting industries, and imports to exports for net importing industries over the period of trade liberalization accompanying the establishment of the EEC. Interindustry specialization—that is, concentration of each nation's industries on fewer products—would predict an increase in these ratios. But intraindustry specialization—or increased product differentiation within national industries—would predict a decrease. He found that in all cases there was a significant substantial decline in the ratios. His results thus indicated that trade liberalization yielded intraindustry specialization. Clearly, a substantial amount of trade in fundamentally similar but nevertheless heterogeneous products developed as the EEC came into being.

MULTIVARIATE TESTS

Instead of testing individual theories, a number of researchers have recently examined simultaneously the effect of a number of influences. Such multivariate tests have the great advantage of assisting us in sorting out the numerous theories which have been put forward.

An ingenious approach was employed by G. C. Hufbauer.[20] He examined the relationship between flows of manufactured goods and economic structure, asking the question: How strong are the links between characteristics embodied in trade and national economic attributes? His tests were designed to evaluate the significance of various

[19] Herbert G. Grubel, "Intra-Industry Specialization and the Pattern of Trade," *Canadian Journal of Economics and Political Science*, **33** (Aug. 1967).

[20] G. C. Hufbauer, "The Impact of National Characteristics and Technology on the Commodity Composition of Trade in Manufactured Goods," in R. Vernon, ed., *The Technology Factor in International Trade* [New York: Columbia University Press (for the National Bureau of Economic Research), 1970].

Table 8.2 Commodity Characteristics, National Attributes, and Trade Hypotheses

Commodity Characteristics Embodied in Exports	*National Attribute Associated with Commodity Characteristic*	*Trade Hypothesis Associated with National Attribute*
Capital per man	Fixed capital per manufacturing employee	Factor proportions
Skill ratio Wages per man	Skilled employees (percent of total)	Human skills
Scale economies	Manufacturing output (percent of total)	Scale economies
Consumer-goods ratio First date traded Product differentiation	Gross domestic product per capita	Technology and product cycle

SOURCE: G. C. Hufbauer, "The Impact of National Characteristics and Technology on the Commodity Corporation of Trade in Manufactured Goods," in R. Vernon, ed., *The Technology Factor in International Trade* [New York: Columbia University Press (for the National Bureau of Economic Research), 1970].

---

hypotheses. In Table 8.2 are listed the commodity characteristics embodied in trade set against various national attributes in order to test the theories associated with those national attributes. For twenty-four countries exporting manufactures, Hufbauer developed data for each of the commodity characteristics and the national attributes. Then testing the significance of the relationship between the two, he found rank correlations between each export commodity characteristic and its associated national attribute to be significant. He also computed simple correlations and found all relationships, except between manufacturing output and scale economies, to be significant. His conclusion: "No one theory monopolizes the explanation of manufactures trade."[21]

Hufbauer's analysis tells us that several forces are at work, but, as he admits, he employs statistical techniques that provide little basis for assessing the extent of the contribution of each determinant. His tests are "little more than a crude screen for eliminating unsatisfactory theories."[22]

Another approach employed has been to use multiple regression analysis to evaluate simultaneously the effect on trade of a number of influences. Typically, the focus has been on explaining some measure of the extent of export activity: exports relative to total sales or exports minus imports.

[21] Ibid., p. 194.
[22] Ibid., p. 162.

An early attempt at this was a study of Canadian trade patterns by Bruce Wilkinson. He employed a multiple regression analysis of several variables in an attempt to explain the ratio of exports to output by Canadian manufacturing industries.[23] On exports of secondary manufacturing industries he found proxies for scale economies, R & D expenditures, and selling costs to be significant. Foreign tariffs and foreign ownership were insignificant explanatory variables.

One of the most extensive tests to date is a study by Robert Baldwin of the commodity structure of U.S. trade.[24] Using 1962 trade figures and 1958 capital, labor, and intermediate input data, he found net U.S. exports to the world to be significantly related to the following:

1. A negative function of the capital–labor ratio, contrary to the Heckscher–Ohlin hypothesis.
2. A positive function of the use of engineers and scientists, a proxy for R & D activity.
3. A positive function of other highly trained and skilled labor.

Baldwin found general measures of human capital (costs of education or years of education) to be insignificant, as well as measures of scale economies. Neither were measures of product or market imperfections (unionization and market concentration) significant. Some of these were significant, however, in explaining net *bilateral* exports.

SUMMARY AND CONCLUSIONS

Our review of empirical tests of international trade theories begins with the striking challenge of the factor proportions theory made by Leontief. According to that theory, the United States, generally presumed to be well endowed with capital but poor in labor, should export capital-intensive products, while its industries competing with imports should be labor-intensive. Leontief's evidence from his input–output tables indicated that just the opposite was true. Further tests of the H-O theory followed. Some supported that theory, whereas others favored Leontief's critical position. Other investigations suggested that if investment in human capital were added to physical capital, it is indeed capital that is the relatively abundant factor in the United States. Still other studies indicated that the large proportion of capital

[23] Bruce W. Wilkinson, *Canada's International Trade: An Analysis of Recent Trends and Patterns* (Montreal: Private Planning Association of Canada, 1968).
[24] Baldwin, op. cit., pp. 126–46.

in U.S. import replacements could be due to heavy use of capital in the production of import substitutes derived from natural resources—industries that require large capital inputs.

The realization that agricultural exports were produced by capital-intensive methods in some countries and by labor-intensive methods in others led to the recognition that factor reversal might be the explanation. Certain production functions could be of such a character that the relative factor intensity of a given pair would not remain the same at all relative factor prices. In such a case, the factor proportions theory would not hold. Each of two countries would be able to produce the same good at comparably low cost. A number of investigations found that, although factor reversals did in fact occur, they were comparatively rare. In a world not of just two countries but of many, some countries can export a commodity produced by capital-intensive methods to compete on the world market with exports from another country produced by labor-intensive methods.

Upon turning to alternative explanations of the basis for trade, tests relating to technology showed a high correlation between R & D expenditure and export performance. Studies relating to the product cycle gave evidence that the United States tends to specialize in newer and more sophisticated manufactured products, other industrialized countries on their more standardized counterparts. An examination of the growth of trade among EEC members as their union became closer indicated a move among these countries toward product differentiation and growing two-way trade in different versions of essentially very similar products.

Multivariate tests of the relations between various commodity characteristics and economic features of national economics gave support to factor proportions, human skills, and the product cycle as bases for trade. A number of tests investigating not just a single theory but permitting simultaneous consideration of different possible causes of trade suggested strongly that no one explanation is adequate.

This is a good note on which to end. The number of commodities traded is too vast and their characteristics are too diverse to make a single explanation credible. Certainly, the number of factors to be taken into account is larger than the labor and capital of the factor proportions theory. Besides physical capital, investment in human capital and in research and development play important roles, and there are many varieties of natural resources. Changes in techniques of production occur at different times in different countries, giving a headstart to new or a resurgence to old export industries in various locations. Product competition gives rise to product differentiation, either real or artificial, generating considerable two-way trade in manufactures. Also to be considered as a cause of some kinds of trade are transportation costs, which largely determine whether an industry will locate near its raw-material base or near its market, and thus whether a country will export a primary or a finished product.

SELECTED REFERENCES

BALDWIN, ROBERT E. "Determinants of the Commodity Structure of U.S. Trade," *American Economic Review* 61 (May 1971). Reprinted in Robert E. Baldwin and J. David Richardson, *Readings in International Trade and Finance.* 2nd ed. Boston: Little, Brown and Company, 1974. Up-to-date evaluation of evidence on the Leontief paradox, plus a new extension of tests.

BHAGWATI, JAGDISH. "The Pure Theory of International Trade: A Survey." No. 7 in *Surveys of Economic Theory*, Vol. 2. New York: St. Martin's Press, Inc., 1965. See especially Sections 1 and 2.

CAVES, RICHARD E. *Trade and Economic Structure: Models and Methods.* Cambridge, Mass.: Harvard University Press, 1960. A comprehensive and critical analysis of international trade theories.

CHIPMAN, JOHN S. "A Survey of the Theory of International Trade." *Econometrica*, **33, 34** (July 1965; Oct. 1965; Jan. 1966). The third of these articles reviews critically the modern theory of international trade; technical and difficult.

HUFBAUER, G. C. "The Impact of National Characteristics and Technology on the Commodity Composition of Trade in Manufactured Goods," in *The Technology Factor in International Trade*, New York: National Bureau of Economic Research, 1970. Contains several statistical tests.

OHLIN, BERTIL. *Interregional and International Trade.* Cambridge, Mass.: Harvard University Press, 1933. Worthwhile reading of the basic Heckscher-Ohlin model, plus Ohlin's observations of empirical support.

ROBINSON, ROMNEY. "Factor Proportions and Comparative Advantage." In American Economic Association, *Readings in International Economics*, Homewood, Ill.: Richard D. Irwin, Inc., 1968. A vigorous critique of the factor proportions theory.

APPENDIX: ELASTICITY OF SUBSTITUTION

Elasticity is a measure of the responsiveness of one variable to changes in an associated variable, the relationship being expressed in relative or percentage terms, to make the outcome independent of measurement units. The price elasticity of demand is probably the most familiar example of elasticity in economics. It is the relative change in quantity demanded in response to relative changes in price, or $dQ/Q \div dP/P$.

Figure 8A.1 Different Elasticities of Substitution

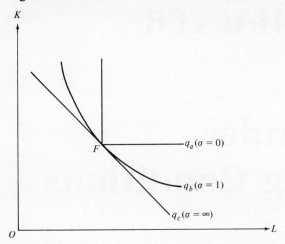

The elasticity of substitution measures the responsiveness of the k/l ratio to changes in the marginal rate of substitution (MRS, or MP_l/MP_k). If we let σ stand for the elasticity of substitution and use Φ as a symbol for the ratio k/l, then

$$\sigma \equiv \frac{d\Phi/\Phi}{dMRS/MRS} = \frac{d\Phi}{\Phi} \cdot \frac{MRS}{dMRS} = \frac{d\Phi}{dMRS} \cdot \frac{MRS}{\Phi}$$

To envision what elasticity of substitution means, consider the examples in Figure 8A.1. The three different isoquants pass through the point F. The isoquant q_c reflects infinite elasticity of substitution. The two factors are perfect substitutes, so that a change in the MRS would be met by a complete switch of the k/l ratio, either to zero K or zero L. The isoquant q_b, however, represents a situation in which a given change in MRS would be met by an equiproportionate change in the k/l ratio; σ is unity. Finally, isoquant q_a represents a situation in which there are no possibilities of substitution; elasticity is zero. In general, the greater the elasticity of substitution, the less is the curvature of the isoquant, and the less is σ the greater the curvature of the isoquant.

9
CHAPTER

Trade Under Changing Conditions

Our discussion of international trade theory so far has been conducted in terms of given conditions of supply, that is, of unchanging factor endowments. It is now time to take into account the possibility that these conditions are not fixed once and for all, but may change either from causes that are internal to a particulary economy or as a consequence of international influences. This chapter considers the effects of such changes on international trade.

There are several relationships that must be taken into account. First, an increase in one or more of the factors will raise the level of production. National income therefore will rise, and expenditures will be affected. These changes alter the nation's offer of exports for imports, with consequent changes in the volume and terms of trade.

Another important set of relationships concerns international factor movements. It is relatively easy to show how, in principle, trade and factor movements are substitutes for each other. Yet there is convincing qualitative evidence that trade and factor movements are often complements. Overall, then, the purpose of this chapter is to move toward a better understanding of the interdependence among internal changes in factor endowments, international movements of factors, and international trade.

GROWTH AND THE TRANSFORMATION FUNCTION

Internal Accumulation of Factor Supplies

No country's supply of the factors is unalterably fixed. Its labor force can, of course, be augmented by population growth. When the natural

144

rate of increase suddenly rises, as it has in recent years in many underdeveloped countries as a consequence of improved public health services, the first impact is on the proportion of children and young people in the population. Only later, as these groups mature, is there a large increase in the work force.

Through the process of saving and capital accumulation, a nation's capital supply is enhanced. The rate of increase may be quite steady, depending on ingrained habits of thrift combined with a slowly rising national income, or it may spurt upward because of institutional change that makes saving safer and more attractive, or (as in western Europe after World War II) because of a sharp increase in productivity and national income. Changes in the distribution of income in favor of groups with a high marginal propensity to save may produce a similar result.

Even natural resources can be increased by exploration and discovery or depleted through exhaustion. We need only mention the discovery in the late 1970s of large new deposits of oil in Mexico and the gradual depletion of the petroleum reserves of the United States during this century. The former greatly strengthened Mexico's export position; the latter transformed the United States from a condition of self-sufficiency in petroleum to one of substantial dependence on imports.

Not only can factor supplies increase or decrease absolutely, it is also possible that the relative factor endowment of a nation may change. For example, the United States during the nineteenth century became transformed from a nation in which natural resources were abundant and labor and capital relatively scarce into one in which capital was the abundant factor.

The effect of such changes in a nation's factor endowment is most easily seen in terms of changes in the transformation function. Consider how this occurs in the case of our hypothetical country II used in previous chapters Food and clothing are the goods produced, with clothing labor-intensive, food capital-intensive. Labor is II's relatively abundant factor, so clothing is relatively cheap and therefore the country's export good. (We continue to use the two-commodity, two-factor model so as to keep the analysis as simple as possible.)

A *balanced* increase in country II's factor endowment is shown in Figure 9.1. The two factors, capital and labor, increase in equal proportions.[1] With input–output relations constant, as determined by unchanging production functions, the output of food and clothing will also increase in equal proportions. This means that, at constant rela-

---

[1] The diagrammatic relationship between factor inputs and commodity outputs is explained in Appendix 1 of Chapter 5, where it is shown how a transformation curve is derived from an efficiency locus.

Figure 9.1   Balanced Growth

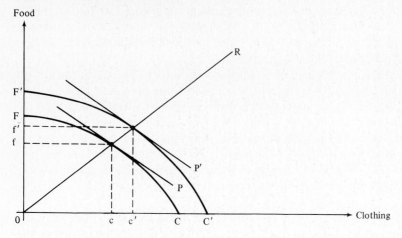

tive prices (shown by the parallel price lines *P* and *P'*), the pattern of production, or the relative output of food and clothing, remains the same.

The situation is quite different when there occurs an *unbalanced* or *biased* change in the supplies of the factors. Thus if there is a relatively large increase in the supply of labor, II's relatively abundant factor, there will be a relatively large rise in the output of clothing, II's export good. Because of this relative increase in the supply of exports, this kind of change in factor supplies is *pro-trade biased.* Diagrammatically, the relative increase in the supply of exports can be seen in Figure 9.2. At constant relative prices, the output of clothing increases (*cc'*) while that of food may decrease as in this instance.

Figure 9.2   Pro-Trade Biased Growth

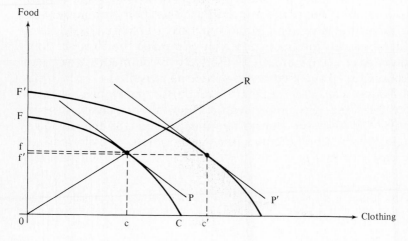

Figure 9.3 Anti-Trade Biased Growth

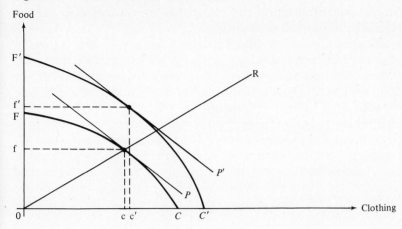

An *antitrade-biased* change in factor supplies is shown in Figure 9.3. There is a relatively large increase in capital, so the new transformation curve, $F'C'$, bulges outward farther in the food direction. At constant prices, there is a relatively greater increase (ff') in the production of import substitutes (food) than of the export good (cc'). The nation's dependence on imports is reduced.

Increases in a nation's factor supplies are one aspect of economic growth. Whether such growth is balanced or biased, and if biased, in which direction and by how much, can have important effects on that nation's supplies of exports and of goods that compete with imports, and thus upon its terms of trade. We shall turn to this topic shortly, but first let us consider another aspect of growth, its impact on income and consumption.

GROWTH AND CONSUMPTION PATTERNS

As the underlying production possibilities of a nation grow, so does the nation's income. We shall assume that population does not increase more rapidly than output, so we can identify growth in aggregate income with growth in per capita income. As income grows, income–expenditure patterns may change, even with constant relative prices. If a rise in incomes results in relatively less of the export good being consumed, this releases some of that good for export, and the income–expenditure pattern is *pro-trade* biased. If, on the other hand, an increase in incomes leads to a relative reduction in the consumption of the *import* good, imports will be replaced by home production and the

income–expenditure pattern is *antitrade* biased. And with no change
in the relative consumption of the two goods as incomes rise, the income–expenditure pattern is neutral.

These possibilities are illustrated in Figure 9.4. We assume a
balanced growth in factor supplies, with the transformation curve FC
and the production point Q_0 moving out to a new position, with the
production point at Q_1 (new transformation curve not shown). Income
rises from the initial budget or income–price line Y_0 to the higher line
Y_1. The initial consumption point is at E_0, the point of tangency of the
relevent community indifference curve U to the income–price line Y_0.
With an unbiased income–expenditure pattern, the indifference curve
for the new income level would be tangent to Y_1 at E_1, on the neutral
income–expenditure line OE. A *pro-trade biased* income–expenditure
pattern, reflecting a reduced consumption of the export good and thus
increased availability of exports, would require a new indifference
curve tangent to the Y_1 line to the left of OE, such as U_x. An *anti-trade
bias* in the income–expenditure pattern would be shown by an indifference curve tangent to the Y_1 line to the right of OE, such as U_m. This
would reflect the replacement of imports by domestic production.

Figure 9.4   Effects of Growth on Consumption

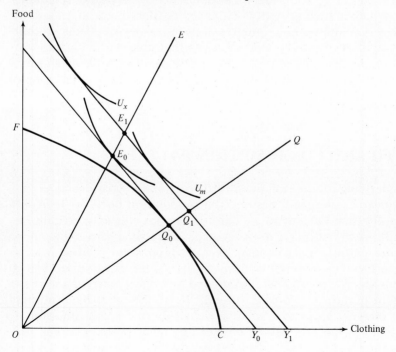

GROWTH AND THE OFFER CURVE

To identify the effect of growth on trade, we must first see what happens to a country's international demand as growth takes place. The easiest way of doing this is to consider the combined effect of growth in production and change in consumption on a nation's offer curve (see Appendix 2 of Chapter 5 for the derivation of an offer curve). We do this for the simplest case: balanced growth in both production and consumption at constant relative prices.

This kind of change is shown visually in Figure 9.5. Balanced growth in factor supplies is illustrated by the uniform outward shift of the production possibilities curve from FC to $F'C'$. Constant relative prices or terms of trade are shown by the parallel lines Y_0 and Y_1, which also indicate real levels of income and consumption. At these constant prices, production of food and clothing increase in equal proportions along the ray OQ from Q_0 to Q_1. The consumption–expenditure pattern is also balanced or neutral, with consumption of each good expanding in the same proportion along the ray OE from E_0 to E_1. The overall result is an expansion of the trade triangle, as shown by the greater length of the export line HQ_1 compared with GQ_0 and the import line HE_1 compared with GE_0.

In the left-hand quadrant we have the constant relative price

Figure 9.5 Effect of Growth on Trade

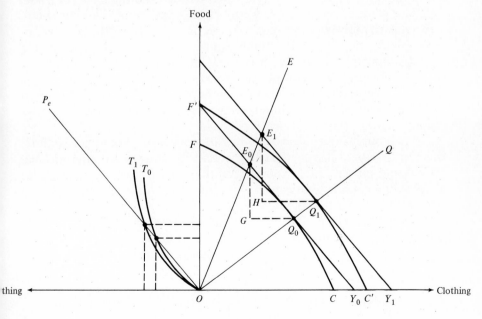

line: OP_e with the same slope as Y_0 and Y_1, and the offer curve OT_0 embodying the exports and imports of the trade triangle E_0GQ_0. The increase in trade indicated by the new triangle E_1HQ_1 requires that the offer curve shift outward to OT_1.

The various possible combinations of production and consumption patterns can yield numerous possible differing results for the trade triangles and the offer curves. Balanced or neutral growth in both production and consumption will always increase trade. If growth in either production or consumption is pro-trade biased while the other is neutral, the increase in trade will be even greater. If one pattern of growth is extremely antitrade biased, it can offset the positive growth effect of the other; trade will decline and the offer curve will shift inward.[2]

THE TERMS OF TRADE

Growth and the Terms of Trade

Once we know what happens to the offer curve, we can readily determine the effect of growth on the terms of trade by examining the shift in the home offer curve vis-à-vis the foreign offer curve. Thus unless the latter is perfectly elastic (i.e., a straight line), an outward shift of the home offer curve caused by growth will worsen the terms of trade. This is the situation in Figure 9.6(a). The initial home offer curve OT_0 intersects the foreign offer curve OT_f so as to establish the relative international price OP_0, with home exports of clothing Oc_0 exchanging for Of_0 imports of food. With growth, the home offer curve shifts to OT_1, establishing the terms of trade shown by the slope of the new price line OP_1. These terms are worse than before. Exports have increased by the amount c_0c_1 while imports have risen only by the much smaller amount f_0f_1.

Although internal growth has increased our country's welfare, this improvement has been partially offset by the reduced international purchasing power of its exports. Another way of looking at it is that the growing country shares part of its gain from growth with its trading partner.

A more extreme case of worsened terms of trade is shown in Figure 9.6(b). Because the relevant portion of the foreign offer curve OT_f is inelastic, the increase in the home country's international de-

[2] See G. M. Meier, *The International Economics of Development* (New York: Harper & Row, Publishers, Inc., 1968), Chapter 3, for a full elaboration of the possibilities.

Figure 9.6 Growth and the Terms of Trade

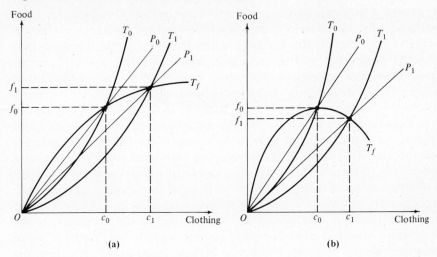

(a)   (b)

mand from OT_0 to OT_1 results in an actual decline in imports in response to increased exports. The overall terms of trade are substantially worsened. Whether such a marked worsening of the terms of
trade would be sufficient to offset the positive effects of growth would,
of course, depend on the relative importance of the internal growth in
production and in consumption and the reduction in the international
purchasing power of the country's exports.[3]

When we consider growth in both countries of our two-country
model, the same issues arise. We need to know the biases on the production and consumption sides, and we need to know the relative rates
of growth in the two countries. The possible combinations become far
too numerous to delineate here. It is, however, possible to consider
particular sets of circumstances, and put the model through its paces
to its logical conclusion.

Such a set of circumstances is one of the reasons put forward by
Prebisch for the alleged secular deterioration of the terms of trade of
developing primary producing countries.[4] Although there is consider-

---

[3] J. N. Bhagwati, "Immiserizing Growth: A Geometrical Note," *Review of Economic Studies*, **24**:201–5 (June 1958), analyzes the possibility in a competitive model that
the terms of trade would deteriorate sufficiently for growth to make a country worse off
in the postgrowth situation than in the pregrowth situation. The possibility, but not
necessity, arises particularly when growth is excessively export biased. If we depart from
the competitive model, several possibilities of immiserizing growth arise. For a summary
statement, see J. N. Bhagwati, "The Generalized Theory of Distortions and Welfare,"
Chapter 4 in J. N. Bhagwati et al., eds., *Trade, Balance of Payments and Growth*
(Amsterdam: North-Holland Publishing Company, 1971).

[4] The argument is set out most clearly in Raul Prebisch, "Commercial Policy in
the Underdeveloped Countries," *American Economic Review*, **49**:26–64 (May 1959).

ably more to the Prebisch thesis than this single element, the analytical point serves to illustrate the workings of our model. The argument rests on the low-income elasticity of demand for primary products. Thus, in terms of our model, the Prebisch argument is that the consumption patterns associated with growth are biased in favor of the manufactured exports of developed countries. Hence the income–expenditure pattern in the developing countries is pro-trade biased, whereas in the developed countries it is antitrade biased. If we add the specification that growth occurs at approximately equal rates in the developed and developing countries, and growth patterns on the production side are neutral, the offer curve of the developing countries shifts outward at a faster rate. Then, because the offer curve of the developing countries is shifting outward faster, the relative price of the developing countries' exports falls. In other words, the terms of trade facing the developing countries tend to deteriorate. Implicit in the model, however, is the assumption that the effect of biased income–expenditure patterns is not swamped by the opposite influences of, say, more rapid growth in the developed countries or antitrade biased growth patterns on the production side in the developing countries. The argument over whether or not the terms of trade of developing countries has in fact deteriorated will be taken up in the next section.

Measuring the Terms of Trade over Time

Because changes in the prices of tradables affect the gains from growth, considerable attention is focused on the international price ratio facing a country. This is usually referred to as its commodity or barter terms of trade. It is the ratio of the prices a country gets for its exports to the prices it pays for its imports. If, as compared with this relation in a given or base year, a country's export prices rise or import prices fall, its commodity terms of trade are said to have improved. The country gains more from trade because a given quantity of exports would not command a larger quantity of imports than before. If, on the other hand, the prices of its exports decline or the prices of its imports rise, its terms of trade are said to have worsened. The country's gain from trade has lessened because now a given quantity of exports would buy a smaller quantity of imports than formerly.

To make these relative price comparisons, index numbers are used. For a selected base year, an average of a country's export prices is computed, with each commodity in the average weighted according to its importance in total trade. For a later year, a similar average is computed; it will reflect the change in average export prices. The same procedure is followed for imports. The country's new terms of trade can then be measured by obtaining a ratio of the new export prices to the new import prices.

$$T_c = \frac{P_{x_1}}{P_{x_0}} \div \frac{P_{m_1}}{P_{m_0}} \cdot 100 \quad \text{or} \quad \frac{P_{x_1}}{P_{m_1}} \cdot 100$$

In this expression, T_c stands for the commodity terms of trade, the subscripts x and m for exports and imports, respectively, and the subscripts 1 and 0 for the given year and the base year ($=100$).

Thus, taking 1975 as the base year and expressing the prices of U.S. exports and imports for that year as 100, we find that in 1980 the index of export prices had risen to 148 and the index of import prices to 181. The terms of trade, consequently, had changed as follows:

$$T_c = \frac{148}{181} \cdot 100 = 82 \text{ approximately}$$

Since U.S. export prices had risen less than its import prices, the terms of trade had deteriorated by 18 percent compared with 1975.[5] This can be interpreted as meaning either that for a given amount of exports the United States could obtain 18 percent fewer imports, or that to purchase a given amount of imports, the United States had to give up 22 percent more exports. The principal explanation for the greater rise in import than in export prices is a sharp increase in petroleum prices. An index of the price of crude petroleum rose in this period from 100 to 335.

Although changes in the commodity terms of trade by themselves indicate the direction of movement of the gains from trade, their implication may be seriously modified by accompanying changes of other kinds. We must reckon with at least three offsetting elements: changes in the character of the statistical data themselves, changes in the volume of trade, and changes in productivity.

1. Index numbers of export and import prices often make no allowance for variations in the quality of the goods traded or for changes in the composition of goods entering into international trade. Unless specifically corrected, a barter terms-of-trade index shows only what has happened to the relative prices of exports and imports that were traded in a certain base year. Yet changes in the quality of goods can be enormous, while new goods are constantly entering the ranks of traded commodities.

This point is particularly important in connection with the re-

---

[5] IMF, *International Financial Statistics*, June 1981. The price indices are indices of unit value.

curring discussions of the terms of trade of primary producing countries. Thus a United Nations' publication shows that according to the price indexes used, the terms of trade between primary products and finished industrial goods deteriorated substantially (from 100 to 64) between 1876–1880 and 1936–1938. This proves, it is claimed, that only 64 percent as large a volume of manufactured goods could be purchased with a given amount of primary products at the end of this period as at the beginning.[6]

Besides other defects, this interpretation of the statistical results completely ignores the fact that, although primary exports of 1938 were substantially the same as primary exports in 1876, manufactured imports had improved tremendously in quality. Compare the nylon stockings of the later date with the cotton stockings of 1876, or the mercury vapor lamp with the kerosene lamp. Moreover, many commodities, such as the automobile, the television set, and the radio, were unknown in 1876 and hence cannot be given any weight in index numbers covering such a long span of years.

Because changes in the quality and the composition of exports or imports are constantly taking place, the conventional conclusion drawn from variations in an index of the commodity terms of trade must be limited to short periods. Even then, the evidence must be treated with care. As for long periods—for example, more than ten years—any statement about changing terms of trade will in all likelihood have to be highly qualified.

2. Subject to the foregoing qualification, a fall in the commodity terms of trade implies that a given quantity of exports will buy a smaller quantity of imports than formerly. Suppose, however, that the volume of exports has simultaneously risen, perhaps as a consequence of lower prices. The exporting country's "capacity to import" may remain unchanged or even improve despite the poorer terms on which it trades.

Such changes in the volume of trade can be taken into account by an index of the income terms of trade, which is simply the commodity or barter terms multiplied by an index of the change in export volume: $T_y = T_c(Q_{x1}/Q_{x0})$. Thus, although Japan's commodity terms of trade fell between 1975 and 1980 from 100 to 76, the volume of exports rose from 100 to 155. This meant that, instead of purchasing 24 percent fewer imports than in 1975, they actually purchased approximately 18 percent more. So the worsened barter terms of trade were more than offset by the increased volume of exports. In the same period, the United States, because of a rise in its export volume to 138, enjoyed a 13 percent rise in its income terms of trade.

[6] United Nations, Economic Commission for Latin America, *The Economic Development of Latin America and Its Principal Problems* (E/CN.12/89/Rev. 1. 1950), Table 1.

The income terms of trade, it should be noted, carry no implication of gain or loss from trade. They do, however, indicate any change in a country's ability to pay for its imports with its exports, which may be very important.

3. A movement in the commodity terms of trade may be partly or wholly offset by a change in the efficiency with which exports are produced. Thus suppose that, while a country's import prices on the average remain constant, the costs and prices of its exports fall 10 percent because of an increase in productivity. An index of the commodity terms of trade would then indicate that these had worsened by the percentage decline in costs. There would be no real worsening of the country's position, however, for although a given value of exports can now command 10 percent less imports, the exports required to obtain the imports can be produced for a correspondingly reduced expenditure of resources. The real costs of imports, in terms of resources used, is unchanged.

An index of the single factoral terms of trade could take such a change in productivity into account. Simply multiply the commodity terms of trade by the reciprocal of an index of the change in cost, expressed in terms of the quantities of the factors used per unit of exports: $T_f = T_c(F_{x0}/F_{x1})$. This gives an index of the physical imports obtained per unit of resources used in producing exports. The use of this measure of changes in the terms of trade is limited by the difficulties in obtaining the data necessary to compute an index of productivity. Very rough approximations may have to be used, amounting to little more than "guesstimates," but the point is important and should always be borne in mind.[7]

INTERNATIONAL FACTOR MOVEMENTS

Instead of growing from an internal accumulation of factors, a country may grow by receiving additional supplies of factors from abroad. This, of course, is contrary to the basic assumption we have used to this point: that factors are internationally immobile. It is now time to consider what happens when we relax that assumption. We do so first in terms of our highly simplified model, so as to bring out clearly the theoretical points involved. We then briefly evaluate the contribution made by a foreign factor, and finally consider the issue of international factor movements more generally.

[7] For a fuller discussion of the terms of trade and additional ways of measuring changes, see J. Viner, *Studies in the Theory of International Trade* (New York: Harper & Row, Publishers, Inc., 1937), pp. 558–70. See also Meier, op. cit., Chapter 3.

Factor Movement in a Simple Trade Model

In the simple competitive model, trade rests ultimately on differences among countries in factor endowments. These are given, they remain fixed, and they cannot move between countries. Trade is free, and given certain rigorous conditions (see p. 86), factor prices in the trading countries will be equalized.

Using this model, we assume, as earlier, that our home country exports the labor-intensive commodity, clothing, in exchange for imports of the capital-intensive good, food. To keep matters simple, we assume further that our country is small, with no influence on world factor or goods prices, which are equal at home and abroad. Figure 9.7 portrays the free trade situation, with P_0 the relative price line, production at Q_0, and consumption at E_0. Autarky production and consumption are presumed to be at A_0.

We now drop the assumption of international factor immobility and allow capital to move freely between countries. But with factor prices equal, there is no incentive for it to move. Some other change

Figure 9.7   Capital Inflow

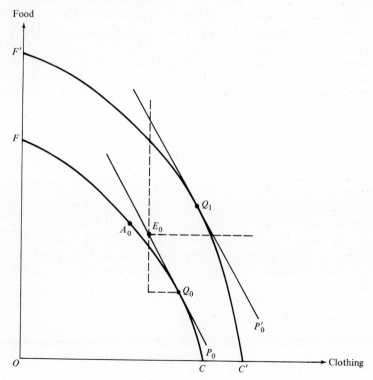

is required to disturb the equilibrium. This we accomplish by arbitrarily prohibiting trade.

By itself, the prohibition of trade would soon cause the price of food to rise relative to that of clothing. This would stimulate a flow of domestic resources—both capital and labor—from clothing to food production, as well as an inflow of capital from abroad. By supplementing domestic capital, the foreign capital would permit an expansion of output in both industries, in proportions that ultimately reflected the community's preferences. Relative prices would gradually approach those obtaining under free trade, with consumption continuing at E_0. Since the production of both food and clothing is increasing, this would cause the transformation curve FC to expand to some such position as $F'C'$. The new production point will lie somewhere on $F'C'$, as at Q_1, above and to the right of E_0. Production of one or both goods would have to be enough greater than domestic consumption to pay for the services of the imported capital.[8]

One final point: Our analysis leads to the basic conclusion that goods movements and factor movements are substitutes for one another. When goods flow freely, but not factors, relative commodity prices are the same everywhere and (under certain conditions) factor prices are equalized, too. When trade is prohibited (subject to the qualification of footnote 8) but at least one factor can move freely, relative commodity prices are equalized and therefore also factor prices.

FACTOR MOBILITY IN THE INTERNATIONAL ECONOMY

Our theoretical analysis has shown that international factor movements can take the place of trade, and thus lead to the same consequences. This is an interesting conclusion, but it is only one aspect of such movements. For just as the accumulation of factor supplies within a country is a source of economic growth, so is the inflow of factors from abroad. The conclusions reached as to the effects of economic growth on national income and upon the terms of trade should be similar. We shall comment briefly on the relations between factor movements and national income, and upon a special aspect of that topic— how the distribution of income is affected. We shall then consider two

---

[8] Here our assumption of the prohibition of trade lands us in a dilemma. How is the foreign capital to be paid for its services? Without trade, there is no means of acquiring foreign currency with which to remit interest or divided payments. Sufficient exports of both goods must be allowed, in the proportions desired by foreign buyers, to transmit the required returns to capital.

especially interesting aspects of international factor movements: how, rather than being a substitute for trade, they have served in many instances to create trade, and how international investment, particularly in recent years, has brought about the internationalization of big business.

Factor Movements and National Income

Whether a nation acquires additional productive resources as a consequence of internal accumulation or as the result of international migration of the factors, its capacity to produce is increased and national income rises. Per capita income will also rise if the rate of growth of national income exceeds the rate of growth of population. Moreover, not only does the income of a nation that acquires factors from abroad rise, but world output and income also rise. For although the nation from which the resources have migrated suffers a decline in production, this loss is more than offset by the receiving country's gain. For the factors would not have migrated (barring politically motivated movements) unless they could earn a higher return abroad. Any movement of a factor from a location where its marginal product is low to a location where it is higher results in a net gain.

The Distribution of Income

Is the gain to a migrating factor, say labor, from the higher return it earns offset by a loss to the labor already employed in the receiving country? If technology remains constant, the answer depends on whether the complementary factors increase in proportion to the migrating factor. If not, the inflow of labor will lower the marginal product of all labor and thus the income of labor already in the country. Even without an inflow of capital and the discovery of sufficient additional natural resources to maintain the previous overall factor proportions, a rapid advance in technology could offset the tendency toward diminishing returns.

There are special circumstances when immigrant labor will not force down the income of resident labor. In western Europe in the 1960s, when employment was high and exports were expanding, the pressure on the domestic labor supply was intense, and West Germany, France, and Switzerland, in particular, permitted the entry of large numbers of workers from southeastern Europe and Algeria. Most came in, however, on visas that could be revoked at any time. Many of the millions who migrated remained for several years. In this instance there was an excess demand for labor, so the influx of foreign labor merely kept wages from rising faster than they did.

In the United States, much of the large inflow of Mexican labor, legal and illegal, has gone into low-wage occupations in the service industries—busboys, waiters, hotel maids, domestic servants, and gardeners—occupations that are shunned by native American labor. Here, there was relatively little direct competition of immigrant with resident labor.

You will recall that in discussing international adjustment to a change in relative commodity prices (pp. 109ff.), we showed that the process was very different in the long and short runs, owing to the fact that in the short run, capital in particular was highly specific in many industries and thus completely immobile for longish periods. In our familiar simple model, a rise in the price of clothing raised the *VMP* of labor in that industry and attracted mobile labor from food production. The return to the immobile capital thus fell in the latter industry but rose in clothing.

Similar reasoning applies to the adjustment to an international movement of a factor. In this instance, however, it seems more appropriate to make capital the specific factor in clothing and land the specific factor in food. Then an inflow of capital, invested in the concrete forms peculiar to the clothing industry, will raise wages by increasing the productivity of labor in that industry. With the increase in the supply of capital, its return would fall. So would the rent of land, since labor would move into the higher-paying clothing industry. A wave of immigration, on the other hand, would lower the return to labor, but raise the return to capital and to land.

Creation of Trade

It is surprising that in spite of the great waves of immigration in the nineteenth century and since, and of the large-scale movements of capital that took place as well, the assumption of international immobility of the factors was a basic premise of international trade theory since the time of Ricardo. Yet it was not until some fifty years ago that John H. Williams of Harvard launched an effective attack on this premise.[9] He contended that international mobility of factors was far greater than had been supposed, often being greater *between* countries than *within* a single one. In particular, he suggested that the very economic backwardness of underdeveloped countries minimized the internal mobility of labor and capital; these factors, particularly capital, moved more

[9] John H. Williams, "The Theory of International Trade Reconsidered," *Economic Journal*, **39** (1929); reprinted in American Economic Association, *Readings in the Theory of International Trade* (New York: McGraw-Hill Book Company, 1949).

freely from the advanced to the underdeveloped countries than within the latter.

This is part of the explanation of great cosmopolitan seacoast cities, foreign trading centers, nearer to Europe in their economic and cultural contacts and characteristics than to their own interiors, and relying upon Europe for finance, transport, and management; of the presence of large-scale foreign enterprise, mainly in the extractive industries, of the existence of problems of immigration or emigration, in countries and continents otherwise comparatively primitive, "pre-economic," to use Bagehot's phrase.[10]

Later work extended Williams' critique to the transformation, during the nineteenth century, of previously isolated subsistence economies into exporters of primary products.[11]

Their entry into international trade was thrust upon them quite suddenly by an invasion of foreign entrepreneurs, who brought with them the necessary capital, managerial talent, technical labor, and (according to Levin) even the major part of the common labor essential to establish a thriving primary export industry. Generally, the only needed factor available in these countries was some natural resource— a rich mineral deposit or fertile or well-located tropical land.

Thus Levin shows how, in the 1840s, the prospective profits to be made from exploiting the rich guano deposits on the Chincha Islands off the coast of Peru attracted British capital and enterprise. Since money incentives had little appeal for the Peruvian Indian, the management was forced to import Chinese coolie labor under contract. Burma's rice industry before World War II depended heavily on seasonal Indian labor, Chettyar money lenders, and British rice millers. Besides these two industries, Levin cites the sugar industry of Queensland, the banana industry of Central America, and tea plantations in Sri Lanaka, among others.[12]

It should be stressed that the foregoing argument in no way contradicts the Heckscher–Oblin theory, but only rejects the long-held assumption of the international immobility of the productive factors. That theory states that if factor endowments are given and held constant, countries will tend to export products that require relatively intensive use of their abundant factors. But if a country's factor endowment is altered by international factor movements, its pattern of trade may change.

[10] Ibid., p. 261.
[11] See Jonathan V. Levin, *The Export Economies: Their Pattern of Development in Historical Perspective* (Cambridge, Mass.: Harvard University Press, 1960).
[12] Ibid., pp. 4–5, Chapter 20.

Services and International Factor Mobility

Specialization in the rendering of services connected with the movement of factors has become an important element in overcoming or coping with the obstacles to international factor movements. A distinction between such services, concerned with factor movements, and commodity-connected services is important in explaining international shifts of factors. Historically, however, the development of both types of specialized international services has been closely linked. With the growth of both domestic and international trade, members of the London business community acquired great skill in the grading and classification of commodities, in the evaluation of market prospects, in the assessment of customer credit-worthiness, in the estimation of risk, and in the performance of all the manifold tasks connected with buying, selling, and transporting goods and in financing these transactions. As the volume of trade grew, the degree of specialization in the performance of these functions increased apace; so did the pool of knowledge essential for informed action. This knowledge and these skills enabled London to become, early in the nineteenth century, the purveyor to the world of services of shipping, marketing, insurance, and banking. (For more details, see pp. 265–68.)

Banking services were at first limited mainly to the provision of short-term credit to finance the international movement of goods. The combination of experience, knowledge, and reputation, however, together with the attracting to London of small and large sums of savings, permitted certain firms to undertake investment banking on an international scale. Relying on their reputation to attract capital, these firms used their skill and knowledge to overcome the obstacles to its international movement. Where returns to international investment were sufficiently high, they discovered these attractive opportunities and engineered a flow of capital.

New York experienced a development similar to that of London, although considerably later. Until after World War I, New York was almost exclusively a national commerical and financial center. Thereafter, with the growing importance of the United States in world affairs, it came to rival London on the international scene. The pull of New York and London as financial and marketing centers attracted to them the head offices of many large corporations. They thus became great pools of managerial talent, and added to the other services they provided that of management. First offered in the form of consultation, managerial services increasingly took the form of the direct export of managerial staff to branch plants and subsidiaries or to foreign firms under contract.

Summarizing our argument, spontaneous factor movements, ruled out by the assumptions of static trade theory, do in fact occur in response to factor price differences. Such spontaneous movements are reinforced by the activities of firms performing banking and management functions. They, too, react to factor price differences, using their knowledge and expertise to overcome the obstacles to international factor movements. Thereby such flows are enlarged, alterations in national factor endowments speeded, and the basis for trade and specialization is changed.

Direct Investment and the Multinational Corporation

From the point of view of ownership and control, two types of international capital movements can be distinguished: direct and portfolio investment. The latter gives the investor a claim to a fixed return on a loan, typified by a bond bearing a specific rate of interest. This kind of investment includes no element of control, which resides in the borrower. Portfolio investment constituted much the larger part of international investment in the nineteenth century; it financed railroads in North and South America and Australia, the provisions of port facilities throughout the world, and other important kinds of capital installations. In contrast with portfolio investment, direct investment results in ownership and thus control of its object, which may be physical assets, or more likely stock in a corporation that owns and controls them. During the twentieth century, direct investment has become the dominant form of the international flow of capital, far exceeding portfolio investment in importance.

Typically, the initiator of direct investment is a business firm, using its funds to build a branch plant abroad or acquiring such a facility by purchasing the stock of an existing foreign firm. Direct foreign investment by individuals through the purchase of stock on various national stock exchanges is large in absolute terms but of minor importance compared with investment undertaken by business firms.

Since direct investment involves ownership and control, and since most of it is undertaken by business enterprise to carry out a deliberate policy of expansion into foreign markets, the flow of capital abroad is usually accompanied by the export of management. And with management goes business practice and industrial technology. Thus the flow of direct investment, especially since World War II, has been the instrument of a substantial internationalization of business. The agents of this development, business firms located in various nations and expanding their operations into others, have been appropriately named *multinational corporations*.

Several features distinguish this type of international business expansion. Most noteworthy is the size of the participants. Multinational enterprises are almost exclusively very large firms, members of a small number of corporations dominant in their respective fields—in a word, oligopolists. The roster includes such names as IBM, du Pont, Imperial Chemical, Michelin, General Motors, Volkswagen, and Royal Dutch Shell. A second feature of the growth of multinational business is that the firms are primarily engaged in manufacturing, which of course covers a wide range of products. Among the industries most favored are chemical, electrical manufactures, transport (mainly automobiles), petroleum refining, and metal fabrication. Some multinational firms are concerned principally with distribution, like several of the great Japanese trading companies, or with a combination of functions, such as the extraction, refining, and distribution of petroleum. Not a few, like Anaconda Copper Co., are engaged in mining of various minerals, and large American, European, and Japanese banks provide worldwide services. But the main area of multinational activity is the broad area of manufacturing. Finally, and the key to their characterization as multinationals, is the geographical reach of these enterprises. The majority of multinational corporations operate in seven to eleven countries, but twelve or more are frequently covered.[13]

Although multinational enterprise became noteworthy and enjoyed its most rapid growth only after World War II, the multinational corporation was present in small numbers even before World War I. Most prominent at that time were such firms as Singer Co. (sewing machines) and Bell Telephone (telephone service and equipment, later Western Electric and ITT) based in the United States, Solvay (chemicals) of Belgium, and BASF (chemicals and dyes) and Hoechst (drugs) of Germany. The number of multinationals increased during the interwar years, especially of U.S. firms, but the most rapid expansion came in the 1950's and 1960's, with the United States, the United Kingdom, western Europe participating and Japan joining in.

What reasons underlay the development and expansion of multinational enterprise? In considering this question, one cannot help being struck by the fact that there is a close association between the size of a firm and its establishment of subsidiaries abroad—that is, becoming a multinational. This is also true of the preceding phase, undertaking the export of its product on its own account. There is little reason for a firm to do this until it has established a dominant position in its home market. Small firms desiring to expand sales beyond their national market can and do rely on the services of professional traders.

---

[13] For a wide variety of quantitative information about the operations of multinational corporations, an excellent source is Lawrence G. Franko, *The European Multinationals* (Stamford, Conn.: Greylock Publishers, 1976).

But when a corporation becomes one of a few dominant firms in an industry, its product is almost certainly differentiated from those of its competitors. This may mean that the product is an innovation, perhaps already copied by imitators, but still distinguished from others by reputation and appearance, reinforced by advertising and packaging. There is substantial evidence to support the view that multinational enterprise is the result of oligopoly based on innovation and its successful commercialization.[14] Among early instances are the sewing machine, telephone service and equipment, anilin dyes, ammonia fixation, and margarine. Later came the assembly line, automatic transmission, penicillin, the computer, and integrated circuitry.[15]

A fairly typical sequence in the emergence of a corporation as a multinational appears to be: first, the establishment of a strong position in the domestic market, then direct expansion into exporting, and finally direct investment in subsidiaries abroad. Entry into the last stage becomes attractive when it promises to increase the profits of the fledgling multinational. As a general rule, establishment of a subsidiary in a specific market would not be a worthwhile alternative to exporting until sales were large enough to warrant a plant of efficient size. Thereafter, among the considerations affecting the decision to act are the possibility of employing relatively cheap labor, reducing transport costs (avoiding gain in weight, etc.), more rapid and effective servicing of customers, easier adaptation of a product to local needs, the ability to keep a close watch on local competitors, and occasionally, jumping over a tariff.

Problems Related to Multinationals   Multinational enterprise attracted little attention until its relatively recent period of rapid growth. This appears to be because in earlier years foreign subsidiaries were set up mainly in advanced industrialized nations: Firms in the United States, the United Kingdom, Canada, and western Europe erected branch plants in one another's territory. Relatively little of this sort of direct investment went to the underdeveloped world. Although foreign investment in such extractive industries as copper and nitrate production in Chile, copper in what is now Zaire, and nickel in New Caledonia was substantial. In more recent times, a great increase in the number of branch plants set up in the underdeveloped countries has taken place. Between 1953 and 1970, western European enterprises alone estab-

---

[14] See Raymond Vernon, "International Trade and International Investment in the Product Cycle," *Quarterly Journal of Economics*, **80** (May 1966); Raymond Vernon, *Sovereignty at Bay* (New York: Basic Books, Inc., Publishers, 1971; and Richard E. Caves, "International Corporations: The International Economics of Foreign Investment," *Economica* (Feb. 1971).

[15] Cited in Franko, op. cit., pp. 26–27.

lished some 700 subsidiaries in the Third World outside Europe, compared to fewer than 100 in the thirty-odd years after World War I.[16]

The introduction of subsidaries of large corporations in other industrialized nations raised few problems, probably because as representatives of an industrial country in another industrial country, the relationship was between more or less equals. The situation is different when the host country is a less developed one; the relative size and strength of the nations involved enter the picture. Considerations of this sort surely lie behind the resentment of host countries in Latin American, Asia, and Africa to the fact that many decisions, especially those relating to the location of research and development activities, are made in favor of the home office. It is hard to see how, on rational grounds, different decisions could be reached, except in unusual circumstances. The dissatisfaction of the host countries is understandable. However, it looks very much like a special aspect of the more general resentment at domination of host governments by multinational corporations and of the "brain drain": the steady migration of trained personnel to the advanced industrial countries that is experienced by the less developed nations.

Another source of resentment at the presence of manufacturing subsidiaries of large foreign corporations is the fear of the host countries that the return of profits of subsidiaries to their home countries constitutes an outflow of capital that should be checked by requiring local participation (often as high as 51 percent) in ownership. But remission of profits is not an outflow of capital but of current earnings, and further, the purchase of a local interest in the foreign enterprise effectively diverts capital from an alternative domestic use.

An often expressed fear is that the competition of a large foreign firm will be injurious to local businessmen, even preventing indigenous industry from getting started. Since one of the features of underdevelopment is a lack of manufacturing industry, this fear would seem to be unwarranted. Generally, the appearance of a manufacturing subsidiary means that something new is being produced in the host country; there is a net addition to the output, employment, and capital of the latter. The introduction of a manufacturing operation, by displacing former imports, may cause losses to local distributors. But there may be offsetting gains, in the form of contracts with suppliers of raw materials, parts, and services, and local distributorships may be retained or even expanded.

A special type of dissatisfaction arises when the foreign firm is engaged in the exploitation of local natural resources, as with Chilean copper, Venezuelan iron ore or petroleum, or Jamaican bauxite. Here

[16] Ibid., Table 5.1.

the foreigner is regarded as taking advantage of the host country by obtaining a high return at low cost from depleting nonrenewable domestic resources. The issue is not whether to develop a nation's natural resources or to let them remain untouched, but what rate of exploitation is in the host country's best interest. There is, of course, a problem of relative power involved here. But the LDCs have increasingly learned to cope with the problem, through such measures as taxation, output limitation, purchase, or obligatory participation, not to mention concerted action, as with OPEC or the declaration of a 200-mile limit on fishing.

Operations of multinationals have also given rise to dissatisfaction in their home countries. Most vocal has been organized labor, which has intermittently expressed its fear that the export of capital is accompanied by an export of jobs to areas of cheap labor. Such empirical evidence as is available is inconclusive. Raymond Vernon cites studies of the United States which indicated that the employment effects of multinationals are, in the aggregate, quite small. The value of these estimates is questionable, however, since they are based on the unwarranted assumption of perfect competition in the industries concerned.

With respect to this issue of employment, it is worth recalling that over the past century, as new relatively capital-intensive industries have emerged in the industrialized countries, the older, labor-intensive industries have tended to migrate to the underdeveloped nations, where labor is relatively cheap. Textiles are the classic example. In more recent years, radio and television assembly, the manufacture of shoes and ladies' purses and handbags, and many other comparatively simple articles and processes have joined the procession. As long as technological progress and growth continue, new industries can be expected to replace the old, as they have in the past, unemployment is a cyclical, not a long-run problem.

Another fear, expressed in some countries, especially the United States, has to do with taxation. It is urged that the operation of multinationals may seriously reduce the tax yield of their home countries. Profits of subsidiaries are taxed in the host countries. These profits are also subject to tax in the home country, generally after subtraction of the taxes paid in the host nation. If the home country levies its tax regardless of whether the profits are left abroad or are repatriated, no problem arises, since home country taxes must be paid wherever the profits come to rest. But if, as in the United States, the foreign earnings of multinationals are not taxed until they are repatriated, there will be an incentive to leave a subsidiary's earnings abroad, provided only that corporate tax rates are higher at home, for then the yield will be higher on whatever earnings are not repatriated. It may even be desirable to increase the subsidiary's apparent earnings by under-charging it for services rendered, such as research and development.

How far to go with respect to repatriation of a subsidiary's earnings will depend on two principal considerations. One is of course the difference in foreign and domestic corporate tax rates. More important, however, is the policy of the multinational with respect to the use of its funds. As the owner of the subsidiary, it is entitled to all its earnings. If expansion of the subsidiary's activities appears desirable, part or all of its profits may be used to finance that expansion. On the other hand, there may be more important uses for them at home. If so, they will be repatriated. In the end, a balance will be struck between the net gain from differing corporate tax rates and considerations of corporate policy. The decision is not a simple one, and is surely unlikely to be always or even predominantly against repatriation of foreign earnings. Fear that tax yields will be seriously reduced because of the activity of multinationals would appear to be unwarranted.

SUMMARY

This chapter has been concerned with various aspects of growth in relation to international trade. First, we left behind the assumption underlying the theoretical factor proportions model, that factor supplies are fixed, and allowed for internal growth from an increase in population, the creation of capital through saving, and the discovery of new natural resources. Balanced growth in such factor supplies results in an equal proportionate growth in output and income. A relatively large increase in a country's abundant factor makes available more export goods, and is pro-trade biased.

With growth in output, income rises, and if income–expenditure patterns remain unchanged, trade is unaffected. If per capita income increases, however, those patterns may change. Such changes may be pro-trade or antitrade biased, depending on whether there is a relative reduction in the consumption of the export or the import good. The combined effects of growth in both production and consumption on the offer curve and on trade are then briefly reviewed, and it is shown that the terms of trade will be worsened, thereby partially offsetting the beneficial effects of growth.

The use of index numbers to measure changes in the terms of trade is explained and illustrated. The importance of allowing for changes in the quality and composition of the goods traded is stressed, as is the need for taking into account changes in the volume of a country's exports or in the efficiency with which they are produced.

Discussion next turns to growth based on international movements of capital and labor, hitherto excluded. Starting with a simple two-commodity, two-factor model in equilibrium with factor prices equalized, a disturbance is introduced in the form of a prohibition of trade. If the international movement of capital is permitted, however, it is shown that goods movements and factor movements are substitutes for one another. Whether a country acquires additional supplies of the factor by internal growth or by inflow from abroad, the effect on national income is the same: it increases. World income also rises as a consequence of international factor movements, for any loss by the factor-exporting country is more than offset by the gain in the receiving country, since (nonpolitical) factor movements take place only if their marginal product is larger at their destination. As for the effect of an inflow of, say labor, on the income of labor already employed in the country of destination, unless complementary factors increase in proportion to the additional labor, the resident labor will suffer a decline in its marginal produce and in its income. This effect could be offset by a sufficient advance in technology.

Contrary to the assumption of theory, large international movements of capital and labor took place during the nineteenth century, leading to the rise of primary product exporting industries in underdeveloped countries, where suitable raw materials were often the only needed factor available. This does not contradict the factor proportions theory, only the realism of its assumption of factor immobility.

During the nineteenth century, the development of specialized services of banking and management reinforced the spontaneous movement of factors. These services, as well as marketing services, became highly developed in London and later in New York.

Two types of foreign investment are distinguished: direct investment, which carries control and portfolio investment, which does not. The latter dominated foreign investment in the nineteenth century, the former in the twentieth. The principal agents of direct foreign investment in this century, especially since World War II, have been multinational corporations (MNCs), which have brought management together with capital and ownership. Most MNCs are large, oligopolistic firms, mainly in manufactures, many operating in a dozen or more countries. The reason for establishing multinationals by acquiring subsidiaries abroad seems to reside in the desire to expand profits by actual physical presence in export markets, where cheap labor may be available, service to customers can be quicker, and products adapted to local needs.

Few serious problems arose in the early days of multinationals; they established subsidiaries in other industrialized nations. Since World War II, MNCs have established branches throughout the Third World, and the difference between the size and economic strength of many multinationals and many host countries came to the fore. Friction developed over the location of research activities, the repatriation of profits to the home country, competition with local industries, the exploitation of natural resources, and fear of domination by the large firms. In the home countries, labor fears the loss of jobs to cheap labor, while problems have arisen with respect to the taxation of subsidiaries.

SELECTED REFERENCES

BERGSTEN, C. F., et al. "Home-Country Policy Toward Multinationals," in Robert E. Baldwin and J. David Richardson, *International Trade and Finance Readings*, 2nd ed. Little, Brown and Company, Boston, 1981, Chapter 16. Reprinted from C. F. Bergsten et al., "American Policy Towards Multinationals: An Overview," in *American Multinationals and American Interests*, The Brookings Institution, Washington, D.C., 1978.

FINDLAY, R., AND H. GRUBERT. "Factor Intensities, Technological Progress, and the Terms of Trade." *Oxford Economic Papers* (Feb. 1959). Reprinted in J. Bhagwati, ed., *International Trade*, Baltimore: Penguin Books, Inc., 1969. Shows the impact of technical progress on production possibilities and hence on the terms of trade.

JOHNSON, HARRY G. "Economic Development and International Trade." In American Economic Association, *Readings in International Economics*, Homewood, Ill.: Richard D. Irwin, Inc., 1968. An original treatment of changes in factor supplies and in technology and their effects on trade. Other articles in the same section of this book of readings will be interesting on special points.

LEVIN, JONATHAN V. *The Export Economies, Their Pattern of Development in Historical Perspective*. Cambridge, Mass.: Harvard University Press, 1960.

MEIER, G. M. *The International Economics of Development*. New York: Harper & Row, Publishers, 1968. Chapter 3 contains a fairly complete review of the effect of growth on the terms of trade.

MUNDELL, R. A. "International Trade and Factor Mobility." Originally in *American Economic Review*, **47** (June 1957). Adaptation appears as Chapter 6 in Mundell's *International Economics*, New York: Macmillan Publishing Company 1968. The original statement of the theoretical model of international factor movements presented in this chapter.

RYBCZYNSKI, T. "Factor Endowment and Relative Commodity Prices." *Economica*, **22** (1955). Reprinted in American Economic Association, *Readings in International Economics*, Homewood, Ill.: Richard D. Irwin, Inc., 1968. The original statement of how an increment in a factor supply affects output.

WILLIAMS, JOHN H. "The Theory of International Trade Reconsidered." *Economic Journal* (1929). Reprinted in American Economic Association, *Readings in the Theory of International Trade*, New York: McGraw-Hill Book Company, 1949. A landmark in the literature, well worth consulting.

PART
3

TARIFFS AND PROTECTION

10
CHAPTER

The Tariff Issue

We have seen that if a basis for international trade exists, its pursuit will enable the participants to enjoy an increase in real income. This gain is not limited to any one of a group of trading nations but is shared by all, since it results from a generally more efficient use of scarce resources. Further, *free* trade permits *full* advantage to be taken of the possibilities of international specialization. This is the essence of the case for free trade.

Protection, on the other hand, reduces, and if sufficiently great wipes out, the gains from trade. By examining the effects of one type of protectionist device, a tariff, we shall see how protection (1) shifts resources from more efficient to less efficient uses, and (2) restricts the consumer's freedom of choice, arbitrarily forcing him to reduce his consumption of things of which he would prefer to buy more if his choice were uninhibited.

The case for free trade has never been successfully refuted, nor even has an intellectually acceptable argument for long-run, enduring protection, based on economic considerations, ever been devised, although much ingenuity has gone into the attempt. We shall see that the arguments for protection that do have validity are either short run or noneconomic in character, or require realization of special conditions. Yet, most of the arguments advanced by protectionists are unqualified, asserted with great conviction, and, what is more important, are widely believed.

EFFECTS OF A TARIFF: PARTIAL EQUILIBRIUM

The effects of a tariff may be examined in terms of the economy as a whole, or in terms of the market for a particular good, say shoes, which is one of many goods. Considerable insight into the effects can be obtained by confining our attention to the latter "partial equilibrium" analysis. To do this, we must assume that demand and supply relationships of the chosen commodity, say shoes, are given and remain constant. On the demand side, tastes, other prices, and consumer's money incomes all remain fixed. On the supply side, technological change, externalities, and other changes in cost conditions are ruled out. In particular, we rule out for the moment any tariffs on material inputs used in the production of shoes.

The Price Effect

The free trade equilibrium situation differs from the usual partial equilibrium demand–supply relationship only in that supply may be domestic, or foreign, or both. We assume a small country vis-à-vis the world, so that changes in its purchases of imports have no effect on their price abroad. In Figure 10.1, S and D represent the domestic supply and demand curves, respectively, and OP_1 is the (constant) price at which foreign supplies are available.

The equilibrium free trade price in the domestic market under these conditions is OP_1, for the availability of identical foreign shoes at OP_1 means that domestic producers are unable to charge a higher price. Domestic producers supply up to the point at which their costs at the margin equal the constant foreign costs: Domestic production is OQ_1.

Figure 10.1   Effects of a Tariff in Partial Equilibrium

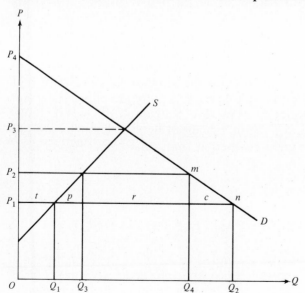

The difference between domestic production and domestic demand (OQ_2) at the price OP_1 is made up by imports (Q_1Q_2). Contrast this with the situation if no imports were available from abroad, yielding a domestic equilibrium price of OP_3.

A tariff of, say P_1P_2 is now imposed on imports of shoes, adding a tax to the price at which the foreign good is offered in the domestic market. Under the assumption of constant costs abroad, the foreign price remains unchanged, but the price in the domestic market now rises by the amount of the tariff to OP_2. Note, however, that if some or all of the tariff is redundant the domestic price will not rise by the full amount of the tariff. For example, a tariff of P_1P_4 would raise the domestic price only to OP_3, the domestic no-trade price.

Domestic Supply Effects

Import Substitution Effect   Domestic producers, now facing the higher price OP_2, are able to cover the rising marginal costs of additional output and expand production to OQ_3. This replacement of foreign production with domestic is called import substitution. The higher per unit costs arising from the expansion of domestic production are reflected in two effects: the protective effect and the transfer effect.

Protective Effect   As the term *protection* suggests, inefficient production is permitted by virtue of the higher price domestic producers are able to obtain. For each additional unit of output it is necessary to pay for the increasing inefficiency of production. The sum of the additional costs due to inefficiency in production of the additional quantity of shoes Q_1Q_3 is the triangular area *p*, and is called the protective effect.

Transfer Effect   The higher price is paid to producers on each unit of their entire output, while the protective effect applies only to that part of increased receipts necessary to pay for the increasingly inefficient production. The transfer effect, measured by the area *t*, is a surplus over costs. This is a transfer of income from consumers of shoes in the form of an economic rent accruing to the producers.

The Revenue Effect

On each unit imported the government collects a duty of P_1P_2. The sum of these duty collections over the quantity of imports Q_3Q_4 is the rectangular area *r:* the tariff times the quantity of imports. This is the revenue effect.

The Consumption Effect

The higher price the consumers face results in a reduction in the quantity consumed and, depending on whether demand is inelastic or elastic, the outlay on consumption of shoes is larger or smaller. The important question is: What has happened to the net satisfaction from consumption of shoes? Net consumer satisfaction is measured by the difference between total satisfaction and the cost of obtaining that satisfaction. Total consumer satisfaction is measured by the area to the left of the equilibrium quantity demanded and below the demand curve. The cost of obtaining this satisfaction, on the other hand, is the value of the outlay: price times quantity demanded. The net consumers' satisfaction or "surplus," then, is the triangular area bounded by the equilibrium price, the demand curve, and the vertical axis.

The imposition of a tariff creates a net loss of consumers' satisfaction amounting to the area P_1P_2mn in Figure 10.1. This loss is far from imaginary, even though it may not be realized by consumers who are unaware of the existence of particular tariffs. It is the difference between the enjoyment consumers would get from having a greater quantity of shoes at a lower price and the enjoyment actually obtained from the smaller quantity at the higher prices.

The Net Loss to the Community

Partially offsetting the loss to consumers is the revenue received by the government (r) and the surplus transferred to producers (t). The net loss to the community as a whole is measured by the two triangular areas, p (less efficient use of resources) and c (loss to consumers not offset or otherwise accounted for).

The fact that these triangular areas are so small relative to the total impact of the tariff on consumers' satisfaction suggests that perhaps the net effect on the community's welfare is of minor importance. A number of empirical studies of the effects of tariffs and related trade restrictions seem to bear out this conclusion. Applied to imports of several commodities in a number of countries, the estimates of the net effect of protection are all low, close to or less than 1 percent of GNP.[1] The effect of any particular import duty, however, is not spread over the entire population, as measures expressed in terms of GNP suggest, but are concentrated on the consumers of a specific good. Their loss depends on the height of the duty and the elasticity of demand for the good, and can be substantial.

[1] These studies are cited in C. P. Kindleberger and P. H. Lindert, *International Economics* (Homewood, Ill.: Richard D. Irwin, Inc., 1978), p. 120, accompanied by an extensive discussion of a number of reasons for suspecting that the estimates are biased.

The question at issue then is: How real are the offsets to the reduction in consumers' satisfaction? As far as the transfer effect (the area *t* in Figure 10.1) is concerned, this does not represent a net gain in income to protected producers over what they would have enjoyed in the absence of the tariff. In the long run, there is no reason to expect that the labor and capital employed in the protected industry would not have found equally satisfactory employment in other sectors of the economy, given only reasonable mobility. It is only in the short run that the transfer of income effected by protection can be said to support income at an elevated level.

Although it is true that the revenue received by the government (the area *r*) is an offset to the loss by consumers, it is important to realize that this revenue involves a cost: the considerable resources required to maintain the customs service. Moreover, in all countries to some extent and in many underdeveloped countries to a major extent, smuggling reduces the revenue of the customs authorities. Although consumers will pay less for smuggled goods than for those that pay the duty, they will still pay more than they would if trade were free.

Tariffs for Protection or Revenue?

Duties on imports are sometimes imposed with a view to raising revenue and at others to give protection to domestic producers. Is it possible to have one effect without the other? A tariff designed to provide revenue only but not protection could in one sense be a duty on imports of a commodity not produced domestically. But even such a tariff has some protective effect by diverting demand to other commodities. A tariff providing protection alone with no revenue must be high enough to exclude all imports; otherwise it is bound to have some revenue effect. In either case the loss of consumer satisfaction occurs. Thus, despite the declared intent of legislators, there is no clear criterion for distinguishing between duties for revenue and duties for protection.

In the foregoing discussion we assumed that our country was too small to affect the foreign price of imports by any change in their volume. We also assumed that no tariffs were imposed on material inputs used in the production of shoes. We now consider some of the consequences of relaxing these two assumptions.

A Large Country

With a country large enough for a reduction in its imports of a commodity to affect its price abroad, the imposition of a tariff will typically cause the foreign price to decline. To the new, lower, price of imports

Figure 10.2   Price Effect of a Tariff with Imports Produced at Increasing Costs

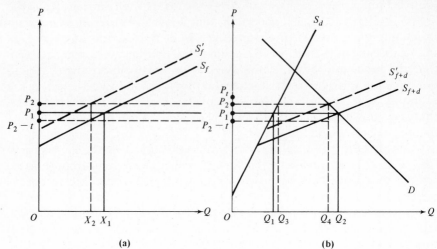

(a)   (b)

the duty is added. The price in the protected market is higher than the foreign price by the amount of the duty, but is not higher than the *pretariff* foreign price by this amount, since the foreign price has fallen.

This may be seen by reference to Figure 10.2(a), which contains the foreign supply curve S_f, part (b) contains the domestic supply (S_d) and demand (D) curves. The total supply of this commodity, shoes, that is available to the domestic market is the horizontal sum of the foreign and domestic supply curves (S_{f+d}) shown in part (b). The equilibrium free trade price at which the sum of domestic and foreign supply equals demand is OP_1, and imports are Q_1Q_2 ($=OX_1$).

The imposition of a tariff means that a tax is added to each unit supplied from abroad, yielding the tariff-laden foreign supply curve S_f' in part (a). The sum of S_f' and S_d is now S_{f+d}'. At the new equilibrium price of OP_2, imports have fallen to Q_3Q_4 ($=OX_2$), and the price at which foreigners supply shoes to our market has fallen to $OP_2 - t$. Owing to this foreign cost reduction, which partially offsets the impact of the tariff, its effects on domestic production and consumption are lessened accordingly. They would, of course, be eliminated only if foreign unit cost were reduced by the full amount of the tariff.

The Tariff Structure: Tariffs on Material Inputs

Now suppose that in addition to a tariff on the finished goods, shoes, a tariff is also imposed on imports of a material input, say leather. Considered by itself, the tariff on shoes (with imports available at constant cost) raises their price by the amount of the duty (from OP_1 to OP_2 in

Figure 10.3). The tariff on the input of leather, however, will raise its price in the domestic market.

The higher price of leather increases the cost of producing shoes domestically, thus raising the domestic supply curve as illustrated in Figure 10.3 by the shift from S to, say, S'. The result is that the net expansion of production from OQ_1 to OQ_3' is less than with the tariff on shoes alone (from OQ_1 to OQ_3). The existence of a tariff on inputs will always cause the output of the final product to expand less than it would if there were a tariff on the latter alone, and it may even cause the output of the final product to contract. This will occur if the tariff on leather raises the costs of producing shoes more than the duty on shoes raises the price of shoes. The domestic supply curve would then shift to a position higher than S'', and the domestic production of shoes would declne vis-à-vis the free trade situation.

The relationship between the tariff on the final product and tariffs on material inputs can be expressed in terms of the *effective rate of protection* enjoyed by the producers who *process the final product*. Note that we distinguish between the finished article, the material inputs, and the processing the latter undergo, for if material inputs are available duty free, it is the processors alone who are protected by a duty on the final product. Thus if inputs comprise 50 percent of the free trade value of the finished article, if the rate of duty on the latter is 50 percent, and if inputs can be imported duty free, the *effective rate of protection* is 100 percent, as against a nominal rate of 50 percent. If, however, importable inputs are also subject to a duty of 50 percent, the

Figure 10.3   Introduction of a Tariff on an Input

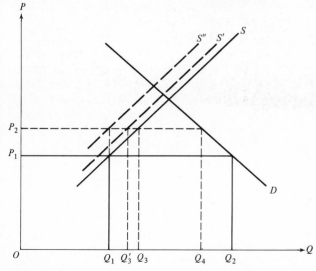

effective rate is also 50 percent, the same as the nominal rate. In general, if the inputs—as well as the final product—are dutiable, the effective rate of protection enjoyed by the processors will be higher the lower the tariff on inputs, and vice versa. The formula for calculating effective rates of protection is

$$t_e = \frac{t_n - t_i \cdot i}{v}$$

where t_e is the effective rate, t_n the nominal rate, t_i the rate on imported inputs, i the proportion the latter are of the value of the commodity, and v the proportion of value added in processing.

The possibility that effective may differ from nominal protection has interesting implications. An industry's net protection can be increased simply by reducing tariffs on the inputs it uses—an objective that is often more easily attained than an increase in its own tariff, for it has the appearance of promoting freer trade. Countries granting tariff concessions may on balance be increasing the protection of their domestic producers. Export industries, facing the world market, cannot generally derive any benefit from a protective tariff but are injured by tariffs levied on material inputs they use; that is, they are subject to *negative* net protection.

Effective protection is often considerably greater than nominal protection on finished goods. Thus, in 1962, the nominal tariff rate on textiles in the United States was 24.1 percent, the effective rate 50.6 percent. In the United Kingdom these rates were 20.7 and 42.2 percent, respectively; in Japan, 19.7 and 48.8 percent. On semifabricated goods, such as steel ingots and other primary steel forms, the nominal and effective rates in these countries were United States, 10.6 and 106.7 percent; United Kingdom, 11.1 and 98.9 percent; Japan, 13.0 and 58.9 percent. On a few products in some countries, notably printed matter and ships, low duties on these goods were more than offset by duties on their inputs, so the effective rates of protection were negative.[2]

ALTERNATIVE INSTRUMENTS OF PROTECTION

We have used a tariff to demonstrate the effects protection has on production and consumption in the domestic market. However, a tariff is not the only instrument that is used to achieve the same results, either

[2] Data from Bela Balassa, "Tariff Protection in Industrial Countries: An Evaluation," *Journal of Political Economy*, **73** (Dec. 1965), Table 1.

deliberately or incidentally. International cooperation under the General Agreement on Tariffs and Trade has restricted the upward movement on tariffs, and has had some limited success in reducing tariffs, particularly among the industrial nations. This has focused the attention of both protectionists and those concerned with reducing impediments to free trade on the question of nontariff barriers.

A nontariff barrier is simply some requirement or regulation that restricts imports. Consider, for example, a quota which limits the quantity of imports to some specified level that is less than the free trade quantity. In Figure 10.1, if, instead of a tariff raising the duty-paid price from OP_1 to OP_2, a quota limiting imports to Q_3Q_4 per period were imposed, the effect would be exactly the same as an import tariff of P_1P_2. At the free trade price of OP_1 an excess demand of Q_1Q_2 is present, and only Q_3Q_4 of imports is allowed, causing the domestic price to rise to OP_2, where the excess domestic demand equals the quantity of imports permitted by the quota.

Quotas represent only one type of an ingenious array of devices that restrict imports. Rather than limit the quantity of imports directly, for example, the same effect if often achieved by limiting the amount of foreign exchange made available for importation of a good. The commodity classification used in administration of an internal excise tax may be designed in such a way as to apply excise taxes to imports only. Customs procedures may impose a cost on the foreign seller that requires him to raise the price at which he offers the good. Similarly, labeling, health, safety, sanitary, and shipping regulations often increase the costs of selling into another market. And so the list goes on. Some barriers are designed for outright protectionist purposes; others are generally accepted as accomplishing other ends. All, however, can inhibit the flow of trade. Further, since the regulations and their administration are variable, there are uncertainties that add to the restrictiveness. In sum, the net effects of nontariff barriers on production and consumption are the same as if a tariff were imposed. And in most cases the government receives no revenue.

EFFECTS OF A TARIFF: GENERAL EQUILIBRIUM

The issue to which the partial equilibrium analysis of a tariff is addressed concerns the effects of a tariff on the market for a particular commodity that is one of many. Rather than concern with a single good, the issue at hand may be whether or not to protect the entire import-competing sector. For this, the effects of a tariff must be considered in terms of general equilibrium analysis. We shall resort to our familiar earlier model of a country producing both food and clothing, which represent the agricultural and manufacturing sectors of an economy, respectively. The fundamental point developed so far that a tariff has both production and consumption effects, remains unaffected, but a wider range of effects, including notably those on welfare, will be taken into account.

World Prices Unchanged

We begin by assuming that our country, which produces both food and clothing but has a comparative advantage in clothing production, is too small to affect world prices by imposing a tariff on food. Figure 10.4 shows our country's transformation curve FC and a series of community indifference curves U_0 to U_4. In isolation, production and consumption would be at E_0. The relative world price of food and clothing is given by the slope of P_e. With free trade, production would be at Q_0, consumption at E_4, with the gain from trade represented by the shift from the indifference curve U_0 at E_0 to U_4 at E_4. (This consists of the

Figure 10.4   Tariff in General Equilibrium: World Prices Unchanged

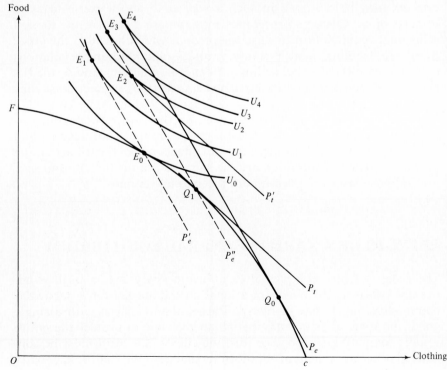

gain from exchange, due to the move first to E_1, and the further gain from specialization by the move to E_4. See page 77.)

Our country now imposes a tariff on imports of food, which raises the price in the domestic market so that the domestic relative price of food and clothing becomes the slope of P_t. This encourages the substitution in production of food for clothing, with the production point moving along the transformation curve from Q to Q'. Since world prices are unchanged, trade will continue to be conducted at those prices, and the trading point will have to be on the international price line P''_e. In consumers were to enjoy those prices, consumption would be at E_3. The fall from E_4 to E_3 measures the loss from reduced specialization due to the tariff. Although trade will be conducted at the international price ratio P''_e, consumers will have to pay the protected price for food, since this is the one ruling in the home market. Consumption will fall still further, to E_2, where the domestic price line P'_t is tangent to U_2. E_2 is the only point which satisfies both essential conditions: that the international exchange must take place on the in-

Figure 10.5   Tariff in General Equilibrium: World Prices Change

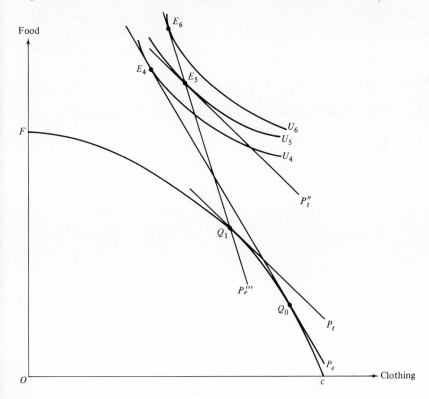

ternational price line P''_e, and that in the domestic market, after the imported goods have paid the duty, consumers must buy them at the protected price P'_t.

World Prices Changed

If we suppose that our country is sufficiently large, its purchases and sales will have an impact on world prices. To provide a basis for comparison, we start in Figure 10.5 with the free trade situation the same as in Figure 10.4. The international price line is P_e, production is at Q_0, and total consumption is at E_4 on indifference curve U_4. The country now imposes a tariff on food imports. This reduces its offer of exports for imports, and because of the country's importance in world trade, raises the relative price of clothing in world markets, as shown by the now steeper international price line P'''_e. Because the country is able to influence the world price, there is a *gain from decreased specialization*. Trade takes place at the new terms of trade P'''_e, but consumption would not be at the high level of E_6, since domestic consumers face the tariff-ridden relative price P_t. Consumption would recede to E_5, still on the international price line, but on the indifference curve U_5 tangent to P'_t. Some of the gain due to trading power is lost by the consumption effect of reduced exchange. Nonetheless, it is possible for the country to realize a *net gain* from the imposition of a tariff in these circumstances. We shall have more to say about this in the discussion of the terms of trade effects that follows.

[For Selected References, see the end of Chapter 11.]

11
CHAPTER

The Case for Protection

SERIOUS ARGUMENTS FOR PROTECTION

There are a number of arguments for protection that must be taken seriously, for in each case protection accomplishes its declared purpose. Some are valid economic arguments which demonstrate that protection in certain circumstances is a means of achieving a level of real income or welfare that is higher than it would be in the absence of protection. There are other, noneconomic arguments for protection that achieve noneconomic objectives deemed worthwhile in their own right. Often there are attempts to confuse the two. We shall consider each type in turn. It will become evident that a protective tariff is seldom the most efficient way of achieving the objective.

Improving the Terms of Trade

As earlier discussion has made clear, a country may be able through the imposition of a tariff to influence the rate at which it exchanges exports for imports. This can happen because, when a country introduces a tariff, its willingness to take imports is reduced. In effect it says to the rest of the world: For any given quantity of our exports, we shall require a larger quantity of imports, part of which (or the proceeds thereof) are to be surrendered to our customs authorities. Since what is involved here is changing international demands, the argument can be considerably clarified if we make use of the international demand or offer curves that were employed before.

Consider the case of the home country imposing a tariff on imports (or a tax on exports). This reduces its offer of exports for imports; the country's demand contracts. In diagrammatic terms, our offer curve would shift upward by an amount proportionate to the tariff. Thus, in Figure 11.1, the imposition by country I of a 50 percent duty on imports of B would be shown by moving each point on the original offer curve OI upward by half its distance from the horizontal axis. This means that for such a point on OI as R, which represents a willingness to offer Oc_1 of clothing in exchange for Of_2 of food, our country now requires the larger quantity of imports Of_1, instead. Of this, one-third, or f_1f_2 would be turned over to the customs authorities in payment of the import duty. Treating all points on OI similarly would yield a new tariff-ridden offer curve OI'.

Suppose that country II's offer curve is as represented by OII. The original position of trade equilibrium would be at T_0, with the terms of trade being shown by the slope of line P_e. After the imposition of I's tariff on imports of F, the new position of equilibrium would be at T_1. The terms of trade for country I would have improved, as indicated by the fact that the slope of P'_e is steeper than that of P_e. Country I is now giving up a substantially reduced amount of C, but receiving only a moderately reduced amount of F.

For a country to be able to improve its terms of trade—the rel-

Figure 11.1 Tariff and Offer Curves

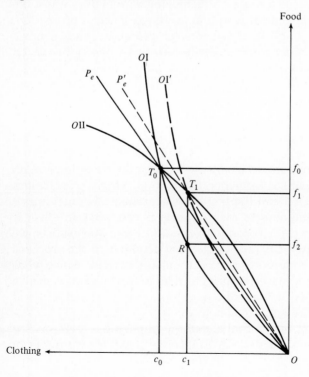

Figure 11.2 Tariff with Foreign Offer Curve Infinitely Elastic

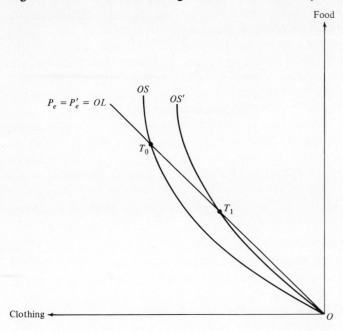

ative price of its exports—it must have some degree of bargaining power. It cannot be in the position of a small nation confronting the rest of the world or even an economically strong trading partner. The small country would have no power to affect prices. Such a country confronts prices that are fixed, unresponsive to any tariff it may impose. Such a situation could be represented as in Figure 11.2, where OS is the offer curve of the small country, while the unyielding, infinitely elastic offer curve of its large trading partner is the straight line OL.[1] If our small country should impose a tariff, raising its offer curve to OS', the terms of trade remain unchanged at P_e.

The situation specified in Figure 11.1, where by imposing a tariff on imports, country II was able to improve its terms of trade, represents a form of *monopsony*, or buyer's domination in the market. By exercising this power, country I is able to force II to give ground as it moves back along its offer curve, accepting less advantageous terms of trade. A necessary condition for this to occur is that II's offer curve, although relatively elastic, shall be less than infinitely so. Price concessions are

---

[1] An offer curve that is a straight line signifies, as stated in the text, a rigid price—an unwillingness to trade except at a given relative price. Such an offer curve is perfectly elastic in the sense that at such a fixed relative price, the country is willing to exchange unlimited quantities of exports and imports.

necessary to entice that country to increase its volume of trade, which in reverse means that under pressure it will accept worse terms of trade, but only at a somewhat reduced volume.

Carry this procedure one step further. When a country's offer curve is less elastic than unity, so that total export outlay declines as the terms of trade improve, then if the country is subjected to economic pressure, the reverse will be true: It will not only accept worse terms of trade, but will also *increase in absolute amount* the exports it gives up. An outcome such as this is illustrated in Figure 11.3, which shows country II confronting an offer curve for country II that is highly inelastic between T_0 and T_1. Imposition of a tariff yields a great improvement in the terms of trade, as shown by the greater steepness of the terms of trade line P'_e. Moreover, this is evident in that the exports country II gives up fall very substantially, while the imports it obtains in exchange actually increase.

The Optimum Tariff   We have now seen how a country can improve its terms of trade by imposing a tariff on imports from a country vis-à-vis which it possesses the advantage of strong bargaining power or

Figure 11.3   Tariff with Foreign Offer Curve Inelastic

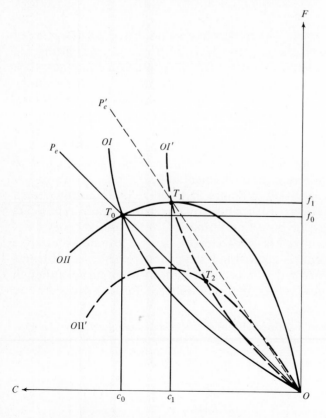

monopsony. We have also seen that, compared with the free trade situation, the improved terms of trade due to the tariff can make the country better off: *can* but not necessarily *will*. Thus we know that if the tariff were so high as to completely stifle trade the country would be back at the autarky position and be worse off than under free trade. Somewhere, then, between free trade and a completely prohibitive tariff there is a point at which there is an *optimum* tariff, where the marginal gain from improved terms of trade just offsets the marginal loss from decreased specialization and exchange.

To see fully the way in which the optimal tariff is arrived at, it is helpful to introduce an additional tool: the trade indifference curve. Such a curve expresses various combinations of a country's exports and imports, each of which enables the community to maintain a constant level of consumer satisfaction. It is thus closely related to a community indifference curve, which registers the community's total satisfaction from consumption, whether provided by domestic production or by foreign trade. Thus a trade indifference curve expresses that part of total satisfaction provided by complementary combinations of imports and exports. We draw a sample of such curves TU_1, TU_2, and TU_3 in Figure 11.4, together with the offer curve OI.

Figure 11.4   Trade Indifference Curves

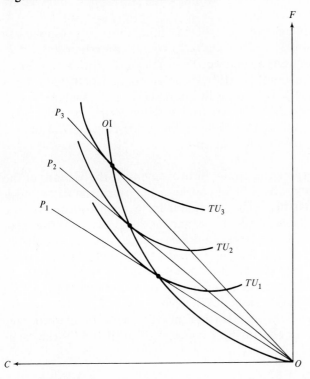

An offer curve is the locus or path of a country's trading points; it represents all combinations of exports and imports satisfactory to it under a given set of conditions. Each such trading point must also be a point of intersection with a trade indifference curve, given the meaning of the latter. Three such points are given by the price lines P_1, P_2, and P_3, with the trade indifference curves tangent to these price lines where they intersect the offer curve OI. Accompanying this equilibrium in the international trade sector is equilibrium in the domestic sector. This domestic equilibrium part of the total picture can be shown diagrammatically, as you will recall from Chapter 4, by the simultaneous tangency of an international price line to the production possibilities curve and to the maximum attainable community indifference curve.

The usefulness of the trade indifference curves is that they focus both on the level of national welfare and on the extent of trade, as does the optimum tariff. Consider the situation depicted in Figure 11.5. The free trade international price line P_e is tangent to TU_0 at point T_0, with exports at Oc_0 exchanging for imports of Of_0. Given the meaning of the trade indifference curve, consumers in country I would find point T_1 just as acceptable as point T_0, although the volume of trade is smaller, but the ratio of imports to exports somewhat higher. This move from T_0 to T_1 could be brought about if country I imposed a tariff sufficient to shift its offer curve to OI'''. This would leave it with national welfare the same as under free trade.

Country I, however, can do better than that. By imposing a small tariff which shifts its offer curve to OI', it can reach a point T_2 on a higher trade indifference curve: TU_1. It can do still better, however. By imposing a tariff to shift its offer curve to OI'', country I reaches its highest possible trade indifference curve consistent with country II's offer curve OII. This is the *optimum tariff*. It is the tariff that moves the country to the trade indifference curve (TU_2) that is tangent to the other country's offer curve.

Retaliation   Corresponding to the improvement in the welfare of the tariff-imposing country there is, of course, a deterioration in the position of its trading partner. The argument for a tariff to improve the terms of trade is thus essentially a "beggar-my-neighbor" one that proposes national gain at the expense of others. Such a policy is unlikely to escape retaliatory action by the injured partner or partners. Thus country II, starting from the tariff-ridden position T_3, would find it to its interest to counter by also levying a duty on imports of C. This would move its offer curve, say to OII', perhaps with T_4 as the equilibrium point. This would induce a further increase in the tariff in country I, followed by a rise in the tariff of country II, until finally the tariff war came to an end.

Figure 11.5   Optimum Tariff

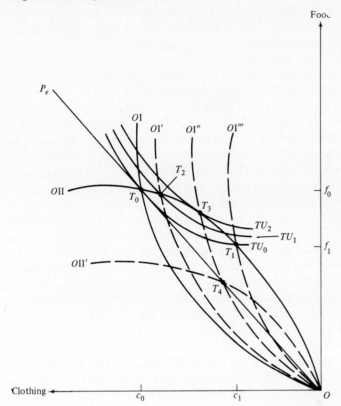

If this is the outcome of country I's initial tariff action, the presumed gain in terms of trade probably goes down the drain. At T_4, for example, both the home and partner countries end up exchanging a smaller quantity of goods at approximately the original terms of trade—clearly an inferior position. Nothing remains but the reduction of consumers' satisfaction and a worsened allocation of resources.

A Tariff for Bargaining

The tariff-laden world is usually one where, in terms of Figure 11.5, both countries have imposed tariffs and both have ended up in a situation inferior to free trade.[2] In such a situation the problem for both

---

[2] It is, however, possible for both countries to have tariffs and one to be better off than under free trade. Thus, in Figure 11.5, if the final equilibrium involved a point on a trade indifference curve above TU_0, country I would clearly be better off than with free trade.

countries is how to move from protection toward free trade. The solution that has been adopted involves a swapping of duty reductions. For example, this was embodied in the U.S. trade agreements program in the 1960s and the subsequent GATT negotiations under the label "Kennedy Round" (see Chapter 13).

Such a course is not open to a free trade country. In Figure 11.5, if the initial situation involved equilibrium at point T_3, it is argued that country II would have to have a tariff as a weapon to use to persuade country I to lower its duty on II's exports. There is some merit to this argument, particularly when a country has some monopsony power in trade, and in view of the institutional bargaining arrangements under the General Agreement on Tariffs, and Trade (GATT). Yet it ignores the reality of the international bargaining in which a country uses non-tariff concessions such as reductions in import quotas or increases in foreign exchange allocations to obtain tariff concessions from its trading partners. Furthermore, the bargaining mentality often focuses attention on the wrong issue: to get as much as possible while giving up as little as possible, rather than on the elimination of the loss to the international community from tariffs.

The argument, sometimes met, that a country with no monopsony power in trade should maintain a tariff for bargaining purposes has no merit. This is simply the small-country case: The country faces a trading partner with a take-it-or-leave-it, fixed-price offer curve, and with a tariff on imports besides. The small country has no power to influence its trading partner to lower its tariff by threatening to raise its own simply because it is small (see Figure 11.2).

Infant Industry

The case for the protection of infant industries rests on the assumption that the country has a latent comparative advantage in the industry or group of industries to be protected. Temporary protection, it is argued, is justified to bring out the comparative advantage that would be stifled in infancy if shelter from established foreign producers were not provided. The case is definitely circumscribed. Protection is only warranted if the industry in question is clearly suited to the country's market prospects, so that it can reasonably be expected one day to stand on its own feet. Moreover, the grant of protection should be for a limited period: until the industry reaches maturity.

Stated in this way the argument conforms to the economic objective of increasing real income via international specialization. Its proponents believe that this result may not be achieved without intervention. Basically, the intervention is justified because one of the assumptions on which the case for free trade rests—perfect competition—is not realized in practice. Imperfections in competition, in the form of unequal access to internal and external economies, make temporary protection necessary to equalize competitive conditions. The careful analyst, however, must carry the economic argument a few steps further.

The argument for infant-industry protection is based on the presence of unrealized internal and external economies. The *internal economies of scale argument* starts by noting that a new producer would have to start on a small and uneconomic scale, unable to meet the low costs of his foreign competitors. But with the shelter of protection he could expand gradually until, having attained optimum size, he could confront the established producers on an even footing.

The internal economies argument is thus essentially a question of comparing the losses that would be incurred in the early stages with the future net benefits. But this is what all firms do, regardless of whether they produce an import-competing good or a nontraded good. If the net return exceeds the rate obtainable on alternative investments, the firm would borrow the funds necessary to cover its early losses. If the net return is less, the investment would of course not be undertaken. Why, then, is protection considered necessary? At this point the infant-industry case has to fall back on the argument that capital markets are imperfect or insufficiently developed to permit the potentially competitive producer to borrow funds. Note, however, that the argument thus ceases to be a case for protection of infant industries. Instead, it becomes a case for improvements in the capital market.

The *external economies argument* for infant-industry protection points out that, although the private rate of return may not justify investment by a particular firm, the social rate of return may. The reason for this is that expansion of the protected industry may lower costs for all firms by creating a trained labor force or by acquiring and spreading knowledge of production techniques. The costs of these activities are borne by individual firms, but the benefits accrue to all firms in the industry; hence the argument for temporary protection until economies external to the firm develop.

But again note how the nature of the argument has changed. In this case the argument is essentially one for improvements in social investments rather than for protection per se. Social investment in labor-force training and making productive knowledge available would make it profitable for firms in the industry to expand output without incurring costs that yield no benefits to themselves alone.

When the infant-industry argument for protection is applied to several industries at once, the possibility of additional external economies develops—in this case economies that are external to the industry. Roads are improved, railways are constructed, power plants erected, and technical and engineering training are provided. These are facilities needed by all industries but that cannot be economically justified for one industry alone. But still the argument is for social overhead investment, not protection per se.

Despite the fact that the infant-industry argument cannot be considered as specifically requiring protection rather than some other intervention in the market, protection is often regarded as equivalent to other devices in attaining the desired objective via the production effect of a tariff. But here too a word of caution is in order, for a tariff also yields consumption effects that reduce consumer satisfaction. In other words, against the net benefits derived from infant-industry protection we must charge the consumption cost of a tariff. Hence a protective tariff involves a cost not incurred when other methods such as production subsidies are used, as is demonstrated in the next section.

In summary, the infant-industry argument boils down to a case for the removal of obstacles to the growth of the infants. It does not demonstrate that a tariff is the most efficient means of attaining the objective.

Distortions in the Domestic Market

The infant-industry argument is based on the presence of distortions that are assumed to disappear with the eventual success of the policy. A similar type of argument cites distortions in the domestic economy that prevent the attainment of the gains obtained in a competitive free trade equilibrium. This argument pushes past the case for temporary infant-industry protection, proposing permanent protection to overcome domestic distortions such as externalities in consumption or production, monopolistic or monopsonistic pricing, or disequilibrium in factor markets. An extensive literature has developed, showing how a tariff is one method of eliminating the domestic distortion.

To leave the argument at this point, however, concedes too much to the protectionist. Without cataloguing the numerous types of distortions, a simple example illustrates the fundamental point: Correction of domestic distortion is better served by the use of taxes or subsidies in the domestic market, for these can offset the effects of the distortion without incurring the consumption effects of protection. Suppose that owing to, say, external economies in production there is a divergence between the private costs of producing a particular commodity, illustrated by the supply curve S_pS_p in Figure 11.6, and the real or social costs of production shown by the supply curve S_sS_s. At the free trade price of OP_1, domestic production is OQ_1, as in the normal analysis. Yet if domestic production reflected real costs, output would be OQ_3. To counteract the distortion, an equivalent tariff (P_1P_2) could be intro-

Figure 11.6   Offsetting a Domestic Distortion: A Subsidy Versus a Tariff

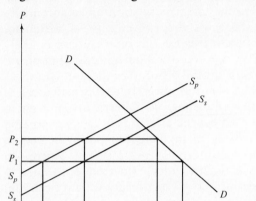

duced. Private producers would expand output to OQ_3, and the effect of the divergence between private and social costs would be nullified.

Note, however that intervention in foreign trade has introduced two effects—on production *and* on consumption. Yet only the production effect is required to counteract the domestic distortion, and this can be obtained by a subsidy on production equal to the distortion, avoiding the consumption effect. Hence, if a tariff is used, against the increase in welfare from elimination of the production distortion must be charged the reduction in welfare from the distortion of consumer choice. Welfare is thus not maximized and may even be reduced when a tariff is used to overcome a domestic distorion.

Employment

During periods of severe unemployment, as in the 1930s, much use has been made of the argument that protection can furnish an effective remedy. This argument also rests on the absence of fully competitive conditions, for the economy is producing at some point within the transformation function. By reducing imports, a tariff stimulates employment directly in the import-competing industries; from this focus, the employment-creating effect spreads to other industries in everwidening though diminishing waves. Investment in facilities for producing substitutes for imports may also result, setting in motion a second force to increase employment.

Taken by itself, the argument is valid. Whether it is the best means of dealing with the problem, however, is questionable. First, it may not be very effective. If one country reduces its imports by a newly imposed tariff, the exports of its trading partners are thereby reduced in like amount. A decline in employment is set in motion abroad; as employment and incomes fall there, less is spent on imports, which are our country's exports. Even though this foreign repercussion is likely to be of smaller magnitude than our country's initial reduction of imports, it may well constitute a substantial offset. Second, our country's exports are almost certain to be reduced, directly and drastically, by retaliation on the part of other countries. A country attempting to increase employment at home by means of a tariff is in effect exporting its unemployment. This sort of beggar-my-neighbor policy is sure to arouse resentment and prompt countermeasures abroad. Third, the stimulation of employment by a tariff involves a permanent reallocation of resources for what is essentially a short-term cyclical problem, for once a tariff is introduced it is seldom easily removed. Finally, recall that a tariff acts not only on the production side, but also reduces consumer satisfaction. The remedy is a costly one.

An alternative is to use monetary and fiscal policy or possibly devaluation of the currency to relieve unemployment. If successful, the accompanying rise in income will bring with it an increase in imports, which may lead to a deficit in the balance of payments and a loss of international reserves. A good deal depends upon whether the unemployment is purely local or is part of a worldwide phenomenon. If the former, and income and employment are merely restored to a preexisting level, there need be no ensuing balance-of-payments difficulties. If the latter, and other countries also adopt expansionary monetary and fiscal policies, incomes and imports of the several countries will rise together and no country need lose reserves. If other countries do not expand and our country has to go it alone, it would still not necessarily mean that a tariff is the solution. The problem is to *restrict the rise in imports* due to the expanding domestic income, *not to decrease imports*, which a tariff would do. It would therefore be preferable to combine an internal policy of expansion with direct quantitative ceilings on imports. For then imports may remain constant, with any tendency to increase with rising incomes being held in check by quotas. A tariff, on the other hand, depresses imports immediately after it is imposed and makes economic conditions worse abroad. Moreover, there is a better chance that direct restrictions can later be removed, especially if they are adopted for the specific purpose of safeguarding the balance of payments. Tariffs, once imposed, are very difficult to dislodge.

Antidumping

The tariffs of many nations contain special provisions against *dumping*, a practice that arouses the indignation, real or feigned, of producers in the market where dumping occurs. What is dumping? Contrary to a widespread impression, dumping is *not* selling abroad below costs of production. It means instead *sales in a foreign market at a price below that received in the home market,* after allowing for transportation charges, duties, and all other costs of transfer. Discrimination between the home and foreign price is the essential mark of dumping. Thus sales abroad below cost of production would not constitute dumping *unless* the foreign were lower than the domestic price.

The problem is complicated by the existence of different kinds of dumping. It may be *persistent* and continue indefinitely because the exporter is in a position to practice discriminating monopoly. When selling in two separate markets, if the elasticity of demand is greater in the foreign than in the (monopolized) home market, he will gain by selling at a lower price abroad. Such dumping may continue indefinitely. On the other hand, dumping may be *predatory*, with price cutting undertaken for the purpose of destroying foreign competition.

From the point of view of the country in which the dumping occurs, it is clear that predatory dumping can be most disturbing, even ruinous, to local firms. The gains of consumers are at best purely transitory, while the effects on business can be lasting. Persistent dumping, on the other hand, is no different in its effects from sales by a low-cost foreign producer. Year in and year out buyers get their supplies at low cost; competing producers, if there are any, can adjust to a stable situation.

To prohibit such dumping would permit domestic producers to charge the foreign monopoly price.

Antidumping duties generally make no distinction between persistent and predatory dumping. Nowadays some of the more flagrant abuses of such duties are curbed under an agreement reached by the members of GATT in 1967. Since sales below the home market price may cause no injury to domestic producers, antidumping duties are permitted only when it can be shown that such injury is involved. This test, however, still permits antidumping duties to be used against a new entrant attempting to engage in persistent dumping.

National Defense

Consider now some arguments for protection based on objectives other than increased real income. The first of these rests on the appeal to national defense. If the products of a particular industry are essential to military strength, it is argued, then if that industry cannot survive without protection it should by all means be maintained by protective duties. The desirability or necessity of providing for the national defense involves ends such as security, power, or even the survival of the nation that lie outside the scope of economics. Yet the cost of this protection does not.

If "essential industries" are defined very narrowly, to include only those engaged in producing technical military goods, such as optical instruments, radar equipment, explosives, and airplanes, we should remember that there are less expensive ways than protection to ensure their survival. The industries in question may be carried on by the government as part of a national defense program, or they may be supported by bounties from the public treasury. The former alternative means that they would be included with other ordnance works that supply the needs of the government. The requirements of the public for optical instruments and the like would continue to be met by imports or by such domestic private enterprise as might exist without protection. Alternatively, bounties might be held down to a level only just adequate to provide for military needs, or expanded to support industries supplying the entire population.

In either case, the national defense argument is essentially a case for a subsidy to obtain the production effects of a tariff, and not for a tariff, which also involves the loss of consumer satisfaction. Furthermore, a subsidy is superior to protection on the grounds of justice, since the benefit of possessing an industry essential to the national defense accrues to the entire population, and it should therefore be paid out of general taxation rather than supported by the consumers, as it would be under a protective policy.

Notice also that, in an economy with a high degree of interdependence between industries, practically any industry necessary for the operation of the economy is essential to national defense. There is scarcely an industry that in some way does not, at least indirectly, produce a commodity that ultimately is required to maintain production in "essential" industries. Hence the argument implies that military security can be guaranteed only by establishing nearly complete self-sufficiency. But this requires protection, protection means inefficiency, and inefficiency is certainly no aid to defense!

International Shocks

The recurrent shocks of international economic disturbances, such as depressions, major industrial changes, crop failures, and wars, are disruptive to domestic economies. It is therefore argued that a nation should reduce its vulnerability to such shocks by instituting protection. Again the issue is fundamentally one of trading off the benefit of reducing shocks against the cost of reduced average real income due to reduced trade. It is important to make explicit that, although national income may be more variable with foreign trade than with self-sufficiency, the mere fact of variability does not imply lower average income. In fact, to show that earnings are lower with trade would merely demonstrate that national specialization is in the wrong goods. Independence sufficient to give effective insulation against international shock would require a substantial reduction of the foreign sector. This means a costly denial of the benefits of international trade.

Given the goal of minimizing shocks from abroad, what is the best way of attaining it? Self-sufficiency via protection is the most effective means of reducing national dependence on imports. The use of tariffs, quotas, or other non-tariff barriers allows the production and consumption effects to act together to restrict imports. Hence, in contrast with most other arguments, this one leads to a recommendation for protection, not subsidies.

Industrialization, Diversification, and Balance

Another objective often desired for its own sake is an industrialized economy that is more "diversified" or "balanced" between primary production and manufacturing. Although often expressed as an argument to achieve increased real income, the case for industrialization must rest on its own desirability. To show that industrialized nations have higher incomes than nonindustrialized nations does not prove that industrialization of a particular country would yield a higher income. On the contrary, it might well entail a misallocation of resources that would cause its real income to fall.

If a different structure of production is preferred for its own sake, this amounts to asserting the primacy of that goal. Protection is one way of achieving it. Here again, however, the argument essentially supports subsidization and not protection. The former achieves the desired production effects without introducing the consumption effects of the latter. Once again, protection is not necessarily the most efficient means of attaining the given objective.

SPECIAL-INTEREST ARGUMENTS FOR PROTECTION

All the protectionist arguments so far considered are relatively sophisticated. So far as any is valid, it is so only under certain well-defined and narrowly circumscribed conditions. Moreover, to deal with the situations toward which most of them are directed, clearly superior alternatives are at hand. Being sophisticated, few are popular. The most popular arguments, except perhaps that for employment, remain to be considered. It is a striking fact that the arguments for protection that carry the greatest political weight refer not to increasing real income, but to redistributing existing income among different groups in society.

The case for protection one commonly encounters is loaded not with arguments about increased real income in the aggregate, but with appeals to the interests of particular groups. This is especially true when a retention or increase of existing duties is at stake, rather than the introduction of new ones. An inefficient industry threatened with more intense foreign competition, either from the removal of duties or the worsening of its competitive position, is bound to suffer. But to translate the individual case into the national interest can only imply that to employ the inefficiently allocated resources in an alternative occupation would be less productive than to leave them where they are. And the argument sometimes gives the impression that the factors of production presently employed in inefficient industries could produce nothing at all if the threatened industries were forced to contract. On the contrary, we can expect a reallocation of factors from inefficient to efficient occupations, which will increase real income. Yet in an effort to avoid the adjustments, the spokesmen for threatened industries invoke the sympathies of their fellow citizens, appealing for support to their special, as opposed to national, interests. Bear these things in mind as you examine the arguments that follow.

Remember too that if the economy wishes to, adjustment assistance can be provided, distributing the burden of the adjustment among all industries, not just those that are affected by the change. Such one-shot assistance is generally cheaper for the economy as a whole than continuing to support inefficient industries by protection year after year. This approach was embodied in the U.S. Trade Expansion Act of 1962, whereby firms and workers that can show serious injury from concession-induced imports are eligible for adjustment assistance (see Chapter 13).

The Pauper Labor Argument

Everyone knows that wages in different countries vary tremendously. The average level in the United States, for example, is about twice as high as in Great Britain, approximately three times that of Italy, and perhaps fifteen times the average Indian wage. With only these facts to go on, it is natural to conclude that the products of "pauper labor" can undersell those of high-wage labor. The tariff is extolled as "protecting the American standard of living" or "sheltering the American worker from the competition of pauper labor."

In contending that a high-wage country cannot compete with a low-wage country, this view is patent nonsense. It is possible to advance it seriously only if one is completely ignorant of both the principles and the facts of international trade. As for the facts, every day, year in and year out, the products of high-wage American labor are sold abroad in competition with goods made by low-paid workers. High wages are clearly no bar to low-cost production, at least in many important lines.

These facts, and the fallacy in the pauper-labor argument, can only be explained by an appeal to the principles underlying international trade. There are two reasons why high-wage labor can without difficulty compete with low-wage labor. One is that labor is not the only factor of production. It is always combined with capital and natural resources. But the proportions in which the different factors are combined vary enormously from one product to another. And we know that the prices of the factors differ greatly among countries. Hence commodities embodying much capital can be produced at low cost in countries where capital is cheap; land-intensive products will be cheap in countries abundantly endowed with land, whereas labor-intensive commodities will be cheap where wages are low.

Low-wage countries, in other words, have an advantage over high-wage countries *only* with respect to commodities whose production requires the combination of much labor with relatively little capital or land, that is, where the wage bill is the preponderant element in costs. It is senseless for a high-wage country to try to compete in the production of such commodities, but it is equally senseless to contend, as the pauper-labor argument does, that a high-wage country is at a disadvantage in *all* lines of production.

There is, however, an additional element of fallacy to deal with. Even if labor *were* the only factor, a high-wage country could still meet the competition of a low-wage country wherever its relative productivity was higher than its relative wages. To take a simple case, suppose that wages in I are three times as high as in II, but that in the manufacture of shoes its labor is three times as efficient as II's. It could then produce shoes at the same cost. If its ratio of efficiency were higher than its ratio of wages, say 4 or 5 to 1, its costs would be lower than II's.

The causes of such superior efficiency could be better management, better-fed or better-educated labor, access to a more advanced technology, or any other forces that affect the productivity of labor. These causes of efficiency would explain labor's higher average wages in I. Wherever they operated with particular force, I's labor efficiency would be relatively high and its costs relatively low. In industries in which I was less than three times as efficient as II, the latter country would have a cost advantage.

Taken together, differing factor combinations and conditions affecting labor efficiency go far toward explaining the ability of a high-wage country such as the United States to meet the competition of low-wage countries. It cannot compete, of course, where labor dominates the factor combination unless its labor is disproportionately productive. But the pauper-labor argument makes no such qualifications. It is a sweeping generalization and, as such, wrong.

A Qualification   In one respect, and one only, is there any merit in the pauper-labor argument that a tariff can support the level of wages in a country. The reason for this is highly sophisticated, and certainly was never comprehended by those who advanced the pauper-labor argument.[3] The qualification is not based on the alleged existence of a comparative disadvantage in all lines of production as in the pauper-labor argument, but arises from the effect of shifts in production brought about by protection.

The effect on factor prices of changing the composition of domestic production owing to the opening of trade was discussed in Chapter 5. Clearly, the same principle applies to the restriction of trade. The real price of the factor intensive in the expanding commodity increases, and the real price of the factor intensive in the contracting commodity decreases. Hence, if the labor-intensive commodity expands with protection, real wages in the country as a whole rise.

Such an effect occurs because, although *total* capital and *total* labor are unchanged, the *proportion* of capital to labor in *each* industry is increased. Hence, with no change in the country's total factor supplies, protection can effect a change in real wages.

Although valid and interesting, the argument is not a protectionist ploy, for it shows only that protection can result in a redistribution of real income in favor of labor. Further, it does not show that the welfare of the community is increased. On the contrary, unless there are terms of trade effects (which is another matter entirely), protection reduced national welfare. Rather than resort to protection to increase the real wage of labor, it is possible to redistribute income in favor of labor by internal means, if this is desired, at the same time garnering the benefits of free international trade.

Furthermore, the argument is purely static: It makes no allowance for such dynamic considerations as the possible effect of a decline in the return to capital on its rate of accumulation and thus on the total

---

[3] The argument presented here was developed in and is taken from the well-known article by W. F. Stolper and Paul A. Samuelson, "Protection and Real Wages," *Review of Economic Studies,* **9** (Nov. 1941); reprinted in American Economic Association, *Readings in the Theory of International Trade* (New York: McGraw-Hill Book Company, 1949).

supply of capital and its proportion to labor in the long run. A relatively high return to capital in the short run might, through its effects on capital accumulation, provide higher wages in the long run. Moreover, labor could also benefit from the stimulus to the introduction of technological innovations provided by a higher level of saving and investment.

Keeping Money at Home

One of the crudest protectionist fallacies is well expressed in the form of a remark falsely attributed to Abraham Lincoln: "I do not know much about the tariff, but I know this much, when we buy manufactured goods abroad we get the goods and the foreigner gets the money. When we buy the manufactured goods at home we get both the goods and the money."

Except for its occasional currency, this argument scarcely deserves consideration. The classically appropriate comment has been made by Beveridge: "It has no merits; the only sensible words in it are the first eight words."[4] The view represents, of course, the crassest form of mercantilism, with its emphasis upon money as a form of wealth. It is only necessary to point out that in international trade goods pay for goods, and that international money moves only to perform the function of adjusting disturbances to trade. Although the U.S. dollar is widely used as a vehicle currency, to carry out international transactions, this does not mean that it is spent in other countries.

Equalizing Costs of Production

Proponents of protection often contend that a truly "scientific" tariff is one which equalizes costs of production at home and abroad. This principle of cost equalization is not, properly speaking, an argument for protection; it is rather a way of dressing up the case to make it more palatable.

> The doctrine has an engaging appearance of fairness. It seems to say, no favors, no undue rates. Offset the higher expenses of the American producer, put him in a position to meet the foreign competitor without being under a disadvantage, and then let the best man win. Conditions being thus equalized, the competition will become a fair one. Protected producers will get only the profit to which they are reasonably entitled and the domestic consumers are secured against prices which are unreasonable.[5]

---

[4] Sir William Beveridge, *Tariffs: The Case Examined* (New York: Longmans, Green & Co., 1931), p. 27, where the preceding quotation is also cited.

[5] In the course of criticizing the argument, F. W. Taussig, *Free Trade, the Tariff, and Reciprocity* (New York: Macmillan Publishing Company, 1920), p. 134.

The doctrine's apparent fairness is only skin deep. To appreciate this, one needs only to realize that a tariff is essentially discriminatory. It picks out for special advantage at the cost of the public precisely the least efficient of a country's industries. By keeping out imports, this protection reduces foreign markets for the country's most efficient (export) industries, and so injures them. Legislation that discriminates in favor of inefficient producers, against efficient ones, and against the general body of consumers can hardly be given high marks for common sense, let alone for fairness.

If there were such a thing as a "scientific" tariff, it should provide an unambiguous set of criteria for determining what commodities to protect and how far protection should be extended in each case. Apply this test to the principle of equalizing costs of production. Should any producers who want to establish an uneconomic industry, or who have already established such an industry, be granted sufficient protection to meet foreign competition even if this requires a duty of 100 percent— or 1000 percent? If not, where shall the line be drawn? Shall cost equalization apply only to the most efficient 10 percent of firms in the industry, to 90 percent, or to all, including the least efficient? Where shall we draw the line? Where *can* the line be drawn except between those who have the political power to exact discriminatory treatment and those who do not?

Upon closer inspection, therefore, this "scientific" principle of tariff making turns out to be a completely unscientific and irrational appeal to national prejudice against the foreigner. Its disarming character, and its lack of any criteria for limiting protection, are its most dangerous features.

SELECTED REFERENCES

BALDWIN, ROBERT E. "The New Welfare Economics and Gains in International Trade." In American Economic Association, *Readings in International Economics.* Homewood, Ill.: Richard D. Irwin, Inc., 1968. A sophisticated discussion of gains under free trade and with tariffs.

BEVERIDGE, SIR WILLIAM. *Tariffs: The Case Examined by a Committee of Economists,* 2nd ed. New York: Longmans, Green & Co., 1932. Still one of the best discussions of the tariff in all its aspects.

YEAGER, L. C., and DAVID G. TUERCK. *Trade Policy and the Price System.* Scranton, Pa.: International Textbook Company, 1966. A very good discussion of many aspects of tariff policy.

12
CHAPTER

Economic Integration

The analysis of this part has reinforced the case initially presented by Ricardo and Mill (Chapter 3) that liberalization of trade has much to commend it. Indeed, in today's industrial economies few would argue for a return to the narrow protectionism of the mercantilist era, or even of the 1930s. Nevertheless, a significant issue remains: whether to liberalize world trade through a general lowering of obstacles thereto, or to link a limited number of countries into regional blocs with similar ends in view. Either policy, it is contended, would yield similar results—a greater volume of trade, a better allocation of the world's resources, and higher standards of living. Either policy would link all or some countries more closely together into a more unified whole. Thus if economic integration means, as in the broadest sense it appears to mean, the unification of distinct economies into a single larger economy, both policies would lead to economic integration. One embodies a universal, the other a regional, approach.

As we shall see in Chapter 26, the movement of freer trade, so strong in the mid-nineteenth century, reemerged in the 1930s and still has many supporters. Its progress, however, is hampered by the difficulty of obtaining agreement among a very large number of countries, and of the weakness and inadequacy of international institutions to police and enforce agreements on trade. Partly because it is easier to obtain agreement among a small number of countries with common economic interests and political ties, the movement for attaining economic integration by the formation of regional blocs has achieved considerable momentum in recent years.

THE CUSTOMS UNION

Various devices for realizing economic integration have been tried or suggested. The least complex and exacting is the *free trade area*, which

205

abolishes tariffs among members but leaves the level of duties against non-members to be determined individually. The *customs union* proceeds further, adopting a uniform tariff against outsiders while eliminating all restrictions on trade among members. These provisions, and the abolition of restraints on the internal movement of capital and labor, characterize the *common market*, whereas *economic union* implies as well the adoption of uniform policies with respect to currency, credit, government expenditures and taxation, and other matters. These distinctions are no doubt too sharp. It can be and is argued that for even a customs union to be successful its policies in these areas must be harmonized, since with complete free trade any serious divergence would be disruptive. Our concern here, however, is primarily with the effects of etablishing regional free trade. To examine these, let us consider the consequences of the formation of a customs union. These may be either static or dynamic in character.

STATIC EFFECTS OF A CUSTOMS UNION

We limit ourselves here to whatever reallocation of resources may be caused by the abolition of barriers to trade among a group of countries. Total resources are assumed fixed, as in the manner of their employment—the technology used. This procedure is somewhat arbitrary, but it contributes to clarity.

Early discussions of customs unions tended to regard them as a step toward freer trade, since they established complete freedom to trade among a few countries, if not among all. This view is incomplete, however, as Viner was the first to show.[1] As far as its members are concerned, a customs union does introduce free trade, but since this action *is* limited to a few, it involves *intensified* discrimination against outsiders because it affords an opportunity for members to displace from their markets imports from those outsiders. This point can be clarified by attending to the direct effects on production of the formation of a customs union.

Production Effects

When members of a customs union dissolve their tariffs on intraunion trade, new sources of supply of many commodities are opened up within the union. Substitution of the new sources of supply for the old occurs. Two types of substitution may be distinguished.

[1] Jacob Viner, *The Customs Union Issue* (New York: Carnegie Endowment for International Peace, 1950).

1. The new supply from within the union may displace high-cost domestic production, hitherto supported by a member's tariff. Thus, if before union French producers of plate glass had been supplying their domestic market at relatively high cost, after union they would be displaced by the low-cost Belgian producers. Where international trade did not exist before, it has now been created. This *trade creation* results in an increase in the efficiency of world production; total world output is greater, since output within the customs union has increased, with no offsetting diminution elsewhere.

2. The new intraunion supply may, however, displace a member's imports from a lower-cost foreign source. If France, for example, had been importing aluminum from Canada and the United States at a price of $100 a ton plus a 30 per cent duty, with the elimination of this duty on intraunion trade, Italian producers with a cost of $120 a ton could now displace the previous imports into France. The actual cost to France of her aluminum is now $20 a ton higher than before. Trade has been diverted from a low- to a high-cost source. This *trade diversion* reduces the efficiency of world production, since to produce the same output as before, a larger quantity of resources has to be used. The French consumer, of course, gains from paying $10 a ton less than before. (Alternatively, one could say that to acquire the same quantity of imports as before, France must now use a larger amount of resources in producing the exports to exchange for the imports.)

A diagrammatic illustration may be helpful. In Figure 12.1, D_h

Figure 12.1   Effects of a Customs Union: Trade Creation

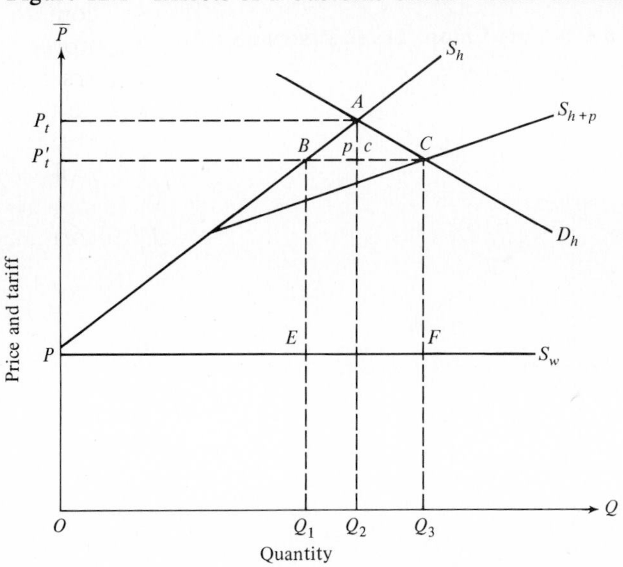

represents demand in the "home" country (H) and S_h its supply from domestic sources. Potential supplies from the "partner" country (P) are indicated by the horizontal distance from the home supply curve S_h to the joint home and partner supply curve, S_{h+p}. The supply from the rest of the world (W) is S_w assumed, to simplify the argument, to be available at constant costs.

We start with a tariff equal to PP_t (or even higher). This effectively excludes competitors both in the partner country and in the outside world, and leaves the home market to be supplied by domestic producers. Price is OP_t, and both consumption and domestic production OQ_2.

Now suppose a customs union is formed between H and the partner country P. Since the tariff is still in effect against W, it is excluded from H's market; supplies from P enter free of duty, however. Price drops to OP_t', consumption expands to OQ_3, and domestic production shrinks to OQ_1. Supplies from the partner country have *displaced* home production in the amount Q_1Q_2, with a saving in cost equal to the area marked p. That is *trade creation*.

To show trade diversion, we eliminate the home supply (as in Figure 12.2) and leave only two potential suppliers, the partner country (S_p) and the rest of the world (S_w). As before, the tariff is PP_t. With the price in H at OP_t, the entire market is supplied in the amount OQ_1 by imports from W.

If now H and P form a customs union, P, hitherto excluded from H's market, will displace W. The price will fall to OP_t' and consumption

Figure 12.2   Effects of a Customs Union: Trade Diversion

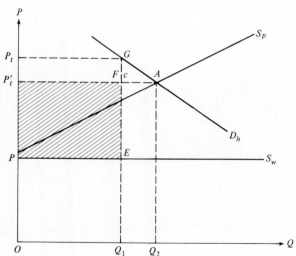

increase to OQ_2. In this instance, however, imports from P displace a more efficient supplier. The original amount of imports, OQ_1, now cost H more, and H must pay for that part of her imports with exports worth $OP_t'FQ_1$, instead of only $OPEQ_1$. She incurs an increased cost in exports equal to the crosshatched area ($PP_t'FE$). (There is an additional loss in customs revenue equal to the rectangular area $P_t'P_tGF$).

Consumption Effects

A consumer attains maximum satisfaction from his expenditures when he equalizes the satisfaction derived from the last dollar spent on all commodities. Then satisfaction obtained from the last unit consumed of each commodity bears the same relation to its price as it does for every other commodity; that is, the ratio of marginal utility to price is the same for all commodities ($MU_a/P_a = MU_b/P_b = \cdots$). This corresponds to equalization of the ratio of marginal utilities of commodities to their price ratios ($MU_a/MU_b = P_a/P_b$), which, as we saw in Chapter 4, is the condition for consumer equilibrium.

   This outcome is assured for all buyers under conditions of perfect competition, for then every buyer confronts the same price for each commodity. Since perfect competition also ensures that price is equal to marginal cost for every commodity, the marginal satisfaction from the consumption of any good—its marginal value product—is just equal to the value of the resources required to produce it.

   The presence of monopoly, of an excise tax, or—on an imported article—of a customs duty, introduces a divergence: It raises the price and marginal value of that article above its marginal cost. Hence a given amount of resources will produce more marginal value or satisfaction in a taxed or monopolistic industry than in the one that is untaxed or competitive. Removal of the tax (or the monopoly) would permit the allocation of more resources to the production of the relatively highly valued good, thereby increasing consumer welfare.

   Now let us apply this argument to the formation of a customs union. When the tariff on intraunion trade is abolished, the price of the commodity now availble duty-free within the union will fall. This is true regardless of whether a low-cost source of supply within the union displaces a domestic high-cost source (trade creation), or whether a relatively high-cost source inside the union displaces a low-cost outside source (trade diversion). In either event, the consumer "gets a break." The divergence between marginal value and (minimum) marginal cost will be entirely eliminated if the lowest-cost producer is in the partner country. If the union supplier is only second best, the divergence between marginal value (the preunion price) and the lowest attainable marginal cost will be reduced. Total consumer satisfaction will increase.

This point is illustrated in Figures 12.1 and 12.2 by the triangular area labeled c in each, which measures the net gain in consumer satisfaction from increased consumption of the commodity in question. (The *total* gain in consumer satisfaction over cost is measured by the larger area $P_t'P_tAC$ in Figure 12.1 and $P_t'P_tGA$ in Figure 12.2. In the first diagram the area p is accounted for by saving in cost from the substitution of low-cost union for high-cost domestic production; the remainder reflects an offsetting loss of income by producers. In the second diagram the area $P_t'P_tGF$ is part of the loss in customs revenue— an offset to consumer satisfaction.)

Substitution Effects   Although it is true that, for every commodity whose price is reduced as a consequence of the establishment of a customs union, there will be a net gain in consumer satisfaction,[2] before we can be sure there will be an *overall* gain on this score, it is necessary to estimate the size of a possible offsetting loss. Such a loss will arise if the commodities whose consumption increases as cheaper supplies are made available within the union displace imported goods that are subject to a tariff. On all such goods, there still exists a divergence between marginal value and marginal cost; they are relatively highly valued. If the now cheaper commodities are good substitutes for such products, then although consumers will enjoy additional (though diminishing) satisfaction from increased consumption of the former, they will suffer an additional loss from reduced consumption of the latter. On each unit of an article whose consumption is reduced, the loss is measured by the divergence between marginal value and marginal cost caused by the duty on imports.[3]

To illustrate, suppose that before the formation of the European Common Market France was importing cameras costing 200 francs from Germany and watches (with the same unit cost) from Switzerland, each commodity being subject to a 50 percent duty. After the removal of the duty on union products, cameras sell for 200 francs, while the price of watches remains unchanged at 300 francs. Let us assume, as in Figure 12.3, that before the Common Market was formed, 100 units each of cameras and watches were sold in France, but that afterward, at the new low price, sales of cameras doubled, to 200, while sales of

[2] This gain will approximate, in money terms, one-half the product of the increase in consumption and the reduction in price.

[3] The loss from reduced consumption of the still dutiable article, however, can never exceed, although it might equal, the gain from increased consumption of the now duty-free commodity. Such an outcome would reflect irrational consumer behavior—a failure to allocate expenditure so as to equalize the *value* of each dollar spent.

Figure 12.3   Consumption Effect of Elimination of a Duty on One of Two Substitutable Imports

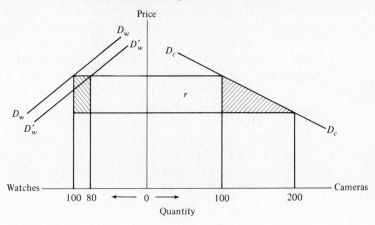

watches (for which cameras are highly substitutable) fell to 80. The elimination of the divergence between the marginal value and marginal cost of cameras yields consumers an increase in welfare represented by the triangular area in the diagram. But there is an offsetting loss from the reduced consumption of watches, represented by the rectangular area on the "watches" side of the diagram. Since the divergence between marginal value and marginal cost for watches remains at the original level, there is a loss of welfare corresponding to this divergence on each unit by which the consumption of watches is reduced. As for cameras, consumer satisfaction is increased on all units purchased— both those bought at the old price and (at a diminishing rate) on the additional consumption at the new, lower price. Offsetting part of this gain, however, there is a loss of customs revenue (represented by the rectangular area r), which must be made up by the new taxation elsewhere.

A Terms-of-Trade Effect

In addition to the effects on production and consumption of a customs union, there is a possible *terms-of-trade effect*. This occurs if foreign supplies of the imports are not perfectly elastic, but are subject to increasing cost conditions. For then, when the partner's supplies are substituted for foreign imports, the price of the latter fall. Therefore, on such external trade as continues, imports are obtained at better terms.

Summary

Certain general conditions determining the gains from an improved allocation of resources and from increased consumer satisfaction may be specified.[4]

1. If the economies merged in a customs union are *competitive* in the sense that they produce a wide range of similar goods, there will be many opportunities for the substitution of the products of one union member for those of another, and thus for trade creation rather than trade diversion. When the lowest-cost supplier is outside the union, this will, of course, constitute an exception causing trade diversion.

On the other hand, the union of complementary economies, producing very dissimilar goods, would provide few opportunities for intraunion substitution. There would be little reallocation of production between high- and low-cost sources of supply, such as would tend to occur with a union of competitive economies. Although elimination of tariffs would increase the trade of existing suppliers, it would do little to *create* trade by causing the substitution of a low- for a high-cost source. A considerable amount of trade might, however, be *diverted* through the substitution of high-cost internal for low-cost external suppliers.

This principle cuts both ways with respect to the European Common Market. The economies of all ten members are competitive in manufactures, which suggests the probability of considerable trade creation. But they are complementary in agriculture. France has partially displaced outside suppliers of wheat and other temperate-zone crops, and the former French and Italian colonies, which receive special treatment under the Common Market agreement, have substituted their bananas and other tropical products for those of Latin America and other suppliers. Dairy products from Denmark and Ireland have certainly replaced some part of those hitherto shipped from New Zealand.

2. Any gain from the union of competitive economies would be augmented by the existence of large differences in unit costs. On the production side, there would be a substantial reallocation of resources from inefficient domestic to more efficient union sources; on the consumption side, there would be a large gain in satisfaction from increased consumption at much lower prices.[5] On the other hand, if ini-

---

[4] The conditions enumerated here are very general. For a more accurate analysis, one would need to consider the elasticities of domestic demand, of partner's and foreign supply, and the substitutability of union for external supplies. See, for example, Harry G. Johnson, *Money, Trade and Economic Growth* (London: George Allen & Unwin Ltd., 1962), p. 57.

[5] This gain in satisfaction is limited, however, to consumers residing in countries whose high-cost producers have been displaced by lower-cost producers in other countries of the union. Consumers in the latter countries will encounter higher prices if these lower-cost producers operate under conditions of increasing costs, with the degree of price rise depending upon elasticity of supply.

tial differences in costs between member countries and outside suppliers are small, this will limit the loss from higher costs resulting from trade diversion.

3. Of prime importance is the level of member's tariffs before and after union: (a) High tariffs before union would favor trade creation, since their removal would tend to cause the substitution of many lower-cost sources of supply within the union for high-cost domestic supplies. Consumer gains would also tend to be larger because of the initial large divergence between marginal value and marginal cost. (b) A low postunion tariff would minimize trade diversion by reducing the likelihood that low-cost outside producers would be excluded from the union market, whereas a high tariff wall around the union would tend to reserve its market for relatively high cost union suppliers. Consumers' interests would be simultaneously served, in that consumption of imports that were good substitutes for commodities now supplied by union producers would be subject to a relatively small divergence between marginal value and marginal cost.

4. Costs of transport act like a natural tariff barrier. Being in the nature of things, they cannot be eliminated, although they may be reduced as technology progresses. Economic union of countries separated by high transport costs would yield relatively little in the way of a more efficient reallocation of resources, for inefficient producers continue to be sheltered by this natural protection.This point applies with particular force to the countries on the east and west coasts of South America, which are separated by the high wall of the Andes, and which find it cheaper to ship goods by the long sea voyage all the way around Cape Horn.

Static Effects Considered

The presumed static gains from a customs union have been challenged on two grounds. First, it is contended that they are likely to be unimportant because of the proportionalities involved. In few countries does the value of foreign trade amount to more than 20 to 25 percent of gross national product. Suppose that it is 20 percent, and that the elimination of barriers to intraunion trade causes that trade to expand by 40 percent, with an average price reduction of 20 percent. If, before union, trade among members was 50 percent of total trade, then in effect total trade has expanded by 20 percent. This is equivalent to a 5 percent growth in gross national product, since total trade comprises 20 percent of GNP. But the net gain is only one-fifth of this—the 20 percent by which average prices were reduced—which yields a figure of only 1 percent. Some consider gains of that order of magnitude as insignificant.[6] But progress generally goes on by small accretions rather than by giant leaps. And trade creation may well continue over time—it need not appear all at once, so the present, discounted value of the gain may be large.

More fundamental than a possible small gain from specialization is a theoretical objection to a customs union as the means to that end. Such gain as may be realized from a reallocation of resources can be attained at less cost by an alternative policy. This amounts to saying that, as far as concerns the static gains from a customs union, that policy is not second best, but at most only third best.

The argument proceeds as follows.[7] Suppose that, instead of forming a customs union, the countries considering this step had lowered their tariffs on all imports by an amount that would yield the same price, quantity consumed, and level of domestic production as would result from the formation of a customs union. In terms of Figure 12.1, this would mean a nonpreferential reduction of the tariff from PP_t to PP'_t. Price in the domestic market would fall to OP'_t, consumption would expand from OQ_2 to OQ_3, and domestic production would shrink to OQ_1, the values realized from establishment of a customs union. But in this instance, imports in the amount Q_1Q_3 would come not from other countries of the proposed customs union, but from outside suppliers. (The relevant import—supply curve would be S_w, not S_{h+p}.) Imports would then be obtained at a unit cost of only OP instead of OP'_t, or a total cost of Q_1EFQ_3 instead of Q_1BCQ_3, and customs revenue would amount to $EBCF$.

Considered by itself, without regard to the possibility of such an alternative, a customs union results in the substitution for high-cost domestic supplies of lower-cost partner supplies (trade creation), with a saving in cost measured by the area p. The alternative policy of a nonpreferential reduction of the tariff by an appropriate amount yields an even greater cost saving and is hence to be preferred.

The Rationality of Customs Unions

This proof that a nonpreferential tariff policy is superior to a customs union as a means toward trade liberalization raises the question of whether the desire to establish a customs union is a rational one. On classical trade theory grounds, if the same economic benefit is attain-

[6] See Tibor Scitovsky, *Economic Theory and Western European Integration* (London: George Allen & Unwin Ltd., 1962), pp. 64–68, where the same conclusion is reached for the probable gains from increased specialization of a union of the six Common Market countries with the United Kingdom and the Scandinavian nations.

[7] The argument presented here is a condensation of that advanced by C. A. Cooper and B. F. Massell, "A New Look at Customs Union Theory," *Economic Journal*, **74** (Dec. 1965).

able at lower cost by a nonpreferential lowering of tariffs as by forming a customs union, the choice of the latter is irrational. Recent literature has devoted considerable attention to this problem.[8]

Justification of the customs union as a rational choice on economic grounds has been attained by characterizing a degree of industrialization as a "public good" that yields a flow of satisfaction to the electorate, just as a private good yields a flow of satisfaction to the consumer. Formation of a customs union then becomes an alternative to a unilateral increase of tariffs as a means of acquiring such a public good. It has been shown that a customs union is a superior means to protection for this purpose because it can do so at lower cost in terms of consumption forgone.[9] This is possible, since a customs union causes domestic resources to be reallocated from the less efficient import-competing sector of industry to the more efficient export sector, which expands due to the opening of the partner's market. A tariff, on the other hand, causes resources to shift to the relatively inefficient import-competing sector. Because of the reduced efficiency, fewer goods are available for consumption.

As Krauss points out, there are dangers in the use of this argument to support the establishment of a customs union.[10] How identify, without ambiguity, what is a public good? How is one to determine the actual need for protection to obtain such a good? And, we might add, how measure the satisfaction yielded by a "public good"?

A more important question to ask is, in what way is this new approach to an old problem in any way superior to the traditional approach? A "public good" of this particular kind is nothing more than a means of ministering to national pride. A nation feels superior if it possesses a steel industry or a national air line that its rivals lack. Viewed in this light the problem is not one of balancing economic benefits and costs, but of achieving a political goal at minimum cost. A customs union may be a cheaper means than protection, but there is a strong possibility that a subsidy would be still cheaper. And cheapest of all would be a program to debunk the highly suspect political goal.

One more point with regard to the motivation for a customs union: in the case of developed countries such as those in the EEC, the

---

[8] See Melvyn Krauss, "Recent Developments in Customs Union Theory: An Interpretive Survey," *Journal of Economic Literature*, **10**:424–30 (June 1972).

[9] Harry G. Johnson, "An Economic Theory of Protectionism, Tariff Bargaining and the Formation of Customs Unions," *Journal of Political Economy*, **73** (June 1965); C. A. Cooper and B. F. Massell, "Towards a General Theory of Customs Unions for Developing Countries," *Journal of Political Economy*, **73** (Oct. 1965).

[10] This argument, it should be noted, is applicable only to less developed countries that lack, but desire, modern industry. In forming customs unions, these countries typically stimulate trade diversion, since they replace low-cost foreign products by high-cost partners' supplies.

reason for choosing to form a customs union could be rational on political or economic grounds. The most important reason may well be political: that customs union is an essential first step on the road to a complete economic and political union. As for its economic rationality, the static gains from trade creation, although small relative to total GNP, could well be significant; in addition, there are likely to be dynamic gains.

DYNAMIC ASPECTS OF UNION

The effects of customs union on production and consumption surveyed up to now are purely static: They involve a reallocation of resources among existing industries, using existing supplies of the factors and existing technology. Some industries expand, others contract, and consumers enjoy lower prices on certain products; otherwise everything goes on as before.

But the dynamic effects of forming a customs union, although by nature nebulous and therefore difficult to measure, may be far more important than the static effects. The basis for dynamic effects is to be found mainly in the presence of imperfectly competitive conditions in the various national markets being united. If such conditions exist, two possibilities emerge: Competition may be intensified, and unrealized economies of scale may become a reality.

Competition and Emulation   If competition in each of the economies being unified were perfect, there would be no opportunity for improvement in production practices, since they would be optimal everywhere. Moreover, competition would be strictly in terms of price, for the quality of any product would be identical for all producers. There would be no expenditure on selling, for this is related to product differentiation, which is a feature of imperfect competition.

In the real world, however, an approximation to perfect competition is found in relatively few markets. In most, it is highly imperfect, especially in manufacturing, where the number of competitors is frequently small and product differentiation is widespread. Firms in separate national markets may differ widely in their conservatism or progressiveness. Those in certain industries in one country may use outdated techniques because of inertia, a desire for the quiet life, tradition, or other reasons; in another country competition in these industries may be intense and industrial and commercial practices thoroughly up-to-date.

Such differences in conditions afford an opportunity, when tariffs are removed, for the "winds of competition" to generate rapid change. Hitherto protected producers, if they are to survive, must either imitate or innovate. Emulation of their competitors leads to the spread of the best practices. There occurs not just a mechanical reshuffling of resources from high- to low-cost firms and industries, but a change in attitudes, habits, and organization. Conservative and traditional industries are forced to adopt improved methods if they are to stay in business. Older men tend to be replaced by younger men, willing and able to change, who with the stimulus of rivalry, improve upon the new practices they are forced to meet.

When a customs union is reinforced by economic integration, with the free movement of capital, labor, and enterprise, and with cooperation in shaping government policies and in establishing common institutions, the competition of ideas generated by product competition is extended over a far wider range. Capital that is free to move shuns repressive or discriminatory tax laws; labor seeks not only higher money wages, but also better working conditions and the most attractive fringe benefits. Given equal prospects of profits, enterprise goes where freedom to operate is greatest. Governments therefore are pressed to reform tax laws, social security provisions, and legislation affecting enterprise—that is, to copy or improve upon the best existing practices. International conventions replace national conventions of engineers, salesmen, executives, and accountants, affording a wider forum for the exchange of ideas. Although its effects are difficult to measure, surely the inauguration of a spirit of emulation is one of the most beneficial effects of economic union.

Emulation may, of course, extend to bad as well as to good practices. If before union national markets were dominated by cartels, these may merely be replaced by larger international organizations, perhaps restricting output and maintaining prices even more effectively. This suggests that in such areas, whether only a customs union or full economic integration is being attempted, a common policy is needed if the welfare of the community is to be served.

Economies of Scale   Under perfect competition, economies deriving from increased size of plant may exist up to a point, but they are sure to be exhausted. For competitive equilibrium requires the attainment of minimum cost, which implies that the scale of the individual firm's operations be optimal. When there is imperfect competition, however, and especially in small markets, plant size may be far from optimal. An increase in the size of any individual producer's plant might yield substantial economies of scale, yet each firm may be inhibited from investing in plant expansion because this will necessitate wresting the market away from rivals. If that market is stationary or expanding only slowly, this may entail such high selling costs as to make the attempt unprofitable. But as Lipsey has observed, if the entire market were to expand so as to allow growth in size without the need to fight for elbowroom, economies of scale could be realized painlessly.[11] Formation of a customs union might then open the door to economies of scale unattainable in segregated markets.

Although a high correlation has been shown to exist between market size and productivity,[12] the causal relationship could reside in the economies of large-scale operations, in external economies, or in the stimulus a large market gives to technological change and to investment. Scale economies are associated with the use of expensive, specialized equipment, the specialization of labor, savings on inventories and from bulk handling, and from relatively smaller outlays for nonoperational activities such as research, planning, and the like (Chapter 7). Although these economies are very real, they are by no means universal. Various studies of German, American, and New Zealand industries, however, indicate that productivity increases with the size of the plant in a substantial proportion of the industries surveyed. In the United States, for example, the production of pig iron, crude petroleum, sugar, paper, electricity, and creameries shows increasing returns to scale, but there is little or no evidence of such economies for fertilizers, bakery products, or tires.[13]

External Economies   As market size increases, economies external to the plant may also arise. Industrial growth creates a pool of skilled labor and managerial talent, and causes technological knowledge to spread and to develop. Expansion of one industry may permit its supplier to introduce more economical large-scale methods. Perhaps the most general basis for external economies is the possibility provided by the growth of an industry for intra-industry specialization. Firms in the expanding industry can concentrate upon certain essential functions, while leaving other tasks to be taken over by newly formed dependent industries, with distinct gains from specialization as a result. A good example of this is the automobile industry, with its widespread subcontracting for parts and components.

More Rapid Technological Advance   In industries in which economies of scale are realized as the market expands, it is likely that large firms will increase their share of the market. Given the combination

---

[11] R. G. Lipsey, "The Theory of Customs Unions: A General Survey," *Economic Journal*, **70** (Sept. 1960).

[12] See the studies cited in Bela Balassa, *The Theory of Economic Integration* (Homewood, Ill.: Richard D. Irwin, Inc., 1961), pp. 109–12.

[13] Ibid., pp. 126, 128.

of economies of scale in research, the larger financial resources and better access to the capital market of the large firm, and its "longer time horizon," then, as Balassa contends, it is probable that the larger firm will spend more freely on research activities.[14] This will tend to promote more rapid technological progress. Moreover, if large producers are relatively more numerous in a large economy, and if they spend more freely on research, the large economy will have the advantage of discoveries over a wider field, for whose application its very size affords more opportunities.

Investment   Economic union tends to stimulate an increase in investment in a number of ways. Introduction of more intense competition forces modernization of plant and equipment, perhaps accompanied by greater product specialization. If products are discontinued, or if entire industries are forced out, there will, of course, be some offsetting disinvestment. For regions with especially high costs, whether due to location or other reasons, this may be serious. But since most firms in a customs union area can be counted on not to lie down and roll over when faced with keener rivalry, a substantial net increase in investment seems almost certain. Moreover, if the forces generating increased efficiency operate as expected, aggregate income will rise, savings will increase, and aggregate investment will be larger. With expanding markets giving a lift to confidence, the *proportion* of income saved and invested may be raised.

To higher savings and investment in the unified community may be added an inflow of foreign funds, attracted by the prospects of producing and selling in the enlarged protected market and by a rising rate of economic growth. Witness, for example, the rise in U.S. direct investment in the six nations of the European Economic Union from $637 million in 1950 to $2,194,000,000 in 1959.[15]

SELECTED REFERENCES

BALASSA, BELA. *The Theory of Economic Integration.* Homewood, Ill.: Richard D. Irwin, Inc., 1961. A most useful survey of the static and dynamic effects of economic integration and of the policy problems raised by integration.

CLEMENT, M. O., R. L. PFISTER, and R. J. ROTHWELL. *Theoretical Issues in International Economics.* Boston: Houghton Mifflin Company, 1967.

[14] Ibid., pp. 174–75.

[15] Office of Business Economics, Department of Commerce, *U.S. Business Investments in Foreign Countries* (Washington, D.C.: Government Printing Office, 1960), Tables 1 and 3.

Chapter 4 is brief and good; it includes general as well as partial equilibrium analysis.

JOHNSON, HARRY G. *Money, Trade and Economic Growth*. London: George Allen & Unwin, Ltd., 1962. Chapter 3 provides a concise statement of the theory of the customs union.

KRAUSS, MELVYN B. "Recent Developments in Customs Union Theory: An Interpretive Survey." *Journal of Economic Literature*, **10** (June 1972). This article provides an extensive bibliography.

LIPSEY, R. G. "The Theory of Customs Unions: A General Survey." *Economic Journal*, **70** (Sept. 1960). A brief summary discussion of theory.

SCITOVSKY, TIBOR. *Economic Theory and Western European Integration*. Stanford, Calif.: Stanford University Press, 1958. Especially good on the dynamic aspects of integration.

13
CHAPTER

Trade Liberalization and Regional Integration

CONTRASTING TRADE POLICIES IN HISTORY

In the course of history we can identify three distinct periods during which the attitude of governments toward international trade has differed widely. The first of these, the mercantilist era, was a phase of close regulation and control, with the regulation undertaken in the interest of supporting the power of the state. In the course of the two and a half centuries during which mercantilism held sway, the middle class of merchants and manufacturers, hitherto small in numbers and of little importance, became increasingly numerous and prosperous. Yet because the restrictive features of mercantilism hampered expansion and enterprise and held down its profits, the new middle class came more and more to oppose and evade its prohibitions and requirements. The merchant–capitalist class, steadily growing in economic and political influence, found its interest better served by economic freedom. Under its pressure, the internal restrictions of mercantilism gradually broke down. Finding wider and wider acceptance, the new laissez faire philosophy was given vigorous expression in the writings of Adam Smith. In Britain it became the dominant point of view, and even on the continent it found increasing numbers of influential adherents.

After the Napoleonic wars, the steady shift in the political strength of conflicting economic interests led to the extension into foreign trade of the liberal ideas hitherto applied only to the internal economy. Trade was freed from its centuries-old bonds by one country after another. The nineteenth century saw trade freer than it had been since Roman times. Both the direction of trade and the character of national specialization became dominated almost exclusively by market forces. Under the new regime, the volume of international commerce expanded by leaps and bounds, making it possible for western Europe to become a highly specialized manufacturing center and thereby to support a huge increase in population.

This remarkable era was marred toward its close by a resurgence of nationalism, which brought with it the beginnings of a return to trade restriction. This movement became intensified with the outbreak of war in 1914 and the inflammation of nationalist sentiments that this entailed. The nostalgia of the 1920s for the comparative simplicity of the Victorian era met only disappointment in the mounting forces of nationalism, in growing economic rigidity, and in a widening range of sensitivity to disturbance. The shock of world depression speeded the disorganization of the world economy and ended in the dominance of nationally oriented policies. Although demand and supply still continued to function, they did so within narrowly constricted areas; the broad world market, which had served so well before 1914 to allocate production and to ensure steady supplies of every imaginable commodity, no longer existed.

COOPERATION TO RESTORE A WORLD ECONOMY

The difficulties encountered during the 1930s showed conclusively that the specialization of the nineteenth century and the growth of population it had engendered had gone too far to permit this disorganization to continue. The dependence of western Europe and Japan on a wide-flung network of trade made efforts to repair that network imperative. Even while World War II was raging, extensive discussions were undertaken and plans laid to reconstruct a wider market area and, at the same time, to effect the minimum essential compromises between the requirements of a multilateral trading system and national demands for reasonable economic stability.

Some of these efforts were on a regional scale, some much broader. The sterling area provided a degree of financial unity, stability and convertibility of currencies, and comparative freedom of trade and payments over a large area. The efforts of the OEEC to liberalize the trade among European nations, and the role played by the European Payments Union in easing their payments problems, should also be noted. And the European Recovery Program not only made the last two institutions possible by assisting European reconstruction, but also set the EPU in operation with a grant of funds. Moreover, in its administration, the European Recovery Program constantly stressed the need for the liberalization of trade and for a closer integration of the European nations (see Chapter 27 for further details).

As institutions serving to restore a more efficiently operating world economy, the contributions of the International Monetary Fund and the International Bank for Reconstruction and Development were particularly critical. The first of these aimed to replace chaotic currency conditions with some degree of stability and, by constant pressure on members, to eliminate exchange controls and encourage a movement toward convertibility. The principal function of the International Bank has been to foster the development of the less advanced nations: It was presumed that economic growth would operate indirectly to enable them to lower their trade barriers and to move toward currency convertibility.

A PROPOSAL FOR AN INTERNATIONAL TRADE ORGANIZATION

At the same time as the discussions leading to the Bretton Woods Conference were initiated, the question naturally arose: If international cooperation might work in the monetary and financial area, why not in the field of international trade? Prolonged discussion of this question resulted in the publication by the U.S. Department of State of a brochure entitled "Proposals for Expansion of World Trade and Employment." These proposals covered a wide range of topics in the realms of commercial policy: tariffs, preferences, quotas and licensing systems, restrictive business practices, the maintenance of full employment, and the establishment of an International Trade Organization to administer any agreements that might be reached.

After endorsement by the executive branch of the U.S. government and the government of the United Kingdom, the proposals underwent discussion at an international Conference on Trade and Employment that first met in London in the autumn of 1946, adjourned to Geneva the following year, and concluded in Havana in the winter of 1947–1948. Fifty-three nations there signed the resulting Charter for an International Trade Organization (ITO), which would go into effect upon its ratification by a prescribed number of nations.

But the ITO never became translated from provisions on paper into a functioning organization. Serious opposition to its wide-ranging provisions developed in the U.S. Congress. It failed ratification and ceased therewith to be a live issue.

THE GENERAL AGREEMENT ON TARIFFS AND TRADE

Anxious to get about the business of reducing trade barriers regardless of what happened to the proposed International Trade Organization, some of the participants in the London Conference urged that extensive tariff negotiations be inaugurated simultaneously with the continuing discussion of the Trade Charter at Geneva. These negotiations, participated in by twenty-three nations, resulted in an extensive set of bilateral trade concessions, which were then extended to all participants and incorporated in a General Agreement on Tariffs and Trade (GATT). Since the initial conference in Geneva in 1947, six additional sets of multilateral tariff negotiations were successfully conducted, terminating with the Tokyo Round in 1979.

Main Principles

To protect the rights and enforce the obligations of the nations signing the original 1947 tariff agreement, the contracting parties of GATT also adopted a set of rules embodying the ITO provisions on commercial policy. To ensure the enforcement of these rules, they provided for annual (later, twice yearly) meetings of the contracting parties, for a modest secretariat, and (after 1954) for a permanent Council of Representatives. Thus although GATT is essentially a contractual arrangement among a number of nations (increased since its inception to eighty-eight), it is also a permanent international organization with continuing duties to safeguard the conduct of international trade. Within the first twenty years of its life, it emerged as the principal force in the world working for the multilateral expansion of trade.

In the rules adopted by GATT, three principles predominate: (1) trade is to be conducted in a nondiscriminatory manner, (2) the use of quantitative restrictions is condemned, and (3) disagreements are to be resolved through consultation.

To ensure against discrimination, the contracting parties agree to apply the most-favored-nation principle to all import and export duties: Each nation shall be treated as well as the most favored nation. As far as quantitative restrictions are permitted, they, too, are to be administered without favor. To meet specific difficulties, however, carefully guarded exceptions to the rule of nondiscrimination are allowed. Thus dumping and export subsidies may be countered by measures limited in application to the offending country. And although the creation of new partial tariff preferences is prohibited, arrangements designed to establish systems of complete preference—that is, customs unions or free trade areas—are permitted, provided that their purpose is "to facilitate trade between the constituent territories and not to raise barriers to the trade of other . . . parties."

As a matter of principle, GATT rules prohibit the use of import quotas and seek to limit restrictions on trade to the less rigid tariff. Although hedged with safeguards, three important exceptions to this prohibition are granted.

1. Countries confronted with balance-of-payments difficulties may use quantitative restrictions. They must, however, be limited to the extent necessary to stop a serious decline, forestall a threatened decline in reserves, or achieve a reasonable increase in abnormally low reserves. Moreover, the International Monetary Fund is to be consulted as to whether quantitative restrictions are really necessary.
2. Underdeveloped countries may apply quantitative restrictions to further their economic development, but only under procedures approved by GATT.
3. Finally, import restrictions may be applied to agricultural or fishery products if domestic production of these articles is subject to equally restrictive production or marketing controls.

In practice, the exception allowed for balance-of-payments reasons has not been seriously abused by the western industrial countries. But many countries, notably the United States and the EEC, have adopted agricultural price-support programs unaccompanied by production controls. To prevent a flooding of their markets, they felt obliged to impose quantitative restrictions on imports. It is not too much to say that, with respect to trade in agricultural products, GATT rules have been largely inoperative.

Besides arranging a series of multilateral tariff negotiations whose comprehensive nature led to a lowering of duties on trade, including more than two-thirds of the world total, GATT's principal accomplishment has been to establish a forum for continuing consultation. Disputes that might otherwise have caused continuing hard feeling, reprisals, and even diplomatic rupture have been brought to the conference table and compromised.

In the early years of GATT, if one member felt that another had violated the rules, withdrawn a valuable concession, or otherwise acted in a manner conflicting with the agreement, it brought its complaint to the annual meeting. The disputants were urged to attempt to settle their difficulties bilaterally. If this failed, the contracting parties formed a working committee, which after studying the matter would make a recommendation or a ruling. If the offending member then refused to change its ways, the aggrieved party could retaliate by withdrawing some concession. More often than not, offending members could and did comply with a recommendation by some change in administrative procedure.

GATT proved so useful in bringing issues to a head and in settling a reasonable proportion of them that, in 1953, the contracting parties set up a panel to act as an informal court to handle disputes. This panel listens to the disputants, formulates and considers the issues, and drafts a report—all the while consulting with the disputing parties. With this change in procedure, the number of complaints brought before GATT and successfuly resolved increased markedly.

As early as 1955, GATT began to take a special interest in the trade problems of underdeveloped countries by establishing in Geneva a training center for officials of these countries. Through formal courses and in-service training arranged with export firms and associations, these officials were given training in various aspects of export marketing. In 1964 the training program became part of a broader trade center, which provided the less developed nations with information on potential export markets and on marketing procedures. Beginning in 1968, the United Nations Conference on Trade and Development (UNCTAD) joined GATT in sponsoring and financing this trade center.

UNITED STATES TARIFF POLICY SINCE 1934

United States tariff policy from 1934 onward can be briefly summarized as paring off the protective fat by negotiation. The Trade Agreements Act of that year, renewed periodically thereafter, authorized the president to reduce existing duties by as much as 50 percent in exchange for similar concessions by other countries. In the series of bilateral negotiations sponsored by GATT in the postwar period, a considerable number of such concessions were exchanged, then extended to other countries by means of the most-favored-nation principle. In 1947 authority to cut duties by 50 percent from the new, lower level was granted; in 1956 further duty reductions were limited to 20 percent.

In the twenty-eight years during which the Trade Agreements Acts shaped U.S. tariff policy, there occurred a very substantial lowering of the average level of U.S. import duties. Responsibility for this reduction was divided about equally between price increases, which lowered the percentage rate of the predominately specific duties in the U.S. tariff, and negotiated duty cuts.[1] Thus in 1934 the average duty

---

[1] Thus, in the 1930 tariff, the specific duty on garlic was 1.5 cents a pound. Converted into an ad valorem figure, it amounted to 40 percent. By 1950 the price of garlic had risen to the point where the 1.5-cent duty amounted to only 22 percent ad valorem.

on dutiable imports was 46.7 percent. At the end of 1952, the duties in effect in 1934 would have amounted to only 24.4 percent at the higher level of prices then ruling. The actual average rate of duties, however, was only 12.2 percent. Trade agreements had therefore brought about a 50 percent reduction of the U.S. tariff level. Between 1952 and 1962 the average duty on dutiable imports was further reduced to approximately 12 percent.

Although this appears to be quite low, and by comparison with the tariff level in the early 1930s is low, an average of a wide range of duties is deceptive.[2] It conceals all duties that are prohibitive, since only duties actually levied on imports are counted. Some duties included in the average are high, although not prohibitive. And many low duties afford substantial protection when international cost differences are slight. It is the consensus of experts that as late as 1962 the U.S. tariff was moderately protective.

Moreover, the Trade Agreements Act in force from 1947 on contained an "escape clause" that practically guaranteed domestic producers against injurious foreign competition. Upon a finding by the Tariff Commission that, due even in part to the concession, a product on which a concession had been granted was being imported in such increased quantities, either actual or relative, as to cause or threaten serious injury to the competing domestic industry, the president was authorized to withdraw or modify the concession. With increased imports defined in relative terms, this meant that protection could be restored even though the output of U.S. industry was growing, provided only that imports were growing faster.

Later extension of the Trade Agreements Act went further by defining an industry as the producers of a single product. This led to the absurdity that an industry producing multiple products could apply for tariff relief even though a relative increase in foreign competition was limited to only one of its several products.[3]

Reinforcing the protectionist policy embodied in the escape clause were two other legislative provisions. One authorized the withdrawal of a concession or the restriction of imports by quotas if imports increased in such quantities as to threaten the national security. Watches, which obtained relief under this provision, are undoubtedly important to a national defense, although the need for maintaining a protected industry as a source of supply is certainly dubious. But the connection between clothespins (which qualify under the national defense provision) and national security would seem to be somewhat indirect. The law (National Defense Amendment of 1955), however, de-

---

[2] In 1962, U.S. duties ranged from 1 to nearly 100 percent.

[3] A finding of injury, coupled with relief, occurred in such individual items of multiple product lines as watches with seven but not more than seventeen jewels, flax toweling, safety pins, clinical thermometers, and garlic.

fines almost any adverse effect on economic welfare, such as increased unemployment, loss of government revenues, or loss of skills or investment, as constituting impairment of national security. A coat of national security paint is a feeble camouflage for the underlying protectionism.

Finally, the "Buy American" Act, passed by Congress during the depression to give preference to American producers, requires federal agencies to award government contracts to American firms unless foreign bids are 6 percent lower (in some cases, 12 percent).

In summary, the Trade Agreements Act and related legislation sought to expand American exports by an exchange of concessions. In the progress of negotiating them, the U.S. tariff was reduced very substantially from its inordinate height of the early 1930s, but it continued to afford protection for most domestic industries encountering foreign competition. Most important, U.S. legislation refused to tolerate injury to domestic producers from such competition. Any such injury, real or threatened, was not to be compensated, but prevented.

The Trade Expansion Act of 1962

The United States had participated from the beginning in the GATT multilateral negotiations for tariff reductions. Apart from the first round, however, the scope and depth of the cuts had been limited. Some rough evidence of this is contained in Table 13.1.

By the time the 1962 GATT round had been concluded, it was clear that some major new initiative would be required to move tariff reduction any further. That initiative came from the Kennedy administration in 1962. President Kennedy advanced to Congress proposals for legislation to replace the expiring Trade Agreements Act that represented, if not a revolution, at least an important shift in American

Table 13.1   U.S. Tariff Cuts Resulting from GATT Negotiations, 1947–1962

GATT Round	Scope of U.S. Tariff Cuts[a] (%)	Depth of U.S. Tariff Cuts[b] (%)
1947	44	35
1949	3	35
1951	9	27
1956	11	15
1962	14	20

SOURCE: First National City Bank of New York, *Monthly Economic Letter*, Sept. 1967, p. 100. Used by permission.

[a] Percentage of dutiable imports on which cuts were made.

[b] Average percentage reduction made, weighted by the value of imports.

tariff policy. Most of these proposals were enacted as the Trade Expansion Act of 1962.

The new law differed from its immediate predecessors in two principal ways: It granted the president much greater authority to lower or even eliminate U.S. import duties, and it substituted for the negative policy of preventing dislocation the positive one of promoting and facilitating adjustment to dislocation caused by foreign competition.

Tariff Reduction   Tariff reduction by negotiation was retained as the basic goal. A more vigorous pursuit of that goal was made possible, however, by more generous provisions for cutting duties. The most important of these allowed the president, through trade agreements, to lower any duty by 50 percent, including duties already lowered through previous trade agreements. In a trade agreement concluded with the European Economic Community, he could reduce or eliminate the duties on any category of commodities in which the EEC or the United States together accounted for 80 percent of the value of world trade. Since Britain was not yet a member of the EEC, this limited the list principally to aircraft, vegetable oils, and perfumes.

Provisions relating to injury resulting from a tariff concession were retained, although far more tightly drawn than the old escape clause. Injury had to be serious and in major part traceable to imports due to the concession.

Adjustment Assistance   Provisions under this heading reflected a refreshingly new attitude toward the dislocation caused by foreign competition. They regarded that competition as essentially no different from domestic competition—a consequence of change and a spur to increased efficiency. Dislocation, or injury to the sluggish competition, is its unavoidable companion and therefore not to be avoided but welcomed. President Kennedy expressed this viewpoint well in a broader context in his message to Congress accompanying his tariff proposals:

> The discipline of the world market is an excellent measure of efficiency and a force to stability. To try to shield American industry from the discipline of foreign competition would isolate our domestic price level from world prices, encourage domestic inflation, reduce our exports still further, and invite less desirable governmental solutions.

There is, however, one major difference between foreign competition promoted by tariff reduction and the familiar domestic competition. The latter is a normal feature of everyday business life; it must always be taken into account by existing firms or by new entrants.

But when an industry has for long been sheltered by protection, businessmen will have been led in good faith to invest large sums in fixed equipment, and employees will have acquired skills that may be of little use in other occupations. Therefore, when the government, in the national interest, alters its established policy of protection, it incurs a responsibility toward those injured by its action. This principle of responsibility underlies the provision in the Trade Expansion Act of 1962 for adjustment assistance. Instead of maintaining the status quo, these seek to promote adaption to the increased competition by stimulating the mobility of resources and their prompt reallocation to more efficient uses.

Thus the government provided firms with technical assistance, financial aid through guaranteed loans, and tax assistance in the form of carrybacks and carryovers of losses. Workers who lost their jobs because of tariff concessions could obtain expanded unemployment compensation and retraining and relocation at government expense.

On the basis of the authority granted in the Trade Expansion Act of 1962, the American administration entered the "Kennedy Round" of GATT negotiations. The round was only concluded in 1967, but the scope of the cuts was greater than any previous GATT round (on 64 percent of dutiable imports), while the average depth of cut was equal to the 35 percent accomplished in the initial GATT round.

Third-seven nations joined in making duty reductions covering approximately $40 billion (four-fifths) of world trade. The major industrial countries in this group applied these cuts about as widely as did the United States, to 64 percent of their dutiable imports. Average reductions ranged in depth from 38 percent (United Kingdom) to 30 percent (Japan) and 24 percent (Canada). They left U.S. and European tariffs on the great bulk of manufactures in the range 5 to 15 percent.

Progress in the Kennedy Round was limited mainly to duty reductions on manufactured goods. With agricultural products the negotiators had less success. They did manage to reach agreements that helped ensure better prospects for American and Canadian wheat in the protected European market. The negotiators also agreed to an average duty reduction of 25 percent on agricultural items protected by normal tariffs. But no progress could be reported on dairy products, subject in many countries to direct quota limitations.

Protectionist Sentiment

The passage of the 1962 Trade Expansion Act was a high point of public support for liberal trading attitudes in the United States. Fueled substantially by the Kennedy tax cut of 1964, imports rose rapidly, especially in steel, synthetic and woolen textiles, television sets, transistor radios, cameras, and compact automobiles. Imports of steel and of textiles from Japan aroused strong resentment from American producers, who exerted heavy pressure on the government to impose quotas. Confronted with threats of severe limitations, Japanese and European steel producers, and Japanese, Taiwanese, and other textile manufacturers agreed to establish "voluntary" quotas on exports to the United States. Between 1962 and 1972, such export limitations grew in number from six to seventy.

This development is only the official side of a much wider swing toward protectionism, which came to a head with the introduction into Congress in 1972 of the Burke–Hartke bill. Its provisions included quotas on almost every category of imports that would have reduced them to approximately 60 percent of their 1971 levels. The bill also would have increased taxes on the operations of foreign subsidiaries of U.S. firms, limited overseas investment, and curbed the flow of technology.

Organized labor, which for many years had been either neutral or relatively liberal on the issue of international trade, strongly supported the Burke–Hartke bill. This was clearly a response to the parallel rise of imports and of unemployment, which labor attributed to European quotas on Japanese imports and the consequent shift of pressure onto the United States, and to the rising importance of multinational corporations domiciled in the United States. It was claimed that these corporations, by erecting plants abroad, exported jobs hitherto providing employment to American workers, and that by exporting technology and capital they undercut American industry's competitiveness.

A study by a U.S. government agency[4] of 298 multinational corporations, however, showed that from 1966 to 1970 the annual increase in employment in the United States by these firms was 2.7 percent compared with only 1.7 percent in total private employment. Exports of multinationals also increased faster than total U.S. exports, and although their imports rose, their exports rose still faster. Moreover, there is no need for a tortured explanation of the 1967–1971 surge in U.S. imports. That can be accounted for by the overvaluation of the dollar relative to the German mark and the yen. The transition from a trade deficit to a trade surplus in the last half of 1973, which reflected the changes in the pattern of exchange rates, lent support to this conclusion.

---

[4] *Multinational Corporation Studies on U.S. Foreign Investment*, Vol. 1 (Washington, D.C.: U.S. Office of International Investment, 1972).

The Trade Reform Act of 1974

The official stance on trade remained comparatively liberal. Submitted to Congress in April 1973, the Trade Reform Act contained many provisions similar to those of the 1962 law. Thus it granted the president authority for five years to negotiate further reductions of tariffs by 60 percent of the levels achieved as a result of the 1962 Act. Authority was also granted to negotiate an elimination of duties of less than 5 percent. The trend was not entirely toward liberalization, however. Escape clause relief for industries adversely affected by trade liberalization was made easier for industry to obtain, and provision for introduction of import surcharges for balance of payment reasons were introduced.

Conclusion of the Tokyo Round Negotiations, 1979

The authority granted the U.S. president in 1974 to negotiate further tariff reductions permitted the United States to participate in the next GATT round of multilateral trade negotiations. These were called the Tokyo Round after the location of the ministerial meeting in the fall of 1973 that launched the new negotiations.

The negotiations ran longer than ever before (to 1979) and covered a far more complex set of issues than simply tariff reductions. This was due, in large part, to the fact that the earlier negotiations had succeeded in reducing most tariffs to a relatively low level, leaving nontariff issues as the outstanding point of dispute. Nevertheless, the industrial countries agreed to a further reduction of their tariffs by about one-third over eight years. Further, those tariffs that were higher were generally cut more, thus reducing tariff escalation.

In an attempt to come to grips with some of the areas where nontariff barriers have been most serious and where world markets have shown considerable instability, the participants in the Tokyo Round agreed to promote the development of certain selected cartel-like arrangements in certain commodities, including meat, dairy products, and some grains. For example, the arrangement for dairy products contains provisions for minimum prices. This represented a significant reversal of previous GATT practice, which had attempted to *remove* restrictions rather than add new restrictions to international trade.

The principal accomplishment of the Tokyo Round was the set of steps taken to control the use of nontariff barriers. The approach taken was to establish codes of good conduct in several areas. The codes are multilateral agreements and contain provisions for consultation and settlement of disputes. These codes are also a major new departure for the GATT and promise to contribute significantly to the *effective* freeing of trade restrictions. For example, the customs valuation code sets out an ordering of acceptable valuation procedures, making it difficult for nations to use arbitrary valuation approaches as protective devices. Other codes deal with government procurement, import licencing procedures, the use of subsidies, and countervailing duties. The final code covers the use of technical standards as a barrier to trade. Various technological standards established by countries for entirely legitimate reasons such as protection of health, safety, environment, and consumers have had the potential, and on occasion have been used, to create trade barriers. The code will restrict such protective use by requiring national technical standards to be based on international standards. The Tokyo Round also made special provision in various codes to assist developing countries. A decade earlier (in 1968) there had been a generalized system of preferences established for developing countries. It had been treated by GATT as an exception to the rules of nondiscrimination and most-favored-nation treatment. The new agreement accepts as permanent the concept of preferential treatment for developing countries. Furthermore, the new agreement accepts the principle of nonreciprocity by developing countries for trade concessions by industrial countries. Developing countries are now permitted, also, to use trade restrictions to attain broad development objectives.

ECONOMIC UNION IN EUROPE

Five years after the establishment of GATT, six western European nations took the first step toward economic unification by forming the European Coal and Steel Community.[5] A bold and imaginative scheme, the ECSC aimed, through the elimination of trade restrictions and the encouragement of the free movement of resources, to stimulate the concentration of the coal and steel industries of the Six in the hands of the most efficient producers. With a common market kept competitive by the policing action of a central authority, it was hoped that members would be assured of abundant and cheap supplies of these essentials of modern industry. Instead of confining itself to the liberalization of trade, the ECSC set up an international authority with substantial powers. It was to do away with all tariffs and other restrictions on trade, eliminate a maze of discriminatory transport rates and establish

[5] The Six include Belgium, Netherlands, and Luxembourg (the "Benelux" countries), and France, Germany, and Italy.

an equitable system, and allocate funds to alleviate the impact of the common market during a five-year transitional period. To police the common market once established, it was authorized to prohibit mergers and even to dissolve existing combinations and to set maximum prices. Finally, the authority was given important powers over investment: It may require the submission of information about plans, forbid a firm to seek outside finances for any project it deems unwise, and make loans to firms for modernization or expansion.

A strong hint that the ECSC was intended only as a first step in economic and political union, together with some indication of the powerful motivation underlying it, is contained in the treaty establishing the ECSC. The six signatories

> Resolved to substitute for historical rivalries a fusion of their essential interests; to establish, by creating an economic community, the foundation of a broad and independent community among peoples long divided by bloody conflicts; and to lay the bases of institutions capable of giving direction to their future common destiny; have decided to create a European coal and steel community.

The European Economic Community

Giving further testimony to the conviction that the traditional national approach to economic problems was no longer consistent with the needs of the area, the six members of the ECSC in succeeding years broadened their attack by considering ways and means of establishing a common market for all commodities and of pooling European resources for the development of atomic power. Their discussions culminated in the drafting of the Treaty of Rome, which set up two new agencies of integration: the European Economic Community and the European Atomic Community. Signed in 1957, these treaties were put into operation on January 1, 1958.

The main economic purpose of establishing the European Common Market was to realize the advantages of increased specialization. It was hoped that a market embracing a population of over 160 million people would permit the more rapid development of the most economical sectors of each industry, as well as the use of the most modern production techniques. Its sponsors contended that existing national markets were too small for economical operation of certain industries except as monopolies. A large market would make possible mass production without this drawback. Attainment of these ends should, it was argued, make the unified area a more powerful unit, ensure continual expansion, increase economic stability, raise standards of living, and develop harmonious relations between its component states.[6]

Provisions of the Treaty of Rome

Customs Union   Central to the Treaty of Rome is the provision establishing a customs union of the original six nations. All tariffs between members on *industrial products* were to be abolished, and a uniform tariff adopted vis-à-vis other nations. To allow time for adjustment, a transition period of twelve to fourteen years was agreed on. During this period, duties on the trade between members were to be eliminated in three stages of four years each, in installments of 30, 30, and 40 percent in the successive stages.

Overseas territories (or former territories) of members were given the option of associating with the European Community. Imports from these territories were to receive the same treatment as those from the metropolitan country, and territorial duties (with exceptions for local overseas industries) were to be gradually reduced to the level applying to imports from the parent country.

The uniform external tariff was to be no higher than the average of the previous tariffs of members. In practice, this meant that it became somewhat higher than the tariffs of Benelux and Germany, somewhat lower than those of France and Italy. As for quantitative restrictions, the treaty provides for their gradual elimination. Although agricultural products are not exempted from these provisions, they raised so many problems as to require special treatment (see pp. 238ff.).

Economic Integration   The European Economic Community is far more than a customs union. Both as a means of ensuring the smooth flow of intraunion trade and as a basis for a closer future political relationship, the Treaty of Rome contains provisions for making the Common Market area into a unified economy. Mere elimination of frontier barriers to trade, it was felt, would be apropriate only for laissez faire economies. But in each of the member nations, government intervention, varying in degree and kind, strongly affected the operation of the economic system. National tax systems, especially those aspects relating to the financing of social security programs, bore with different weight on different industries. Both taxes and subsidies were used to support certain industries in one country, but not in others. And national policies for dealing with inflationary and defla-

[6] Organization for European Economic Cooperation, *Report Prepared by the Heads of Delegations of the Intergovernmental Committee Set Up by the Messina Conference to the Ministers of Foreign Affairs* (Paris: OEEC, Aug. 28, 1956).

tionary conditions could differ with respect to their character, intensity, and timing.

Unless these national policies were "harmonized," a labor-intensive industry subject to abnormally high social security charges would operate at a disadvantage; unsubsidized but efficient producers would be at the mercy of their subsidized rivals, and unsynchronized monetary and fiscal policies could provoke unwanted balance-of-payments disturbances. Moreover, monopolistic organizations in one country might, with the opening of the gates of trade, lead to the domination or possibly the extinction of competitive industry in another. Therefore, "to promote throughout the Community a harmonious development of economic activities," and "closer relations between its Member States," the community undertook a "progressive approximation" of their economic policies.

To accomplish this, the Treaty of Rome (Article 3) provided for

(1) the abolition, as between Member States, of the obstacles to the free movement of persons, services and capital;
(2) the inauguration of a common agricultural policy;
(3) the inauguration of a common transport policy;
(4) the establishment of a system ensuring that competition shall not be distorted in the Common Market;
(5) the application of procedures which shall make it possible to coordinate the economic policies of Member States and to remedy disequilibria in their balances of payments;
(6) the approximation of their respective legislations to the extent necessary for the functioning of the Common Market.

These provisions are very general. They were left to be worked out through hard bargaining around the conference table.

Special Aid Funds   It was foreseen that as tariffs were gradually abolished, industries hitherto dependent on protection might well be injured, even though they might be able to adjust over time by intensifying their specialization, improving efficiency, or converting to other lines of production. To help workers in these industries over their difficulties, a European Social Fund was established that meets half the costs of retraining employees and, if necessary, of moving them to new locations. In 1972, this fund was reshaped and enlarged for the better attainment of these objectives.

Aid to industrial proprietors is part of a larger project. This is the European Investment Fund, which has one primary function and two secondary functions. Its most important task is to furnish aid to improve conditions—as by financing basic community facilities—in the underdeveloped regions of member states. In addition, it helps finance projects of European importance that are too large to be handled alone by the individual states, and advances funds to firms encountering difficulties in reconversion. The fund had an initial capital of $1 billion, supplemented by loans raised in international capital markets.

Organization of the Community

With the entry into effect of the Treaty of Rome in 1958, the European Economic Community immediately confronted a great variety of tasks—establishing administrative agencies and their procedures, determining rules for the regulation of competition and agriculture, and preparing for the first installment of duty reductions. Since the community was to be a sort of supergovernment with respect to economic affairs, it needed specific agencies to act, legislate, and settle disputes. The treaty provides for a full complement of the necessary agencies.

The principal administrative body is the European Council, a sort of economic cabinet of the community. It consists of one member from each state and is the executive agent of the community, making daily decisions, formulating rules of conduct, preparing new legislation, and prodding members to carry out the provisions of the treaty. Aiding the council in its work is a fourteen-member European Commission, which oversees the application of the treaty, studies special problems, and makes recommendations to the council. As advisory bodies, there is a Monetary Committee to watch over balances of payments, examine disturbing developments, and recommend remedies, and the European Economic and Social Committee. The latter consists of representatives of industry, workers, farmers, retail trade, and the liberal professions; its area of concern is virtually unlimited.

The "legislative" branch consists of an assembly of 198 members, which does not as yet legislate but acts as a consultative body on recommendations of the Council. It performs the same function with respect to the European Coal and Steel Community and Euratom, the organization created to plan and administer the development of atomic energy resources for the six states.

Finally, there is a Court of Justice to adjudicate disputes, also shared in common with the ECSC and Euratom.

Implementation of the Treaty

Customs Union   In dealing with its most important single purpose, the establishment of a customs union, the original six members exceeded their target of eliminating all industrial duties on mutual trade and of erecting a common external tariff in twelve to fourteen years.

After only slightly more than eleven years, on July 1, 1968, the last of the series of duty reductions became effective: Full customs union was a reality.

That the gradual elimination of tariff barriers on intraunion trade had a substantial effect is suggested by the more rapid growth of imports from members than from nonmembers: 17.1 percent as against 9.2 percent between 1958 and 1965. Moreover, the share of EEC imports from member countries increased in the same period from 29.5 to 45.1 percent.[7]

Agriculture   For historical reasons, too many people remained on the land in France, Germany, and Italy as those nations became industrialized. National politics reinforced inertia to keep them on too numerous farms of uneconomic size. This legacy was reinforced by severe postwar shortages of foodstuffs, lack of foreign exchange to pay for imports, and demands of farmers for increased incomes, which led these nations to impose complex import restrictions and to adopt differing kinds and degrees of price supports. There resulted in each nation a pattern of agricultural production unsuited to its resources, an increase in output to satisfy domestic needs in many products, and much uneconomic production.

Harmonization of the widely divergent policies, essential if trade in agricultural products was to be freed, presented the most difficult obstacle for the community to overcome. Matters were not helped by the fact that the goals of agricultural policy laid down in the Treaty of Rome were themselves potentially inconsistent. These included an increase in productivity by means of technical progress and optimal use of resources, the establishment of reasonable prices for consumers, and higher earnings for farmers. All three could be reconciled through a long-range program of agricultural improvement, but farmers' earnings could also be raised by a short-run program of increasing prices. Severe conflict developed in the Council of Ministers, which was resolved only after protracted negotiations and the shelving of a long-range policy in favor of a short-run attack. This took the form of marketing arrangements to increase agricultural prices.

For products encountering foreign competition, which included most temperate-zone crops, target prices were to be established that were to be uniform throughout the community after allowing for transport charges. These are maintained by variable import duties that completely offset any price advantage enjoyed by competitive imports. For commodities whose production exceeds Common Market require-

---

[7] Lawrence B. Krause, *European Economic Integration and the United States* (Washington, D.C.: The Brookings Institution, 1968), pp. 22–23.

ments, subsidies are available to finance exports or additional community consumption. Funds for these subsidies come from import levies and, temporarily, from contributions by members.

These arrangements went fully into effect on July 1, 1968, establishing a single unified market for agricultural products simultaneously with the elimination of all duties on internal trade in manufactures. The target prices for grains set at that time were approximately 50 to 70 percent above 1964 landed import prices.

Other Aspects of Integration   Formal restrictions on the movement of labor ended with the establishment of the EEC, and, in practice, labor mobility has been high. Large numbers of Italian workers, in particular, have helped counteract labor shortage in Germany. In more recent years, workers from nonmembers, notably Greece, Yugoslavia, Spain, and Algeria have contributed substantially to supplement the native work force in France, Switzerland, and Germany.

With fixed exchange rates and no formal obstacles to its mobility, both short- and long-term capital have moved among community members with relative ease. But the international monetary disturbances of recent years led to the imposition of national restraints on capital movements of varying severity; presumably these will be short-lived. A notable effect of the formation of the EEC has been the attraction of its large, protected market for U.S. investment. This increased sharply after 1958 and caused alarm and opposition because, although it amounted to a small part of total European investment, it was concentrated in a few of the more advanced, research-intensive industries.

Monetary Union   At a summit conference in 1969, the EEC decided to establish monetary union, with either a common currency or irrevocably fixed exchange rates. This was to be accomplished by stages over a period of ten years, but has not come about (see Chapter 29).

Opinion within the community with respect to the requirements for monetary union has been sharply divided between those who insist that coordination of macroeconomic policies must come first and those who believe that the adoption of a common currency will bring policy coordination in its train. It seems dubious that monetary integration could occur before a thorough integration of capital markets and coordination of macroeconomic policies. Without the latter, any difference in national preferences with respect to rates of inflation and unemployment would lead to severe balance-of-payments problems. At the heart of the problem is the old conflict between national goals and a fixed exchange rate adjustment mechanism. A community member adopting a more inflationary set of policies could be forced, if a common currency or absolutely fixed exchange rates were to be preserved, to introduce exchange restrictions. This outcome can be avoided by policy coordination before monetary integration, or by accepting painful adjustment.[8]

Monopoly   Provisions with respect to monopolistic practices are stated in the Treaty of Rome in very general terms. Certain practices likely to interfere with competition are prohibited, but with exceptions when they contribute to technical progress or improved production or distribution of goods. Taking "unfair" advantage of a "dominant" position by one or more firms is also prohibited, but the crucial terms are not defined. Formulation of concrete antimonopoly policy began with the compulsory registration of cartel agreements and their subsequent approval or disapproval. As this procedure continues and as court cases are decided, the actual shape of EEC policy in this area will be determined.

Political Integration   In the earlier years of the EEC's existence, it was thought that political integration would follow closely upon economic integration, if only because many economic policies would have to be "harmonized" and this would require political decisions. It is true that such decisions have constantly to be made. But as the EEC has evolved, these decisions are made separately in the individual capitals of the member nations and reported back to Brussels. They are not made collectively in Brussels by a group of Europeans thinking as Europeans. What we see today is not political union, but agreed community policies in the economic area reached by negotiation and compromise.

Associated Countries   Agreements with eighteen former French and Belgian colonies establish free entry for their imports, and provide certain preferences to exports of community members. Kenya, Tanzania, and Uganda, as former countries of the Commonwealth, are associated with the EEC under similar provisions. As already noted, the EEC also accords the generalized system of preferences to all less-developed countries. In addition, association agreements have granted trade preferences to practically all countries bordering the Mediterranean. (These agreements run counter to the rules of GATT, which forbid discrimination among suppliers, except for members of a free trade area or a customs union.) The net result of all these preferential arrangements is that the United States, Japan, and Canada are the only im-

---

[8] On this issue, see J. Marcus Fleming, "On Exchange Rate Unification," *Economic Journal*, **81** (Sept. 1971); M. Hall and D. Tanna, "On Exchange Rate Unification: A Comment"; and J. R. Presley and P. Coffey, "On Exchange Rate Unification: A Comment in Relation to the EEC," *Economic Journal*, **82** (Dec. 1972).

portant industrial countries whose products are dutiable at standard, nonpreferential rates in the larger part of western Europe.

Gains from Integration

The architects of the EEC anticipated that economic integration would yield substantial benefits, both of a static and dynamic variety. Despite the statistical pitfalls that surround any attempt to isolate the effects of integration from those of normal growth, changes in consumer preferences, conditions of supply, or general trade liberalization, a number of studies of the static effects of integration—of trade creation and trade diversion—have been made. If we use various techniques to get around the statistical difficulties, they all show the same direction of change and the disparity in their magnitudes is not excessive. Trade creation was substantial and far in excess of trade diversion. Taking an unweighted average of three comprehensive estimates, including his own, Kreinin[9] arrives at the following results. For the years 1967–1968, annual trade creation in manufactured goods amounted to $3.9 billion, or three times the annual trade diversion of $1.3 billion. For 1969–1970, trade creation was $8.9 billion, nearly eight times trade diversion of $1.1 billion. "On balance, the static effects of EEC have been highly favourable to world efficiency."[10]

Dynamic effects, due to the creation of a much larger market and its stimulus to growth through economies of scale, greater investment, and intensified competition, are almost impossible to distinguish from the effects of normal growth. Probably they, too, were positive.

Expansion of the European Community

After prolonged negotiations between four members of the European Free Trade Association (see the next section) and the EEC, accompanied by lively public debate within those nations, the United Kingdom, Ireland, and Denmark joined the European Community on January 1, 1973. During a five-year transition period, trade barriers between these nations and original EEC members were abolished. The common agricultural policy was adopted within four years, and capital movements also gradually liberated. As for Britain's special relations with the Commonwealth, the status quo continued until 1975, when the larger Commonwealth countries negotiated trade agreements with the enlarged EEC; the smaller countries were given various options. Owing to their special importance, imports into Britain of Commonwealth

[9] Mordecai E. Kreinin, "Effects of the EEC on Imports of Manufactures," *Economic Journal,* **82** (Sept. 1972).
[10] Ibid., p. 916.

sugar and New Zealand dairy products were reduced gradually until the common community tariff became applicable. The membership grew to a total of ten when Greece joined on January 1, 1981. Like other new members, Greece was given a transition period of five years for reducing tariffs with other members and the application of farm policy. Longer transition periods were permitted for implementation of full freedom for the movement of workers and for some sensitive agricultural products.

Waiting in the wings are Portugal and Spain, both of which underwent transitions to democratic government in the 1970s. Negotiations began in 1978 and 1979, and continue in early 1983.

The European Free Trade Association

During the years before the signing of the Treaty of Rome, Britain showed little interest in joining the endeavors of the Six, but instead proposed the formation of a larger Free Trade Association whose scope would have been limited to the elimination of tariffs between members on industrial products. At that time, the British government declined to consider any union encompassing agricultural commodities because its own agricultural policy gave consumers the benefit of prices kept low by duty-free imports from the Commonwealth, while it supported domestic agriculture by direct payments from the Treasury.

In 1959, faced with the Common Market as an established fact, unwilling to join, and fearful of its effect on her trade, the British government, with six other nations, formed the rival European Free Trade Association. A gradual, step-by-step reduction of duties on intra-area trade in industrial products culminated in their complete elimination at the end of 1966, one year and a half before the EEC reached the same stage.[11] Each member of the EFTA retained its own external tariff; agricultural products continued to be governed by each member's individual set of policies.

Despite great differences in the size and economic status of members—the United Kingdom in economic terms constituted more than half the entire association—and despite their geographical dispersion, the EFTA enjoyed considerable success. Intra-area imports rose sharply in the six years after 1958 compared to trade with other countries, by 11.3 percent as against 7.6 percent. The share of member-country imports also increased, from 17.6 percent to 21.2 percent. This latter figure contrasts with the much larger one for EEC imports from members of 45.1 percent.

There seems little doubt that the EFTA was intended initially as

[11] Krause, op. cit., p. 17.

a counterweight to the European Common Market, to endure only until its members could obtain admission to the latter. The first such effort came in 1961, when Britain, followed by all the other EFTA countries except Portugal, applied for membership in the EEC. Negotiations continued for over a year until January 1963, when de Gaulle slammed the door shut with his veto. French opposition continued through 1967, but later was dissipated. With the entry of the United Kingdom, Ireland, and Denmark into the community at the beginning of 1973, the EFTA became truncated into a five-member organization (Austria, Sweden, Switzerland, Portugal, and Norway). This shrinkage, however, would appear to be but temporary. A Special Relations Agreement among Sweden, Switzerland, Austria, Portugal, and the EEC went into force simultaneously with the entry of Britain, Ireland, and Denmark into the community. It provided for gradual tariff reductions on industrial products and an eventual free trade area of fifteen nations. Finland and Iceland, which had been associated with EFTA through special arrangements, also joined the new agreement.

As EFTA entered its third decade, the 1980s, it consisted of the four Nordic countries—Iceland, Norway, Sweden, and Finland (an associate member)—plus Austria, Switzerland, and Portugal. The access obtained to the EEC market, together with their own free trade arrangements, means that the EFTA members are part of the biggest industrial market that exists, some 300 million high-income people. The principal difference between the EEC and EFTA is that the latter have not moved beyond free trade in industrial goods, and in particular have made no attempts to integrate themselves monetarily or politically. The relative political neutrality has been especially important for Finland, Sweden, Switzerland, and Austria. Portugal, and to some extent Norway, continue to feel the need to integrate themselves further with the European Economic Community on the political level, for they feel more akin politically to the nine NATO members of the ten-member EEC than to the neutralist-dominated EFTA.

ECONOMIC UNION IN LATIN AMERICA

The Latin American Free Trade Area

With their wide differences in governmental structure and in political temper, the nations of Latin American have not had a comparable political basis for forming an economic union. They share, however, a common interest in protecting and expanding their trade and in promoting their economic development. Although their trade has been growing, its rate of expansion has been slow. During the 1950s, Latin America's share of free world exports actually fell from 11 percent to 8 percent. Moreover, one-fourth of Latin American exports went to the European Common Market, and of this, half consisted of commodities adversely affected by European preference for the products of associated African nations. The low level of intra-Latin American trade, too—only about 10 percent of total trade—has been a cause for concern.

Discussion of the possibility of establishing arrangements that would strengthen the Latin American trade position—in particular, any that would stimulate increased intra-area trade and contribute to regional economic development—began in 1954. For several years, ideas on this topic were exchanged, with the Economic Commission for Latin American playing a leading role. Finally, seven countries—Argentina, Brazil, Chile, Paraguay, Peru, and Uruguay in South America, and Mexico—reached sufficient agreement to formalize their views in the Treaty of Montevideo, which was signed on February 18, 1960, and entered into force on July 1, 1961. Three additional countries, Colombia, Ecuador, and Bolivia, later joined the original seven.

The declared purposes of the treaty were the liberalization of intra-Latin American trade, the promotion of complementarity of industrial production, and the coordination of agricultural development and trade. It was hoped that trade liberalization would be achieved through the gradual elimination, over a period of twelve years, of all duties and restrictions on mutual trade. Although there was no provision for a common external tariff, the treaty urged members to work toward uniform treatment of imports of capital, goods, and services from third countries, with the prospect at some later date of establishing a common market of all twenty Latin American countries.

Hope was also expressed that a more economic allocation of manufacturing industries might be realized, with accompanying internal and external economies, through national specialization. To this end, the treaty authorized "complementarity agreements," which would presumably reserve certain industries to some countries, others to different countries.

The goal of coordinating agricultural development and trade policies was expressed in very general terms. Much more specifically, the opposite goal of national insulation was then supported by a provision that enabled a member to limit agricultural imports to the amount by which customary consumption exceeds home production.

The Treaty of Montevideo provided a framework that could, given the will to make it work, have lead to the formation of a true common market for all Latin America. There were, however, many obstacles to be overcome: the vested interests of national producers, both industrial and agricultural; the continuance of bilateral trading and payments arrangements by many countries; and a vague feeling of distrust and uncertainty among the members of negotiating bodies. The participants, it is true, agreed to duty reductions on several thousand items, but few if any of these cuts were large enough or on sufficiently important products to register any significant progress. Provincial nationalism continued to dominate the scene; it has yet to give way to a widespread conviction as to the benefits of community action. Twenty years after its inception, the Latin American Free Trade Area died.

A subgroup of the LAFTA that survives is the Andean pact. It now consists of Bolivia, Colombia, Ecuador, Peru, and Venezuela. Chile, once a member, withdrew in 1976. It has succeeded in negotiating some specialization arrangements, but has been unable to agree on mutual tariff reductions, and has been hurt by the outbreak of fighting in a border dispute between Ecuador and Peru in 1981.

Central American Economic Integration

Integration moved much faster in Central America. Three separate agreements were signed by five countries (Costa Rica, El Salvador, Guatemala, Honduras, and Nicaragua) in 1958 and 1959, but in the following year these were incorporated in a more comprehensive document, the General Treaty of Central American Economic Integration. Aiming at the creation within five years of a customs union with a common external tariff, it established free trade immediately in all products originating in the five member countries, barring a rather large number of exceptions to be liberalized gradually.

There was also provision for economic integration through the agreed assignment of certain industries to specific countries. A Central American Economic Integration Bank was established in May 1961 with capital of $16 million to support closer economic union by helping to finance agricultural, industrial, or social overhead projects of interest to the entire community.

Considering the relatively low stage of development of the Central American republics, even their union into a group with a population of 10 million, will not guarantee a prosperous market for industrial production. Exports consist, to the extent of approximately 80 percent, of coffee and bananas; there is little industry in the area and that small in scale; and economic growth is inhibited by illiteracy, primitive agricultural methods, a small and comparatively unenterprising middle class, poor communications, and a general power shortage. Yet there are few efficient light industries; greater competition could stimulate others to improve; and with financial help still others may emerge. The least one can say is that the union of five small countries into a single market might afford some additional stimulus to growth, a stimulus that would increase as basic economic development proceeds.

However, years after its establishment, the Central American Common Market began to come apart. Political frictions developed after the brief armed conflict between Honduras and El Salvador in 1969. El Salvador began in 1970 to regulate its trade with the other countries; a year later, Honduras imposed duties on Central American Common Market imports. Trade between Costa Rica and three of the members was suspended briefly because of foreign exchange problems, but resolved by devaluation of Costa Rica's currency.

Twenty years later, the growing political frictions in the region do not give grounds for optimism about the future economic integration of the region. Political stability and consensus are a necessary condition for economic integration.

SELECTED REFERENCES

BALDWIN, R. E. "The Tokyo Round of Multilateral Trade Negotiations." Chapter 15 in R. E. Baldwin and J. D. Richardson, *International Trade and Finance: Readings,* 2nd ed., Boston: Little, Brown and Company, 1981. An analysis of the results of the Tokyo Round of GATT.

CLINE, W. R., and E. DELGADO, eds. *Economic Integration in Central America.* Washington, D.C.: The Brookings Institution, 1978. A collection of papers on the subject.

———, et al. *Trade Negotiations in the Tokyo Round.* Washington, D.C.: The Brookings Institution, 1978. A review of the issues on the negotiating table in the Tokyo Round.

COFFEY, P., ed. *The Economic Policy of the Common Market.* London: Macmillan Publishers Ltd., 1979.

CURZON, G. *Multilateral Commercial Diplomacy.* London: Michael Joseph Ltd., 1965. A thorough history of commercial policy negotiations.

JENSEN, FINN B., and INGO WALTER. *The Common Market: Economic Integration in Europe.* Philadelphia: J. B. Lippincott Company, 1965. (Paperback.) A good earlier work on details of the structure and working of the EEC.

KRAUSS, MELVYN B. "Recent Developments in Customs Union Theory: An Interpretive Survey." *Journal of Economic Literature,* **10** (June 1972).

SAVAGE, K. *The History of the Common Market,* 2nd ed. London: Kestrel Books, 1976.

14
CHAPTER

Developing Countries and the International System

In the second half of the twentieth century the family of nations expanded dramatically. The 51 soverign nations that had formed the United Nations in 1945 had expanded to 157 members by 1982. The remarkable expansion of the sheer number of members of the international community also changed the nature of the international economy. Most of the newly formed countries are also relatively poor, often newly independent after a colonial experience, and many are producers of primary commodities.

The new members of the international economy have accepted the tenets of the international political system, but the climate of the economic relationship between rich and poor states is cool, if not antagonistic. The difference in the economic sphere springs in part from the absolute income gap between rich and poor nations, and in part from the fact that many of the leaders of the new members of the international community do not share the belief in the value of a competitive international economy fettered by commitments to freedom of trade and payments.

This chapter takes up the issue of the international economic relationship between the rich and poor nations.

THE NATURE OF POVERTY IN THE POOR COUNTRIES

To set the stage it is important to understand the nature of poverty in the poor countries of the world. In the 1980s very large numbers of the

Table 14.1 Selected Indicators, Rich and Poor Nations, 1950–1980

I. **Income:** Real GNP per capita, 1980 U.S. dollars	*1950*	*1960*	*1980*
Industrialized countries	3841	5197	9684
Middle-income countries	625	802	1521
Low-income countries	164	174	245

II. **Health:** Life expectancy at birth, years	*1950*	*1960*	*1978*
Industrialized countries	66	69	74
Middle-income countries	52	54	61
Low-income countries	35	42	50

III. **Education:** Adult literacy rate, percent	*1950*	*1960*	*1975*
Industrialized countries	95	97	99
Middle-income countries	48	54	71
Low-income countries	22	29	38

SOURCE: World Bank, *World Development Report, 1980*, Washington, D.C., 1980, Figure 4.1, p. 34.
NOTES: The data exclude centrally planned economies. The industrialized countries range from Ireland through Finland, the United States, to Switzerland. The middle-income countries range from Egypt through Chile to Singapore, Spain, and Israel. The low-income countries include Bangladesh, Mali, Togo, and Indonesia.

world's population remain in absolute poverty. Some simple indicators give a stark picture: about 600 million adults illiterate; 550 million people living in countries where the average life expectancy is less than 50 years; 400 million people living in countries where the death rate of children aged one to four is 20 times that of industralized countries. In all, about 780 million people live in absolute poverty.[1]

Since World War II there has been some significant progress in the fight against poverty, but the absolute gap between rich and poor nations has widened. Thus the selected indicators contained in Table 14.1 reveal that in real terms per capita income in the low-income countries grew absolutely between 1950 and 1980. The improvements in life expectancy at birth and in adult literacy rates have been dramatic reflections of this improvement. The faster real growth in income in the industralized countries, nevertheless, has increased the absolute difference in per capita income.

[1] The data are from the World Bank, *World Development Report, 1980* (Washington, D.C.: World Bank, 1980), and exclude China and other centrally planned economies.

It is against this backdrop that the spokesmen of the poor countries have entered the debate on the role of their nations in the international economic system. Another important part of the issue is the question of whether or not international trade contributes to alleviation of poverty and growth of real incomes.

TRADE AND ECONOMIC DEVELOPMENT

From our study of the theory of international trade, we learned that nations can maximize their incomes by specializing in production and exchanging their specialized products with one another. Free trade, by promoting the most efficient worldwide allocation of resources, effects the equivalent of an upward shift in the production possibilities curve of each nation. Protection, which interferes with this efficient resource allocation, can be justified only under limited and highly restrictive circumstances.

This analysis, although valid, has its own limitations: It applies to a given moment or a short interval of time; it reflects a cross-sectional, static point of view that makes no allowance for the passage of time and the changes that it brings. Economic development, however, is a process, a dynamic unfolding of interrelated events, that contrasts sharply with the static character of the traditional doctrine of comparative cost.

There are, however, elements of a dynamic theory in some of the classical literature of international trade, elements that strongly suggest that trade exerts an important influence on economic development. Thus it has been noted that trade opens up markets for a country's specialized production, increasing employment, raising profits, and providing the basis both for larger savings and their investment in expanded output. As production grows, economies of scale may be realized, innovations stimulated, and productive efficiency raised. Without trade, the importation of capital goods, so essential to a nation's growth, would be impossible. Trade also acquaints people with new and attractive goods that act as incentives to greater effort. According to a later but not inconsistent view, trade may even induce capital, enterprise, and labor to migrate to the site of natural resources, there to develop a thriving export industry. In all these ways, trade acts as an "engine of growth," in Sir Dennis Robertson's phrase, that powerfully stimulates a country's development.[2]

---

[2] D. H. Robertson, "The Future of International Trade," *Economic Journal*, **48** (Mar. 1938).

During the nineteenth and early twentieth centuries, this "engine" functioned efficiently. Large and growing markets in Britain and Europe led to rapid expansion of the exports of primary producing countries, principally the newer countries in the temperate zones: the United States, Canada, Australia, New Zealand, Argentina, Uruguay, and South Africa. Opportunities to improve their lot attracted a high flow of immigrants, bring with them skills, the culture of western Europe, and some capital. By 1870 one-third of British capital exports went to these regions to build railways, sink mine shafts, and finance cattle and wheat ranches; by 1913 it amounted to two-thirds.[3] As the new nations grew in population and wealth, local markets became large enough to justify the rise of manufacturing industries.

Since World War I, international trade has been far less effective in transmitting growth from an expanding center to outlying areas. For one thing, the rate of growth of trade has slackened off. The focal center of world advance, although still progressing vigorously, has emitted a stimulus of diminishing intensity to the rest of the world. Whereas between 1850 and 1880, the volume of world trade rose by 270 percent, and between 1880 and 1913 by 170 percent, from 1928 to 1958 it increased only 57 percent.[4] Until after 1953, instead of expanding more rapidly than world output, it grew more slowly.

The reasons for this development can be found in a combination of forces tending to depress the demand for primary products.[5]

1. Technical change has reduced the relative industrial use of raw materials; improved processes have achieved large economies in raw material consumption; synthetics have increasingly displaced natural raw materials (silk, wool, nitrates, rubber, hides, and skins); heavy industries (engineering and chemicals), whose raw-material consumption is relatively low, have grown faster than light industries in the industrial countries.
2. As incomes have risen in the industrial countries, an increased proportion has been spent on services.
3. The income elasticity of demand for many agricultural commodities is low.
4. High duties in western Europe have impeded the import of agricultural products.

If the stimulus to growth that operated so effectively in the nineteenth century has waned, it is also true that the character of the economies stimulated is different today. The new nations that grew so rap-

---

[3] R. Nurkse, *Patterns of Trade and Development* (Oxford: Basil Blackwell Publisher Ltd., 1961), p. 17.
[4] Ibid., p. 19n.
[5] Ibid., p. 23.

idly before World War I were in the temperate zones; they inherited the culture, the skills, and the institutions of a dynamic civilization. The emerging nations of the mid-twentieth century are mainly in the tropics; they consist of traditional peasant societies, countries that inherited and still retain in large part a feudal system of great landed estates and isolated tribal economies. Their nature is such that they respond with far less vigor to a stimulus that has weakened. It is therefore no mystery why international trade is a less effective engine of growth than in earlier decades, why the underdeveloped nations of today remain stagnant, while continued progress in the advanced countries further widens the gap in standards of living.

Instead of relying on trade as an engine of growth, the careful analysis of W. Arthur Lewis suggests that the engine of growth for today's developing countries is more appropriately technological change, "with international trade serving as lubricating oil and not as fuel."[6] Those developing countries that continue to depend on trade per se as engines are doomed to frustration of their ambitions.

The analytical economic debate does not, however, resolve the political debate. Developing-country spokesmen remain adamant in their demands for some form of new international economic order. It is to the latter debate that we now turn.

THE NEW INTERNATIONAL ECONOMIC ORDER

There emerged in the 1970s a set of demands for what was termed a "New International Economic Order." The low-income countries contended that the international economy was *not* functioning in their interests and that it should be changed to do so. What were some of the major bones of contention? What is the evidence about these issues? These matters lie at the heart of the relationship—actual and proposed—of the low-income countries to the international economy.

Bases of Contention

The case for a New International Economic Order rests in the first instance on the allegation that the actual order of the 1970s and 1980s was inappropriate or unjust. The evidence cited includes many elements, but rests principally on a comparison of the shares of income and population of the industrial countries relative to those of the Third

---

[6] W. Arthur Lewis, *The Evolution of the International Economic Order* (Princeton, N.J.: Princeton University Press, 1978), p. 74.

World countries, such as we cited in Table 14.1. The discrepancy in per capita incomes between the rich industrialized countries and the rest, and the absence of any hope of closing the gap, is the real issue. This difference, of course, manifests itself in many different ways.

First, most international economic agencies such as the IMF and the World Bank distribute voting power on the basis of economic power. Hence a coalition of the majority of the world's population or a majority of the number of countries is unable to force decisions that favor the Third World countries. The rich countries have the votes.

Second, the distribution of international monetary reserves does not reflect the "need" for those reserves. In the early 1980s the industrial countries, representing less than a fifth of the world's population, held over half of the world reserves, while the non-oil developing countries held about one-fifth. Furthermore, creation of new reserves remains in the hands of the reserve currencies and the IMF. Hence, to obtain more reserves, the poorer countries must, in effect, pay seigniorage to the industrial countries (see Chapter 30).

Third, assistance from industrial countries to Third World countries has declined as a proportion of the GNP of the former group. In 1960 official development assistance amounted to one-half of 1 percent of GNP of the industrial countries. In 1970 the proportion had fallen to just over one-third of 1 percent, and remained virtually constant into the early 1980s.[7] Particularly noteworthy in this respect has been a decline of U.S. official development assistance to less than one-fifth of 1 percent of GNP in the early 1980s.

This decline in the proportion of GNP allocated as aid, the Third World proponents argue, demonstrates that necessary support will not be forthcoming voluntarily and therefore requires a formal change of institutional arrangements to ensure a more appropriate level of income transfers from the rich to poor countries. It should be noted, however, that the *absolute real* value of aid has continued to rise, growing by about 40 percent in the period 1970–1981.

Fourth, the so-called free international economy is far from free. Many barriers to poor country access to markets in the industrial countries continue to exist. Successful exporters in Third World countries find their products quickly subjected to restrictions imposed to protect inefficient industries in the importing countries. The structure of protection also discriminates against processing in developing countries, with the frequent result that they have to ship primary products to

---

[7] The Development Assistance Committee of the OECD annually collects and publishes a consistent set of data on official development assistance disbursed by the OECD's twenty-four member countries. The latest data are usually featured in an article in *The OECD Observer*, bimonthly, Paris.

industrial countries for further processing, then buy back the processed products at inflated prices.

Fifth, the developing countries have built up an enormous debt to private and public agencies in the industrial countries. Recent data show a nearly sixfold increase in debt of non-OPEC developing countries from 1971 to 1981, and a tenfold increase in the debt service burden.[8] The borrowing countries regard this burden as excessive and often unfair becuse it was incurred by exploitative contracts, or was undertaken by ineffective or even corrupt former governments.

Finally, it is argued that the multinational corporations have taken unfair advantage of developing countries in the past. Because of their relatively weak bargaining position, and desperate need for investment capital and new techniques, developing countries believe they have granted excessively generous concessions to multinationals (MNCs). Furthermore, MNCs are accused of internal political interference to maintain those concessions. MNCs are also accused of having an unwarranted control over technology, and of using that control to limit the transfer of technology to developing countries.

The UN Program for Action on a NIEO

Proponents of a New International Economic Order argue that such a state of affairs should not be allowed to persist. Yet demands in the political arena for a NIEO had relatively little effect until the successful action by OPEC in 1973 to raise world oil prices. This action created both a serious problem for the non-oil developing countries and at the same time served as a symbol for all developing countries that joint action could alter the substance of economic relationships. The latter realization led to the adoption by the United Nations, at a Special Session of the General Asembly in the spring of 1974, of a "Declaration and Programme of Action on the Establishment of a New International Economic Order." The U.N. program addressed rich–poor country issues.[9]

Trade

The principal focus was on trade matters, especially on improving access to world markets and on exerting some control over those markets in the interest of the developing countries. The vehicle for achieving such trade reforms was an "Integrated Commodity Program" directed at trade in both primary and manufactured products.

[8] "Aid in 1981," *The OECD Observer*, No. 117, July 1982.
[9] See E. Laszlo and J. Lozoya, *The Objectives of the New International Economic Order* (Elmsford, N.Y.: Pergamon Press, Inc., 1978).

In the primary commodity sphere the NIEO proposals seek not only to improve the terms of trade of developing countries' primary commodity exports, but also to stabilize their prices and earnings. These objectives would be achieved by establishing international buffer stocks and managing supplies of primary commodities. To accomplish this, a Common Fund was proposed to act as a banker to finance the various schemes. The cost of such a fund, however, proved so great that it has not been established. Just as fundmental as the cost is the potential benefit. This depends very much on the nature of the commodity, the nature of the disturbances affecting its market, and whether or not *price* instability results in *earnings* instability. Some commodities cannot be stored (e.g., bananas), while others are so heterogeneous that it is impossible to specify the precise type that should be used to buffer the market (e.g., leather hides). Moreover, if disturbances are primarily in supplies, a stabilized price would *destabilize* earnings because price fluctuations would no longer offset quantity fluctuations.[10]

The long-standing objective of improving the terms of trade of primary commodities was also a major focus in the U.N.'s approach. The vehicle for accomplishing this objective was to restrict the supply of primary exports. The validity of such an approach has been contested in the industrial countries on the grounds that the income transfer would not be related to need: The poorer countries would not necessarily be the principal gainers, and the poorer people within those countries would not necessarily receive the benefits. In fact, any effective price *increasing* scheme must restrict supply and is likely to create unemployment, to the benefit of the owners of the primary resources (land or mineral). Criticism has also been leveled at the proposals on other grounds: (1) that many industrial countries which are also primary producers, such as Canada, would also receive income transfers; (2) that demand elasticity for many commodities is relatively high, so that a price increase would induce a self-defeating switch to substitutes; and (3) that producers who do not participate in the restriction of supply would receive a free ride and could in the end sabotage the cartel arrangements.

The developing countries, and more especially, those among them that have been labeled recently as the "Newly Industrializing Countries," such as Taiwan, Brazil, and Argentina, have also been concerned about their access to international markets in manufactures. In the First U.N. Conference on Trade and Development (1964) the idea of a general system of preferences for developing countries was urged on the industrialized nations. Although many accepted the arrangement,

[10] See D. T. Nguyen, "The Implications of Price Stabilization for the Short-Term Instability and Long-Term Level of LDCs' Export Earnings," *Quarterly Journal of Economics*, **93**, 1979.

the degree of preference granted has been relatively limited. A large proportion of developing country exports, being primary products already enter duty free, and of the remainder, many were excluded from the "generalized" schemes or limited by quotas.

Although the degree of preference granted has not been large, the growth in manufactures of the industralizing nations and the generalized liberalization of international trade have together resulted in a remarkable transformation in the composition of developing country exports. A World Bank study in 1977 estimated that manufacturing as a proportion of non-oil exports of developing countries had grown from but 10 percent in 1955 to 21 percent in 1967 and to 41 percent in 1977.[11]

Aid and Debt

A second major thrust of the NIEO concerned assistance to developing countries. Each industrial nation was called upon to meet the official U.N. development assistance target of a minimum of seven-tenths of 1 percent of GNP in foreign aid. Further, in recognition of the fact that many developing countries were carrying a substantial debt load, the NIEO contained a controversial proposal for the renegotiation of those debts.

Prior to the first great oil price increase in 1973, individual developing countries had on occasion found themselves facing insurmountable debt problems. Sometimes this had even led to occupation of their customs houses for several years by a foreign government to collect the debt, as illustrated by U.S. occupation of the Dominican Republic from 1916 to 1930. On other occasions this debt problem has been resolved by mutual agreement to reschedule debts, as with Ghana after the overthrow of Nkrumah in 1966. The first great oil price rise of 1973, however, led to such a massive and widespread increase in debt and debt service obligations as to bring this problem into the limelight. The 1974 NIEO Program focused attention on the debt issue, while the UNCTAD conference in 1975 proposed generalized debt relief for all developing countries, especially for the poorest. Several industrial nations have converted past loans to the poorer developing countries into grants. Such total cancellation amounted to over $6 billion. To put this into perspective, note that this amounted to about 15 percent of outstanding official debt of the poorer developing countries in 1977.

The problem of debts of developing countries continues in the 1980s. If we take 1973 as the last year before the great oil price rise

---

[11] World Bank, *Prospects for Developing Countries 1978–1985* (Washington, D.C.: World Bank, 1977).

affected debts, we observe the long-term external debt of non-oil developing countries rising from less than $100 billion in 1973 to more than $500 billion in 1982.[12] Yet that absolute increase embodies a significant amount of both inflation and real economic growth. The ratio of external debt to GNP over the same period grew from nearly 17 percent to just over 25 percent, and now amounts to a little more than one year's exports.

In some respects the problem is not a governmental problem at all. Over 60 percent of the debt in 1982 was to private creditors, thus reflecting a growing success of the international economy in facilitating financial intermediation between lenders and borrowers. Nonetheless, the worldwide recession of 1982, combined with high real interest rates, brought into sharper focus than ever before the burden of the debt. Debt service, consisting of interest and amortization, rose in 1982 to over 22 percent of exports of the non-oil developing countries, compared with a proportion hovering around 14 percent in the period 1973–1977. Meanwhile, the oil-exporting developing countries were struggling, not always successfully, to meet payments on their debts which had been contracted in a much more optimistic era.

The sheer size of the burden brought renewed calls for some official form of relief. In the NIEO proposals in the 1970s attention had been focused on the roles and voting powers in the World Bank and the IMF. The principal complaint has been about conditions the IMF attaches to its assistance. Critics argue that the IMF has unwarranted leverage over the policies of the debtor country, and should be prepared to grant massive unconditional assistance to debt-ridden countries. Its leverage arises because other official as well as private creditors generally take the IMF's evaluation of a debtor's internal program as evidence of financial soundness.

The Fund, while remaining committed to the principle of conditionality, has been remarkably responsive to the needs of the developing countries by creating new borrowing facilities that reflect their problems. The buffer stock financing facility, the oil facility, the extended fund facility, and the creation of the trust fund with the proceeds of the IMF gold sales have all been primarily for developing countries (see Chapter 30).

Conclusion

The developing countries have not succeeded in persuading the industrial nations to accept their proposals for a "New International Eco-

[12] International Money Fund, *World Economic Outlook* (Washington, D.C.: IMF, 1982).

nomic Order." Nevertheless, what has emerged in the period since World War II has been a remarkable integration of the developing countries into the international economy. The resulting interdependence is aptly illustrated by the fact that one-fourth of U.S. exports go to developing countries, and the United States relies extensively on developing countries for her imports.[13] Hence *both* the developing and the industrial countries have an interest in the growth and effective functioning of the international economy.

SELECTED REFERENCES

BHAGWATI, J., ed. *The New International Economic Order: The North–South Debate.* Cambridge, Mass.: The MIT Press, 1977.

CLINE, W. R., ed. *Policy Alternatives for a New International Economic Order.* New York: Praeger Publishers, 1979.

CORDEN, W. M. "The NIEO Proposals, A Cool Look." In R. E. Baldwin and J. D. Richardson, *International Trade and Finance: Readings,* 2nd ed., Boston: Little, Brown and Company, 1981. A careful analysis by an economist who is sympathetic to the goals of the developing countries but skeptical about the efficiency of the means proposed.

KREININ, M. E., and J. FINGER. "A Critical Survey of the New International Economic Order." *Journal of World Trade Law* (Nov./Dec. 1976).

LEWIS, W. A. *The Evolution of the International Economic Order.* Princeton, N.J.: Princeton University Press, 1978. A set of lectures on how the evolution of the existing international economic order came into existence and how it has been changing.

MACBEAN, A. *A Positive Approach to the International Economic Order,* Part I: *Trade and Structural Adjustment,* and Part II (with V. N. Balasubramanyam): *Non-Trade Issues.* London: British–North American Committee, 1978 (Part I) and 1980 (Part II). A clear basic analysis from a sympathetic viewpoint.

MURRAY, T. *Trade Preferences for Developing Countries.* London: Macmillan Publishers, Ltd. 1977. A study of the generalized system of preferences.

WORLD BANK. *World Development Report,* annual, since 1978. A very useful review of development issues and a ready source of reference data.

---

[13] William R. Cline, ed., *Policy Alternatives for a New International Economic Order* (New York: Praeger Publishers, 1979).

PART
4

INTERNATIONALISM AND ITS RIVAL

15
CHAPTER

The Growth of an International Economy

The body of theory whose study we have just completed explains the bases on which international trade rests and indicates in what ways nations can benefit from the specialization trade makes possible. In pointing to these gains, the theory serves as a policy prescription that has found wide, though not universal, acceptance. As a model that describes reality, however, it can be valid only if a number of critical assumptions are at least approximated in practice.

The more important of these are that capital and labor shall be highly mobile within a single country, substantially less so between countries; and the production and merchandising shall be effectively competitive. But for competition to be effective, buyers and sellers must be able to communicate readily with one another. This implies that trade shall be free, especially of direct quantitative restrictions, which impose a rigid limit on the amount of goods traded, and that currencies shall be at least partially convertible into one another, for without convertibility contact between national markets is lost.

Europe in 1815

Conditions in the real world of the early nineteenth century were far different from those postulated in the theoretical model. Only in Great Britain and Holland was it comparatively easy for capital and labor to seek out those industries or occupations in which returns were highest, owing to the fact that in these countries alone had thoroughgoing national unification been achieved. Internal barriers to trade were non-

261

existent. The feudal order was a thing of the past; in Holland a good canal system and in England canals, coastal shipping, and recently improved roads quickened the movements of goods and people. Men of commerce had long dominated the political and economic affairs of the Netherlands. In Great Britain, energetic and enterprising businessmen had already revolutionized the production of iron and cotton textiles and were spreading the new techniques over an everwidening range of industry. Although the landed aristocracy still dominated Parliament, the political influence of the business class was steadily increasing. British agriculture, too, had but recently undergone a revolutionary change in technology and provided a prosperous and efficient model for others to copy.

On the Continent, on the other hand, local tariffs, dues, and tolls impeded commerce, even in countries as united as France. Germany and Italy were still divided into petty kingdoms and principalities. ("Germany" consisted of some 300 independent territories, each with its own customs and currency system, and using a bewildering variety of weights and measures.) The mercantilist system retained feudal remnants binding the peasant to the land and concentrating its ownership in the hands of a favored few. Capital was scarce and the enterprise to use it even scarcer.

As for international trade, the complex mercantilist structure of tariffs, prohibitions, bounties, and shipping regulations continued unimpaired. Even in Britain, the Navigation Acts were still in force, and what Adam Smith said in 1776 could have been repeated in 1815 with little change.

During the nineteenth century all this changed. Northwestern Europe became industrialized; its agriculture was improved; people and investment funds flowed from Britain, France, and Germany to the Americas and other regions new and old; and the mercantilist structure was thoroughly dismantled. From about 1860 until the outbreak of World War I, one could say that the world of fact reasonably approximated the world of our theoretical model. It will be the task of this chapter to trace the main changes that occurred and to sketch the principal features of the international economy that they brought into being.

Three aspects of change in the ninteenth century will be stressed. First is the rise of Great Britain to a position of economic and political preeminence, and the accompanying emergence of London as the world's economic nerve center. Second is the rapid economic growth of western Europe and then of the overseas regions settled by Europeans. And finally, there is the demolition of the surviving remnants of mercantilism, the restrictions on foreign trade. These strands of history were, of course, closely interwoven; it is possible to distinguish them only for purposes of analysis. Together they produced the institutions and the forces that constituted a truly international economy.

THE RISE OF BRITAIN

Industry

During the sixty years between 1815 and 1875, the Industrial Revolution continued its work of transforming the predominantly agrarian economy of Britain into the workshop of the world. The weaving of cotton textiles, still a handloom operation at the turn of the century, gradually gave way to machinery. By 1875 the handloom was extinct. A few years later the woolen industry, too, succumbed to mechanization. With this technical progress, costs fell, and British textiles, even with expanding output in Europe and the United States, dominated markets from Shanghai to Buenos Aires. Iron had become liberated from its dependence on charcoal and was now processed with coke from the rich British coalfields; it found expanding uses as new machines were perfected and took over more and more operations. From less than a quarter of a million tons in 1800, pig-iron production expanded fifty times in the next seventy-five years. By 1875, Great Britain accounted for more than all the rest of the world put together. The factory system, with its clanking machines, soot and smoke, and sprawling slums, but also with its cheaper and more abundant stream of cottons, woolens, glass, pottery, leather goods, and the tools and machines to make them, attracted more and more workers from farms and fields. From a mere 31 percent in 1801, city dwellers came by 1871 to comprise 61 percent of the population. Although rivals were emerging, they presented as yet no serious challenge. Britain stood out alone as the world's sole industrial nation.

It was the displacement of manual by mechanical operations in industry after industry that mainly accounted for the phenomenal growth in the output of coal and iron, the dominant materials of the age. No other product of the nineteenth century even began to compare with machines as a consumer of iron and steel. And the greatest pressure on these resources came when the steam engine acquired mobility by land and sea with the appearance of the locomotive and the steamship. These early nineteenth century inventions[1] not only required iron and steel to build them and coal to drive them; far larger quantities of

---

[1] Although preceded by earlier experimental models, the first successful steamboat was Robert Fulton's *Clermont* (1807) and the first successful locomotive, George Stephenson's *Rocket* (1825).

iron and steel were needed for rails, wheels, carriages, and miscellaneous gear, and later (especially after 1850) in the construction of ships.

Transportation

Although the railway and the steamship gave a tremendous impetus to the growth of the iron and steel industry, their real importance lay in their true function—that of providing rapid, reliable, and cheap transport of goods and people. Within a quarter century after the first short line opened in 1825, Great Britain had acquired its main trunk lines. The dray, the carriage, and the canal boat became, instead of the sole means of transport, supplements to the railroad—supplements of ever-declining importance. By 1880, 18,000 miles of lines crisscrossed the country with a dense network.

Though the steamship antedated the railway as a new form of transport by some twenty years, technical problems delayed its extended use by several decades. Not until 1865 did steamships become quantitatively important; they then comprised 15 percent of total British shipping tonnage. In the meantime, greatly increased numbers of sailing vessels served the needs of expanding world trade. British ships and sailors maintained and extended their earlier lead; by 1850, about 60 percent of world shipping tonnage was of British registry. Toward the end of the century, when steamer tonnage far exceeded that of sailing vessels, Britain's share of the world's merchant fleet reached a peak of 73 percent.

Trade

As her railways ensured speedy and cheap delivery of raw materials to processors and of finished goods to shipping ports, as her expanding fleet furnished ready means of carrying her industrial products to overseas markets and of bringing back raw materials and foodstuffs of every kind, Britain's trade mounted ever higher. Exports tripled in the first half of the nineteenth century and almost tripled again in the second half. Imports grew even more rapidly, reflecting the country's increased dependence on foreign raw materials and foods; they expanded nearly fivefold by 1850 and trebled again by 1900. Textiles and textile products continually exceeded all other exports; in the early 1880s they accounted for just over half the value of total exports. Taken together, coal, iron and steel, and their products comprised another quarter. The remaining exports were scattered among a wide variety of industries.

As Britain's population moved into the cities and as the nation specialized increasingly in the production of manufactures, her dependence on foreign farms, plantations, and mines grew constantly. At the end of the Napoleonic Wars, the country was still largely self-sufficient as to foods; as for raw materials, it needed no foreign wood nor iron ore, but had to import all its cotton and most of its timber. With the needs of her growing population (15 million in 1800, 44 million in 1900) constantly rising, and with her expanding exports, Britain rapidly lost most of her relative independence. By the close of the century, close to 60 percent of the wheat and flour consumed in the country came from overseas. Imports of meat began in the 1870s; with the introduction of refrigeration after 1876, cheap Argentine beef and Australian mutton steadily displaced the products of local slaughter houses. To evergrowing imports of cotton and timber were added wool from Australia, which with later supplies from Uruguay and South Africa eventually furnished practically all this fiber. After 1860, imports of rich Spanish iron ores began to supplement those of native origin; by 1885 imports amounted to almost a quarter of domestic ore production. In addition to these most basic imports, purchases of innumerable other products—hemp, jute, and flax; tin, copper, lead, and nickel; tea, coffee, and cocoa—also reflected the growing specialization of Britain and of her suppliers.

Specialized Market Facilities

An interesting and important result of expanding imports of highly specialized products was the emergence one after another of specialized marketing facilities. Some of these were of long standing, such as the markets for spices and sugar, in which specialized dealers and brokers had carried on an active import and reexport business since at least Elizabethan times. After 1846, with the steady increase in wheat imports that followed the repeal of the Corn Laws, specialized trading in this and other grains coming from Russia centered in the Baltic Coffee House in London, long a rendezvous for general traders. Simultaneously, Liverpool began to develop specialized facilities for dealings in imports from America. With the flood of cheap American wheat after 1870, when railways opened up the western states, Liverpool came to outrank London as a market. Liverpool, as the port nearest the cotton manufacturing towns, also became the outstanding cotton market, with organized exchanges dealing in both "spot" and "future" transactions in standardized grades. London had long been the country's chief market for transactions in wool; as imports outdistanced domestic production in importance, it became the great distributing center for the world.

The London Money Market

Of all the specialized markets that developed in Great Britain as the nation rose to a position of commercial and industrial preeminence, none was as important in its contribution to the country's leadership as the London money market; for it was the gradual perfection of London's banking and financial facilities that made the pound sterling a true world currency, and the entire world a sterling area.

London had for centuries been the commercial and financial metropolis of the kingdom. By the end of the Napoleonic Wars, its banking business was conducted by over 800 private, unincorporated banks, the sixty strongest being located in London, the rest scattered throughout the country. To finance the stream of commodities moving to London for local use, for redistribution to other parts of the nation, or for export, provincial traders and manufacturers drew bills of exchange on their London customers, ordering them to pay the sum due to some city bank. These bills they discounted with a local country bank, from which they received the amount owed less a discount. The country bank then forwarded these bills of exchange to the London bank of its choice, which either held the bill for collection, say thirty or sixty days later, or rediscounted it immediately for cash itself or with some other bank with funds to invest. Immediately or later, the country bank acquired deposits in London to compensate it for its payments to local clients.

Simultaneously, goods moved from London to the provinces. For these, provincial buyers had to make payment in London. They did so by purchasing bills of exchange drawn on its London correspondent by a local bank. These ordered the former to pay the sum specified to the London merchant. In this way the deposits built up in London by country banks were constantly being depleted. Buyers and sellers in the provinces paid their bills to and received payment from local banks; their opposites in London received or paid London funds. Little gold or currency had to move in either direction, the great bulk of transactions being cleared against one another.

Bill Brokers and Dealers   If this mechanism was to work efficiently, someone had to stand ready to discount the large numbers of country bills of exchange constantly being drawn, ordinarily not for immediate but only for later payment. As the volume of this business increased, specialized agencies arose to put up the money, or to find someone who would. The first to appear, just as the struggle with Napoleon ended, was the bill broker. For some time, he was just what his name implies—a financial go-between, seeking out the bills of country merchants and bankers, locating banks with surplus funds, and persuading the latter to invest in the bills in his care. For his trouble and his knowledge, he exacted a small commission.

About fifty years later, the bill broker began to give way to the dealer. The bill dealer was himself a principal, not just an agent. Using sizable funds of his own or borrowing for short periods at the big London banks, he took up bills on his own account. Still later came the discount house, which was simply the dealer writ large; it had more capital of its own, took deposits from the public and paid interest on them, and did a greater volume of business.

Acceptance Houses   The acceptance function, the second task to be taken over by a highly specialized group, was from the latter part of the eighteenth or the early part of the nineteenth century performed by various leading London mercantile firms. Because of the great knowledge they acquired as to the credit-worthiness of an immense number of merchants and manufactures with whom they did business, they could afford to underwrite, as it were, the bills of exchange of reliable individuals and firms whose names were less well known than theirs. This they did by simply writing "accepted," together with their signature, across the face of a bill. For this act, which amounted to guaranteeing the bill, they received a small commission. The effect was that:

> In plain English the man with second-class credit paid a commission to the possessor of first-class credit and thereby secured an improvement in the discount terms which was equal to an amount far in excess of the small commission paid for the accommodation.[2]

As the volume of their business increased, and as England waxed wealthier and began to invest in the securities of foreign governments and railways, some of the more prominent of these trading firms dropped their mercantile transactions and specialized in the business of acceptance and of security issues. Because of their foreign connections and of the phenomenal growth of British foreign trade, the bulk of their acceptance business had to do with international transactions. Down to about 1850, these great acceptance and issue houses also had a near monopoly of the foreign exchange business, that is, the purchase and sale of bills and drafts running in terms of foreign currencies. Later they began to leave this part of their operations to be carried out by a new class of financial institutions, the branches of foreign banks that appeared in London after the Franco-Prussian War.

[2] Ellis T. Powell, *The Evolution of the Money Market* (London: The Financial News, 1915), p. 374.

At the same time that some of these more important houses were turning their attention increasingly to the issue of securities, others, together with newcomers, specialized entirely in the acceptance business. By the end of the nineteenth century, the function of accepting, as well as that of discounting, was very largely in the hands of highly specialized firms and companies. Some part of each type of business, however, was undertaken by the commercial banks, particularly by the branches of foreign and colonial banks that came to London after 1870.

The Bank of England   Occupying a central position in this banking system was the Bank of England. Privately owned, its directors insisted on regarding it as in no essential different from any other private bank. Nonetheless, it had even by the end of the eighteenth century come to perform certain of the functions typical of a central bank: (1) It carried on all the banking business of the government, and during the Napoleonic Wars had been its financial right hand; (2) it maintained the only gold reserve of importance in the kingdom; and (3) it kept in the form of deposits a large part of the reserves of all other London banks.

Nowadays it is a commonly accepted duty of a central bank to provide commercial banks with additional reserves in time of need by rediscounting certain types of commercial paper. This duty the Bank of England came to accept only grudgingly and reluctantly. In a whole series of early crises, when extraordinary demands for currency or gold caused a drain on the reserves of the commercial banks, refusal of the Bank to play the role of "lender of last resort" forced the government to take the initiative. It did so either (as in 1793 and 1811) by advancing Exchequer bills to merchants against the security of goods, or (as in 1847 and 1857) by promising the Bank legislation indemnifying it for issuing its notes liberally, in excess of the legal limit.

Finally, in 1866 the Bank on its own initiative lent freely to meet the demands upon it, and in a letter to the Chancellor of the Exchequer laid the facts before him. His reply authorized free lending to stem the crisis. Following this action, there was considerable dispute as to the wisdom of the Bank's accepting the duty of acting as "lender of last resort." The issue was finally settled by the publication of Bagehot's *Lombard Street*, whose

> lucid common sense . . . was itself decisive. Since then the responsibilities of the Banking Department as the lender of last resort have been unequivocally recognised.[3]

[3] R. G. Hawtrey, *The Art of Central Banking* (New York: Longmans, Green & Co., 1932), p. 126.

Summary   We are now in a position to see the London money market as a whole and to examine its operation. The London banks, including the branches of foreign and colonial banks, furnished the principal source of funds for financing the short-term requirements of industry and commerce. This was supplemented to some extent by the capital of bill dealers and discount houses and by money deposited by the public with the latter. The ultimate borrowers of these funds were traders and manufacturers in London, in various parts of the United Kingdom, and—increasingly as the nineteenth century wore on—exporters and importers all over the globe. British borrowers obtained part of their short-term working capital by direct loans from one or more of the London or country banks; the rest they raised by offering their bills of exchange on the discount market, which furnished practically all the funds supplied to foreigners. Bills coming on the discount market, if from a well-known and established firm, whether domestic or foreign, would either be discounted directly by a bill dealer or a discount house, or parceled out among the banks by the bill brokers. If the borrowing firm was not outstanding, it had its credit validated by one of the specialized acceptance houses before placing it on the discount market.

In normal times the supply of funds lent at short term by the banks to their clients, together with those available in the discount market, was adequate to finance smoothly the conduct of Britain's domestic and foreign trade, as well as a large part of the foreign trade of the rest of the world. All the loans and bills discounted ran for short periods of time, usually from sixty to ninety days, and since some were coming due every day, there was a steady stream of repayments and issuance of new credits. The entire resources of the London money market were therefore a gigantic revolving fund, constantly being depleted and as constantly, replenished.

Of course, the demands varied from time to time in relation to the supply of funds available; these changes were reflected in movements of the discount rate. When the demands became exceptionally large, or when the capacity of the London banks to make advances was strained by having to draw upon their reserves to ship gold abroad or to meet unusually heavy internal needs for currency, it became necessary for the market to have recourse to the Bank of England. Then the discount houses, rather than the banks, obtained the additional reserves necessary to avoid a disastrous contraction of credit.

We have already referred to the fact that dealings in foreign exchange proper—that is, the purchase and sale of bills of exchange drawn in foreign currencies—came to be concentrated in the hands of foreign banks. The volume of this business was never large in London before World War I. British exports were in demand everywhere; the pound sterling was as good as gold and more convenient; and British exporters and importers preferred to draw and to be drawn upon in pounds sterling. Hence sterling bills of exchange were used to finance the exports and imports of the United Kingdom and those of a large part of the rest of the world as well.

The volume of sterling bills constantly coming into the London money market was immense. They arose, as we have seen, out of the financial requirements both of purely domestic economic activities and of foreign trade, including in the latter remittances for shipments that never saw English shores. The reasons for this worldwide preference for the pound sterling as a vehicle of international payments were numerous. In part it was Great Britain's paramount position as exporter of manufactured goods and importer of raw materials and foodstuffs and her equally great preeminence as international investor. In part, also, it was the stable value of the pound sterling in terms of gold, resulting from the rigorous adherence to the gold standard from 1821 until 1914. But certainly of great importance was the high standing of the British acceptance houses and the assurance that any bill receiving their endorsement could be readily discounted, at the world's most favorable rates, on the London discount market. As Powell expressed the matter,

> The effect of this system, from the point of view of our national economy, is that we are able to take toll of a vast aggregate of foreign trade in which we have no direct concern whatever, by lending our acceptances to finance it. A draft on New York or Berlin may be imagined as negotiable in Canton against shipments of silk to New York itself; but if the silk exporter is to get the best rate for his drafts, he will see that they are drawn on London.[4]

From the operation of these compelling forces, London became the world's great financial center, furnishing short-term credits to foreign as well as to British importers and to overseas borrowers needing funds to meet a temporary excess of foreign claims over foreign credits, and providing, through the capital-raising activity of the security-issuing houses, sterling loans for foreign long-term capital requirements.

WESTERN EUROPE CATCHES UP

With a lag of several decades, western Europe went through a phase of development similar to Britain's, although with certain important differences.

[4] Powell, op. cit., p. 375.

Agriculture

Before appreciable progress could be made, the feudal landholding system had to be abandoned. The Revolution had freed the peasant in France. His inbred conservatism remained, however, and it required both official prodding and the competition brought by the railway to persuade him to adopt new crops and new methods. In Prussia, the defeat at Jena in 1806 forced the large landholders to recognize the need for reform. Emancipation edicts followed, which, by freeing the serfs and permitting land transfers and choice of occupations, created the mobility essential for progress. Similar reforms spread to other parts of western Europe.

Improvements in agriculture now became possible. Leadership in some countries, notably Prussia, came from the more progressive landowners, who saw in the modernized large-scale commercial farms of England a model to emulate. With population increasing and the towns and cities growing, markets were good, and new crops—especially potatoes, sugar beets, and linseed—afforded good returns and required a break with old methods. Government sponsorship of change helped, both in France and Germany; agricultural societies were formed, new techniques and new machinery demonstrated, and competitive exhibits organized. After 1840, the expansion of the railway network added the stimulus of intensified competition to force the abandonment of antiquated methods and the less profitable crops.

Industry

European industry in 1815 remained almost completely in the handicraft stage. Its progress thereafter varied widely. Change was negligible in Italy and Spain until late in the century. In France, for a variety of reasons, it lagged badly until about 1860, when railway mileage was substantial. Advance came sooner and was most rapid in Germany and Belgium.

German industrialization exhibited a sharp contrast with that of Britain. There was no revolution in thought or attitudes such as occurred in England between the fifteenth and nineteenth centuries. Prussia, the dominant state, carried down into modern times a spirit of medieval submission to authority and of looking to the state for leadership. From the very first, the state took an active part in fostering the growth of industry, both from choice and necessity.

In 1816, a staff member of the Prussian Department of Commerce, Industry, and Public Works established the Industrial Institute (*Gewerbeinstitut*), which began training engineers and machine builders in 1821. Both Prussia and other German states sent industrial spies to England, where they used various stratagems to evade the numerous

British laws (repealed in 1842) restricting the export of machines, models, and blueprints. Prussia also displayed a keen interest in and careful attention to education, with special solicitude for the teaching of science.

Lack of a numerous class of enterprising businessmen concerned with manufacture, as well as a shortage of capital, also handicapped industrial development on the Continent. As additional remedies for these deficiencies, Prussia granted a number of subsidies to industry, admitted imports of machinery duty free, and encouraged the migration of skilled British workers and engineers. After the formation in 1834 of the German Customs Union (*Zollverein*), which brought the German states behind a single tariff, new industries were sheltered by protective duties. The Prussian State took an active part in the planning and construction of railways. Their stimulating effect became especially important after 1860, when Germany possessed nearly 7000 miles of track.

Any account of the early stages of industrialization on the Continent would have to give an important place to the aid provided by British capital, labor, and enterprise. It was less in Germany than elsewhere, but even here British workers and engineers installed machinery and demonstrated its operation in the cotton, woolen and jute industries, in machine manufacture, gas works, mines, and railways. In France and Belgium, most of the early railways were built by British engineers and navvies, manned by British engine drivers, and financed in part by British capital. Many industrial plants, too, owed their origin or modernization to British skills and capital.

By 1870, the leading nations of western Europe had gone through the first stages of the Industrial Revolution. They had a well-developed railway system, factory methods of production were well entrenched in the textile industries, and modern engineering establishments were producing most of their own requirements of machinery. They still lagged far behind Great Britain, however. Measured by the output of pig iron, the most important industrial raw material, Britain was for out in front, with over 6 million tons. Germany produced a little less than a quarter of this amount (1.4 million tons), with France somewhat behind with 1.2 million tons. Britain also stood far ahead in manufactures, with almost one-third of world production. The United States was coming to the fore, accounting for about a fifth; Germany was responsible for 13 percent; France, for about 10 percent.

ECONOMIC DEVELOPMENTS OVERSEAS

Many volumes have been written about the economic development of the United States. Canada, Australia, Argentina—the "regions of recent settlement" outside Europe. It would be impossible to deal in brief scope with this phenomenon—to trace the effect of differing government policies, the relative importance of specific natural resources, and the exertions by which the citizens of these areas peopled the empty spaces, built cities, and founded and developed important industries. We shall, therefore, limit ourselves to an account of the international contributions to overseas growth—the tremendous migration of labor and capital of the nineteenth century—and to some of the more important social conditions surrounding that growth.

Overseas Investment

British capital not only helped to get the Industrial Revolution under way in Europe, but it also aided greatly in inaugurating the process of economic development overseas. Here its main contribution was to provide what has come to be called *social overhead capital*—the facilities without which specific industries and even agriculture cannot function efficiently, but which they are incapable of furnishing themselves: railways, roads, harbor works, power plants, telephone and telegraph systems. Of a total British foreign investment of $18.5 billion outstanding in 1913, 40 percent was in railways, 5 percent in other utilities, and 30 percent in loans to governments, most of which probably went into one form or another of social overhead capital. This is three-fourths of the total. The rest was scattered in mining, finance, manufacturing, and plantations. Moreover, about two-thirds of all British overseas investment went to the newly settled lands; only one-fourth was directed to the tropical or semitropical economies with large populations and widely differing cultures. Europe obtained the rest, mainly before 1870.

British capital began to move abroad in sizable amounts soon after the Napoleonic Wars. By 1850, it amounted to £200 million, most in western Europe and the United States, and the larger part in railways. During the next twenty-five years, the destination of Britain's surplus funds remained the same; the rate of flow increased. Between 1875 and 1913, Canada and the Empire came to the fore, though the United States and Latin America also received substantial amounts. At the end of this period, nearly $9 billion was invested in the Empire (principally in the great Dominions); the United States and Latin America shared $7.5 billion almost equally.

Beginning with the second half of the nineteenth century, France and Germany also became foreign lenders. Both countries at first invested mainly in Europe; political considerations strongly influenced the direction of their loans. Thus France, with strong diplomatic ties with Russia, lent heavily to the Russian government. Germany, to counter Russian expansion, concentrated on southeastern Europe.

Later investments of both countries helped finance overseas development. France directed large sums to Latin America and the French Empire; Germany, to Latin America and the United States. By 1914, French investments abroad totaled approximately $9 billion, of which about 60 percent was in Europe. Germany had lent $6 billion, half of it to European borrowers, and one-sixth each to the United States and Latin America.[5]

Results of Investments

Although some of the funds invested came from governments, the great bulk derived from private savings. The decisions that directed them to their destinations were made by individuals, banks, and business firms. Frequently, these decisions were strongly influenced by fanciful misrepresentation by the banks that distributed the securities. With few exceptions, however, their motivation was gain. Investors expected a higher return than they could get at home. By and large, in spite of numerous defaults, they do not appear to have been disappointed. On comparable home and foreign investments (government bonds or railway securities, for example), British investors did rather better on their foreign ventures.[6] Frenchmen came off worse; any advantage on the side of foreign investments was very small, for French banks gave bad advice, and the native caution of the French investor was outweighed by his credulity.

The most important gains from international investment were not those received by the investors themselves, but those accruing to the entire community, both at home and abroad. In the lending countries, export industries enjoyed larger markets and bigger orders; their expansion permitted them to achieve economies of scale. Investments in foreign mines, plantations, and means of transport assured the industrial countries of needed supplies of raw materials and foodstuffs; they also, especially those in railways and shipping, made them cheaper. In the borrowing countries, foreign investment provided the social overhead capital so necessary for economic growth. It opened up new regions, thus making possible the combination in more effective proportions of labor and hitherto unexploited resources, while freeing domestic capital to provide such direct aids to labor as farm implements

[5] Figures from William Ashworth, *A Short History of the International Economy 1850–1950* (New York: Longmans, Green & Co., 1952), p. 173.

[6] Excluding about one-tenth of total British investments between 1870 and 1880 in government bonds on which losses from defaults outweighed gains from interest payments, returns from foreign government bonds exceeded those on British consols by amounts ranging from 0.7 to 10.7 percent. The differentials on railway stocks and bonds were comparable. Figures are from A. K. Cairncross, *Home and Foreign Investment, 1870– 1913* (New York: Cambridge University Press, 1953), pp. 229–30.

and machinery, factory equipment, and all the array of producers' goods so badly needed in a growing economy.

People on the Move

One outstanding feature of nineteenth-century investment was that it was accompanied by, even correlated with, a large migration of labor. Between 1820 and 1930, gross migration amounted to 62 million people, three-fourths of it occurring in the half-century before World War I. Europe contributed much the greater part of these immigrants. Until 1890, most of them came from Ireland, Germany, and the Scandinavian countries; thereafter south-eastern Europe, especially Italy, supplied the majority. The United States exerted the greatest drawing power; it attracted over three-fifths. Another fifth went in about equal proportions to Canada and to Australia, New Zealand, and South Africa; Argentina and Brazil between them claimed most of the remainder.

In the earlier stages, the immigrants moved from relatively unproductive farms in the old countries to more productive agricultural employment in the newer countries, or they provided the labor to open mines and build railways. Later, an increasing proportion went into industry; in the United States, the steel, the women's dress, and building industries took large numbers.

With a few exceptions, factors—both labor and capital—moved from areas where they were abundant and cheap to regions where they were scarce and dear. (It will be recalled that the movement of goods, which may be regarded as a substitute for factor movements, is similar in character.) In the nineteenth century, too, the migration of labor and capital was complementary; both entered the new countries together, to be combined with the relatively rich, virgin resources of the new lands in proportions that were more productive than those formerly attainable either there or in the old countries. Economic growth resulted—the appearance of new industries, better communications, the settlement of empty plains, the emergence of new towns, and all with rising per capita incomes—probably at a faster rate than ever before witnessed.

Conditions Favorable to Development

One aspect of the economic development of western Europe and of the regions of recent settlement overseas merits special attention. This is the *social environment* in which that development took place. Feudalism had been destroyed early, either before or on the threshold of the great economic changes of the nineteenth century. With the elimination of the relatively rigid social relations of feudalism, class structure became fluid, ensuring the social mobility and the freedom to exploit resources so essential to the new industrial society. (The contrast is sharp between the rate of economic development in Latin America, where a feudal land tenure system and social structure were imported by the Spanish and Portuguese, and in the United States, Canada, and Australasia.)

More positively, western Europe and the regions settled mainly in the nineteenth century by its emigrants possessed a set of institutions uniquely favorable to rapid economic growth. High on the list is a tradition of orderly government and all that implies: the supremacy of the law and a corresponding willingness to abide by the decisions of courts, respect for prescribed methods of transferring political power between contending parties, and a reasonably efficient and honest bureaucracy. Given this tradition, changes in government could be peaceful, continuity and stability were assured, and transactions involving the government could be guided by reason and common sense.

As a result of the stimulus to secular and scientific interests given by the Renaissance, of the emphasis on individual efforts generated during the Reformation, and of the vigorous political, economic, and philosophical disputes of the eighteenth-century Age of Enlightenment, western Europe also acquired a high respect for the role of the individual, for the experimental approach, and for the material rewards of effort. The importance of these considerations for the successful operation of a private enterprise system is clear.

Finally, the prior accumulation of capital in England, the creation in London of an international capital market open to European borrowers, and its later widening to include western Europe itself, provided financial resources vital to rapid overseas development. The tradition of order and stability carried overseas by the settlers in turn guaranteed their access to these sources of capital.

TRADE IS MADE FREE

An efficiently functioning international economy would have been impossible without the third of the great changes of the nineteenth century—the release of trade from its burden of mercantilist restrictions. Here, as in the growth of industry and the creation of an international market for goods and capital, Britain led the way. We have repeatedly called attention to the increasing numbers and wealth of the English manufacturing and mercantile class, whose desire for economic freedom resulted in the gradual repeal or nullification of various domestic regulations of mercantilism. After the Napoleonic Wars they were ready for an attack on its still intact foreign ramparts. Both their interests in, and their ideas on, foreign trade had been altered by recent or current developments.

The Need for Wider Markets

Although the long years of war with France had intensified rather than relaxed the regulation of trade, they had also speeded the growth of Britain's newer industries—cotton, iron and steel and coal, and engineering. After Waterloo, although their position was unchallenged abroad, their markets were in a state of collapse. The government stopped buying firearms, cannon, and naval vessels. Supplies of uniforms, blankets, and tents were no longer needed. Nor was continental Europe, for years overrun by marauding armies, likely for some time to be a heavy buyer of British goods. Concern for markets, therefore, led merchants and manufacturers to look more favorably on measures to increase the freedom of trade.

Changing Ideas

At the same time that sagging sales aroused an interest in broader markets, ideological weapons useful in the coming fight against trade barriers were being sharpened. Adam Smith had made a good beginning with his exposure of the absurdities of mercantilism and his limited demonstration of the gains from trade. Now Ricardo, himself a businessman and a recognized spokesman for business groups, strengthened the argument for the liberalization of trade with his famous doctrine of comparative costs. Followers in England and France, and popularizers too, soon took it up, clarified it, and developed a well-reasoned case for free trade. This became part of the standard intellectual equipment of liberal statesmen and crusading reformers. One of the former, Huskisson, brought some order into the chaotic jumble of Britain's mercantilist and wartime duties, paring down the most exorbitant duties, substituting moderate tariffs for import prohibitions, and abolishing bounties. The Corn Laws, the core of British protectionism, remained sacred as long as an archaic distribution of Parliamentary seats gave unqualified political control to the landed gentry.

The Reform Bill of 1832 abolished at a stroke the numerous rotten or pocket boroughs that permitted many great landowners to appoint members of Parliament, and at the same time enfranchised half the middle class. Although still far from representative, Parliament reflected more accurately the views of the governed. Its reform furnished an essential ingredient for repeal of the Corn Laws.

Repeal of the Corn Laws

Sir Robert Peel (Prime Minister, 1841–1846), who became the great parliamentary leader of the free trade movement, began the dismantling of protection by obtaining adoption of the income tax. This provided assured revenues hitherto derived from a mass of duties on exports of manufactures and imports of raw materials, which with the support of the manufacturing class were now dropped or greatly reduced. On the issue of agricultural protection, however, he at first sided with his party. But a rising tide of opposition to the Corn Laws outside Parliament, together with eloquent representation of the free trade interest within, finally caused him to desert it.

The opposition was the work of the Anit-Corn Law League, an organization of manufacturers founded in 1839 to promote repeal. The prospect of cheaper bread had a strong appeal to the laborer, whether on the farm or in the factory, while the manufacturer saw in cheaper food, according to the Ricardian theory of the day, the possibility of lower money wages and higher profits. Backed with plenty of money, organized with extraordinary efficiency, and supported with the eloquence of Richard Cobden and John Bright, the League

> accomplished the miracle of uniting capital and labour. It combined argument and emotion, bringing both to perfection in meetings that began with Cobden and ended with Bright. It appealed equally to self-interest and to humanity. In an age when political literature was limited in quantity and inferior in quality, the League, in 1843 alone, distributed nine million carefully argued tracts by means of a staff of eight hundred persons. In an age when public meetings were rare, when finance and government were regarded as mysteries appertaining to the political families and to well-born civil servants, the League lecturers taught political economy, and criticised the year's budget, to vast audiences of merchants and clerks, artisans and navvies, farmers and agricultural labourers.[7]

Within Parliament, Cobden's lucid economic arguments, combined with Peel's own study of the facts, finally converted the Prime Minister to free trade. In 1845 he seized the opportunity afforded by the Irish potato blight to suspend the Corn Laws. Popular opposition to their restoration was so strong that in 1846 repeal was inevitable.

The Spread of Freer Trade

In ensuing years, Great Britain completed her movement toward free trade and other countries followed her lead. In 1860, Parliament re-

---

[7] G. M. Trevelyan, *British History in the Nineteenth Century* (London: Longmans, Green & Co., 1922), p. 270.

moved all but sixty of four hundred articles from the dutiable list; gradually, even these fell by the wayside and the British market became and remained open to imports without restriction until 1914. France, under the leadership of the liberal emperor Napoleon III, replaced her highly protective tariff with a very moderate one in a series of international negotiations beginning with the Cobden–Chevalier Treaty of 1860. After 1850, Holland and Belgium adopted distinctly liberal tariffs. Even the United States, which had pursued a protective policy since 1816, substantially moderated its duties in the tariff of 1857. And during the 1860s the German *Zollverein*, whose original mild tariff of 1834 had been raised thereafter, succumbed to free trade pressures and lowered its duties from protective to revenue levels.

In addition to their liberality, two features of these mid-nineteenth-century tariffs that were to endure until after 1914 are well worth noting. These were their stability and their generality. Even though rates of duty tended to move upward again after 1870, tariffs changed very gradually, usually being left in force for a decade or more. By reducing the risks and increasing the calculability of trade, this feature facilitated its steady expansion. And by the insertion into commercial treaties of the now famous "most-favored-nation" clause, which extended to all treaty partners concessions granted in each treaty, the benefits of tariff reductions were generalized throughout the world.

Stimulated by its release from restrictions, international trade grew apace. Rough estimates, which are all that are available, suggest that its value doubled between 1830 and 1850. In the next thirty years world trade at least trebled and may have nearly quadrupled. From being a relatively unimportant adjunct of domestic activity, foreign trade loomed increasingly large where it did not dominate economic life altogether. Australia, New Zealand, Argentina, and Uruguay became specialists in the production of wheat, wool, and meat. Britain, their principal market, permitted its agriculture to go through a sharp phase of contraction while the nation concentrated its energies on specialized manufactures. In the face of cheap supplies of western wheat, Denmark transformed its economy from a grain-growing and exporting basis to one that imported grain and exported bacon, ham, eggs, and dairy products. All over the globe, specialization matched the growth of trade.

AN INTERNATIONAL ECONOMY

With the adoption of the gold standard in the early 1870s by all the important countries of Europe and by several Latin American nations, currencies became firmly linked at stable exchange rates and were made fully convertible.[8] The expanding needs of the rising industrial countries for imported raw materials and foodstuffs and for markets for their manufactures could be met by purchases from one group and sales to another, the balances being cleared through a complex multilateral network centering in London. There the highly developed and efficient money market attracted funds from all over the world and made them available to finance the major part of the world trade and an important share of the capital requirements of growing national economics.

Disturbances and consequent adjustments were inevitable. Yet, because it was an era of rapid growth, the disturbances could be assimilated without too great dislocation. For such as remained, the gold standard provided an effective mechanism of adjustment, which, although it tended toward deflation, was politically acceptable and therefore allowed to work.

Although socialist doctrines, both "utopian" and Marxist, had their adherents, neither they nor any other rival seriously challenged the combination of industrial capitalism and political democracy that spread throughout the Western nations. Reliance could be and was placed upon market forces to regulate production, the flow of raw materials and finished goods, the movement of capital and even, in large part, of labor. By the late nineteenth century, an international economy not too unlike the theoretical model actually existed.

[For Selected References, see the end of Chapter 16.]

---

[8] The United States had legally established the gold standard in 1873, after being on a paper currency basis since 1861. Specie payments, however, were not resumed until 1879.

16
CHAPTER

The Revival
of Nationalism

From the vantage point of the late twentieth century, there can be no
doubt that the nineteenth century, or more accurately the hundred
years between the Napoleonic Wars and World War I (1814–1914), constituted a unique period in many respects. From our own focus of
interest, it stands out as the century during with deliberate governmental regulation of trade gave way to regulation by market forces.
Nations became free to specialize in production according to the dic-
tates of relative costs, and did so. A large and constantly growing
volume of international trade linked the various regions of the world
into a smoothly functioning, integrated economy of global scope. The
developments that brought this about began soon after 1815 and
reached a crescendo in the 1850s and 1860s in the free trade movement.

By the early 1870s, the liberalizing forces reached their peak of
accomplishment. From then on, although far from spent, they had to
fight a rearguard action against a rising tide of nationalism. Although
most of the gains remained intact, events of the late nineteenth and
early twentieth centuries established a trend that foreshadowed the
future. These include a revival of nationalism with its anticosmopol-
itan policies and a great shift in the balance of economic power. This
chapter will examine these developments.

THE CHALLENGE TO BRITAIN'S LEADERSHIP

The Rise of Germany

At the time Germany achieved political union in the Empire (1871), she
was no better than a poor third in economic weight, whether this be

measured in manufacturing production, the output of iron and steel, or the volume of trade. But within forty years, she outdistanced the United Kingdom, became the strongest European power, and made a bid for world domination.

Germany's rapid economic growth began immediately after the Franco-Prussian War and the attainment of political unity. With a strong central government replacing the numerous small and ineffectual principalities, a coordination of hitherto independent and sometimes conflicting policies became possible. The billion dollar indemnity from France enabled Germany to adopt the gold standard; the acquisition of Alsace–Lorraine, with its textile mills and iron ore deposits, provided additional resources for expansion. Coal and iron production, which had increased slowly until now, rose sharply. Between 1870 and 1900, the output of both minerals grew fivefold. Still behind at the turn of the century, in the next decade Germany rushed forward, surpassing Britain in the production of pig iron and coal and outranking her in her share of world manufacturing output.

Nor was Germany's growth exclusively internal. Her exports grew steadily, but more slowly than industrial production up to 1900, then increased sharply. In 1872 they totaled $500 million; in 1900, $1132 million; and in 1913, $2494 million. The principal export items were manufactures—hardware, chemicals, cotton textiles, beet sugar, and one major mineral, coal. The leading imports were raw materials and foods—grain, wool, cotton, and timber.

Because of the similarity of Germany's exports to those of Britain, their expansion depended partly upon the ability of German producers to undersell the British. Germany's advance unquestionably introduced a strong element of direct competition. But these exports were by no means wholly competitive. There was considerable specialization within products; Germany concentrated on the coarser textiles, Great Britain on the finer grades; German producers made principally cheap watches and clocks, the British (and later the Swiss) the more expensive types. Some German goods, too, were noncompeting in nature, even being exported to England; among these were chemicals and electrical equipment. Moreover, in eastern Europe, Germany found a market to which British exporters had paid little attention and in which Germany had the advantage of location. The increase of her exports in this area, especially, represented a net increase in world trade rather than a loss to Britain.

Lulled into complacency by their long enjoyment of an unchallenged position, the commercial interests of Britain were stunned when confronted, in the 1880s and 1890s, by German and to a lesser degree by French, Belgian, Swiss, and Austrian rivalry. British goods had always been superior. They had required little pushing. If they were not precisely suited to the foreigner's needs, the foreigner had had to adapt himself to what was available.

To get a foothold in foreign markets in the face of British dominance, the German trader exploited his rival's every weakness. He adapted products to his customers' wishes; he packaged his wares attractively; he took pains with even the smallest orders, hoping that larger ones might follow. His representatives abroad became more numerous than the British, and, unlike the latter, learned the local language and often married local girls and took root in the community. Cash on demand, or at the most, sixty to ninety days' credit, was sound British practice. But the upstart Germans did not hesitate to give six to nine months or even longer.

These new, unpleasant facts aroused acute alarm, notably in the mid-1880s and mid-1890s, years of severe depression. But as world trade recovered, it became apparent that although British manufactures had lost ground in some markets, especially on the Continent, the development of new, together with the growth of old, provided more than an offset. Expansion overseas required steadily increasing imports, and exploitation of the mass market for cheap textiles in Asia furnished a new outlet. The net result of the new competition was not, as some had feared, England's collapse as an industrial power. British traders had to work harder and producers had to relinquish some lines of production to new, low-cost rivals, and to specialize where their resources and skills counted most.[1] Channels of trade altered some diminishing, some swelling. And with the emergence of Germany and other western European nations as important producers of manufactures, an increasing proportion of trade took the form of an exchange of manufactured specialties—German electrical and mining machinery for English agricultural and textile machines, coarse grades of textiles for finer, dyestuffs for heavy industrial chemicals.

The United States

The economic progress of Germany was far exceeded by that of the United States. The contrast was but natural, considering the fact that the transition from a predominantly agrarian to a modern industrial nation took place in a country of continental size, possessing immense resources of land, minerals, power, and timber. Rapid development of these resources was assured by their very richness, which gave the profit-seeking businessman the prospect of high returns; by the prevalence, as in England, of an individualist philosophy; by the rapid

---

[1] Some branches of British industry met sharp German competition in the home market, notably sugar refining, chemicals, iron and steel, and cotton and woolen textiles. Exports of woolen fabrics declined absolutely, from 324 million yards per annum in 1870 to 174 million in 1909–1913.

growth of population; and by the relatively high level of incomes attributable to a favorable ratio of population to resources.

The high proportion of resources to population, or the relative scarcity of labor, together with the rapid growth of population, played a most important role in the speedy development of American industry. With abundant fertile land available almost for the asking down to the end of the nineteenth century, farming offered rich rewards for the enterprising and provided a growing market for products of industry. Continued expansion of this market was assured by the phenomenal growth of population, which nearly doubled between 1870 and 1900.

Not only did the high productivity of American agriculture furnish a large and growing market for industry among the farming population, but also by offering an attractive alternative to work in mine or mill it forced the payment of high wages in industry. And because of the basically democratic character of the American people, they were ready to spend their high per capita earnings on mass-produced goods. Thus the tendency toward the production of standardized commodities with a broad, mass market received a strong impetus from the nature of the buying public.[2]

The economies attainable when industry can concentrate upon the production of large quantities of identical goods were partly responsible for the rapidly increasing efficiency of American industry. Probably of equal importance was the high level of wages caused by the scarcity of labor. This forced manufacturers to adopt laborsaving devices, the invention of which has been a unique feature of "Yankee ingenuity."[3] Thus necessity compelled the use and stimulated the de-

[2] This explanation of the prominence of mass-production industries in the United States was advanced by Erwin Rothbarth in a brilliant and suggestive article, "Causes of the Superior Efficiency of U.S.A. Industry as Compared with British Industry," *Economic Journal*, **56**:383 (1946). By way of contrast with the United States he cites the United Kingdom, where "there remains an aristocracy and a middle class impregnated with aristocratic ideas, who reject mass-produced articles and insist on articles with individual character" (p. 386).

We may add to what Rothbarth says, that in addition to the relative abundance of land, America's comparatively enlightened land policy (as embodied in the Homestead Act of 1862), by making land accessible to would-be-buyers, "put purchasing power in the hands of those . . . ready to buy large quantities of standardised goods." Had the concentration of landholdings been permitted on a wide scale, as in many Latin American countries, great extremes of income distribution such as characterize those nations might have resulted in the United States as well.

[3] "The American display of machinery at the Vienna International Exhibition of 1873 was, according to the contemporary reporter, 'the richest in new forms of apparatus, and contained by far the most striking examples of the special adaptation of machines to peculiar varieties of work, and of what is commonly described as "labor-saving machinery." ' . . . As an English observer noted in 1885, 'The tools and processes which we are inclined to consider unusual are the commonplaces of American shops, and the determination to do nothing by hand which can be done by machinery is the chief characteristic.' " Samuel Reznick, "Mass Production Since the War Between the States," in Harold Williamson, ed., *The Growth of the American Economy* (Englewood Cliffs, N.J.: Prentice-Hall, Inc., 1944), p. 502.

Table 16.1   Pig-Iron Production in Leading Countries (Millions of Metric Tons)

	Great Britain	United States	Germany	France	Russia
1870	6.1	1.7	1.4	1.2	0.4
1900	9.1	14.0	7.6	2.7	2.9
1910	10.2	27.7	13.1	4.0	3.0
1920	8.2	37.5	6.4	3.3	0.1
1930	6.3	32.3	9.7	10.0	5.0
1940	8.4	43.0	21.0	4.6	15.5

SOURCE: W. Nelson Peach and Walter Krause, *Basic Data of the American Economy* (Homewood, Ill.: Richard D. Irwin, Inc., 1948), p. 59; reproduced from G. A. Roush, ed., *The Metal Industry During 1941* (New York: McGraw-Hill Book Company).

velopment of the most advanced technology of any of the industrial nations.

The presence of mass markets and the need for labor-saving machinery made their effects evident early. Before 1850, guns and pistols were manufactured from interchangeable parts. After the Civil War, this system was applied to sewing machines, clocks and watches, agricultural machinery, the typewriter, and the bicycle. The machine-tool industry, located first in the eastern states and later spreading to Ohio, furnished the technical basis for the precision manufacture of interchangeable parts.

In spite of the early introduction of mass-production methods, American industry remained until the very end of the nineteenth century well behind British, although advancing rapidly. The figures for both pig-iron production and share of manufacturing production reflect this fact (see Tables 16.1 and 16.2). In 1870, U.S. output of iron was just over one-fourth of British. It is doubtful if manufactures at this date amounted to more than half the production of the United Kingdom.[4] By 1900, the United States ranked first as a producer of pig iron and coal. It also apparently was the premier manufacturing nation. By 1913, there was no question as to relative position. United States output of pig iron was as large as that of the United Kingdom, Germany, and France together, while its share of world manufactures (35.8 percent) was only slightly less than that of these three industrial nations (36.1 percent). In other words, just before the outbreak of

[4] Although Table 16.2 shows the United States in 1870 as accounting for 22.3 percent of world manufacturing production, as against the United Kingdom's 31.8 percent, the figure for the United States is almost certainly too high. It includes a large proportion of articles produced by handicraft and neighborhood "industries." In addition, prices were very low in 1870, and there is no indication that this factor is taken into account. Even the 1900 figure for the United States is probably too high, owing to the fact that almost one-fourth of total manufactures were of the handicraft variety.

Table 16.2   Percentage Distribution of the World's Manufacturing Production

	U.S.	Germany	U.K.	France	Russia	Italy	Belgium	Sweden	Japan
1870	23.3	13.2	31.8	10.3	3.7	2.4	2.9	0.4	—
1896–1900	30.1	16.6	19.5	7.1	5.0	2.7	2.2	1.1	0.6
1913	35.8	15.7	14.0	6.4	5.0	3.1	2.1	1.0	1.2
1926–1929	42.2	11.6	9.4	6.6	4.3	3.3	1.9	1.0	2.5
1936–1938	32.2	10.7	9.2	4.5	18.5	2.7	1.3	1.3	3.5

SOURCE: League of Nations, *Industrialization and Foreign Trade*, p. 13.

World War 1, the United States had replaced Britain as the world's principal industrial power.

A large growth in American foreign trade accompanied America's phenomenal expansion. Just after the Civil War, U.S. exports barely exceeded $300 million (1866–1870 average). A few years before the outbreak of World War I, they were nearly six times as large, or $1750 million (1906–1910 average). Despite their growth, however, U.S. exports were much more complementary to, than competitive with, British production. As late as 1910, nearly three-fourths consisted of crude materials and foods, manufactured foods (of which flour is by far the most important), and semimanufactures, and only about one-fourth (26.7 percent) of finished manufactures. Moreover, although U.S. exports exhibited rapid growth, they remained a relatively small proportion of total U.S. production. In 1870, exports were 7 percent of gross national product; in 1913, 8 percent.

Americans were so busy developing a continent and satisfying the needs of an immense free trade area that the development of export markets, except as an outlet for the abounding production of farms, forests, and mines, was comparatively unimportant. As production of manufactures grew, the United States became, it is true, more capable of taking care of its requirements for finished goods. This is reflected in the decline in imports of finished manufactures from over 40 percent in 1866–1870 to just under 25 percent in 1906–1910. In spite of this trend toward industrial self-sufficiency, reinforced by rising tariff rates, total imports increased so rapidly—from $408 million to $1345 million—that imports of finished manufactures doubled in the period under review. Europe, moreover, remained by far America's greatest market and its principal source of imports. In 1870, that continent (including the United Kingdom) as a major customer took 80 percent of U.S. exports; in 1910 the figure was still 65 percent. As for imports, the United States obtained 55 percent of these from Europe in 1870; by 1910, its share had dropped only to 52 percent.

Britain's Position in 1913

Although the economic growth of Germany and the United States had vital implication for power politics, as the events of 1914–1918 were to show, it made little difference to the average citizen of the British Isles. Real wages increased steadily throughout the last half of the nineteenth century, owing to the fact that money wages either rose more rapidly than prices or fell less rapidly. From 1901 to 1914, the rise of real wages was reversed; they fell an average of 0.7 percent per annum during this period. Prices were now rising rather rapidly, and especially the prices of raw materials and foods. Yet even then, hours of labor continued to be shortened, and the extension of social services worked to labor's advantage. According to another estimate, which covers not only labor but all gainfully employed, real income continued to rise right up to 1913, although less rapidly than during the last half of the nineteenth century.[5]

The British balance of payments had been under no strain from 1870 onward. Not only was a large and somewhat irregular growing excess of imports over exports paid for out of the earnings of British foreign investments, the merchant marine, and insurance and banking establishments, but there was also a substantial surplus available each year for additional investment overseas. For the period 1873–1896, it is true, investment turned more toward internal improvements, and the rate of foreign lending declined. It increased again, however, after 1900, and by 1913 British total foreign investment stood close to £4000 million, yielding an annual income of £210 million. At the close of our period, the balance of payments surplus was larger than ever before, and still growing.

There was, in short, nothing unsound about Britain's position on the eve of World War I. Although forced by world economic expansion to share markets with relative newcomers, she herself benefited from this expansion. Some adjustments to competition had been necessary, but the industries that had been the backbone of her own development were still growing and were still the world's largest exporters. Real income per head of the population had been rising for two generations and was exceeded only moderately by that of the United States and Canada. A huge stake in foreign investment yielded a substantial an-

---

[5] From 1850 to 1873, when prices and wages were both rising, the annual increase in real wages, after allowing for unemployment, was 1.3 percent. From 1873 to 1900, the annual increase averaged 1.85 percent. [W. W. Rostow, *British Economy of the Nineteenth Century*, (Oxford: Clarendon Press, 1948), Chapter 4.] The data for the period after 1900 show that income per head of the occupied population, in constant prices, stood at £175.8 in 1894–1903; by 1913 it was £195.4, or 11 percent higher. [Colin Clark, *The Conditions of Economic Progress* (New York: Macmillan Publishing Company, 1940), p. 83.]

nual revenue. Together with large earnings from services, this enabled the country to import each year far more than it exported, and in addition to export a large sum of capital.

NATIONALISM AND PROTECTIONISM

The rivalry for markets that arose in the 1880s and 1890s reflected the attainment of maturity by continental industry and its consequent release from British tutelage. Since this successful industrial development had been achieved during an era of relatively low tariffs, one might have expected the liberal attitude toward trade to persist. Indeed, in view of the challenge to Britain's exports and the invasion even of her domestic market, a revival of protectionist sentiment in the United Kingdom would have been understandable. And although there was such a revival, it never acquired sufficient strength to alter Britain's commitment to free trade. On the contrary, it was on the Continent that a rising spirit of nationalism took root, one of whose fruits was a renewed campaign for protection that reversed the earlier downward trend of tariffs.

The resurgence of nationalism appears to have been partly the perverse outcome of liberal doctrine and partly the aftermath of wars. Liberalism, the dominant political philosophy of the nineteenth century, stressed the supremacy of the individual and the natural harmony of individual and social interests under a regime of free competition. It took the existence of national states for granted—they were the necessary agency for eliminating obstructions to economic and political freedom and for establishing the minimum rules of a free society. But if the individual was to be free, he must not only be free from excessive government intervention; his freedom implied also freedom from foreign oppression. National self-determination was an essential ingredient in the liberal system of thought.

Enforcement of the doctrine of self-determination by local leaders resulted in the formation, by peoples who were by and large homogeneous as to language and culture, of several new nations. Greece, with British aid, threw off Turkish rule in 1829. Belgium became an independent nation in 1830. In the 1850s, Garibaldi led the Italian people against their Austrian oppressors, and with the help of French troops and British diplomacy, Italy achieved national unity in 1860. Self-determination had little to do with the creation of the German Empire, which was more the result of the assertion of Prussian military hegemony; yet the Empire did bring together peoples who were linguistically and culturally similar. When a new nation is born, it tends to assert its newfound nationality. This is especially true when it is large and powerful and when its birth is attended by military struggle. Germany and Italy provide good examples. One of the characteristic forms of nationalist self-assertion is the imposition of protective duties on imports. In the revival of nationalism in the mid-nineteenth century we have a force providing at least a predisposition toward protection.

History also records that protection is a legacy of war and a common expression of national rivalry. We have already noted the growing rivalry of the 1880s and 1890s; as for war, there was the Crimean War, the bitter struggle between the Northern and Southern States of the American Union, and conflict between France and Prussia. All these influences together were surely enough to generate a reaction against the earlier, liberal trade policies.

What actually set the protectionist movement under way was, however, none of these broad political factors, but two specific economic developments of the 1870s. One was the invasion of the Continent by cheap American and Russian grain, made accessible by the activities of railway builders. The other was the depression of 1873–1879, the longest and deepest period of stagnant trade the world had yet experienced. Peasants and manufacturers alike were full of lamentations; their clamor for relief gave the initial stimulus to protection.

Another influence was at work over the whole latter half of the nineteenth century. To meet rising expenditures on armaments, education, public health, and social insurance, greater revenues became necessary. And since customs duties provided, during the nineteenth century, the larger part of the revenue of many nations, it was natural to turn the screw a bit tighter.

Once the swing to protection started, the deeper force of nationalism supported and maintained it. There is also a tendency for a rise in duties to continue as vested interests grow and gather political strength. They also tend to spread over an ever wider range of commodities, since it is difficult to deny to others what has already been granted to some. The operation of these forces is illustrated in the history of tariff policy from 1870 to 1913.

Tariff Policy to 1913

Even in the face of serious depression, German tariffs continued to fall in the 1870s. Duties on grain had been abolished in 1865; those on iron and on shipbuilding materials followed in 1873; and the tariff on iron manufactures was to go in 1877. Despite the pressure of distressed farmers and worried industrialists, Bismarck resisted; the iron duties were dropped according to schedule. His need for funds, however, helped win him over. In the tariff of 1880, moderate duties were imposed on various iron products, while grains and a number of other items received considerably more protection. Further upward revision of the iron and food duties occurred in 1902, when rising tariffs elsewhere and the lapse of various treaties that had frozen German duties furnished the motive and the opportunity. Even then, although the tariff on grains was highly protective, that on manufactures averaged only a rather modest 25 percent.

In France, inability of agricultural and industrial groups interested in protection to unite promptly postponed for two decades any action to reverse the low-duty treaties of the 1860s. Not until 1892, when these groups controlled Parliament, was tariff revision undertaken; but when it came, it was thorough. Duties on agricultural products were set at new high levels, and those on manufactures were raised to an average of about 34 percent. Another increase came in 1910, when protection was also extended to many newly developed products, among them chemicals and electrical and rubber goods.

For the beginning of that policy of protection always associated with the Republican party in the United States, we have to go back to the eve of the Civil War. Victory in the elections of 1859 brought the Republicans to power on a platform calling for the encouragement of industrial development by tariff protection. The tariff of 1861 embodied this principle; it repealed the low duties of 1857 (24 percent on most imports, with maximum rates of 30 percent) and restored those current in 1846, when most dutiable articles paid 30 percent, a few 40 percent, and brandy and spirits, alone, a maximum of 100 percent. Rising financial requirements of the Union government led to further increases and extensions until 1864, when rates averaged 47 percent, a record level. After a brief lowering of duties by a flat 5 percent in the 1880s, owing to a constant surplus in government revenues, the tariff was hiked twice in rapid succession, in 1890 (average rate of duties, 50 percent) and in 1897 (average rate of 57 percent).[6]

Some idea of the intellectual level of tariff discussion of these times may be gained from the following excerpt from the Republican platform of 1896, which wrapped the tariff in the American flag and propounded most of the conventional arguments in its support:

> We renew and emphasize our allegiance to the policy of protection as the bulwark of American industrial independence and the foundation of American development and prosperity. This true American policy taxes foreign products and encourages home industry; it puts the burden of revenue on foreign goods; it secures the American market for the Amer-

---

[6] These percentages are very approximate, owing to the difficulty of estimating the ratio of duties to dutiable imports when some rates effectively prohibit imports. Nonetheless, they probably give a fairly accurate impression of the upward trend.

ican producer; it upholds the American standard of wages for the American workingman; it puts the factory by the side of the farm, and makes the American farmer less dependent on foreign demand and price; it diffuses general thrift, and founds the strength of all on the strength of each.[7]

No further change of general importance in the U.S. tariff occurred until 1913, when the new Democratic administration, the first since 1892–1896, undertook in the Underwood tariff a thoroughgoing revision. Over 100 items, including sugar and wool, were added to the free list; rates on nearly 1000 classifications were reduced, and relatively few were raised; the ratio of duties to dutiable imports fell to the extremely low average of 16 percent. Unfortunately, this new tariff had little opportunity to be tested; within a year, war broke out in Europe.

With the exceptions of Great Britain and the Netherlands, European countries generally followed the lead of Germany and France by adopting protective tariffs. Russia even preceded them. Before 1868, the Russian tariff had been comparatively moderate, aiming chiefly at revenue. That year, however, marked the introduction of a deliberate policy of protection. Recurrent and substantial increases in the duties from then until 1914 gave her one of the highest, if not the highest, tariffs in the world.

Upon the unification of Italy in 1860, the moderate tariff of Sardinia became the law of the new kingdom. Parliament adopted a policy of industrial protection in 1878, extending the program to agriculture in the following year. In 1887, rates were raised to a high level and remained in effect until after the war. Switzerland first embarked upon a policy of mild protection in 1891, then stepped the rates up sharply fifteen years later.

Although increasing foreign competition stimulated the rise of strong internal opposition to Britain's liberal trade policy, its practical effect was to divide the Conservative party and to unite the free trade forces. In the election of 1906 the Liberals enjoyed an overwhelming victory, and little more was heard of protection as a general alternative to free trade until the economic collapse of the 1930s.

IMPERIALIST EXPANSION, 1880-1913

Just as during the liberal era governments showed an antipathy toward protection, so too they exhibited at least a passive attitude toward col-

---

[7] Cited in Asher Isaacs, *International Trade: Tariff and Commercial Policies* (Homewood, Ill.: Richard D. Irwin, Inc., 1948), pp. 207–208. See also Chapter 11 for a discussion of these arguments.

onies. There was little interest in subjugating native peoples and thus extending the dominion of the metropolitan countries. If the practice of governments thus coincided with the liberal doctrine of self-determination, it is doubtful if this resulted from deliberate intent. More likely, it was the consequence of preoccupation with internal problems of growth and development, as well as recent experience with colonies. Thus, in Britain, the value of colonies was seriously questioned, partly as a reaction perhaps to the rebellion of her American possessions, partly because larger and more accessible markets for her rising production were available in Europe and abroad. To England's experience of 1776, buttressed by claims for and achievement of self-government by Canada and Australasia, was added that of Spain and Portugal, which between 1810 and 1825 witnessed the loss of all but shreds of their former empires. Even Bismarck as late as 1868 regarded the advantages of colonies as illusory. Small wonder, then, that "colonies were looked upon as an antiquated encumbrance from the past."[8] France alone sought overseas possessions, acquiring Algiers in 1830 and parts of Indochina and Somaliland in 1862.

All this changed suddenly. Beginning in the 1880s, a wave of colony grabbing began that continued right down to the outbreak of war in 1914. Its principal results were the division of Africa among the European powers, the spread of Britain's dominion over Burma and Malaya, the extension of France's Indochinese empire over an area half again as large as the mother country, and the economic, if not the political, partition of China. The Americas were exempt from this land-grabbing fever—apart from the earlier, ill-fated attempt of Louis Napoleon to conquer Mexico—because of the Monroe Doctrine, the presence of the British fleet, and the growing strength of the United States.

How shall we explain this burst of imperialist expansion? Although it was a manifestation of the intensified national rivalry of the late nineteenth century, it can no more be explained by nationalism than can protection. Nationalism is a pervading sentiment that is conducive to certain types of action, but it contains no mechanism capable of generating change. It may provide the intellectual climate needed for change, but it is not itself a moving force.

It would appear that the planting of national flags in alien territory was closely related to the industrial growth of the metropolitan countries. This growth created a voracious appetite for raw materials—for copper, tin, and manganese; for sisal, hemp, and jute; for ivory, teak, and mahogany; for palm oil, copra, and rubber. Demand for these and other raw materials was high and rising; traditional

[8] L. C. A. Knowles, *The Industrial and Commercial Revolutions in Great Britain During the Nineteenth Century* (London: Routledge & Kegan Paul Ltd., 1922), p. 321.

sources of supply were inadequate, and new ones needed to be opened up.[9] Traders on the spot at the source of raw materials could make handsome profits—profits that were enhanced by the superior knowledge and sophistication enjoyed by the trader in his dealings with unsophisticated people.

But to obtain the raw materials on which his profits depended, together with sales to the native population of cotton cloth, liquor, beads, and trinkets, the trader required trading ports with an assured food supply, protection for his own and his employees' lives, and safe conduct for his goods to and from the interior. And when, as with rubber, cacao, tea, and palm oil, careful cultivation of crops in large plantations became necessary, substantial funds had to be invested.

All this implied a reasonably stable and effective government, capable of keeping the peace, disciplining outlaw and criminal elements, and providing assurances against the destruction or expropriation of property. Since backward and warring tribes could provide none of this, the trader had to do it himself. Very often the first political penetration of an area came about in this way, as an additional function of private enterprise in primitive surroundings. Later, as traders of rival nationalities threatened to invade his preserves, he appealed to his government. Supported by the industrial interests to which he ministered, and reinforced by the pervading sense of national rivalry, his appeals seldom fell on deaf ears. The "white man's burden" was accepted; and like protection, once started, landgrabbing tended to continue of its own weight, since unappropriated territory probably contained resources of value that someone else might get first. This sequence of events could be observed in many parts of the world, but nowhere more clearly or consistently than in Africa.

The Partition of Africa

Africa stood alone as a comparatively empty, vast, and defenseless area, and it was in Africa that the new imperialism found its main outlet. Before 1875, nearly nine-tenths of this continent was unknown to outsiders. The Ottoman Empire controlled, after a fashion, a fringe along the Mediterranean coast including Egypt, with the French-conquered

[9] Although the London prices, both of finished manufactures and of raw materials and foodstuffs, followed a downward trend from 1875 to about 1900, there is considerable evidence to show that, at the source, primary products remained constant or even rose. They fell in London owing principally to the large reduction in transportation costs brought about by the extension of railways, the substitution of steam for sailing vessels, and improvements in warehousing and handling facilities. See P. T. Ellsworth, "The Terms of Trade Between Producing and Industrial Countries," *Inter-American Economic Affairs*, **10** (Summer 1956).

territory of Algeria to the west. At the extreme southern tip, Great Britain had acquired the Cape Colony (1806) and Natal (1843). Apart from these substantial European and Turkish possessions, there was no trace of foreign domination except for scattered and largely forgotten trading posts established long before by the Spanish, Portuguese, French, and British along the west coast and by the Portuguese and French on the east.

The new imperialism began, strangely, as an international venture. After Stanley's exploration of central Africa brought news of its wealth in 1878, Leopold II of Belgium formed an international company that sent Stanley back into the Congo basin to stake out claims and establish trading posts. In 1885, the company transformed itself into the Congo Free State, with Leopold as its private sovereign and business manager. Later, in 1908, after mounting indignation over the brutal methods of exploitation used in the ivory, rubber, and slave trades, it was taken over by Belgium.

Simultaneously with Stanley's activities, the French got busy. De Brazza pushed inland from the French coastal settlement at Gabon, preceded Stanley's arrival at a point that later became Brazzaville, and established claims that were rapidly enlarged into French Equatorial Africa.

On the heels of de Brazza's and Stanley's exploits, rivalry between French, English, and German trading companies began in and around the basis of the Niger, which lies at the base of the west African bulge. The Germans also, with the support of Bismarck, who by now had been converted to imperialism, made a start in carving out German Southwest Africa, far down the coast next to Cape Colony. Typical methods were to buy small tracts or to make treaties (containing unintelligible text but accompanied by appropriate gifts) with local chiefs, and then to set up trading and missionary posts. Later the areas were extended by a wider network of "treaties" or by outright conquest; railways were built; and direct rule over large territories became a reality.

The partition of east Africa occurred simultaneously with that of the west, and by identical methods. Cecil Rhodes built an empire in Rhodesia and Bechuanaland, while other Englishmen were busy acquiring British East Africa and British Somaliland. Germany absorbed Tanganyika, France picked a quarrel with the queen of Madagascar and added this huge island to its domain. Even the Italians entered the race, gaining their slice of Somaliland, together with Eritrea.

Meanwhile Britain, after a period of joint supervision of Egypt's finances with France, had taken control of the country in the process of putting down a nationalistic revolt (1882). Using dubious Egyptian claims to the Sudan as a legal basis, Lord Kitchener pushed up the valley of the Nile, conquering the dervishes as he went, until he reached Fashoda in 1898. There he met a Captain Marchand, who after a two-year trek across the jungle from the French Congo, had hoisted the French flag. A diplomatic wrangle in London and Paris settled the question of sovereignty in favor of the British; the Sudan became nominally an Anglo-Egyptian condominium, and the British were well on their way to establishing their rule over a solid belt of territory from Cape to Cairo. Thus, after two decades of exploring, land purchase or conquest, and economic assimilation, all Africa except Abyssinia and the Negro Republic of Liberia had fallen under foreign "protection" or rule.

Imperialism in the Far East

French imperialism, checked at Fashoda, found more scope in the Orient. The acquisition in 1862 of Cochin China, at the tip of the Indochinese peninsula, had only whetted France's appetite. By intervention to avenge the murder of (non-French) Christians, by conquest, and by war with China, the French during the decade of surging imperialism extended their rule over all of what came to comprise Indochina. After an ultimatum to the king of Burma (demanding revocation of trading rights granted the French), followed by invasion, British India annexed Burma in its entirety (1886).

At the end of the 1880s the era of imperialistic land-grabbing was almost at a close. There was little unpopulated or weakly held territory not already under the dominion of one or another of the major powers, except in China. It was to China that the scene of imperialistic rivalry shifted in the 1890s.

Both China and Japan had been forcibly opened to commerce between 1840 and 1880. And even though Britain, as a result of the Opium War (1839–1842), had obtained Hong Kong, as well as five "treaty ports" where traders were to be free to reside and do business under their own laws, the rights so acquired were not to be exclusively British, but were to be enjoyed equally by other nations. The liberal principles of trade, not imperialistic exclusiveness, became the rule.

It was Japan, rapidly modernizing on western lines, that in 1894 began the race for foreign domination of the mainland. Rivalry in Korea between Japanese and Chinese factions unleashed the Sino-Japanese War, which resulted in Korean "independence" under Japanese tutelage, and the cession to Japan of Formosa and various smaller islands. Fearing Japan's expansion Russia, joined by France and Germany, intervened to prevent her taking south Manchuria. For their "friendship" and at their urging, China granted important concessions. The battle for concessions was on, and with the concessions came economic penetration and trade dominance as the preludes to possible territorial partition.

Thus matters stood when in 1904 Japan challenged the presence of Russian troops in Manchuria. The success of the well-trained Japanese troops in the war which followed gave Japan bases in Port Arthur and Dairen, together with important railway and mining rights hitherto held by Russia.

After the Russo-Japanese war, the parceling out of the earth had about come to an end. Only a few changes occurred before the frictions bred of imperialism broke out in World War I.

Dollar Diplomacy

Somewhat belatedly, the United States also became caught up in the wave of nationalist expanson beyond the areas already acquired. During the Spanish-American War, military strategy had dictated the seizure of the Philippine Islands. Since there was danger that they might fall into Germany's hands, since they had great economic and strategic value, and since there was also the "white man's burden" to consider, it was decided to keep them. In the same year, 1898, sugar interests in the Hawaiian Islands fomented a rebellion, established a Hawaiian Republic, and succeeded in getting it adopted by the United States as a territory. Hawaiian sugar thereby became a domestic American product, with duty-free entry to the mainland.

Barring these two episodes, the American imperialist phase involved no acquisition of foreign real estate, but what came to be called "dollar diplomacy"—intervention in the affairs of near neighbors in support of previous commercial or financial penetration. Thus in Mexico a struggle between British and American oil interests for control of the Mexican oil fields brought their governments to their support, with each backing a rival Mexican political group. The outcome was not too happy for either of the big powers, however, since the Mexican constitution of 1917 vested all subsoil rights in the Mexican people and furnished the legal basis for Mexico's expropriation, in 1938, of all foreign oil holdings. A similar conflict between British and American oil interests in Costa Rica led to U.S. support of a rebellion which established in power a regime that recognized American oil concession and canceled British ones.

Threatened losses to American bondholders led to direct armed intervention in the Caribbean republics. In 1905, the U.S. government insisted that the Dominican Republic appoint an American receiver-general to collect customs and to allocate to American and foreign bondholders the amounts necessary for interest payments. Political interference followed a few years later and culminated in 1916 in armed intervention and the establishment of an American military dictator-ship, which lasted until 1924. In Haiti, other means of imposing an unwelcome treaty having been unsuccessful, American armed forces in 1915 took over administration of the country.

Strategic rather than commercial or financial interests lay be-hind American armed support of the Panamanian "revolution" of 1903, which pried Panama loose from Colombia and gave the United States a perpetual lease on the Canal Zone. In Nicaragua, strategic and fi-nancial interests merged in American support, by loans and by armed intervention, of a rebellion (1909) friendly to American purposes. In the end, a treaty gave to the U.S. government the right to build a canal and a naval base; it also gave to American bankers control over Nica-ragua's finances, banking, and railways.

SELECTED REFERENCES

ASHWORTH, WILLIAM. *A Short History of the International Economy.* London: Longmans, Green & Co., 1952. An excellent brief study of the spread of the Industrial Revolution during the past century, of the emergence of an international economy, and of the course of international economic relations since 1914.

BAGEHOT, WALTER. *Lombard Street,* 14th ed. London: John Murray (Publishers) Ltd., 1915. A nineteenth-century work that had great influence on the formation of central banking policy.

BUCHANAN, NORMAN S., and HOWARD S. ELLIS. *Approaches to Economic Devel-opment.* New York: The Twentieth Century Fund, Inc., 1955. Chapters 7 and 8 contain a good, brief account of the expansion of the Western economy.

CLAPHAM, J. H. *An Economic History of Modern Britain,* Vol. 2. New York: Macmillan Publishing Company, 1932. A standard work on the subject.

FEIS, HERBERT. *Europe, the World's Banker 1870–1914.* New Haven, Conn.: Yale University Press, 1930. The best single source for data on inter-national investment in this period.

HENDERSON, W. O. *Britain and Industrial Europe, 1750–1870.* Liverpool: Liv-erpool University Press, 1954. Contains much illustrative material on Britain's role in the industrial expansion of Europe.

JONES, G. P., and A. G. POOL. *A Hundred Years of Economic Development in Great Britain.* London: Gerald Duckworth & Co. Ltd., 1940. An interesting and readable account of Britain's economic growth in the nineteenth century.

KNOWLES, L. C. A. *The Industrial and Commercial Revolutions in Great Britain in the 19th Century.* London: Routledge & Kegan Paul Ltd., 1922. Note-worthy for its emphasis on the role played by transportation in Britain's development.

PART
5

INTERNATIONAL
MONETARY
RELATIONS

17
CHAPTER

Income, Expenditure, and the Balance of Payments

Up to this point the main theoretical concern has been with the forces that determine how the world's resources are allocated to the production of different commodities, the specialization of production among countries that results, and the consequent pattern of international trade. This was a world of barter trade with balance in the value of exports and imports at the equilibrium price determined by the interaction of reciprocal demands. The problem of balancing a country's international transactions did not arise. This was because we assumed that all markets for goods and factors cleared and that the national income and national expenditure[1] were equal.

In this part we relax that restriction. We allow for the fact that, in the short or medium run at least, desired national expenditure may not equal national income. When national expenditure does not equal national income, the difference must be a change in the national asset position.[2] We need to consider simultaneously desired national expenditure, national income, and the desired national asset position.

A variety of issues is immediately opened up when we allow for

---

[1] For the reader familiar with the literature of the 1950s and 1960s, the term "absorption" is the relevant concept. We have chosen to employ the more descriptive term "national expenditure" to convey to the reader the sense that individuals *choose* to spend their income or to accumulate assets. The term "absorption" seems to suggest that it is a passive residual. As the discussion develops, it will become clear that "national expenditure" is not a residual category. Rather, it is part of the simultaneous determination of three variables: income, expenditure, and asset holdings.

[2] For the most part the national assets are financial assets. For completeness we should also note that inventory accumulation could also be the balancing item.

this simultaneous three-way relationship among income, expenditure, and assets. First, each country's income, expenditure, and assets are denominated in its own currency. Hence, what determines the value of each national currency in terms of another currency? Second, what determines the desired and actual national asset holdings, and how do changes in the national asset holdings interact with national expenditure and national income? Third, more than one type of asset usually exists. There is, of course, money. In addition to money there are claims on individuals, on corporations, and on governments. How do choices among these different types and choices among different countries affect the outcome? Fourth, desired changes in national asset holdings may run contrary to perceived or actual national interests. Governments sometimes intervene to impose controls. What are the consequences? Fifth, the system of international monetary relations may affect the outcome. What is the role of international monetary institutions? Are there different national interests involved?

These are the broad issues that are addressed in the second half of the book. And they will be taken up roughly in the order listed. The importance of these issues is evident to even the most casual observer of twentieth-century economic history. The spreading circle of restrictions on international trade and payments during the Great Depression is widely recognized as having contributed to a deepening of that depression. The massive U.S. balance of payments deficit of the late 1970s and the dramatic decline in the value of the U.S. dollar relative to the currencies of several other industrial countries, and the subsequent reversal of the U.S. dollar's value, are important milestones in the economic relations between the United States and the other industrial countries. Consequently, we will attempt to place our economic analysis in its historical perspective, both to illuminate the analysis and to help interpret the history.

THE BASIC RELATIONSHIP: INCOME AND EXPENDITURE

Let us begin by exploring briefly the basic relationship between income and expenditure. This is fully general and does not depend on the simple model we will employ shortly to lead the reader through some of the details of the analysis. Thus, in general, national money income is the total of receipts from the sale during a year of all goods and services produced by a nation, and national expenditure is the total of all payments made for the final purchase of all types of goods and services.[3] Those receipts that make up national income (Y) can be divided into two categories: receipts from residents and receipts from foreigners. National expenditure (E) can also be divided into two types of payments: payments to residents and payments to foreigners. Thus

Y = receipts from residents and receipts from foreigners

E = payments to residents and payments to foreigners

But receipts by residents from residents are identical with payments by residents to residents. Hence if we subtract E from Y,

$Y - E$ = receipts from foreigners − payments to foreigners

Thus if income exceeds expenditure, receipts from foreigners will exceed payments to foreigners by the same amount, whereas if expenditure exceeds income, payments to foreigners will exceed receipts from foreigners by the same amount.

Let us take this one step further. Since receipts from foreigners and payments to foreigners include all foreign transactions of a nation, the difference between them constitutes its net balance on current international account. In other words

$Y - E$ = net balance on current international account

or

$$Y - E = B$$

The balance can also be expressed in a more familiar manner. Receipts from foreigners arise from a nation's exports of goods and services, while its payments to foreigners are due to its imports of goods and services,[4] so we can transform the equation for the balance on current international payments to

$$B = X - M$$

The simple categorization of exports and imports should not mask the fact that there are many many different kinds of goods and services involved in the aggregrates. Commodity trade alone is highly

[3] This section is an adaptation of an analysis used by Harry G. Johnson in "Towards a General Theory of the Balance of Payments," Chapter 6 of *International Trade and Economic Growth* (London: George Allen & Unwin Ltd., 1958).

[4] As we shall see in the next chapter, the current payments and receipts must also account for transfers.

complex, comprising tens of thousands of goods ranging all the way from basic raw materials through semimanufactures to a great variety of finished manufactures. As for services, these are numerous and varied: transportation, communications, banking and insurance, government support of diplomatic missions and military establishments abroad, and economic aid, among others.

This large array of widely different and uncoordinated transactions that give rise to receipts and payments among well over 100 nations of varying size and character means that the possible sources of disturbance to any given country's international balance is large indeed.

Among the most vivid illustrations of such disturbances is the sharp increase in the price of petroleum engineered in 1973 and 1974 by the Organization of Petroleum Exporting Countries (OPEC), followed by a repeat in 1979 and 1980. Increases in the price of this vital source of energy had serious effects on the import bills of many nations. Switzerland, for example, found its bill for petroleum imports increase by more than threefold from 1972 to 1974. Besides the immediate impact of these actions on import bills and the price of gasoline and fuel oil, the price effects spread over a wide range of products: all petrochemicals and their derivatives, such as human-made fabrics, plastics, and innumerable products into which they entered as components. Another related disturbance to the trade balance of the United States and of certain western European nations was the surge of Japanese exports of their fuel-efficient automobiles in the late 1970s. As these illustrations suggest, the balance of payments of any nation can be subjected to unforeseeable disturbances whose effects may be seriously disruptive to its economy.

We are now ready to explore the details of the underlying analytical framework. Our approach is to begin with a highly simplified model and to complicate the model one step at a time so that it is clear what role each new complication has on the results. Of course, the highly simplified model will not "describe" the real world, and even our full model will remain an abstraction. This approach will, however, enable us to gain some powerful insights into the underlying forces and thus help us to interpret the course of history.

A VERY SIMPLE MODEL OF NATIONAL EXPENDITURE, INCOME, AND THE BALANCE OF PAYMENTS

In this section we set out a very simple model of how national expenditure is related to national income and to asset holdings, in order to discover some key feature of the simultaneous relationship among the three variables. We consider a small country that is completely specialized in production of one good only, clothing.[5] The quantity of clothing produced per year is fixed. This is determined by the underlying factor supplies and the production functions. Residents of the home country consume some of the clothing they produce and sell some on the world market in exchange for imports of a second good, food.

World prices of clothing and food are determined in world markets, and the volume of the home country's trade has no effect on those world prices: Residents of the home country are able to buy and sell as much as they wish without having any effect on the world market. This is the standard small country assumption frequently employed in international economics. It permits us to keep the analytical framework simple, for we are able to focus on the home country without having to worry about what is happening in the rest of the world. For a country such as the United States it is *not,* clearly, a "realistic" assumption, but it does permit the reader to grasp some important concepts. We will take up the interrelationships with the rest of the world in later chapters.

We also assume that international payments and receipts are made in some common means of payment used in all parts of the world. This permits us to leave the complication of foreign exchange to Chapter 19.

We assume further that all goods and factor markets are cleared each period. Hence there is no excess demand or supply for any factors or goods, and the income of the factors is the value of the domestic production. This means that all the fixed quantity of clothing produced each period is sold for the fixed world price, and that the factors producing clothing receive the full value of clothing production (price times quantity) as their incomes.

If we now add the assumption that all incomes are spent each period, we have a very simple model of balanced international trade. This is because each period the factors producing clothing receive the value of the clothing produced. They spend all of their income, partly on clothing and partly on food. The value of expenditure on clothing plus the value of expenditure on food thus equals the value of clothing output (income). The *difference* between the value of domestic expenditure on clothing and the value of output of clothing is the value of exports. But it is clear that this difference between income and expenditure on clothing is also equal to the value of expenditure on food

<hr/>

[5] The reader will recall that this complete specialization in production was a feature of the models of Ricardo and Mill discussed in Chapter 3.

imports. Therefore, there is balanced international trade. In summary, the following holds.

income = value of clothing production

expenditure = value of clothing expenditure plus value of food expenditure

exports = value of clothing production minus value of clothing expenditure

imports = value of food expenditure

Since by assumption, excess demand for goods is zero and there is no asset,

$$\text{income} = \text{expenditure}$$

Then substituting from above,

value of clothing production = value of clothing expenditure plus value of food expenditure

or, rearranging,

value of clothing production minus value of clothing expenditure = value of food expenditure

Therefore,

$$\text{exports} = \text{imports}$$

Let us now illustrate these relationships diagrammatically. We map quantities of clothing and food per period in Figure 17.1. Domestic production is specialized in clothing, producing OC_0 of clothing. The country is able to trade from the point C_0 at fixed international prices of P_c/P_f, with the ratio P_c/P_f equal to the slope of the line passing through C_0. This line then is the country's income line. When we constrain expenditures to equal income, the expenditure point is also on the income line at a point such as E_0. (The precise location depends on tastes and relative prices.) This means that the quantity OF_{e0} of food is imported, in exchange for exports of $C_{e0}C_0$. Since income and expenditure are equal, the value of exports equals the value of imports.

Figure 17.1   Income–Expenditure Equilibrium

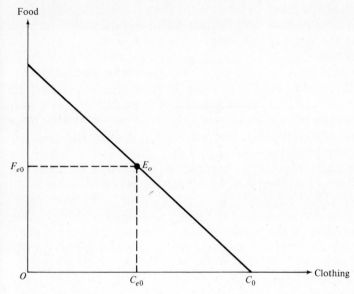

ONE ASSET

The reason income and expenditure are precisely equal each period is that by assumption we have not permitted any change in the national asset position. Unintended inventory changes in this model are ruled out by our assumption that excess demand for goods is zero, and no financial asset exists.

Let us now abandon that very simple model in one respect only. We introduce one asset into the model. There is no need at present to identify the asset. We assume simply that the asset is held by individuals because it yields useful services to its holders. Individual economic agents value those services in the same way they value the consumption of nondurable goods or the services of durable goods. If actual asset holdings match the desired asset holdings, then agents consume the services of the actual stock of the asset and they consume the value of their current income. Hence income and desired expenditure are equal. If, however, economic agents hold, say, more than the desired amount of the asset—or what is the same thing, they wish to consume more goods in the current period than their income permits—they will adjust their holdings of the asset until they reach the desired holdings. This they do by spending more than they earn. While such excess expenditure continues, their stock of the asset is being reduced.

On the other hand, if actual holdings of the asset happen to be less than desired holdings of the asset, *or* what is the very same thing, if desired spending is less than income, individuals spend less than their income and accumulate the stock of the asset.[6]

To summarize:

1. Individuals do not change their asset position when desired asset holdings equal actual asset holdings and hence desired expenditure (E) equals income (Y).
2. Individuals accumulate the asset when desired holdings exceed actual holdings, and therefore desired E is less than Y.
3. Individuals reduce asset holdings when desired holdings are less than actual holdings, and therefore desired E exceeds Y.

For the moment we make the further assumption that there is only one type of asset in the world. The small country we are considering has the very same type of asset as the rest of the world.

Consider what happens when domestic residents wish to accumulate the asset, or wish to spend less than they earn. Desired *ex-ante* expenditure plus desired asset accumulation equals income. Domestic residents receive as income the (fixed) value of the good they produce. They spend some on the export good, and of the rest they accumulate some as the asset, and they spend the remainder on imports. The difference between the value of the exports and the value of the imports is equal to the accumulation of the asset. Hence in each period the asset accumulation is equal to the net export surplus.

This situation continues only as long as individuals have some reason to spend less than their income. For example, once the asset balances have reached their desired level, to be consistent, domestic residents would no longer have any reason to spend less than their income, and expenditure once again equals income, the value of exports equals the value of imports, and the flow accumulation of the asset is zero.

Diagrammatically, the situation just described means that the expenditure point will temporarily lie below the income line, and hence the value of exports exceeds the value of imports. This is depicted in Figure 17.2, where E_1 lies below the income line passing through C_0. (We shall use the dashed line to depict the expenditure line and the

---

[6] It is worth emphasizing that it makes no difference to the argument if one looks at the worth of the consumption forgone by holding the asset rather than the worth of the services of the asset. At the margin these are the same. Hence if the worth of the consumption forgone by holding the asset rises, rational individuals will want to increase their expenditure until they have adjusted. But this is the very same thing as saying that the desired holdings of the asset have fallen and hence individuals spend in excess of their income until equilibrium has been restored.

Figure 17.2 Asset Accumulation

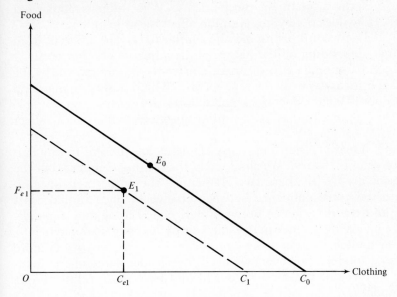

solid line to depict the income line.) The difference between income and expenditure is asset accumulation. The value of the asset accumulation per period is the value of the excess of income over expenditure. The asset accumulation is accomplished by selling exports of C_0C_{e1} per period, and buying a lesser value of imports, in this case of OF_{e1}, and taking the difference, which amounts to the value of C_0C_1, in the form of the asset. The accumulation of the asset and the corresponding export surplus continues until the desired stock of the asset is equal to the actual stock, or what is the same thing, until such time as the domestic residents decide to spend all of their current income. (Recall that the rest of the world is assumed to be so large, relative to the home country, that the export surplus and the change in the asset stock are absorbed without affecting the willingness of the rest of the world to continue to absorb or give up goods and assets at existing prices.)

CONCLUSION

The process just described contains two important elements that are worth emphasizing because they will be noted repeatedly throughout our analysis. First, the disturbance sets in motion adjustment forces that ultimately result in a new equilibrium. We will be interested in the nature of the adjustment mechanisms. What adjusts, and what does not? How does policy intervention affect the adjustment process? Note that the new equilibrium may be similar to or very different from the original, depending on the nature of the adjustments that occur.

Second, national expenditure differs from national income by the flow change in assets—all in real terms. Which assets change and which do not? What effect does policy intervention have on the outcome? The answers to these and similar questions will crucially affect the results.

Note, however, that both these elements are present in any balance-of-payments theory. We shall see in the coming chapters that the issues associated with these two elements—the adjustment mechanism, and the correspondence between change in the national asset position and the divergence between national income and expenditure—are recurring themes in our analysis of the balance of payments, even as the models become more complicated. Before we turn to more complicated models, however, we need to consider some of the institutional features of the modern world and how these relate to our simple model.

SELECTED REFERENCES

ALEXANDER, S. S. "Effects of a Devaluation on a Trade Balance." *IMF Staff Papers,* **5** (Apr. 1952). Reprinted in American Economic Association, *Readings in International Economics.* Homewood, Ill.: Richard D. Irwin, Inc., 1968. The original presentation of the real expenditure (or absorption) approach to the analysis of balance of payments.

JOHNSON, H. G. "Towards a General Theory of the Balance of Payments." Chapter 6 in his *International Trade and Economic Growth.* Cambridge, Mass.: Harvard University Press, 1958. A lucid statement of the basic approach regarding the balance of payments as the difference between *aggregate* receipts and payments.

MEADE, J. E. *The Balance of Payments.* New York: Oxford University Press, 1951. The classic modern treatise on the balance of payments. Chapter 1 on the meaning of the balance of payments is well worth consulting.

TSIANG, S. C. "The Role of Money in Trade Balance Stability: Synthesis of the Elasticity and Absorption Approaches." *American Economic Review,* **51** (Dec. 1961). Reprinted in American Economic Association, *Readings in International Economics.* Homewood, Ill.: Richard D. Irwin, Inc., 1968. Reintroduces into the literature the role of the asset money in balance-of-payments analysis.

18 CHAPTER

The Balance-of-Payments Accounts

Most countries maintain statistical records or accounts of their international transactions, often with great detail and elaborate discussion of their implications. These are called the balance-of-payments accounts. More formally, the balance-of-payments accounts may be defined as

> a systematic record of all the economic transactions between residents of one country and the residents of the rest of the world during a given period, usually one year.[1]

To better understand these accounts, and to see how they relate to our economic analysis, we want to examine the principal features of balance-of-payments accounting. Since the economic activity pursued in our simple model generates a prototype set of accounts that reflect the fundamental features of all balance-of-payments accounts, we begin there, and then turn to the more complex real world.

THE BALANCE-OF-PAYMENTS ACCOUNTS IN THE BASIC MODEL

There are two types of transactions that give rise to international payments and receipts: (1) those that take place in the market for goods

[1] Residents, whether individuals or organizations, are considered as having their residence where they normally live. A tourist is a resident of his home country, but a businessman living abroad more than some specified period (as defined by the laws of the country where he lives) is regarded as a resident of the foreign country. International organizations (the International Monetary Fund, the World Bank, the United Nations), are "foreign" regardless of location, whereas their employees are not. In addition to an annual balance of payments, a number of countries report on a quarterly basis.

and services and thus arise out of the production of expenditure of current incomes; and (2) those that involve the purchase and sale of assets. The former include exports and imports of goods and services, and are recorded in the *current* account of balance of payments. The latter relate to changes in ownership of items that already exist, and comprise the *capital* account.

To illustrate in terms of our simple model, let us assign numerical values to the situation described in Figure 17.2 To do so we need to specify a currency in which the transactions are recorded. We assume that it is a "dollar," symbolized by $. (Issues arising from the existence of different currencies are taken up in the next chapter).

production of clothing = 1000 units per year
price of clothing = $1.00 per unit
price of food = $2.00 per unit
expenditure on clothing = 400 units = $400
exports of clothing = 600 units = $600
expenditure on food
    (= imports of food) = 175 units = $350
total expenditure = $750
total income = $1000
asset accumulation = $250 per period

The corresponding balance-of-payments accounts are shown in Table 18.1.

Notice two important balances that will always occur in balance-of-payments accounts. First, the net current balance (+ $250) exactly offsets the net capital account balance (− $250). Second, the total of all receipts (+ $600) is exactly offset by the total of all payments (− $600), leaving a net balance of zero on all international transactions.

Table 18.1 Hypothetical Balance of Payments

Item	Receipts	Payments	Net
Current account			+ $250
Exports	+ $600		
Imports		− $350	
Capital account			− $250
Asset		− $250	
Total	+ $600	− $600	0

THE BALANCE-OF-PAYMENTS ACCOUNTS OF NATIONS

The actual transactions of nations are far more complex than those of our simple model, but the basic ideas remain the same. To illustrate, consider the balance of payments of the United States for two recent years in Table 18.2. First, the entries have netted out the receipts and payments so that under each entry we are looking at the equivalent of the net column in Table 18.1.

Receipts from the rest of the world are commonly called "credits" in the balance-of-payments accounts and are plus (+) items. The receipts are for such things as exports of goods, provision of services to foreigners, provision of the services of capital to foreigners (in other words earnings by domestic residents on their investments abroad), and transfers from foreigners to domestic residents.

Payments to the rest of the world are called "debits" in the accounts and are entered as minus (−) items. Payments are made by domestic residents for the purchase of imports, the purchase of foreigners' services, the payment of income to foreign investors, gifts to foreigners, the purchase by domestic residents of foreign assets, and short-term lending by domestic residents to foreigners.

Table 18.2 U.S. Balance of Payments, 1978, 1981 (Billions of U.S. Dollars)

		1978	*1981*
A.	Current account	− 14.31	4.19
	A.1. Goods, services, and income	− 8.76	11.39
	A.2. Transfers, donations	− 5.55	− 7.20
B.	Capital account	2.13	− 25.77
	B.1. Direct investment	− 8.17	12.88
	B.2. Other long-term capital	− 3.62	0.26
	B.3. Short-term capital	− 16.90	− 43.41
	B.4. Foreign official assets in United States	30.82	4.50
C.	Other	10.61	26.21
	C.1. Counterpart items	− 0.84	0.74
	C.2. Net errors and omissions	11.45	25.47
	Total A + B + C	− 1.57	4.63
D.	Changes in official reserves	1.57	− 4.63
E.	Net balance A + B + C + D	0	0

SOURCE: IMF, *Balance of Payments Statistics*, **33**, No. 8 (Aug. 1982).
NOTE: Short-term capital *includes* "exceptional financing" items.

In addition, note the basic distinction between current and capital accounts. The *current account* includes exports and imports of both physical commodities and various kinds of services, plus transfers (taken up below). The services include transportation, tourism (all services to travelers outside their home country), interest and dividends (representing the service of capital), government services (supplied to diplomatic, military, or other government agencies by the host country), and a variety of other services, which include banking, insurance, and motion pictures, among others. These services are sometimes referred to as "invisibles," since unlike the flow of goods they cannot be seen crossing the border. Nevertheless, they are fundamentally the same as the sale or purchase of physical commodities simply because they relate to the generation or expenditure of current income.

The *capital account* records all the purchases and sales of existing assets between domestic residents and foreigners. This includes direct investment abroad (a debit or minus entry) and by foreigners in the home country (a credit or plus entry). It also includes portfolio investment, and transactions by deposit money banks. Finally, it includes changes in the official reserves held by the home government.

Another distinction sometimes made is between long-term and short-term capital. The distinction is arbitrary: financial assets with maturities of less than one year are classified as short term. In a well-developed financial system, the maturity of the asset makes little difference to the holder in his decision with respect to whether or not to move his investment from one country to another.

It should always be remembered, but is often forgotten, that *all* international transactions, whether in the current or in the capital account, are carried out by individual economic entities and not by an abstraction such as a nation. It is people acting as individuals, as agents of a corporation, or as government officials who carry out international business. It is convenient, however, to refer to these transactions as *if* it were nations rather than individuals that are involved.

BALANCE-OF-PAYMENTS ACCOUNTING CONVENTIONS

In principle, a balance of payments is built up according to the rules of double-entry bookkeeping, of which the most fundamental is that every business transaction has two sides, both of which must be recorded. This simply reflects the economic principle underlying all business dealings: You pay for what you get; or one never gets something for nothing. (Gifts require special treatment, to be explained shortly.)

It is a convention of bookkeeping to charge, or debit, the owner of an account for everything he gets, and to credit him for everything he gives up. Thus a merchandise export would be entered in a country's balance of payments as a credit; the corresponding debit would show the manner in which payment was made. For most countries, which carry out their international transactions through one of the major foreign exchange markets, this would be in the form of an addition of dollars or sterling or some other foreign currency to the foreign currency holdings of the exporter's bank. There would be a debit to "foreign exchange" or "foreign balances" amounting to the value in domestic currency of the export. Imports, on the other hand, would be a debit entry in the country's balance of payments; the corresponding credit would be to "foreign exchange." This would indicate a reduction in foreign currency holdings of the country's banks.

Countries with important financial centers, such as New York and London, conduct most of their foreign business in terms of their own currencies. This is because the cost of the credit importers normally require is least in the larger and more efficient financial centers. With such trade, although exports will of course show up as a credit in the balance of payments and imports as a debit, the corresponding entries for the payments made will be to foreign-owned balances in domestic currency. Thus the bulk of U.S. exports will be paid for not by an increase in New York banks' foreign exchange holdings, but in a reduction in U.S. balances owned by foreigners. Most U.S. payments for imports would take the form of dollar payments into foreign-owned New York balances.

DONATIONS

Special mention should be made concerning the treatment of donations or gifts. These differ from ordinary business transactions in that they do not reflect an exchange of goods or services for money or for evidence of debt. Donations involve no *quid pro quo*. A person or a government transfers commodities or services or money to some other person or government, but receives nothing tangible in exchange. That fact must be recorded if the account is to balance. This is done by substituting for an entry recording a payment received, one which indicates that a donation has been made.

Thus suppose that the U.S. government extends economic aid amounting to $2 billion to certain less developed countries. If this aid takes the form of exports of machinery and equipment, the export figure on the credit side of the balance of payments is entered. The debit side, however, would have no record of a $2 billion payment since none of the aid recipients' foreign exchange holdings would be drawn upon to pay for these exports. Instead, the exporters would have been paid by the U.S. government. To record this in the balance-of-payments statistics, a debit entry entitled "donations" is made. This not only records the fact of the donation, but also preserves the balance in the international account required by the principles of double-entry bookkeeping. Private donations, such as immigrants' remittances and charitable contributions, and such compulsory "donations" as reparation and indemnities are recorded in the same way. Consequently, a country that on balance is giving away some of its current income to the rest of the world will have a negative entry appearing under the current account item "transfers and donations."

Some countries report their balance of payments accounts with particular foreign countries—usually countries with which they have especially close economic relationships. For example, Canada reports balance of payments accounts with the United States, the United Kingdom, and the rest of the world. The U.S. balance-of-payments accounts disaggregations include Canada, the European Economic Community, Eastern Europe, Latin America, and Japan.

ESTIMATES VERSUS ACCOUNTS

If governments kept a set of accounts showing international transactions, with every transaction recorded, construction of a balance of payments would be a simple matter of closing the account books. At the end of the year, a summary of the accounts—the balance of payments—would show the total flow through each type of account giving rise to receipts and through each type of account giving rise to payments. But the account or accounts in which actual receipts and payments are recorded—bank balances at home or abroad—would show only the net change.

But no such complete set of accounts is kept. Instead, an attempt is made to estimate each individual debit or credit item by methods of varying degrees of accuracy. For merchandise exports and imports, the figures are usually reasonably accurate, since reports are made to customs authorities as goods enter or leave a country, although smuggling is ever present and in some countries substantial. Leaving aside the smuggling problem, there remain substantial inaccuracies in reporting of seemingly obvious trade flows.[2]

---

[2] For an account of an interesting attempt to reconcile substantial differences between Canadian and U.S. merchandise trade accounts, see Statistics Canada, "Reconciliation of Canadian–U.S. Current Account Balance of Payments Statistics, 1970," in *The Canadian Balance of International Payments* (Ottawa: Information Canada, 1973).

The remaining items must be estimated somewhat less directly. Thus many countries estimate foreign travel expenditures of their own residents by generalizing from a sample survey based on questionnaires filled out by returning tourists. An estimate of the receipts from foreign travelers in the country can be derived from statements by entering and departing travelers as to their initial and final holdings of domestic and foreign monies, or from reports required of banks as to the value of travelers' cheques cashed. A country's banks can also be required to report changes in foreign-held balances, in balances they hold abroad, and other transactions under their surveillance. Obviously, there are many possibilities of error in these estimates. It is very unlikely that the two sides of any balance of payments will in fact be equal. This makes it necessary to include a balancing entry for "errors and omissions" (line C.2 in Table 18.2).

Despite the inevitable errors, a nation's international account can be discussed and analyzed as if it were a true double-entry record, for the facts it records are an approximation to what a complete accounting summary would show and can be treated in the same manner. Sometimes we may have clues as to the source to which errors and omissions should be attributed. Since short-term capital transactions are the most difficult to ascertain when reported evidence indicates that these are large, failure to count them all is likely to be responsible for a major part of "errors and omissions."

For the sake of completeness, we should also note line C.1 in Table 18.2, "Counterpart items." This entry is designed to account for changes in the stock of assets that are not attributable to flows of assets. The entry includes items such as the changes in valuation of foreign exchange reserves due to exchange rate changes, and the monetization or demonetization of gold.

MEASURES OF BALANCE

Recall that the total of all international payments and receipts with all foreigners must yield a net balance of zero. This is simply because a balance of payments, as an *ex-post* accounting record, must always balance if it is kept according to the basic rule of accounting. Individual subcomponents need not balance to zero, however. For example, the current account balance, which is the sum of all current payments and receipts, may be positive or negative. In fact, analysts are likely to be interested in a variety of subbalance measures because of the information conveyed. First, the *current account balance* itself is a useful measure because it tells the extent to which countries' current expenditures correspond to its income. A current account deficit, for example, measures the amount by which a country's current expenditure (including transfers) exceeds its current income. The difference, recall, must be financed by *asset* changes. Hence in 1978 the United States ran a current account deficit of $14 billion, which was financed by a corresponding sale of assets which aggregated to an identical amount. By contrast, in 1981 the current account ran a surplus (Table 18.2).

Subdivision of the current account balance may cast light on some issues. For example, the current balance *before* transfers and donations (A.1 in Table 18.2) tells the extent to which a country is currently "paying its way." All too often news reports will draw on artificial distinction between the "merchandise" or visible trade balance and the balance on goods, services, and income (A.1 in Table 18.2). Since there is no *economic* difference between a visible and an invisible, such a distinction is pointless.

A second balance that is sometimes reported is called the "basic" balance of payments. This balance looks at the total of the current account plus the long-term capital account on the grounds that these reflect the long-run influences that work on a nation's balance of international transactions. The remaining transactions—short-term private and official capital and changes in reserves—are all regarded as transitory. Further, as we shall see when we examine interest-sensitive capital flows in Chapter 21, government policy may deliberately act on interest rates to offset short-term capital flows. When this is the case, the short-term capital flow is acting to offset an *ex-ante* excess demand for foreign exchange that is deemed undesirable by the national policymakers. This balance for the United States in 1978 amounted to a deficit of U.S. $26.10 billion, while in 1981 the "basic" balance ran a surplus of U.S. $17.33 billion (see Table 18.2; add A + B.1 + B.2).

There are, however, two serious problems with this measure. First, the components of the basic balance itself—trade and long-term investment—are highly responsive to short-term developments. Hence it is entirely possible to have current account and/or a direct investment flow change because of short-term business cycle developments which have nothing to do with "basic" forces at work on the nation's balance of payments. Second, it is difficult to separate short-term from long-term capital in statistics; they are often intermingled. And short-term capital frequently is used to finance trade and hence can influence the so-called basic balance In addition, as we noted earlier, the length of maturity of an asset need not affect the permanence of its ownership. For these reasons, many economists do not regard the basic balance as a useful summary indicator of the overall balance of payments.[3]

---

[3] See, for example, the Bernstein Review Committee Report, *The Balance of Payments Statistics of the United States*, Report of the Review Committee for Balance of Payments Statistics to the Bureau of the Budget (Washington, D.C.: Government Printing Office, 1965).

A third balance that is frequently of interest is the official reserve transactions balance (line D in Table 18.2). This measures the extent to which domestic official authorities have entered into international transactions with purchases or sales of reserves. Such intervention, as we shall see later, is designed to offset an *ex-ante* excess demand for or supply of foreign exchange. In other words, if the total of all autonomous transactions were to yield an outcome that the authorities considered undesirable, they could draw on reserves (broadly interpreted) or add to reserves, depending on which way they wished to offset the outcome. The *ex-post* record in the balance-of-payments statistics records the *net* results of such transactions.

The reserves available to a country include (1) previously accumulated official holdings of gold and foreign exchange, and (2) established drawing rights at the International Monetary Fund (see Chapter 30). In addition, a country may engage in official borrowing, which would simultaneously increase its capital account credits and its stock of reserves.

It is important to note that the official reserves transactions balance refers to *domestic* intervention. The United States also records the extent to which foreign officials have purchased or sold U.S. assets. Foreign countries do this because they use U.S. dollar-denominated assets for their own official reserves. Thus in 1978 foreign official entities were net purchasers of U.S. assets amounting to U.S. $30.8 billion, while in 1981 they were net purchasers to a much smaller extent of U.S. $4.5 billion (see Table 18.2, item B.4).

To help fix ideas, we recommend that the reader review the balance-of-payments experience of a variety of countries in recent years, paying particular attention to the current account/capital account distinction as well as the official reserves transactions balance. The best source for such statistics is the IMF's *Balance of Payments Statistics*, (annual).

THE BALANCE OF INTERNATIONAL INDEBTEDNESS

One thing that a balance of payments does not show, but which may be important to know, is a country's overall balance of indebtedness. This is the total of its investments in securities and property in other countries, less the total of such investments by foreigners in the country in question. Such information can be useful for estimating a country's net earnings from overseas investment income or for calculating what liquid funds it could raise in a crisis, as on the outbreak of war. Together with known investment income, it provides a check on the average yield on the country's foreign investments. Such information has to be obtained through a separate inquiry or inventory of foreign long-term assets and liabilities, and is compiled much less frequently. We cannot expect to get it from the balance of payments, since the balance of payments includes, on the one hand, that part of the gross national product derived from net sales abroad and, on the other hand, changes in the country's foreign assets and liabilities, both short term and long term. The balance of payments is thus a flow per period of time, whereas the balance of international indebtedness refers to the stock position at some particular point in time.

We have reproduced in Table 18.3 the summary data for Canada's balance of international indebtedness in 1976 (the latest year available at the time of writing) and for comparison purposes, 1967. The gross indebtedness (liabilities) of Canadians to the rest of the world in 1976 was substantial. Nevertheless, noting the significant Canadian ownership of foreign assets means that the net indebtedness was about one-half of the gross indebtedness. Note further that the short-term assets and liabilities were approximately the same size, and a relatively small proportion of the total liabilities. This meant that Canadians were not faced with an immediate prospect of having to repay the net debt. Rather, on balance foreign-owned assets were being used by Canadians, and foreigners were being paid, net, for the use of those assets. Note that these *payments* for the use of foreigners' assets show up in Canada's balance of payments on current account as current account payments.

Table 18.3   Canada's Balance of International Indebtedness (Year End, Billions of Canadian Dollars)

		1967	*1976*
A.	Assets	15.2	48.8
	A.1. Long-term investments abroad	9.0	23.5
	A.2. Short-term assets	6.0	14.5
	A.3. Net errors and omissions	0.2	10.8
B.	Liabilities	40.5	97.3
	B.1. Long-term investment in Canada	34.7	81.4
	B.2. Short-term liabilities	5.8	15.9
C.	Net indebtedness A − B	25.3	48.5

SOURCE: Statistics Canada, *Canada's International Investment Position,* Catalogue No. 67-202 (Ottawa: Statistics Canada, 1980), Table 1.

SELECTED REFERENCES

INTERNATIONAL MONETARY FUND. *Balance of Payments Manual,* 4th ed. Washington, D.C.: IMF, 1978. This details how the IMF members should compile and report their balance of payments data in a uniform manner. One part focuses on basic concepts and underlying principles, another part deals with definitions and classifications, while a final chapter describes various analytic balances that can be constructed, but the manual eschews theoretical analysis.

————. *Balance of Payments Statistics.* Washington, D.C.: IMF, annual (with monthly numbers). This reports balance-of-payments accounts for all the member countries of the International Monetary Fund.

PESTIEAU, CAROLINE. *A Balance of Payments Handbook.* Montreal: Canadian American Committee, C.D. Howe Research Institute/Washington, D.C.: National Planning Association, 1974. A guide to understanding balance-of-payments accounting concepts and measures. The analytical portion is somewhat dated by the emergence of flexible exchange rates in the world economy.

STERN, ROBERT M., et al. *The Presentation of the U.S. Balance of Payments: A Symposium,* Essays in International Finance No. 123. Princeton, N.J.: International Finance Section, Princeton University, 1977. A presentation of some differing views by individuals well informed on the topic concerning the format adopted for presentation of U.S. balance-of-payments accounts in 1976.

MEADE, J. E. *The Balance of Payments.* New York: Oxford University Press, 1951. Chapter 2 takes up problems of the international consistency of definition of balance of payments.

19
CHAPTER

Foreign Exchange

The balance-of-payments records described in Table 18.1 were all kept in a currency called a "dollar." Which of the many different dollars of this world—the Hong Kong dollar, the Canadian dollar, the U.S. dollar, or some other dollar—was not specified. Moreover, it could just as easily have been some other currency—a peso, or a mark, or a franc, or a sol, or a cedi. Virtually every country of the world has its own currency.[1] It is now time to allow for the fact in our analysis.

When each country has its own currency, international transactions are distinct from purely domestic transactions in that they will generally involve at least two currencies. This immediately raises a great variety of issues. One issue, and in many ways the simplest, is the "translation" of prices in one currency into another. This is done by the *exchange rate*. The exchange rate at which dollars are translated into, say, pounds sterling also translates prices denominated in pounds into prices denominated in dollars. For example, suppose that a British exporter sells a bolt of cloth to an American buyer. The price per yard in sterling is £10. The American purchaser pays a price in terms of dollars that is the product of the price in sterling and the rate of exchange of dollars per pound. In other words,

price in dollars = exchange rate of dollars per
pound × price in pounds

or in symbols,

$$P_\$ = r_{\$/£} \cdot P_£$$

---

[1] The exceptions are former colonies or groups of former colonies that maintained some form of monetary relationship either among themselves or with the metropolitan country in the postcolonial era. For example, a group of Francophone countries of West Africa all use the CFA franc as their common currency.

Hence, if the exchange rate at the time of the transaction happened to be $1.50 per pound, the dollar price per yard would be

$$P_\$ = (\$1.50/\pounds) \times \pounds10.00 = \$15.00$$

Beyond the simple translation, a more significant issue arises from the fact that the domestic and foreign currencies are not the same. The earnings of domestic residents from the sales of goods and services and the sale of assets to foreigners mean that domestic residents receive currencies that are of no use to them in domestic transactions. To pay their employees or suppliers or to purchase their own day-to-day needs, domestic residents require domestic currency. Similarly, when domestic residents wish to purchase imports or foreign-owned assets, the home currency needs to be transformed into foreign currency.

The vehicle to carry out this transformation is the foreign exchange market. To help fix ideas, let us assume that the home currency is called a dollar, while the foreign currency is called a pound.[2] Consider two types of foreign transactions: one that gives rise to a receipt from a foreigner (a balance of payments credit) that is denominated in another currency; and one that requires a payment to a foreigner (a balance of payments debit) also denominated in another currency. Each case requires a transformation from one currency to another.

A Receipt from a Foreigner, Denominated in a Foreign Currency. When a home country resident sells goods, services, or an asset to a foreigner, and the foreigner pays in a foreign currency, the home resident would normally wish to sell the foreign-denominated currency on the foreign exchange market in order to obtain home currency. For example, an exporter from the U.S. sells an order of 1000 units of a good. The foreign buyer pays £40.00 per unit or £40,000 in total. The exporter now has £40,000, which he wishes to transfer into dollars. He offers the pounds on the foreign exchange market. At the going exchange rate of $1.50/£, the exporter receives

$$(\pounds40,000) \times (\$1.50/\pounds) = \$60,000$$

The same sort of transformation is involved for any other foreign-denominated receipt such as interest earned on a foreign-denominated bond or the sale of a security to a foreigner. They all give rise to a sale of foreign exchange.

---

[2] For the reader concerned that the home country is assumed to be "small," think of it as being the Barbados dollar.

A Payment to a Foreigner, Denominated in a Foreign Currency. Suppose that a home country resident buys a good, service, or an asset from a foreigner and pays in a foreign currency. To obtain the necessary amount of foreign currency to carry out the transaction, the home resident will have to buy the foreign exchange using the equivalent in home currency. For example, an importer purchases 500 units of a good at a price of £7000 per unit. The importer pays £3,500,000. To obtain the £3,500,000, the importer purchases the pounds on the foreign exchange market with the equivalent amount in dollars. At the going exchange rate of \$1.50/£, the importer pays

$$(£3,500,000) \times (\$1.50/£) = \$5,250,000$$

Any other payment in foreign currency, such as to pay interest to a foreign lender or to purchase a security from a foreigner, would give rise to a similar need to transform home currency into foreign exchange.

It is worth noting that it makes no difference whether the transaction is initiated by the domestic resident or the foreigner. In the first case, sale of pounds for dollars is the same thing as a purchase of dollars with pounds. Similarly, in the second case, the purchase of pounds with dollars is the same thing as the sale of dollars for pounds.

More generally, for *each* currency there are purchases and sales originating in a wide variety of international transactions from various locations around the world. For example, U.S. trade with the United Kingdom gives rise to dollar–pound transactions but such transactions are part of the entire world market for sterling and part of the world market for U.S. dollars. Thus, from the standpoint of the dollar, the sales and purchases of dollars which these transactions with the United Kingdom represent are part of the total world sales and purchases. In addition to this particular portion of the world market purchases and sales of dollars, there are those other portions originating in the New York foreign exchange market which although expressed as purchases and sales of Canadian dollars, German marks, French francs, Italian lira, Japanese yen, and so on, when looked at from abroad consist of sale and purchases of dollars in terms of these other currencies. All these contributions to the world purchase and sale of dollars coming from all parts of the globe make up the world market for dollars. What is true for the dollar is true for each of several other major currencies of the world.

Like any market, the foreign exchange market makes available to buyers and sellers the specialized services of intermediaries. In the foreign exchange market, where the object of exchange is national monies and claims thereto, the intermediary service is provided by special departments of banks, supplemented by highly specialized brokers. To see how such a market operates, consider one of the largest and most active.

THE NEW YORK FOREIGN EXCHANGE MARKET

The central core of this market consists of the foreign exchange departments of about twenty-five banks and their commercial customers "who are the ultimate users and suppliers of foreign exchange".[3] Exporters and others who have received payment or who have claims to payment in a foreign currency sell these claims to the trading banks, which thereby acquire bank balances in some foreign currency, of which pounds sterling and the Canadian dollar are by far the most important. Out of the balances so established, these banks sell foreign exchange to importers and others who have payments to make abroad. To the extent that such purchases and sales of any given currency are equal, payments in that currency are cleared within the trading bank. Normally, of course, each bank attempts to maintain an "inventory" of each principal currency traded, to be able promptly to meet the needs of its customers.

This segment of the entire foreign exchange market, encompassing direct dealings between banks and customers, is only its most visible portion. A second level of operations is conducted among the various foreign exchange banks. If a given bank's sales of a particular currency to customers exceed its purchases, seriously depleting its inventory, it may be able to acquire additional amounts of the needed currency from another bank whose purchases exceed its sales. These interbank transactions are not effected directly, but through the mediation of specialized foreign exchange brokers, who not only arrange the exchange funds, say dollars for sterling, between banks, but also the terms of that exchange—the current or spot rate of exchange.[4] Fi-

[3] Alan R. Holmes and Francis H. Schott, *The New York Foreign Exchange Market* (New York: Federal Reserve Bank of New York, 1969), p. 12. The description given here is based on this source.

[4] Brokers are also used in London, while in Switzerland with only a few banks dealing in foreign exchange, dealers of banks are in direct contact. Some continental countries have a foreign exchange bourse where dealers make their bids in public at daily meetings that "fix" a rate for the day. For a description, see Rudi Weisweiller, "How the Foreign Exchange Market Works," Chapter 2 in *Foreign Exchange.*(London: George Allen & Unwin Ltd., 1972). In Canada there is a single broker in each of Toronto and Montreal, employed by the banks as a group. See S. A. Shepherd, *Foreign Exchange and Foreign Trade in Canada*, 4th ed. (Toronto: University of Toronto Press, 1973).

nally, at times when either supply or demand in the entire market is in excess, New York banks correct the imbalance by direct trading with foreign banks through international telephone calls, cables, and teletype messages.

The New York banks with foreign exchange departments serve not only the New York area, but through correspondent relations, serve banks in other parts of the United States. A number of banks in other large cities, however, also maintain inventories of major foreign currencies and engage in foreign exchange transactions on their own account.

The New York foreign exchange market deals mainly in pounds sterling, the Canadian dollar, other European currencies, the major Latin American currencies, and the Japanese yen.

Most other currencies enjoy only a thin or irregular market. When a demand arises for a currency in which the New York banks do not maintain balances, they can nonetheless obtain such a currency in any amount desired. For banks in most countries maintain balances in New York; by making a payment in dollars to such an account, the New York bank can acquire the currency needed by its customer.

It is precisely the position of the dollar as a world vehicle currency that mainly accounts for the fact that most foreign exchange transactions involving the United States are carried out in terms of dollars, with the initiative for foreign exchange transactions originating abroad. Banks in major financial centers, principally London, Montreal–Toronto, Paris, Frankfurt, Zurich, Amsterdam, Brussels, Milan, Geneva, and Tokyo, maintain dollar balances in the United States, buy dollars from and sell them to customers, and deal with one another in much the same maner as do banks in the New York market. The result is a loosely connected worldwide network of financial centers making up the market for dollars.

INSTRUMENTS OF FOREIGN EXCHANGE

A number of different instruments are used to effect transfers in foreign currency. The commonest of these is the cable or telegraphic transfer. Thus an exporter in the United States may have received payment from a British importer in the form of a deposit to his credit in a London bank of, say, £100,000. He cables that bank to transfer this sum to the account of his New York bank, which pays him the equivalent in dollars at the going rate of exchange. Or he could cable the importer to make the sterling payment directly to the London branch of the New York Bank. An importer in the United States with a payment to make abroad would pay dollars to the New York bank, which would cable its branch or its foreign correspondent to make the payment in foreign currency to the exporter abroad. Foreign exchange transactions initiated in foreign markets are carried out in precisely the same manner. The only difference is that the cable is denominated in dollars, while the payment to the exporter or by the importer is made in local currency.

Bank drafts, which are simply checks drawn by one bank on another, are sometimes used instead of telegraphic transfers. When the importer on either side needs time to pay, the instrument used must provide for the extension of credit. The commonest instrument of this type is the bankers' acceptance.

A bankers' acceptance may be denominated and made payable in the currency either of the exporter or the importer. Generally, the currency chosen is that of the country with the most ample credit resources. Consider, for example, the use of a bankers' acceptance in connection with an import of Brazilian coffee into the United States. The importer in New York obtains from his bank a letter of credit, which authorizes the Brazilian exporter to draw a bill of exchange on his bank—say the Chase Manhattan Bank—for the value of the shipment, say $100,000, payable in sixty days. Upon receiving this letter of credit, the Brazilian exporter draws a bill ordering the Chase Manhattan to pay that sum to a specified New York bank. This he takes, with the letter of credit, bill of lading, and other documents, to his own bank in São Paolo, which pays him the cruzeiro equivalent of $100,000 less the discount rate in New York for sixty days. The Brazilian exporter has received his money and is out of the transaction. The bill (with attached documents) goes to the correspondent of the São Paolo bank in New York (say the Citibank), which presents it to the Chase Manhattan Bank for acceptance. It can now be discounted in the New York money market or held to maturity, depending upon whether the São Paolo bank wants to augment its dollar balance immediately or earn the discount. In either event, at the end of sixty days, the bill's holder presents it to the Chase Manhattan Bank for payment. This institution, having the previous day received a check for $100,000 from the importer, has the money in hand to close the transaction.

American exports as well as imports can be financed in a manner that permits the importer abroad to use the facilities of the New York money market. Thus a Brazilian importer of U.S. farm equipment would arrange through his bank to have its correspondent (the Citibank) issue a letter of credit to the American exporter, authorizing him to draw a bill of exchange in dollars upon it for, say, $100,000. This would order the Citibank to pay this sum at the end of sixty days to the bearer. When signed by an official of the bank, it becomes a bankers' acceptance. Normally, the exporter would discount it at his bank, which could recover the payment made to the exporter by discounting the bill in the money market, or earn the interest by holding it until maturity. Just before the sixty days expired, the importer in Brazil would have to provide the Citibank with funds to meet its acceptance. The simplest way for him to do so would be for him to buy a telegraphic transfer from his home bank, transferring title to $100,000 of its balance with the Citibank to that institution.

THE ROLE OF INTERNATIONAL FINANCIAL CENTERS

We have noted that the major portion of U.S. international transactions are carried out in dollars with the initiative for obtaining or making payment assumed by the exporter or importer abroad. To an even greater extent the international transactions of the United Kingdom are executed in terms of the pound sterling. The reason is that London and New York are great financial centers, with abundant and expert banking facilities and ample funds for the discounting of bills of exchange at comparatively low rates of interest. London became such a center in the nineteenth century, with the emergence of a variety of specialized brokers, dealers, and bankers. New York became a major financial center only after the establishment of the Federal Reserve System in 1915, which strengthened the financial structure and aided the growth of a market for bankers' acceptances.

For any group of nations whose banks have balances in a center such as New York, it is a simple matter to carry out their transactions, not only with the United States, but also with one another, in dollars. Thus Brazil can export to Greece and receive payment in dollars, while paying for its imports from that country in the same currency. Both Brazilian and Greek exporters, under letters of credit issued by correspondents of their banks in New York, draw bankers' acceptances on these New York banks and discount them at their local banks, which then have them rediscounted when they reach New York. When the time comes for the respective importers in each country to pay, each buys a dollar bank draft or cable transfer from his local bank, and therewith transfers Brazilian or Greek-owned dollars in New York to the banks in that city which have to meet the acceptance as they come due. The Brazilian and Greek exporters receive payment in cruzeiros and drachmas, respectively, the importers pay in these currencies, and to the extent that the exports of the two countries offset one another, they are cleared in dollars in New York. As far as Brazilian–Greek trade is concerned, the country whose exports are larger will wind up at the end of a given period with an increased dollar balance, the other with a diminished one.

ARBITRAGE

An interesting issue arises when we contemplate the simultaneous existence of more than one physical location for the purchase and sale of the various currencies of the world. For each, there is a world market that is not geographically centralized, but widely dispersed in various submarkets, yet is effectively a true world market because of the close linkage of these submarkets. This linkage is provided by arbitrage operations of foreign exchange traders.

Arbitrage operations link different foreign exchange markets together into what is, in effect, a single market in the following manner. Suppose[5] that the pound were quoted in New York at $2.40/£, while in London it stood at $2.45. Arbitrage dealers would then buy pounds in New York with dollars at the lower rate, sell these pounds in London at the higher rate, and make 5 cents profit on each pound bought and sold. The increased demand for pounds in New York would raise the rate there, while the additional supply of pounds sold against dollars in London would lower it, and the two rates would converge. They could differ only by the very small cost of carrying out these operations, which is low per pound because transactions are in large sums.

But arbitrage is not limited to operations in two currencies, or to two-point arbitrage. Three-point (and even wider) arbitrage is also common when currencies are free from controls. Thus is the dollar/sterling rate were $2.40/£ and the dollar/mark rate $0.60/mark, the implied cross rate between the mark and the pound is 4 marks/£. Suppose, however, that the actual rate in Frankfurt was only 3.8 marks/£. Arbitragers would then buy dollars with pounds in London (obtaining $2.40 with each pound), use the dollars so acquired to purchase marks in New York (obtaining 4 marks for each $2.40), and buy pounds in Frankfurt with these marks. With the exchange rate there at 3.8 marks/£, with each 4 marks acquired in New York for £1, they could obtain £1.05. Thus for each pound invested at the start of the circle, arbitragers would earn a profit of £0.05. Assume, to simplify the arithmetic, that the dollar/sterling and the dollar/mark rate remains unchanged. Then arbitrage will continue until the value of the pound in marks is consistent with its value in dollars. This will be when the mark/pound

---

[5] For the sake of illustration the size of the discrepancy in this example is far greater than would ever occur in a real situation.

rate is 4 marks/£. Continuing purchases of pounds in Frankfurt would drive up the value of the pound, which means increasing the number of marks required to buy a pound. The result of arbitrage is to link the three exchange markets virtually into one, and to bring into being consistent cross rates.

When the purchase and sale of foreign exchange are subject to effective and tight control, arbitrage becomes impossible. Exchange controls usually require the surrender to the authorities of all foreign currencies acquired by residents and limit purchases thereof to specific approved purposes. If, in our illustration, Germany had such controls, arbitragers would be unable to buy pounds with marks at the cheap mark/sterling rate. The rate between the mark and the pound could then be inconsistent with the dollar/sterling and the dollar/mark rates. Such "disorderly" cross rates are a common accompaniment of exchange controls.

We can use either exchange rate, for instance, the dollar/mark rate or the mark/dollar rate, to express the value of the dollar or the mark. This is because two-point arbitrage keeps the value of a currency the same in each of a pair of markets. Moreover, the dollar rate of exchange on any currency, say the German mark, is the reciprocal of the mark rate of exchange on the dollar. When the dollar/mark rate is $0.60/1 mark, the mark/dollar rate must be $1^{2}/3$ marks/dollar. And with three-point or wider arbitrage establishing harmonious or consistent cross rates, we can take any free rate of exchange on a currency as representative of all rates.

THE FOREIGN EXCHANGE MARKET AND THE BALANCE OF PAYMENTS

If all business transactions between one country's residents and the rest of the world during a given year were carried out in the foreign exchange market, there would be a one-to-one relationship between the sum of daily market transactions for the year and the balance of payments. This identity is approached in some countries, but never quite realized. As we noted in the preceding chapter, certain transactions do not give rise to a purchase or sale of foreign exchange. These include donations, direct barter exchange of goods, and private compensation arrangements under which the importer in each of two countries pays an exporter in his own currency. In addition, goods or services bought or sold on credit that remains unpaid at the end of the year must be counted among the transactions carried out during the year, and must accordingly be recorded in the balance of payments. But since such transactions require no payment to be made during the period in which they are executed, they will not appear in the foreign exchange market during that period. Contrariwise, at the beginning of the year, some foreign exchange transactions will be unaccompanied by simultaneous balance-of-payments entries, the entries having occurred in the preceding year.

These exceptions mean that we cannot identify total foreign exchange transactions with the balance of payments. However, since only in exceptional times do barter and special compensation arrangements appear, then, unless unilateral transfers are quite large, purchase and sale of foreign exchange and balance-of-payments debits and credits should approximate to one another fairly closely. Liquidation of previous-year transactions early in the year and postponement of payments at the end of the year should also not differ greatly in normal times. Thus we can say with rough accuracy that all transactions entering the foreign exchange market during a given year will affect the balance of payments of that same period.

FOREIGN EXCHANGE DEMAND AND SUPPLY

The foregoing description of the processes of foreign exchange transactions and the market does not tell us why people want to engage in these transactions (i.e., why they might demand and supply foreign exchange). To clarify our analysis it is helpful to return to the simple model introduced in Chapter 17.

Suppose that the domestic currency of our small open economy is called the *crown*, symbolized by "kr." If we take the dollar as a representative foreign currency, then the exchange rate is stated as crowns per dollar:

$$r = \text{kr}/\$$$

It can be used to translate dollar-denominated prices into crown-denominated prices in the same way that the exchange rate between pounds and dollars was used to translate pound-denominated prices into dollar-denominated prices. Hence the world prices of the two goods in our simple model, clothing and food, are translated from dollars into crowns as

$$P_{c\text{kr}} = r_{\text{kr}/\$} \cdot P_{c\$}$$
$$P_{f\text{kr}} = r_{\text{kr}/\$} \cdot P_{f\$}$$

Let us assume there is perfect commodity arbitrage so that these relationships hold at all times.

Consider initially the situation described in Figure 19.1(a). Since income and expenditure are equal, the value of exports equals the value of imports—both in terms of local currency and in terms of foreign exchange. Sales of foreign exchange amounting to the quantity of exports times the dollar price of exports are exactly matched by purchases of foreign exchange to pay for imports equal to the dollar price of imports times the quantity of imports.

Figure 19.1   Income–Expenditure and Foreign Exchange Market Equilibria

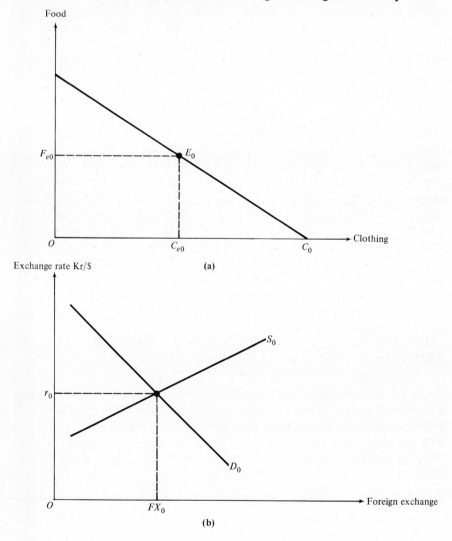

Table 19.1 Balance Sheet, Consolidated Banking System, Country X (Units of Local Currency)

Assets	Liabilities
Net foreign assets	Currency and bank deposits
Domestic credit	Net worth
Claims on governments	
Claims on private sector	

We know also that since income and expenditure are equal each period, the stock of the asset remains unchanged. To see this more precisely, consider the balance sheet of the consolidated banking system at the beginning of a typical year. The principal items are set out in Table 19.1. Note that, as with any balance sheet, these items are all stocks of assets and liabilities at the same date. The net foreign assets include foreign exchange working balances held by the banking system.

During the course of the year exporters will be receiving foreign currency which they deposit with their bankers, thus simultaneously increasing the banking system's foreign assets *and* liabilities to the exporters in the form of bank deposits. At the same time, importers will be purchasing foreign exchange from the banks. The banks' foreign assets and the banks' liabilities in the form of the importers bank deposits decline by identical amounts. As long as imports equal exports, it is clear that the banking system's purchases and sales of foreign exchange are equal, and hence there is no change in the banking system's net foreign asset position and no corresponding change in its liabilities.

A DIGRESSION: THE FOREIGN EXCHANGE MARKET DIAGRAM

It is helpful to think of these purchases and sales of foreign exchange as coming together in the foreign exchange market in the financial center (or centers) of the country. In this example, we have offers of sales exactly matching purchase requests. In other words, we have a point of equilibrium in the foreign exchange market whose demand for foreign exchange equals supply of foreign exchange at the current exchange rate of kr/\$ $= r_0$.

Pursuing, for a moment, the market approach, we can depict the market using the tools of demand and supply schedules relating the volume of foreign exchange to the exchange rate. Such an approach is a useful heuristic device, and for that reason we will make some limited use of it. The reader is warned, however, that the precise form and the shifts of the curves in response to various disturbances depend critically on the model employed. The partial equilibrium demand and supply curves for foreign exchange traditionally used in undergraduate text-books have the obvious shortcomings of any partial equilibrium measure applied to what is fundamentally a general equilibrium issue: Other things, such as income and expenditure levels, cannot be treated as unaffected by changes in the foreign exchange market. The foreign exchange demand and supply curves used here have no relationship whatsoever to such partial equilibrium curves. Rather, the demand and supply curves depicted here should be thought of as derived from the general model we are employing. Thus it is possible to derive for-eign exchange demand and supply curves from either the Keynesian model or the monetary model introduced in the next chapter.

A foreign exchange market is depicted in Figure 19.1(b), together with the corresponding production, consumption, and trade diagram [Figure 19.1(a)]. With domestic expenditure at E_0, and the income line passing through C_0 the value of imports equals the value of exports [Figure 19.1(a)]. With an exchange rate of r_0, the value of foreign exchange purchases and sales are equal to FX_0.

In addition to the exchange rate, what are some of the important influences on the equilibrium value of foreign exchange transactions? First, the volume of domestic production of the export good is positively related to the value of foreign exchange transactions. For a given set of preferences, which at the margin includes consumption of the import good food, the larger the domestic production of clothing, the larger the volume of imports and exports. Economically, this is simply be-cause a larger production of clothing amounts to a higher income. Part of that increased income is spent on imports of food, which is paid for by greater exports of clothing production (at fixed world prices). In terms of Figure 19.2 this amounts to production of clothing rising to C_1 and equilibrium expenditure moving to E_1: The extra foreign exchange volume appears as FX_1 rather than FX_0.

Second, the preferences of domestic residents for the foreign good relative to the home good affect the volume of foreign exchange trans-actions. If the home residents have little interest in consuming foreign goods, foreign exchange transactions will be low. Thus, at an income level given by the production of OC_0 clothing, if preferences were such that domestic residents preferred to consume at point E_0', the volume of exports and imports, and hence foreign exchange transactions (FX_0'), would be less than the volume when preferences placed the consump-tion point at E_0.

Figure 19.2   Adjustment to Increased Income

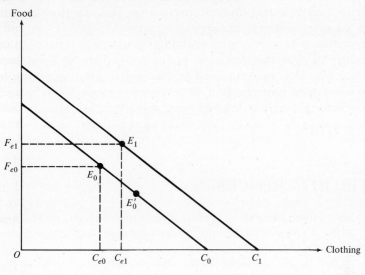

(a)

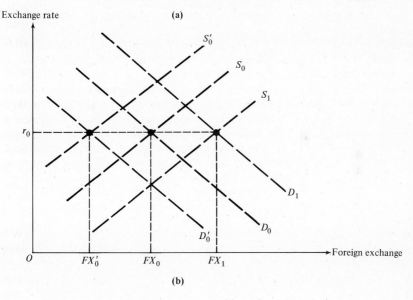

(b)

Third, the relative prices of exports and imports (i.e., the terms of international trade) will affect the equilibrium volume of foreign exchange transactions. For example, a high world price of the export clothing increases the volume of foreign exchange transaction due to both an income and substitution effect. The income effect raises the equilibrium volume because domestic residents spend some of their increased income on the foreign good food. The substitution effect also increased the equilibrium volume of international transactions because the foreign good is relatively cheaper.

The workings of the foreign exchange market are critical in our understanding of how the domestic economy and the international economy interact. We can now consider the interrelationships in more detail as we examine how the domestic economy responds to international disturbances, and how international disturbances impinge on the domestic economy. That is the task of the next chapter.

SELECTED REFERENCES

CONINX, R. G. F. *Foreign Exchange Today.* Cambridge: Woodhead-Faulkner, Ltd., 1978. An outline of current foreign exchange practices and views by professional dealers.

EINZIG, P. *The History of Foreign Exchange,* 2nd ed. London: Macmillan Publishers, Ltd., 1970. Describes the origin and evolution of foreign exchange markets, practices, and techniques from ancient times to the 1960s.

HOLMES, A. R., and F. H. SCHOTT. *The New York Foreign Exchange Market.* New York: Federal Reserve Bank of New York, 1969. A useful description of the workings of the foreign exchange market.

MANDICH, D. R., ed. *Foreign Exchange Trading Techniques and Controls.* Washington, D.C.: American Bankers' Association, 1976. Intended to inform bankers and financial analysts how foreign exchange markets work, the risks involved, and the "how to" of coping with the risks.

RIEHLAND, H., and R. M. RODRIGUEZ. *Foreign Exchange Markets: A Guide to Foreign Currency Operations.* New York: McGraw-Hill Book Company, 1977. A practical guide to the nature of exchange markets and their close relationship to money markets, including a discussion of many specific problems encountered in exchange market operations.

20
CHAPTER

Balance-of-Payments Adjustment

"France devalues the Franc—again." "The Canadian dollar hit a new all time low yesterday." "The adjustments necessary to eliminate the balance-of-payments deficit will be painful." These are but a few of the headlines that appear in the world-financial press in any given year or even week. They reflect two types of concern. One is that the balance of payments affects the rest of the economy. A balance-of-payments deficit or surplus, or an exchange rate change, can have a substantial impact on the domestic economy—and vice versa. The other concern is that a balance-of-payments problem or an exchange rate problem is one that must be dealt with. If it is not, other adjustment mechanisms will come into play. Are there policy choices here, and if so, what is there to choose among the options?

In this chapter we deal with the balance of payments and macroeconomic adjustment. We assume first that the country employs a *fixed exchange rate*. This system was the dominant system among industrial countries in the post–World War II period until the early 1970s. It is still employed by numerous other countries and hence is of considerable significance in the world today. The flexible exchange rate regime currently in use among many of the major currencies (or currency blocs) will be taken up next. A later chapter (Chapter 24) on the system still employed by most countries of the world—exchange control—will complete the list of possible options.

The focus of our discussion is on the relationship between the international and the domestic economies, and how a disturbance in one affects the other. We will want to know how some common domestic disturbances affect balance-of-payments adjustment, and, of course, how international disturbances affect the domestic economy.

In all cases we will be asking how equilibrium is restored to the balance of payments.

The nature of the adjustment that occurs depends very much on what is assumed or permitted to adjust and what is not, on the avenues through which the adjustment forces work, and on the time horizon being considered. The possible combinations of these elements are numerous and complex. International economists are still debating vigorously many of these issues. Consequently, it is impossible to present the reader with a definitive body of theory and empirical evidence. Rather, what we will do in this chapter is present two quite distinct models that have emerged in the literature: the Keynesian model and the monetary model. By working through those models the reader can expect to develop a more thorough understanding of how the balance of payments interacts with the domestic economy under fixed and flexible exchange rate regimes.

FIXED EXCHANGE RATES

What do we mean by a fixed exchange rate, and how does it stay fixed? Formally, a fixed exchange rate or a "pegged" exchange rate occurs when the monetary authority announces that it stands ready to buy and sell foreign exchange at some predetermined price of foreign exchange.[1] Hence if an excess supply of foreign exchange emerges, the authority must purchase that excess (using local currency). If an excess demand occurs, the authority must provide that excess demand (from reserves it holds for the purpose, or by borrowing from abroad).

The Keynesian Model

Recall that the key to understanding the balance of payments, in any model, is to determine what creates a divergence between expenditure by domestic residents and income of those domestic residents. One model where such a difference can arise is in the well-known Keynesian model of the open macroeconomy. The reader is undoubtedly familiar with the model, so we will simply sketch it here.[2]

The principal insight of the Keynesian approach is that output of goods and services varies with the aggregate demand for that output. For this to occur there must be some degree of excess capacity in the

---

[1] In most actual cases, the announcement is of some central rate plus or minus some small margin such as 1 percent, around the pegged rate.

[2] Any basic textbook of the principles of economics covers this material. The notation used here is standard, so the reader should have no difficulty using the model developed in a basic textbook.

economy that is not in production for want of adequate aggregate demand. The Keynesian approach assumes further that prices are given and do not adjust as aggregate demand changes. For these assumptions to be at all plausible we must assume that the equilibrium levels of income under consideration are sufficiently far from what might be thought of as the full-capacity or full-employment output of the economy to ensure that there is no pressure on the price level.

The most useful place to start in describing the Keynesian model is with the equilibrium condition: Income equals desired expenditure on home production by domestic *and* foreign residents. Typically, two categories of expenditure by domestic residents are identified: consumption expenditures (C) and investment expenditures (I). Since those expenditures do not distinguish between expenditures on home produced and foreign produced goods and services, to obtain the desired domestic expenditure on home production, imports of goods and services (M) must be deducted. Thus expenditure by domestic residents on home produced goods and services by domestic residents is

$$C + I - M$$

Expenditure by foreign residents on home production is simply the value of exports of goods and services (X). Putting all this together, we are able to write the Keynesian equilibrium condition

income = expenditure by domestic
and foreign residents
on home production

$$Y = (C + I) - M + X \tag{1}$$

To give the model some analytical content, we need to explain the forces that determine the various expenditure types. In the very simple Keynesian models, consumption and import expenditures are taken to be positive functions of income

$$C = C(Y), \qquad O < \frac{\Delta C}{\Delta Y} < 1 \tag{2}$$

and

$$M = M(Y), \qquad O < \frac{\Delta M}{\Delta Y} < 1 \tag{3}$$

while exports and investment expenditures are assumed to be determined autonomously.

There are several ways the Keynesian model is depicted graphically. The most common is simply to sum the expenditure categories vertically, as in Figure 20.1(a). The equilibrium condition (1) is graphed by drawing the 45° line along which expenditures by domestic

Figure 20.1   Keynesian Equilibrium Determination

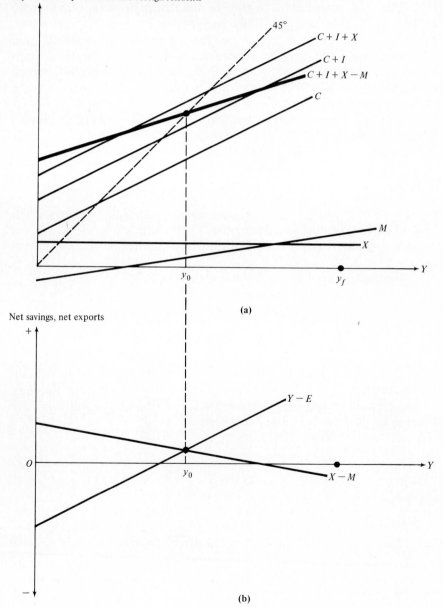

Expenditures by domestic and foreign residents

(a)

Net savings, net exports

(b)

and foreign residents on domestic production exactly equals income. Equilibrium income, then, is where desired expenditure by domestic and foreign residents on domestic production is just equal to income: at Y_0 in Figure 20.1(a). At a lower level of income, desired expenditures exceed output, placing upward pressure on output, while at a higher income level, desired expenditures are less than output, placing downward pressure on output. Hence, at Y_0, domestic output just matches desired purchases of it.[3]

To focus on the international dimension of the model it is useful to rearrange the equilibrium condition

$$Y - (C + I) = X - M \qquad (1')$$

On the left-hand side we now have income less expenditures by domestic residents on *all* goods (both domestic and foreign). The latter, of course, is the familiar E we have employed previously. Another way of looking at the left-hand side is to recognize that $Y - C$ equals savings (S). Hence the left-hand side is $S - I$, which is "net savings," or in other words $Y - E$. The right-hand side of ($1'$) is the value of exports minus imports of goods and services or the net balance on current account. The equilibrium condition (1) may be rewritten, therefore, in a variety of equivalent ways:

$$Y - E = X - M \qquad (1'')$$

$$S - I = X - M \qquad (1''')$$

Focusing on ($1''$), we see that in equilibrium the difference between income and expenditure by domestic residents is equal to the difference between the volume of exports and imports.

It is important to recognize that the *determination* of the equilibrium difference between Y and E is the result of the simultaneous working of the entire Keynesian system: The endogenous variables C and M plus the exogenous variables I and X *together* determine Y and E.

The equilibrium arising from ($1''$) is readily depicted by mapping $(Y - E)$, which is a positive function of income, against the current account balance $(X - M)$, which is a negative function of income. This we do in Figure 20.1(b). The equilibrium income level is at Y_0, where net income minus expenditure (i.e., net savings) equals the next export surplus. As we have drawn it, the economy is in equilibrium where the country is running a net export surplus and is therefore a net saver. The country is, consequently, accumulating assets in some form. The

---

[3] Note that in drawing Figure 20.1(a) we have specified some "full-capacity output" level Y_f somewhere to the right of our equilibrium.

Keynesian model does not directly concern itself with the issue of *why* residents of the home country accumulate assets. It focuses instead on the determinants of income and expenditure. Asset changes are thus the balancing residual.

Sterilization: A Brief Digression   An important issue remains. In a fixed exchange rate system, when an export surplus exists, the authorities are purchasing the excess supply of foreign exchange, and are paying for those purchases with domestic currency. Hence, unless the authorities act to offset this effect, domestic residents are in fact increasing their holdings of domestic currency each period. As we shall see when we take up the *IS–LM* model (which is still a Keynesian type model), such an asset accumulation can affect the Keynesian equilibrium.

To avoid this possibility we assume here that the authorities deliberately *sterilize* the effect on the domestic stock of assets of their foreign exchange market intervention. They do this by contracting domestic credit by an amount equal to the expansion of the net foreign assets of the monetary system. Thus, in terms of Table 19.1, the composition of the assets of the monetary system changes but the *net* left-hand side remains constant, and hence the monetary assets of the banking system are unchanged.

Disturbances and Adjustment in the Keynesian Model   One of the major features of the Keynesian model is that it helps us understand how changes in expenditure by domestic or foreign residents disturb the equilibrium domestic income. Such a disturbance could arise from any number of forces that are at work on the international and the domestic economies. It could arise simply because of a shift in tastes (e.g., for France, a greater preference in North America for German white wine over French red wine). Or it could arise because of some third force which alters the relative usefulness of the domestic and foreign goods (e.g., a change in the price of gasoline affects the relative attractiveness of the North American gas guzzlers vis-à-vis the fuel-efficient foreign automobiles). It could arise because of some deliberate action by the foreigner such as the imposition of a trade restriction on exports (e.g., a foreign tariff raised against our exports). Above all, disturbances to home exports are likely to occur because of changing business conditions in a country's trading partners. Expanded output among our trading partners is likely to result in increases in their imports (i.e., our exports).

The effect of these disturbances on income is the subject of the familiar multiplier analysis. Of most interest in the present context is the foreign trade multiplier. It is readily derived by noting that in the initial situation and after any change, the equilibrium condition (1) must be satisfied. Hence the changes must add up, too:

$$\Delta Y = \Delta C + \Delta I - \Delta M + \Delta X \qquad (4)$$

To illustrate this point, while keeping the analysis as simple as possible, let us assume that there is *no* autonomous shift in any of consumption, investment, or imports. Hence the relevant effects are simply the changes in consumption and imports induced by changes in income. Those changes are

$$\Delta C = c \, \Delta Y$$

and

$$\Delta M = m \, \Delta Y$$

where c and m are the marginal propensities to consume and import. Substituting into (4) and assuming that $\Delta I = 0$, we have

$$\Delta Y = c \, \Delta Y - m \, \Delta Y + \Delta X \qquad (5)$$

Rearranging, we obtain

$$\Delta Y - c \, \Delta Y + m \, \Delta Y = \Delta X$$
$$\Delta Y(1 - c + m) = \Delta X$$

Therefore,

$$\Delta Y = \frac{1}{1 - c + m} \cdot \Delta X \qquad (6)$$

The relationship (6) tells us that the size of the impulse to income from an autonomous increase in exports depends on the size of the "leakages" from the spending stream—the marginal propensity to import and the marginal propensity to save $(1 - c)$. The smaller those leakages (into savings and imports), the greater will be the income multiplier.

A graphical illustration of the effect of an export shift is contained in Figure 20.2. From an initial equilibrium at Y_0 with a current account surplus of CA_0, consider an autonomous increase in exports of ΔX. This shifts the current account function upward to $(X - M)_1$. At the initial level of income Y_0 there is total expenditure on domestic output by domestic and foreign residents that is in excess of that output. Con-

Figure 20.2 Export Expansion Effect on Income

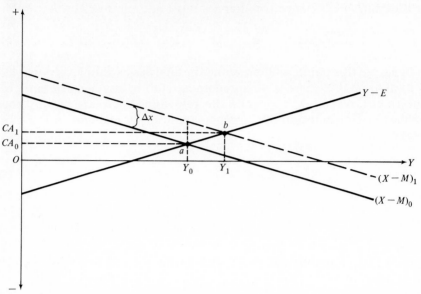

sequently, in the Keynesian model, output expands until that excess is eliminated. Equilibrium moves from point *a* to point *b*.

Notice two important points about the effect of this disturbance: (1) The effect of the size of the leakages may be seen graphically. The smaller the marginal propensity to save (and hence the flatter $Y - E$), the greater the effect of the export disturbance on income. The smaller the marginal propensity to import (and hence the flatter $X - M$), the greater the effect of the export disturbance on income. (2) In the new equilibrium the current account surplus is greater than initially, but because some of the increased export income is spent on imports, the increase in the surplus is *less* than the increase in exports.

Foreign Repercussions Recall in the preceding analysis that the foreigner's demand for home goods affects the equilibrium. Now if home imports are a significant portion of the foreigner's total exports (which is certainly the case for a large country such as the United States), then changes in the home country can affect the demand for foreign goods, which in turn will feed back on the foreign demand for the home country's exports.

To be more explicit, a fall in domestic expenditure would tend to reduce domestic income, and increase the current account surplus— meaning fewer net purchases from foreigners. This reduction in purchases from foreigners would tend to reduce their incomes, which

Table 20.1 Percentage Change in Real GNP Induced by a Sustained Autonomous Increase in U.S. Real Expenditure Equal to 1 Percent of U.S. GNP, Selected Industrial Countries

Country	After Two Quarters	After Six Quarters
United States	1.43	1.39
Canada	0.18	0.55
Japan	0.04	0.12
Belgium	0.02	0.10
Denmark	0.03	0.01
France	0.01	−0.07
West Germany	0.09	0.14
Italy	0.03	0.21
United Kingdom	0.06	0.10

Source: R. C. Fair, "Estimated Output, Price, Interest Rate, and Exchange Rate Linkages Among Countries," *Journal of Political Economy*, **90**, No. 3 (June 1982).

would then cause them to reduce their purchases from us. Our reduced exports would, as a result, create an additional income loss to the home economy due to repercussions from abroad.

In the short run such a spiral of effects can be quite important both to the foreigners and to the home country. This is certainly a significant element in the international transmission of the 1982 recession. In each country the severity of the recession was due primarily to the nature and magnitude of the domestic policies followed. The international linkages undoubtedly contributed to the spread of the recession, just as they contribute to the spread of expansionary pressures on the world economy.

The magnitude of these international linkages has been estimated recently by R. C. Fair.[4] Using an econometric model that takes into account the international linkage relationships, Fair found that substantial effects do exist, as shown in Table 20.1. Thus expansionary fiscal policy in the United States has a relatively major impact on Canada, amounting to over one-third of the effect it has in the United States. Note also the contrast between the effects on Germany and France. The former has significantly closer trade links with the United States than the latter.

Devaluation in Keynesian Model In a fixed exchange rate regime, perhaps the most potent instrument of all to affect the balance of payments on current account is the exchange rate itself. The key to understanding the effect in a Keynesian model is to note that the foreign

---

[4] Ray C. Fair, "Estimated Output, Price, Interest Rate, and Exchange Rate Linkages Among Countries," *Journal of Political Economy*, **90**, No. 3, 507–35 (June 1982).

goods prices are assumed to be given *in terms of foreign currency*. A devaluation of the home currency raises the price of foreign exchange. Hence the prices of foreign goods, in terms of *domestic currency*, rise. Exporters find it more attractive to sell abroad, and importers find home goods more attractive buys. Both of these effects work in the same direction as far as the current account in concerned: They tend to increase the current account surplus for a given level of income.[5] Hence, in terms of Figure 20.2, this is equivalent to the upward shift in the $X - M$ curve from $(X - M)_0$ to $(X - M)_1$. The equilibrium of the current account balance and income are both increased. Notice, then, that part of the effect of devaluation in the Keynesian model is to increase pressure on domestic output.

Conflicts in the Keynesian Model   The Keynesian model of the balance of payments points to a potential short-run conflict between the balance of payments and income. Suppose a country has a balance of payments deficit such as CA_0 in Figure 20.3. One avenue to elimination of the deficit would be to reduce expenditure. As long as income is below full-employment income, this would be regarded as undesirable because it would also reduce the equilibrium level of income. The deliberate creation of unemployment implied by such a policy to solve the balance-of-payments deficit is a choice most policymakers would find intolerable. Rather, the policymaker is faced with pressures to *increase* expenditure to reduce unemployment. This, of course, would exacerbate the balance-of-payments deficit. Consequently, countries that find themselves in a situation of unemployment and balance-of-payments deficit often choose to continue to run a deficit for as long as it is possible to draw on foreign exchange reserves, and perhaps incur substantial debt. Should the country be in the situation of inflationary pressure and balance of payments deficit, there is no policy conflict: A reduction of aggregate demand will solve both the inflationary and the deficit problems.

Returning to the case where there is a conflict between unemployment and the balance-of-payments deficit, the choice may be to restrict imports. Diagrammatically, this would shift the $(X - M)$ curve upward because for a given level of income, imports would be less. [The shift is not drawn in Figure 20.3, but the reader can readily perform the exercise of drawing a line $(X - M)_1$ that is parallel to but above $(X - M)_0$, passing through Y_2.] This gives the appearance of solving the balance-of-payments deficit with no accompanying income

---

[5] For completeness, we must recognize the possibility that the higher price of foreign exchange will reduce the volume of exports while having a relatively limited effect on the volume of imports such that the value of the net current account is not increased. We rule out such a case here.

Figure 20.3   Expenditure Increase Creates a Balance-of-Payments Deficit

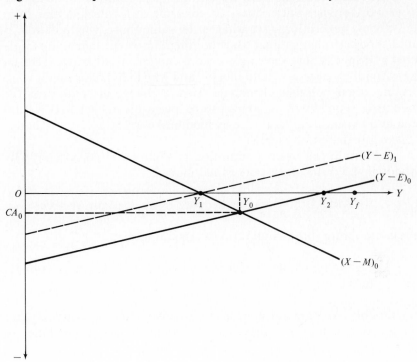

loss, but rather a gain from Y_0 to Y_2. In the long run, however, this reduces the country's gains from international trade (see Chapter 11), and if accomplished via exchange control may generate even more serious consequences for the domestic economy (see Chapter 24). Thus such a solution of a short-run problem is likely to cause long-run damage to the home country, as well as repercussions on one's trading partners. For the latter reason, such solutions have been referred to as "beggar-my-neighbor policies." The label was coined in the era of trade restrictions of the 1930s, but is equally applicable today.

The Monetary Approach

The monetary approach to the balance of payments, in its simplest form, takes income as given and focuses on the determinants of holdings of a single asset, money. As a result, expenditure levels adjust as necessary to permit asset levels to change. Recall that the Keynesian model treated assets as the residual that adjusted in some undetermined way to differences between income and expenditure.

Recall also the simple model developed in Chapter 17, where we had one unspecified asset and we did not concern ourselves with the *reason* individuals would choose to consume at a rate different from their income generation—or, what is the same thing, why individuals would choose to change their asset holdings. Now we take that simple model and specify that the single asset is money. Further, we focus on why individuals choose to hold money, and why individuals might want to change their holdings of money. Such a change in holdings of the single asset money will, of course, introduce a divergence between income and expenditure, and a corresponding current account balance-of-payments deficit or surplus.

We retain the basic assumption of Chapter 17 concerning why individuals hold the asset; now called money.

1. Individuals hold money because it yields useful services.

We can elaborate that assumption by assuming that

2. The value of the services of money is directly proportionate to the stock of money held.

Finally, we keep our analysis relatively simple by assuming that the desired real stock of money is a fixed proportion of real income. In formal terms, this may be stated as

$$\frac{M^D}{P} = k \cdot Y \qquad (7)$$

where M^D is the desired stock of nominal money, P is an index of the domestic price level, Y is real income, and k is the desired proportion. This relationship may, of course, be transformed into a nominal relationship, multiplying through by the index of the domestic price level, P.

$$M^D = k \cdot Y \cdot P \qquad (7')$$

Given (7), anything that changes real income will change the desired holdings of real money proportionately. Further, if we start from a position of equilibrium where the actual real money stock equals the desired real money stock, then anything that changes the price level, or the nominal stock of money, or real income will disturb the equilibrium and bring into play adjustment forces.

To illustrate how the monetary approach works, let us pick up the framework of the simple model of income, trade, and expenditure employed in Chapters 17 and 19. The analysis there focused entirely on the features of the equilibria. Desired expenditure equaled income, and desired asset holdings equaled actual asset holdings. In terms of Figure 20.4, the expenditure point E_0 is on the income line passing through the production point C_0.

From this state of equilibrium, consider how the adjustment mechanism works in the monetary approach under a fixed exchange rate. What adjustments occur in response to the disturbance? How is equilibrium restored? What does the new equilibrium look like?

We will consider three of the most common disturbances: a world price-level change, a domestic credit change, and a world terms-of-trade change.

A World Price-Level Disturbance Consider the effect of a uniform increase in the world price level: The world market prices of both clothing and food rise in the same proportion. Given the fixed exchange rate, the local currency prices of clothing and food also rise by the same proportion, as, of course, does nominal but not real income.

With higher nominal income, domestic residents will want to hold a higher nominal stock of the asset, money. How do they accomplish this desire? They reduce their expenditure, shifting the expenditure line inward, resulting in an actual expenditure point such as E_1 on the dashed expenditure line in Figure 20.4. Another way of putting

Figure 20.4   Price-Level Disturbance in a Monetary Model

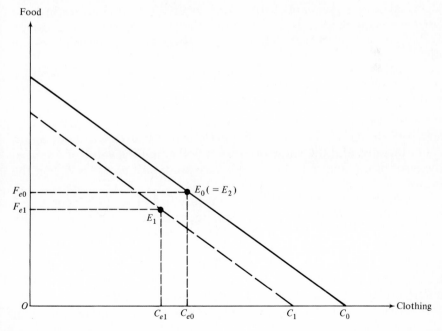

it is that the *real* quantity of money and hence the *real* flow of services of the money have been cut, but that since the real income is unchanged and since the relative prices of goods and money services are unchanged, the domestic residents wish to consume the same *real* money services as before. To accomplish this, they must restore their previous real money balances and can do so only by temporarily consuming less than their income.

Consuming less than income means that the expenditure point, E_1, is below the income line in Figure 20.4. This involves a larger volume of exports than initially, yielding a larger volume of foreign exchange earnings. At the same time the lower expenditure level reduces the volume of imports, to C_{e1}, which results in a lower volume of purchases of foreign exchange. Since in the initial situation the volumes of foreign exchange purchases and sales were equal, there must now be an excess supply of foreign exchange.

This excess supply of foreign exchange, under a fixed exchange rate, as we noted earlier is purchased by official intervention in the foreign exchange market. To keep the exchange rate fixed each period, the authorities must enter the foreign exchange market to purchase the excess supply. If they fail to do this, the excess offers of foreign exchange would bid the price down.

The official purchases of foreign exchange are made by paying out local currency. Thus domestic residents receive local currency payments equal to the excess of their exports over their imports, an amount identical to the excess of their income over their expenditure in local currency each period. In other words, the official purchases of foreign exchange finance the accumulation by residents of money balances in each period.

The accumulation of money balances restores the desired stock thereof. Domestic residents will continue to accumulate money balances—spend less than their income—only as long as their actual stock of money is less than the desired. When they no longer wish to accumulate money balances, domestic expenditures will once again equal income, and the value of exports will equal the value of imports. In terms of the diagram the expenditure point will be E_2 ($= E_0$) on the income line.

The process of adjusting expenditure from less than income (E_1) to equal income (E_2) at the fixed exchange rate means that the quantity of imports rises, and hence the quantity of foreign exchange demanded expands. Similarly, as the expenditure level rises, the quantity of exports falls and the corresponding supply of foreign exchange shrinks. Equilibrium in the foreign exchange market is restored, with the demand and supply of foreign exchange once again equal.

This process of adjustment of the money stock can be set out in

Table 20.2 Adjustment of the Balance Sheet, Consolidated Banking System

Assets	*Liabilities*
Net foreign assets—increase	Currency and bank deposits—increase
Domestic credit—unchanged	Net worth—unchanged

terms of changes in the balance sheet of the consolidated banking system—including the official entity that buys and sells foreign exchange. The items are the same as in the balance sheet shown in Table 19.1. Both the official agency and the commercial banks hold foreign assets and liabilities in the form of currency and deposits. As long as exporters' sales of foreign exchange exceed importers' purchases, the difference is purchased by the official agency. Meanwhile, the deposits by exporters of their local currency proceeds from the sale of foreign exchange have exceeded the payments by importers to purchase the foreign exchange. Consequently, during the adjustment process, there are two equal *flow* changes in the consolidated balance sheet: net foreign assets, and currency and bank deposits, both increase by the amount of the export surplus. This is illustrated in Table 20.2.

Finally, when equilibrium has been restored, annual demand for and supply of foreign exchange are equal, income and expenditure are equal, and domestic residents have accomplished what they set out to do when they reduced expenditure to a level below their income: They have restored their holdings of the asset money to the desired level. Consequently, they are enjoying both the services of money and the consumption of goods at desired levels that are consistent with their tastes and incomes.[6]

In the new equilibrium, nothing *real* has changed, but *nominal* values have. The domestic prices have risen to match the higher foreign prices. In order to stick to the "rules" of the fixed exchange rate system, the authorities have had to (1) permit the domestic price level to rise to the higher foreign price level, and (2) accept the increase in the domestic nominal money stock.[7]

In the new equilibrium, note also that nothing *real* has changed vis-à-vis the original equilibrium. The levels of real incomes, real expenditures, and real money stock are the same. The composition of real expenditure is unchanged.

[6] It is worth noting that the authorities could have achieved the same effect by expanding domestic credit rather than intervening directly in the foreign exchange market. The domestic resident's desire for greater nominal money balances could have been satisfied without the necessity of temporarily spending less than their incomes.

[7] As we shall see below, neither of these consequences needs to follow when we permit the exchange rate to change.

A few things have changed, however. The volume of the nominal money stock and the composition of the corresponding assets of the monetary system have changed. This is because in the process of restoring money stock to a level consistent with the higher price level, there was an accumulation of foreign exchange assets by the monetary authorities. Hence the assets of the banking system now consist of an increased stock of foreign assets and the same stock of domestic credit. Further, the volume of nominal foreign exchange transactions has increased. This is because the quantities of exports and imports are the same as initially, but the foreign currency prices have risen, with the result that foreign exchange transactions have increased by the proportion that world prices have risen.

A Domestic Monetary Disturbance   To strengthen our grasp of the fundamentals of this model, consider now one of the most common domestic disturbances to balance-of-payments equilibrium, an increase in the money stock that is not matched by an increase in demand for that money. The additional money is unwanted: Residents put a low value on its services relative to the value they attach to the consumption forgone by holding the money. Hence they choose not to hold the extra money but to spend it on goods.

The rate at which domestic residents choose to spend their excess money holdings establishes the amount by which their expenditure exceeds their income, and hence the excess demand for foreign exchange per period. This is readily seen in terms of the basic diagram we employed earlier. In Figure 20.5 we show the initial equilibrium expenditure at point E_0, given production of OC_0 and trading at given world prices of clothing and food to point E_0. Equal quantities of foreign exchange are generated by exports and used for imports.

From this equilibrium consider the disturbance of an increase in domestic credit. New loans are made by the monetary system to either the private sector or to the government. Corresponding to the loans are increased holdings of money in the economy in the form of currency and/or bank deposits. Faced with the relatively unwanted increase in the single asset, money, domestic residents increase their expenditure. In terms of Figure 20.5, expenditure moves to a point such as E_1, the value of the difference between E_0 and E_1 being the rate at which domestic residents draw down their excess money balances. Domestic residents have increased the volume of their imports of food and decreased the volume of their exports of clothing.

In the foreign exchange market, at the fixed exchange rate (and since world prices of clothing and food are unchanged), the volume of foreign exchange demanded increases and the volume of foreign exchange supplied decreases. To maintain the fixed exchange rate the

Figure 20.5   Adjustment to Domestic Monetary Disturbance

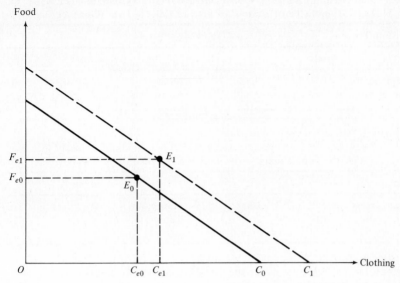

monetary authorities have to meet the excess demand for foreign exchange. They do so by selling foreign exchange from their exchange reserves. This decline in foreign exchange reserves also means a corresponding decline on the liabilities side of the consolidated balance sheet of the banking system: Currency plus bank deposits are falling, too. This, of course, is how the domestic residents are financing their excess of expenditures over income.

The gradual decline in money balances means that domestic residents are restoring these to the desired levels (determined by the services derived from money, given the real income and price levels). How fast this process occurs depends on how they feel about the state of disequilibrium. Ultimately, however, the excess money balances will have been spent, and there will no longer be any reason to finance expenditure in excess of income. Then the expenditure point will again be back on the income line at E_0 and the volume of foreign exchange demanded for imports will equal that supplied from exports.

As noted, these adjustments have an effect on the consolidated balance sheet of the banking system. The numerical illustration in Table 20.3 shows those changes simply. In the end, actual currency plus bank deposits (i.e., money stock) equals desired. Net foreign assets have declined by the amount of the original excess money stock, which was the amount by which domestic credit had been increased in the first place. In other words, the final equilibrium in this simple monetary model of the fixed exchange rate finds the money stock restored

Table 20.3 Numerical Illustration, Consolidated Banking System Balance Sheet Effects, Hypothetical Country (Millions of Units of Local Currency)

I. Initial Equilibrium

Assets		Liabilities	
Net foreign assets	2000	Money	5000
Domestic credit	3100	Net worth	100
	5100		5100

II. Disturbance: Domestic Credit Expansion

Monetary authorities increase domestic credit by 500 (which simultaneously increases the money stock by the same amount). The impact of the disturbances then yields:

Assets		Liabilities	
Net foreign assets	2000	Money	5500
Domestic credit	3600	Net worth	100
	5600		5600

III. Adjustment Process

Since nothing has happened to change the desired money stock, the adjustment process described in text begins. The excess of expenditure over income in this open fixed exchange rate economy involves a trade deficit, and hence an excess demand for foreign exchange at the fixed exchange rate. The cumulative <u>changes</u> in the consolidated balance sheet relative to the <u>initial</u> equilibrium are:

Assets		Liabilities	
Net foreign assets:			
decrease	500	Money	unchanged
Domestic credit:			
increase	500	Net worth	unchanged
Net changes	0		0

IV. Final Equilibrium

Hence, in the final equilibrium, the balance sheet of the consolidated banking system will be:

Assets		Liabilities	
Net foreign assets	1500	Money	5000
Domestic credit	3600	Net worth	100
Total	5100	Total	5100

to its original quantity, while the composition of corresponding assets has changed because the original attempt to create assets in excess of desired money stock led to a substitution of one type of asset for another.

An Improvement in the World Terms of Trade A different sort of disturbance to equilibrium occurs when *relative* world prices change, thus altering the terms of trade facing a country. We continue to assume that the country is small and cannot affect world prices, and that its volume of production of the exportable is given. Hence we can focus our attention on how the balance of payments of a small open economy adjusts to an exogenous change in the terms of international trade.

Consider the case of a rise in the world price of the country's export, clothing, while the world price of the import good, food, remains constant. Diagrammatically, the initial equilibrium is depicted in Figure 20.6. Expenditure at E_0 is on the income line passing through C_0 at the initial world prices of clothing and food. A rise in the world price of clothing increases the amount of food a unit of clothing will command, thus causing the income line to become steeper (C_0F_1 versus C_0F_0).

What determines the nature of the final equilibrium expenditure (E_2 in Figure 20.6)? We know that it will be equal to the new income level (on line C_0F_1). Exports may rise or fall, depending on whether the substitution effect or the income effect dominates. Since real income is higher, there is a tendency to consume more clothing at home, thus reducing exports of clothing. But since the relative price of

Figure 20.6 Adjustment to a Rise in the World Price of Export

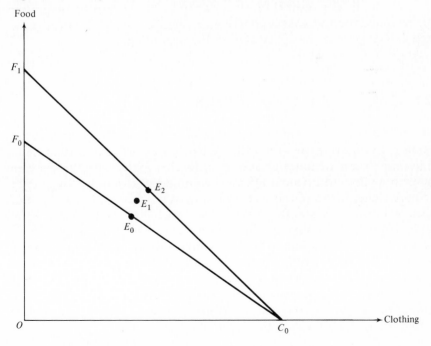

clothing has risen, there is also a tendency to substitute food for clothing, thus releasing more clothing for export. For most countries the income effect is likely to dominate simply because the export good and the import good are not usually close substitutes in domestic consumption. If so, export volume will decline. On the import side, both the income and substitution effects act to increase imports. Since in our example the world price of food is unchanged, we can say that at the new equilibrium expenditure, the amount of foreign exchange demanded that each period is greater than the initial equilibrium amount. And since in equilibrium the supply of foreign exchange must equal the demand, the foreign exchange derived from exports must also have risen.

What about the transition from the initial to the new equilibrium? Having a higher real income, residents will want to spend more on consumption and also add to their money balances. To accomplish the latter, expenditure must, temporarily, be less than income. In terms of the diagram, the temporary expenditure point must be *below* E_2.

During the transition, imports exceed exports in value, so the supply of foreign exchange exceeds the demand. The monetary authorities buy up this excess supply so as to maintain the fixed exchange rate, thereby causing the balance sheet of the banking system to show equal increases in the domestic value of foreign assets and money liabilities.

In the final equilibrium, income and expenditure are equal (at E_2). Demand for and supply of foreign exchange are equal, at the same fixed exchange rate that prevailed in the beginning.

FLEXIBLE EXCHANGE RATES

The second major system governing a country's exchange rate is the *flexible exchange rate*, in which the exchange rate adjusts in the face of an *ex-ante* excess demand or supply of foreign exchange. We want to known how that adjustment affects the domestic economy. Since 1973 the major currencies of the world (and currency blocs such as the European Monetary System) have been on flexible exchange rates. The list in 1980 included the United States, the United Kingdom, Japan, Canada, and the European Monetary System. In addition to major currencies employing fully flexible exchange rates, a number of smaller countries employ a device that very closely approaches it—the *crawling peg*, in which the exchange rate is adjusted almost continuously in order to maintain balance of payments equilibrium. Countries such as Brazil and Peru had such regimes in use in 1980.

Adjustment in the Keynesian Model

The key feature of a fully flexible exchange rate regime is that by movement of the exchange rate, supply and demand for foreign exchange are maintained equal at all times. Consequently (in the absence of capital flows which we have assumed away for the present), the balance of payments on current account $(X - M)$ will be zero. Diagrammatically, in a figure such as our representation of the Keynesian model in Figure 20.1 (b), this means that the $(X - M)$ curve coincides with the horizontal axis. This is how we have drawn Figure 20.7. The current account balance will always be zero, regardless of the level of income. Note further that because the current account balance always equals zero, in equilibrium income and expenditure by domestic residents must be equal to each other.

Consider now some disturbances to the equilibrium. First, let us examine a foreign source disturbance such as an increased demand by foreigners for home exports. Such a shift cannot affect the current account balance because the flexible exchange rate maintains the balance equal to zero. Hence there is no effect transmitted to the domestic

Figure 20.7 Flexible Exchange Rate Adjustment in a Keynesian Model

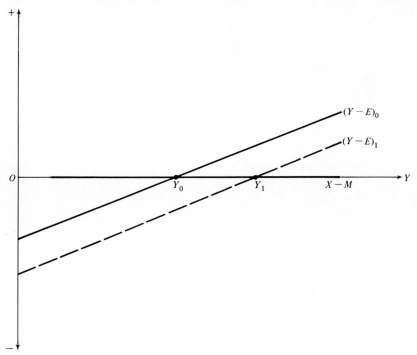

expenditure or income under a flexible exchange rate in this basic Keynesian model.

Second, we can examine the effect of a domestic-source change, such as an increase in domestic expenditure. [Diagrammatically, this would shift the $(Y - E)$ curve to the right.] The increased expenditure would not have a net spillover into the foreign sector. Rather, it would vent its full effect on domestic output.

The mechanism for this adjustment is illustrated by reference to the foreign exchange market (see Figure 20.8). Before the disturbance, demand and supply for foreign exchange are equal at the initial exchange rate (FX_0 at the exchange rate r_0). The increased domestic expenditure, at the initial exchange rate, would tend to increase domestic purchases of all goods and services. This would mean, in the absence of any adjustment mechanism, that desired purchases of foreign exchange for imports would increase (to a point such as DFX_1 in the diagram). At the same time, the increased domestic purchases of exportable goods would tend to reduce export offerings at the initial ex-

Figure 20.8   Foreign Exchange Market Adjustment to Increased Domestic Expenditure

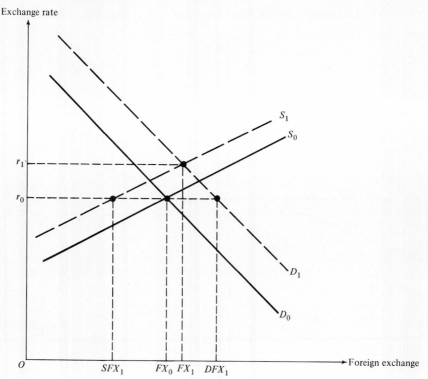

change rate (resulting in SFX_1). In other words, the increase in domestic expenditure has generated an excess demand for foreign exchange at the initial exchange rate.

Because the exchange rate itself is flexible, this excess demand situation will not in fact emerge in the market. Instead, the exchange rate tends to rise, encouraging domestic purchasers to switch away from purchases of the now higher-priced imports and exportables. The higher prices may also encourage people to spend less in general because the relative attractiveness of services from goods has fallen in relation to assets. The amount of the rise in the exchange rate necessary to restore equality between the demand and supply for foreign exchange depends, of course, on the size of the excess demand generated by the expenditure increase and on the responsiveness of the economy to the exchange rate rise.

Continuing with the illustration in Figure 20.8, we let the new equilibrium exchange rate be r_1. At this rate, the demand for foreign exchange (for imports) is once again brought into equality with the supply of foreign exchange (from exports) at a flow per period of FX_1.

Adjustment in the Monetary Approach

Regardless of the analytical approach employed to examine the effects of a disturbance, when the economy has a fully flexible exchange rate, supply and demand for foreign exchange are kept equal by letting the exchange rate adjust. In the monetary approach, as with the Keynesian approach, the contrast between the fixed and flexible exchange rate cases lies in the variables that adjust. In the fixed exchange rate case, the stock of money adjusts; in the other case, the exchange rate and hence the price level adjust.

First, what happens when an equilibrium situation is disturbed by an increase in domestic credit? Corresponding to the greater domestic credit is a greater stock of money. Domestic residents want to spend the excess money stock. Hence, if nothing else changed, there would be an excess demand for foreign exchange at the original exchange rate. With the exchange rate free to move it is the exchange rate that adjusts, rising in this case. This must occur because there is no mechanism to maintain the exchange rate at its previous level.

Underlying this process, it is important to note just what is, in fact, adjusting. The creation of an excess money stock disturbed the equilibrium between actual and desired money stock. To restore equilibrium either the actual nominal money stock or the desired money stock must change. Yet there is no mechanism for the actual nominal money stock to change.

Recall from equation (7') that the desired nominal money stock is assumed to be a fixed proportion of nominal income:

$$M^D = k \cdot Y \cdot P \tag{7'}$$

Now since the domestic price of each of clothing and food is the product of the foreign price and the exchange rate, the domestic price index (P) must also be such a product. In other words,

$$P = P_\$ \cdot r \tag{8}$$

Then, substituting into (7'), we have

$$M^D = k \cdot Y \cdot P_\$ \cdot r \tag{9}$$

Hence, since k and Y are exogenously given, and we continue to assume, as we did in Chapter 17, that world prices are given, only the exchange rate r can adjust (see Figure 20.9). The entire adjustment is borne by the exchange rate. To restore equilibrium, the exchange rate must rise—or what is the same thing, the value of the local currency in terms of foreign currency must depreciate. The size of the exchange rate change in this model is the same proportion as the initial monetary change.

At the higher exchange rate real domestic expenditure remains identical with the initial situation (in Figure 20.9, $E_1 = E_0$). The volume of foreign trade and hence foreign exchange transactions is unchanged ($FX_0 = FX_1$). The exchange rate and hence the domestic price level have carried out the complete adjustment ($r_1 > r_0$).

In contrast with the foregoing domestic change, consider now what happens when the foreign price level rises. At the initial exchange rate, local currency prices would be higher by the same proportion as the foreign prices had risen. The desired money stock would be greater and the domestic residents would want to reduce expenditure in order to restore equilibrium between actual and desired money stock.

In the same way as in the preceding example, there is no mechanism available to maintain the disequilibrium that would emerge in the foreign exchange market. Consequently, instead of remaining at the initial exchange rate, the exchange rate must fall, thereby causing local currency prices to fall by the same proportion. Monetary equilibrium is maintained because the increase in the foreign price level has been precisely offset by the exchange rate fall, leaving domestic residents in monetary equilibrium and hence in income–expenditure equilibrium.

Figure 20.9 Flexible Exchange Rate Adjustment in a Monetary Model

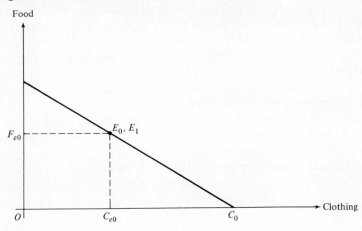

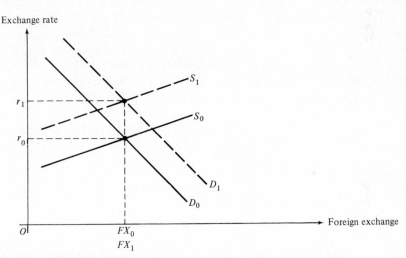

A SUMMARY CONTRAST BETWEEN FIXED AND FLEXIBLE EXCHANGE RATES

The foregoing analysis suggests a simple contrast between the properties of a fixed exchange rate and a flexible exchange rate regime.

We have seen that with flexible exchange rates a foreign price rise left the domestic economy unaffected. Similarly, a change in foreign expenditure on home exports did not affect the domestic economy. This suggests a basic proposition: A flexible exchange rate insulates the domestic economy from a foreign disturbance.

In contrast, under a fixed exchange rate regime, we saw that a foreign disturbance such as a foreign price rise in the monetary model or a change in foreign expenditure on home exports in the Keynesian model does affect the domestic economy. The maintenance of the rigid fixed exchange rate acts to transmit the foreign disturbance to the domestic economy.

What can we say about a domestic disturbance? With a flexible exchange rate regime we saw the domestic economy receiving the full brunt of either a monetary or a Keynesian expenditure disturbance. However, with a fixed exchange rate regime, the domestic disturbance is in part absorbed by the foreign sector.

This analysis suggests a general policy prescription—a country facing predominantly international disturbances could employ a flexible exchange rate to insulate itself from those shocks, and a country facing predominantly domestic disturbances could employ a fixed exchange rate to gain the help of the foreign sector as a shock absorber. However, one must interpret these results with some care. First, a real change in the economic circumstances of a nation ultimately must be accepted. The choice of exchange rate regime cannot possibly shield a country from such a change. An example may prove helpful. An improvement in the international terms of trade facing a country—such as an increase in the world price of petroleum for a petroleum exporter—must mean that the country is better off. As we saw with the monetary model, the exchange rate regime affects how fast a country moves to its new situation. It cannot affect (directly at least) the fact that its real income has changed.

Second, capital flows have not yet been included in our analysis. We will find that they usually act to dampen the effect of other disturbances, but can in themselves be a source of disturbance.

Third, there is more—much more—to the choice of economic policy instruments than an analysis of their effects. For example, suppose that a country chose an exchange rate regime on the basis that it expects to face international disturbances more frequently than domestic disturbances. It would then be well prepared for the disturbance that it expects, and ill prepared for the disturbance that it does not expect. And if the costs associated with the less frequent disturbance are substantially greater than the costs associated with the more frequent one, it is far from clear which should be offset, and consequently which policy should be in place.

Considerations such as these have led some countries to seek an intermediate form of exchange rate policy involving a flexible exchange rate combined with official exchange market intervention. It is often referred to as a *dirty* or *managed float*. We shall examine this policy option after we have included capital flows in our analysis (see Chapter 22).

THE CHOICE BETWEEN THE KEYNESIAN AND MONETARY APPROACHES

We have presented the Keynesian and monetary approaches as alternatives. We have done this largely because the literature has developed that way. Proponents of each invite us to choose one over the other. Is such a choice possible, let alone desirable?

The simple Keynesian model takes prices as fixed and focuses on income adjustment as the equilibrating mechanism in the economy. The monetary approach takes income as fixed and focuses on the money stock (fixed exchange rate) and the price level (flexible exchange rate) as the equilibrating variables.

One possible basis for choice between the Keynesian and monetary approaches, then, is to consider what one takes as fixed and what one believes adjusts. A fully general approach would take into account the principal features of both. That is the task that awaits us in Chapter 22. Before we move to that, however, we need to add a very important element in any discussion of international economic adjustment—international capital movements. That is the purpose of the next chapter.

A further possible basis for choice is to turn to the empirical literature. Unfortunately, as the authors of a recent survey of the literature observe: "With rare exceptions the empirical studies undertaken so far test the (monetary) theory 'in isolation'; in no way is it pitted against the traditional approaches."[8] The results of the empirical literature, then, are generally inconclusive. However, one of the specific predictions of the monetary approach has been found generally valid. The monetary approach maintains that as income grows, the demand for money grows. In the absence of any increase in the stock of money to accommodate this, the balance of payments tends to run a surplus (or the exchange rate appreciates). This prediction has been confirmed in several empirical studies. In contrast, the prediction that an expansion of domestic credit would be offset by an equal and opposite contraction of foreign assets has not been borne out in the empirical tests.[9]

---

[8] M. E. Kreinin and L. H. Officer, *The Monetary Approach to the Balance of Payments: A Survey*, Studies in International Finance No. 43 (Princeton, N.J.: International Finance Section, Princeton University, 1978), p. 76.

[9] See Kreinin and Officer, op. cit., for details.

SELECTED REFERENCES

ARTUS, J. R., and J. H. YOUNG "Fixed and Flexible Exchange Rates: A Renewal of the Debate." *IMF Staff Papers*, **26**, No. 4 (Dec. 1979). Reprinted in R. E. Baldwin and J. D. Richardson, *International Trade and Finance: Readings*, 2nd ed., Boston: Little, Brown and Company, 1981. Takes a critical approach to the claims made by proponents of both fixed and flexible exchange rates.

BLACK, S. *Flexible Exchange Rates and National Economic Policy.* New Haven, Conn.: Yale University Press, 1977. Relates the theoretical issues to the policy discussion.

FLEMING, J. M. "Domestic Financial Policies Under Fixed and Flexible Rates." *IMF Staff Papers*, Nov. 1962. A classic article on the subject.

FRENKEL, J. A., and H. G. JOHNSON, ed. *The Monetary Approach to the Balance of Payments.* Toronto: University of Toronto Press, 1976. A collection of the major papers associated with the revival of the monetary analysis of the balance of payments, edited by two of the major proponents of the approach.

KREININ, M. E., and L. H. OFFICER. *The Monetary Approach to the Balance of Payments: A Survey*, Studies in International Finance No. 43, Princeton, N.J.: International Finance Section, Princeton University, 1978. A reasonably critical review of the literature.

RABIN, A. A., and L. B. YEAGER. *Monetary Approaches to the Balance of Payments and Exchange Rates*, Essays in International Finance No. 148. Princeton, N.J.: International Finance Section, Princeton University, 1982. A nontechnical analysis which argues that although shifts in demand for or supply of money to hold may not necessarily affect the balance of payments, they can be and usually are.

WILLETT, T. *Floating Exchange Rates and International Monetary Reform.* Washington, D.C.: American Enterprise Institute, 1978. A policy-oriented discussion of the issues.

21
CHAPTER

International Capital Movements

Early in 1982 capital was fleeing Japan at around $1.8 billion a month. With the interest rate differential between America and Japan now much smaller, the net outflow slowed to $420 million in September. . . . foreigners began to find relatively underpriced Japanese stocks and bonds more seductive. Foreign capital started to move into Tokyo. . . . Helped by further cuts in the American Federal Reserve's discount rate, Japan's net capital outflow was only $290 million in November. So the yen rocketed by more than 10% in three weeks.[1]

Such a description involving capital flows, interest rate differentials, and exchange rate changes is commonplace in the international financial press. The forces at work are substantial. It is important, therefore, to incorporate such phenomena in our analytical framework. That is the purpose of this chapter.

The model we have employed up to this point has explicitly assumed that individuals hold only *one* kind of asset—money. It is now time to relax that assumption. The wealth of individuals and of nations consists of more than just money. It includes the capital stock—buildings, machinery, and other productive facilities as well as the stock of housing and durable goods such as automobiles, antiques, and art.

Although in most advanced industrial countries there are active markets for the purchase and sale of these assets, even more active are markets for *claims* on a share in those assets such as stocks (claims that include rights to share in the profits) and bonds (claims that are a promise to pay certain agreed-upon amounts at specified dates in the

[1] *The Economist*, Dec. 4, 1982, p. 73.

future). These markets enable individuals to exchange ownership of claims on the assets, and in the course of their functioning reflect the values placed on those assets. We know, too, that capital ownership is often international. The stocks and bonds issued by Exxon, General Motors, and Xerox, for example, are held by residents of dozens of different countries.

We now need to include in our analysis the fact that there exists more than just money as an asset. We will still maintain a highly simplified model to permit us to consider major issues with as much analytical clarity as possible. We will discover that even these highly simplified models can appear rather complicated, but by introducing one complication at a time it will be relatively easy to see the fundamentals.

The first complication introduced in this chapter is a second asset in addition to money. The immediate issue that arises is the determination of the composition of asset portfolios. How much of one asset versus the other do people wish to hold? What happens when the relative attractiveness of holding the two assets changes?

Once we are able to handle two assets, we will need to consider whether or not the second asset can be traded on the international capital markets. If the second asset is tradeable, then international capital flows become an issue. International capital flows, in turn, create a further link among the economies of the world. The nature of the link depends on the exchange rate regime. A capital flow under a fixed exchange rate means that participants are able to take the exchange rate as given both at the time they make a decision about what currency to hold or security to purchase, and in the future when they intend to hold a different currency or dispose of a security. When the exchange rate is flexible, the participants must also take into account the fact that change in the exchange rate could alter significantly the profitability of intended actions. The international financial institutions have created several mechanisms to assist the participants in coping with the exchange rate flexibility.

Capital flows also require the national economies to adjust. A fixed exchange rate means that changes in the distribution of the stock of assets between countries bears the major part of the burden of adjustment. When the exchange rate is flexible, much of the adjustment occurs via the exchange rate. Either type of adjustment has significant effect on the rest of the domestic economy.

A Second Asset

Individuals hold their wealth in many forms. Money is a convenient form for many reasons, but largely because money provides a service to the holder. Money is not, however, the only possible asset that people might hold. To keep the analysis simple, we will assume that in addition to money there is a second type of asset called *bonds*. A bond is simply a promise to pay the holder certain agreed-upon amounts of money at specified dates in the future. Usually, it is the payment of interest on certain dates and repayment of the principal at the terminal date.

Now, as soon as we allow an individual to hold a second asset, the person has to choose how to allocate his total wealth between money and the second asset. Since we are allowing only two assets, and given total wealth, as soon as the person chooses how much of one asset to hold, the amount held in the other form is automatically determined. For example, a person with assets totaling $10,000 in value may decide to hold $2000 in the form of bonds. This means that he has *also* chosen to hold the remainder, $8000, in the form of the alternative asset, money. In other words, the portfolio decision on how much money to hold is really the same decision as how many bonds to hold.

This fact greatly simplifies our analysis. We do not have to look simultaneously at the money market and the bond market. Given total assets, in equilibrium when individuals hold their desired stock of money, they must also be holding their desired stock of bonds. Hence if the money market is in equilibrium, the bond market must also be in equilibrium. Consequently, we are able to concentrate our attention on the money market.

By introducing a second asset we do have one significant complication, however. People must make a choice between the two assets. That choice we assume is based on the relative returns to holding the two assets. The return from holding bonds is the interest that is paid (assuming the bond is held to maturity). If we make the convenient definition of money as currency plus demand bank deposits (which do not pay interest), then the choice the individual faces is between the interest-bearing asset—bonds—and the non-interest-bearing asset—money.[2]

What can we say about the effect of the interest rate on the desired holdings of money? The greater the return on the competing asset, (i.e., bonds), the *smaller* the proportion of their assets individuals would like to hold as money. This permits us to specify a desired money holdings schedule that is a *negative* function of the interest rate on the competing asset. Figure 21.1 illustrates such a relationship. Of course, the other elements that we have already considered, such as the price

---

[2] Of course, the inclusion of interest on money does not fundamentally alter the issues. One simply has to think in terms of the net difference between the interest paid on money and on bonds.

Figure 21.1 Demand for Money

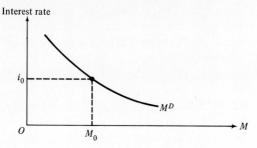

level, income, and wealth, all enter into the determination of the *position* of the curve describing desired money holdings.

It is clear from this that if all the determinants of the demand for money are given and if the interest rate on the competing asset is given, the desired distribution of wealth holding between money and bonds is also given. In Figure 21.1, given the position of the M^D curve, the interest rate (i_0) determines the equilibrium holding of money (M_0) and hence of bonds.

Money and Bonds in an Open Economy

We have not yet said anything about the international dimension of the issue. Let us continue to assume, as in our earlier models, that the country is small in the sense that world prices are given to it.

A critical distinction is between tradeable and nontradeable bonds. *Tradeable bonds* can be sold at the same price to either domestic residents or foreigners, equally easily. *Nontradeable bonds* can be sold only to domestic residents.

Several elements enter into the determination of whether or not a bond is tradeable. The key feature of a tradeable bond, that the holder can sell it just as easily in a foreign capital market as in the domestic capital market, means that the issuer must be known in the world capital market and the issuer's rating monitored by the international capital market institutions. For many issuers, such as small corporations and municipalities, it is not worth the trouble of establishing their credentials in the international market. However, for large corporations, national governments, many state and provincial governments, and even some city governments, it is worth the trouble, because the local capital market may not be thick enough to satisfy their needs.

The literature has developed in two strands, based on the distinction between tradeable and nontradeable bonds. The early literature made the insular assumption that domestic bonds are *not* tradeable, even though domestic goods are. We will begin our analysis with that assumption, turning later to the case where bonds are tradeable in the international capital markets.

As in the preceding chapter, the exchange rate regime will make a considerable difference in the analysis. We must, therefore, divide our discussion into the cases of the fixed exchange rate and the flexible exchange rate.

FIXED EXCHANGE RATES

Nontraded Bonds

Now consider the asset–expenditure equilibrium we established in Chapter 20, and include bonds in the stock of assets. Desired holdings of money depend now on both income and the interest rate. Suppose that from an initial situation of asset–expenditure equilibrium there is an addition to the stock of domestic bonds. How does the adjustment occur, and what effect does this have on the income–expenditure–international trade equilibrium? By assumption the excess stock of bonds cannot be sold to foreigners. Instead, the domestic price of bonds must fall to restore equilibrium. Bondholders are forced to accept the capital loss due to the excess issue of the nontraded bonds.

The excess issue of nontradeable bonds forces people to change the *composition* of their portfolios. Holding relatively more bonds means holding relatively less money. This, of course, is consistent with what we would expect from the fact that the price of bonds is the inverse of the interest rate. The fall in the price of bonds means that the interest rate has risen, and at a higher interest rate we have posited that the desired holdings of money is less. In brief, then, the excess issue of bonds creates, *indirectly*, an excess money stock. The excess money stock is vented just as if it were directly created: It is spent, until the (foreign) assets of the monetary system are reduced by the amount of the excess. In other words, even though the disturbance was not an increase in money stock, part of the *adjustment*[3] has been via a

---

[3] Part of the adjustment has been in the bond market also. The price of bonds has fallen, inflicting a capital loss on the nontraded bondholders.

reduction in the money stock because money and bonds are both assets that the public holds.

A numerical example may help to fix the idea. Let us use the country with the crown (kr) as its currency. Suppose that in the initial equilibrium the assets consisted of line 1 in Table 21.1. Then if the stock of (nontraded) bonds is increased by, say, 10 percent, the *initial (disequilibrium)* situation would be described in line 2.

Before any adjustment occurs, the situation described in line 2 is obviously a disequilibrium. What are the adjustments? There are two. First, the bondholders have more bonds than they wish at the existing price of bonds. To persuade them to hold this larger volume of bonds, the *price* of bonds must fall—which is the same thing as that the interest rate on bonds must rise. The value of the outstanding stock of bonds falls. Second, the higher interest rate to persuade people to hold a higher proportion of their assets in bonds means, correspondingly, that holding kr 500 in money has become relatively less attractive. Hence holders of money will spend their excess holdings of money until the desired distribution between money and bonds is restored. If income is unaffected, this means that the excess expenditure emerges as a balance-of-trade deficit until the cumulative trade deficit draws down the initial excess money stock created by the higher interest rate. The final equilibrium could be such as is described in line 3 in Table 21.1: The value of money holdings is less than in the initial equilibrium and the value of bond holdings is less than the initial plus increment of bonds. Note that even though bonds are not tradeable, because of the interdependency between the money market and the bond market, the excess issue of bonds meant that *some* of the adjustment had to be borne by the money market.

The result for the foreign assets was *just as if* there had been an excess issue of money of kr 15. The balance of trade deficit had to run until the kr 15 of excess money holdings had been spent. One of the reasons we have considered the case of nontraded bonds is that there is associated with them a literature that is largely in the Keynesian tradition—we shall take this up in the next chapter.

Table 21.1

Situation	Money	+	Bonds	=	Total Assets
1. Initial equilibrium	kr 500	+	kr 200	=	kr 700
2. Impact of additional bonds	kr 500	+	kr 220	=	kr 720
3. Final equilibrium	kr 485	+	kr 215	=	kr 700

Tradeable Bonds

Let us now introduce internationally tradeable bonds into the picture. To keep the analysis simple, let us assume that the bonds of domestic issuers are just as acceptable on the international capital market as they are by domestic residents. Assume further that the country is also small in the sense that it takes the interest rate on world capital markets as given. Now, consider a disturbance to the asset–expenditure equilibrium we had initially set out in Chapter 20. Suppose that total assets are increased by an issue of bonds, creating an excess of actual bond holdings over desired. Domestic residents will spend more than their income in order to restore their asset holdings to the desired level. The component of their excess assets that they are selling is tradeable bonds. When they sell these on the domestic market, instead of depressing the price of bonds domestically, at the first sign of depression of the domestic price of bonds, foreigners will buy the domestic bonds (which are tradeable) and will continue to do so until domestic residents have restored asset equilibrium.

Notice that two things happen simultaneously;

1. Domestic residents spend more than domestic income, thus creating a current account deficit.
2. Foreigners buy the domestic bonds that are sold to finance the excess of expenditure over income, thus creating a capital account surplus that exactly offsets the current account deficit.

The *net* effect on the balance of international payments and receipts in this case is *zero*. However, the *composition* of the balance of payments has been changed. The sale of bonds to foreigners increases the supply of foreign exchange, while the net excess of expenditure increases the demand for foreign exchange by exactly the same amount. Thus, while income remains the same, expenditure rises above income, the excess being financed by the sale of bonds to foreigners. In terms of Figure 21.2, expenditure rises to E_1 (above the income line passing through E_0). The volume of foreign exchange transactions rises. Despite the level of expenditure in excess of income, there is no loss of foreign exchange reserves because the trade deficit exactly equals the capital account surplus.

Notice also that the *transfer* of real resources from foreigners to domestic residents, corresponding to the sale of the bonds to the foreigners, has been accomplished by the process of expenditure in excess of income. Similarly, in the opposite case of a foreign sale of bonds to domestic residents, the domestic residents must give up to the for-

Figure 21.2   Adjustment to the Issue of Tradeable Bonds

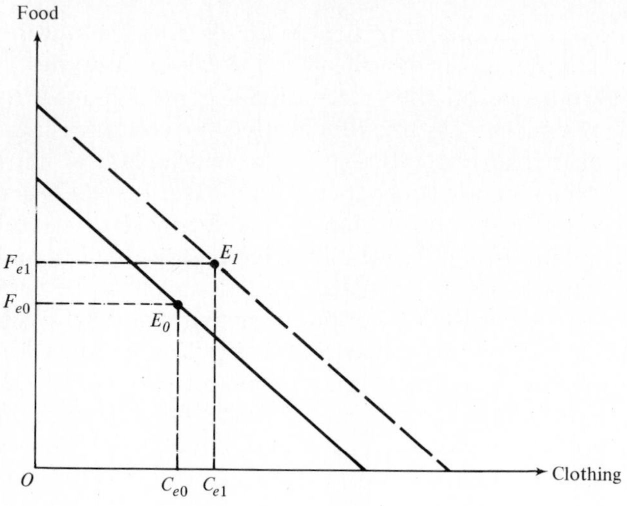

eigners real income equal in cumulative value to the value of the assets the domestic residents purchase.

In this analysis of tradeable bonds we have used the relatively simple example of a single financial instrument. The basic point applies to the international sale of *any* financial asset. The owner of the financial asset finds it marginally advantageous to sell it to the foreigner. The proceeds of the sale, in turn, are used to finance the original asset owner's expenditure in excess of his income. It may be that the financial asset is in the form of a bond such as we have assumed so far, or it could be any one of the many other different types of internationally exchanged financial assets mentioned in our discussion of the balance-of-payments accounts.

In fact, we must recognize that any highly developed capital market provides a variety of instruments which differentiate among lenders and borrowers on various economic bases, such as risk, size, and term of investment. This is the result of a competitive market for financial services working to meet the needs of a great variety of lenders and borrowers. All the different types of instruments and maturities are linked closely, however, because of the competitive nature of the financial markets.

This complex, yet highly integrated capital market structure applies both domestically and internationally. The international dimension can be interpreted simply as an extension of efficient domestic capital markets, but usually beyond the web of domestic regulators.

We shall return to this theme later in our discussion of the Eurocurrency markets.

Stocks Versus Flows   When an existing financial asset changes hands domestically there is no change in the total national ownership of financial assets. When a financial asset is purchased or sold internationally, however, the stock of nationally owned financial assets changes. It is this *change* in the national financial asset position in a given period that is referred to as a capital *flow* during the period. In much of our analysis we focus on the *flow* aspect of international financial capital. We must, nevertheless, keep in the back of our minds that there is a corresponding change in the *stock* position, and that it is generally a change in the actual stock position vis-à-vis the desired stock position that triggers the flow.

FLEXIBLE EXCHANGE RATES

A city treasurer has to float a bond issue. He looks at the domestic capital market and discovers that interest rates are considerably higher than are currently being charged in another currency. He quickly calculates that he could cut the interest cost of borrowing in half if he were to arrange to borrow in some other currency. Fortunately for the city taxpayers, the treasurer has on his staff someone who points out that this calculation is accurate only if the exchange rate is the same at the time of borrowing *and* repayment. If the exchange rate were to move in the interim, the entire calculation would be thrown awry.

A wholesaler is placing orders for next season's stock, to be delivered six months from now. He receives quotes from a domestic supplier and a foreign supplier. Payment terms are cash on delivery, but while the local supplier quotes in the local currency, the foreign supplier quotes in the foreigner's currency. When the quotes are compared, at the current exchange rate, the foreigner's quotation is 15 percent below the local supplier's. Which supplier is the lowest-cost source? The answer clearly depends on what happens to the exchange rate between the local currency and the foreigner's currency between now and the date of payment.

These two illustrations suggest a general point. When we cannot count on a permanently rigid exchange rate, both the short-term and long-term international capital transactions are concerned not only with interest rate differentials, but also with the exchange rates at different times, such as at the time of investment and repayment, as well as the denomination of the transactions.

For the short-term, the international financial markets have developed very useful mechanisms to help the parties cope with this additional dimension—exchange rate variability between date of commitment and date of transaction. The principal mechanisms work via the forward market in foreign exchange. Through this market the interest rates and changes in the exchange rate are linked. That linkage is critical and therefore warrants detailed examination.

Forward Foreign Exchange Market Mechanisms

Banks that deal in foreign exchange buy and sell foreign currencies for current delivery and for future delivery. A contract for future delivery is known as a forward foreign exchange transaction. The parties contract to buy or sell a definite amount of a given currency some later date, to be paid for then at a rate specified now. Contracts for one, three, or six months are the commonest for interbank transactions; those with customers may run for intermediate or longer periods, some for a year or more.

The existence of a forward market is a great convenience for traders and others with transactions involving a foreign currency. It enables them to cover themselves against the risk of exchange rate fluctuations, which is called *hedging*. Not everyone wishes to have their risks covered. Some prefer to take an open position in effect betting that the exchange rate will move in a particular way. This is called *speculation*.

Hedging   Hedging is undertaken by international traders who wish to guard their anticipated profits against the risk of a change in the exchange rate. An exporter with a shipment to be made and paid for in, say, three months is concerned that if the spot exchange rate were to fall, the proceeds of his shipment in his own currency would be less than he now expects. On the other hand, an importer worries about a possible rise in the rate of exchange, in which case his purchase will cost him more than he now anticipates. Especially for traders in bulk commodities, whose margin of profit may be very small, avoiding such a risk can be very important.

Both exporter and importer can eliminate this exchange risk through the use of the forward market. Dealers will quote, and contract to sell or buy at a firm forward exchange rate. After the conclusion of such a contract, no money changes hands until the contract matures. At the time, the bank would turn over to an importer or take from an exporter the amount of foreign currency specified in the forward contract, in exchange for local currency at the specified forward rate.

Not all commercial transactions (export and imports of goods and services) are always covered, however. Some traders may simply be ignorant of the existence or usefulness of the forward market; others may feel confident either that the spot rate is unlikely to change appreciably or that they can call the direction of its movement accurately. The latter group is obviously speculating; such an action merges with that of the professional speculator.

Speculation   Speculators, who hope to gain from betting on the future value of a currency, also find the forward market a convenient vehicle for their operation. They could, of course, carry out their speculations by purchasing spot exchange in a currency they believe will appreciate, holding it for the necessary period, and then, if their forecast is correct, selling it for a profit. This procedure, however, requires putting up the entire sum ventured. Instead, the speculator can purchase a forward contract from a bank, which requires no immediate outlay other than a margin deposit on the order of 10 percent. When the forward contract matures, the speculator hopes that the spot rate will be higher than the forward rate he contracted to pay, for he can then sell the currency delivered by the bank at a profit. A speculator anticipating depreciation of a currency would go short of that currency; that is, he would sell a forward contract and hope to cover at its termination at a spot rate below the forward rate of the contract.

The Role of Banks in the Forward Market   It is the banks that provide the forward contracts, selling forward exchange to importers and to "bull" speculators, while buying from exporters and "bear" speculators. There is no particular reason to expect that the forward exchange requirements of the banks' customers will exactly balance. Exports may exceed imports, or vice versa; the proportion of each that is covered may differ; and speculative opinion is certain to be preponderantly bullish or bearish, except when there is no incentive to speculate. Unless the needs of the two sides of the market happen to be equal, banks will find themselves forced to take an "open" position; collectively, at least, they will be undertaking to deliver more foreign exchange at later dates to buyers than they are acquiring from sellers, or it may be the other way around. Some banks may be willing to take an uncovered position if it corresponds to their dealers' opinion, based on expert knowledge and long experience, as to the probable appreciation or depreciation of the currency involved. Yet the size of the open position any bank can take is limited by the amount of its working capital and the proportion that management is willing to venture in a speculative situation.

For any bank that wishes to avoid taking a "long" or a "short" forward position in any currency, that is, an excess amount of that currency to be taken in or paid out, two alternatives are available. First, it may be able to match its excess forward commitment by dealing with a bank that is in the opposite position. Suppose that New York bank A is long in sterling, while bank B is short. Bank A could arrange to sell sufficient forward sterling to B to even out a long position, or buy if it is short.

In the absence of this alternative, a bank can cover its forward position by a spot purchase or sale. If bank A is short in three-month sterling by, say, £100,000, it can buy spot sterling, lend it out in the London money market at the going interest rate for three months, and when the loan is repaid, use the principal to meet its excess obligation to deliver sterling. Were it long by the same amount, it would borrow £100,000 in London, buy dollars to invest in the New York money market, and at the end of three months use the proceeds of this investment to buy sterling. This action meets its forward obligation to buy sterling, and with the pounds purchased it pays off its borrowings in London.

By this technique of evening out long or short forward exchange positions, a bank eliminates the risk attached to changes in exchange rates, since both its forward and its spot transactions were made at known rates. The bank forgoes making a potential profit from a change in the future spot rate, and limits its gain to its trading profit on its foreign exchange dealings (arising out of a very small difference between the price it pays sellers and the price it charges buyers) and to any difference in interest rates in the two money markets.

Interest Arbitrage The covering operations we have just described are clearly short-term capital movements. A bank covering a short forward position in sterling by using dollars to purchase spot sterling and investing it in the London money market is moving part of its liquid capital from New York to London. Covering a long forward position requires borrowing in London and lending in New York, a short-term capital movement in the opposite direction. Obviously, the relative level of short-term interest rates in the two markets will be of major importance in determining whether a capital movement results in a profit or a loss, and will therefore affect not only capital movements undertaken to cover an open forward position, but also the movement in general of short-term funds seeking a higher return.

The source of capital for any money market consists of funds of individuals, corporations, and governmental units not immediately needed for longer-term investment in plant and equipment or for such pressing short-term needs as meeting payrolls or carrying inventories. In addition, banks contribute a major portion of such funds because of the necessity of maintaining an appropriate balance between their short- and long-term investments. Outlets for these funds include domestic Treasury bills and various short-term commercial securities. Banks apportion their funds among these investments with an eye for maximum return, taking into account relative risk. When foreign exchange markets are free from rigorous controls, there exists the alternative of investing in comparable foreign securities, an alternative that will tend to be exercised provided it offers a higher return.

Any investor choosing to switch a portion of his funds from domestic to foreign short-term investments because of a favorable interest differential will want to avoid the possibility of loss should the exchange rate change before the time comes to bring his money home. He will therefore want to cover his purchase of spot exchange, made to transfer his funds abroad, by the simultaneous sale of forward exchange.

To illustrate, and to bring out clearly the critical variables involved in covered interest arbitrage, let us begin with a situation in which there is no incentive for capital to move. Consider one of the most important pair of forward foreign exchange markets, New York and Toronto. Assume initially that the short-term interest rate is the same in New York and in Toronto, and speculators see no reason, on balance, for the exchange rate between the U.S. dollar and the Canadian dollar to change.

Now allow us to introduce notionally an interest rate differential without changing either the spot or the forward exchange rate.[4] Assume that the short-term interest rate in New York is 8 percent and in Toronto is 10 percent per annum. This creates an incentive to move short-term funds from New York to Toronto. There is an opportunity for profitable covered interest arbitrage. The arbitrageur takes the following steps.

1. He borrows U.S. dollars.
2. He buys Canadian dollars spot with the borrowed money.
3. He buys Canadian bonds with the Canadian dollars.
4. He sells forward Canadian dollars to take delivery of U.S. dollars at a known exchange rate to repay the U.S. dollar loan.

Every time the arbitrageur engages in such a round of transactions he will effectively be lending at 10 percent money he is only

<hr />

[4] We are deliberately setting a differential that is far greater than could exist in practice, simply to illustrate the point.

paying 8 percent to borrow.[5] Needless to say, such an opportunity would not persist for long; a substantial volume of funds is potentially available for such a riskless round of transactions. The actions of the arbitrageurs would:

1. Push up U.S. interest rates due to the increased borrowing in the United States.
2. Push up the spot price of Canadian dollars in the foreign exchange market.
3. Push down Canadian interest rates due to greater lending in Canada.
4. Push down the forward price of Canadian dollars.

In fact, arbitrageurs would continue to make such rounds of profitable transactions until the net profit of going on such a round of transactions is zero. If we ignore transaction costs, this zero profit situation is met when 1 unit of domestic currency is notionally sent on the round just described and comes out at a value equal to 1 unit of domestic currency. In terms of the algebra of the transactions, it is when

$$\frac{1}{r_0} \cdot (1 + i_f) \cdot r_t \cdot \frac{1}{1 + i_d} = 1$$

or, rearranging, we have the condition that has been labeled the *interest rate parity theorem:*

$$\frac{r_t}{r_0} = \frac{1 + i_d}{1 + i_f}$$

where

r_0 = spot exchange rate
r_t = forward exchange rate
i_d = domestic interest rate
i_f = foreign interest rate

and the periods considered are identical.

The validity of this relationship may be seen by following the transactions of the arbitrageur noted above (assume that the United States is the home country).

[5] If the rounds were made in *reverse,* arbitrageurs would be lending money at 8 percent which they had borrowed at 10 percent.

1. Borrow U.S. $1.00 means that there is a commitment to repay U.S. $1.00 plus interest at the end of the period. This has the present value of

$$\frac{\text{U.S. } \$1.00}{1 + i_d}$$

2. With the proceeds buy Canadian dollars spot; divide by the exchange rate:

$$\frac{\text{U.S.\$}}{1 + i_d} \cdot \frac{1}{r_0} = \text{Canadian dollar equivalent}$$

3. Lend in Canadian dollars at the Canadian interest rate. Hence multiply by $(1 + i_f)$:

$$\frac{\text{U.S.\$}}{1 + i_d} \cdot \frac{1}{r_0} \cdot (1 + i_f)$$

4. Sell Canadian dollars forward. Hence multiply by the forward exchange rate:

$$\frac{\text{U.S. } \$1.00}{1 + i_d} \cdot \frac{1}{r_0} \cdot (1 + i_f) \cdot r_t$$

5. If the proceeds amount to U.S. $1.00, no further profit is possible.

By way of illustration, consider the U.S. dollar vis-à-vis the Canadian dollar on December 30, 1982. The noon midmarket quotations for Canadian dollars in U.S. financial markets were[6]

spot	U.S. $0.80952/Cdn$
3 months forward	U.S. $0.80821/Cdn$

In other words, the forward foreign exchange market was slightly discounting the Canadian dollar. This reflected the fact that Canadian interest rates were slightly higher than U.S. interest rates. The three-month Treasury bill yields on that same day were quoted as

U.S.	1.975% for 3 months
Canada	2.160% for 3 months

[6] Interest rate and exchange rate data are from *Globe and Mail, Report on Business*, Dec. 31, 1982.

From this information on American arbitrageur would note that he could buy Canadian dollars spot, invest in Canadian Treasury bills at the higher interest rate, and sell Canadian dollars forward at a discount that offsets the interest premium. Since the interest rate parity condition was satisfied,[7]

$$\frac{\text{U.S. \$0.80821}}{\text{U.S. \$0.80952}} \simeq \frac{1 + 0.01975}{1 + 0.02160}$$

he would *not* find it profitable to engage in arbitrage.

Spot and forward exchange rates are intimately related to interest rate differentials. Interest rates need not be equal between countries as long as authorities permit forward and spot exchange rates to differ. If forward and spot rates are identical, however, then as long as capital is free to move, interest rates on financial instruments of similar maturity and risk must also be identical.

Official Intervention   The link between spot and forward exchange rates provides an opportunity for official intervention in the forward foreign exchange market. How does this intervention work? The officials act as speculators, taking a position in the forward market. Suppose that they wish to depress the spot foreign exchange rate. They could do this by selling foreign exchange forward, which would tend to depress the forward rate, and hence, for given interest rates, would invite arbitrageurs to bid down the spot foreign exchange rate. In terms of the equilibrium relationship

$$\frac{r_t}{r_0} = \frac{1 + i_d}{1 + i_f}$$

if r_t is bid down by official intervention, for given interest rates, arbitrage would tend to bid down r_0 to restore the equilibrium.

The data on forward intervention are not usually published immediately in the way that foreign exchange reserve data are published monthly. However, ultimately, data on net outstanding official forward contracts are published. The Canadian data reveal an interesting episode of this type.

In the spring of 1962 the Canadian dollar, which had been floating since 1950, was under considerable downward pressure. Official intervention to halt the slide included a significant temporary entry into the forward market. In the month of June 1962 over U.S. $500 million was sold in forward contracts.[8] The Canadian Exchange

---

[7] The precise equality can seldom be shown from market quotations because transactions costs mean that there is a difference between buying and selling rates.

[8] Bank of Canada, *Review*, June 1978, Table A.13.

Fund Account, in this way, was able to sell foreign exchange forward without at the time having to reveal the fact that it was doing so. Had the authorities chosen to deplete reserves by this amount, the monthly publication of this information would undoubtedly have strengthened the consensus of speculators against the official intervention.

Conclusion   We have seen that the existence of a well-developed forward exchange market assists traders of goods, of securities, and of currencies in arranging their desired foreign exchange transactions. Those who wish to avoid an exchange rate risk (hedgers) may do so, and those who wish to expose themselves to an exchange rate risk (speculators) may do so. The forward foreign exchange market also serves to integrate interest rate differentials with the spot and forward exchange rates via covered interest arbitrage. This integration may be employed by the monetary authorities to intervene indirectly in the spot foreign exchange market.

Capital Flows and Adjustment

The integration of foreign exchange markets, both spot and forward, with the capital markets adds a further potential avenue for adjustment to a disturbance. In Chapter 20 we saw how either a change in foreign exchange reserves or a change in the exchange rate provided avenues of adjustment to various kinds of disturbances. To that list of options we may now add a third—international borrowing. Capital flows are able to finance transitory short falls and excesses in the net international transactions, with the result that neither the foreign exchange reserves nor the exchange rate is forced to bear the full burden of adjustment.

The mechanism is straightforward. Suppose, for example, that there is a delay in the annual harvest of an export crop, with the result that exports are temporarily less than imports. The resultant current account deficit would tend to result in either (1) a loss of foreign exchange reserves and hence a reduction in the money stock, or (2) a fall in the value of local currency on the foreign exchange markets. Either mechanism *could*, as we have seen before, carry out the full adjustment. However, the initiation of either would tend to create a capital flow that would reduce the need for adjustment. The loss of foreign exchange reserves and the reduction in the domestic money stock would tend to drive up to local interest rates, and hence attract an inflow of capital. The fall in the spot value of the local currency on exchange markets would attract arbitrage funds at given domestic and international interest rates to maintain the covered interest arbitrage equality.

Such an inflow of capital reduces the size of the adjustment that must occur via either the money stock or the spot exchange rate, and is automatically triggered by the appearance of a transitory disturbance. In this sense, then, capital flows may be regarded as a source of adjustment to a disturbance. However, capital flows may also turn out to be disturbances requiring adjustment. Recall from Chapter 20 that although exchange rate adjustment is a particularly attractive mechanism of adjustment to a foreign disturbance, for the exchange rate adjustment can act to insulate the domestic economy from the foreign disturbance, our conclusion was carefully hedged with the observation that a real change in the economic circumstances facing a nation, such as a change in the terms of international trade, must be accepted sooner or later.

A change in the real rate of return from assets denominated in the home currency is also a change in the real economic circumstances of the country. Wealth holders will want to move their assets accordingly. The result in the long run must be a movement of real purchasing power transferred between nations. This is accomplished ultimately by the investing country spending less than its income and the borrowing country spending more than its income. When such a transfer is attempted under a flexible exchange rate, the exchange rate changes. The transfer is accomplished by the exchange rate change generating a divergence between expenditure and income in the very same way that a currency depreciation temporarily reduces expenditures below income.

Consider a country experiencing a capital outflow—for whatever reason. From an initial situation of equilibrium between expenditure and income, and between demand and supply for foreign exchange, the capital outflow increases the demand for foreign exchange. Since we have a flexible exchange rate, the exchange rate must rise. This has the effect of a currency depreciation, which we have examined earlier (see pp. 358ff.). It reduces expenditure to a level below the income. Thus, in terms of Figure 21.3, expenditure falls from E_0 to a point such as E_1. The difference between E_1 and E_0, of course, corresponds to the flow of capital out of the country. Correspondingly, the receiving country has an expenditure in excess of its income in order for it to absorb the capital inflow.

We can now see why the existence of capital flows might be regarded as a disturbance. An individual person or corporation attempting to move capital between countries certainly does not regard it as a disturbance, but the collective public must certainly regard it as a disturbance if it is forced to reduce its expenditure to accommodate a capital outflow.

This sense is further strengthened when the possibility of real income losses from a capital outflow emerges in a Keynesian short-run model. Due to rigidities in the system, the fall in expenditure to achieve a real capital outflow could also result in a fall in real income. If, to avoid the capital outflow, the country instead accepts a higher interest

Figure 21.3 Adjustment to Capital Outflow

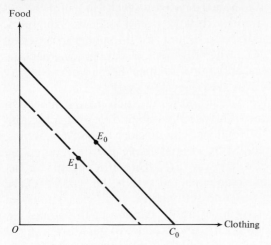

rate, real income may also suffer. We shall take this up in the next chapter.

It is because of the potential real income effects that policy-makers are especially concerned about capital flows. That concern is often focused on the international speculator, who may be seen as forcing a country to adjust at a time when the policymakers would prefer not to.

Speculative Capital Movements

A speculator believes that he knows better than the current market consensus. When he anticipates the depreciation of a given currency, whether its exchange rate is officially pegged or free to vary, he will move funds out of that currency into one that he believes is stronger. He can do so by selling the weak currency forward at any rate above the expected future spot rate. If his estimate is right, he will be able to cover his sales in the spot market at a rate below what the buyers have undertaken to pay, thereby making a profit.

Under a fixed exchange rate system, a situation can arise that is particularly favorable to speculators. If a currency is weak, perhaps because domestic inflation has caused it to become overvalued at the fixed exchange rate, and the country's balance of payments has been in chronic deficit, the spot rate will have been pushing steadily against the upper intervention point. If reserves are low and falling, devaluation may become a virtual certainty, although government officials will deny that it is even being contemplated. Speculators obtain a one-way option: The spot rate is most unlikely to fall—all the signs point to a rise. (With a strong currency, speculators may have a similar but opposite single option.) The limited funds normally available to professional speculators may be greatly augmented at such times by the action of international corporations with large liquid assets to safeguard. Forward sales of the weak currency mount, as do spot purchases of strong currencies. The speculative movement of capital can become massive, as it did in February and again in June 1973, when one day over $3 billion (U.S.) moved into West German marks.

In the flexible exchange rate situation no such nearly one-sided bet is available to a speculator. The normal ebb and flow of trade and finance result in constantly shifting *net* demands for various currencies, which in the absence of speculation, would move the exchange rate temporarily away from its equilibrium rate. Thus if a speculator believes that he knows what the true expected rate is, he will purchase when the rate is below that rate, and sell when it is above. The effect of such speculation is first, to reduce the fluctuation of the actual exchange rate around the expected rate, and second, to generate a profit for the speculators.

Speculators are, by and large, experienced and shrewd observers of phenomena affecting foreign exchange markets. They have to be, since their livelihood depends on it. With a powerful incentive to exercise accurate foresight, and with ready access to relevant information and experience in using it, the operations of speculators should normally move the actual exchange rate toward rather than away from the long-run equilibrium rate. Speculation should be stabilizing. If some persistent influence causes a currency to depreciate, speculators will try to anticipate that depreciation. In doing so, they will drive the exchange rate toward its new equilibrium level rather sooner than if they did not act. As that level is approached, their activity will tend to taper off.

The task facing the speculator is not trivial. Whenever there is a change in the exchange rate, he must decide if it is a permanent or a transitory change. He must also make some assumption about the nature and degree of official intervention that is likely to occur. Finally, to stay in business the speculator must be able to make a return on his funds at least equal to the return he could obtain if the funds were employed in other activities.

Evidence   The available evidence seems to support the view that, in all but exceptional circumstances, speculation is stabilizing under a regime of flexible exchange rates. Most important is the experience of Canada. On a fixed exchange rate, and in 1950 faced with a persistent balance-or-payments surplus, reinforced by a large speculative capital inflow from the United States, appreciation of the Canadian dollar appeared essential. Rather than fix a new par value arbitrarily, the Canadian government decided to rely on the market and allowed the dollar to float. Until 1961, intervention in the foreign exchange market by the monetary authorities was minimal, being undertaken only to offset sudden gusts in private demand and supply. During most of the time from 1950 to 1960, the Canadian dollar floated at a premium against the U.S. dollar of 2 to 4 percent, with a maximum variation of 6 percent. This experience contributed to the view that a stable flexible exchange rate is possible.

The experience also cast light on some significant problems that can arise with a flexible exchange rate. With the appearance in 1961 of rising unemployment the country's financial management became "schizophrenic."[9] Instead of using its freedom from balance-of-payments constraints to adopt a liberal credit policy, the central bank insisted on maintaining high interest rates, thus attracting short-term capital. This, of course, tended to support the Canadian dollar's value and thus to stimulate imports and depress exports. In 1961 the government announced its intention deliberately to depreciate the currency, and in May 1962 it pegged the Canadian dollar at a discount of 7.5 percent against the U.S. dollar.

Additional evidence is available from the period immediately after World War I. In several countries with freely floating exchange rates and with relatively stable internal economic conditions, after a brief period of abnormal scarcity and inflation in 1919 and 1920, exchange rate fluctuations were comparatively moderate, remaining fairly close to a computed equilibrium rate.[10] This was true of the United Kingdom from 1921 to 1925, when the country went back on the gold standard. Norway had a similar experience except for approximately one year, when the exchange rate rose faster than the price level, suggesting speculative capital movements. But with the imposition of a vigorously restrictive monetary policy, the krone soon began to appreciate. In France, inflation was more serious and exchange rate fluctuations were considerably greater, departing further from the computed equilibrium rate. The main operative force appears to have been a lax monetary policy, which fueled inflation as well as speculative demand for foreign exchange. That demand, however, although reinforcing the effects of a rapidly rising money supply, did not become self-aggravating: Exchange rate movements were repeatedly checked.[11]

---

[9] A. W. Wynne Plumptre, *Exchange Rate Policy: Experience with Canada's Floating Rate*, Essays in International Finance No. 81 (Princeton, N.J.: International Finance Section, Princeton University, 1970), p. 6.

[10] This computed rate was purchasing power par; see Chapter 29.

[11] This information on the post-World War I period was obtained from S. C. Tsiang, "Fluctuating Exchange Rates in Countries with Relatively Stable Economies," *IMF Staff Papers*, **7**:244–73 (Oct. 1959).

Widespread Floating, 1973–1974   From May 1973 on, following a period when it became apparent that the new parities set in December 1971 were unsuitable, most major currencies of the world were allowed to float. Although some currencies, notably the U.S. and the Canadian dollars, were subjected only to mild intervention to iron out short-run fluctuations and to moderate large swings in exchange rates, others, in particular the German mark, the French franc, and the Japanese yen, were held more firmly in line with various types of interference with the operation of a free exchange market. Therefore, this period was not really a fair test of floating rates. For what it is worth, however, the evidence gives no support to the view that speculation is likely to be a destabilizing element under a flexible rate system. Speculation was frequent and sometimes of large proportions, yet in no instance did it prove to be self-reinforcing. After a speculative flurry had worn itself out, rate fluctuations subsided within relatively narrow limits.

In the period since 1973–1974, during which there has been widespread use of floating exchange rates, there has been substantially more variation of exchange rates then the earlier Canadian experience in particular would have suggested. This is partly due to the nature of repeated new shocks that have plagued the international system such as the OPEC oil price changes in 1973 and 1979. In addition, however, there does not seem to have been a substantial volume of funds available for speculation. Two significant institutional explanations for this situation have been offered by McKinnon.[12] Banks have an overriding aversion to the risk of insolvency. Consequently, they have developed internal operating rules which ensure that they limit their exposure to speculative risk. A few cases of bank insolvency arising from currency exposure have reinforced this concern. The other potential major source of speculative funds are multinational corporations. Whereas they have demonstrated their willingness to make one-sided bets for short periods under the fixed exchange rate era, they have been remarkably unwilling to make long-run commitments of substantial funds to exchange rate speculation—something in which, quite correctly, they do not regard themselves as being expert.

Lying in the background, and largely explaining this reticence of the major private financial powers to commit resources to routine speculation, is the fact that foreign exchange markets and the national financial markets have become subject to unpredictable massive official intervention. The careful calculations of expected profit by the speculator are easily wiped out by an official decision to alter radically the course of their intervention. Hence potential speculators are unwilling to expose themselves unless the expected return is substantial.

[12] See Chapter 7 of R. I. McKinnon, *Money in International Exchange: The Convertible Currency System* (New York: Oxford University Press, 1979).

Hyperinflation and Speculation   The main thrust of the foregoing argument has been that when economic conditions in a country are stable—in particular, when its monetary authorities pursue a policy that prevents severe inflation, thus providing a basis for reliable prediction—speculation in foreign exchange will be stabilizing. A sound foundation for the exercise of judgment exists. Since the evidence points to a stable trend in monetary conditions, which strongly influence the direction of exchange rate movements, speculators will judge accordingly. Concretely, they anticipate that the future spot rate will not vary widely from the current rate. This describes a stable rather than a speculative situation. There will be no speculative attack on the currency and no speculative movement of capital, but only such movement as is warranted by any interest differential that may exist.

When economic conditions are highly unstable and inflation is rampant, as in Germany after World War I, there is nothing on which one can depend. A basis for reliable prediction simply does not exist, thus setting the stage for speculation. Yet surprisingly, the evidence from this period shows only two intervals during which the rise in exchange rates led or coincided with the rise in internal prices.

From the end of the war until the spring of 1920, exchange rate movements preceded those of internal prices. Although this typifies a speculative situation, the cause in this instance appears not to have been professional speculation, but a flight of capital generated by the pessimism of defeat, reinforced by a rush to buy commodities long unattainable in blockaded Germany.[13]

In 1923, Germany's hyperinflation reached such a pitch that the currency became virtually worthless, with the U.S. dollar quoted at 1 trillion marks. Certainly, at times in this period, speculation was a factor in forcing up exchange rates and in aggravating inflation. At bottom, however, the prime mover was a total loss of control over the supply of money.

CONCLUSION

We have now added a major new dimension to our analytical framework. In earlier chapters individuals chose between spending their incomes and accumulating an asset. We have now allowed for a three-way choice facing individuals: (1) spending, (2) money accumulation, or (3) income-earning asset accumulation. The rate of return on in-

---

[13] Frank D. Graham, *Exchange, Prices, and Production in Hyper-inflation: Germany, 1920–23* (Princeton, N.J.: Princeton University Press, 1930), especially Chapter 6.

come-earning assets—the interest rate—has become a key variable in our analytical framework. Some important market mechanisms integrate financial and currency markets.

Consideration of this dimension now permits us to examine international capital movements and their role as sources of adjustment and disturbance. The basic issue has been broached in this chapter. The full-blown analysis is taken up in the next chapter.

SELECTED REFERENCES

GRASSMAN, S. *Exchange Reserves and the Financial Structure of Foreign Trade.* Westmead, England: Saxon House, 1973. An extensive empirical study of hedging and invoicing practices in Sweden's foreign trade.

McKINNON, R. I. *Money in International Exchange: The Convertible Currency System.* New York: Oxford University Press, 1979. Chapters 4, 5, and 7 have excellent discussions of hedging, arbitrage, and speculation.

TSIANG, S. C. "The Theory of Forward Exchange and the Effects of Government Intervention on the Forward Market." *IMF Staff Papers*, **7** (Apr. 1959). The seminal analytical article dealing with forward exchange.

———. "Fluctuating Exchange Rates in Countries with Relatively Stable Economies." *IMF Staff Papers*, **7** (Oct. 1959). Deals with the post–World War I experience cited in the text.

Canada's Experience with Floating Exchange Rates

PLUMPTRE, A. W. WYNNE. *Exchange Rate Policy: Experience with Canada's Floating Rate*, Essays in International Finance No. 81. Princeton, N.J.: International Finance Section, Princeton University, 1970. This pamphlet provides an excellent brief survey of events in this period. Plumptre also notes that when the Canadian dollar floated in the 1930s, when world conditions were highly unstable, it "did not behave in an unstable fashion and short-term capital movements were self-correcting, not self-aggravating" (p. 5).

SOHMEN, EGON. *International Monetary Problems and the Foreign Exchanges*, Special Papers in International Economics No. 4. Princeton, N.J.: International Finance Section, Princeton University, 1963. Another excellent brief account of the Canadian experience in the 1950s.

WONNACOTT, PAUL. *The Canadian Dollar, 1948–62.* Toronto: University of Toronto Press, 1965. A more complete examination of the Canadian experience.

Princeton Studies in International Finance

Several studies in this series are particularly concerned with international capital market issues. The following are of special relevance:

No. 17. SOHMEN, EGON, *The Theory of Forward Exchange*, 1966.
No. 32. BLACK, S. W., *International Money Markets and Flexible Exchange Rates*, 1973.
No. 39. KENEN, P. B., *Capital Mobility and Financial Integration*, 1976.
No. 44. WIHLBORG, C., *Currency Risks in International Financial Markets*, 1978.

22
CHAPTER

The *IS–LM* Model and Tradeable Bonds

The world's currency and financial markets are linked by the availability of capital ready to shift from one country to another in search of the maximum return. The efficient operation of both the currency markets and the capital markets which this generates is a great advantage for all participants in the international economy. Nevertheless, we saw in the preceding chapter that a capital movement could well be a significant disturbance for a country. The reason is that when there is a net capital flow, there is a corresponding *real* difference between income and expenditure to accomplish the capital transfer. For example, to achieve a capital outflow, expenditure must fall below income. In the short run, there may be rigidities in the domestic economy so that not only expenditure but also income falls. We must be concerned, therefore, about the possible interaction of relative asset equilibrium, expenditure, and income.

In the post–World War II period, there developed a substantial literature dealing with these interactions. The literature uses the basic ideas of relative asset stock equilibrium between money and bonds which we developed in Chapter 21, together with a version of the Keynesian income–expenditure model developed in Chapter 20 modified to include the interest rate as an important direct determinant of expenditure.

To explore fully the ideas that emerge from this literature, it is helpful to develop a simple version of the model. Again the distinction between the case when the bonds are tradeable and not tradeable is crucial. We begin with a model where domestic bonds are sold only in the domestic financial market, and subsequently develop the other extreme case, where the bonds are perfectly tradeable. Finally, in the next chapter we develop an intermediate case. The reader will observe that in the process of developing this model we are, effectively, integrating the Keynesian and monetary approaches to the balance of payments. The adjustment processes will involve *both* income and the stock monetary assets.

This literature developed in the context of fixed exchange rates, and assumes that the domestic price level is given. We will extend the model in one small way into the flexible exchange rate world. However, a full treatment in the context of flexible exchange rates is beyond the scope of this book. With not only interest rates and income as variables, but prices and exchange rates (spot and forward) also adjusting, and where the relative speeds of adjustment matter, the reader can appreciate that the issues become extremely complex.

DERIVATION OF THE *IS–LM* MODEL: NONTRADEABLE BONDS

Consider first the asset side of the model. Recall that with money and bonds as the only two possible assets, the distribution of the total stock of assets between money and bonds is determined by the interest rate. The choice between holding money and bonds is based, therefore, on the interest rate. Consequently, the money demand function includes not only nominal income, as in earlier chapters, but also the interest rate as one of its arguments. In other words,

$$M^D = M^D(Y, P, i)$$

To simplify, we assume that in the Keynesian model the price level is fixed, and that

$$M^D = M^D(Y, i)$$

Diagrammatically, given some income level such as Y_0, the desired money stock is a downward-sloping function of the interest rate as $M^D (Y_0)$ in Figure 22.1. A higher income must mean a higher desired money stock (for a given interest rate). Indeed, there is an entire family of M^D curves, each member corresponding to a different income level:

$$Y_0 < Y_1 < Y_2$$

If we now impose a given money stock (and assume in the background that there is a given stock of bonds), we can derive a locus of monetary equilibrium of the two key variables of income and the in-

Figure 22.1   Money Demand at Various Income Levels

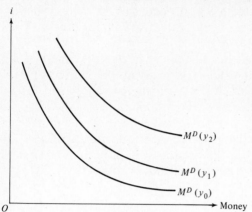

terest rate. This we do diagrammatically in Figure 22.2. The left-hand side [Figure 22.2(a)] reproduces Figure 22.1 and also specifies a given money stock M_0^s. Monetary equilibrium for a specified income level such as Y_0 is where the desired money holdings equal the given stock. This is the intersection of the M_0^s curve and the M^D curve for that income level $M^D(Y_0)$. Asset equilibrium in this situation would be achieved with an interest rate of i_0, for that is the interest rate given Y_0 that would keep the public just satisfied with holding the stock of money M_0^s.

Repeating this exercise for higher incomes, we are able to trace

Figure 22.2   Derivation of the *LM* Curve

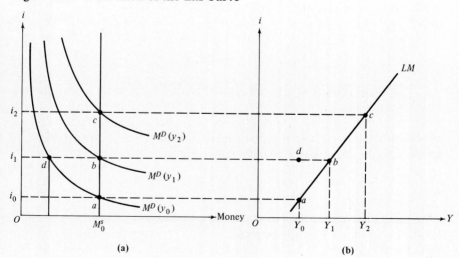

out the locus of monetary equilibria for alternative income levels. In Figure 22.2(a) this is the series of points *a*, *b*, *c*. Notice that at higher income levels individuals want to hold more money, but since they have to be satisfied with the same amount of money, at the higher demand for money, they are satisfied only by the fact that the opportunity cost of holding money is greater. In other words, the higher interest rate is necessary in order to reduce the desired money stock to a level compatible with the available supply.

The locus of the equilibria *a*, *b*, and *c* in interest rate–money space can also trace out a locus of equilibria in interest rate–income space. This is done in Figure 22.2(b), also as points *a*, *b*, and *c*. Thus in part (a), given M_0^s and $M^D(Y_0)$, we see that equilibrium is achieved at point *a*, where the interest rate is i_0. The corresponding point of Y_0 and i_0 in part (b) is also point *a*. Similarly, point *b* represents that combination of income and interest rate at which there would be monetary equilibrium, given the money stock M_0^s, and the stock of bonds.

The careful reader will note that it is not just *any* combination of *Y* and *i* that traces out the locus *LM* in Figure 22.2(b). For example, the combination of $M^D(Y_0)$ and i_1 at point *d* is *not* an equilibrium in Figure 22.2(a), and consequently point *d* in part (b) is off the *LM* curve.

Now turn to the income–expenditure relationship. We are concerned here about equilibrium in the market for currently produced goods and services. In Chapter 20 we did not include the interest rate as a determinant of the equilibrium. However, a moment's reflection will suggest that the interest can affect the level of desired expenditure. This is so for a variety of reasons, but it largely has to do with the relative desirability of spending now versus later. Thus the lower the real interest rate, the more desirable it is to borrow to spend now rather than wait. The higher the real interest rate, the more attractive it becomes to postpone current expenditures. This is true particularly for durables, such as investment in new plant and equipment or durable consumer goods. Hence it is appropriate to make domestic expenditure not only a (positive) function of income, but also a (negative) function of the real interest rate.

$$E = E(Y, i)$$

The income–expenditure model from Chapter 20 is thus expanded by the inclusion of an interest rate argument in the expenditure function. The principal change is in the diagrammatic representation of the expenditure equilibrium. The upward-sloping curve $Y - E(Y)$ in Figure 20.1(b) becomes a *family* of curves, depending on different interest rate levels. The lower the interest rate, the greater the desired current expenditure and hence the farther to the *right* the curve $Y - E$

lies. This is illustrated in Figure 22.3(a), where we have drawn the curves $Y - E(i_0)$, $Y - E(i_1)$, $Y - E(i_2)$ corresponding to successively higher interest rates.

    For a given interest rate, equilibrium in the current goods and

Figure 22.3   Derivation of the *IS* Curve

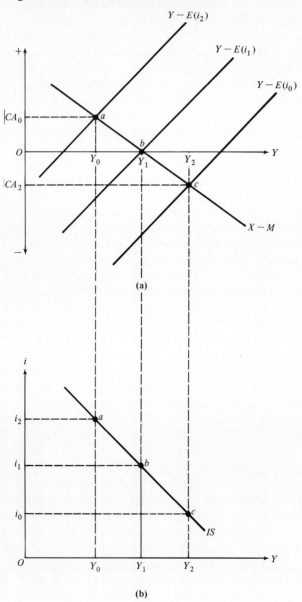

services market is achieved where the current account balance exactly matches the difference between income and expenditure. The locus of such equilibria for different interest rates and income levels is the well-known *IS* (for income–spending) curve. It traces out the combinations of interest rates and incomes that yield equality between, on the one hand, the excess (shortfall) of income over expenditure, and on the other hand, the current account surplus (deficit). Thus, in the income–expenditure diagram for an interest rate i_0, equilibrium is at point c, where $Y - E(i_0)$ intersects $X - M$ at Y_2. The corresponding point c in Figure 22.3(b) is a point on the *IS* curve of i_0 and Y_2. Similarly, points b and c are equilibria in i and Y space, and thus together trace out sample points on the curve *IS*.

The *IS* curve and the *LM* curve are each insufficient alone to determine equilibrium in either the money or goods markets: Each could be in equilibrium at various combinations of the interest rate and the income level. Consequently, neither can be determined independently of the other. To complete the system we must put them together in order to find that combination of the interest rate and income level that *simultaneously* satisfies equilibrium in the money market and the goods market. This we do in Figure 22.4. The level of i and Y that *simultaneously* satisfies equilibrium in both is i_1 and Y_1.

To remind the reader of the underlying workings we have also linked the *IS—LM* equilibrium with the money market equilibrium and the income–expenditure equilibrium. Thus in the money market we can see that at i_1 and Y_1 the desired money stock (M^D) equals the actual money stock of $M^s{}_0$. In the income–expenditure diagram we see that at Y_1 the current account balance of CA_1 is exactly equal to the difference between income and expenditure with Y_1 and i_1: in this case, $CA_0 = 0$. (Of course, the equilibrium current account need *not* be zero in the Keynesian model.)

The Current Account Balance and the IS–LM Model

As we derived the *IS–LM* model, we did nothing to change the basic negative relationship between the current account and the level of income that is common to Keynesian-type models. The greater the income, the smaller the current account surplus—or the larger the current account deficit.

We happened to draw Figure 22.4 in such a way that at the equilibrium i_1 and Y_1 the current account was just balanced. What happens if the authorities were not satisfied with Y_1 as a level of income? Instead, assume that the authorities have selected Y_F as a target "full-employment" level of income. Suppose that they choose an expansion of the money stock to reach Y_F? This would shift the *LM* curve down-

Figure 22.4 *IS–LM* Equilibrium

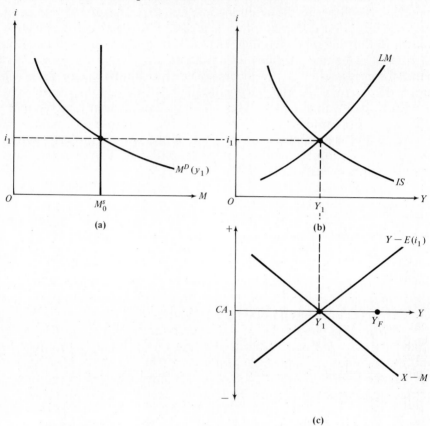

(a)

(b)

(c)

ward and to the right, for in order to persuade people to hold the greater money stock the opportunity cost of holding that money (i.e., interest forgone on bonds) would have to be less (Figure 22.5). At the initial levels of interest (i_1) and income (Y_1) there would no longer be simultaneous equilibrium in the goods market and the money market. To persuade individuals to hold the excess money stock, income would have to rise or the interest rate would have to drop. The drop in the interest rate would affect the goods market equilibrium encouraging individuals to spend more. To restore equilibrium in both the goods market and the money market would require a combination of a higher income at a lower interest rate. The expansionary policy would have the desired effect, for the simultaneous equilibrium would shift in Figure 22.5 from point *a* to point *b*—the intersection of the new curve LM_2 and the original IS_1 curve—with the equilibrium value of Y_F, and i_2. However, the authorities would also discover the principal draw-

Figure 22.5   Monetary Expansion in an *IS–LM* Model

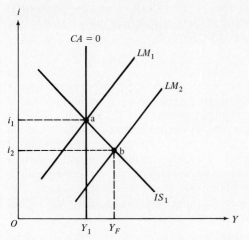

back of such a policy. Increased expenditure has outpaced increased income; at the higher income level there is a current account deficit.

The deficit would have to be financed by drawing down the country's foreign exchange reserves, as long as we retain the assumption that bonds are nontradeable. Clearly, this would feed back to reduce the domestic money stock—an effect that would *continue* until the *LM* curve had returned to a point where its intersection with the *IS* curve yielded an income level with a *zero* current account balance: in Figure 22.5 at point *a* on the *CA* = 0 curve. In other words, a temporary equilibrium away from *CA* = 0 is possible, but such a situation puts into play monetary adjustment forces that tend to restore the equilibrium income to a level consistent with a zero current account. The authorities may choose to sterilize the effect of the reserve loss by expanding domestic credit to replace the foreign exchange reserves. Such a policy would enable the income to continue at a level in excess of that compatible with current account balance, but in the end could not be sustained. Ultimately, foreign exchange reserves would be exhausted, and the authorities would be forced to let the adjustment occur.

The immediate lesson from this analysis is that *at the existing exchange rate* the achievement of external balance (*CA* = 0 in this case) is incompatible with the achievement of the target income level Y_F. A persistent attempt to achieve one goal will frustrate the achievement of the other unless the authorities are willing to employ an additional policy instrument.

Many countries have learned to their sorrow the consequence of such a policy approach. Foreign exchange reserves have been exhausted in order simultaneously to protect an overvalued exchange rate and to maintain expenditure at a level in excess of what is consistent with balance in international payments. We shall return to this theme in a later chapter. An example will serve to illustrate the nature of the problem; the West African country of Ghana in the first few years after independence is all too forceful an example.

> In 1959, responding to the desire to speed development, the government incurred a substantial deficit, creating an excess of total expenditure over output. With a fixed exchange rate and a relatively free system of international trade and payments, the adjustment came about largely in the form of increased imports of goods and services, which jumped by more than one-third in 1959. The excess demand for real resources in general was thus turned into a demand for foreign goods and services. This demand was met via a current account deficit, which was accommodated by drawing on foreign exchange reserves and external capital account borrowing, largely on the part of the government. . . .

> The capital account balance turned strongly negative in 1961, while the current account balance moved into an even larger deficit position. In that year reserves dropped from N¢ 297 million to N¢ 147 million. Such a reserve loss was clearly not sustainable. . . .

> For the home government, . . . failing a change in the official exchange rate, some device had to be found to close the deficit.[1]

Many others have followed the same path and have rediscovered the same truth.

IS–LM WITH PERFECTLY TRADEABLE BONDS

With a Fixed Exchange Rate

The IS–LM model just developed can be used to analyze the case when domestic bonds are tradeable in the international financial markets. Such a possibility significantly alters the IS–LM analysis. It effectively means that the home country can finance a current account deficit via the sale of bonds to foreigners. To see this, consider the same initial IS–LM equilibrium that we dealt with before (Figure 22.4): The equilibrium income Y_1 and interest rate i_1 are such that $CA = 0$ and there is asset equilibrium both in terms of the level of asset holdings and the *composition* of assets. We will consider two distinct cases: an expansionary expenditure policy, then an expansionary monetary policy.

[1] J. Clark Leith, *Foreign Trade Regimes and Economic Development: Ghana* (New York: National Bureau of Economic Research, 1974), p. 38.

An Expansionary Expenditure Policy   Suppose that domestic policymakers chose to engage in an expansionary expenditure policy,
thereby shifting the *IS* curve to the right—to IS_1 in Figure 22.6. If the
domestic bonds were nontradeable, the equilibrium would shift to
point *b*, for the interest rate would have to rise in order to persuade
domestic residents to hold the same stock of money even though their
incomes had risen. However, because bonds are tradeable, as soon as
the downward bond price (i.e., upward interest rate) pressure emerges,
foreigners start buying home bonds, thereby preventing the price of
bonds from falling (the interest rate from rising).

The fact that the interest rate cannot rise means that the expansionary effect of the expenditure stimulus is amplified—not dampened.
Instead of moving *up* the *LM* curve, the sale of bonds to foreigners
creates a situation where the current account deficit is more than covered by the capital inflow, resulting in an accumulation of foreign exchange reserves. That accumulation of course increases the money
stock, shifting the *LM* curve rightward. This process continues until
the increase in *the money stock*, via the capital inflow, restores monetary
equilibrium consistent with the higher income–expenditure goods
market equilibrium. In Figure 22.6 this is where the *LM* curve has
reached LM_1 and is now in a flow equilibrium at i_1, Y_2. Notice, however,
that the situation at Y_2 involves a *continuing* current account deficit
that is continually financed by the sale of bonds to foreigners. To maintain income at Y_2 the country must continue to increase its debt to
foreigners each period.

This policy approach is one that has been followed at various
times by many different countries. Perhaps the most clear-cut example

**Figure 22.6   Expansionary Expenditure Policy with Perfectly Elastic Foreign
Capital: Fixed Exchange Rate**

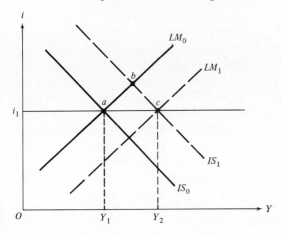

Table 22.1 Sweden's Balance of Payments, 1977–1981 (Millions of SDRs)

		1976	1977	1978	1979	1980	1981
A.	Current account	−1427	−1875	−205	−1861	−3446	−2603
	A.1. Goods, services, and income	−780	−1124	764	−994	−2432	−1682
	A.2. Transfers, donations	−647	−751	−969	−867	−1014	−921
B.	Capital account	850	2563	1162	1445	4400	3282
	B.1. Direct investment	−512	−561	−276	−391	−294	−467
	B.2. Other long-term capital	832	1352	−280	−215	−43	−383
	B.3. Short-term capital	520	−91	660	355	617	1404
	B.4. Foreign official assets in Sweden	—	—	—	—	—	—
	B.5. Exceptional financing	10	1863	1058	1696	4120	2728
C.	Other	140	209	−611	−94	−955	−276
	C.1. Valuation changes	11	−46	−193	13	81	261
	C.2. Net errors and omissions	129	255	−418	−107	−1036	−537
	Total A + B + C	−437	897	346	−510	−1	403
D.	Changes in official reserves	437	897	−346	510	1	−403
E.	Net balance A + B + C + D	0	0	0	0	0	0
	Conversion rate: kroner per SDR	5.0290	5.2324	5.6571	5.5389	5.5049	5.9706

SOURCE: IMF, *Balance of Payments Statistics*, **33**, No. 8 (Aug. 1982).

NOTE: Lines may not add to totals because of rounding.

has been the case of Sweden in the period 1977–1981. The Swedish balance-of-payments accounts identify capital account transactions that are specifically to finance the balance of payments. A summary of the Swedish balance-of-payments accounts for 1976–1981 is presented in Table 22.1. (The special capital account borrowing is line B.5, "Exceptional Financing.") From 1977 through 1981 the cumulative current account deficit was over $10 billion, which was more than financed by borrowing. Further, during the period end 1976 through the end of 1979, the money stock increased by 50 percent while the real GDP increased by less than 3 percent for the entire 3 years.[2]

In other words, the automatic monetary adjustment mechanism that would have come into play with a current account deficit had been

[2] IMF, *International Financial Statistics*, May 1981.

offset deliberately by foreign borrowing. Consequently, the country had actually accumulated net reserves. The increase in reserves had been monetized, which had resulted in even greater growth of the money stock.

An Expansionary Monetary Policy   An expansionary monetary policy with a perfectly elastic supply of foreign capital can be analyzed relatively easily using Figure 22.7. Such a policy may be thought of as shifting the *LM* curve outward to LM_1. The tendency to put downward pressure on the interest rate would mean that a capital outflow would occur, offsetting the monetary expansion. Equilibrium would, in fact, be restored only when the capital outflow had precisely offset the monetary expansion, returning the *LM* curve to LM_0. Monetary policy in such a situation—of perfect capital mobility and a fixed exchange rate—succeeds merely in changing the *composition* of the monetary assets. It is totally ineffective in affecting the interest rate or income.

With a Flexible Exchange Rate

What happens if there is perfectly mobile capital and the exchange rate is flexible? Capital flows, which result from any disturbance to the interest rate equilibrium, will be offset by the exchange rate adjustment that acts on the current account balance. (Recall that a depreciation of the home currency increases the current account surplus for any given income level. From Figure 22.3 it is evident that it would shift the *IS* curve upward to the right. An appreciation shifts the *IS* curve downward and to the left.)

Figure 22.7   **Expansionary Monetary Policy with Perfectly Elastic Foreign Capital Supply: Fixed Exchange Rate**

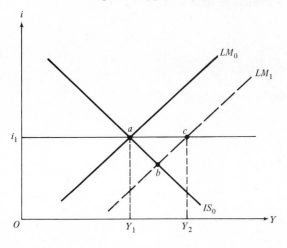

An Expansionary Expenditure Policy   Consider the case of an expansionary expenditure policy examined previously (Figure 22.6). The expansionary expenditure policy had raised the interest rate–income level at which the goods market would be in equilibrium. Diagrammatically, this had shifted the IS curve to IS_1. Now, with the exchange rate flexible, the upward pressure on domestic interest rates would generate a capital inflow that would result in an appreciation of the currency (see Figure 22.8). The currency appreciation, in turn, would have a contractionary effect on the current account and shift the IS curve downward and to the left. The system would return to equilibrium when the current account contraction effect due to the appreciation of the currency has exactly offset the expansionary expenditure policy. Diagrammatically, this is when the IS curve has returned to IS_0 and equilibrium is restored at point a.

Note the contrast with the fixed exchange rate case where the expansionary expenditure policy was reinforced by the capital inflow, leading to a higher equilibrium income level (Y_2 in Figure 22.6).

An Expansionary Monetary Policy   For completeness we note the case of an expansionary monetary policy when the exchange rate is flexible and capital is perfectly mobile. The pressure of excess money stock would tend to depress the interest rate (see Figure 22.9), resulting in an outflow of capital. The capital outflow would result in a depreciation of the home currency, which, in turn, would tend to generate a current account surplus, thereby reinforcing the effect of the expansionary monetary policy. The ultimate equilibrium would occur when the effect of the capital outflow on the exchange rate had resulted in

Figure 22.8   Expansionary Expenditure Policy with Perfectly Elastic Foreign Capital: Flexible Exchange Rate

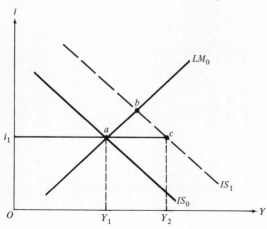

Figure 22.9 Expansionary Monetary Policy with Perfectly Elastic Foreign Capital: Flexible Exchange Rate

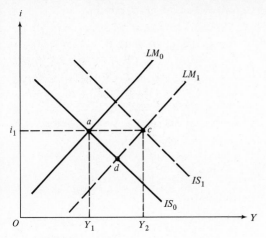

an increased aggregate expenditure that precisely accommodates the initial monetary expansion. (In Figure 22.9 this is at point *c*.)

A Foreign Interest Rate Disturbance: Fixed Versus Flexible Exchange Rates

Countries that are integrated into the international capital markets face a dilemma when confronted by higher international interest rates. The dilemma is readily illustrated by using this framework.

Consider the consequences of an upward shift of international interest rates [illustrated in Figure 22.10(a) by the move from i_0 to i_1]. The maintenance of interest rate at the initial level in the face of the higher international interest rate would result in major capital out-flows, and could not be sustained. The options open to the country are (1) to adapt an expansionary expenditure policy, or (2) to permit a contractionary monetary policy. In either case it must accept the higher interest rate as long as it wishes to remain integrated in the international capital market. The choice of whether or not to permit the exchange rate to adjust determines which way the adjustment will occur.

If the authorities maintain the exchange rate fixed [Figure 22.10(b)], the incipient capital outflow occurring at the initial equilib-rium (point *a*) will show up as a loss of foreign exchange reserves. The resulting reduction in the money stock would continue until the money stock had adjusted to equilibrium at the higher level of interest (the curve LM_1 passing through point *b*). The economy has adjusted to the

Figure 22.10 Foreign Interest Rate Disturbance

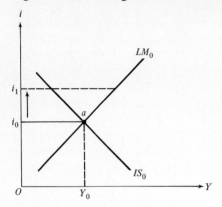

(a) Initial disturbance: interest rate in world capital market rises.

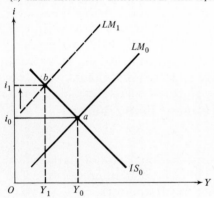

(b) Adjustment under fixed exchange rate

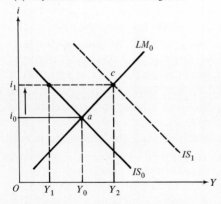

(c) Adjustment under flexible exchange rate

higher world capital market interest rates by reducing its income (to Y_1).

If, instead, the exchange rate is flexible [Figure 22.10(c)], the incipient capital outflow at the initial equilibrium would generate an exchange rate depreciation. The lower value of the domestic currency would create an export surplus, so that the trade surplus exactly offsets the capital outflow. The new equilibrium (point c) with a higher income level (at Y_2) gives the appearance of an improvement over the initial situation. A very important qualification must be noted. The ongoing situation (at point c) is sustained by a continuing export surplus to offset the capital outflow. Thus the country has been forced to refrain from spending some of its (admittedly higher) income and loan that to the foreigners.

This choice—between a fixed exchange rate and the consequent deflation of the domestic economy versus a flexible exchange rate and the forced loaning to the foreigners—was the choice facing the leaders of the seven largest industrial countries as they met in Versailles in early June 1982. High real interest rates[3] in the United States were spreading to the capital markets of the other countries (see Table 22.2). The diplomatic language did not mask the grave concern the other leaders had about the implications of U.S. policy for their own economies. "Success in our continuing fight against inflation . . . will also help to bring down interest rates, which are now unacceptably high. . . ."[4]

The Managed or "Dirty" Float Policy Option

The difference between fixed and flexible exchange rate cases has caught the attention of policymakers. Many, while nominally following a floating exchange rate, have in fact chosen a managed or "dirty" float policy. While virtually all countries on a floating exchange rate intervene to smooth out day-to-day variations, many countries have intervened massively at one time or another to alter the course that the flexible exchange rate would have otherwise taken. In the example cited in Figure 22.8, instead of permitting the capital inflow to result in an exchange rate appreciation that would thwart the expansionary fiscal policy, a managed float would simulate the fixed exchange rate: Keep the exchange rate at its initial level by buying up the excess supply of foreign exchange, and monetize that excess supply. This in-

---

[3] The real interest rate is the difference between the nominal interest rate and the rate of inflation. For example, if the nominal interest rate is 10 percent and the inflation rate is 7 percent, the real interest rate is 3 percent.

[4] Final communique, Versailles summit meeting, June 4–6, 1982, quoted in *IMF Survey*, **11**, No. 12, 189 (June 21, 1982).

Table 22.2 Real Interest Rates in Selected Industrial Countries, Quarterly 1980–1982 (Percent)

	1980				1981				1982			
	I	II	III	IV	I	II	III	IV	I	II	III	IV
United States	−2.52	−3.92	−1.85	−0.27	1.54	3.69	3.60	5.54	6.67	6.94	7.14	5.25
United Kingdom	−4.66	−7.48	−3.06	−1.96	1.14	2.47	4.07	3.78	3.58	4.34	4.28	4.12
France	−0.81	−0.72	−0.76	0.03	1.49	2.94	3.01	2.11	1.99	1.99	4.38	5.75
West Germany	3.30	2.90	2.60	3.30	4.30	5.00	5.00	3.50	3.90	3.60	3.80	3.38
Italy	−5.47	−5.12	−5.28	−4.30	−0.80	1.96	4.75	4.90	4.01	5.62	4.15	3.98
Japan	1.77	0.92	0.76	1.41	2.03	3.77	4.93	4.31	4.66	5.65	5.68	5.67
Canada	3.43	1.97	1.97	1.87	1.07	2.52	4.47	3.12	3.84	3.67	3.75	2.51

SOURCE: IMF, *International Financial Statistics.*

NOTE: The interest rates taken are those corresponding to the government bond yields (line 61). The relevant inflation term subtracted is that one corresponding to the percentage change in the Consumer Price Index (with respect to the same quarter a year before).

tervention would continue until capital-inflow-created monetary expansion had accommodated the expansionary expenditure policy. In terms of the diagram this would occur when the *LM* curve had shifted rightward to yield an equilibrium where the authorities had initially hoped to be with their expansionary fiscal stimulus—namely, at point *c* in Figure 22.8, with an equilibrium level of income Y_2.

More often than not, a dirty float is indicted when the flexible exchange rate adjustment process would yield a depreciation of the domestic currency. Perhaps the easiest way to see this is by examining the case of monetary expansion with a flexible exchange rate and perfectly mobile international capital. An expansionary monetary policy would put downward pressure on the domestic interest rate. In terms of Figure 22.9, the equilibrium between IS_0 and LM_1 in such a situation would be at point *d*. The downward pressure on the interest rate would tend to generate a capital outflow. This, in turn, puts pressure on the exchange rate, resulting in a depreciation of the home currency to create a current account surplus that offsets the capital outflow. Equilibrium would be restored when the current account surplus exactly offsets the capital outflow. (Diagrammatically, the money stock associated with LM_1 prevails at point *c* in Figure 22.9.)

The effect of expansionary monetary policy in this case has been magnified by the currency depreciation. Note the contrast with the fixed exchange rate case, where expansionary monetary policy was completely ineffective because the monetary reserve loss offset the monetary expansion. Now, if a policymaker is facing a situation in which the monetary expansion is regarded as excessive, instead of permitting the exchange rate to float downward and thereby exacerbate the excess expenditure by depreciation of the currency, a policy that mimics the fixed exchange rate could well be preferable. In this case, the defense of the exchange rate would result in a loss of foreign exchange reserves and a monetary contraction (from LM_1 to LM_0 in Figure 22.9).

Before the reader concludes that all our policy problems have been solved, we must note that this approach is very much dependent on the continued flow of interest-sensitive short-term capital to maintain some particular policy stance. We shall consider the consequences of this feature in the next chapter. We need merely note at present that the dependence on a *continued* flow of short-term capital makes the policy approach inherently short term, one that is unsustainable in the long run.

CONCLUSION

In this chapter we have developed the standard *IS–LM* model in a way that integrates the Keynesian and monetary models of balance-of-payments adjustment. Income, the stock of assets held by individuals, and the interest rate all interact to achieve adjustment when an equilibrium is disturbed. At the same time, each could be the source of a disturbance, requiring the other elements of the system to adjust. The model was developed initially under the assumption that capital could not move internationally. We then introduced tradeable bonds, which permitted international capital movements.

The analysis of the model also depends on whether or not the exchange rate is fixed or flexible. We found that in a pure fixed exchange rate an expansionary expenditure policy is reinforced by the capital flow, while in a pure flexible exchange rate case expansionary expenditure policy is offset by the capital flow.

In considering the effect of expansionary monetary policy, on the other hand, we found that just the opposite holds: Under a fixed exchange rate an expansionary monetary policy is offset by the capital flow, whereas under a flexible exchange rate the expansionary monetary policy is not offset by the capital flow.

Because national policymakers may not wish to have to choose between a fixed versus a flexible exchange rate, frequently the managed float approach has been adopted, permitting policymakers to blend the various adjustment mechanisms.

The extreme assumptions that domestic bonds are either nontradeable or perfectly tradeable facilitated our analysis of the adjustment process. A somewhat more realistic intermediate assumption— that there is *some* but *not perfect* sensitivity of capital flows to the domestic interest rate—awaits development in the next chapter.

[For Selected References, see the end of Chapter 23.]

23
CHAPTER

External and
Internal Balance

Exchange rates, interest rates, trade flows, capital flows, income, and expenditure; all are intimately related, we have learned. In the preceding chapter we developed the *IS–LM* model to help us handle the essential features of these interrelationships. In doing so we considered the *IS–LM* model under two extreme assumptions concerning the interest sensitivity of the capital account. In the first case we assumed that domestic bonds could not be sold to foreigners. In the second case, we assumed perfect substitutability of domestic and foreign bonds.

In this chapter we develop the intermediate case, in which there is some, but not perfect, substitution between domestic and foreign sources of capital. In doing so, we employ a "foreign balance" curve in the *IS–LM* framework.

The development of this analytical framework enables us to address one of the major policy issues of the postwar period: What is the appropriate policy approach to achieve simultaneous internal and external balance?

THE *IS–LM* MODEL WITH A FOREIGN
BALANCE CURVE

In the *IS–LM* model, when we assumed that domestic bonds could not be sold to foreigners, the net balance of international transactions was synonymous with the current account balance. If we were to draw a curve describing such a state of net international balance in the *IS–LM* space of *i* and *Y*, it would be a vertical line passing through the

Figure 23.1   *IS–LM–FB* Model

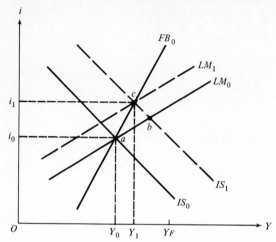

level of Y at which $CA = 0$. At levels of Y greater, there would be net foreign deficits, and at levels of Y smaller, there would be net foreign surpluses.

In the second case, where we assumed perfect substitutability of domestic and foreign bonds, the current account deficit or surplus was exactly offset by the foreign sale or purchase of bonds at the given international interest rate. Hence, in the $IS–LM$ space, the line describing a state of net international balance is *horizontal* at the world interest rate.

These two cases of net foreign balance curves describe the extremes. The intermediate situation is one in which there is some, but not perfect, substitution between domestic and foreign bonds, or more generally between domestic and foreign sources of capital. This involves some flow response of international capital to the level of the domestic interest rate, relative to the interest rate prevailing in international capital markets. This is depicted in Figure 23.1 as FB_0, which is a net foreign balance curve that is upward sloping in the interest income space. Above the net foreign balance curve the net balance of payments would be in surplus: For example, the capital inflow more than compensates for the current account deficit. Below the curve, the net foreign balance would be in deficit.[1]

The initial equilibrium in Figure 23.1 of IS_0 and LM_0, intersecting

[1] A detailed derivation of the FB curve is contained in the Appendix to this chapter. In drawing the FB curve we depict it as steeper than the LM curve. This is a convention followed by many authors, but need not be the case. If FB happens to be flatter than LM, the reader will observe that very different results can occur.

at a point on the FB_0 curve, indicates that the current account balance is exactly offset by the capital flow, meaning that there is no net change in the foreign assets of the banking system, and hence no flow change in money stock.

This general model may now be used to analyze the consequences of various types of disturbances that affect the economy. We continue to assume that the price level is fixed in the domestic economy. This may seem incompatible with the possibility that we may alter the exchange rate or aggregate expenditure without affecting the price level and warrants particular mention. The approach is consistent with the Keynesian tradition, which assumes, at least implicitly, that the domestic economy is relatively "insulated" from the international economy.[2] In particular, it means that the prices of goods in the domestic economy can diverge significantly from those in the international economy. A devaluation, by raising the price of a unit of foreign currency in terms of local currency, raises the price of imports facing domestic residents, and reduces the high price of home exports facing the foreigners. And as long as the domestic economy is not pressing the "full-employment" output, the domestic price level may reasonably be taken as fixed.

We now disturb the initial state of equilibrium of Figure 23.1 by a fiscal stimulus that increases expenditure. This shifts the *IS* curve rightward to IS_1. The result is to create a temporary equilibrium at a higher income level and interest rate (at point *b*, the intersection of IS_1 and LM_0). However, because the initial position involves a higher income and a *lower* interest rate than are compatible with net foreign balance, there is a net balance-of-payments deficit, meaning that foreign exchange reserves are being lost. The drawing down of foreign exchange reserves, in turn, means that the money stock is falling. (Diagrammatically, this is shifting the *LM* curve leftward.) This process continues as long as the net balance of payments is in deficit (moving the *LM* curve from LM_0 to LM_1, where, at the equilibrium indicated by point *c*, the economy is once again in net foreign balance). Note that in this case—under a fixed exchange rate—the fiscal stimulus has had a positive effect on income.

Contrast this with the attempt at monetary stimulus under a fixed exchange rate. As a mental exercise, consider what happens if the authorities increase domestic credit and hence the money stock. The temporary equilibrium would result in a net balance of payments deficit. The loss of foreign exchange reserves draws down the money

---

[2] The phrase is R. I. McKinnon's in "The Exchange Rate and Macroeconomic Policy: Changing Postwar Perceptions," *Journal of Economic Literature*, **19**, No. 2, 535 (June 1981).

Figure 23.2   Foreign Capital Market Disturbance

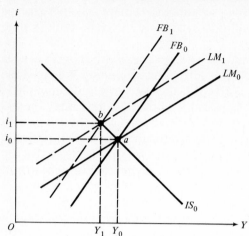

stock. The reserve loss continues to reduce the money stock until the initial equilibrium is restored.

Finally, suppose that the disturbance were due to the fact that the foreigners' capital markets have tightened, and hence the interest rate at which they borrow and lend on international markets has risen. The result would be an upward shift of the FB curve, from FB_0 to FB_1 in Figure 23.2.

The initial equilibrium (IS_0 and LM_0 at point a) would now involve a balance-of-payments deficit. The resulting loss of foreign exchange reserves would draw down the domestic money stock (shifting the LM curve leftward). This process would continue until the balance-of-payments deficit is eliminated and equilibrium restored (at point b). The adjustment process in this case has resulted in a *higher* domestic interest rate and a *lower* domestic income level.

EXTERNAL VERSUS INTERNAL BALANCE IN THE *IS–LM–FB* MODEL

The monetary adjustment mechanism in this analytical framework, given sufficient time and if permitted to work, will act to restore external balance after a disturbance. However, the *IS–LM–FB* framework contains no mechanism that will ensure the new equilibrium will correspond to what might be termed "internal balance." The equilibrium level of income may be at a level substantially less than the authorities desire. The policy response, then, might well be to engage in a combination of policies that would stimulate domestic expenditure and sterilize the balance of payments adjustment.[3] Hence to achieve what the authorities regard as a desired state of "internal balance," they find that they must sacrifice external balance.

This observation of a possible conflict between external and internal balance led to the development of a substantial volume of literature concerned with the question of how best to achieve simultaneous internal and external balance. To understand the essential features of that literature does not require the development of elaborate new diagrams. We can use the *IS–LM–FB* diagram to see the key points. In all of this literature, it is assumed that sterilization of foreign exchange reserve changes occurs. This means that the *LM* curve remains fixed unless authorities explicitly act to shift it via a deliberate policy.

A preliminary related issue should first be noted: the problem of numbers of targets and instruments, which was first elaborated by Tinbergen.[4] If there are two interdependent targets—such as internal and external balance—to be achieved, the authorities will generally require at least two independent policy instruments in order to achieve exactly both targets. Thus, while a given target might be achieved by either instrument, only by chance will the setting of a particular instrument that achieves one target result in the achievement of the other target.

The second issue concerns the appropriate assignment of instruments to targets. Mundell's work suggests a simple rule: "An instrument should be matched with the target on which it exerts the greatest relative influence."[5] In the specific context of internal–external balance, let us compare the relative effectiveness of fiscal and monetary policy in achieving internal and external balance.

To begin, consider a situation of internal imbalance such as that illustrated in Figure 23.3, with equilibrium income at Y_0 and target income at Y^F. The initial choice is between expansionary monetary policy (shifting the *LM* curve to achieve equilibrium at point *b*) and expansionary expenditure policy (shifting the *IS* curve to achieve equilibrium at point *c*). By using expansionary expenditure policy it is clear that the movement to the target level of income is achieved with *less* external imbalance because interest rates rise and attract foreign capital inflow. Given the higher income level achieved by an expansionary expenditure policy it is then possible to assign to monetary policy the

---

[3] Recall from Chapter 20 that sterilization is the action by the monetary authorities to *offset* the effect of foreign exchange reserve changes on the domestic money stock.

[4] J. Tinbergen, *On the Theory of Economic Policy* (Amsterdam: North-Holland Publishing Company, 1952).

[5] R. A. Mundell, *International Economics* (New York, Macmillan Publishing Company, 1968), p. 8.

Figure 23.3 **Assignment of Fiscal and Monetary Policy to Internal and External Balance**

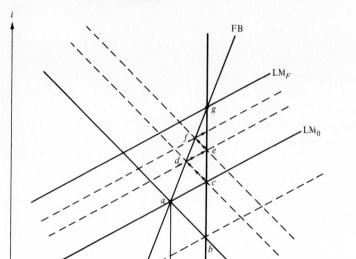

task of moving in the direction of external balance. Diagrammatically, this combination would move the economy from point *a* to *c* to point *d*, which is on the external balance curve (but now short of target *Y*). Continuing this assignment—monetary policy to external balance and expenditure policy to internal balance—will gradually move the economy to a situation where *both* internal and external balance prevail. The reader can readily verify that the opposite assignment would have taken the economy explosively away from both internal and external balance. Note that there is no need for the monetary and fiscal authorities to follow the alternating approach we have just employed, or even for them to act as if either knows of the other's existence. If each takes its mandate to act with *its instrument* when the economy is off *its target*, the effect will be to move the economy toward both internal and external balance (point *g* in Figure 23.3).

The approach to economic policy that this analysis suggests is open to a number of serious criticisms. It presumes a knowledge that the authorities may not in fact possess: that they know with some precision how far the economy is from both internal and external balance. It presumes further that they know the quantitative results and timing to be obtained from the application of each policy and that they are able to apply their instruments that way. We shall have more to say shortly about the extent of justifiable policy intervention.

A more immediate difficulty with the approach of assigning to monetary policy the task of achieving external balance concerns the effect it has on the *composition* of the balance of payments. Although the net balance of payments may be zero, one possible result may be substantial current account imbalances offset by opposite short-term capital account imbalances. Such a situation would not be sustainable for extended periods. Only a country that was acting as banker to the world such as the United States in the post–World War II period up to about 1970 could hope to, and even then ultimately must be concerned about a policy that involves a net negative long-run balance of short-term capital flows.

Not only might the situation be unsustainable, it could give the result that an interest rate policy chosen for external balance may have no relationship whatsoever with the appropriate long-run scarcity value of capital, or the appropriate home country policy toward its long-run capital borrowing. Capital-rich countries might well end up as long-run borrowers, while capital scarce countries could turn out to be net lenders in the long run under such an approach to external balance.

Another angle on the compositional problem, quite simply, is that this policy does not permit a country to choose a policy mix in which its current account balance is positive, or negative, depending on whether the country wishes to accumulate or decumulate its assets.

Finally, some critics attack the entire foundation of this policy stance: the integration of a nation's capital market into the international capital markets. The ability to attract a large volume of capital, they argue, also increases the nation's vulnerability to economic policy decisions taken elsewhere. Those policy decisions, although taken in the best interests of the owners of the capital, can be detrimental to the national interest, the critics claim.

Reliance on capital flows is not, then, a complete answer to the policy problem. A further instrument may be needed as a means of attaining external balance. The instrument that immediately suggests itself is the exchange rate. We saw in Chapter 19 how a rise in the exchange rate could generate an excess supply of foreign exchange. The mechanism in a Keynesian model (such as the IS–LM model) is that a devaluation raises the price of imports facing domestic residents and lowers the price of exports facing foreigners. Hence both domestic residents and foreigners *switch* their expenditure from foreign to domestic goods, thereby reducing the current account deficit. In terms of Figure 23.4 a devaluation shifts the X–M curve upward from $(X$–$M)_0$ to, say, $(X$–$M)_1$. Note that at the new equilibrium Y_1, the excess of expenditure

Figure 23.4 Devaluation in a Keynesian Model

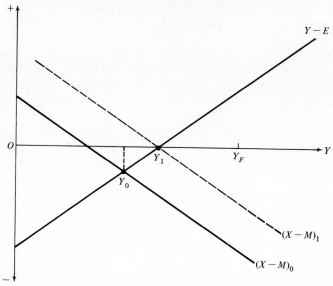

over income has been reduced, which of course is what the devaluation must do under any approach if it is to achieve a reduction in the curent account deficit.

The results just described are readily translated into two effects on our $IS-LM-FB$ diagram (Figure 23.5). From an initial deficit equi-

Figure 23.5 Devaluation in IS-LM-FB Model

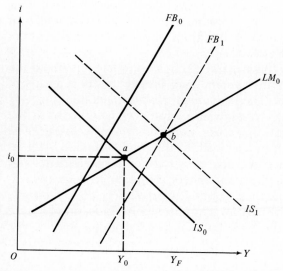

librium at *a*, a devaluation shifts the *IS* curve rightward, because the current account deficit is reduced for given levels of income. The foreign balance curve is shifted rightward for the same reason. The post-devaluation equilibrium will generally be somewhere northeast of point *a*, such as point *b*.

A discrete devaluation in such a model can move equilibrium toward external balance. Note, however, that it also tends to increase expenditure on domestic income. This means that policymakers still face an assignment problem in this framework. The assignment problem is, however, readily resolved. Because the exchange rate is relatively more potent in affecting external balance, and expenditure policies are relatively more effective in controlling income, it is appropriate to assign the exchange rate the task of achieving external balance, and the expenditure policies the task of internal balance.

ACTIVIST VERSUS PASSIVIST ADJUSTMENT TO INTERNAL AND EXTERNAL BALANCE UNDER FIXED EXCHANGE RATES

The Keynesian approach to macroeconomics takes as its starting point the existence of some rigidities in the economy that result in an equilibrium level of income that is independent of the full-employment level. However, in the later 1960s, following Friedman's influential presidential address to the American Economic Association,[6] a different strand of literature emerged in which it is argued that there exists a "natural" level of output that the economy tends to produce in the long run, although in the short run, shocks may move the economy away from this natural rate of output. Consequently, as long as the natural rate of output is not affected by macroeconomic influences, macroeconomic policy intervention may act to shock the economy away from its natural output, but the effect of the shock eventually dissipates and the economy ultimately returns to its natural rate of output. While microeconomic "supply-side" policies may change the natural rate of output attainable from given resources, aggregate demand or exchange rate policies cannot permanently move the economy away from its natural rate of output.

This approach then suggests that there is an automatic adjustment mechanism at work internally. Recall also the automatic monetary adjustment of balance-of-payments deficits or surpluses under a fixed exchange rate. The existence of a balance-of-payments deficit is

[6] M. Friedman, "The Role of Monetary Policy," *American Economic Review*, **58**, No. 1, 1–17 (Mar. 1968).

a flow adjustment designed to restore asset stock equilibrium. In other words, external imbalance is inherently an adjustment mechanism itself. Furthermore, the adjustment process is self-extinguishing. The flow deficit serves eventually to eliminate the stock monetary disequilibrium. When stock monetary equilibrium has been restored, the flow deficit has been eliminated and external balance achieved.

When we integrate these two automatic adjustment mechanisms we have the result that *chronic* internal or external imbalance (or both) exists only if adjustment mechanisms have been blocked or persistently offset. Otherwise, the economy will, in time, achieve both internal and external balance.

This conclusion does *not* mean that there will never be a state of imbalance internally or externally. Nor does it necessarily mean that such imbalances are not a matter of policy concern. Rather, we may think of an economy that is subject to shocks of varying kinds and intensities that can result in internal and/or external imbalance. The long-run adjustment mechanisms, given sufficient time to work and allowed to work, could eliminate the imbalances.

There are two significantly different policy approaches open to the authorities. One approach—which could be labeled *activist*—argues that it is possible to improve upon the workings of the marketplace, especially when it comes to macroeconomic policy issues such as full employment, inflation, and the balance of payments. The other approach—which could be labeled *passivist*—argues that policymakers cannot possibly do as well as the workings of the automatic adjustment mechanism.

The activist case starts from the analytical framework we have developed in this chapter, and argues that this framework provides policymakers with powerful insights into the working of an open economy. It argues further that these general analytical effects of policy actions can be quantified with a reasonable degree of precision so as to permit an activist policymaker to apply the appropriate policies with the correct size and timing of the intervention. To that end enormous efforts are expended in the development of quantitative macroeconomic models for the use of policymakers. The models have developed an ability to track the key economic variables and in simulating the effects of policy alternatives.

The passivist response to this line of argument is that a permanent policy change is inappropriate if a disturbance is transitory and that at the time of any disturbance no one can know whether it is permanent or transitory. Consequently, no one can know whether or not adjustment is appropriate. Both the private sector and the politician-cum-policymaker face this difficulty equally, for they both have the same set of information. Consequently, there is no compelling reason to believe that policy intervention will improve on the adjustment path the private sector would follow in any case. The most effective role the policymaker could play would be to design the system to assist the automatic adjustment processes rather than intervene in a way that more often than not slows the adjustment process because the attempt to alleviate the perceived adverse effects of the adjustment.

The activist responds that while we are waiting for the automatic adjustment to occur, the economy may suffer unnecessarily from the disequilibrium adjustment process. Prolonged periods of unemployment and/or balance of payments deficits with monetary deflation are simply too big a price to pay to rely on the automatic processes, the activist concludes. The passivist's only response is to cite the record of activist policy intervention and argue that we *would* have been better off without that intervention.

What is the correct answer? The debate is far from settled. The activists and passivists will continue to differ as long as the evidence remains inconclusive or capable of different interpretations.

SELECTED REFERENCES

DORNBUSCH, R., and S. FISCHER. *Macroeconomics,* 2nd ed. New York: McGraw-Hill Book Company, 1981. Chapters 18 and 19 contain derivations of the open-economy *IS–LM* model and related analyses under fixed and flexible exchange rates.

LEITH, J. CLARK. "On the Assignment of Policies to Achieve Internal and External Balance." In G. L. Reuber, *Canada's Political Economy.* Toronto: McGraw-Hill Ryerson Ltd., 1980.

MEADE, J. E. *The Balance of Payments.* New York: Oxford University Press, 1951. The classic early analysis of the effects of various disturbances on income and the balance of payments, and of the use of policy to attain internal and external balance.

MUNDELL, R. A. *International Economics.* New York: Macmillan Publishing Company, 1968. Contains much of the author's early seminal work on internal–external balance and the problem of targets and instruments.

VON NEUMANN WHITMAN, M. *Policies for Internal and External Balance,* Special Papers in International Economics No. 9. Princeton, N.J.: International Finance Section, Princeton University, 1970. A useful analytical survey of the literature.

APPENDIX: DERIVATION OF THE *FB* CURVE

Foreign balance is defined as equality of international receipts and payments in the absence of any official reserve transactions. This is the case when the current account deficit (surplus) is exactly offset by a capital account surplus (deficit) for a net foreign balance of zero.

In Figure 23A.1(a) we draw the familiar $X–M$ schedule that was first introduced in Chapter 20 [Figure 20.1(b)]. The balance of payments on current account is a negative function of the level of income. As income rises, domestic expenditure on imports rises and (perhaps) the level of exports falls for a net negative relationship.

The second function is the relationship between international capital *flow* and the domestic interest rate. The capital inflow is taken to be a *positive* function of the domestic interest rate. For given foreign

Figure 23A.1 Derivation of the FB Curve

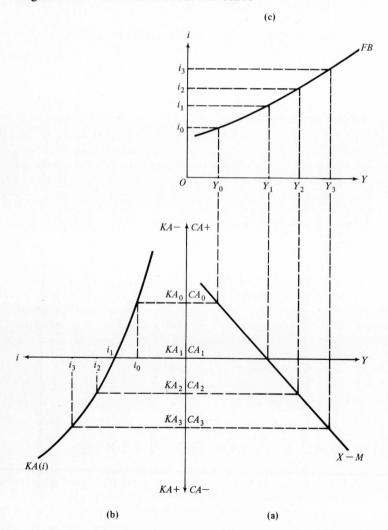

(c)

(b)   (a)

interest rates and given evaluation of "country risk" by the foreigners, they are willing to make more new loans and domestic borrowers are wanting to arrange more new borrowings from foreigners, the higher the domestic interest rate. We assume the exchange rate is fixed for the foreseeable future. At some interest rate net borrowing from abroad is zero. No new borrowing *net* is occurring, although the existing *stock* of outstanding loans remains outstanding. Below that interest rate, the net flow of lending is out of the country. Domestic residents on balance are lending to foreigners because of the relatively more attractive return obtainable from foreigners.

We map the net capital account flow vertically in Figure 23A.1(b), the capital *inflow* measured downward from the origin and the capital outflow upward. The interest rate is measured leftward from the origin.

Putting the two accounts together, for a net foreign balance of zero, we must have the current account plus the capital account sum to zero. Thus at Y_0 there is a current account surplus of CA_0, which to achieve a net foreign balance of zero must be offset by a capital account outflow of KA_0. This would be achieved by an interest rate i_0. Consequently, the *combination* of i_0 and Y_0 is a point on the *FB* curve. Repeating the exercise for alternative levels of income, determining the current account for that income and the interest rate necessary to exactly offset that current account, we can find the locus of the combinations of Y and i that will yield a net foreign balance of zero: Some further sample combinations are Y_1 and i_1, Y_2 and i_2, Y_3 and i_3. We map the resulting curve *FB* in Figure 23A.1(c).

In drawing *FB* we must recognize that its slope and position depend on the underlying functions. Any *change* in those underlying conditions will change the *FB* curve. For example, in the Keynesian model, the $X-M$ curve will shift upward and to the right if there is a devaluation. This would mean that for a given level of income, a greater current account surplus would occur, and consequently a *lower* interest rate would be required to achieve a net foreign balance of zero. In brief, the *FB* curve would shift downward and to the right.

If foreign interest rates changed, the net foreign capital flow curve and hence the *FB* curve would shift. For example, if foreign interest rates rise, individuals would want to lend more to foreigners at a given home interest rate, and the offsetting current account surplus would be greater, and hence a lower income would be required to achieve a net balance of zero: The *FB* curve would be shifted to the left.

In summary, the *FB* curve is the locus of combinations of the domestic interest rate and income that yield current account deficits (surpluses) and capital account surpluses (deficits) that just balance each other. The *FB* curve is drawn for a given set of underlying domestic policies and external conditions.

24
CHAPTER

Exchange Control

In the foregoing chapters we have examined two policies that a nation might adopt when faced with a deficit in the balance of payments: either to permit a decline in foreign exchange reserves, or alternatively, a rise in the price of foreign exchange. There is, however, a third option: to ration the excess demand for foreign exchange. This option is in fact the one employed by a majority of all countries, including most developing countries.

Exchange control differs fundamentally from either exchange reserve or exchange rate adjustment. In essence, exchange control disregards market forces and substitutes for them decisions of government officials.

Authorities institute exchange control when an excess demand for foreign exchange has emerged at the actual fixed exchange rate and they dislike or are unable to adopt the other options of adjustment. The options they confront are threefold:

1. They could attempt to satisfy the excess demand from their foreign exchange reserves, but if the reserves are running low, that option is good for a limited time only, and in any case cannot be a permanent solution unless accompanied by domestic expenditure reduction.
2. They could allow the exchange rate to rise, but that would be admitting that expenditure (and probably income) would have to be cut.
3. Most policymakers-cum-politicians prefer the third option, which is to distribute the flow of available exchange among the various uses represented by the potential buyers and continue to charge the undervalued price of foreign exchange to those who are the favored purchasers. This option, as we shall see, is especially attractive when the imported goods are

Figure 24.1   Excess Demand for Foreign Exchange

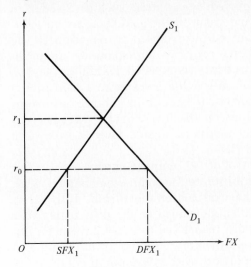

major mass consumption items or are important to the country's industrialization strategy.

The initial problem faced by the authorities may be seen from a diagram of the foreign exchange market (Figure 24.1): DFX_1 is demanded, while only SFX_1 is available at the exchange rate r_0. The market cannot satisfy all those who wish to purchase foreign exchange at r_0. Hence the authorities must *ration* the earnings SFX_1 among the greater uses, DFX_1. To do this, the authorities must first of all obtain control of all the foreign exchange earnings SFX_1. Then they must decide *which* of the uses represented up to DFX_1 is to receive an allocation and *how much* to allocate to each.

Such a system is clearly different from either of the adjustment mechanisms that rely on the market. Because it is so different, and also because it is so widespread, it warrants a detailed examination. In this chapter we consider why a country might choose at adopt exchange controls, and describe the anatomy of an exchange control regime. We then evaluate its consequences and consider possible avenues of escape from exchange controls.

WHY COUNTRIES CHOOSE EXCHANGE CONTROLS

The reasons why countries adopt exchange controls are as diverse as the countries themselves. Of the 131 members of the IMF, some 100 had one form or another of payments restriction in the early 1980s.

There are relatively mild forms of exchange control, usually over capital transactions alone, employed by countries such as Sweden in the 1980s or Great Britain after it went off the gold standard in 1931. The former attempts to look at each proposed transaction to see whether or not it benefits the home country. For example, "direct investment abroad by Swedish residents requires individual authorization, which normally is granted only if the investment is considered likely to promote exports or otherwise to benefit the balance on current account, irrespective of the return on the investment."[1] Yet Swedes continue to be significant direct investors outside Sweden even on a net basis (see line B.1, Table 22.1).

The British exchange control of 1931 banned capital exports but left the enforcement of this prohibition to the commercial banks. Such mild forms of exchange control have often been short-lived: Either they have been removed with the disappearance of the difficulties that brought them into being, or more restrictive controls have been imposed. These involve detailed approval of all foreign transactions and are used today by a large proportion of the developing countries of Africa, Asia, and Latin America.

The underlying case for the mild form of exchange control is that the excess demand for foreign exchange is attributable entirely to one category of demand such as private short-term capital. If the authorities deem the satisfaction of that category of demand to be relatively unimportant, and certainly not worth the adjustments required elsewhere in the economy, they use exchange control to prohibit that type of payment. Certainly, it is arguable that it would be preferable to deny access to a few to avoid imposing a significant adjustment burden on the entire economy. As we saw in the preceding chapter, short-term capital flows may give rise to such adjustment burdens.

This type of disturbance is illustrated in Figure 24.2. An initial equilibrium at r_0 with $SFX_0 = DFX_0$ is disturbed by a short-term capital outflow equal to $SFX_0 - DFX_1$. Rather than either (1) draw down exchange reserves by that amount and hence deflate the economy, or (2) let the exchange rate rise to r_1 pushing up the domestic price level, the authorities prefer to *block* the short-term capital outflow. If they are successful, the remaining demand is described by D_0, eliminating the excess demand for foreign exchange and avoiding the necessity of adjustment.

As a short-term device, this might prove effective. Note, however, that as soon as the authorities decide that a particular type of foreign exchange use is inappropriate, *someone* has to intervene in the

---

[1] International Monetary Fund, *Annual Report on Exchange Arrangements and Exchange Restrictions* (Washington, D.C.: IMF, 1980), p. 384.

Figure 24.2   Short-Term Capital Disturbance

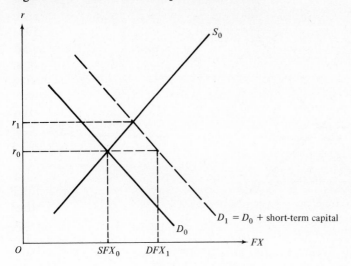

market to distinguish between acceptable and unacceptable uses. As we shall see, this is where the troubles from exchange controls begin. If the mild controls are not quickly abandoned, it frequently happens that the balance-of-payments problem remains, often exacerbated by exchange control. Individuals discover ways of evading surrender requirements and invent new claims on the available foreign exchange. The authorities then find it necessary to expand controls. To maintain constant effectiveness of the controls, they must do so at a rate that exceeds the rate at which people find ways of getting around controls. Limited restrictions give way to comprehensive and rigorous controls. This is because exchange control deals with the problem by suppressing the symptom of excess demand without addressing the cause. Controls may also contribute to a worsening of the excess demand for foreign exchange.

Besides the feeling of being in charge that exchange controls give, their popularity is closely bound up with the desire for economic planning. In a country where the government believes that it has a mandate to control as much of the economy as possible, setting the foreign exchange rate is regarded as critical in fulfilling that mandate. The exchange rate is the single most important price in the economy that the government is able to set by decree.[2] Hence it is a major instrument to be used to direct the economy. Having set the exchange rate, usually below an equilibrium rate, the authorities find that rationing is essen-

---

[2] The most important price is, of course, the price of domestic money in terms of goods. That price, however, cannot be set by a single decree.

Figure 24.3 Exchange Control

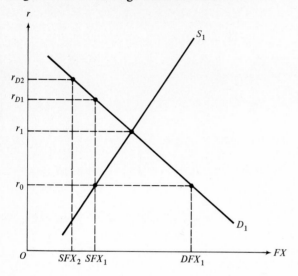

tial. This fits well with the predilection to control the economy, for the authorities believe they can now direct the allocation of foreign exchange among its many possible uses. We shall see how the elaborate system develops and what its consequences are.[3]

THE ANATOMY OF EXCHANGE CONTROL REGULATIONS

When the authorities choose to adopt permanent foreign exchange control, two types of regulations must be developed: (1) regulations governing the surrender of foreign exchange earnings, and (2) those governing their allocation among competing uses. The first set of regulations is necessary for the control system to work at all. To see this, it is helpful to think of what would happen if there were no effective surrender requirements (see Figure 24.3). At the controlled exchange rate all of the potential users (DFX_1 in Figure 24.3) would be competing for the smaller foreign exchange earnings flow (SFX_1). If those earnings

[3] One argument favoring exchange controls which frequently emerges in developing countries that are dominant suppliers of particular exports is that to allow the exchange rate to change would merely result in a decline in the world price of its exports. To the extent that this is true, of course, it is an argument in favor of an optimum import tariff or export tax, not exchange controls per se. An appropriate optimum export tax can be set much more explicitly and precisely, whereas the incidence of exchange controls depends on the degree of excess demand in the domestic economy, something the authorities have found it impossible to control.

were sold to the highest bidders, the exchange rate paid by buyers would have to rise (to r_{D1}), at which rate the excess demand would be eliminated. In other words, the scarcity value of the available foreign exchange earnings (SFX_1) is greater than the equilibrium price of foreign exchange (r_{D1}, not just r_1). To prevent the suppliers of the limited amount of foreign exchange generated at the low price from selling to the highest bidder, which would mean, effectively, that the exchange rate would rise, the authorities must institute some form of control to force the surrender of exchange earnings to them.

Note that the authorities must do more than simply decree that foreign exchange must be surrendered. They must *force* its surrender. Some would-be buyers of exchange at the controlled exchange rate will not obtain it. Buyers willing to pay more than the controlled rate will move outside the formal foreign exchange market to buy directly from the suppliers at a higher rate. Without forced surrender, the official foreign exchange channels would quickly dry up.[4]

Second, regulations governing the allocation of foreign exchange must be developed. Since the very decision to employ rationing implies that some uses of foreign exchange are more worthy than others, the problem is to set up a method of deciding *which* uses should be allocated foreign exchange at the price, r_0, below the market-clearing price.

Most exchange control countries develop a complex system that incorporates several different criteria to determine which users get how much foreign exchange and how they can spend it. Perhaps the most common criterion is the allocation of foreign exchange by end use. This permits the authorities to allocate more foreign exchange for so-called "essential" commodities, such as wage goods or raw materials for local industry, and correspondingly less to other uses, such as imported luxuries or goods that compete with local production.

It is apparent that the authorities may attempt to achieve more than one goal with the single instrument—income redistribution and industrialization. Inconsistencies readily develop. Yet this is only the beginning. In addition to allocation by end use, the authorities may find it necessary or desirable to discriminate among the applicants on the basis of the applicants themselves. Is the applicant a large or a small firm? In some countries large firms are preferred because of their *reliability*, whereas in others small businessmen are given preference. Is the applicant from a preferred region, such as a depressed area? Is

---

[4] Of course, even with forced surrender, some find devices to avoid it. One very common and simple device is to underbill exports or overbill imports. An export shipment in fact worth $10,000 may be billed to the foreigner at $8000, with the side agreement that the difference will be paid to a foreign bank account in the exporter's name. Or, by prior agreement, the foreign supplier bills the local importer at an excessive value; on the basis of this invoice the importer obtains the foreign exchange and pays the exporter, who deposits the excess in the importer's foreign bank account.

the applicant a private or a publicly owned entity? Is the applicant a foreign-owned or a locally owned firm?

The exchange control authorities may also discriminate among applicants on the basis of how the purchase is to be financed. Preference may be given to purchase from foreign vendors offering lengthy credit or who are willing to engage in barter transactions.

The exchange control authority that follows many of these criteria is likely to find itself in an impossible position. It may, for example, have to choose between an application for foreign exchange from a large foreign-owned firm engaged in a favored industrial activity in a depressed region versus a small, locally owned firm wishing to import an essential consumer good that competes with a local industry.

The end result may be interpreted in terms of Figure 24.3. The available foreign exchange is now less than SFX_1, say SFX_2, because of erosion of surrender requirements and because domestic cost pressures are making it increasingly difficult for exporters to earn SFX_1 in the world markets. The exchange control authorities distribute the available foreign exchange in a manner that bears little relationship to the marginal scarcity value r_{D2}. At best the distribution among potential users is random from the origin to DFX_1. At worst the distribution is perverse, with allocations going to specially favored buyers who would not even be in the market at an equilibrium exchange rate such as r_1.

DOMESTIC CONSEQUENCES OF EXCHANGE CONTROL REGIMES

Most countries find it very easy to let themselves slide into a system of exchange controls. Once the controls are in place, the authorities discover that they now have considerable freedom of action with respect to internal policies that might affect the balance of payments.

No government is apt to delay very long using this newly found freedom, usually in a way that increases the supply of money and credit. Monetary and fiscal disciplines are difficult and unpopular, and there are many attractive national goals—maintenance of full employment, economic development, postwar reconstruction, raising the standard of living—whose pursuit inevitably leads along the path of monetary expansion. Some countries will follow this primrose path reluctantly and slowly, some rapidly.

Given the apparent isolation of the domestic economy, attention is diverted from the balance of payments. Imbalances, which in the absence of exchange control and licensing would have required immediate attention, are ignored because the restrictive system makes them appear to be inconsequential. The result is that the domestic economy moves substantially out of line with the international economy. The restrictive system of controls and licensing has to bear increasingly greater pressure. The pressures often prove to be more than the control mechanisms can handle, and avoidance and evasion of the regulations become serious. To cope with these, a proliferation of restrictive instruments is employed to shore up the control system. The web of regulations and restrictions becomes so complex that the effects of both old and new policies are virtually impossible to evaluate. Once caught in such a web, few countries find it possible to extricate themselves without a long and arduous dismantling of the system accompanied by deflationary measures.

Once entangled in a complex web of controls, most countries find it very difficult to extricate themselves. Instead, they remain caught for extended periods, with very serious consequences for the domestic economy.[5]

First, the control system creates massive production inefficiencies. Favored activities can incur production costs several times world levels, while other activities receive negative effective protection (see pp. 178ff.).

Second, the control system induces excessive use of imported machinery and raw materials. By keeping such inputs relatively cheap, the domestic productive structure tends to be dominated by activities intensive in the use of imported inputs. Techniques of production tend to substitute in favor of greater use of imported inputs. Excessive reliance on imported machinery and raw materials makes the economy more dependent on imports, thus magnifying the adverse affects of an export shortfall.

Third, a control regime frequently creates domestic monopolies by prohibiting imports where a domestic producer already exists. This results in a loss from a higher price, due partly to the exclusion of imports and partly to the creation of a domestic monopoly.

Fourth, a control regime often encourages the creation of excess capacity by allocating import licenses according to the size of the ex-

---

[5] Many of these consequences have been documented in *Foreign Trade Regimes and Economic Development* [Cambridge, Mass.: Ballinger Publishing Co. (for the National Bureau of Economic Research)], a major study of several developing countries that have resorted to exchange controls for extended period. The overall results are presented in two synthesis volumes: J. N. Bhagwati, *Anatomy and Consequences of Exchange Control Regimes*, Vol. XI, 1978; and A. O. Krueger, *Liberalization Attempts and Consequences*, Vol. X, 1978. The individual country studies are: A. O. Krueger, *Turkey*, Vol. I; J. C. Leith, *Ghana*, Vol. II; M. Michaely, *Israel*, Vol. III; B. Hansen and K. Nashashibi, *Egypt*, Vol. IV; R. E. Baldwin, *Philippines*, Vol. V; J. N. Bhagwati and T. N. Srinivasan, *India*, Vol. VI; C. R. Frank et al, *South Korea*, Vol. VII; J. R. Behrman, *Chile*, Vol. VIII; and C. F. Diaz-Alejandro, *Colombia*, Vol. IX.

isting capital investment. Further, control regimes frequently support both efficient and inefficient firms by allocating foreign exchange to all of them on a pro rata basis. This, together with bottlenecks and shortages due to import controls, tends to generate excess capacity whose potential output is difficult to sell abroad because various costs of selling (travel, etc.) are subject to exchange rationing.

Fifth, controls give rise to enormous administrative costs of operating the system as well as of reacting to it. Both the regulators and the regulated have to devote significant managerial resources to these ends, thus depriving such productive activities as innovation of needed talents.

Sixth, controls establish artificial sources of gain from the sale of import licenses, from smuggling to evade import duties, and from the creation of domestic monopolies. Pursuit of these opportunities for profit diverts substantial resources from productive activities.

Finally, as noted earlier, exchange control systems make a nation more vulnerable to bouts of inflation, for they prevent a trade deficit from contracting the money stock, and they reduce import tax receipts by restricting imports. In this way, controls eliminate two important automatic budget stabilizers, giving freer rein to inflationary pressures.

Although the effects just enumerated are serious, if a control regime were to accelerate economic growth, its net effect could be beneficial. Yet in no recorded instance has prolonged and thorough exchange control led to accelerated growth.

CONSEQUENCES FOR THE INTERNATIONAL SYSTEM

By maintaining an overvalued currency, exchange controls cause a nation's exports to be overpriced abroad, while its imports are underpriced and in short supply at home. Other countries with exchange controls are doubtless in the same fix. What is more natural than that two or more such countries should get together? All have a common interest in augmenting both imports and exports; they merely require some device making it unnecessary to pay in a convertible currency.

Out of such shared difficulties and interest various forms of bilateral trading arrangements tend to arise, the essence of which is agreement to accept one another's inconvertible currencies in payment for exports and to use them to acquire imports. (We shall examine some of these arrangements in more detail shortly.)

If only one country adopts controls, its currency becomes inconvertible by the very fact that use of that currency is restricted. This inconvertibility is nondiscriminatory, for restrictions apply equally to the purchase of any other currency. But with the spread of exchange control and of its inevitable companion, bilateral trading arrangements, restrictions quickly become discriminatory. Applications for foreign exchange are granted readily if the currency desired is that of a bilateral trading partner, where balances can be easily acquired. But if it is a free or convertible currency, applications are rigidly restricted. The world becomes divided into "hard"- and "soft"-currency areas, one with convertible currencies, the other regulating convertibility with varying degrees of discrimination.

This division of the world encourages the further spread of exchange controls; for a country still adhering to convertibility finds that although its balance of payments, as a total, is in balance, it has a surplus with the soft-currency bloc and a deficit with the hard-currency area, but it cannot use the surplus to settle the deficit. To deal with the deficit, depreciation or deflation would be appropriate, but either policy would tend to increase its surplus in inconvertible currencies. The country needs to reduce exports to, and increase imports from, the soft-currency area—and the reverse with respect to the hard-currency countries. It may find that to do this it is obliged to introduce exchange controls itself, in order to participate in bilateral trading arrangements.

Bilateral Trading Arrangements [6]

The potential variety of bilateral trading arrangements is almost limitless. In the history of the international economy three types, in descending order of restrictiveness, can be distinguished.

Private Compensation Among the earliest forms of bilaterial trade were barter deals undertaken by private firms. These were common in the 1930s; although largely superseded by more formal arrangements, they continued to be used after the war. Thus, in the early 1930s, German coal producers arranged for the export to Brazil of 9 million marks' worth of coal, obtaining in exchange an equal value of coffee. German fertilizer was similarly exchanged for Egyptian cotton.

Somewhat more complicated arrangements, having the advantage of releasing the exporter from also performing the unaccustomed functions of an importer, involved an export and import firm in each country. Agreement had to be reached on what commodities would be exported, in what quantities, and at what values. Upon receipt of the goods, the importer in each country paid his fellow exporter in local currency, and the transaction was completed.

[6] This section provides important historical elaboration of the experience with exchange controls, but may be skipped without loss of continuity.

All such arrangements required the approval of the exchange control authorities, even though they avoid the need to apply for an allocation of foreign exchange. Not only are exports and imports both subject to license, it is also the duty of the authorities to see that exports than can, in spite of difficulties, be sold for scarce, free currencies are not needlessly diverted from these markets. Hence it has generally been necessary for firms engaging in such deals to show that their exports were "additional"—that is, except for some special arrangement, they could not be sold. This tends to give weight in this type of trade to relatively unimportant or fringe items in the exports of each partner.

Private compensation requires that the individual exports and imports of each transaction offset each other. This puts upon the exporter wishing to consummate such a deal the responsibility of ascertaining what imports are acceptable both to the exchange control authorities and to buyers in his country. Even when a fellow countryman among importers is drawn into the arrangements, it is still necessary for the two parties to find one another. To overcome such difficulties, specialized brokers emerged before the war in Germany and other countries, devoting their energies to uncovering possibilities of mutually advantageous and permissible trade, and to finding and bringing together potentially interested parties.

Implicitly, private compensation arrangements involve a departure from the official exchange rate. The export good, which would not otherwise be sold because it was too expensive on the world market at the official exchange rate, does find a market. Or the import, which was not otherwise available, can now be brought into the country. The implicit price of foreign exchange in such transactions is higher than the official rate: The country has, in effect, devalued for that transaction, while other transactions continue at the undervalued official price of foreign exchange.

Clearing Agreements   A more generalized approach to bilateral trading was found with the development of *exchange clearing*. In bilateral clearing, each country agreed to establish, usually in its central bank, an account through which all payments for imports and exports between the two countries shall be cleared.[7]

Argentina and Italy in 1952 entered into a five-year agreement of this type. For all imports from Italy into Argentina, payments by importers had to be made into the Argentine clearing account in pesos. Similarly, Italians importing Argentine goods made payments into the Italian clearing account in lire. Exporters in each country were in turn paid in local currency from the balances deposited by importers.

[7] Some clearing agreements are limited to certain categories of commodities, the rest of the trade being carried out in the normal manner.

As long as exports and imports are equal in value, clearance is complete and there is no problem of keeping the account in balance. Since precise equality is not to be expected, some provision to meet such a divergence is necessary. The commonest method is to establish a "swing" credit of a fixed amount. Thus in the Italian–Argentine agreement, exports could exceed imports in either direction by as much as $100 million. Any further excess had to be settled in gold or dollars. Another device is to alter the exchange rate applied to the clearing transactions, which is always specified in the agreement. Since it is an arbitrarily determined rate, it may overvalue one of the currencies and thus be responsible for the trade imbalance. Before World War II, Germany deliberately used its superior bargaining power vis-à-vis the Balkan nations to force their acceptance of an overvalued rate for the mark. This gave Germany advantageous terms of trade and led to the accumulation of mark balances by the Balkans. To liquidate the mark balances, which implicitly involved a loan to Germany, the Balkan countries had to accept relatively unwanted commodities at high prices: hence the large Balkan imports of aspirin and harmonicas.

Without a "swing" limit to the net excess of trade in either direction, not only might large unusable balances accumulate, but the monetary effects in each country could be serious. In the country with an excess of imports, substantial net payments of local currency would be made into the clearing account, thus retiring money from circulation. As with any excess of imports over exports, this is deflationary. In the country whose exports exceeded its imports, in-payments by importers would be insufficient to compensate the exporters. If the central bank were willing to advance credit to pay them, the money supply would be increased immediately by this amount, and ultimately, after these central bank funds had been deposited with commercial banks, perhaps by the full amount made possible by reserve requirements. Without such advances, the exporters would have to wait for payment until their turn came, which would dampen their enthusiasm to export.

Payments Agreements   Another type of bilateral arrangement, somewhat wider in scope than the clearing agreement, is the payments agreement. It is no different from the clearing agreement in principle or in mechanism, but simply extends clearing facilities to additional categories of payments. The most important of these is outstanding debts, although the various service transactions, including the service of debt, are usually included.

Countries that build up substantial credits in exchange control countries, either prior to the introduction of controls, as a result of the operation of bilateral accord, or simply because of the rashness of exporters, acquire a frozen asset. A payments agreement provides the means to thaw it by prescribing that a certain percentage of payments for imports into the creditor country's clearing account shall be earmarked for the liquidation of accumulated debt. The creditor country need exercise no control over imports from the debtor, since only if imports exceed exports can accumulated debt be paid off. The debtor country, on the other hand, must hold imports from the creditor down sufficiently so that the agreed proportion of the value of its exports actually becomes applied to debt retirement.

In the decade following World War II, most bilateral agreements in Europe were of this broader type, including provisions not only for the settlement of debt, but also for payments for shipping charges, debt service, tourism, and the whole range of service items. With the gradual liberalization of trade, strictly bilateral accords gave way more and more to arrangements that permitted a considerable degree of multilateral clearing, as in the European Payments Union (see p. 493).

While the industrial countries were moving away from narrow bilateral arrangements toward multilateral clearing, and eventually the resumption of convertibility, many developing countries were moving in the other direction. Both because of exchange control and because they found that bilateral trade pacts were often the only way to engage in significant trade with socialist countries, numerous developing countries have bilateral trade pacts with a long list of partners. In the early 1980s, fifty to sixty of the IMF members had such bilateral trade and payments arrangements.[8]

Disorderly Cross Rates

In addition to causing a bilateral channeling of trade, exchange control tends to disturb the orderly relationship between exchange rates, replacing it with disorder.

As long as currencies are convertible, the whole system of interrelated exchange rates among different currencies must remain consistent. Any tendency for the cross rate between the franc and the pound to diverge from the rate between the dollar and the pound and between the franc and the dollar will be promptly corrected by the activity of exchange arbitragers (see pp. 329ff.). With the introduction of exchange control and inconvertibility, exchange arbitrage—the simultaneous purchase and sale of exchange in different markets—becomes impossible. Since the rate on any currency is arbitrary—being set by the authorities and maintained by quantitative restrictions—then, unless consistent cross rates are consciously sought, they will generally be-

---

[8] See International Monetary Fund, op. cit.

come disorderly or disparate. This is particularly true if a country has a deficit with one trading partner and a surplus with another; for then it will be tempted to depreciate its currency vis-à-vis the first and appreciate it vis-à-vis the second. This, in effect, establishes multiple exchange rates among countries.

To take an illustration from the period just after World War II, suppose that, with the dollar/pound rate as $2.80, the rates on the dollar and the pound in French francs were consistent, at fr 350/$1 and fr 980/£1, respectively. Encountering a deficit in its balance of payments with the United States and a surplus with the United Kingdom, the French exchange control authorities now depreciate the franc against the dollar to a 400-franc rate, and appreciate it relative to the pound to 960 francs. The corresponding cross rate is $2.40/£1 (960/400 = 2.40), which is inconsistent or disparate as compared with the actual cross rate of $2.80/£1).

This inconsistency provides an opportunity for Americans (or perhaps the nationals of other countries) to purchase sterling cheaply. At a fr 400/$1 rate, they could buy 960 francs for $2.40, and with these francs acquire £1, a saving of 40 cents over the rate on sterling in New York. Even though the British exchange control authorities permitted sterling so obtained to be used only for goods shipped to France, these could be transhipped to the United States, or the destination could be changed after they had left a British port.

Situations of this kind arose frequently in the years after World War II and were the basis for official protests against the establishment of inconsistent exchange rates that led to the emergence of disorderly cross rates.

Multiple Exchange Rates Among Classes of Transactions [9]

In our discussion of exchange control, we have repeatedly stressed how an overvalued exchange rate depresses exports and requires the strict regulation of imports. In the search for relief from this constriction of trade, Germany in the 1930s originated and developed to a high degree bilateral arrangements which soon became widespread.

Another device serving the same purpose, multiple exchange rates among classes of transactions—also originated in Germany in the early 1930s. Its effectiveness in opening up hitherto closed markets, together with other advantages that appeared as time went on, led to its rapid extension, especially in Latin America. In the years immediately after World War II some twenty-odd countries used multiple ex-

---

[9] This section provides important historical elaboration of the experience with multiple exchange rates, but may be skipped without loss of continuity.

change rates in one form or another. In the early 1970s, thirty to forty members of the IMF reported this practice.

Dual-Rate Systems   The simplest, though not historically the earliest, of multiple exchange rate systems is one employing only two rates, an official rate (usually an overvalued one) for permitted transactions and a free rate for all others. Ordinarily, the official rate is confined, on the supply side, to exports assumed to be capable of holding their markets even at an overvalued rate. These are typically commodities in which the country's position as a supplier is strong, even semimonopolistic, as with Brazil in coffee or Chile in copper. Part or all of the foreign exchange from these exports must be surrendered at the official rate. Under Thailand's postwar exchange control system, for example, 100 percent of rice proceeds had to be turned over to the government; for rubber, the surrender quota was 20 percent; and for tin was successively, 50, 40, and 20 percent.

On the demand side, to provide low-income consumers with "essentials," imports of basic necessities are usually permitted at the official rate. If the list of these commodities is narrowly restricted and if sufficient foreign exchange is allotted to satisfy demand, their prices can be held down. If, however, the exchange made available is insufficient, low prices can be maintained only by means of rigorous price controls accompanied by black markets. Otherwise, importers will charge prices high enough to ration the scarce supplies and will gain a windfall profit.

All transactions other than those permitted at the official rate take place at the free rate. These include exports needing encouragement, nonessential and luxury imports, and usually all invisibles, including capital exports and imports. With a truly free rate, the competition of these various demands and supplies establishes a rate that clears these transactions. There is, it should be noted, a possibility that this competition may drive the rate up to the point where costly luxuries are imported at the expense of semi-essentials needed by the lower- and middle-income groups. This is especially true where, as in some underdeveloped countries, income distribution is highly uneven, with a large share in the hands of the wealthier classes.

If the free rate fluctuates violently, the government may attempt to stabilize it by entering the market as a buyer or seller. To avoid the need for this, or to limit depreciation thought to be excessive, it may restrict the transactions allowed at the free rate. This is almost certain to lead to the emergence of a black market, where deals excluded from other markets are transacted. Because they are difficult to detect, these transactions are usually confined to such invisible items as tourists' expenditures, remission of profits, and transfers of capital.

Fixed Multiple-Rate Systems   Complex multiple exchange rate systems emerged from the trial-and-error procedure of prewar days, when many countries were seeking relief from the restrictiveness of an overvalued official rate buttressed by exchange controls and import licensing. Unwilling to devalue their currencies at a single stroke, largely because exchange control had permitted the equilibrium rate to move so far from the actual rate that a devaluation of the size contemplated would be unacceptable, they tried a piecemeal approach, establishing a number of distinct exchange rates, one for each of several categories of transactions. The lowest rates were commonly applied to exports in the strongest competitive position, or perhaps to only part of them, and to imports of the greatest importance to the economy, the importance being defined in terms of a variety of objectives, such as income distribution and industrialization policies. On the ascending scale of higher rates, the position of any export depended on the degree to which it was felt necessary to stimulate it, of any import, upon its relative unimportance. The highest of all rates usually applied to invisibles, including capital transfers.

Effects of Multiple Rates   Compared with the average of all the various exchange rates used by a given country, those below the average overvalue the currency. They have the effect of a tax on exports and a subsidy on imports. Higher-than-average rates, on the other hand, undervalue the currency. They resemble a subsidy on exports and a tax on imports.[10]

Overvaluation (low exchange rates) tends to discourage the use of a country's more productive resources, both in export and in import-competing lines. With respect to exports, only the strongest export producers, that is, those whose resources have the greatest international advantage, are able to sell at these low rates. The subsidy to imports provided by low rates of exchange discourages domestic production of substitutes that could easily compete at the average rate.[11] On the other hand, undervaluation (higher-than-average rates) encourages the use of inefficient resources through the subsidization of mar-

[10] Unless we assume that, under a free exchange rate system, the average of multiple rates would be the equilibrium rate, there is a difficulty here. If, as has sometimes appeared to be the case, the equilibrium rate would approximate the highest of the multiple rates in effect, then all lower rates would provide varying subsidies to imports and impose taxes of varying severity on exports.

[11] The scheduling of imports of essential foodstuffs at subsidy rates greatly handicapped Chile's agriculture. From being a net exporter of agricultural products in the 1930s, by the late 1940s the country had become a net importer. Although this shift was partially due to growing domestic demand for agricultural products not suited to Chile, it was aggravated by rising imports of such commodities as wheat and meat, whose production was made unprofitable by the low export and import exchange rates applied to those products.

ginal exports and the protection of inefficient import-competing industries.

The effects of multiple rates are also similar in their revenue implications to import and export taxes and subsidies. Clearly, an import or export tax raises revenue for the government, whereas an import or export subsidy is a fiscal drain on the government's funds. With multiple exchange rates among commodities, purchase of foreign exchange at low rates and resale at higher rates also produces revenue for the government, and is similar to a system of an export tax plus an import tariff. And purchase of foreign exchange at high rates and resale at lower rates is a fiscal drain similar to an export subsidy plus an import subsidy.

Partial Devaluation   Multiple exchange rates are in essence a form of partial devaluation. Consequently, foreign exchange is less scarce than it would be with a single but overvalued rate. Imports not permitted at a low, overvalued rate can be obtained, but only at some higher rate and at higher prices. Rationing by price thus replaces rationing by quantitative restrictions. The whole complex apparatus of quantitative control can be dismantled.

This reintroduction of rationing by price greatly reduces the area of administrative decision—the need for determining the amount of each commodity to be imported, the source from which it may be obtained, and which importer is to get the business. The huge bureaucratic staff required to carry out such detailed regulations can be heavily pruned, to the substantial benefit of the government budget.

Since the efficiency of the control apparatus depends on the honesty and ability of the administrators, elimination of quantitative restrictions is a particularly great boon to a country lacking a first-rate civil service. Incompetence compounds errors in judgment, serious enough in the best of circumstances; corruption means that exports and imports will be determined largely on the basis of graft and favoritism.

Complexity and Uncertainty   Despite these advantages over exchange control with no devaluation whatever, multiple exchange rates have their own shortcomings. They introduce an additional element of complexity, and if either the rates themselves or the transactions permitted at each rate are frequently changed, as has often been true, further uncertainty is created. Moreover, unless positive action is taken to prevent it, disorderly cross rates are very likely to emerge.

Inefficient Use of Resources   The increased ease of importing and the stimulus to favored exports are, of course, a gain to the country adopting multiple rates. Against this must be set the inefficient use of resources resulting from the combination of taxes and subsidies implicit in such a system. This effect can be quite serious;[12] it is, moreover, haphazard, in that the various subsidies and penalties are not determined with reference to prospects of long-run industrial efficiency but by balance-of-payments considerations.

Discriminatory Effects on Competitors   Also to be taken into account is the effect of multiple exchange rates on other countries. Particularly important in this respect is the fact that when a subsidy rate is introduced for exports, it applies only to a limited number of exports and thus concentrates its impact on a few competing countries. This is rightly regarded as a form of unfair competition, which is aggravated by resort to further changes in such rates. With uniform, comprehensive depreciation, on the other hand, the impact on competitors is spread "as broadly as the diversity of the economy of the depreciating economy permits."[13]

CONCLUSION

Reviewing the option of exchange control as an adjustment mechanism, we find it to have serious consequences for the economy immediately affected. When use of the option becomes widespread, as both before and after World War II, the world economy as a whole becomes disrupted.

Due to the insulation it provides against outside forces, the nation practicing exchange control is free to adopt policies with an inflationary bias. The emerging distortions can be disastrous for the country. Quantitative controls on foreign transactions are forced to bear greater and greater burdens as the effects of other balance-of-payments support policies are eroded. The burden is often more than the administrative system operating the controls can bear.

The combination of domestic inflation and complex controls often leads to economic atrophy. Poor export performance, low domestic savings rates, discouraged foreign investment, and low productivity of what little investment is mobilized combine to retard economic performance severely.

[12] Thus, not only Chilean agriculture, but also that of Peru and Ecuador (and doubtless of other countries as well), suffered serious contraction after World War II because of the penalty rates on certain foodstuffs. Before Peru introduced multiple rates, domestic production of meat was sufficient for home consumption; with imports of meat permitted at the (low) official rate, home production fell to less than half of total consumption. Ecuador had a similar experience with wheat flour. E. M. Bernstein, "Some Economic Aspects of Multiple Exchange Rates," *IMF Staff Papers*, **1**:230 (Sept. 1950).

[13] Ibid., p. 234.

When exchange controls extend to a number of countries, their trade is forced into bilateral channels. With the spread of bilateralism and the consequent destruction of the gains from trade of a truly international trading system, both for the uncontrolled and the controlled regions, are greatly reduced. Goods can no longer be bought freely where they are most efficiently and cheaply produced, nor can they be sold where the prices are highest. Ability to buy, as always, is determined by ability to sell. Exports from controlled currency nations have limited access to free markets; disproportionate amounts must be exchanged for the similarly overpriced exports of other nations that have hedged themselves in with restrictions.

With trade determined in considerable part not by comparative costs, but by availability of means of payments, the allocation of resources becomes more and more uneconomic. Export industries come into being or are expanded not because they are efficient, but because their markets are sheltered. Quantitative restrictions on imports give protection to high-cost substitutes. Both export and import-competing production are subject to random and often unpredictable discrimination. Instead of contributing to the strength of the national economy, the foreign sector becomes a drain.

To the reduction in the gains from trade must be added the direct cost of supporting a sizable bureaucracy, and the more intangible, indirect costs of errors of judgment, magnified manyfold if the administrators are incompetent and corrupt.

Resort to multiple exchange rates can mitigate some of these deficiencies. Multiple rates are, however, only a partial solution to devaluation and introduce uncertainties and distortions of their own.

A country facing a balance-of-payments disequilibrium and forced to choose between depreciation, deflation, and exchange controls should weigh carefully the desirable and undesirable consequences of each. Exchange control furnishes no solution to the problem. It deals only with the deficit, not its causes, and it exacerbates those causes, tending to create a more basic disequilibrium.

Unless restrictions can be kept moderate or are to be used as a temporary stopgap while other, more fundamental adjustments are made, resort to exchange control is likely to be a costly and disappointing choice, and one from which extrication proves difficult if not impossible.

The serious consequences of widespread exchange control systems, both for individual countries and for the world economy, suggest substantial gains if a way out could be found. A satisfactory solution involves, for individual countries, three major ingredients:[14]

[14] Krueger, *Liberalization Attempts and Consequences*, op. cit., Chapter 10.

1. A nation's authorities must adopt an appropriate exchange rate, thus eliminating the excess demand for foreign exchange at the controlled rate. This, however, may prove to be a very difficult decision for a government to take. Many former recipients of foreign exchange allocations will find themselves worse off at the higher exchange rate. Their political power, either in parliament or in the military, has often been enough to mean the downfall of governments that attempted to take the first step out of exchange control.
2. The authorities must establish severe limits on the growth of domestic expenditure. Often this means especially strict control over government expenditures. Again the political risks are enormous. Those adversely affected are certain to voice their displeasure, while the beneficiaries of a healthy economy are likely to be less visible and less organized.
3. To ensure success, the country should also have available an external cushion during the transition period.[15] This permits it to avoid relapsing into controls in the event of a temporary setback such as a crop failure. Moreover, effects of the readjustment on real living standards may be moderated.

For the international economy to find its way out of exchange control after World War II required the construction of an international institutional framework which permitted the major industrial countries to liberalize simultaneously. That framework is one of the major subjects of Part VI.

SELECTED REFERENCES

BERNSTEIN, E. M. "Some Economic Aspects of Multiple Exchange Rates." *IMF Staff Papers*, **1**, No. 2 (1950). A brief theoretical discussion of the effects of multiple exchange rates.

BHAGWATI, J. N. *Anatomy and Consequences of Exchange Control Regimes*, Vol. XI of *Foreign Trade Regimes and Economic Development*. Cambridge, Mass.: Ballinger Publishing Co. (for the National Bureau of Economic Research), 1978. A synthesis of the experience documented in a major study of several developing countries. See also the Krueger volume below.

BLOOMFIELD, ARTHUR I. *Speculative and Flight Movements of Capital in Postwar International Finance*. Princeton, N.J.: Princeton University Press, 1954. In addition to much factual material, this book considers methods of

[15] In this, the support of the IMF and foreign aid agencies may prove particularly crucial.

avoiding exchange controls and possible means of dealing with capital flight.

ELLIS, HOWARD S. *Exchange Control in Central Europe.* Cambridge, Mass.: Harvard University Press, 1941. Examines the operation of control schemes in the 1930s.

KRUEGER, A. O. *Liberalization Attempts and Consequences,* Vol. X of *Foreign Trade Regimes and Economic Development.* Cambridge, Mass.: Ballinger Publishing Co. (for the National Bureau of Economic Research), 1978. A companion synthesis to the Bhagwati volume noted above.

LIEFTINCK, P. "Currency Convertibility and the Exchange Rate System." *Finance and Development,* **8,** No. 3 (Sept. 1971). An explanation in nontechnical terms of some of the factors involved in extending the freedom of currency convertibility.

MEADE, JAMES E. *The Balance of Payments.* New York: Oxford University Press, 1951. Part V contains a good discussion of direct controls, both financial and commercial.

MIKESELL, RAYMOND F. *Foreign Exchange in the Postwar World.* New York: The Twentieth Century Fund, Inc., 1954. The best source for a general discussion of the immediate postwar system of controlled trade payments, with much illustrative material.

PART
6

THE INTERNATIONAL MONETARY SYSTEM IN THE TWENTIETH CENTURY

25
CHAPTER

Structural Weakening of the World Economy

THE WORLD ECONOMY OF 1913

The hundred years between the Napoleonic wars and the war of 1914–1918 witnessed the creation of a true world economy, with most of its member nations closely integrated through a highly developed network of trade and finance. The numerous facilities essential to the operation of this complex system of interrelated markets were centered in London, but their influence was spread throughout the globe by means of branch offices, correspondents, and contractual relationships. These facilities include specialized export and import firms, commodity brokers, commercial banks and investment banks, acceptance and discount houses, insurance companies, shipping lines, and a worldwide system of telegraphic communications.

Specialization of national production, based on widely varying factor endowments, was intense. Although tariffs to some extent obstructed trade and retarded specialization, their effect was not too serious, for they were changed infrequently and only a few were high. Because each of the various kinds of specialized production was concentrated in a very few geographic localities, multilateral trade was essential. Fortunately, since all the principal and many of the less important countries were on the gold standard, there existed the universal convertibility of currencies so necessary for the operation of a multilateral trading system.

This was not a static world, but one of rapid change. Technology advanced with great speed, bringing into existence new methods of production and totally new products. Heavy migration of labor and large movements of capital progressively altered relative factor endowments, the very foundation of much international trade. Nor were these

445

movements themselves constant—they ebbed and flowed and changed their direction without warning. Intermittently, too, the channels of trade were interrupted and diverted by changes in the commercial policy of nations.

All these phenomena introduced disturbances of varying severity, to which the balance of payments of each nation affected had somehow to become adjusted. The means to that adjustment was furnished by the automatic mechanism of the gold standard, which operated smoothly because the institutional environment—notably the close relations between London and other financial centers—was favorable. Through its operation, the many and recurring changes were assimilated with a remarkable smoothness and lack of friction.

FORCES OF DISINTEGRATION

The happy combination of economic institutions, market forces, and harmonious climate of opinion was rudely shattered after 1914. The balance of power in Europe, carefully nurtured by a century of British diplomacy, ended abruptly with the challenge of German expansionism. Four years of bitter war, with entire nations in arms, wrought terrible destruction and loss of life.

Despite all the damage and disruption, within a few years the worst of Europe's wounds had healed. Production recovered to prewar levels and then began, after a brief interruption, a steady climb. A deep nostalgia for the past bred a sincere attempt to reconstruct the international framework. The gold standard was restored; the wartime restrictions on trade were abandoned; trade connections were reestablished; and a new agency, the League of Nations, was created to ease international tensions and to facilitate agreed solutions for common problems.

For a time, success appeared within reach. The middle and later 1920s were years of great prosperity; production and trade advanced steadily and standards of living improved. Yet the international structure on which all this rested had been greatly weakened in ways little appreciated at the time, ways that made the world economy less resilient and less capable of smooth adjustment to further change. Moreover, that structure was subjected to a series of disturbances far greater than any it had hitherto been forced to face. Even before the great upheaval of World War II, the impact of these developments destroyed the highly articulated but feebler successor to the world economic system of the late nineteenth and early twentieth centuries.

In this chapter we depict the sources of weakness in the international economy of the interwar years, indicate the structural and other changes to which adjustment had somehow to be made, and show how failure to meet this challenge brought about collapse.

A WEAKENED INTERNATIONAL STRUCTURE

Monetary Developments After World War I

The pressures of war had caused most of the belligerents and many of the neutral nations to abandon the gold standard. Although the sharpness and extent of the break varied from one country to another, free movements of gold ceased during the war and for some years after it. Thus the close link between national price systems was broken, and prices in different countries were free to move independently. Inflation went to varying lengths, depending upon the balance-of-payments situation confronting each nation and the fiscal policies it followed. It was most intense in Germany, Russia, and Austria–Hungary, where currencies became, within a few years after the war, virtually worthless and had to be replaced by new issues. In France, wholesale prices rose to more than eight times the 1913 level; in Italy, the rise was about sevenfold. Even the United Kingdom and the United States witnessed a postwar peak of prices of 330 and 272, respectively, also relative to 1913 = 100.

To bring some order into this chaotic situation was one of the first postwar concerns. Except where currencies had become virtually worthless, the earlier long attachment to the gold standard bred a strong desire for its restoration. Its abandonment during and after the war was generally regarded as but a temporary break with the past.

If gold was again to be the base, there arose immediately the question of what the metallic content of each currency should be, and thus the level of exchange parities. The United States, which during the war had modified its attachment to the gold standard only to the extent of requiring licenses for the export of gold, merely abolished this requirement in 1919 and returned to gold at the old parity. With ample gold reserves, it could do so. Germany and Austria scrapped their worthless currencies and adopted new ones—the Reichsmark, with the prewar gold parity relative to the dollar of 23.8 cents, and the schilling, with the relatively high parity of about 14 cents. Rigorous controls over the supply of money in both countries kept the internal value of these new currencies in line with their external or gold value, and international loans provided the reserves needed to meet adverse swings in the balance of payments. Many countries, however, had to make do with their existing but badly depreciated currencies. For them to have restored the relatively high prewar gold parities would have meant exchange rates that seriously overvalued their currencies. It would have required ruinous deflation to bring down internal costs and prices sufficiently to effect an appropriate balance between exports and imports. The only alternative for these countries was to devalue their currencies in terms of gold—to bring their external value into line with the existing and depreciated internal value. Some nations—notably the United Kingdom—stood in an intermediate position, with prices and costs high in relation to 1913, but not so much higher than in the United States that the gap could not be eliminated by moderate deflation.

Restoration of the Gold Standard

Great Britian, the center of the prewar gold standard, approached the problem of restoration gradually, yet with its course set in advance. The British decision rested on a report (in 1918) of the famous Cunliffe Committee, which assumed that the gold standard still existed in Great Britain, that its continuance was imperative, and advocated its restoration "without delay."

The Committee's recommendations were followed, however, only slowly and tentatively. Exchange restrictions were removed gradually; the Bank of England pursued a cautious deflationary policy; and British prices became more closely aligned with prices in the United States. As a result, the dollar/sterling exchange rate recovered from a low of $3.18 in early 1920 to $4.36 two years later. An embargo on the placement of foreign loans in Britain, and American credits of $300 million, gave sufficient support to the pound to permit Parliament in 1925 to put the currency back on gold at the prewar parity of $4.866.

At this time the index of wholesale prices in the United Kingdom stood at 159 and in the United States at 155 (1913 = 100), a fairly close correspondence. But because the wholesale index is heavily weighted with the prices of internationally traded commodities (which must meet foreign competition and therefore cannot differ much across national boundaries), it failed to reflect adequately the fact that British costs remained relatively high. Restoration of the old parity is generally conceded to have overvalued the pound by at least 10 per cent and to have subjected the island's economy for the next seven years to continuous deflationary pressure. Because prices and costs were quite rigid, they failed to decline appreciably. Instead, Britian suffered from chronic unemployment, which throughout the twenties never fell below the figure of 1 million.

Between 1925 and 1928, more than forty countries returned to gold, some at their prewar parity, others at a devalued level. Switzerland and the Netherlands were among the former group; France and Italy, on the other hand, where even postwar deflation left prices far higher than in 1913, cut the gold content of their currencies by approximately four-fifths and three-fourths, respectively. By the end of 1928, an extensive international currency system based on gold had been recreated.

Hopes and Expectations

With the reconstruction of a broadly inclusive international gold standard, that prewar pillar of stability and cohesion, it was widely assumed that the most essential aspect of reconstruction had now been achieved. The world, it was felt, could look forward once more to the attainment of a stable international equilibrium, subject of course to temporary disturbances or even to changes of a deeper, more enduring character, but sufficiently limited or gradual so as to permit adjustment by the old familiar processes. It is hardly surprising that statesmen, weary of the burden of unaccustomed problems, should have regarded with relief the restoration of an automatically functioning mechanism. That mechanism, it was believed, would take from their shoulders the responsibility for thought and for difficult decisions.

As it turned out, their hopes rested in large part on illusion. They had, they thought, reconstructed a well-understood and efficient piece of machinery. They overlooked the fact that parts of this machinery beyond their control had changed in ways that seriously hampered its operation. They could not foresee the excessive burdens to which it would be subjected.

Formal Changes in the Gold Standard

The gold standard established in 1925–1928 differed somewhat from that of 1914. To alleviate an impending shortage of gold, its coinage had been generally discontinued, except in the United States, and assets in the form of balances in gold-standard countries were permitted to count as reserves of a country's central bank. These changes, known as the gold bullion system and the gold exchange system, were comparatively unimportant. Under the former, currencies were convertible into gold bullion rather than coins, and vice versa, at a fixed price; under the gold exchange system, local currencies could be used to acquire the currencies of gold-standard countries. Gold exports and imports were unrestricted.

It was in the basic or vital, rather than in the purely formal or external, characteristics of the system that serious change had taken place. The prewar efficiency of the gold standard had depended upon the centralization of international transactions in London and upon adherence to well-established rules of international conduct. These essential foundations had been eroded.

Prewar Features of the Gold Standard

Before the war, the gold standard had centered in London. By the simple process of adding to and subtracting from the sterling balances owned by the banks of practically every nation, the great bulk of international transactions was *cleared*. The London market also played the role of a world central bank. When other countries suffered an adverse balance of payments, the London market advanced short-term loans that supplemented their dwindling gold reserves. When Britain lost gold, the London market borrowed from the entire world. These short-term capital movements were supplemented by changes in the ownership of outstanding long-term securities. With gold movements in part replaced by capital movements, the extent of the accompanying contraction or expansion of credit was moderated. If the underlying disturbance proved short-lived, this was all to the good; if, however, a fundamental readjustment were needed, London's lending or borrowing interposed no obstacle, but merely gave more time for deep-seated forces to assert themselves.

Finally, London had for long been the principal source of long-term investment abroad. From experience in this exacting business, her bankers developed a high degree of skill and judgment. Moreover, the well-organized London investment market was very sensitive to international influences. When exports exceeded imports, foreign balances were transferred to British ownership and gold moved in, easing the money market. For a time, short-term foreign lending might absorb part of the additional funds now available. But the scope of such lending is limited; if the balance-of-payments surplus continued, the lending would come to a halt, with a resumption of gold movements and a further easing of the money market. The continuance of easy credit conditions would now stimulate long-term foreign lending. An inward movement of foreign securities replaced the flow of gold, and the purchasing power put at the disposal of foreigners supported and made possible the continuance of the large volume of exports. International investment thus played an essential part in, and greatly facilitated, the adjustment mechanism.[1]

---

[1] This account is confirmed by direct evidence. "In London interviews granted the writer it was repeatedly stated by investment bankers that before the war they never concerned themselves with the position of the balance of payments, but that when money was knocking around, looking for employment, they felt that to be a good time for bringing forward foreign issues." William Adams Brown, Jr., *The International Gold Standard Reinterpreted* (New York: National Bureau of Economic Research, 1940), p. 55.

Substantive Change: Divided Responsibility

Because of events transpiring during and after the war, these substantive aspects of the gold standard had undergone radical change. The Federal Reserve System, established in 1915, gave the United States a central banking structure that stabilized the hitherto erratic money markets, as well as an acceptance market which soon came to rival that of London. The growing importance of this country as a source of supplies, both during and after the war, supported this market and also made increasingly necessary the maintenance of substantial dollar balances in New York. Although negligible in 1914, these balances as early as 1926 amounted to nearly $1.5 billion. Moreover, the New York Stock Exchange at no time imposed restrictions on trading in foreign securities, whereas the United Kingdom at various intervals had to place an embargo on foreign issues. This fact, together with the availability of credit for long-term borrowing in New York, brought additional deposits and a large and growing business of distributing securities.

Two heads may be better than one, but two clearing centers certainly are not, for the efficiency of a clearing center is in direct proportion to its centralization of transactions. When there is more than one, after the transactions are cleared in each center, those between the centers must be offset. More foreign balances must be maintained, and more labor devoted to the clearing function.

Two *financial centers*, on the other hand, can strengthen the international economy if they work in harmony, not at cross purposes. The additional resources, both short and long term, that the rise of New York made available were all to the good, the more so since London's ability to finance foreign investment was declining. On the debit side, however, must be set the inexperience of New York bankers and the greater sensitiveness of its money market to domestic and speculative forces than to the pressures of a changing balance of payments. It is to be expected that the financial center of a nation continental in extent and comparatively self-sufficient in production, whose foreign trade is a small fraction of its total turnover, should be relatively unaffected by surplus and deficits in its international accounts. Less predictable was the dominating influence in New York of the rate of interest on stock market loans (the call loan rate), which responded to speculative influences rather than to movements of trade.

In such a money market, if active speculation drives up the call loan rate, commercial interest rates, including that on acceptances, will also rise, for competition for funds is pervasive. If at the same time there exists a surplus in the U.S. balance of payments (which means deficits in those of other countries), short-term international lending by New York would be appropriate to the international needs. Yet a contrary inward movement of funds may take place, attracted by the high return on stock market loans. Precisely this combination of circumstances arose during the 1920s. The stock market boom made it impossible for New York to perform its function of short-term international lender.

Despite this contradiction, the United States did engage in substantial *long-term* foreign lending. Yet these loans (totaling nearly $5 billion between 1922 and 1928) were not closely related to the state of the U.S. balance of payments, but to inflationary forces within the country. Moreover, the inexperience of New York bankers had unfortunate results: excessive attention to the immediate gains from bankers' commissions rather than to the underlying soundness of the loans themselves. Hence there were many loans to dubious borrowers and for unproductive purposes. Financing of foreign investments also tended to be sporadic rather than steady.

Most important of all, however, the disappearance of the close integration of the world's capital markets eliminated the rapid shifts in long-term securities that had contributed so much to the smooth operation of the prewar gold standard. For that standard to work after the war, much greater reliance would have to be placed on the contraction and expansion of credit.

Changes in Goals

Before the war, the maintenance of a currency's convertibility had been the ultimate criterion of monetary policy in the leading countries, and the condition of a nation's reserves had been the main guide to action. In the favorable environment of the late nineteenth century, the monetary authorities seldom had to use their powers vigorously, but they took decisive action in accord with this criterion when necessary.

All this changed after the war. Each nation insisted on determining its supply of money independently; the state of its reserves became a secondary consideration. Inward movements of the metal were neutralized by central bank sales of securities to the market; the additions to commercial bank reserves from abroad were offset by domestic withdrawals. Losses of reserves due to a gold outflow were similarly replaced by central bank funds devoted to the purchase of open market securities. Thus, between 1920 and 1924, the Federal Reserve authorities offset a considerable part of the large gold receipts of these years, attributing their action to the need (1) to maintain sound credit conditions (*domestic* stability), and (2) to ensure that this gold would be available for export again when the need arose.[2] The Bank

[2] The gold came from countries that were off the gold standard, and whose trade was still disorganized; its movement was therefore regarded as abnormal. For an official explanation of the policy on neutralization, see the *Tenth Annual Report of the Federal Reserve Board* (1923), pp. 20–22.

of England, too, after 1925, followed a systematic policy of gold neutralization by varying its security holdings inversely with gold movements—a policy whose net effect was deflationary. Although, in view
of all the circumstances, and especially in view of *domestic* conditions
in both countries, these actions may have been wise, they clearly went
counter to traditional gold-standard practice.

Many reasons underlay this substitution of national goals for reliance on the automatic operation of an international monetary system.
Among them was a growing concern for internal economic stability,
induced by increasing industrialization and urbanization, which subjected more and more people to the hazards of unemployment. The
advance of economic knowledge also played a role. Confronted with
the monetary disturbances of the war and postwar years, economists
had studied these phenomena intensively; out of their studies came
greater understanding and increased powers of control. In particular,
schemes for the stabilization of prices and therewith of economic activity through central bank action acquired a wide following. Furthermore, the means to make these schemes effective increased apace. Central banks, formerly confined to a few countries, now arose all over
Europe, in several Latin American nations, and in Australia and South
Africa.

The Changing Climate of Opinion

The trend toward independent national action in monetary affairs was
only an eddy in a much broader current. Especially since World War
I, but starting much earlier, there has been an unmistakable movement
toward increasing government intervention in economic life. This was
an inevitable reaction against some of the unfortunate consequences of
laissez faire.

Economic freedom brought striking increases in productivity and
therewith in standards of living. It released the energies of businessmen
to amass capital, form new enterprises, and adopt new techniques, and
thus to expand output at a phenomenal rate. But it also enabled the
strong and well informed to take advantage of the weak and ignorant.
The result was long hours of labor, widespread employment of children,
dangerous working conditions, insecurity, and filthy slums. These consequences had not been foreseen by the early supporters of laissez faire,
for they assumed all participants in economic activities to be equal—
equal in bargaining power, in knowledge of their interests, in capacity
to distinguish good wares from bad, and equal, too, in available alternatives as to occupation, place of work, or housing. Since this necessary equality was patently absent, individual and social interest failed
to coincide. The actual situation was aptly suggested by an oft-quoted
parody of the mid-nineteenth century: " 'Every man for himself and

God for all of us,' as the elephant said when he danced among the chickens."[3]

The response to the antisocial effects of industrial change in a framework of individualism varied widely. Some thoughtful and sensitive people, such as the Tory humanitarians in Great Britain, introduced specific reforms for particular evils such as child labor and long hours of work. Others rejected the individualist philosophy in its entirety and sought to formulate a new and more adequate social theory. These included Utopian socialists such as Robert Owen in England and Saint-Simon and Fourier in France, Christian Socialists such as Charles Kingsley, and most important of all, Marx, Engels, and their followers.

With the spread of industry and the growth of cities and an urban working class, the numbers subjected to the hazards of unemployment, industrial accidents, a weak bargaining position, and slum living constantly rose. There developed a basis of mass support for reforms directed toward these deficiencies and for the new collectivist ideas. Political parties broadened their appeal by introducing reform measures; trade unions organized the workers for more effective bargaining; and socialist and labor parties emerged to promote their political interests. Legislatures enacted laws to regulate public utilities, outlaw child labor, regulate the conditions of work, and protect the consumer. Generally somewhat later to appear were the various forms of social insurance: workmen's compensation, old-age insurance, unemployment insurance, and, finally, health insurance. Also to be included under the heading of social legislation are slum clearance and public housing and our old acquaintance, central banks, established to permit the more effective control of credit.

These new laws all had two things in common: they aimed at improving conditions of life in modern industrial society, and to accomplish this they required more intervention by the state in the operation of the economy. The role of the state took on ever-increasing importance. In changing social conditions and the response made to them, there existed a solid foundation for an ever-larger exercise of national authority.

Economic Nationalism

Reinforcing this trend toward independent national action were the forces of nationalism bred of economic rivalry. We have shown how they led, after about 1870, to rising tariffs and to colonial expansion. After World War I, economic nationalism was reinforced, quite natu-

---

[3] Attributed to Charles Dickens by W. Jethro Brown, *The Underlying Principles of Modern Legislation* (New York: E. P. Dutton, Inc., 1915).

rally by the inflammatory effects of war itself, artificially by the creation of Poland and the Baltic states and of the succession states of the Austro-Hungarian Empire. Moreover, during the war, in belligerent and nonbelligerent nations alike, new industries arose or old ones expanded to replace supplies cut off by the war. With the war's end, motives of security and of self-interest combined to exact protection against the original and more economical centers of production.

Thus free trade Britain continued duties established in wartime on certain luxuries and inaugurated the "key industries" duties (with rates of 33¹/₃ and 50 percent) on a number of militarily important items. The United States abandoned the policy of low duties embodied in the Underwood Tariff of 1913, and in 1922 enacted a new high tariff. In Japan, India, Australia, and Latin America, the disappearance of European competition for four years in many lines of industry called forth local production. Some of these war infants died a natural death as trade was reopened, but many clamored for and obtained protection.

Resurgent economic nationalism not only raised barriers to trade, but it also interfered with the international movement of labor. The United States, although it remained the principal destination of immigrants, restricted immigration sharply, and in 1924 introduced quotas based on national origin. These quotas favored immigrants from northern Europe and discriminated against those from southern Europe and the Orient where population pressure was greatest. The total numbers entering the United States, which had averaged 880,000 a year in the decade ending with 1910, fell to an annual average of 411,000 in the 1920s.

All the developments to which we have drawn attention in the last few pages—the rise of New York as a second and less-experienced world financial center, the national determination of monetary policy, the increased role of the state in economic affairs, and the resurgence of economic nationalism—weakened the delicately balanced international economic system, making it more rigid and less sensitive to changes calling for adjustment. Our next task is to examine the increased burden this mechanism was called upon to meet.

THE BURDEN OF STRUCTURAL CHANGE

War Debts and Reparation

Prewar capital movements, at least since the Franco-Prussian war, had been the result of the free choice of individual investors and were mainly in response to the attraction of a more promising yield. Although they varied from year to year and altered their direction as time passed, these shifts were seldom violent. Between each lender and borrower, too, the current of lending generally began slowly, rose gradually to a peak, and then tapered off, thus giving time for balances of payments to adjust to the flow of capital, or the flow itself contributing effectively to that adjustment.

The situation was very different after 1918, for the war left a heavy legacy of international debt. At the end of the paying line was Germany, saddled (in 1921) with a reparation burden of $33 billion, most of which was to be paid to Great Britain and France. Italy, France, and Belgium were in debt to one another and to Britain. All these countries, together with several others, owed the United States at the time of the armistice a principal sum of a little over $7 billion.

For the chain of payments to move smoothly all along the line, two requirements had to be met: Large sums in marks had to be extracted annually from the German people, and these sums had to be transferred regularly into other currencies—ultimately a large proportion into dollars.

The first of these problems was one of taxable capacity, an internal problem. The capacity of Germany to pay reparation from this point of view would amount to the difference between the maximum taxable capacity of the country and the minimum needs of government. In the late 1920s, German taxes were 25 percent of the national income, and reparation obligations comprised 10 percent of these taxes, or 2.5 percent of the national income. Although heavy, the burden would not appear to have been insuperable.

The transfer problem was more complex and difficult. After the sums in money had been raised in Germany, they had to be remitted to the reparation recipients. Over any but a brief period of time and for relatively small amounts, such international transfers could only be made in the form of goods and services. Under the restored gold standard, it was essential to set in motion an expansion of spending and a rise of prices in the creditor countries and a decline of spending and prices in Germany sufficient to cause Germany's exports to exceed its imports by the amount of annual reparation to be transferred.

To some extent, the extraction of additional taxes from the German people helped set this mechanism in operation. By reducing their personal consumption, this taxation released goods, or the factors to produce goods, for export, and also caused some diminution of imports. In addition, however, an expansion of spending was needed in the creditor countries. This could have been started had Germany been able to make a sizable transfer of funds. Had the receiving governments then spent these sums on reconstruction, in addition to similar expenditures out of domestic resources, a rise in spending would have resulted. Imports would also increase, to the direct or indirect benefit of German exports.

The catch was that Germany had insufficient reserves of gold or foreign exchange with which to make the needed initial transfers of purchasing power. Moreover, the Dawes Plan protected Germany against any serious loss of international reserves, and also prohibited any devaluation of the newly stabilized mark as a means of making her exports more attractive. The essentials for setting the transfer mechanism in motion were therefore lacking.[4]

The problem of war debts and reparation continued to plague both creditors and debtors thoughout the 1920s and early 1930s. Although the British government owed the United States only about half as much as was due it from its allies, at the peace conference in 1919 it unsuccessfully urged the cancellation of all war debts. Three years later, the British offered to scale down payments from their debtors to what they in turn had to pay the United States. But the American government met these overtures with stubborn resistance, and steadily refused to concede the existence of any connection between allied war debts and German reparation. Its attitude was tersely expressed in President Coolidge's famous dictum: "They hired the money, didn't they?"

Not until 1927, some three years after the Dawes Plan arranged a settlement of German reparation, did all the countries involved finally reach agreement on the amounts owed and terms of payment.[5] Capital sums were scaled down considerably, and annual payments were to be spread over a period of sixty-two years. At least, some degree of certainty replaced the earlier bickering and confusion. Yet the former European belligerents were left with a burden of payments reflecting a debt not based on productive assets, but representing a sheer dead weight.

---

[4] The fullest discussion of the German transfer problem is to be found in the controversy between Keynes and Ohlin, which appeared in 1929. Keynes stressed the need for a fall in German costs and prices to make her exports more attractive—the classical aspects of the adjustment mechanism—while Ohlin emphasized the effect upon international demands of initial transfers of purchasing power. But as Keynes finally pointed out in a reply, the means of starting the transfer of purchasing power were lacking. "If Germany was in a position to export large quantities of gold or if foreign balances in Germany were acceptable to foreign Central Banks as a substitute for gold in their reserves, then it would be a different matter." J. M. Keynes, "Mr. Keynes's Views on the Transfer Problem: III. A Reply," *Economic Journal*, **39**:404–408 (1929). The two original articles, although not the subsequent discussion, have been reprinted in American Economic Association, *Readings in the Theory of International Trade* (New York: McGraw-Hill Book Company, 1949).

[5] No settlement was ever reached between the USSR and its major creditors, owing to the Soviet unwillingness to assume debts incurred by the Czarist government.

International Investment

International investment revived after the war; by the end of the decade, the United States, the United Kingdom, and France had each lent substantial sums. Between 1919 and 1929, the United States invested abroad approximately $7 billion, France about $600 million, and Britain restored her foreign investments, which had fallen about a quarter, to the prewar level of some $19 billion.

Although this international lending of the 1920s provided foreign exchange needed by many countries, it was not as large in proportion to income as in prewar days, nor directed to as productive uses. Instead of going mainly into railways, public utilities, and other capital equipment to increase the output of the relatively undeveloped areas, a major share went to European national and municipal governments, notably in Germany, where it was used for buildings and other public works. Although serviceable, these investments did little to increase productivity, nor did they yield a salable output that could earn foreign exchange with which to meet interest payments. Moreover, particularly after 1925, to these long-term investments was added a large volume of short-term lending, much of which was actually used to finance long-term projects. These short-term loans created an unstable situation in which the danger of default was serious.

In one important respect, international lending of the 1920s created an illusion of soundness and stability that simply did not exist. Some countries used the proceeds of new loans to pay the interest on past loans. It was only in this way that Germany, which borrowed almost three times as much abroad as it paid in reparation, was able to transfer the required payments. These, in turn, enabled European governments to meet their war-debt payments to the United States.

The Changing Structure of Industry and Trade

The postwar years also witnessed a change in the relative industrial strength of different countries, which both imposed an additional burden of adjustment and rendered the international economy less capable of meeting that burden. These developments were the consequence partly of the war and the economic disruption that followed in its wake, partly of differences in long-run trends of economic growth.

Industry in the European belligerents, faced with the implacable demands of war, had to convert from the production of peacetime goods to the manufacture of munitions and military supplies. Exports naturally suffered, in the case of Britain declining to about half the prewar volume. Even this reduced volume was more precarious and uncertain, being subjected to constant interruption by Germany's unrestricted submarine warfare. After the conflict ended, to the difficulty of restoring broken trade connections were added the uncertainties caused by inflation and by the losses in shipping.

In this interval of some eight years or more, many countries began themselves to produce goods no longer available, or available only intermittently and uncertainly, from Europe. We have already noted this development; suffice it to say that it was very widespread. Another alternative was to place orders with neutral suppliers, especially those outside the area of combat. Japan benefited particularly from such sales; her output of manufactures doubled between 1913 and 1921–1925. This was not a total loss to European countries, since the economic growth of their customers meant higher incomes and a greater ability to import than before. But if this opportunity was to be met, it required rapid adaptation of supplies to the new types of goods for which demand was increasing.

Pressure on Britain

The effects of industrial expansion abroad were felt with particular severity in Britain. Japanese and Indian production of cotton piece goods increasingly displaced British sales in Far Eastern markets. By 1937, these were less than 10 percent of the 1913 figure. Like cotton, the woolen textile industry lost heavily to protected domestic industries in foreign markets, and to a lesser extent to rising Japanese competition. Exports of woolen tissues fell from 219 million square yards in 1913 to 156 million in 1929. In the same interval, coal exports declined almost 20 percent. This industry faced additional competition from newly opened mines in Russia, China, India, and South Africa at the same time that fuel conservation and the use of petroleum and hydroelectric power were reducing the demand. The iron and steel industry barely held its own; to do so, it was forced to concentrate more and more on finished products, where its disadvantage was least, while pig iron lost ground to the new, larger plants in Germany and the United States.[6]

Faced with declining demand for her traditional staples and with many markets lost to new competitors, Britain clearly had to undertake a major shift of resources. This she did with considerable success— even though hampered by an overvalued currency and the restrictive credit policy this implied. While output of cotton and woolen textiles and of coal were lower in 1930 than before the war, a rapid expansion took place in the production of motor cars and motorcycles, electrical

[6] Data in this paragraph are from Alfred E. Kahn, *Great Britain and the World Economy* (New York: Columbia Unversity Press, 1946), Chapter 6.

machinery and equipment, and chemicals. Exports of these and other products replaced coal and textiles, with the result that in 1929 the total values of exports was some 15 percent greater than in 1913.

Even so, Britain—and to a lesser degree, other European countries as well—lost ground relatively. Between 1913 and 1929, the total value of world exports increased by two-thirds. The British increase of only 15 percent is small by comparison; so is that of Belgium—22 percent. Germany fared somewhat better, with her exports rising 33 percent. France almost held her own with a 50 percent increase. In contrast with Europe, Canada, Japan, and the United States forged ahead. Canada's exports multiplied three and one half times between 1913 and 1929, Japan's increased threefold, and those of the United States doubled. Expressed in terms of percentages for continents, the distribution of world exports had changed as follows:

> 1913: North America, 15.8; Europe, 50.9; Asia, 12.5; other, 20.8
> 1929: North America, 19.5; Europe, 47.4; Asia, 14.9; other, 18.2

Although Europe remained the world's greatest exporting region, it was losing ground. Moreover, the changes that occurred in the 1920s were, as we shall see, only the beginning of a continuing trend.

The Increasing Dominance of the United States

A particularly interesting and important feature of the industrial change going on in the world was the increasingly important position occupied by the United States. We have already noted that in the interval 1870–1913, that country came to surpass Great Britain as a manufacturing power, its share of world manufactures rising from 23 percent to almost 36 percent, while Britain's declined from nearly 32 percent to only 14 percent. (Germany's share of manufacturing output also rose from a little over 13 percent to just under 16 percent.) This phenomenal increase reflected the rapid economic growth of a young country; its roots are to be found in a steady natural increase in population, supplemented by a large volume of immigration, and in a high rate of capital accumulation and investment. Between growing numbers and rising incomes, more and more opportunities for the domestic production of manufactured goods appeared and were exploited.

Immigration and the natural increase in the population added less to growth in the 1920s than formerly, although total population increased from 106 to 123 million during the decade. Investment, that dynamic factor in economic expansion, continued at an extremely high level. Gross capital formation averaged 20 percent of gross national product from 1919 to 1929. Technology, most visible in new and improved products, also continued its advance. Thus it is not surprising to find that industrial production simultaneously rose by 51 percent. This was the period when the automobile industry grew from infancy to adulthood, carrying with it petroleum extraction and refining and tire production. This decade also saw the output of electrical equipment and of the power to drive it more than double. This rate of industrial growth was unmatched by any other country, although Canada, Japan, and South Africa, each starting from a much smaller base, came close.

As a result, the United States increased its lead as a producer of manufactures still further. In 1926–1929 it accounted for 42.2 percent of the world total, as against 11.6 percent for Germany and 9.4 percent for the United Kingdom. Other estimates tell a similar story: of the consumption by the fifteen most important commercial nations of the nine principal raw materials and foodstuffs, the United States accounted for 39 percent. Its national income was equal to that of twenty-three other nations, including its most important rivals. When we add to these facts that in the 1920s the United States became the world's first exporter and its principal investor, although still second to Great Britain as an importer, its dominant position is striking.

The meaning of these facts is clear. As the world's outstanding manufacturing power, its largest creditor, and one of its two largest traders, the economic health and the economic policies of the United States were of the greatest significance to the suppliers, customers, and debtors of that world.

Ready access to the U.S. market, stable U.S. income and employment, and a steady flow of U.S. lending were not only important but vital. Sudden changes in the U.S. tariff, capriciousness in its lending, or instability in its business could disrupt economic life in most of the rest of the world. Its position of leadership, so suddenly achieved, imposed responsibilities. These, unfortunately, the nation was not prepared to assume.

Agricultural Overproduction

If the expansion of industry in various new lands created an unbalanced situation, even greater instability resulted from the growth of agricultural production. The 1914 war greatly increased the demand for many raw materials, as well as for some foodstuffs, while it removed from production or from contact with world markets important sources of supply, especially of wheat and sugar. Consequently, production in accessible regions bounded upward. With the return of peace, supplies from older producing areas gradually reappeared. But the newer producers did not retire from the field. The result was an accumulation of stocks, downward pressure on prices, and agricultural discontent.

Producers of rubber, wheat, sugar, and coffee attempted to deal with the situation by establishing various types of control schemes. Although details of these projects varied, they all shared one common weakness: The controls could be made effective over only a portion, although usually a major share, of the producers. Each scheme foundered because it made expansion profitable outside the area under control. Thus rubber restriction applied only to Malaya: Additional plantings in the Netherlands East Indies brought its ruin. Coffee control was limited to Brazil, but production in Colombia, Venezuela, and other regions increased rapidly. Cane sugar producers tried restriction, but beet sugar output, aided by tariffs and subsidies, continued to rise.

Thus, at the end of the 1920s, overproduction of important agricultural products, and of such raw materials as timber, copper, and nitrates, as well, both contributed to world instability and presented a problem of structural disequilibrium that would take years to correct.

The World Situation: 1929

Reviewing the developments of the decade 1919–1929, we may put on the credit side the re-creation, after the disruptive effects of World War I, of a working international system. Although the world's monetary arrangements were less effective than formerly, they were still truly international in character. Currencies practically everywhere where fully convertible into one another, thus making possible the continued existence of a truly open or multilateral trading system. It is true that tariffs were considerably higher than in prewar days and that, therefore, less advantage was taken of the possibilities of international specialization. Yet trade was large and growing, and it continued, with minor exceptions, to be free of those particularly repressive barriers, direct quantitative controls. International lending was once again providing, in large volume, badly needed foreign exchange.

Yet the painfully reconstructed international economy labored under great difficulties. The new gold standard was less efficient than the old, and the goal of currency convertibility into gold had been discarded in favor of nationally more congenial, but internationally more questionable, practices. The same forces that had led nations to assert greater monetary independence—the increasing role of government and the rising tide of economic nationalism—also led to greater self-assertion in policies concerned with employment, taxation, trade, and immigration. A huge dead weight of war debts and reparation had somehow to be collected and fitted into balances of payments, and although the large volume of international lending contributed to the momentary solution of this problem, it did relatively little to increase the capacity of debtors to service these loans. Major shifts in the location of industry required a vigorous response in the older countries; although this adjustment had begun, it was proceeding at a rather sluggish pace. The increasing dominance of the United States forced it into a position of leadership for which its isolationist tradition equipped it most inadequately. And to the structural changes in industry were added serious maladjustments in important sectors of agriculture.

It is possible that, given time, even the weakened international structure could have carried through the necessary adjustments and that some difficulties would have yielded to sensible negotiations, if only a reasonably high level of world demand had been maintained. The gradual and piecemeal changes that normally occur, involving the transfer of labor and capital from unprofitable to profitable lines of production, would have had a chance to operate.

Such a gradual solution of its problems, however, was denied the world by the outbreak of the worst depression in history. Even the most profitable industries became unprofitable. There was nowhere for surplus resources in the overexpanded industries to go, no incentive to build up new fields of employment, and no opportunity for lending to improve by continued experience.

[For Selected References, see the end of Chapter 26.]

26
CHAPTER

Forces of Disintegration

Beginning with 1929, new difficulties piled on top of old. The precariously balanced international economy collapsed under their weight.

THE GREAT DEPRESSION OF THE 1930s

Its Origin and Spread

The great depression of the 1930s throws a strong light upon the dominant economic position of the United States, and reinforces the view that economic conditions in that country go a long way toward determining the level of activity in the rest of the world. There can be little doubt that the major forces that transformed the prosperity and optimism of 1929 into the unemployment and pessimism of 1932 had their origin in the United States, and that declining activity and demand there spread outward in all directions until they encompassed most of the globe.

Although it is true that a downturn in economic activity got under way in half a dozen of the less-developed countries (and in Germany) at various points in time between late 1927 and the middle of 1929, their collective economic weight was not sufficient to spark a worldwide collapse. It was not until the downturn of industrial activity in the United States in July 1929, followed by the stock market collapse in October, and therewith the puncturing of the bubble of overoptimism, that conditions became rapidly worse in ever-widening circles.

The main support of generally prosperous conditions over most of the world had been a high level of income, employment, and production in the United States, dating from 1922. Underlying and making possible this eight-year stretch of prosperity was an investment boom of record proportions. Investment, the dynamic factor in any modern economy, attained unprecedented heights. Besides this large and continuing investment, induced principally by the rapid growth of industries related to the automobile and to the use of electric power, the country enjoyed its greatest building boom in history.

What brought this era of good times to an end? There can be little doubt as to the principal factors responsible for the onset of depression, even though any brief explanation is bound to involve serious oversimplification. It was simply that major fields of investment, whose activity primed that of the whole economy, had become saturated. The capacity of the automobile industry to produce cars, by 1929, far exceeded its ability to sell them. The tire industry too, was overbuilt. Many other producers of durable goods faced a similar situation and encountered serious sales resistance early in 1929. Investment in additional plant and equipment to produce still more of all these goods was not needed and was unlikely to be needed until demand had caught up with existing capacity.

Ever since the beginning of 1928, residential construction had been falling off sharply; it was clear that the supply of houses and apartment buildings, whose numbers the building boom had immensely augmented, was adequate to meet even a growing demand for some time to come.

The decline in activity was swift, especially after the shock to confidence administered by the stock market collapse. With only brief interruptions, investment, industrial production, employment, and national income plummeted downward for three disastrous years. Investment, the key to industrial activity, virtually ceased. In real terms, the gross national product shrank by one-third; in current prices, by nearly half. Industrial production fell to less than half the 1929 level, and that of durable manufactures, reflecting both industrial goods and consumer goods such as automobiles whose consumption could be long postponed, to less than one-fourth.

The collapse of the huge American economy reacted swiftly and violently upon other countries. As income declined, so did outlay on imports. Indeed, as Figure 26.1 shows, the quantity of imports went down almost precisely in accord with U.S. industrial output. Over the entire period covered by the chart, there is a close correspondence between physical imports and the level of industrial production, understandable because two-thirds of U.S. imports consist of primary products and semimanufactures used in industry.

In terms of purchasing power directed toward foreign countries, outlay on imports fell from $4.4 billion in 1929 to $1.3 billion in 1932.

Figure 26.1 Industrial Production and Imports of the United States, 1925–1939

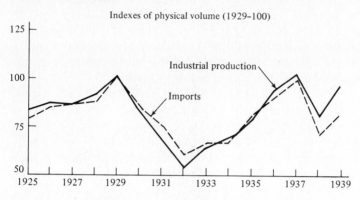

Indexes of physical volume (1929=100)

This meant reduced activity in the export industries of U.S. trading partners, and by the well-known mechanism of the multiplier, a decline in their incomes and levels of employment. But this was not all. Payments by the United States for service transactions were cut almost in half—from just under $2 billion in 1929 to $1 billion in 1932. Even more important, American long-term lending not only ceased entirely, but turned into an import of capital (mainly a repatriation of American funds). Long-term foreign loans by the United States averaged $978 million from 1927 to 1929; in 1932, there was an inflow of $251 million of long-term funds from abroad.

Taken together, the amount of dollars spent or invested abroad by Americans

> dropped from a level of about $7,400,000,000 for the 3 years 1927 to 1929 to a mere $2,400,000,000 in 1932 and 1933—a reduction of 68 per cent over a span of only 3 years.[1]

This in itself was a terrific shock to the economies of other countries. Added to the difficulties already encountered by agricultural producing nations, it sufficed to pull the entire world (outside the insulated and planned Russian economy) down with the U.S. economy.

The Smoot–Hawley Tariff of 1930

To the depressing effect on world trade of a sharp decline in U.S. national income there was added, in June 1930, a substantial increase in

---

[1] Hal B. Lary and associates, *The United States in the World Economy*, Economic Series No. 23 (Washington, D.C.: U.S. Department of Commerce, 1943), p. 173. This excellent study is also the source of the data cited previously.

the American tariff, whose effects extended well beyond the years just cited.

Discussion of tariff revision had been underway in Congress for some time. It started as a means of providing relief to agriculture, many branches of which, because of declining prices, did not share fully in the general prosperity of the 1920s. The general argument seemed to be that, since industry was prosperous and industry had protection, agriculture would be made prosperous if it were granted protection. Quite aside from the fact that the prosperity of industry depended mainly upon the high level of investment and the high level of production induced thereby, and hardly at all on protection, this naive argument overlooked the fact that many farm products (wheat, cotton, tobacco, lard) for which protection was being urged were export commodities, which customs duties could not possibly protect.

As was to be expected, limitation of the tariff revision to agricultural commodities, where it would do little good but also little harm, proved impossible. The temptation for senators and congressmen from industrial regions to use the technique of vote-trading or log-rolling to obtain increases on products of interest to powerful constituents was too great. So the range of commodities considered broadened from a few to 25,000; the end result was an increase in over 800 rates, covering a wide variety of both agricultural and industrial goods.

This gratuitous and totally uncalled-for raising of an already high tariff produced nothing but unfortunate results. It evoked widespread protests and precipitated prompt tariff increases in a dozen nations, notably of duties on products of particular importance to the United States.

How much the Smoot–Hawley Tariff reduced U.S. imports is impossible to judge, although there is no doubt that it had an appreciable effect. At least as serious was that it nullified completely the efforts of the League of Nations, in progress since 1927, to halt the upward trend of tariffs, and instead accelerated that movement.

Why Not Insulation?

With the shrinkage in U.S. imports and foreign lending, in each of a large number of countries there set in a decline of production and employment. Reinforced by the operation of the multiplier, their incomes and imports fell sharply, spreading depression in ever-widening circles. Because of the lag between the initial decline in exports and the induced fall in imports, these countries experienced an adverse shift in their balances of payments that caused a large outflow of gold. To the primary deflation of income due to falling exports there was added a secondary deflation of response to the contraction of reserves.

With the wisdom of hindsight, we might now recommend as a preferred policy for these countries the prompt introduction of exchange control, coupled with discriminatory restrictions on imports aimed at the source of depression. These external measures should have been combined with increased government outlays to sustain income and employment. Removal of the import restrictions could then have been made conditional upon the adoption by the United States of similar expansionary policies.

There are many reasons why such action was impossible at the time. It was a type of policy that would have required international agreement, and this agreement would have been impossible to achieve. Moreover, devotion to the principles of laissez faire was still too strong. In spite of the enlargement of the area of state action, no government as yet accepted responsibility for the level of economic activity and employment. At most, it was felt that government should attempt through central banking policy to check booms and to moderate depressions. The very fact that no depression comparable in severity to that of 1929–1933 had been experienced in the memory of living man tended to reinforce this view, as also did the rapidity of recovery from the postwar slump of 1920–1921 and the success attending the use of monetary policy in the 1920s.

Finally, there existed as yet no general agreement, even among economists, as to the principal causes of the business cycle or as to means of combating it. It was the great depression of the 1930s that directed attention forcibly to the problem, and led to the development of the modern theory of employment and income, with its stress on policy intervention.

Varying Reactions

Instead of acting together to insulate the depression and counteract its effects, each nation was left to face its mounting difficulties as best is could. One alternative was to adhere to the gold standard and allow the deflationary forces to tighten their grip, while perhaps restricting imports by higher tariffs. Another was to abandon the gold standard and permit the currency to depreciate. Still a third was to subject the balance of payments to direct control, either by quantitative restrictions on imports or by outright exchange control.

Each nation's response varied with its financial strength, its dependence on foreign loans, and the degree of its attachment to the gold standard. The countries of western Europe without exception chose fixed exchange rates plus deflation. They allowed their balances of payments to deteriorate, their gold reserves to shrink, and the level of economic activity to contract.[2] This solution proved impossible for certain primary producing countries whose export prices had been under severe pressure and which were hard hit by the decline in foreign lending. Thus even before the end of 1929, Argentina, Brazil, Paraguay, and Uruguay all depreciated their currencies. Australia, New Zealand, Boliva, and Venezuela followed them in 1930. Only Turkey and Iran introduced exchange controls.

By the spring of 1931, it looked as though deflation, even if a painful method of readjustment, was doing its work. The gold standard was still intact in western Europe and the United States. Exchange depreciation had not spread beyond the original nine countries, nor had controls been extended. There were even some hopeful signs on the horizon: in the early months of 1931, industrial production recovered slightly in Germany and the United States. Money rates were low even in Germany, and credit was easy in all the principal centers. There was some prospect that recovery might finally take hold.

The International Financial Crisis of 1931

The hesitant optimism of the spring of 1931 was shattered by the outbreak of an international financial panic. It began not in a major financial center, but in little Austria. A revaluation of the assets of the Credit-Anstalt, the largest commercial bank in Vienna, showed that they had depreciated to the point where the bank was technically insolvent. This revelation led immediately to the withdrawal of foreign short-term credits. A "standstill" agreement with creditors, followed by restrictions on withdrawals, stopped the run on Austria, but did nothing to stem the anxiety that lay behind it.

Worried creditors shifted their withdrawals to Germany, which was a net short-term debtor (see pp. 457ff.) to the amount of 5 million marks (over $1 billion dollars). Although a one-year moratorium on reparation payments, initiated by President Hoover, caused withdrawals to slacken, it did not end them. An important German bank failed early in July, the run intensified, and by the end of the month nearly 3 billion marks of short-term funds had been transferred abroad. Rather than see the gold and foreign exchange reserves of the Reichsbank exhausted, the government introduced exchange control by a

[2] Contrary to the general trend, France throughout the period 1928–1932 added heavily to its gold holdings. This may be explained largely in terms of the calling back to France of overseas balances, the liquidation of French security holdings, and the attraction to France of foreign short-term capital in search of a safe haven. Germany's imports declined more rapidly than its exports, thus giving rise to a surplus in its current international account, which made possible the continuance of reparation payments and the service of foreign debt.

series of decrees, a step followed by eleven other countries in eastern and northern Europe before the year ended.

Germany's choice of exchange control was dictated by the fact that the public had been schooled to believe that exchange depreciation would lead to extreme inflation. Also, exchange control was especially suited to blocking capital flight. The traditional weapon, a high discount rate, had proved its ineffectiveness, for the Reichsbank had raised it to 15 percent without producing the slightest result.

Britain Abandons Gold

Capital withdrawal now shifted to England. It was known that British bankers had lent heavily to Germany and other central European countries and that now these credits were tightly frozen. On the other hand, foreigners had claims on London totaling £560 million. Adding to the uncertainty of Britain's position was the probability of a large government deficit, as well as the steady worsening of the country's balance of payments.

Foreign withdrawals mounted rapidly. Despite advances of £130 million from the Bank of France and the Federal Reserve System, these and more were soon paid out. With further credits unavailable, on September 21, Parliament suspended the Bank's obligation to sell gold.

During this crisis, Bank Rate had been raised only to $4^{1}/_{2}$ percent. Critics claimed that had a rate of 8 to 10 percent been established, the run on London might well have been halted. This argument was nonsense. In the circumstances of 1931, a Bank Rate of 10 percent would far more likely have been interpreted as a sign of weakness than as the exercise of a bygone power "to pull gold from the earth."

With the abandonment of gold, sterling exchange rates were freed to reflect the country's weak balance-of-payments position. Gradually, sterling depreciated, reaching a point 30 percent below the old parity in December. Within five months, the pound began to rise again. In June 1932, with the establishment of the Exchange Equalization Account, Britain inaugurated a period of managed, rather than freely fluctuating, exchange rates. The Account, or stabilization fund, received certain foreign assets from the Bank of England, together with £150 million in Treasury bills (in 1933 increased by £200 million) that it could sell in the market for sterling, using the proceeds for the purchase of gold or foreign exchange. By alternately buying and selling foreign currencies, it could keep fluctuations of the pound within bounds, subject to a limit on support imposed by previous accumulations of gold and foreign exchange.

Formation of Currency Blocs

In abandoning gold, Britain carried with her a large number of countries that, because Britain was their major market and London their reserve center, could not afford to see sterling depreciate against their currencies. They too left the gold standard, tied the value of their currencies more or less closely to the pound, and continued to keep the major part of their international reserves in the form of sterling assets. Here we have the beginning of a formally organized sterling area.[3] London, as the principal reserve center of the members, also performed most of their clearing, although until the outbreak of war, their currencies remained on the whole freely convertible. Each member kept the value of its currency stable in terms of the pound by official purchases and sales of sterling; and the British Exchange Equalization Account moderated fluctuations of the pound against the dollar and other gold currencies. Stability of the pound was also enhanced by an informal but very effective control of foreign lending by the Treasury, which confined capital exports to sterling-area members.

After the depreciation of sterling and the formation of the sterling area, only five countries remained solidly on the gold standard. These were the United States, France, Switzerland, Belgium, and the Netherlands.

Most other nations adopted some form of exchange control, whereupon their currencies immediately became inconvertible. The European members of the exchange control bloc kept their exchange rates stable at the old gold parities; others, especially in South America, allowed their currencies to depreciate heavily, then held the new exchange rates absolutely or relatively fixed.

Disintegration of the World Trading System

The introduction of exchange control and inconvertibility over a rather large area set in motion the tendency toward the bilateral channeling of trade to which we drew attention in Chapter 24. Depreciation by the sterling area and by certain countries outside it (notably Japan) reinforced this tendency, especially among nations that used exchange controls to maintain unchanged the nominal gold value of their currencies. For quite independently of monetary developments within these nations, their currencies now became overvalued relative to those that had depreciated. Their exports were depressed and their imports

---

[3] With later additions to the membership, the prewar sterling area included all British Commonwealth countries except Canada, plus the Baltic nations, Egypt, Eire, Iraq, Palestine, Portugal, the Scandinavian countries, and Thailand.

stimulated. Controls had therefore to be tightened, and alternative markets for exports and sources of imports sought by means of bilateral trading arrangements.

The members of the gold bloc were, of course, similarly affected. As their balances of payments became increasingly adverse, they attempted to check rising imports by raising tariffs or by introducing quantitative restrictions. France, in particular, relied heavily upon import quotas.

Even Great Britain, in spite of the relief from the pressure of falling world prices afforded by depreciation, embraced protection. Earlier duties, imposed during and immediately after World War I, had been limited in scope. In 1931 and 1932 the Conservative party, now dominant in a coalition government and since the onset of the depression strongly committed to a protective policy, pushed through a comprehensive tariff. Duties ranged from 20 percent on a wide variety of manufactures to 30 percent on many luxuries and $33^{1/3}$ percent on the products of "key" industries.

For a long time the Conservative party had cherished the ambition of uniting the Empire more firmly by a system of *imperial preference*. Since the new tariff did not apply to Commonwealth countries, a basis now existed for the negotiation of mutual concessions. The Ottawa Conference of 1932 was called to explore the possibilities.

Being mainly an exporter of manufactured goods, Britain wanted freer access to dominion markets for these products. But the Dominions were keenly interested in developing further their growing manufactures. These objectives appeared irreconcilable. They could only be realized, in part, if the Dominions raised the duties on foreign goods, while leaving them more moderate, although still protective, on British goods. In general, this is what they did. For her part, Britain maintained a number of existing preferences and imposed new "Ottawa" duties on foreign supplies of certain products of particular interest to the Dominions. Thus, after Ottawa, Commonwealth tariffs were higher against the foreigner.

We can summarize the effects of the international financial crisis by saying that it led, first, to the breakdown of the international currency system and its replacement by three fairly distinct blocs, consisting of five countries still on the gold standard, a much larger group with fluctuating but convertible currencies, and another large group subject to exchange controls. Second, largely because of the effects of this division, but partly for extraneous reasons, the world trading system itself began to disintegrate as tariffs multiplied and climbed, quantitative restrictions spread, and trade became increasingly diverted into bilateral channels.

The World Economic Conference: 1932

By summer of 1932 the opinion was widespread that general and lasting recovery required measures to combat the breakdown on international trade and finance, and that such measures could only be undertaken through intergovernmental cooperation. Plans were laid for a World Economic Conference to be held in June 1933. A Preparatory Commission of Experts worked out an elaborate draft agenda dealing with tariffs, quantitative trade restrictions, agreements on raw materials and foodstuffs, and a wide variety of monetary problems including, particularly, currency stabilization. It was hoped that by restoring stable currency conditions, the revival of international trade would be facilitated, through "making it possible to abolish measures of exchange control and remove transfer difficulties." Shortly after the Conference had convened in London, however, and before it could achieve any concrete results, these hopes were dashed by the destabilization of the American dollar.

Devaluation of the Dollar

Deflation in the United States had been especially severe. Between 1929 and 1932, wholesale prices fell 32 percent, while the national income was cut in half. As prices fell, the banks liquidated commercial loans rapidly. Total loans of all banks had by the end of 1932 been contracted by 42 percent. Real estate loans, however, shrank only 10 percent. As property values declined, the security behind this paper evaporated, and more and more banks were forced to close their doors. Some 5100, about one-third of the total, did so between 1930 and 1932.

As the weak position of the banks became more apparent, a wave of currency and gold hoarding got under way, rising to panic proportions early in 1933. President Roosevelt declared a national banking "holiday" on March 16. At the same time he imposed an embargo on gold and silver exports except under license from the Treasury. A month later, the President announced that the departure from the gold standard would continue indefinitely. Simultaneously, Congress passed legislation permitting him to lower the gold content of the dollar by 50 percent. The dollar was left to fluctuate uncertainly.

The reason for this drastic step had nothing to do with the U.S. balance of payments, which was stronger than that of any other country, but reflected an obsession with the credit and price squeeze. Some of President Roosevelt's advisers held the naïve veiw that, if the price of gold were raised, commodity prices would automatically rise in direct proportion. Won over to their position, he was determined to put their policy into effect. Therefore, he rejected a specific proposal of the World Economic Conference aimed at exchange stabilization; the Conference dragged on in futile discussion for some three weeks more, but accomplished little.

For a time, depreciation of the dollar and rising prices went hand in hand. At first, speculators, anticipating further government action, bid up foreign currencies. Then the Reconstruction Finance Corporation used its newly acquired authority to buy gold, gradually raising its price. By July a weighted average of exchange rates had risen 32 percent over the February level, export prices had climbed 33 percent, import prices 27 percent, and purely domestic prices 12 percent.

The rise of export prices was considerably more than theoretical considerations would appear to justify, for in the existing conditions of depression, the supply of exports was very elastic. Moreover, a large proportion of U.S. exports being consumed at home, any appreciable increase in their dollar price would reduce home purchases and divert production aboard.[4] As for U.S. imports, these were predominantly raw materials and crude foodstuffs whose supply is inelastic in the short run. And the huge U.S. market was highly important to their producers. For both these reasons, foreign suppliers of U.S. imports would tend to cut their prices as the dollar depreciated, thus leaving prices in the United States relatively unchanged.

The apparent contradiction between theoretical expectation and what actually happened can be explained by other contemporary developments. The National Industrial Recovery Act of 1933 prohibited price cuts and set floors under wages and raised them. In anticipation of higher wages, manufacturers expanded output halfway to the 1929 level. Agricultural legislation paid farmers to reduce output, generating speculative buying of farm products. In these purely domestic events, not in exchange depreciation, is to be found the main explanation of the rise of export prices. Reinforcing the rise of export prices and stimulating an increase in the price of U.S. imports was a temporary improvement in the world situation, accompanied by an upward movement of the wholesale price level in several important countries.

During the next several months, the picture changed. Between July 1933 and February 1934 export prices rose only two points, to 135. Import prices climbed a bit more, from 127 to 131, while the average of exchange rates went on up from 132 to 146. Without any firm support, the earlier expansion ceased and turned into a slump. Industrial

---

[4] Since the United States is a large country, exporting only a small part of its production, increased foreign sales resulting from lowered foreign prices would add relatively little to total demand. Also, the U.S. economy contributed a relatively large proportion to the total world supply of many goods; any increase in its exports would therefore tend to have a seriously depressing effect on prices abroad.

production, income, and consumption fell. Foreign prices stopped rising and moved downward, probably in part reflecting the deflationary influence abroad of exchange depreciation in this country.

It is difficult to justify the depreciation of the dollar by the results. This policy served badly the price-raising objective of the administration. Nor is that objective itself above criticism, for it represented a treatment of a symptom rather than the cause, which was the collapse of private investment expenditure. Later recovery measures relied much more heavily upon government outlays to replace this shrunken component of income and were more successful.

In any event, on January 31, 1934, the U.S. experiment with currency depreciation came to an end when the price of gold was fixed at $35 an ounce, as compared with the predepreciation price of $20.67. The dollar was now definitely devalued relative to gold and gold-standard currencies by approximately 41 percent.

THE RESULTS OF EXCHANGE DEPRECIATION

Effects on Trade and Production

Devaluation of the dollar, added to the depreciation of sterling and related currencies, intensified deflation in the remaining gold-standard countries and increased the pressure on the balances of payments of those with overvalued currencies supported by exchange controls. As the ability of the gold countries to resist devaluation became more doubtful, a speculative flight of capital developed, reinforced by growing fears of war. With the dollar stabilized, most of these funds sought safety in the United States. Between 1934 and 1936, the inward flow of gold, closely paralleling the inflow of capital, surpassed $4 billion, almost half of this amount coming from the reserves of the gold standard nations.

At first these countries responded by raising tariffs and tightening quantitative restrictions on trade. Then, early in 1935, Belguim devalued her currency 28 percent; Switzerland, France, and the Netherlands followed in September 1936 with devaluations of approximately 30, 25, and 19 percent, respectively. France, with gold losses continuing, found herself unable to hold the fort. Two further downward readjustments of the franc were succeeded, in 1938, by abandonment of gold altogether and stabilization of the franc in terms of sterling. Germany and other exchange control countries in eastern Europe and South America stiffened their controls and, to stimulate exports, began to experiment with multiple exchange rates.

Although world industrial production mounted steadily from 1933, reaching at the end of 1936 a level 20 percent above 1929, world trade recovered but haltingly. In December 1936 it was still 10 percent below 1929, reflecting the intensification of restrictions in both the gold-standard and exchange control areas.

Partially offsetting these adverse developments was the stimulus exchange depreciation and abandonment of gold gave to internal expansion. By releasing countries following this policy from the fear of losing reserves, it permitted them to introduce more liberal credit and fiscal policies. Early in 1932 the Bank of England lowered its Bank Rate from 6 percent to 2 percent and added to commercial bank reserves by open market security purchases. Sweden also adopted a cheap-money policy and stepped up government expenditures. In these and other sterling-area countries that took similar steps, industrial production recovered rapidly, by 1936 reaching levels substantially above the previous peak of 1929. Rising production and incomes in these countries also brought an increase in trade, especially with one another.[5]

Insulation against outside forces permitted a comparable internal expansion where exchange controls were in force, as in Germany, although these same controls held the advance of trade in check. But in those nations that still adhered to gold, economic recovery was but slight; 1936 production levels remained well below those of 1929.

THE WORLD ECONOMY PRIOR TO WORLD WAR II

Although the trend toward higher tariffs, the wider use of quantitative restrictions, and the intensification of exchange controls continued after 1932, thus tending further toward the disintegration of the world economy, the picture just before the outbreak of World War II was not one of unrelieved gloom.

Exchange Rate Equilibrium Approached

Although three distinct currency areas still existed, the period of recurring revaluation and exchange rate instability was at an end. Since final devaluation of the dollar, the dollar/sterling rate had varied within a range of approximately 3 percent ($4.90 to $5.05), and about sixteen other currencies were pegged to sterling. Exchange rates, except on the controlled currencies, had approached equilibrium levels, and even

---

[5] The temporary abandonment of gold by the United States, but not the forced depreciation that followed, can be defended as a precondition of expansion, for efforts earlier in 1932 and 1933 to expand the credit base had been accompanied by outward movements of gold.

those subject to controls were being brought more in line with reality by the fractional depreciation that goes with the introduction of multiple exchange rates.

The Trade Agreements Program

Even in the field of trade policy, a modest program of tariff liberalization got under way. Sponsored by Cordell Hull, the U.S. Secretary of State, a bill to permit gradual tariff reduction was passed by Congress in 1934. Known as the Reciprocal Trade Agreements Act, it authorized the President to sign commercial agreements with other countries, reducing existing U.S. duties by as much as 50 percent in exchange for parallel concessions. Since the study of proposed concessions and counterconcessions, as well as the actual negotiations in which they became realized, were to be carried out by committees made up of representatives of executive departments, this measure removed the making of tariffs from the political arena of Congress and made possible the beginning of a rational approach to this problem.

Especially in the depressed conditions of 1934, the bill could probably never have been sold to Congress had it not stressed the expansion of American exports by reduction of foreign duties. And since the Trade Agreements Act transferred from Congress to the executive responsibility for alterations in the tariff, there can be little doubt that this abdication of power was made attractive by the memories that many congressmen had of their nightmarish experience in the year-long legislative tussle preceding the enactment of the Smoot–Hawley Tariff Act of 1930. For then they were subjected to the constant pressure of innumerable lobby groups and were "asked to pass judgment on the wisdom of thousands of different rates defined in the esoteric jargon of hundreds of different trades."[6]

In no sense did the Reciprocal Trade Agreements program contemplate the abandonment of protection, for a provision known as the "peril point clause" specified that duties were not to be cut if such action threatened serious injury to American industry. Moreover, an "escape clause" required an upward adjustment of a duty reduced as a result of negotiations if serious injury were shown to have resulted from that reduction. In spite of these limitations, the Trade Agreements Act was a step toward the liberalization of trade—as Sumner Welles later characterized it, "one spot of sanity in a world outlook that seemed wholly and hopelessly dark."[7]

[6] Raymond Vernon, *America's Foreign Trade Policy and the GATT*, Essays in International Finance No. 21 (Princeton, N.J.: International Finance Section, Princeton University, 1954).

[7] Sumner Welles, "Postwar Trade Policies of the United States," *International Conciliation*, May 1943, p. 394.

Originally enacted for a span of three years, the Trade Agreements Act was periodically reenacted (although modified somewhat after the war) until replaced by the more liberal Trade Expansion Act of 1962. Before war broke out, twenty-one agreements had been signed under which average rates of duty on dutiable imports into the United States were substantially reduced, with corresponding reductions on its exports granted by other parties to these agreements. By setting in motion a reversal of the trend toward even-higher barriers, the program furnished the basis for a renewed and broader attack upon the problem in the years immediately after the war.

SELECTED REFERENCES

ASHWORTH, WILLIAM. *A Short History of the International Economy, 1850–1950.* London: Longmans, Green & Co., 1952. Chapters 7 and 8 provide, in brief compass, an excellent review of the major events between 1914 and 1950, together with an evaluation of their significance.

BANK FOR INTERNATIONAL SETTLEMENTS. *Annual Reports* (Basel). For a review and evaluation of current developments, these reports are extremely useful.

BROWN, WILLIAM ADAMS, JR. *The Gold Standard Reinterpreted, 1914–1934.* New York: National Bureau of Economic Research, 1940. A thorough study of the gold standard that focuses upon the changes it underwent after World War I.

HARROD, R. F. *The Life of John Maynard Keynes.* New York: Macmillan Publishing Company, 1952. The middle chapters of this book provide a vivid account of events of the interwar period from the point of view of one who was an active and influential participant.

KAHN, ALFRED E. *Great Britain in the World Economy.* New York: Columbia University Press, 1946. A well-documented and readable account of the post-1914 changes in the British economy and how they affected Britain's international position.

27
CHAPTER

From Reconstruction to Payments Problems

Our review of the interwar period (Chapters 25 and 26) showed it to have been dominated by the legacy of war and by the impact of the depression. World War I brought in its train disruption and disequilibrium. Looking back nostalgically to the simplicity and certainty of a world firmly bound together by a gold standard centering in the London money market, the world's political and economic leaders struggled uncertainly to reconstruct the past. Their efforts, however, were overbalanced by structural and political changes as yet imperfectly understood. They restored the gold standard, but not London's position of preeminence nor the close financial integration of prewar days. They sought to free trade from its increasing shackles, but were repeatedly balked by the irresistible forces of nationalism unleashed by the war.

Because its great economic strength was now apparent, the United States might have led in forging a world economy more suited to the changed circumstances. Yet its people, having just completed a long period of internal development, shrank from the responsibilities their new position thrust upon them. The automobile age had arrived, and they exploited to the limit the opportunities it afforded.

From the point of view of what forces were to be allowed to determine the course of trade, the decade of the 1920s was inconclusive and contradictory. Impulses and efforts toward establishing greater freedom for comparative costs competed with nationalistic policies with respect to money, trade, and immigration. Less free than in the Victorian age, far more free than under mercantilism, the world economy moved uncertainly toward reliance on the impersonal price mechanism.

This phase ended suddenly with the onset of the Great Depression. One of its chief manifestations, the sharp decline in income, now seized the center of the stage. Imports followed the curve of production; the ranks of the unemployed swelled everywhere. To combat unemployment and to safeguard its currency, one nation after another adopted more and more stringent controls. With few exceptions, goods or capital could move only when governments gave their permission. The forces of nationalism dominated almost all channels of international trade and payments.

Again during World War II, the channels of trade and even its composition were shaped by the division of the world into warring blocs and by the insatiable needs of the armed forces. Because more nations and more people were drawn into this struggle, and because the complexity and costliness of armaments had greatly increased, the demand for goods to feed the war effort was far greater and more disruptive to the peacetime structure of production than in 1914–1918. On the other hand, to obtain the needed supplies became more difficult, because the Axis powers dominated most of Europe, North Africa, and the East beyond India. The consequent search for substitutes for rubber, tin, quinine, hemp, and a long list of strategic materials furnishes a vivid illustration of the vital role played by international trade.

Despite the scope and destructiveness of World War II, within two years of its termination, production had staged a fuller recovery than in the same period after World War I. Industrial production reached 80 percent of prewar production and agricultural production, 75 percent. Comparable figures for the earlier recovery were only 76 and 63 percent, respectively. Yet because of the greater destruction of industrial plant and transportation facilities wrought during World War II, Europe's dependence on the outside world had become greater and made more enduring recovery far more difficult.

INTERNATIONAL PAYMENTS DIFFICULTIES

It is in western Europe's balance of payments that the international consequences of subnormal production and other war-induced changes are mirrored (see Table 27.1).

Production efforts were channeled primarily toward reconstruction. Governments, under heavy pressure to restore living standards, financed domestic expenditures in excess of incomes. However, consumer goods and many raw materials were still in short supply. Further contributing to the problem was an overvaluation of European currencies relative to the U.S. and Canadian dollar.

For the first three years after fighting stopped, Europe's trade

Table 27.1 Europe's Balance of Payments on Current Account, 1938 and 1946–1950 (Billions of Current Dollars)

	1938	1946	1947	1948	1949	1950
Imports, f.o.b.	$5.8	$9.4	$13.7	$14.4	$13.5	$12.5
Exports, f.o.b.	3.7	4.3	6.4	8.8	9.4	9.6
Balance on trade account	−2.1	−5.1	−7.3	−5.6	−4.1	−2.9
Income from investments (net)	1.4	0.5	0.4	0.4	0.4	0.5
Other current invisibles (net)	0.7	−1.2	−0.5	0.3	−0.1	−0.1
Balance on services account	2.1	−0.7	−0.1	0.7	0.3	0.4
Balance on current account (goods and services)	0.0	−5.8	−7.4	−4.9	−3.8	−2.5

SOURCES: United Nations, *A Survey of the Economic Situation and Prospects of Europe*, p. 54; *Economic Survey of Europe in 1949*, p. 109; *Economic Survey of Europe in 1950*, p. 114.

deficit exceeded $5 billion; in the three years before World War II, the trade deficit had been only $2 billion. Whereas the current account as a whole was in balance in 1938, for five years after the war it showed a large, although gradually diminishing deficit.

Fortunately for western Europe, there were resources initially available to finance the current account deficits. By drawing on reserves, borrowing what it could, and seeking extraordinary grants, Europe was able to maintain expenditures in excess of incomes for a few years.

During 1946 and 1947, the means of meeting Europe's huge excess payments came from an assortment of loans and grants and from further drafts on her badly depleted reserves. Some $4 billion was provided by the short-lived United Nations Relief and Recovery Administration (UNRRA), established during the war to prevent starvation, disease, and economic collapse in the immediate postwar period of maximum disruption. Under the Anglo-American Financial Agreement, the United States and Canada together advanced $5 billion to the United Kingdom. Additional stopgap aid came from various sources: $400 million to Greece and Turkey for military and economic assistance; American Export-Import Bank loans of approximately $2 billion; and nearly another $1 billion from the International Bank for Reconstruction and Development and the International Monetary Fund.

THE EUROPEAN RECOVERY PROGRAM

By the summer of 1947 it had become clear that relief works and emergency loans were totally inadequate means for coping with Europe's difficulties. Mounting international deficits, inadequate supplies of fuel and raw materials, slackening industrial production, and shortage of foodstuffs intensified by the worst harvest in years—all pointed to the need for a more drastic and far-reaching attack. This the European Recovery Program (ERP), or the Marshall Plan, aimed to provide.

In his commencement address at Harvard University on June 5, 1947, Secretary of State Marshall, after reviewing the breakdown of the European economy, stated the concern of the United States for this condition and its willingness to cooperate fully in a coordinated recovery effort. Insisting that "the initiative . . . must come from Europe," and that they should agree on requirements and on the action they would take, he pledged United States aid in drafting a program and in later financial support thereof.

The response was immediate. Out of a conference lasting all summer, there emerged a committee, later crystallized as the Organization for European Economic Cooperation (OEEC), whose report analyzed Europe's problems and formulated a program of recovery to extend over the four years 1948–1951. Financial aid needed was estimated at $22.4 billion, most of which would have to come from the United States. As their contribution, the participating countries undertook to do everything in their power to make Europe productive, so that it could sell enough to pay its way in the world. This meant raising output and increasing efficiency of production, both of exports and of articles hitherto bought outside the European trading area. As means to this major goal, OEEC members were to cooperate in every way possible, in particular to eliminate restrictive trade barriers, and each was to check inflation as a precondition to the effective use of Europe's resources.

Parallel committees in the United States wrestled with cost estimates, the availability of American resources for aid, and the probable impact of a major aid program on the U.S. economy. From $12 billion to $17 billion was suggested as the necessary American contribution to a really effective undertaking. Congress passed legislation providing interim aid and $4 billion for the first year's operations of the Economic Cooperation Administration (ECA), the administrative counterpart of the OEEC in Europe.

The story of the ERP is a fascinating one. A flood of American administrators and experts, including businessmen, college professors, industrial and agricultural technicians, and publicity agents, crammed into offices in the European headquarters, Paris, and in the capital of every OEEC member country. Their job was to schedule Europe's needs in cooperation with the OEEC, to approve orders for goods ranging from wheat to tobacco, from tractors to locomotives and freight cars, and to see that these goods got to where they were needed.

By late 1951, although the recovery program was not yet completed, mutual defense against communist aggression overshadowed economic aid and the ECA was merged in a new organization, the Mutual Security Administration, which administered both military and economic assistance. The cause of this change in direction and in organization was, of course, the outbreak of the Korean war in June 1950 and the resultant emphasis on rearmanent.

Up to mid-1951, the ECA has spent a total of $10.3 billion. Approximately 90 percent of this was in outright grants, only $1.1 billion being advanced as loans.

EUROPE'S RECOVERY

Production   With the crucial aid supplied by the United States, Europe made rapid progress. Industrial production in the OEEC countries, some 17 percent below prewar production in 1947, almost closed this gap in 1948. From then on it rose about 10 percent each year until 1951, when it stood 35 percent above the level in 1938. Agricultural production behaved similarly, although it moved at a slower rate.

Control of Inflation   Inflation, which was open and unrestrained in some countries, notably France and Italy, and suppressed by price controls and rationing in England and the Netherlands, was brought rapidly under control. The increasing abundance of goods as production rose helped substantially to slow down the rise of prices, but deliberate use of monetary and fiscal policy was at least equally important. Drastic currency reforms in Germany and Austria, where inflation had progressed farthest, canceled the larger part of the old and excessive currency issues and replaced them with new ones. By early 1950 a decade of rapidly rising prices had given way to price stability, interrupted only briefly by the Korean war.

Intra-European Trade   Trade among western European nations stood in 1947 at about 60 percent of its prewar volume. Reduced production, both in industry and agriculture, partially accounted for this sharp decline. More important was an imbalance in production and therefore in the ability to supply exports. Industrial output was especially low in Germany, whose large export surplus with other European countries formed the basis on which the prewar trade pattern rested. With this pattern disrupted, there developed a general tendency toward the close bilateral balancing of accounts between European trading partners. By 1948 some 200 bilateral agreements, backed up by rigorous quantitative restrictions, governed intra-European trade.

With growth in production came the physical means to restore intra-European trade. But the bilateral arrangements and trade restrictions remained stubborn obstacles. To combat the latter, the OEEC adopted a Code of Liberalization, under which each member obligated itself progressively to eliminate restrictions on private trade. By 1955 the greater part (84 percent) of quantitative restrictions on trade had disappeared. At least equally important was the establishment of the European Payments Union, which provided an effective means of clearing intra-European payments and thus of doing away with the bilateral channeling of trade. These collective measures, together with the steady increase in production, resulted in an increase in intra-European trade (by 1955) to almost 90 percent above the prewar level.

Devaluation   A combination of eager buyers and handicapped suppliers created a typical sellers' market during the immediate years after the war. By 1949, with the increased availability of goods both in Europe and in North America, this suddenly became transformed into a buyers' market. Price considerations again came to the fore. Overvalued European currencies, not a serious hindrance to exports as long as supplies of all kinds were short, now become a primary obstacle. It became increasingly clear that currency values simply must be revised.

On September 18, 1949, Britain took the plunge, devaluing the pound by 30.5 percent. Within a few days twenty-seven nations followed her example, including all the sterling area (except Pakistan) and eleven western European nations. Most of the countries devalued by the same amount; a few—notably Belgium, France, West Germany, and Italy—chose a substantially smaller figure.

The Balance of Payments   Each aspect of European recovery so far considered singly—the increase in production, the ending of inflation, the resurgence of intra-European trade, and the correction of currency overvaluation—worked jointly with the others to restore balance in Europe's international accounts. By 1950 the huge 1947 current account deficit had been cut by two-thirds to $2.5 billion. Thereafter, progress was steady, with rising U.S. military expenditures in Europe contributing increasingly to Europe's dollar receipts. Including these expenditures, the OEEC countries from 1952 through 1955 had a surplus on current account. Since economic aid continued, although in diminishing amounts, it was possible to add to reserves of gold and foreign exchange. These climbed steadily from $9.8 billion at the end of 1951 to $15.3 billion in 1955.

By the end of that year, eleven of the OEEC group felt sufficiently sure of themselves to restore full currency convertibility for nonresidents, although residents remained subject to certain restrictions with respect to capital transfers and travel expenditures.

It is interesting to recall that even as late as 1957 there were few who believed that western Europe's payments problem had been solved. It was widely urged that the balance achieved was temporary and apparent rather than lasting and real, since it rested in considerable part on uncertain U.S. foreign expenditures and was supported by quantitative restrictions on dollar imports. With any significant decline in these expenditures, or with the removal of these restrictions, a persistent tendency toward dollar shortage would reassert itself.

This view undoubtedly underestimated the strength and vigor of Europe's recovery. Instead, many economists expressed a basic pessimism by contending that the problem of dollar shortage extended back at least to 1914, and that it rested on the previous and continuing superiority in the competitive position of American industry, based on more rapid technological progress in the United States.[1]

THE U.S. BALANCE OF PAYMENTS TO 1968

The U.S. trade balance ran surpluses most years through the late 1960s (see Table 27.2). Those American trade surpluses were fairly closely matched by corresponding transfers and capital account deficits, leaving relatively little in the way of net changes in official reserves. However, by 1968, the thirst of the rest of the world for American capital was satiated. The so-called "dollar shortage" had been eroded. (We shall pick up the narrative of the emerging U.S. balance of payments problem in the next chapter.)

RECOVERY IN GERMANY AND JAPAN

Among the most remarkable phenomena of the post−World War II international economy is the recovery of Germany and Japan. At the end

---

[1] G. D. A. MacDougall, "Does Productivity Rise Faster in the U.S.?" *Review of Economics and Statistics,* **38** (May 1956), showed that U.S. productivity increased more rapidly than elsewhere only during the two world wars.

Table 27.2   **U.S. Balance of Payments at Five-Year Intervals, 1953–1968 (Billions of U.S. Dollars)**

	1953	1958	1963	1968
Current account	−1.37	+0.77	+4.41	+0.59
Trade balance component	+1.29	+3.31	+5.22	+0.64
Capital account	+0.11	−3.06	−4.79	+0.30
Changes in official reserves (+ = decrease)	+1.26	+2.29	+0.38	−0.89

SOURCE: IMF, *International Financial Statistics.*

of the conflict, parts of German and Japanese industry lay in ruins. Industrial production in Japan in 1946 was nearly 28 percent below the prewar level, in Germany about the same. Within five years, the prewar figure had been reached in both nations. At the end of ten years (1955), Japanese industrial output was more than 50 percent above prewar production, and in Germany, 60 percent. In the next ten years, Japanese industrial production soared to almost six times (570 percent) the 1938 figure, and Germany's reached a level three times higher. In terms of annual rates of growth of GNP, Germany achieved a figure of 7.6 percent in the 1950s; in the 1960s it had slackened off to 4.8 percent per annum. Japan's accomplishment was outstanding: GNP rose 9.5 percent per annum (1950–1960) and 11.1 percent (1960–1970). In the meantime, the United States expanded production at the relatively modest rates of 3.3 percent in the 1950s and 4.0 percent in the 1960s.

The increased efficiency that underlay rapidly rising production in Germany and Japan and the improved international competitiveness that resulted showed up in the growing share of German and Japanese exports in world trade (see table 27.3). Note the decline in the U.S. share of world exports, from over 21 percent in 1953 to 16 percent in 1968, and the parallel decline of the British share. In the same period, Germany doubled its share of world trade, from under 6 percent to

Table 27.3   **Exports as Percent of World Exports**

	1953	1958	1963	1968
United States	21.33	18.83	17.20	16.24
United Kingdom	10.06	9.98	8.99	7.24
West Germany	5.92	9.25	10.71	11.65
Japan	1.72	3.03	4.01	6.16

SOURCE: IMF, *International Financial Statistics.*

nearly 12 percent, and Japan, with less than 2 percent of world exports in 1953, nearly equaled those of the United Kingdom by 1968.

Many factors combine to explain the economic performance of Germany and Japan; of these, the most conspicuous were high rates of saving and investment. In Japan during the 1960s investment amounted to approximately one-third of GNP. For Germany the figure was close to 25 percent; for the United Kingdom, 17 percent; and for the United States, about 16 percent.[2] With these high rates of investment, Japan and Germany were able to rebuild their industrial plant, replacing old equipment with the most modern types. Japanese manufacturers, large and small, introduced technological innovations at a rapid rate, especially in the late 1950s.

Personal savings in the four countries contrasted in a similar fashion. In the mid-1960s they were Japan, 20.2 percent; Germany, 12.2 percent; United Kingdom, 7.6 percent; and the United States, 7.6 percent.[3] In both Germany and Japan a high rate of saving was promoted by a low burden of defense underspending, imposed by the terms of the peace treaties. Other forces that would have to be taken into account in a more thorough explanation of Japan's phenomenal economic growth are the generally high educational level of its labor force, the unusual mutual loyalty of labor and employer, and the leadership provided by government.

Whatever the full explanation, it is clear that by the mid 1960s the economies of Japan and Germany, as well as Europe more generally, had fully recovered from the ravages of World War II.

SELECTED REFERENCES

AUBREY, HENRY G. *Behind the Veil of International Money*, Essays in International Finance No. 71. Princeton, N.J.: International Finance Section, Princeton University, 1969. A thorough discussion of political and economic considerations related to the U.S. balance-of-payments problems of the 1960s.

ECONOMIC COMMISSION FOR EUROPE. *Economic Survey of Europe in [Year]*. New York: United Nations, annual from 1949. Analytical discussion of economic developments in postwar Europe.

————. *Economic Survey of Europe Since the War*. New York: United Nations,

---

[2] *The Economist*, Mar. 31, 1973, Survey, p. 15.

[3] Miyohei Shinohara, *Structural Changes in Japan's Economic Development*, Economic Research Series No. 11 (Tokyo: The Institute of Economic Research, Hitotsubashi University, 1970), p. 43. This book contains a wealth of material related to Japan's economic growth.

1953. A thorough review of Europe's progress through 1952, and an analysis of its problems of trade, payments, and industrial development.

LARY, HAL B. *Problems of the United States as World Trader and Banker.* New York: National Bureau of Economic Research, 1963. A study of the U.S. balance-of-payments problem in the early 1960s that evaluates elements of strength and weakness in the country's position at that time.

MAKIN, JOHN H. *Capital Flows and Exchange-Rate Flexibility in the Post-Bretton Woods Era,* Essays in International Finance No. 103. Princeton, N.J.: International Finance Section, Princeton University, 1974. Overvaluation of the dollar in the 1960s is shown to have contributed not only to a deficit in the U.S. current account, but also to an excessive outflow of long-term capital.

SALANT, WALTER, S. *Financial Intermediation as an Explanation of Enduring Deficits in the Balance of Payments,* Brookings Reprint 249. Washington, D.C.: The Brookings Institution, 1972. A carefully reasoned application of portfolio theory to the analysis of chronic U.S. deficits in the 1950s and 1960s, stressing financial intermediation by the United States as a major cause.

28
CHAPTER

Development of the Postwar International Monetary System

When World War II ended, and for many years thereafter, the world's currency system was in disarray. Two currencies—the U.S. dollar and the Swiss franc—stood out as the only stable and fully convertible monetary units. True, the sterling area provided free transfer of payments among members through changes in reserve deposits held in London. But payments to other countries, especially to the dollar area,[1] were subject to strict though varying exchange controls and import restrictions. As for the rest of the world, each country pursued its own goals independently. In western Europe, the general shortage of goods, inadequacy of export capacity, and excess of purchasing power forced the maintenance of fixed exchange rates at overvalued levels, backed up by extensive systems of controls and trade restrictions. Many other countries faced a comparable situation and adopted similar measures. Bilateral trading arrangements, adopted as a device to ensure minimum essential imports, were widespread.

From this situation of trade and payments restrictions there emerged a remarkably free and efficient international monetary system. At the heart of it was the set of institutional arrangements formally created at Bretton Woods in 1944 but only brought into play gradually over the next 15 years. A second institutional arrangement that began to take shape in the 1950s is called the Eurocurrency market. Unlike the Bretton Woods system, it was not formally designed and

---

[1] The United States, Canada, and countries (primarily in Latin America) that financed their trade through New York banks.

created with the signature of a document. Rather it grew up on its own as an institutional response to the needs of the international financial system. This chapter concerns the development of these two systems.

THE BRETTON WOODS SYSTEM

Establishment of the International Monetary Fund

Even while the war was still in progress, it was apparent that in view of the disruption and dislocation certain to exist upon its termination, deliberate and strenuous efforts would be necessary to bring some degree of order out of the threatened chaos of worldwide restrictionism. Sharing such convictions, experts in the United States and the United Kingdom during the war prepared comprehensive plans for postwar international monetary cooperation. At first working independently, then together with representatives of other countries, they drafted the elements of a common plan for the establishment of a new and unique institution, the International Monetary Fund (IMF). At an international conference held at Bretton Woods, New Hampshire, in July 1944, the delegates hammered out the Articles of Agreement, together with another agreement establishing the International Bank for Reconstruction and Development.

The creation of the Fund represents a major effort at international cooperation. Although by no means the first in its field, it is the most detailed attempt deliberately to organize the conduct of international monetary affairs. Before World War I, there was international cooperation, but it relied on impersonal market forces and not on the establishment of specific institutions with directors, staff, and powers of action. The cooperation between central banks of the 1920s and 1930s was informal and relatively loose. The IMF, however, strikingly embodied the trend that developed after the war of deliberate and conscious organization to achieve certain agreed international goals.

Purposes   The three main purposes of the IMF clearly reflected the lessons of the interwar period.

1. Perhaps most apparent was the need for full and worldwide convertibility of currencies in the foreign exchange markets, for this would recreate a multilateral system of payments and therewith a trading system that would permit the fullest advantage to be taken of the possibilities of international spe-

cialization. Therefore, the Articles of Agreement made the "elimination of exchange controls" a major objective of the IMF.

2. To guard against the unsettling effects of unstable exchange rates and especially against competitive depreciation which had been conspicuous in the 1930s, another task was to restore "reasonable stability of exchange rates."

3. Most difficult of all, the IMF was to undertake to reconcile the apparently irreconcilable—"to combine exchange rate stability with national independence in monetary and fiscal policy."

Powers   To realize these difficult objectives, the agreement establishing the IMF replaced freewheeling national exchange and payments policies with a code for international cooperation by which members agreed to abide. This code consisted of detailed provisions specifying the means available to the IMF to realize its assigned objectives.

Elimination of Exchange Restrictions   To eliminate foreign exchange restrictions and thus eventually to restore convertibility, new exchange restrictions on current international transactions required the approval of the IMF. After 1952, members still retaining exchange restrictions were to consult with officers of the IMF with respect to their continuance.

An exception was made, however, for unwanted capital movements—that is, speculative or politically motivated flights of capital. Members could be requested to introduce controls to prevent such movements.

Stability of Exchange Rates   In approaching the twin problems of restoring stable exchange rates and providing an acceptable means of international adjustment, the IMF agreement aimed at stability as a norm, but flexibility in the event of severe disequilibrium. Normally stable rates were ensured by requiring each member to declare a par value for its currency, expressed in terms of gold or the U.S. dollar, and to allow spot rates of exchange to vary from that value by no more than 1 percent.

Adjustment: A Compromise Solution   To deal with the less serious short-run disturbances or with the early stages of more deep-seated difficulties, the IMF acquired sizable resources upon which members could draw. As a condition of membership, each country had to subscribe an individual quota based on its relative size and economic strength, of which 25 percent had to be in gold and the remainder in its national currency. From these subscriptions, the IMF acquired by 1957 resources totaling $9 billion ($1.7 billion in gold). Any member could, in effect, borrow from these resources up to 25 percent of its quota each year for a period of five years.[2] These *drawing rights* provided readily accessible credit to supplement members' own international reserves. Later, the IMF furnished an additional means of supplementing reserves whereby it undertook to make available sums in excess of the regular drawing rights.

Finally, in 1969, the establishment of Special Drawing Rights (SDRs) provided an additional sizable increment of reserves for financing payments disequilibria. To the extent of 70 percent, SDRs are "owned" reserves, like an international fiat money acquired by members. When drawn upon to settle international transactions, only 30 percent have to be repaid, whereas all the drawing rights in the General Account are repayable. Three initial distributions of SDRs were made, in 1970, 1971, and 1972, totaling $9 billion (in 1969 dollars).

For combating serious or "fundamental" types of disequilibrium, the IMF agreement in principle abandoned the objectionable deflation–inflation mechanism required by rigid exchange rates and turned to supervised flexibility of exchange rates. The articles of agreement established the principle that a member confronting a "fundamental disequilibrium" in its balance of payments must consult with the IMF. If the latter agrees that fundamental disequilibrium[3] exists, and that a change in par value is necessary (likely to prove appropriate and effective), then the IMF must concur with any proposed devaluation or revaluation not in excess of 10 percent. Greater changes were intended to be subject to negotiation between the Fund and the member.

Monetary and fiscal independence of members is guaranteed in the Bretton Woods agreement: If the IMF is satisfied that a change in par value is necessary, it "shall not object to a proposed change because of the domestic social or political policies of the member." Can a member, then, follow an inflationary monetary policy, even though it may neutralize the corrective effect of a devaluation? Not necessarily, for members also undertake "to collaborate with the Fund to maintain exchange stability," with which internal inflation would clearly be inconsistent. In practice, the IMF has attempted with considerable success to persuade members to follow domestic policies consistent with external stability; it has also provided them with technical assistance in designing and applying appropriate policies.

The participants at the Bretton Woods Conference clearly in-

---

[2] Literally, a member does not borrow, but purchases with additional deposits of its own currency the currencies of other members with which it is running a deficit.

[3] This concept is not defined in the Articles of Agreement, but presumably means disequilibrium of a serious and enduring character.

tended that the "adjustable peg" they established would be used relatively freely, to avoid the need for heavy reliance on the universally disliked mechanism of internal deflation–inflation. But the commitment to fixed exchange rates won out in practice. In the early years changes were infrequent, and usually came so late that an exchange rate change was the last resort.

Emergence of a Multilateral Payments System

Establishment of the International Monetary Fund gave the free world a respected international institution dedicated to the restoration of a fully multilateral payments system. During the early years of its operation, the IMF was able to achieve relatively little, but after the lapse of the five-year transition period in 1952, more and more countries abandoned rigid exchange controls and moved toward the operationally simpler and less restrictive system of multiple exchange rates. For this and for a general relaxation of restrictions, the IMF can certainly take part of the credit.

For almost a decade after the war, the sterling area, although it permitted free transfers among members, severely limited transfers to other areas, especially to the dollar area. In 1954 the system was greatly simplified and liberalized; this liberalization continued in piecemeal fashion until 1958, when only a limited number of restrictions on payments by residents remained in effect.

Certainly, the most striking move toward convertibility and free international payments came in Europe with the inauguration, in 1950, of the European Payments Union. This short-lived institution did away, at one stroke, with the bilateral balancing of trade into which the nations of Europe had been forced by postwar shortages. Backed by a grant of $350 million in U.S. currency, the Payments Union undertook to advance limited credits to members with deficits in their balances of payments, while members with surpluses agreed to extend credit to the Payments Union. As the size of these credits increased, it was provided that a rising proportion were to be liquidated in gold or dollars. With this important supplement to their own inadequate reserves, members could and did gradually replace the stringent restrictions on intra-European trade. Nations with considerable exporting capacity had hitherto limited their exports to avoid the accumulation of unusable currencies of countries with low export capacity. Now they could relax their restrictions, receiving a stipulated portion of increased exports in European Payments Union credits, the rest in gold or dollars.

Liberalization of exports had a sort of multiplier effect on intra-European trade. Those nations, now enabled to buy essential goods more freely, could recover their economic potential more rapidly, while the nations with larger exports could afford to spend an increasing part of their receipts even on luxuries. This furnished countries that produced such commodities (wines, perfumes, subtropical fruits) with the means of acquiring—perhaps in a third market—basic industrial supplies needed for their reconstruction.

Aided greatly by the European Payments Union, intra-European trade grew rapidly, while the economies of Europe increased in strength and competitive ability. By the end of 1958, the EPU was disbanded and fourteen European countries felt sufficiently sure of themselves to restore full currency convertibility for nonresidents, although residents remained subject to certain restrictions with respect to capital transfers and travel expenditures. The Bretton Woods system was now fully operational.

An enormous amount had been accomplished. The foundations for a relatively free system of international trade and payments had been established. At the end of 1958 the IMF's Annual Report on Exchange Restrictions revealed that the major industrial economics of the noncommunist world[4] had relatively free international payments systems. While there remained restrictions on payments by many of the nonindustrial countries, most of these were relatively mild or limited in range with single exchange rates and nearly free payments.

The foundation was in place. What remained to be seen was whether or not the creation of a relatively free system of international payments would have a pay off for the international economy.

From the Gold-Exchange Standard to the Dollar Standard

Bretton Woods reestablished gold as the basis for par values of currencies, but since the agreement did not prescribe gold as the sole form in which reserves could be held, it did not usher in a true gold standard. Many nations permitted their central banks to hold part of their reserves in currencies convertible into gold. From the point of view of a central bank, such foreign exchange holdings were superior to gold; if invested in highly liquid securities, they earned interest, whereas gold reserves entailed storage costs.

Because of the economic predominance of the United States after World War II in terms of production, wealth, and a huge gold reserve, the U.S. dollar became the logical candidate for reserve currency status. With liquid liabilities negligible, the dollar was readily convertible into

---

[4] The USSR was a signatory at Bretton Woods, but did not join the IMF. Three other member countries, which subsequently became members of the Soviet bloc, withdrew from the Fund: Poland in 1950, Czechoslovakia in 1954, and Cuba in 1964. Not all communist countries are excluded. Romania and Yugoslavia are members. The People's Republic of China took up the Chinese membership in 1980.

gold, and the large and sophisticated New York money market afforded a wide choice of liquid assets for the profitable investment of reserve holdings. Like the pound sterling of the nineteenth century, the dollar was not only as good as gold, but better.

The U.S. dollar also proved attractive to private international users. Commercial banks, multinational firms, and trading companies from around the world added steadily to their liquid assets in New York. The U.S. dollar was becoming a currency of convenience, or a "vehicle" for carrying out international transactions. There was one very simple reason for this. Bilateral markets between most of the world's 100-odd currencies simply did not exist: such a multiplicity of markets would be far too costly to maintain and too thin to be effective. Hence it was convenient for most to make the transactions via a "vehicle currency."[5] Thus, although many transactions might never involve the United States in any way, the U.S. dollar came to be used in transactions between most pairs of currencies.

In the postwar decades, then, for both official and private use, there was a significant growth of U.S. dollar liquid liabilities willingly held by foreigners (Table 28.1). Note that those who chose to hold those U.S. dollars did so because they valued the services to be obtained. That is why, in the first place, they willingly gave up real goods and services in exchange for the dollars.

The ability of the United States to obtain real goods and services in exchange for the creation of new U.S. dollars, in effect to capture the seigniorage, naturally created some resentment on the part of the official international community. It has led to a number of proposals to permit the seigniorage to be captured by others (see Chapter 14).

The net benefit to the United States from a world dollar standard was far from clear, however. The United States, by allowing the world to adopt the U.S. dollar as the standard, was now far more constrained in its policy options. Under the gold exchange standard, the U.S. balance of payments became the *residual* of policy decisions of the rest of the world. Thus if the sum of the rest of the world's policies result in a surplus for the rest of the world, then the United States must accept the verdict: A deficit with a resultant gold loss is dictated for it. For the United States to attempt to choose some other net position would, of course, overdetermine the world system.

The United States took on a further responsibility when the U.S. dollar emerged in widespread use as a world currency. Holders of the U.S. dollar would expect it to maintain its real value. If it did not, and if inflation emerged in the United States, the consequences not only for

---

[5] See A. Swoboda, *The Euro-Dollar Market; An Interpretation*, Essays in International Finance No. 64 (Princeton, N.J.: International Finance Section, Princeton University, 1968), for a development of the "vehicle currency" theme.

Table 28.1	U.S. Liquid Foreign Liabilities, 1951–1977 (Year End, Billions of U.S. Dollars)
Year	*Liability*
1951	8.24
1952	9.53
1953	10.55
1954	11.71
1955	12.22
1956	13.99
1957	14.40
1958	15.66
1959	17.42
1960	18.80
1961	20.73
1962	22.07
1963	23.29
1964	25.62
1965	25.50
1966	27.12
1967	29.91
1968	30.96
1969	39.45
1970	41.39
1971	55.18
1972	60.70
1973	69.07
1974	94.77
1975	94.34
1976	108.99
1977	124.31

SOURCE: IMF, *International Financial Statistics*, line 4d.d. (Series terminates at the end of 1977.)

the country itself, but also for the world economy, could be very serious. We shall have more to say about this issue shortly.

THE EUROCURRENCY MARKET

Origin

In the early 1950s a fortuitous set of circumstances gave rise to what became known as the Eurodollar market, or more broadly, the Eurocurrency market. During those cold-war days, eastern European banks had earned dollar balances they wished to retain denominated in U.S. dollars. Fearing a possible blocking of deposits held in New York in the event of a crisis, they arranged for European banks (largely London) to accept deposits of dollars. To distinguish such deposits, denominated in dollars, from their regular accounts kept in domestic currency, the European banks had to establish separate books for their Eurodollar business. As the practice spread to other currencies and other banking centers of the world, the definition of this type of deposit broadened to include *deposits denominated in a currency of a country other than where the bank is located.*

Having accepted deposits of liquid assets (in the form of claims on deposits in the currency of denomination), the European banks began to make loans, with the liquid assets as reserves against those loans. They had now taken on the role of financial intermediation. Those who wished to loan and those who wished to borrow did not have to seek each other out to find a match. Just as in the domestic financial markets, gains to both lenders and borrowers could be provided.

The Eurocurrency market was stimulated initially in this financial intermediation role by the existence of two sets of limitations imposed on competition in financial markets. In the United States, a Federal Reserve regulation (Regulation Q) imposed a limit on interest rates payable on time deposits; in Europe, monopolistic features of the national banking systems pushed interest rates above the competitive level. When those interest rates were higher in Europe than in the United States (as they generally were in the 1950s), and while exchange controls made short-term capital movements through the foreign exchanges difficult if not impossible, the emergence of an intermediate money market, where dollars could be deposited and loans contracted, proved most attractive to lenders and borrowers alike. Both U.S. residents and foreigners who acquired dollars in excess of their needs for transactions balances, instead of investing them in short-term assets (including time deposits and certificates of deposit) in New York, could transfer them to what came to be known as Eurobanks, which accepted deposits denominated in dollars and paid an interest rate superior to that in New York. European borrowers could obtain dollar loans from these banks without the need to go into the foreign exchange market.

For a brief period during and after 1957, balance of payments troubles caused the British to restrict the use of sterling to finance trade outside the sterling area. This gave a sharp impetus to the growth of the Eurodollar market: London banks continued to finance nonsterling trade, but used Eurodollars to do so.

Thus, because of special circumstances that were present in the

1950s, there came into being a banking system distinct from but supplementary to the banking system of Europe. Like any banking system, its elements consisted of reserves, deposits, and loans, all denominated in dollars and recorded in dollar acounts in certain European banks, called Eurobanks. The reserves were the New York deposits to which these Eurobanks acquired title when their previous holders switched them into Eurodollar deposits. Being outside the regular banking system, the reserve ratio banks maintained became a matter of private prudence rather than official regulation.

From a total of only about U.S. $1 billion in 1960, Eurodollar deposits grew rapidly, reaching a level of about U.S. $20 billion at the end of 1965.[6]

A Fallacy

It is convenient at this point to deal with a fallacy that has been widely held and from time to time still reappears. This is that the growth of the Eurodollar system depends on the presence of deficits in the U.S. balance of payments. In fact, there is no relation between them. Any foreign entity, bank or nonbank, that acquires a claim against the United States and thus obtains dollars can deposit those dollars with a Eurobank. This applies to any debit item in the U.S. balance of payments, whether that balance of payments as a whole is in deficit or surplus. Thus, in 1968, when the volume of Eurodollar deposits increased by almost $9 billion, every segment of the U.S. balance of payments was in surplus: the current account, the private capital account, the basic balance, and the official settlements balance.[7]

The Size of the Market

In the years since the first Eurodollar deposits were accepted and loans were made, the market has grown to enormous proportions (see Table 28.2). The rate of growth has continued to be very high throughout the years considered. It is particularly striking that in the seven years 1973–1980 the size more than quadrupled. The current magnitude of the market is readily comprehended when placed in comparison with the size of the U.S. money stock. At the end of 1980, the stock of Eurocurrency funds was valued at $575 billion, while at the same time the value of the U.S. money stock (M-1) was $404 billion.

[6] Bank for International Settlements, *Annual Reports*, Basel, various years.
[7] Given by F. Machlup in *International Monetary Problems*, a conference sponsored by the American Enterprise Institute for Public Policy Research (Washington, D.C.: The Institute, 1972), p. 7.

Table 28.2	Estimated Eurocurrency Funds, 1965–1980 (Year End, Billions of U.S. Dollars)
Year	*Deposits*
1965	(about 20)
.	.
.	.
.	.
1973	132
1974	177
1975	205
1976	247
1977	300
1978	377
1979	475
1980	575

SOURCE: Bank for International Settlements, *Annual Reports*, Basel.

Financial Intermediation

The growth of the market has occurred largely because it has proven to be an efficient source of financial intermediation. The market is confined largely to short-term (less than one year) wholesale interbank business.[8] It has been able to offer very low spreads between borrowing and lending rates—much lower than in domestic banking. This is because there are economies of specialization and economies of scale. The market has also been able to offer both depositors and borrowers a wide range of maturities—from a day or so to, in some cases, over a year. While there is reportedly little *net* transformation of maturities by the market, the intermediation function is nevertheless significant for the individual depositor or borrower who is able to obtain an appropriate maturity without having to seek out an exact match to his desired maturity. Finally, the intermediation function provides a range of risks and returns to lenders, while financing a similar wide range of quality of activities at appropriate premia.

The financial intermediation role of the Eurocurrency market was put to its severest test in 1974, when as a result of the OPEC oil price increase, many consuming countries chose to draw down their assets rather than adjust immediately to the higher oil prices. The

[8] There has emerged alongside the currency market a *bond* market in which banks act as underwriters rather than as intermediaries. The bonds are for the longer term.

OPEC members, on the other hand, wanted to accumulate assets, a large portion in the form of Eurocurrency deposits. The trouble was that the portfolio of assets being dissaved by the oil importers did not match the desired portfolio of the OPEC members. The former was largely long term, and had a full range of risk diversification, while the OPEC members preferred to put their new found wealth in short-term low-risk deposits. The existence of the Eurocurrency market permitted the "recycling" process to transform the currency and country mixes of oil-deficit countries into the currency and country mixes that the OPEC members wished to hold. This recycling proved to be an enormous task, but by the end of the 1974, the Eurocurrency markets had absorbed nearly U.S. $23 billion. In addition, deposits *within* national banking systems plus Treasury bills of the United States and the United Kingdom accounted for nearly $13 billion more, and another $20 billion was placed in long-term investments.[9]

Issues

The emergence of such a large currency market, not subject to regulation by any national or international authority, has raised significant concerns and controversies in the world of international finance.

Regulation   Concern over the absence of regulation arises because there is no protection of individual depositors from Eurobank default, and no protection for the system as a whole against a "bank run" which might generate financial collapse.

Individual depositors, it should be remembered, are themselves banks. Hence the "consumer protection" motive for regulation need not apply. While the risk is not large, the possibility of collapse of the system as a whole is a potential cause for concern. As is clear from the foregoing, collapse of the Eurocurrency system would be a significant blow to the international financial system. With nations, the central bank normally acts as lender of last resort. Who is responsible in the Eurocurrency market for a bank whose head office is in one country, perhaps located in a second country, that is dealing in currency of a third country? At present, the principal protection lies in the "name" of the banks and the *potential* intervention of the central banks in the financial centers and in the home countries of the participating banks. The latter particularly find that they must consider the worldwide consolidated financial position of their banks in order to minimize the risks to the domestic financial institution and system.

---

[9] These data are from the Bank for International Settlements, *Annual Report*, 1976–77, Basel.

Foreign Exchange Markets   The Eurocurrency markets are closely related to the foreign exchange markets. The existence of this large pool of funds contributes significantly to the smooth functioning of the foreign exchange markets. Since the Eurocurrencies are "vehicle" currencies, the massive Eurocurrency pool permits an evening out of demands and supplies across currencies and across maturities in the forward exchange markets without requiring large swings in exchange rates or official intervention. The existence of that large pool, however, has turned out to be a major constraint on governments wishing to maintain an undervalued or overvalued exchange rate. Given the one-sided bet inherent in the adjustable peg system, once a currency was identified as a prime candidate for a change in its peg, the speculators combined to put enormous pressure on the target exchange rate. Few governments were able to resist for long, and none permanently. This was particularly true in the latter days of the Bretton Woods system, 1970–1973.

The Eurocurrency market was not the only source of such speculative funds. The entire cash and short-term funds of the world's capital markets are potentially available. In the current system of general floating among the major currencies of the world, the existence of this large pool of funds has been critical, contributing to the smooth functioning of the forward exchange markets, by providing a ready source of funds for covered interest arbitrage.

Capital Market Integration   The Eurocurrency market has contributed to the effective functioning of the international economy by moving capital quickly and easily when needed. The existence of a massive market that welcomes new deposits and provides a pool of funds that could be drawn upon also means that unless a country has exchange controls, it is not able to move independently its national interest rate–forward exchange rate configuration. As we saw in Chapter 22, this has important implications for the independence of national monetary policies.

Inflation   Finally, a contentious issue concerns whether or not the Eurocurrency system is an independent source of excess credit creation that consequently contributes to inflation. This is readily dismissed by noting that the Eurocurrency deposits are (1) interest bearing, and (2) not capable of being spent without moving out of the Eurocurrency market, into a national currency, perhaps through a foreign exchange market. For a Eurocurrency deposit to create inflationary pressure it would have to be *withdrawn* from the Eurocurrency market and transformed into a national money ready to be spent on that nation's output. The size of Eurocurrency deposits has not more effect on, say, German inflation than the size of interest-bearing time deposits in France. Thus the mere growth of the Eurocurrency markets does not create in national economies an addition to the stock of "currency plus demand deposits," which could then contribute to inflationary pressures.

CONCLUSION

All in all, the Eurocurrency market development has become one of the unique inventions of the second half of the twentieth century. As with most major inventions, we wonder how we could have done without it, even though its introduction has not been perfectly smooth.

SELECTED REFERENCES

GARDNER, R. N. *Sterling–Dollar Diplomacy.* New York: McGraw-Hill Book Company, 1969. A very interesting study of how international policies and institutions were created and shaped. Especially relevant to this chapter are Chapters 5, 7, and 15, which relate the story of Bretton Woods.

HORSEFIELD, J. K. et al. *The IMF, 1945–1965: Twenty Years of International Monetary Co-operation,* Vols. I, II, and III. Washington, D.C.: IMF 1969. The official history and documentary record of the Fund.

DE VRIES, M. G. *The IMF, 1966–1971: The System Under Stress,* Vols. I and II. Washington, D.C.: IMF 1976. Sequel to the above.

KERLIK, J. R. "Some Questions and Brief Answers About the Eurodollar Market." Chapter 33 in R. E. Baldwin and J. D. Richardson, *International Trade and Finance: Readings,* 2nd ed. Boston: Little, Brown, and Company, 1981. A useful, nontechnical set of questions and answers about what the market is and how it operates.

MCKINNON, R. I. *Money in International Exchange: The Convertible Currency System.* New York: Oxford University Press, 1979. Chapter 9 discusses the Eurocurrency market.

MEIER, G. M. *Problems of a World Monetary Order,* 2nd ed. New York: Oxford University Press, 1982. Part I reviews the background development and collapse of the Bretton Woods System.

TEW, B. *The Evolution of the International Monetary System, 1945–77.* London: Hutchinson Publishing Group, Ltd., 1977. A useful nontechnical description of the postwar evolution of the world's monetary system.

TRIFFIN, R. *Gold and the Dollar Crisis.* New Haven, Conn.: Yale University Press, 1960. The classic identification of the instability of the gold-exchange standard.

29
CHAPTER

From Fixed
to Floating
Exchange Rates

FIXED RATES

Gold, Inflation, and the U.S. Dollar

In the years following Europe's move to convertibility (1958) the U.S. dollar continued to grow in use as the major vehicle currency for international transactions. The world as a whole increased its holdings of U.S. liquid assets (see Table 28.1). Development of the Eurodollar and its growth in the 1960s, which is in addition to the growth of U.S. liquid foreign liabilities, confirmed the usefulness of the U.S. dollar-denominated assets to the international financial community.

One of the ironies of the modern financial history is that while this growth in use of the U.S. dollar was occurring, at the very same time the U.S. dollar was running into "trouble." The trouble in this case was decline in U.S. reserves of gold (see Table 29.1).

For the explanation of this phenomenon, especially for the years 1965 and onward, we have to look to the fact that the United States had pegged the price of gold at U.S. $35.00 per ounce since 1934. Although this price had undoubtedly overvalued gold at that time, wartime price inflation had generally wiped out the overvaluation. In the first two decades after World War II, the United States had had remarkable price stability. In 1965, however, following the famous Kennedy tax cut of 1964, the U.S. wholesale price index started to move upward—not rapidly at first, but nevertheless perceptibly. The index,

Table 29.1   Industrial Countries' Official Holdings of Gold, 1949–1980 (Year End, Million Fine Troy Ounces)

	1949	1950	1951	1952	1953	1954	1955	1956
United States	701.8	652.0	653.5	664.3	631.2	622.7	621.5	630.2
Germany		—	0.8	4.0	9.3	17.9	26.3	42.7
Switzerland	43.0	42.0	41.5	40.3	41.7	43.3	45.6	47.5
France	15.5	18.9	17.1	16.6	17.6	20.2	26.9	26.4
Italy	7.3	7.3	9.5	9.9	9.9	9.9	10.1	9.7
The Netherlands	5.7	9.0	9.1	15.6	21.2	22.9	24.8	24.3
Belgium	20.0	16.8	18.2	20.1	22.2	22.2	26.5	26.4
Japan	0.1	0.2	0.3	0.5	0.5	0.6	0.7	0.7
Canada	13.9	16.6	24.1	25.3	28.2	30.7	32.4	31.5
United Kingdom	37.8	81.8	62.1	44.3	64.6	72.2	57.5	50.6
Gold price, end of period U.S. dollar per ounce (London)	34.71	34.71	34.71	34.71	34.71	35.04	34.97	34.91

	1957	1958	1959	1960	1961	1962	1963	1964
United States	653.1	588.1	557.3	508.7	484.2	458.8	445.6	442.0
Germany	72.6	75.4	75.4	84.9	104.7	105.1	109.8	121.4
Switzerland	48.7	55.0	52.3	62.4	73.1	76.2	80.6	77.9
France	16.6	21.4	36.9	46.9	60.6	73.9	90.7	106.5
Italy	12.9	31.0	50.0	63.0	63.6	64.1	66.9	60.2
The Netherlands	21.4	30.0	32.4	41.5	45.2	45.2	45.8	48.2
Belgium	26.2	36.3	32.4	33.4	35.7	39.0	39.2	41.5
Japan	0.7	0.7	7.0	7.1	8.2	8.3	8.3	8.7
Canada	31.4	30.8	27.4	25.3	27.0	20.2	23.4	29.3
United Kingdom	44.4	80.2	71.8	80.0	64.8	73.8	71.0	61.0
Gold price, end of period U.S. dollar per ounce (London)	35.00	35.08	35.07	35.60	35.15	35.07	35.08	35.12

	1965	1966	1967	1968	1969	1970	1971	1972
United States	401.9	378.1	344.7	311.2	338.8	316.3	291.6	276.0
Germany	126.0	122.6	120.8	129.7	116.6	113.7	116.5	117.4
Switzerland	86.9	81.2	88.3	75.0	75.5	78.0	83.1	83.1
France	134.5	149.7	149.5	110.8	101.3	100.9	100.7	100.7
Italy	68.7	69.0	68.6	83.5	84.5	82.5	82.4	82.4
The Netherlands	50.2	49.5	48.9	48.5	49.2	51.1	54.5	54.2
Belgium	44.5	43.6	42.3	43.5	43.4	42.0	44.1	43.1
Japan	9.4	9.4	9.7	10.2	11.8	15.2	19.4	21.1
Canada	32.9	29.9	29.0	24.7	24.9	22.6	22.7	22.0
United Kingdom	64.7	55.4	36.9	42.1	42.0	38.5	22.2	21.1
Gold price, end of period U.S. dollar per ounce (London)	35.12	35.19	35.20	41.90	35.20	37.37	43.63	64.90

	1973	1974	1975	1976	1977	1978	1979	1980
United States	276.0	276.0	274.7	274.7	277.6	276.4	264.6	264.3
Germany	117.6	117.6	117.6	117.6	118.3	118.6	95.3	95.2
Switzerland	83.2	83.2	83.2	83.3	83.3	83.3	83.3	83.3
France	100.9	100.9	100.9	101.0	101.7	102.0	81.9	81.9
Italy	82.5	82.5	82.5	82.5	82.9	83.1	66.7	66.7
The Netherlands	54.3	54.3	54.3	54.3	54.6	54.8	44.0	43.9
Belgium	42.2	42.2	42.2	42.2	42.5	42.6	34.2	34.2
Japan	21.1	21.1	21.1	21.1	21.6	24.0	24.2	24.2
Canada	22.0	22.0	22.0	21.6	22.0	22.1	22.2	21.0
United Kingdom	21.0	21.0	21.0	21.0	22.2	22.8	18.3	18.8
Gold price, end of period U.S. dollar per ounce (London)	112.25	186.50	140.25	134.75	164.95	226.00	512.00	589.50

SOURCE: IMF, *International Financial Statistics.*

which in 1958 had stood at 54.1 (1975 = 100), was 54.1 in 1964. In 1965 it moved to 55.2 and in 1966 to 57.1.

Now, by standards of the later 1970s, this scarcely appeared to be a serious problem. Nevertheless, as a reserve asset, gold was beginning to lose its value relative to other assets, including reserves denominated in the U.S. dollar itself, for the financial markets continuously adjusted the return paid on U.S. dollar-denominated reserves. The U.S. government responded to this not by abandoning the fixed relative price of gold, nor by attempting to restore *absolute* price stability. Instead, the U.S. government persuaded other governments not to convert their dollar balances into gold. By the end of 1965, the U.S. dollar, although legally convertible into gold, in fact was not. The world was effectively on a dollar standard.

In the next few years, the significance of the change became apparent. Fueled by the escalating U.S. involvement in the Viet Nam war, and other expenditures, expansionary fiscal and monetary pressure in the United States spilled over into the rest of the industrial world. This led to fears that the United States would devalue, or other currencies revalue, and began to let loose the speculative flows of funds that eventually brought the downfall of the Bretton Woods fixed exchange rate system.

Despite the fact that gold no longer really mattered, the United States remained concerned about the formal price of gold. In 1968, the United States, the United Kingdom, and the EEC of the day (except France) joined in a Gold Pool to intervene in the private gold market to hold down the price of gold. Finally, to avoid further losses of gold to the private market (and thus admitting the futility of the policy) members of the Gold Pool divorced the official from the private gold market by establishing a two-tier price for gold. They agreed to stop buying or selling gold on all private markets, to maintain the official price of $35 in official transactions, and to refuse to replace gold leaked into private markets by nonmembers. The two-tier gold price arrangement endured until late 1973.

The Collapse of the Bretton Woods System

The international economy was on a *de facto* dollar standard from 1965. As long as the United States maintained a reasonable degree of internal balance, the system of fixed exchange rates against the dollar, rather than gold, could work. The automatic adjustment mechanisms under fixed exchange rates appeared to function well. The balance of payments of the industrial countries other than the United States showed reasonable degrees of external balance. A major contribution to this effectiveness of the working of the system was the increased integration of the international capital markets, which served to enhance the mobility of capital.

A critical degree of freedom in the system had been lost, however. By eliminating the adjustment mechanism of the U.S. dollar against gold, the U.S. dollar became the final determinant of the system's nominal size. The pre-1965 gold-exchange standard had meant that the loss of gold by the United States would curtail the U.S. monetary base at the same time as there was an *increase* in the monetary base of the surplus country. Such symmetry was no longer the case. Hence a U.S. deficit or surplus on official settlements would affect the rest of the world, but not the United States. It became all the more critical then for the dollar to "set the standard" of international values.

Fortunately for the United States, in the first few years of the pure dollar standard, pressure from the United States on the world system abated somewhat. In 1968 and 1969 the balance of payments on official settlements ran a small surplus.

In a few individual cases some countries were forced to adjust their fixed exchange rates because they had gotten out of line themselves. Thus, in November 1967, sterling had been devalued (and was followed by several countries with close ties to sterling). In August 1969, France devalued, and in the fall of that year, Germany revalued.

The major pressure on the international dollar standard began in 1970. As we saw in our analysis of the *IS–LM* model (Chapter 23), expansionary fiscal and monetary policy put pressure not only on internal balance but on external balance as well. Increasing internal pressure in the United States spilled over in 1970. The United States ran a balance of payments deficit (on official settlements) of nearly U.S. $10 billion. Canada was among the first to feel the pressure, and not wanting to inflate, floated upward in June 1970.

In the coming months, the pressure of balance of payments surpluses continued to mount on the Europeans. The appearance of these surpluses encouraged speculators to take more and more of those one-sided bets against fixed exchange rates, moving into a currency which they expected to revalue and out of a currency they expected to devalue.

The final assault on the Bretton Woods fixed parities system began in early 1971 as upward speculative pressure on the German mark heightened. The Bundesbank spent billions of marks buying up dollars to maintain the fixed exchange rate at the par value set in late 1969. In May 1971, the German mark and the Dutch guilder were allowed to float and the Swiss franc was revalued. The next target was the U.S. dollar itself. In 1971 the United States had a deficit on official settlements of nearly U.S. $30 billion, spurred mostly by about U.S. $20 billion in short-term funds that moved out of U.S. dollars and into other major currencies. The asymmetry of the U.S. position in the international financial system made this problem far more serious than the previous cases of other individual currencies getting out of line. The U.S. balance-of-payments deficit served to expand the monetary base of the countries receiving the speculative flows, but a corresponding contraction of the U.S. monetary base did not occur automatically.[1] Consequently, the U.S. deficits contributed to an expansion of the total world monetary base.

During the summer and fall of 1971, the international financial community was in a state of great confusion: In August, President Nixon had announced the official suspension of convertibility of gold into U.S. dollars at $35.00 per ounce—which had been, in fact, the practice since 1965. Most of the major currencies, except France, floated. A political consensus developed on the need for realignment of the exchange rates among the world's major currencies. The problem was which currencies should be changed and by how much.

The United States took the position that overvaluation of the dollar was not general and uniform vis-à-vis other currencies, but that the mark and the yen in particular were substantially undervalued. Hence a uniform devaluation of the dollar would be inappropriate; Germany and Japan should revalue. Those, and others, contended that the United States should contribute to the needed realignment by devaluation of the U.S. dollar. After much inconclusive bargaining, a Group of Ten countries agreed to meet at the Smithsonian Institution in Washington to attempt to resolve their problem.

The Smithsonian Agreement

Out of this meeting came the Smithsonian Agreement of December 18, 1971, which arranged a two-part compromise that the participants hoped would restore some kind of order: (1) Seven nations agreed to change the par value of their currencies in terms of gold and SDRs. *The dollar was to be devalued appreciably,* and the lira and the Swedish krona slightly; four other currencies were to be revalued by varying amounts. (2) The permitted margin above and below parity within which a currency must be defended was raised from 1 percent to 2¼ percent, creating a band for fluctuations of 4½ percent. Table 29.2 shows the changed currency relationships resulting from the agreement.

President Nixon hailed the outcome of this Washington meeting as "the most significant monetary agreement in the history of the

---

[1] The reasons for this are spelled out by R. I. McKinnon, *A New Tripartite Monetary Agreement on a Limping Dollar Standard?* Essays in International Finance No. 106 (Princeton, N.J.: International Finance Section, Princeton University, 1974).

Table 29.2 Exchange Rate Relationships Resulting from the Smithsonian Agreement

Country	Percentage Change in Terms of Par Value (in Gold or SDRs)	Percentage Change in Terms of the U.S. Dollar
Belgium	+ 2.76	+ 11.57
Canada (floating continued)		
France	—	+ 8.57
West Germany	+ 4.61	+ 13.58[a]
Italy	− 1.00	+ 7.48
Japan	+ 7.66	+ 16.88
The Netherlands	+ 2.76	+ 11.57[a]
Sweden	− 1.00	+ 7.49
United Kingdom	—	+ 8.57
United States	− 7.89	—

SOURCE: IMF, *Annual Report*, 1972, p. 39.
[a] Based on par value in effect prior to May 9, 1971, when these currencies were allowed to float. The changes are relative to the values current prior to December 18, 1971.

world." The assessment of the London *Economist* was more realistic: "The most important point about the new pattern of exchange rates is that it will not last for long."[2] Within six months, the new set of rates came unstuck when the United Kingdom announced that it would allow the pound to float. In *February 1973, the United States devalued the dollar by another 10 percent*, leading Switzerland, Italy, and Japan to resort to (controlled) floating. In March the European Economic Community established what became known as "the snake in the tunnel" by undertaking a joint float of their currencies against the dollar, while limiting fluctuations among the participating currencies within a band of only 2¼ percent.[3] This was, some hoped, a step in the direction of eventual European monetary union.

FLOATING RATES: 1973 ONWARD

The advent of floating exchange rates among the industrial countries revived fears and concerns about whether or not such a system could work. Would some countries resort to the "dirty float" option to attempt to gain some national advantage? Would the other major achievement of the Bretton Woods system—convertibility among the

[2] *The Economist*, Dec. 25, 1971, p. 10.
[3] The United Kingdom, Ireland, and Italy declined to participate in this scheme, so the currencies to be confined within the "tunnel" were those of Belgium–Luxembourg, Denmark, France, Germany, and the Netherlands.

world's major currencies—also fall victim to the collapse? Certainly, the precedent of the 1930s would suggest a very strong likelihood. How would the new system cope with major disturbances?

The remarkable fact is that it has worked, tolerably well, for over a decade. During that first decade there were some substantial shocks to the international economy. The world economy has adjusted to those shocks, assisted to a significant degree by the integrated international financial system.

Perhaps the most notable feat has been the maintenance of convertibility among the major currencies of the world. As we saw in Chapter 26, the breakdown of the gold standard in the 1930s led both to floating *and* to an ever-widening web of exchange controls which lasted for a quarter century. Several factors may help explain the difference between the 1930s and the 1970s.

The international political community, through the medium of the IMF, has developed for itself guidelines of appropriate behavior in a managed float system. Surveillance of that behavior is maintained by the Fund (see Chapter 30).

The leaders of the seven major industrial countries meet annually in a summer summit. The ever-present risks of one country adopting beggar-my-neighbor policies seem to be minimized by the necessity of meeting face to face with the other leaders.

In a similar vein, the central bankers of the "Group of Ten" major IMF countries plus Switzerland meet regularly in Basle at the Bank for International Settlements.

Overall, there appears to be a commitment by the industrial countries to the maintenance of an integrated international economy. The working of a system of floating exchange rates raises some very interesting issues, however.

The First Great Oil Price Increase, 1973

The move to a system of floating exchange rates in mid-1973 was soon to have a severe test. In late 1973, the Organization of Petroleum Exporting Countries (OPEC) announced a fourfold increase in the price of petroleum.

Because of its vital importance as a source of energy and as a widely used raw material, especially in fertilizers and plastics, this exercise of monopoly power confronted most industrial nations, notably Japan and those of western Europe as well as a large part of the less developed world, with massive balance-of-payments problems. The consensus of experts appeared to be that in the year 1974 alone, the oil deficits of importing countries would range from $60 billion upward with corresponding surpluses accruing to OPEC members.

Here we have not merely a disturbance to balance-of-payments equilibrium of a fundamental character, but rather a violent disruption of trade, production, balances of payments, and monetary conditions throughout much of the world. Because of its role as the most important source of energy and as an exceedingly important raw material, the quadrupling of the price of imported oil immeasurably complicated the adjustment problem for practically every country of the world.

The terms of trade change imposed by OPEC created a classic "transfer problem." How could the real resources be released from oil-importing countries and absorbed by the oil-exporting countries? Floating exchange rates could not, of course, protect the industrial countries from such a real phenomenon. Somehow total domestic expenditure in oil-importing nations had to be reduced to conform with their lower real income (see Figure 20.6). Many nations chose, quite reasonably, to make this adjustment gradually, and drew down their assets to pay for their current account balance of payments deficits. The oil-exporting countries initially chose also to accumulate assets rather than spend all their increased income. This massive transfer of assets from oil-importing to oil-exporting countries created the so-called "recycling" problem. As we noted above (pp. 499ff.), the international financial system, especially the Eurocurrency market, played a crucial role in facilitating that transfer of asset ownership and transformation of its structure to that desired by the new owners.

The transition of adjustment to the new terms of trade was reasonably short. Within a couple of years many of the OPEC countries were running balance-of-payments deficits on official reserve transactions (see Table 29.3).

The critical feature of this experience was that the members of the international economy—both oil importers and OPEC members—chose to adjust to the oil price shock rather than to block adjustment. While blocking adjustment cannot work in the end, for no nation can continue to spend in excess of its income permanently, the choice made in the 1970s to avoid trade and payments restrictions was crucial. It would have been relatively easy in the face of the oil-price-induced current account deficits for the industrial countries to have attempted to meet the problem by direct restrictions on nonoil imports. The existence of an effective integrated international financial system made it possible for the industrial countries to choose to adjust gradually, but nevertheless to adjust. The fact that they chose that route led the international economy away from the path of restrictionism that had been chosen in the 1930s.

In the next few years following the great oil price rise of late 1973, OPEC raised its nominal price of oil moderately, but found it was being outpaced by worldwide inflation (Table 29.4). Consequently,

Table 29.3 Selected Oil-Exporting Countries' Net Balance of Payments on Official Reserve Transactions Basis (Millions of SDRs)

	1973	1974	1975	1976	1977	1978	1979	1980
Algeria	489	469	−275	539	−297	74	374	1030
Indonesia	285	573	−1696	541	856	120	1116	1726
Iran	−40	+5842	91	380	2918	n.a.	n.a.	n.a.
Iraq	557	1590	−410	1616	2117	n.a.	n.a.	n.a.
Kuwait	n.a.	n.a.	3180	2778	4176	1913	8608	9446
Libya	398	−824	1446	−1359	963	1663	−356	1987
Nigeria	101	4253	154	−328	−705	−1702	2472	3567
Saudi Arabia	770	8639	7468	3220	2310	−9644	181	3033
Venezuela	511	3715	2217	−13	−132	−1523	748	−17

SOURCE: IMF, *Balance of Payments Statistics.*
NOTES:
1. Lines A through D, including counterpart items, exceptional financing, and changes in foreign authorities' reserves.
2. n.a., not available.

again in 1979, OPEC moved to substantially increase its price. Thus, although by 1981 the industrial countries' CPI level was nearly double that of 1974, the nominal oil price was more than triple that of 1974, representing a further *real* increase of the petroleum price. This presented a new disturbance to the international economy which again faced severe adjustment problems, but this time complicated by an increasingly complex set of capital market and aggregate demand dis-

Table 29.4 Nominal and Real Prices of Crude Petroleum, 1973–1982 (U.S. Dollars per Barrel)

Year	Nominal Price[a] (Average Export Price, Exporting Countries)	CPI, Industrial Countries[b] (1973 = 100)	Real Price in 1973 Dollars
1973	3.22	100.0	3.22
1974	10.49	113.3	9.26
1975	11.03	125.9	8.76
1976	11.73	136.3	8.61
1977	12.82	147.8	8.67
1978	12.83	158.4	8.10
1979	19.08	173.0	11.03
1980	30.91	193.6	15.97
1981	34.31	212.9	16.12
1982	33.30	229.5[c]	14.51

[a] IMF, *World Economic Outlook,* April 1982.
[b] IMF, *International Financial Statistics.*
[c] Derived from the average price increase in the first three quarters of 1982.

turbances. This time OPEC had gone too far to retain internal agreement. Eventually in the summer of 1982, OPEC's control over prices and production began to crumble, and in 1983 the OPEC's control over the world price of petroleum fell apart completely.

Real Exchange Rates and Purchasing Power Parity

With floating exchange rates of the 1970s it soon became apparent, as it had in the 1920s and 1930s when exchange rates had floated, that nominal exchange rates held little meaning when both price levels and exchange rates are changing. Two issues emerge. The first concerns what is happening to the price of foreign exchange relative to the domestic price levels between any two countries. A second issue, to be considered in the next section, concerns what happens to the value of the home currency relative to all other currencies. The first is generally referred to as the *real* exchange rate, and the second as the *effective* exchange rate. The point of the *real* exchange rate is readily seen in the following example.

Assume that the exchange rate with a major trading partner rises by 20 percent over the course of a year. To evaluate the significance of this we also want to know what has happened to the domestic price level in the home country relative to the trading partner. If the price level of the home country has risen by 15 percent more than in the trading partner, we would be able to say that the *real* price of foreign exchange has risen relative to that trading partner.

To make this comparison we construct an index of the real relative price of foreign exchange, or the real exchange rate for short. In symbols, where we use I to represent an index of the current period relative to some base period, the superscript prime (') to represent the foreign country; and where r is the index of the price of foreign exchange and P is the domestic price index,

$$\text{real exchange rate index} = \frac{Ir}{IP/IP'} \cdot 100$$

Consider a numerical example showing the real exchange rate index. Let the home country be the United States, the foreign country Britain. In the base period the exchange rate of U.S.\$/£ was \$2.00/1£. In the current period the exchange rate is \$1.75/1£. The exchange rate index is

$$Ir = \frac{1.75}{2.00} \cdot 100 = 87.5$$

The U.S. price index in the current period relative to 100 at the base period is

$$IP = 110$$

The British price index in the current period, relative to the same base period as in the United States is

$$IP' = 145$$

The result is

$$\text{real exchange rate index} = \frac{87.5}{110/145} = 115.34$$

In other words, even though the dollar price of pounds has fallen, it has not fallen by as much as the British prices have risen relative to American prices. As a consequence the *real* exchange rate of dollars per pound has risen by just over 15 percent.

Recognition that domestic price levels change at different rates in different nations led to the development of the purchasing power parity concept. In the years following World War I, there was need for a simple workable rule of thumb to determine appropriate levels of exchange rates after the war. Trade had been disrupted, inflation had proceeded at widely different rates in different countries, and innumerable restrictions had been placed on trade. Clearly, a return to the prewar exchange rates would have been impossible. A new set of rates could be established on the basis of calculations of relative degrees of inflation, claimed Gustav Cassel of Sweden.

Cassel's proposal was to choose the exchange rate that would exactly compensate for the differential inflation in the intervening years. While he did not put it in these terms, the essential point of the proposal may be interpreted in terms of the real exchange rate index: The "purchasing power parity" exchange rate would be the exchange rate that makes the real exchange rate index exactly equal to 100. In other words, the purchasing power parity exchange rate at time t ($PPPr_t$) would be

$$PPPr_t = \frac{PI}{PI'} \cdot r_0$$

where the price indexes also refer to time t and use time zero as the base period.

Two practical difficulties are evident. First there is the problem of selecting an appropriate base year. If one is attempting to restore a situation of equilibrium, the base year should be one of equilibrium. Second, what is the appropriate index to use? If only export and import prices are included, the purchasing power parity index calculation would be a mere truism since changes in international prices (allowing for changes in transport charges and tariffs) must be the same in related markets. The prices of nontraded goods obviously affect the relative attractiveness of traded goods. Hence a broadly inclusive price index is desirable.

More than statistical problems have confronted the purchasing power parity approach to exchange rates. The heart of the matter is whether real or monetary forces dominate in the determination of exchange rates. In earlier chapters, we saw in a simple monetary model that a monetary disturbance would alter exchange rates and price levels by the same proportion and thus the purchasing power parity prediction would apply. However, once we introduce capital flows into our model, even that simple prediction need no longer apply. Further, if we take into account such real disturbances as might lead to terms of trade changes, we recognize that there is more to exchange rate determination than absolute price levels. These considerations suggest that the principal case where purchasing power parity could be expected to work would be in a situation of hyperinflation, but that in other, more normal situations, the presence of other nonmonetary disturbances is likely to mean that the purchasing power parity calculation will not be very useful. The first point is borne out by the evidence concerning prices and exchange rates in the early 1920s, when exchange rates were flexible, Jacob Frenkel has found.[4]

The second point is supported in a variety of studies of the floating rate period from 1973. Hans Genberg, for example, found that during the early years of generalized floating after 1973, short-run variations in exchange rates did not match relative price-level movements.[5]

Effective Exchange Rates

The widespread use of floating exchange rates also raises an interesting conceptual issue. When the currencies of some countries are rising, and those of others falling, can we say anything about the relative movement of any one currency? The issue is readily seen in Figure 29.1, where hypothetical exchange rates among the U.S. dollar, the

---

[4] J. A. Frenkel, "Purchasing Power Parity: Doctrinal Perspective and Evidence from the 1920's," *Journal of International Economics*, **8**, No. 2, 169–91 (May 1978). This number of the journal contains a symposium on purchasing power parity.

[5] H. Genberg, "Purchasing Power Parity Under Fixed and Flexible Exchange Rates," *Journal of International Economics*, **8**, No. 2, 247–76 (May 1978).

Figure 29.1   Effective Exchange Rate Problem

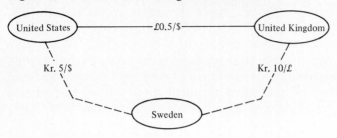

Panel 1. Initial Situation.

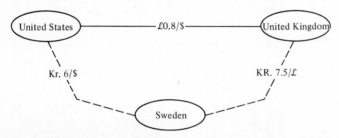

Panel 2. Subsequent Situation.

pound sterling, and the Swedish krona are set out. In the initial situation all three rates are consistent with each other, so there is no opportunity for arbitrage (see Chapter 21). Consider the issue of how Sweden quotes its "exchange rate." Under a fixed exchange rate regime it matters not whether the rate quoted is kr/$ or kr/£. If Sweden were to change its exchange rate it would do so equiproportionately in terms of dollars or pounds. Thus a 10 percent increase in the krona price of foreign exchange raises the kr/$ rate and the kr/£ rate by 10 percent each. It is possible to say unambiguously that Sweden has devalued, and by how much: 10 percent. Now consider what can happen under floating rates. Suppose that the krona price of a U.S. dollar rises, but meanwhile the pound price of a U.S. dollar is appreciating even more relative to the pound. To remain consistent, the krona price of a pound must fall. Once cross rates are consistent again, we can then ask: Has the Swedish krona depreciated or appreciated?

The answer clearly depends on how "important" the two exchange rates are. If Sweden had no economic relationships with the United Kingdom, she could safely ignore the change in the krona price of a pound. In this case, as in most cases, however, some form of average must be devised to indicate what is happening to the foreign exchange rate. That average has come to be referred to as an *effective exchange rate.*[6]

More formally, we may state the effective exchange rate index is a weighted average of the relevant exchange rate indexes. Thus where w_i refers to the weight of a particular exchange rate in the index and Ir_i is the index of the exchange rate i,

$$\text{effective exchange rate index} = \Sigma_i w_i(Ir_i) \cdot 100$$

Return to the example of Figure 29.1. The krona/dollar index is (kr 6/$)/(kr 5/$) × 100 = 120. The krona/pound index is (kr 7.5/£)/(kr 10/£) × 100 = 75. Suppose that we assign a weight of $2/3$ to the krona/dollar rate and $1/3$ to the krona/pound rate. Then the effective exchange rate index in the new situation is

$$\text{EERI} = (0.667)(120) + (0.333)(75) = 105$$

In other words, the effective krona price of foreign exchange has risen. Note, however, that had the weights been reversed, the conclusion would also have been reversed.

The last observation points out how critical the weights can be. As with any index number problem, there is no such thing as a "perfect" set of weights. One possible set of weights, to continue our example, could be the importance of each of the United States and the United Kingdom in Sweden's trade and investment flows. That, however, could leave out the effects that changes in exchange rates of Sweden's competitors might have. Thus the yen/dollar rate could readily affect Sweden's competitive position in steel in the U.S. market, while the Canadian dollar/pound rate could affect Sweden's competitive position in forest products in the United Kingdom.

The latter considerations led the IMF to devise a *multilateral* set of weights using a model of multilateral international trade and payments. This set of weights from the multilateral exchange rate model (MERM) is now widely used for computing effective exchange rates. The result for the seven major industrial countries is reported in Table 29.5.

Note, however, that in particular situations, the MERM may *not* provide the appropriate set of weights. For example, the 8 percent rise in the U.S. dollar/Canadian dollar exchange rate in early 1982 could have a significant affect on U.S.–Canadian trade and payments. Yet the relatively small weight of this trade in the global trade picture

---

[6] This is not to be confused with other concepts that had previously employed the term "effective exchange rate," for example, in the series *Foreign Trade Regimes and Economic Development*, op. cit.

Table 29.5 Effective Exchange Rate Index (Average Exchange Rate, 1975 = 100)

	1970	1971	1972	1973	1974	1975	1976	1977	1978	1979	1980	1981	1982
United States	83.9	86.1	92.8	101.2	98.9	100.0	95.1	95.5	104.5	106.7	106.5	94.6	84.7
Canada	95.1	92.8	93.8	98.6	95.4	100.0	94.2	102.0	113.9	118.6	118.3	115.1	112.9
United Kingdom	77.6	77.6	80.8	89.8	92.3	100.0	116.8	123.2	122.7	114.7	104.1	105.4	110.5
France	110.0	112.1	109.1	103.8	110.5	100.0	104.6	109.5	109.5	107.1	105.9	118.5	130.4
Italy	77.6	78.1	78.9	87.2	96.2	100.0	121.5	132.5	140.8	144.1	148.8	171.5	185.5
West Germany	127.4	123.5	120.5	108.1	102.0	100.0	95.4	88.5	83.3	78.4	77.6	83.8	80.5
Japan	107.5	105.7	95.4	90.1	96.4	100.0	96.0	86.8	70.6	76.0	79.1	70.0	74.2

SOURCE: IMF, *International Financial Statistics*.
NOTE: The index is EERI defined in the text. A rise in the index reflects a rise in the average price of foreign exchange. This is the inverse of the rate reported by the IMF.

meant that the MERM weights would understate the effect of this change for both Canada and the United States (but probably not for Europe).

Optimum Currency Areas

Flexible exchange rates have been adopted by several countries. This system has a great deal to recommend it. Perhaps most important in the complex world of international financial transactions, the foreign exchange market itself is the most efficient means for bringing international payments and receipts into balance. Policy makers are able to employ fiscal and monetary policies primarily to achieve internal balance, while external balance can be achieved by the exchange rate.

The applicability of the flexible exchange rate does not, however, necessarily extend to *every* currency or political unit in the world. Such an extreme would mean that Mauritius, with an area of 720 square miles and population of less than 1 million, would have its exchange rate floating against the rest of the world. And if an independently floating currency provided a simple solution to balance-of-payments problems, why should not regions within a nation, such as West Virginia or Newfoundland, which have encountered frequent and severe regional payments difficulties, establish independent monetary systems with floating exchange rates? The extent to which currencies should be independent, with flexible exchange rates, is a matter of degree. The question at issues is: What is an optimum currency area?

One clue to an answer is provided by considering the relative ease of adjustment among the various regions of a single country. Adjustment among the regions of a single country is made relatively easy, first, by a high degree of factor mobility. If a region is a part of a well-integrated nationwide capital market, a disturbance to its balance of payments calls into play accommodating capital movements that make unnecessary any loss of bank reserves and thus a multiple contraction of the money supply, with consequent deflation. If labor is also free to move, any unemployment caused by the adjustment process can be moderated by migration from deficit to surplus regions.

A second characteristic of a region within a nation that contributes to ease of adjustment is that the entire country is ruled by a common government whose policies can be used to soften the impact of a local balance-of-payments disturbance. Public expenditures can be directed by the national government to combat unemployment in local areas, and national unemployment insurance provides central funds for local use. Moreover, if adjustment causes regional income to fall, both personal and corporation income tax payments to the central government fall, reducing the size of any balance-of-payments deficit.

Factor Mobility   The first of these—factor mobility—suggests that a single currency area should be limited to one within which that mobility is high. But this condition holds true of most nations; labor and capital generally move more freely within a nation than internationally. Moreover, since national policies blanket an entire nation, even if factor mobility were low between two regions, such policies as have been mentioned, and monetary policy, too, can be used to offset regional payments difficulties. Thus consider two regions, I and II: If demand in I shifts away from II, causing unemployment and downward pressure on prices in II, monetary expansion, although causing inflation in I, would ease II's problem. If II were a relatively small region economically speaking, the amount of inflation in I could be mild. This line of argument takes us back to our starting point: An optimum currency area is the existing nation-state! If its capital market is not well integrated, or if labor mobility is limited, these shortcomings could be corrected by institutional changes or income transfers, which would be less formidable tasks than dividing the country in two.[7]

Dependence on Trade   But there is another aspect of a region's economy that has a vital bearing on whether it would benefit from monetary independence and flexible exchange rates. This is its degree of openness, or dependence on trade.[8] A good measure of this is the ratio of its production of tradeable goods (exportables and importables) to nontradeables. If this ratio is high, an adverse change in international payments will drive up the exchange rate, raise domestic prices of exportables and importables, and, by shifting demand onto nontradeables, quickly raise their prices, too. The increase in production and the decrease in consumption of exportables and importables, which is required to improve the trade balance, will be minimal. In the extreme case, when all production consists of these goods, the internal price level would rise in step with the exchange rate, and the latter would make no contribution to improving the trade balance.

If, on the other hand, the ratio of tradeables to nontradeables is low, a rise in the exchange rate would affect directly the prices of but a small proportion of total output. The prices of nontradeables would therefore be but little influenced by the induced shift in demand. The rise in the price of tradeables would stimulate increased production

---

[7] Factor mobility as an aspect of an optimum currency area has been developed most fully by Robert A. Mundell, "A Theory of Optimum Currency Areas," *American Economic Review*, **53** (Sept. 1963).

[8] This aspect of an optimum currency area was noted and discussed by R. I. McKinnon, "Optimum Currency Areas," *American Economic Review*, **53** (Sept. 1963).

and reduced domestic consumption and thus improve the trade balance. In sum, "if we move across the spectrum from closed to open economies, flexible exchange rates become both less effective as a control device for external balance and more damaging to internal price-level stability."[9]

Such price repercussions of flexible exchange rates could have significant monetary implications. This would be true for a nation heavily dependent on foreign trade and subject to frequent balance-of-payments disturbances. For the value of money as a liquid asset results from its acceptance as a medium of exchange and its usefulness as a store of value. But that acceptance and usefulness are diminished if the domestic price level is unstable. Nationals might prefer to hold, even for transactions purposes, a currency that was more stable in value. This would create a capital outflow when, with an adverse international payments condition, a capital inflow would be helpful. For such a country, it would be better to peg its currency to that of a stronger (less open) country. If it were permanently pegged at an absolutely fixed exchange rate (with no "band" for fluctuations whatever), it would in effect become part of the latter country's currency.

How dependent on trade can a nation be and still benefit from allowing its currency to float freely? This is a question that can perhaps be answered only by trial and error. The United States, with its exports and imports together amounting to about 20 percent of its gross national product, is an obvious candidate. Canada's experience with floating its dollar from 1950 to 1962 and again since 1970 has on the whole been satisfactory, yet the sum of its exports and imports amount to over 55 percent of gross national product.

The concept of an optimum currency area suggests that some countries (or other units) should be linked by rigidly fixed exchange rates, or even a common currency, while between others the exchange rate should carry a significant portion of the adjustment process. A common currency would be most desirable when:

1. The degree of factor mobility among the participants is high.
2. The degree of intra-area trade is high, and the extra-area trade is low, as a proportion of GNP.

These characteristics clearly apply to the United States and similarly to other federated countries. Do they apply equally to some of the

[9] Ibid., p. 719.

recently formed economic unions such as the EEC? A partial answer comes from the experience of the European Monetary System.

The European Monetary System

With the advent of widespread use of floating exchange rates, several of the countries of Europe sought to establish a zone of monetary stability among themselves. Initially, this took the form of a scheme for narrowing the margins of fluctuations among the currencies. It involved not only the members of the EEC (except the United Kingdom) but also Austria, Switzerland, Norway, and Sweden. This joint-float arrangement was relatively short-lived, losing member after member as some found themselves either unwilling or unable to employ the complementary monetary and fiscal policies necessary to stay within the group.

In the later 1970s, the so-called "snake" was down to only five of the EEC countries plus Norway. The EEC then sought once again to create its own monetary system. In March 1979, the EMS was launched by all of the then members except Britain.

The arrangement consists of three parts:

1. *The ECU*. At the center of the system is the European Currency Unit, an ECU, which is also the name of an ancient French silver coin. The ECU is the numéraire of the system, consisting of a certain number of units of each currency.
2. *The exchange rate system*. Each currency is pegged to the ECU with a range of variation of ±2.25 percent permitted. This means that the members are maintaining the values of their currencies vis-à-vis other members, but not relative to those outside the EMS. When the limits are approached by a specified amount, all members are required to intervene, while the country itself is to institute complementary monetary and other policies to defend the fixed parity.
3. *Credit facilities*. To assist in the maintenance of the fixed parities, the EMS has a variety of loan arrangements among its members which provide for substantial amounts of automatic credit. Ultimately, the EMS intends to establish a European Monetary Fund.

The motives of the Europeans in establishing the EMS are by no means uniform among the participants. Nevertheless, one can detect in the statements of the various European commentators a belief in the value of stable exchange rates, and the discipline that such rates would provide national policymakers.

The record in the first few years has not borne out the hopes of the proponents. Periodic currency realignments have been necessary.

CONCLUSION

The international monetary system in the postwar period was built on two major foundations: fixed exchange rates and convertibility of currencies. When the former collapsed, it was replaced by a system of floating exchange rates that enabled the system to retain convertibility despite major international financial disturbances.

The system of floating exchange rates poses for each country the question of whether or not to fix its exchange rate—and if so to what— or to float—and if so alone or jointly. To formulate an appropriate answer requires an understanding of what is an optimum currency area. The actual sorting out of which countries should float and which should fix their exchange rates continues.

The transformation of the international monetary system has brought about significant changes in one of the major institutions, the International Monetary Fund. Its current role and functioning are the subject of the next chapter.

SELECTED REFERENCES

COHEN, B. J. *The European Monetary System: An Outsider's View*, Essays in International Finance No. 142. Princeton, N.J.: International Finance Section, Princeton University, 1981. A useful outline of the principal features and evaluation of the EMS.

KATSELI-PAPAEFSTRATIOU, L. T. *The Reemergence of the Purchasing Power Parity Doctrine in the 1970's*, Special Papers in International Economics No. 13. Princeton, N.J.: International Finance Section, Princeton University, 1979. Examines competing interpretations and evidence on PPP.

McKINNON, R. I. *Money in International Exchange: The Convertible Currency System*. New York: Oxford University Press, 1979. Chapter 8 reviews fluctuating exchange rates 1973–1978, and Chapter 10 examines monetary unions and fixed exchange rates.

OFFICER, L. H. "The Purchasing Power-Parity Theory of Exchange Rates: A Review Article." *IMF Staff Papers*, **23**, No. 1 (Mar. 1976). A comprehensive survey of the literature.

RHOMBERG, R. R. "Indices of Effective Exchange Rates." *IMF Staff Papers*, **23**, No. 1 (Mar. 1976). Examines and compares several types of indices of effective exchange rates.

TOWER, E., and T. D. WILLETT. *The Theory of Optimum Currency Areas and Exchange-Rate Flexibility*, Special Papers in International Economics No. 11. Princeton, N.J.: International Finance Section, Princeton University, 1976. Develops a comprehensive framework for identifying optimum currency areas.

TREZISE, P. H., ed. *The European Monetary System: Its Promise and Prospects*. Washington, D.C.: The Brookings Institution, 1979. Papers by both officials and academics on the creation of the EMS.

30
CHAPTER

The IMF and the International Monetary System

The establishment of the IMF put in place what has proved to be one of the most durable and adaptable international institutions ever. Despite the collapse of the system created at Bretton Woods, the Fund, which had been designed as the centerpiece of the Bretton Woods system, still plays a significant role in the international financial world.

The IMF retains as its principal objective the creation and maintenance of an open system of international trade and payments. Members are now free to choose an appropriate exchange rate arrangement; the principal bases for determining a member's "good conduct" is the degree of exchange restrictions employed. As a consequence a wide variety of exchange rate arrangements exist; most countries continue to peg, but many float, and others are on a crawling peg.[1]

To maintain the open system of international trade and payments, the Fund provides balance of payments assistance to its members, but it does so only with conditions attached. Members of the Fund are required to follow rules of good behavior that proscribe trade and payments restrictions. The basic assistance available from the Fund was found to be insufficient for the size of the balance-of-payments

---

[1] In early 1982 some ninety-three members pegged their currencies, four employed a crawling peg, eight made up the EMS, and the remaining thirty-eight were either floating or, as the IMF put it, "cannot be properly classified under other categories." Among those pegging by far the largest single group, some thirty-eight, continued to peg to the U.S. dollar, and thirteen francophone countries of Africa pegged to the French franc, while some thirty-seven chose a composite basket to peg against, the most popular basket being the SDR (some fifteen members).

problems facing members. Imaginative new policy initiatives led to the expansion of Fund resources and the creation of a new reserve asset called the SDR. These developments meant a growth in the power of the IMF, and inevitably led to debate over whether or not the Fund is evenhanded in dealings with its members. In this chapter we examine these issues to understand better the role of the IMF in the international economy.

ORGANIZATION AND FUNCTIONING

The International Monetary Fund is formed by over 140 members. The membership includes all the industrial countries (except Switzerland), most developing countries, and some of the communist countries (but not the USSR).

Each member has a quota that establishes how much it has to pay into the fund, its rights to draw from the fund, and its voting power in the organization. The basis for the quota initially included national income, reserves, import volume, export variability, and the share of exports in national income. Over the years since the initial quota distribution, reviews of quotas have resulted in changes in the weights and the absolute size of quotas.

Typical quotas established for December 1980 are illustrated by the following distribution (percent of total):

Afghanistan	0.11%
Canada	3.41%
France	4.83%
Germany	5.43%
Grenada	0.01%
India	2.88%
Japan	4.17%
Mexico	1.35%
United Kingdom	7.36%
United States	21.15%

Each member pays a subscription equal to the quota assigned to it. Initially, the quota had to be paid 25 percent in gold and 75 percent in the member's own currency. The 25 percent portion is now paid in SDRs (an IMF—created reserve asset, explained on pp. 535ff.). The total value of the resources immediately available to the Fund is almost 60 billion SDRs (or nearly U.S. $70 billion at 1982 exchange rates).

Assistance to Members

To assist countries in maintaining or restoring convertibility, the Fund offers a wide variety of assistance. The various "facilities" under which the Fund makes available its assistance differ on the basis of source of the balance-of-payments problem facing the country, and in the degree of conditionality associated with the assistance.

The original arrangement, which still constitutes a major portion of Fund assistance, involves a member country drawing from the Fund on the basis of the member's quota. The drawings are thought of as five equal slices or "tranches" each amounting to 25 percent of the member's quota. The total available under this regular facility thus amounts to 125 percent of the member's quota. A member is able to draw the first "reserve" tranche without any restriction whatsoever. This amounts to the right to draw on the member's own contribution of gold or convertible currencies. Beyond that, however, drawings on the four remaining credit tranches become increasingly restrictive. For the initial credit tranche the member is expected to show reasonable efforts to overcome the balance-of-payments problem. The upper credit tranches require more elaborate undertakings by the member in the form of a stabilization program. The member undertakes to meet certain performance criteria, including credit policy, government borrowing, and external debt. The restrictiveness of these conditions is one of the principal sources of friction between the Fund and its members, yet it constitutes the principal leverage the Fund has on its members to correct the problems that led to the need for drawing.

Usually, a member does not draw outright on the Fund, but instead arranges a standby drawing. This gives the member the ability to draw up to a predetermined amount without further review of its policies, as long as it can demonstrate that it has met the conditions initially agreed upon. It is now possible to have a standby arrangement for up to three years.

A member is obligated to repay its credit tranche drawings from the Fund. Such repayments must begin after three years, and by eight quarterly installments the drawing is fully repaid five years after drawing.

In addition to the ordinary facility, the Fund has developed a variety of other facilities. One group provides credit *in addition to* the regular facility, principally on the basis of some special reason for a balance of payments difficulty. Thus the Compensatory Financing Facility is designed to assist members that have balance-of-payments difficulties arising from export shortfalls. Since such drawings are due to problems that are deemed beyond a member's control, conditions are not severe, beyond establishing the fact of the shortfall. This facility is used largely by developing countries that experience large swings in the prices of their primary product exports.

In part to help members organize schemes that might dampen fluctuations in primary product prices, the Fund established a Buffer Stock Financing Facility in 1969. This enables a member to draw additional resources to participate in approved buffer stock schemes.

A further facility that provided additional credit to members was the temporary oil facility established for 1974 and 1975 to permit members to cope with the great oil price increase of 1973–1974. The total credit provided under this facility at its peak was over half of total drawings on the Fund.

Another additional facility is the Extended Facility, introduced in 1974, to permit a member country to map out a long-term solution to its balance-of-payments problems and to obtain credit for considerably longer term: Repayment begins four and one half years after drawings and is completed ten years after.

In recognition of the fact that some members have had balance-of-payments problems that were large in relation to their quotas, the Fund developed ways of providing supplementary finance. In 1981 this was embodied in the Enlarged Access Policy. It is now possible for a member's cumulative access to the Fund to be up to 600 percent of quota.

These various sources of assistance to Fund members have been used in varying degrees. The changing patterns of use are sketched in Figure 30.1.

The fund charges its members for the credit it provides. There is a basic service charge on all transactions, a commitment fee for standby arrangements, and interest on outstanding credit. The interest rate in 1981–1982 was fixed at 6.25 percent per annum, except for the enlarged access policy, which is financed by Fund borrowing and a floating rate reflecting the borrowing cost is charged.

Conditionality

The idea that a member would have to follow certain policies and meet certain quantitative indicator criteria in order to gain access to Fund credit was not embodied in the original articles of agreement of the Fund. The conditionality approach arose from the effort to establish the revolving nature of the Fund's resources. The drawings on the Fund would have to be temporary, and some means would have to be found to ensure that characteristic. If during the temporary period of a drawing nothing had been accomplished to correct the need for the drawing, the requirement to repay would leave the member country in a difficult position. The logic of conditionality, therefore, was to ensure

Figure 30.1   Use of the Fund's Resources as at April 30, 1971–1981 in Billions of SDRs (from IMF, *Annual Report*, 1981, p. 83)

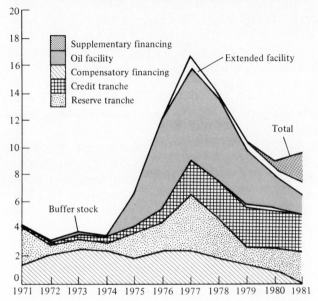

that when the time for repayment had arrived, the need for the drawing would have disappeared because the country had adopted a practical program of policy action. As it evolved, conditionality became directly related to the size of the drawing on the Fund.

Conditionality involves the Fund in influencing domestic policy in the member country, and consequently raises significant concerns by the drawing countries. The implication that balance-of-payments difficulties are attributable to "mismanagement" is difficult for any sovereign country to admit or accept. This basic difficulty is exacerbated by the fact that typical programs contain policy measures designed to control the growth of nominal aggregate demand. Further, the tradition emerged that a program had to be precise and specific, thereby making compliance measurable. The attainment of specific performance criteria became the basis for judging the appropriateness of national policies, and ultimately failure to meet certain criteria could automatically interrupt a member's drawings from the Fund.

The specific nature of the performance criteria is aptly illustrated by the Fund's agreement with Mexico in December 1982 to provide a total of SDR 3.6 billion over three years in support of the Mexican government's economic program.[2]

[2] Details reported in *IMF Survey*, **12** (Jan. 10, 1983).

The highlights of the agreed program involved:

1. Reduction of the public sector deficit from the equivalent of 16.5 percent of GDP in 1982 to 3.5 percent in 1985.
2. Reduction of the rate of inflation from the range of 90 to 100 percent during 1982 to about 55 percent during 1983 and to lower levels in succeeding years.
3. Application of an incomes policy.

The Mexican authorities made substantial concessions to obtain the assistance of the Fund.

The Fund's attitude is that collaboration between the Fund and the member is good for the member because it helps the member develop a comprehensive program of action. This, in turn, assists the member in gaining access to international capital markets. Furthermore, technical and financial assistance from the Fund encourages donors to provide funds to aid receiving countries.

Regulation of Members' Behavior

Beyond providing access to funds to assist in overcoming balance of payments difficulties, the IMF Agreement places certain obligations of good behavior on its members. First and foremost, as we noted in Chapter 28, the Fund outlawed the introduction of new exchange restrictions, and required members to consult annually with the Fund on remaining exchange controls. This provided the Fund with an opportunity to examine a wide range of the member's policies on the grounds that they were relevant to determining whether or not it might be feasible to remove the restrictions.

Even as more countries established full external convertibility of their currencies, the Fund continued the practice of annual consultations, but in the cases of countries adhering to the commitment to convertibility, the Funds makes no judgment about the members' policies.

The results of the consultation become "decisions" of the Executive Directors of the Fund. A sample is reproduced in Table 30.1. As the reader can appreciate, the detailed way in which the Fund comments on the economic policies of a member certainly makes the member think twice about those policies that are drawing fire. Further, the process of regular consultation gives a basis for understanding between the Fund and a member should the need arise for drawing on the Fund. To the extent that the consultation is successful in early detection of problems and leading to corrective action, the consultation process may contribute to the improvement of the economic performance of the member countries.

Table 30.1 Sample Consultation Result

An actual conclusion (omitting the name of the member) on a recent Article IV consultation was as follows:

Executive Directors have congratulated the . . . authorities on the success of their stabilization efforts, which in the past two years have led to a marked improvement in the balance of payments and to a lowering of the underlying rate of inflation; while allowing a level of economic growth higher than the average for (similarly placed) countries. This remarkable success was seen as largely reflecting the adoption of exchange rate and interest rate policies directed at improving competitiveness and restoring the relative attractiveness of domestic financial assets. The moderation of wage increases and a strong increase in the private savings ratio were seen as important and successful contributing forces.

    The Directors were gratified that the stabilization effort has laid the basis for a more sustained rate of growth, and they encouraged the authorities in their efforts to promote a further recovery of investment. Taking into account the recent deterioration in the external current account and in the overall balance of payments, it was important, in the view of Directors, that the exchange rate remain competitive and that interest rates be maintained at levels adequate to attract continued inflows of workers' remittances and foreign capital and to mobilize an increasing volume of domestic savings.

    Many Directors observed that the situation of public finances, including the unsustainably high public sector deficit as a ratio of GNP, continued to be a cause of concern. They welcomed the efforts currently being made by the authorities to bring about a more equitable distribution of the tax burden, to reduce tax evasion, and to improve productivity in the public enterprise sector. They also stressed the importance of tightening controls over expenditures, especially the social security system, and the local authorities, and of pursuing appropriate pricing policies, particularly in the public enterprise sector and in the energy field, in order to contain the growth of subsidies. Furthermore, they emphasize the importance of increasing the nonmonetary financing of the budget deficit.

    Most Executive Directors felt that the authorities' goal of reducing inflation would require a somewhat tighter stance of financial policies. In this respect, concern was expressed about the rapid growth of domestic bank credit in recent months, which was regarded as excessive, and the Directors welcomed the authorities' intentions to keep close scrutiny of policies in this area.

    Directors expressed satisfaction with the recent measure to liberalize the trade and payments system and the hope that further steps in that direction would be taken.

    Finally, Executive Directors expressed their gratification concerning the very positive and fruitful relationship between . . . and the Fund and their confidence that this collaboration will continue to strengthen in view of the medium-term aspects of . . . economic strategy.

SOURCE: *Finance and Development*, **18**, No. 4, p. 16 (Dec. 1981).

Nevertheless, one should not attribute too much to the consultative process. Most member governments are entirely aware of the policies they are following and the consequences that flow from those policies. Their unwillingness to take the steps recommended by the Fund is attributable to their unwillingness to accept the political consequences of the proposed policies.

    The other major power of the IMF to regulate its members' behavior was in the area of exchange rate par values. The Fund Agreement imposed on members an obligation to select and maintain a par value exchange rate, and to hold the rate to that value plus or minus 1 percent. The memories of the chaotic exchange rates of the 1930s were a powerful influence on the founders of the IMF. The Fund would create some discipline in the setting of exchange rates, by restricting members from changing their rates except to deal with "fundamental disequilibrium." Further, if the proposed change were large (more than 10 percent), the advance approval of the Fund should be obtained. At the same time the Fund staff would make it clear when an exchange rate adjustment was considered desirable.

The Fund's experience with adjustment of exchange rate par values proved to be difficult. Repeatedly crises were associated with dramatic and hurried consultations of varying degrees of effectiveness and influence by the IMF. In the end the collapse of the par value system in 1973 left the Fund without any role in setting exchange rates. This proved to be something of a godsend for the Fund as an institution because it permitted the emergence of an alternative role for the Fund, and one that could be played more effectively by the Fund.

From the collapse of the Bretton Woods system in 1973, there emerged a renewed sense of need for international financial collaboration among the major industrial nations. Further, it became clear that the floating rate system required, to some degree, "management," and that the Fund was the only global authority capable of undertaking such a role. The Articles of the Fund Agreement, consequently, were amended, effective April 1, 1978. The amendment both legalized the *de facto* floating exchange rate system and assigned to the Fund the task to "exercise firm surveillance over the exchange rate policies of members."

In setting up its surveillance arrangements,[3] the Fund enunciated three principles a member is expected to follow.

1. Avoid manipulating exchange rates to prevent balance-of-payments adjustment or to gain an unfair competitive advantage over other members.
2. Intervene in the exchange market where necessary to counter disorderly conditions.
3. Take into account the interests of other countries.

The consultative mechanism is the vehicle whereby the Fund carries out its surveillance. So far the experience with the system of surveillance has been remarkably free of serious problems.

[3] "Surveillance over Exchange Rates," Appendix II in *Annual Report of the Executive Directors for the Fiscal Year Ended April 30, 1977.* (Washington, D.C.: International Monetary Fund, 1977).

THE NEED FOR GREATER LIQUIDITY AND THE SDR

The decade of the 1960s was characterized by active and sometimes heated discussion of the need for reform of the international monetary system and of means of achieving it. A landmark in this discussion was Robert Triffin's book, *Gold and the Dollar Crisis*,[4] which stressed the inherent instability of the gold-exchange standard and predicted its collapse. In his program for reform, he saw the principal need to be the provision of an acceptable and internationally controlled reserve money. To fill this role, he suggested the use of deposits with the IMF, which would replace national currencies and perhaps eventually also gold. Triffin's plan would have preserved the Bretton Woods system essentially intact in other respects, with fixed, although occasionally changeable, exchange rates.

Sharply in contrast to Triffin's insistence that an international money displace national currencies among reserve assets is the proposal, made during the mid-1960s, that the dollar standard be made official, with gold forced into a role of relative unimportance. This result could be achieved, according to the proposal of Emile Despres, if the United States stood ready to sell gold without limit in defense of the dollar and strictly limited its purchases at the official $35 price. The United States would also make additional dollar reserves available through lines of credit.[5]

Some economists, most notably Jacques Rueff of France, took quite a different position, advocating a return to a true gold standard. This would have required raising the price of gold sufficiently to make existing gold reserves adequate in money value for the world's needs.

Much of the debate was overtaken by events in the 1970s as the Bretton Woods system crumbled and was replaced by the mixed system of floating major currencies. Nevertheless, the emergence of the new international monetary system was not without difficulty, and required the attention of the international community in general and the IMF in particular. Furthermore, not all the problems of the system were yet solved. In the early 1980s, the system continued to face the long-standing problem of capital flows and had to face a problem that had not been present in the 1930s: worldwide inflation.

To give the reader a sense of how the system coped with and adjusted to the unfolding events, it is useful to review the emergence

---

[4] New Haven, Conn.: Yale University Press, 1960.

[5] See the statement by Emile Despres in *New Approach to United States International Economic Policy*, Hearings Before the Subcommittee on International Exchange and Payments of the Joint Economic Committee, 89th Congress, 2nd sess., Washington, D.C., 1966; reprinted in L. D. Officer and T. D. Willett, eds., *The International Monetary System* (Englewood Cliffs, N.J.: Prentice-Hall, Inc., 1969).

and subsequent evolution of the Special Drawing Right created by the IMF in 1969.

During the first decade of general convertibility of European currencies, there emerged a concern over the adequacy of the resources available to IMF members in relation to the potential total calls on those resources from members to finance temporary payments disequilibria. Countries need to have adequate reserves to permit maintenance of currency convertibility while adjusting to a balance-of-payments disturbance. Failure to ensure adequate reserves, then, could result in a reversion of the system to a plethora of controls.

One avenue available to an individual country to increase its reserves would be to accumulate foreign exchange reserves by running balance-of-payments surpluses. Such an approach, however, would work for the system only if the corresponding deficit country were a reserve currency such as the United States. A surplus in one country with the corresponding deficit in another, nonreserve currency, country would merely redistribute reserves. If the system as a whole were to run a surplus vis-à-vis the United States, the rest of the system would be giving up real goods, services, and assets, net, in exchange for American money to hold. Needless to say, such a solution did not appeal to many countries who regarded the rate of return on holding U.S. dollars in their reserves as inadequate compensation for the real goods, services, and assets forgone. Furthermore, such an approach placed the expansion of reserves on a tenuous basis should the United States—as was widely believed at the time—soon eliminate its deficit with the rest of the world.

An alternative to the growth of reserve currencies was to rely on the traditional reserve asset, gold. However, it is impossible to ensure that the quantity of gold could increase at a rate appropriate to the world's need for additional reserves. Consequently, the possibility of increasing the *value* of gold was embodied in the Bretton Woods agreement. It would have been a simple uniform devaluation of all currencies vis-à-vis gold; leaving the relative values among individual currencies unchanged. However, this solution was never tried, largely because the system that did emerge in the second half of the twentieth century was a gold plus currency reserve system rather than a pure gold reserve system. A uniform devaluation of all currencies would mean that the effect on the value of individual countries' reserves would depend on the gold–currency composition of their reserves on the date of the revaluation. Anticipation of such an event could have created enormous speculative pressures, especially against the U.S. dollar, as countries tried to increase holdings of gold prior to the revaluation date. Furthermore, the fact that such a move would have created a windfall for gold-mining countries such as South Africa and the USSR simply reenforced resistance even to consider such a move. In any event, the revaluation of gold was never attempted.

Instead of attempting to increase reserves per se, the system could expand borrowing rights. This, in fact, has been done by the increases in members' quotas (see Table 30.2). The cumulative result of the increases in quotas combined with larger membership has been to expand the total value of quotas from an initial value of SDR 7.155 billion to SDR 60.026 billion in 1980.

In early 1983 the policy-setting committee of the Fund approved a further increase in quotas of 47 percent to SDR 90 billion. This would augment the resources of the Fund somewhat earlier than the scheduled 1985 general review of quotas would have dictated. The need for the additional resources was dictated primarily by substantial commercial debts of several newly industrializing countries, most notably Mexico, Brazil, and Argentina.

Creation of the SDR

Expansion of borrowing rights is not regarded by Fund members as exactly equivalent to increases in owned reserves. Borrowing from the Fund, beyond the initial 25 percent tranche, has conditions attached to it, and must be repaid, neither of which applies to owned reserves. Consequently, unless the return on owned reserves is very high, members will rely on owned assets first, before resorting to borrowing rights in the Fund. Further, if the conditionality and repayment requirements are too strict, a member may choose to resort to payments restrictions rather than borrow from the Fund.

These circumstances led the Fund members to agree to create in 1969 a new reserve asset called a "Special Drawing Right." The SDR is a cross between an owned asset and a borrowing right.

Table 30.2   Changes in IMF Quotas, 1945–1980

Effective Year (Month)	*Change*
1945 (Dec.)	Fund agreement entered into force
1950 (Dec.)	First general review, no major change
1956 (Jan.)	Second general review, no change
1959 (Sept.)	Increase of 50%
1965 (Mar.)	Increase of 25%
1971 (Apr.)	Increase of 25% and special increases for some members
1978 (Apr.)	Increase of 32.5%
1980 (Nov.)	Increase of 50.9%

SOURCE: IMF, *Annual Report*, various years.

Neither the allocation nor the use of the SDR is subject to conditionality: Further, when the SDR was established, 70 percent of each SDR could be used as an owned asset that does not have to be repaid the way ordinary IMF drawings must be. In 1981 this restriction was abolished, so that now holders of SDRs are able to sell *all* of their holdings should they choose.

The initial allocation totaled SDR 9.3 billion, spread over three years (1970–1972). The second allocation of an additional SDR 12 billion accrued over the period 1978–1981. While the Fund may withdraw or cancel SDRs, this has not yet been done.

Distribution of the SDRs among members is in proportion to members' quotas. This is designed to distribute the assets on the basis of potential need for reserves in the same way as the regular tranche drawing rights are distributed.

The Link Proposal

Other possible bases for distribution were debated at the time the SDRs were established. Perhaps the most important alternative was the "link" proposal. Instead of paying out newly created reserve money to individual nations according to an estimate of their balance-of-payments needs, which is what a quota-based distribution represents, some part, say 30 to 50 percent, could be allocated to the less developed nations as a supplement to national allocations of economic aid. Alternatively, and perhaps preferably, these new reserve funds could be turned over to international development agencies such as the World Bank and the various regional development banks for allocation to countries according to established criteria of feasibility and economic soundness. After being spent, these SDRs would show up in the reserve holdings of the nations selling the real resources needed for development.

The establishment of a link between reserve creation and development aid has a history that goes back to the Keynes Plan submitted to the Bretton Woods Conference.[6] Both support for and opposition to such a link have been vigorously advanced. The arguments start from the common ground that new international reserves such as SDRs are created at no resource cost, but give command over resources to the first recipients. Opponents to the link contend that short-term balance-of-payments financing and long-term development are separate problems. Furthermore, if SDRs are distributed as aid, a resource cost is

[6] See Y. S. Park, *The Link Between SDRs and Development Finance*, Essays in International Finance No. 100 (Princeton, N.J.: International Finance Section, Princeton University, 1973), for the history of these proposals and a detailed statement of the arguments pro and con.

imposed on the developed countries that supply the real resources on which these funds are spent. This cost can be avoided and an optimal distribution of reserves attained if the new reserves are allocated so that they will be held and not spent. Holding reserves provides a liquidity yield, in the form of slowing down the speed of adjustment through income changes, exchange rate realignments, and the imposition of controls, which can in principle be expressed as a rate of interest. Spending reserves, on the other hand, provide a yield either in consumer satisfaction or as a return on investment. The ideal position is attained when the marginal liquidity yield (plus any interest earned on reserve holdings) equals the marginal yield of consumption or investment. If SDRs were supplied so as to conform to this criterion, they would be held and not spent. Optimal reserve creation would be realized and any cost to the developed countries avoided.

Proponents of the link take the position that reserve creation provides an opportunity to realize a collective goal: the provision of additional development aid, which is as rational as an optimal distribution of reserves. Although allocating SDRs as aid does impose a resource cost on developed nations, this cost is warranted by the social desirability of an international redistribution of wealth. Moreover, as a practical matter, it is improbable that the theoretical optimal distribution of reserves could be attained by any concrete proposals likely to be adopted.

In any case, the link proposal was not adopted initially, nor has it been used subsequently as a basis for distributing SDRs.

Valuation of the SDR

What is an SDR worth? The value was calculated initially in terms of gold: SDR35 = 1 ounce of gold. However, with the emergence of floating exchange rates, in 1974 the SDR was established as a basket of sixteen members' currencies. The particular group of sixteen was chosen on the basis that each had a share of world exports greater than 1 percent in the previous five years. The valuation is determined daily.

In 1981, to simplify the valuation, the number of currencies in the basket was reduced to the five countries with the largest shares of world exports. The weights and U.S. dollar equivalents are presented in Table 30.3. The weights were translated into units of each currency on the date of valuation, and those currency amounts remain fixed. Then the currency amounts are converted into U.S. dollar equivalents at the market exchange rates prevailing in the London foreign exchange market. Adding up the U.S. dollar equivalents yields a U.S. dollar value of 1 SDR. The SDR value of any other currency is then determined by

Table 30.3   SDR Valuation on January 2, 1981

	(1) Currency Amount	(2) Exchange Rate on January 2, 1981	(3) U.S. Dollar Equivalent	Weight (%)
Currency				
U.S. dollar	0.5400	1.00000	0.540000	42.46
German mark	0.4600	1.97400	0.233029	18.32
French franc	0.7400	4.56000	0.162281	12.76
Japanese yen	34.0000	202.87000	0.167595	13.18
Pound sterling	0.0710	2.37800	0.168838	13.28
Total			1.271743	100.0
U.S. dollar value of SDR			1.27174	

SOURCE: *IMF Survey*, **10**:6 (Jan. 12, 1981).
NOTES:
Column (1): the currency composition of the basket.
Column (2): exchange rates in terms of the currency units per U.S. dollar, except for the pound sterling, which is expressed as U.S. dollars per pound sterling.
Column (3): the U.S. dollar equivalents of the currency amounts in column (1) and at the exchange rates in column (2); that is, column (1) divided by column (2) except for the pound sterling, for which the amounts in the two columns are multiplied.

the market exchange rate with the U.S. dollar, and the U.S. dollar/SDR value.

To encourage holdings of SDRs by members, the Fund established the asset as interest bearing. Initially, the rate of interest was substantially below the return on currency reserve assets because the Fund did not envision SDRs replacing other reserve assets. However, from 1981 onward, the Fund pays the average of interest rates on short-term domestic obligations in the five countries included in the SDR valuation basket. The Fund charges members for their use of SDRs at the same rate it pays interest on holdings of SDRs. Hence what matters is a country's *net* holdings of SDRs. A net debtor pays interest, while a net creditor earns interest. Payments of interest and interest charges thus balance out as a whole for the system. However, since the Fund itself is a net creditor, as an organization it earns interest on SDRs, thus, in effect, collecting seigniorage from the users of the SDRs.

LIMITING DISEQUILIBRATING CAPITAL FLOWS

Another major issue facing the international monetary system has been the problem of disequilibrating capital flows. In the classical model of balance-of-payments adjustment, with prices and wages flexible in both directions, short-term capital movements are always accommodating or equilibrating. The deficit country loses reserves, interest rates rise, investment and output contract, and prices fall, while opposite developments occur in the surplus country. The consequent adjustment in the balance of payments is given more time to operate, however, and the harshness of the adjustment mechanism is moderated by the inflow of capital into the deficit country, stimulated by the relative changes in interest rates. There is no collision with domestic policy because there is no policy.

But in modern-day conditions short-term capital flows, instead of easing adjustment, *may* make it more difficult. This occurs when an existing deficit is enlarged by an outward flow of capital. Then the capital movement is disequilibrating. Such a situation arises when the deficit country, suffering from severe unemployment because prices and wages adjust downward only with great difficulty, enforces an easy-money policy to sustain investment and employment. If interest rates are higher in the surplus country, capital moves to this money market, adding to the pressure on the deficit country's balance of payments. Both Britain and the United States struggled with such situations in the 1960s. With the growth of multinational banks and manufacturing corporations, the increased mobility of capital is likely to make similar circumstances even more disturbing in the future.

Possible Solutions

Disequilibrating capital flows and the means of dealing with them were on the agenda of the Committee of Twenty of the IMF, which debated these issues in 1974. A number of suggested remedies were mentioned. These included greater harmonization of national monetary policies, "subject to the requirement of domestic demand management;" prompt exchange rate adjustment; wider margins; temporary floats; and controls.

As to the first of these, if demand management in deficit and surplus countries calls for monetary policies that are complementary, there is no problem. But it is in the difficult cases that policy and adjustment conflict, and the prospects of policy harmonization are minimal.

The three possible remedies for short-term capital movements having to do with exchange rates—prompt exchange rate adjustment, wider margins, and floating rates—all rely on effecting more rapid payments adjustment, thus making capital flows unnecessary or of shorter duration, or, as with wider margins and floating rates, they diminish capital movements by making them more risky.

Many countries have attempted with varying success to stem unwanted capital flows by numerous control devices. In the 1970s, Japan and Germany and several other European nations imposed higher reserve requirements on foreign than on domestic bank deposits and refused to pay interest on such deposits, and some have even introduced negative interest rates. Several countries, including Switzerland and Japan, limited the amount of nonresident deposits that their banks could accept.

Belgium for some time, France (1971), and Italy (1973) employed a two-tier foreign exchange market, one limited to commercial (current account) transactions and the other for financial (capital account) business. Dealings in the commercial market took place at a fixed rate of exchange, whereas the rate for financial transactions was free to float. It is impossible by this device to screen and limit only short-term capital flows; it is even very difficult to prevent evasions that bring capital transactions into the commercial sector of the market.[7]

Capital Flows Under Flexible Exchange Rates

The adoption of floating exchange rates by the major currencies (or groups of currencies such as the EMS) has not eliminated the problem of interest-sensitive capital flows in the international economy. Under a flexible exchange rate the investor must consider not only the rate of return and the risk of default, but also the future path of the exchange rate. The relationship between the exchange rate and the interest rate thus becomes a central issue.

The covered interest arbitrage parity condition derived in Chapter 21 is worth recalling in this regard:

$$\frac{r_t}{r_0} = \frac{1 + i_d}{1 + i_f}$$

If both the domestic and foreign nominal interest rates incorporate expected rates of inflation, and the real interest rates do not change, then the premium–discount on the forward exchange rate will reflect those differences in expected rates of inflation. Further, any *change* in the expected rate of inflation at home will affect the nominal interest rate. Thus a rise in the domestic inflation rate would increase the domestic nominal interest rate and result in a decrease in the spot price of foreign exchange relative to the forward (i.e., an increase in the expected depreciation of the home currency).

[7] See, for example, The German Council of Economic Experts, *Toward a New Basis for International Monetary Policy*, Studies in International Finance No. 31 (Princeton, N.J.: International Finance Section, Princeton University, 1972).

The analysis is further complicated when we recognize that capital flows depend also on expected *real* rates of return. Suppose, for example, that the domestic real interest rate rises as the domestic inflation rate and nominal interest rates fall. While the higher real interest rate tends to attract a capital inflow and a fall in the price of foreign exchange, the lower nominal interest rate tends to encourage a capital outflow. Thus interest rate changes may generate exchange rate changes that are either in the same direction or the opposite direction.

IS THE IMF EVENHANDED?

A major debate continues concerning the evenhandedness of the Fund in dealing with rich and poor countries. Critics of the Fund argue that it imposes conditions on the poorer countries that are tougher than it imposes on rich countries. Defenders of the Fund argue that strict conditions need to be imposed in order to maintain the revolving credit nature of the Fund.

The arguments are often complex, but boil down to the following. There is, first, an asymmetry in the treatment of Fund members. Those in surplus, even if they have achieved the surplus by resort to mercantilistic policies, do not have adjustment forced upon them. Thus the deficit countries are forced to bear all or most of the burden of adjustment. More than that, those in deficit have increasing degrees of conditionality imposed on their Fund drawings, based not on the extent to which they have been responsible for their current predicament, but merely on whether or not they are drawing on the credit tranches. Furthermore, the critics argue, the size of a member's access to Fund credit depends not on the magnitude of the member's problem, but on the size of the quota, which, in turn, depends on the member's economic role in the international economy.

It appears to the poor countries that their need for Fund resources is much greater, relative to their economic power in the world economy, than is the need of the richer members. Yet the latter, because of their greater role in the international economy, have greater quotas and thus greater access to Fund resources. It is the richer members that have least need of Fund resources. They are able, if they choose, to draw vast sums from the private international capital market.

Defenders of the Fund respond that access to credit in the world's financial markets has always been based on credit worthiness, which in turn reflects the creditors' expected ability to repay. The Fund is a significant supplementary source of credit which is in addition to arrangements that rely solely on the private capital market. Further, the Fund has established special facilities based largely on need. The Fund's staff assists countries to develop ways of getting out of difficulty, and then provides the resources (on the condition that the agreed-upon program is followed) to assist recovery.

The critics of the Fund respond to this by vigorously asserting that in developing its prescriptions for recovery, the Fund's staff relies on an analytical framework that is too doctrinaire, which in the light of the current intellectual debate about the effects of alternative models (e.g., monetary versus Keynesian approaches) is using the Fund's resources to impose a particular economic policy approach on the poor countries. Since the culprit in the eyes of the Fund frequently is government spending in excess of tax revenues, the Fund insists that excess spending be cut back. Since much of the spending is on social or development programs, the Fund's insistence on conditions frequently casts it in the role of villain in the eyes of spokesmen for developing countries. Villain or not, the Fund persists in establishing conditions for credit to its members.

SELECTED REFERENCES

ARTUS, J. R., and A. D. CROCKETT. *Floating Exchange Rates and the Need for Surveillance*, Essays in International Finance No. 127. Princeton, N.J.: International Finance Section, Princeton University, 1978. Development of the use for surveillance of IMF members' exchange rate practices.

CHRYSTAL, K. A. *International Money and the Future of the SDR*, Essays in International Finance No. 128. Princeton, N. J.: International Finance Section, Princeton University, 1978. Argues that unless the SDR is transformed into a potential real money, it has a very limited future.

GUITIAN, M. "Fund Conditionality, and the International Adjustment Process." *Finance and Development* (Dec. 1980, Mar. 1981, June 1981). A series of articles examining the Fund's experience of applying conditionality in access to Fund resources.

MEIER, G. M. *Problems of a World Monetary Order*, 2nd ed. New York: Oxford University Press, 1982. Parts II and III consider the floating exchange rate regime and reforming the international monetary system.

NOWZAD, B. *The IMF and Its Critics*, Essays in International Finance No. 146. Princeton, N.J.: International Finance Section, Princeton University, 1981. An evaluation of the main lines of criticism directed at the Fund from Third World countries.

SOUTHARD, F. A. *The Evolution of the International Monetary Fund*, Essays in International Finance No. 135. Princeton, N.J.: International Finance Section, Princeton University, 1979. Reviews the institutional characteristics of the Fund that enabled the Fund to survive and adapt to changing international circumstances.

TEW, B. *The Evolution of the International Monetary System, 1945–77*. London: Hutchinson Publishing Group, Ltd., 1977. Contains a thorough description of the IMF.

AUTHOR INDEX

SUBJECT INDEX